DEMOCRACY IN URBAN AMERICA

DEMOCRACY IN URBAN AMERICA

Readings on Government and Politics

Edited by

OLIVER P. WILLIAMS

*Fels Institute of Local and State Government,
University of Pennsylvania*

CHARLES PRESS

Michigan State University

RAND MCNALLY & COMPANY

CHICAGO

RAND MᶜNALLY POLITICAL SCIENCE SERIES
Morton Grodzins, *Advisory Editor*

To Marion and Nancy

PREFACE

IN ASSEMBLING this collection of readings we have tried to build around a common theme without doing violence to the authors' ideas. Our selections are mainly from the writings of political scientists, sociologists, and those in related disciplines in the social sciences. We have informed our academic colleagues of our reasons for editing and in a few cases have received suggestions from them which were incorporated into our plans. In one or two instances, authors wished to add materials to their selections. With the permission of copyright holders, such additions were made and have been indicated. We have also indicated clearly in the printed copy where we have deleted materials and hope that such breaks are not too distracting for the student reader.

The book was conceived as a new way of teaching local government. In many respects it is a course, for it is not designed to parallel the existing texts with "outside" readings. Rather, it has a logical development of its own. Only in a few instances have we sacrificed the basic theme of the book to include materials which seemed logically part of every local government course.

The assumption of this approach is that the "facts" about municipal government (i.e., charters, forms, etc.) are those matters most easily learned and most easily forgotten. Courses may never go beyond these "facts" to the traditional "outside" materials which potentially contain the ideas which are most essential. Our effort has assumed that the facts may be the marginal matters learned only to aid in understanding the broader questions.

Therefore, the teacher using this volume is embarking on an experiment—one that hopefully will add to his own insights and will quicken the interest of his students in the policy-making process at the local level and in the relevance of this process to democratic values.

We wish to thank the contributors to this volume and their publishers for their assistance. We also wish to express special thanks to Charles Adrian and Morton Grodzins who reviewed the outline of our proposed selections and gave us valuable comments and suggestions. Finally, we wish to thank our wives for their assistance and we would like to dedicate this volume to them.

OLIVER WILLIAMS
CHARLES PRESS

TABLE OF CONTENTS

CHAPTER THREE: COMMUNITY, POLITICAL PARTICIPATION, AND DEMOCRACY

CHAPTER FOUR: METROPOLITANISM

CHAPTER FIVE: GOVERNMENT STRUCTURE AND FORMS OF ELECTIONS: AN ASSESSMENT OF THE MUNICIPAL REFORM MOVEMENT

DEMOCRACY IN URBAN AMERICA

INTRODUCTION: DEMOCRACY

IN URBAN AMERICA

THIS READINGS BOOK is designed to ask both old and relatively new questions about democracy in urban America. The old ones pertain to the values of local self-government which have long been a part of our national political catechism; the new ones to the condition of local democracy as it exists in the cities of America today. By raising both at the same time, it may be that new answers to some of the old questions may emerge.

One of the old questions concerns the necessity for local self-government in a democratic society. The traditional answer has been that local self-government is the foundation of our democratic system. It is still a popular answer, and it may well be a good one, but too often it is a glib response based on limited reflection or observation.

The idealization of strong local self-government began with the very inception of our national system. Jefferson is usually considered the theoretician who first exalted the idea of republics in miniature. But, given his stress on agrarian democracy, his remarks are, in most respects, inappropriate for the experience of our subsequent national life. Alexis de Tocqueville, writing after the new democracy had been in operation only two generations, supplied us with the clearest statement of what may be considered the classic view of local democracy in America. De Tocqueville was not blind to the shortcomings of local self-government, but he saw in it a major source of strength for American democracy Here democratic men were truly equal, where neighbors could sit down with neighbors, and through negotiation, common sense, and a feeling for the needs of the common community could work out the policies for building roads, schools, gathering taxes, and providing essential services. It was here that the sense of membership in a democratic society was instilled in all citizens, and membership in this primary group served as a protective buffer for the citizen in resisting advances of a centralized bureaucracy. Local governments were, therefore, the "democratic building blocks" created through face-to-face relations. Thus they furnished the foundation for representative democracy at the national level.

1

The De Tocqueville conceptions are familiar to us, for his arguments have retained great vitality in public expression. His ideas undoubtedly have been sustained by the experience of many citizens in
governing small communities, in handling school district issues, in
attending PTA meetings, and in participating in community chest drives.
However, it is a model which is somewhat threadbare if it is used to
characterize generally the political life in urban, or even small town,
America today. The model has been inappropriate for a long time for
large cities. It was possible to dismiss these cities as being atypical of
our political way of life as long as they were filled with recent immigrants and had corrupt and evil reputations. Such bracketing of the
densely populated urban areas as special cases at this late date is, of
course, totally unwarranted.

To many people, the most attractive portion of the classical model
has been the idea of universal citizen participation. But it is just this
aspect of the model that has troubled many contemporary observers
of local politics. The most redundant remarks on the subject refer to
"voter apathy" toward local affairs. Frequently the implication is that
the idealized participation pattern observed by De Tocqueville could
take place in the urban setting if all of the lazy citizens would inform
themselves and vote. But it must be recognized that democracy and
large voter participation are not equivalents. In addition, nonvoting may,
under some circumstances, be a rational method of expressing a policy
preference.

It is not simply the number of participants, but rather the kinds
of participation, which provide the basis for more meaningful questions
about local democracy. Indeed, many analyses of qualitative participation raise doubts about the ability of local government to supply a
foundation for national democracy. Let us cite a few examples.

Some observers have found in the suburbs the development of
values and patterns of daily living which prevent the exploitation of
issues, make elections a formalistic ritual, consign government to an
appointed bureaucracy, and, at the same time, fail to make citizens
face up to the decisions that have to be made. All of this, these critics
argue, takes place amidst much citizen "participation," if by this word
we mean voting, personal contacts with officials, attending meetings,
or serving on advisory boards.

Another author points to the flight of effective leadership from
the local community as a result of the growth of the *national* private
corporation. At one time in the history of many communities, the local
industrial executives were a chief source of civic leadership talent. Their
modern equivalents, the branch managers, are less likely to be interested

in the community—their values and aspirations are expressed through the company bureaucracy. Furthermore, since they are frequently transients, they are likely to participate only in those aspects of community life that either directly serve their corporations' interests or in certain nonpolitical areas, where the corporation believes the executive may gain desirable training. Thus instead of local participation serving as a training ground for state and national leadership, it becomes a proving ground for aspirants within a corporate hierarchy.

Two generations of sociologists, delving into the political structures of local communities, have produced case studies which contradict the classic democratic model. They report the existence of hierarchical regimes in which the important decisions of communities are made by relatively few people. These reports do not refer to instances of "boss rule" or to forms of the political party machines, but rather to systems of political control which are exercised in a much less obtrusive fashion. Whether these "power structures" imply the existence of local political oligarchies or merely more accurately describe democratic leadership is a point which is strongly debated. In either case, the De Tocqueville model of local governmental participation needs drastic revision.

There have, in addition, been studies which raise the question as to whether, even in voting, patterns of behavior in local elections have emerged which have undemocratic implications. This research involves descriptions of the "alienated" voter. Our urban culture may be creating a situation in which many citizens feel powerless and frustrated in relation to the effective political decisions influencing their lives. Such individuals may vote only in blind protest, in a groping attempt to punish the unknown "they" (the conspirators assumed to be in control). The result is a negative vote on all proposals or a vote for the demagogue who may express the anguished feelings of the alienated, but who offers no program of action aimed at realistically solving local problems.

Finally, some reports on communities outwardly resembling De Tocqueville's model indicate that all is not well for local democracy even in the small village. These findings demonstrate that the small town in our mass society is being bypassed. So many decisions are made outside these communities that local democracy has little opportunity to assert itself. Even in areas where local control is possible, the calcifying effects of long-established customs may have made the democratic process a ritual, rather than an effective method of fashioning answers to common problems.

Lest it be felt that this book of readings is merely a chronicle of despair, it should be added that writers are also included who view the situation with some optimism. This optimism is not based upon a revivalistic spirit which sees a "reawakening" of the American public, however. Rather, it is based on the belief that the simple De Tocquevillian model is an improper standard for a viable theory of local democracy in a contemporary context.

There are deep roots of democratic control and direction that may be uncovered by the astute observer if he is not blinded by outworn conceptions. Perhaps the simple model of neighbor-to-neighbor participation obscures the fact that urban dwellers help mold their environment by a manifold system of participation through work, church, club, and family institutions, in addition to the more obvious forms of political participation. One observer has uncovered a surprising number of community ties within districts of a large city through a study of community newspapers and their relation to the politics of the ward. Another has insisted that a large city political organization with a machine reputation actually did do a good job of representing its constituents.

Perhaps the number of such "positive" studies and proposals are few because of the academic penchant for being critical. To a certain extent, however, this dissident role is assumed simply because the defenders of the local government myths are legion among the practitioners and participants in local decision-making, and the academician feels bound to develop a more realistic perspective. Thus, the views capsulized in this introduction and which are developed in the readings probably present a less than complete true cross section of local government in America today. They probably neglect many situations where time-honored democratic traditions retain their vitality. But our purpose is to address ourselves to problems, and it is our thesis that no type or size of American community is immune to the kinds of problems suggested above.

There is nothing unique in pointing to shortcomings in local government; civic reform is a national institution. But civic reform has been little interested in theory. Its major contribution has been to insist that governmental forms be simplified so that the voter's burdens would be lightened and he could more readily determine who was responsible for decision-making. Essentially, however, the civic reformers have embraced the De Tocqueville model and have exhorted citizens to "get out and agitate." The movement has also furnished the active citizens some mechanisms for administrative improvements. The result has been that a great many cities are more efficient and provide better services, though urban politics has not necessarily become more interesting or policy-making more "democratic." Many reformers have assumed that the municipal operation is a kind of administrative state in miniature whose object is to provide certain well-defined services. Thus, the problem has been only to see that services were provided honestly and efficiently. The "democratic" portion of the problem was solved when the city bosses were slain.

Although the classicists and the reformers can be easily chided for their rather naive theories of democracy, it remains a difficult matter to improve on them. Some observers have attempted to do so by transferring to the local level the institutions that appear to sustain our national democracy. The two most significant of these institutions are political parties and interest groups, although neither of these are capable of supporting local democracy in most cases. While it is not difficult to introduce one party to the local scene, there have been few communities that have been able to sustain a two-party or multi-party system. The political geography of our national parties has usually rendered cities and towns into one-party areas. While some experimentation with local or nonpartisan forms has yielded results, a competitive party model does not accurately describe the system of representation in most local jurisdictions.

Outside our largest cities, competition among formally organized interests is relatively unknown. The great array of letter-head organizations in national and state capitols dwindles down to a mere handful in the medium and small cities. The Chamber of Commerce, the labor unions, and the Board of Realtors practically exhaust the list. Even these groups are frequently not organized for influence in the local arena. Zoning ordinances, housing codes, city plans, and health regulations are usually passed after the testimony of a small knot of alert citizens and the business or residential interests most immediately involved. The fact that there are interests active in molding local policy will be readily granted. However, no existing study has verified the claim that the interplay of these interest groups sustains many viable local democracies.

We do not propose to set forth a new theory or model of local democracy. Actually, such a possibility is precluded by the very nature of this collection of diverse readings. We have, however, through selection and editing, been able to present a point of view. It is a "negative" view in that it often qualifies the shibboleths of local democracy.

Some may object to the fact that in re-examining the De Tocqueville model we have attacked a straw man. We can reply that the shibboleths have been drawn upon the De Tocqueville model for a reason and that, therefore, the model itself deserves examination. Also, as an educational aid, this readings book must begin with things familiar to the beginning student—a second reason we have chosen to deal with the classical model of local democracy.

Obviously it is our hope that the readings will encourage the for-

mulation of a better model. Let us discuss two ground rules for exploring the actual world of local government and for re-examining the
problem of local democracy.

1. American communities differ widely from one another in size;
in function (small shopping center, residential suburb, industrial center, mining town, etc.); in their social, ethnic, and racial composition;
and finally, politically. Some may be truly oligarchical, others more
broadly representative. But even within these two catagories there are
further variations. In one town, the old families may be powerful; in
another, the factory owners; and in a third, the Main Street merchants.
Among those local governments which are broadly representative, there
are a great range of institutions and mechanisms for participation and
representation.

As a result, we should not search for or seek to create a single,
simple model for democratic local government. For example, intelligible
alternatives may be supplied in one community by the traditional two
parties, in another by local factions, and in another by a single faction
or group which, through unique local circumstances, is kept responsive
in the process of retaining office.

2. We should stop viewing local government in isolation. Instead
of talking about building blocks of democracy, it might be better to
talk of interdependent, co-operative systems of local, state, and national
governments. Demands which are frustrated at one level of government often find response at another. State and national governmental
power may not pose threats to local democracy, but rather may furnish a
source of strength and support for it. Cities for generations did little
about slums until the national government entered the picture. The
present activities of the current national program do not depend, however, solely on the Washington bureaucracy, but also on the new interest
and leadership that has been stimulated at the local level.

Chapter ONE

THE VARIETY AND CHANGE IN

THE AMERICAN URBAN PLACE

Introduction
1. *The American Urban Place*, Max Lerner

ONE OF THE MOST IMPORTANT FACTS to bear in mind when studying urban government and politics is the absence of a neat symmetry in the character of urban places. In parlance, the term "urban" may refer to communities that range from wide spots along the highway having a population of a few hundred persons to the giant population centers such as New York. The legal term "city" is similarly applied to a variety of communities. All of these are urban America.

The effect of scale or size on the urban governmental process is still largely an undefined area of study. Some obvious generalizations about political behavior can be made concerning the effects of increasing city size: individual action tends to give way to public action, opportunities for face-to-face relationships in politics diminish, and the degree of bureaucratization and professionalization of government increases. Since most people in the United States live in large urban places or their immediate environs, this book concentrates on such communities. But even if we held our attention narrowly to cities of a specific size, rigorous generalization on political behavior would often be risky, for other factors such as the economic base, ethnic and racial composition, local traditions, governmental structure, and informal political arrangements also affect the manner in which local decisions are made.

For this reason, the selection from Max Lerner has been chosen to introduce this book of readings. The conventional classification of the American community employs the four-part breakdown of rural, small town, big city, and suburbia, and Lerner reminds us that this division is, to a certain extent, historically derived. Each place once dominated the American scene and each remains associated with a particular set of values and style of life. While each type of community "had its day," each still continues to exist. Thus, in addition to the differences in communities listed above, these historical survivals add another dimension to the variety in American urban places.

1. The American Urban Place

MAX LERNER

The American place started with small population units, rapidly grew to big ones, and has ever since been under the double tension of moving from the small unit to the big one and at the same time moving from the center of the bigger unit outward toward the rim. Traditionally the small town has been held to embody the American spirit better than the larger frame. De Tocqueville affirmed that the township as a unit both of government and of living had preceded the state and nation in America and was more important than either. In New England the township has lasted over three hundred years, and while it has been battered by heavy pressures from state, nation, and economy, it still retains traces of the two goods that Americans have always seen in it—the friendliness of face-to-face relations and the concern about the town's affairs felt by all its citizens.

De Tocqueville had a reason of his own for his tub-thumping about the New England township—his hatred for French centralization, which made a person "a kind of settler, indifferent to the fate of the spot which he inhabits. The greatest changes are effected there without his concurrence. . . . The condition of his village, the police of his street, the repairs of the church or parsonage, do not concern him; for he looks upon all these things as unconnected with himself and as the property of a powerful stranger whom he calls the government." He saw American town government as the ideal contrast to this lugubrious picture. For all his bias he was nonetheless right about the "provincial independence" of the American small town and the fierce identification of even its

Reprinted from *America as a Civilization* (New York: Simon and Schuster, Inc., 1957), pp. 148–56, 159–60, 167–68, 176–82 by permission of the author. Author's footnotes omitted. Professor Lerner teaches history at Brandeis University.

poorest citizens with the disputes and rivalries that raged about its affairs. This intensity still prevails in many New England towns, governed by three "Selectmen," who draw up annual budgets that are examined, item for item, by the entire citizenry sitting in the primary democracy of the town meeting. In the early days of the Republic the small town was the tap spring of the revolutionary spirit and of cultural strength. There were few Presidents from Lincoln and Grant to Truman and Eisenhower who were not the products of small town culture. During most of American history, until the turn of the twentieth century, it was the basic community form for most Americans.

But the growing point of American life is scarcely to be found in the small town today. Latterly the important lines of growth have been elsewhere. It is partly that all the small units in American life are having to wage a losing fight—not only the small town but the small farm, the small business firm, the small college, even the neighborhood within the big city. Somewhere between the turn of the century and the New Deal the small town felt the withering touch of the Great Artifact that we call American society, and in the quarter century between 1930 and 1955 the decisive turn was made, away from small-town life. The currents of American energy moved around and beyond the small towns, leaving them isolated, demoralized, with their young people leaving them behind like abandoned ghost towns.

What happened was that the small town lost its economic and cultural base. Partly this happened in the areas most badly scarred by soil erosion, where the destruction of the rural hinterland stripped away the substance of small-town existence. But actually this was a marginal force. Everywhere, even in the most prosperous areas, the small town was undercut by the big changes in American life—the auto and superhighway, the supermarket and the market center, the mail-order house, the radio and TV, the growth of national advertising, the mechanization of farming—so that it turned its face directly to the centers of technology. It was the city and the suburb—the cluster-city complex—that became the focus of working and living, consuming and leisure. "None of the kids ever come back here to live after they've gone away to school," said an older man from Shannon Center, Iowa, which had lost almost half its population in the 1940s. The young people go on to find jobs in factories or businesses far from where they grew up, or they go away to college or technical school and get the kind of training for which the small town, with its limited opportunities, simply cannot offer a demand. . . .

What happened to the small town was not only that the big social changes undercut it and swirled around it, leaving it isolated, but they also drained it of its store of power. The power of America today is to be found largely with the business and community leaders of the city, who initiate policies for corporate empires, trade-unions, national pressure groups, and big-audience media. Knowing this, we tend to forget that in an earlier America the decisions that expressed the American will were largely made by small-town lawyers, bankers, merchants, editors. As merchandising, transport, and recreation shifted, the locus of power shifted. The town could no longer perform most of its functions alone—roadbuilding, relief, education, taxation, public works— and it came to depend on subsidies from the Federal and state governments. As the power diminished, however, the intensity of the feuds and rivalries did not always subside, and the small town sometimes offered the unreal spectacle of an intensified struggle over dwindling stakes of power.

To the outward eye, the town of the 1950s, with its church spires, its Town Hall, its Main Street stores, its bank, its weekly newspaper, seemed what it always was. But its decay was unmistakable, taking the form of a displacement of its power and a disorganization of its traditional ways of life. Charles Francis Adams had seen it generations earlier, in his poetic description (in *Three Episodes of Massachusetts History*) of the disappearance of the New England village. Even the close controls which the code-makers of the town once exerted on its moral standards had to be relaxed in the face of the general moral confusion. George Homans pointed out, in commenting on a study of the social disorganization of "Hilltown"—a Massachusetts farming town of about 1,000 people—that a town clerk who absconded with community funds was no longer dealt with draconically as in similar cases in the past, that girls being dated were expected to "come across" sexually, and that virginity before marriage was no longer stressed or counted upon. Few would argue today that the condition of mental health in the small town is better than in the city, or that there is less alcoholism or a better family situation. Nor can one any longer underplay the seamier sides of American localism—the heartbreaking inertia, the presence of corruption and greed even at the grass roots. Human meanness and human generosity are widely distributed in a culture, and the pursuit of the cultural life goals goes on with little reference to the unit of living. There may be greater tranquillity in the small town but no more happiness; there are face-to-face relations but no deeper understanding of the human situation; there is a more compassable universe to grasp, physically and socially, but in reality it is no less bewildering.

If I have been unsparing here in dealing with the legend of small-town superiority, I do not mean to belittle the enduring although lesser place the small town is likely to have in American life. The growth of a highly urban and mechanized Great Society has by-passed not only the town itself but also some of the values with which it was historically linked. Emerson's Concord, Lincoln's Springfield, William Allen White's Emporia, Truman's Independence, and Eisenhower's Abilene must have borne along on their current a way of life strong enough to shape the men they produced. Some of America's towns, especially in New England and in the prosperous areas of the Middle West, are still conscious of being the carriers of a tradition and a philosophy. When Harry Truman, commenting on the problem of juvenile delinquency, wrote that "our children need fewer gadgets and more chores," he was expressing a recognizable small-town philosophy—the direct, no-nonsense, keep-life-simple philosophy of small-town mores. Truman's own personality—informal, downright, salty, with its strong sense of task, its stress on personal loyalties and obligations, its rejection of cant, its shrewd assessment of men and issues, and its built-in moral code—is the distillation of what is healthiest and most pungent in the surviving values of small-town culture. Although most small-town politicians (and much of American politics still derives from the small town) would shy away from Truman's identification with majority aspirations and minority causes, with labor interests and civil liberties and Negro civil rights, enough of them are enough like Truman to make a fusion of urban and small-town values conceivable. If the small town is wholly sacrificed there will be sacrificed along with it some continuity of face-to-face relations, an awareness of identity, a striving to be part of a compassable whole, a sense of counting for something and being recognized as a person and not a cipher.

A number of recent American writings indicate that the nostalgia for the small town need not be construed as directed toward the town itself: it is rather a "quest for community" (as Robert Nisbet puts it)—a nostalgia for a compassable and integral living unit. The critical question is not whether the small town can be rehabilitated in the image of its earlier strength and growth—for clearly it cannot—but whether American life will be able to evolve any other integral community to replace it. This is what I call the problem of place in America, and unless it is somehow resolved, American life will become more jangled and fragmented than it is, and American personality will continue to be unquiet and unfulfilled.

If the small town survives at all in a future America, it will have to survive within this frame and on a new economic base—not as the minor metropolis of a farming area, or as a mill town or mining town, but as a fusion of farming and industrial life along with the residential spill-over from the city and the suburb. I shall deal with both these forms in what follows, but it is worth saying here that neither the mammoth city nor the dormitory suburb is as it stands an adequate solution of the problem of place in America. Neither is the small town as it stands. But it can diversify its economic base, especially with the trend toward decentralizing industry. With the new modes of transport it can reach even the distant big city easily—for work or recreation, school, medical facilities, or friends. And it can build a way of life which forms a continuity with the small town of the past but without its cluttering accompaniments of provincialism and torpor.

America was formed in its present mold in the process of city building, and it is still true—even in the era of the suburban revolution—that wherever American places are being shaped anew the new forms irrepressibly move toward becoming cities. While making goods and making money, the American has become in the process a city maker as well.

Lewis Mumford, in his *Culture of Cities,* has traced with learning and passion the historical rise of the city as shelter, fortress, industrial center, mechanical way of life—the stages toward "Megalopolis." In every civilization the rise of the big city has been a by-product of technical and industrial development. This has been true not only in Europe, whose cities grew big earlier than America's and whose population density is higher, but also in Asia, where the recent upsurge of population and the ferment of new forces have raised the size of the big cities staggeringly high. It is truer of the American city, however, that the rise of megalopolis has meant the accumulation not only of masses of people but of masses of power. The growth of the American city has gone along with—and been the product of—revolutions in production, motive power, transport, communications. Every transformation in the economy, including the rise of new industries and the changes from roads to canals to railroads to autos and aviation, and from steam to gasoline to electric and atomic power, has further complicated the web of city life. Yet the changes move inexorably, and as they occur they keep transforming the outer sky line and the inner structure and life of the city. Every new step in technology tends to destroy the inner forms of the cities on which they rest and which have made them possible, and on their ruins new forms arise. . . .

As a result of city living, Americans are becoming a people whose earliest memories are less apt to be of the farm or village or the main street of a small town than of pavements, and movies, and swimming at the docks, and running in gangs, and "going downtown." They have had to get accustomed to the jangle of city sounds striking on the nerve centers, to new ways of dodging city traffic or of waiting it out patiently, to the complexity and pavements of the "asphalt jungle."

Why do they stand it? The answer is that many don't, hence the Great Exodus to the suburbs. For those who do, the city has become more than a convenience: it is a necessity. This is true for workers who must be near factories, railroad yards, and offices; for businessmen who must be near their markets and customers; for writers and artists, advertisers, workers in the big media, who must be near the centers of the nation's life.

The city is no longer a mode of comfort, as it was in earlier phases. In some ways it has become the acme of discomfort—congested, traffic-stalled, smog-filled, shut out from sunlight, with scarcely space for breathing and no feel of soil beneath one's feet and no sense of the rhythm of the seasons. Any subway rider during the rush hours in New York can testify that city life has rigors challenging the frontier. This *ascesis* is made endurable (at least for the eggheads) because of the excitement of theaters, concerts, night clubs, restaurants, sports events, universities, art schools, which only the city can furnish and for which even the big media and the modern arts of mass reproduction are no substitutes. Beyond these amenities the core attraction of the city as a way of life is tension, movement, opportunity, and a swarming kind of warmth. A recent survey of Detroit, into which waves of workers have swept from farms and small towns, shows that most of them do not share the fashionable despair about city living. They like living in Detroit. It is as if there were an unlocalized yearning for what is big in size, dense in numbers, varied in type and stock of people, mobile, responsive. The cities are fed by this restlessness and grow through it.

Thus the American city as a way of life is the product not only of technical and economic factors but also of loneliness. It is here that the byzantine aspect of American city culture becomes important. What is involved is not only the quest for liquor and night clubs, late hours, sexual excitement and sexual opportunity. These are the more obvious garments of a Faustian hunger and an almost pathetic fear of being left out of things. The city is at once the product and symbol of human alienation and the longed-for antidote against it. It is the sum of all the signatures that a restless spirit has left on a people sensitive to experience. "This city," as E. B. White put it in a prose hymn to New York which is the distillation of the urban mood, "this mischievous and marvelous monument which not to look upon would be like death." . . .

The new urban personality which is emerging in America is the product of the machine—but also of a good deal more. The machine aspects of city living are obvious enough. Who can forget the swift tunneling of the machine-as-subway in the earth, the scurrying of the machine-as-automobile over its surface, the exacting regularity of the machine-as-traffic-light, the droning of the machine-as-television, the stream of print emerging from the machine-as-press, the silent power and precision of the machine-as-dynamo? Who can escape the tempo of the mass city—hurrying to work, to appointments, to crises, to pleasure, to tragedy?

Yet what gives the city its character as living is not the tempo or discipline of the machine but the effort to reach for values beyond it. The youngster becomes a member of the city gang, partly at least because the gang gives him a chance for a sense of belonging and feudal allegiance. Similarly with mechanized sports and amusements in the big city. Prize fighters pummel each other like gladiators before thousands; baseball contests are commercial events staged on schedule, with team standings calculated down to the fourth decimal point; movies and TV project the same image on thousands of screens to the accompaniment of millions of fluttering pulses; choruses of dancing girls tap out their rhythms in night clubs with machinelike precision. Yet the big fact about all of them is not that they are mechanical, which is true enough, but that they furnish channels for mass emotion which relieve the tension of machine living.

Within this frame the city has developed a type of American character different from the type that De Crevecoeur, De Tocqueville, or even Bryce depicted. It is less conditioned to the soil and the seasons, less religious, more skeptical about motives and chary of being "played for a sucker," less illusioned in the sense in which illusions—about friendship, work, sex, love and God—provide an internal sustaining force for the personality. It has been psychologically hardened by innumerable brief encounters—in public schools, on subways and busses, in restaurants, in the course of shopping—which would become intolerable if one did not sheathe oneself against them with a constricted response. It is precocious about money matters and sex, since so many people grow up in crowded quarters where few things are concealed from them. It is stoical in the face of hardship and the man-made catastrophes of economic life. It is not "urbane" except in the small groups in which one can afford to be generous, but it is much more likely to strip the jungle life of the city down to the nakedness of the human animal. It economizes time with an almost manic earnestness during the hours of business, only to waste it with equally manic intensity during the hours of pleasure and recreation. It lays stress (within limits) on individual traits of personality, on uniqueness in dress and sophistication in taste, on awareness, on the dramatic impact that the individual makes in his brief meetings with others. It has replaced fear by anxiety, and the concern about danger from elemental forces with a vague concern about security, safety, and the opinions of others.

What this means is that city living has carried men and women ever further away from their instinctual endowment. The city is not the root of the planlessness, the tensions, and the conformism of American life, but it is the envelope that encloses them. Or, to change the figure, the city is the battleground of the values of the culture. . . .

The shift to the new suburbs . . . meant a shift in class composition. The suburbs used to be the residential areas for wealthy businessmen, bankers, and lawyers who wanted the manorial touch. But now the "rich" suburbs, like Bronxville (near New York) and Winnetka (near Chicago) or the Quogue that Fitzgerald celebrated in his *Great Gatsby* (it was set in what he called West Egg, on Long Island), have been outstripped by others. There were the rented or purchased homes in the big "developments," like the Levittowns and the Park Forests, which were filled by professional people and by technicians and junior executives of the big corporations; there were the suburbs of skilled workers, usually mushrooming around aviation plants and other defense industries that had to be built in open territory or near power sources, as in the Buffalo-Niagara Falls area; there were even trailer courts for retired middle-class couples as well as for war workers.

Suburban America was mainly middle-class America. It was recognized as such by the builders who laid out the houses at middle-class prices for middle-class incomes and living, and also by the department stores and chain stores which hastened to set up suburban branches. In fact, there are some who discuss the American suburbia largely as a business market which came into being as a prosperous middle-class appendage to the new marketing methods. But the truth was that the new middle class, comprising corporate and government bureaucrats, advertising and sales executives, technicians, professional people, and white-collar workers represented the growing point of the American class system. Anxious to live under better conditions than the crowded apartments in violence-ridden neighborhoods of the city, they sought "warmer" living in communities which would be within striking distance of the cultural services of the metropolis. It gave them the sense of status that was crucial to their self-respect. It enabled them to have the best of both worlds—of the big city and the small town.

Thus the suburban movement was an effort of the new middle classes to find a garment for their living that would express outwardly the changes that had already taken place inwardly in their image of themselves and in their relation to their society. They no longer wished to be identified with the "city masses," nor could they stand the anonymity of urban life where the lonely are terribly lonely and no one knows anybody else who happens to live in the same big apartment house. They were the transients, living in an era of transiency, and therefore they were all the more seized by the panic of temporariness: thus they wanted a home of their own, whose mortgage they could at least in part pay off, with whose lawn and garden they could mix their sweat. and where they could putter in a toolshed or garden and have a garage with a car of their own that could carry them away from it all. This was class in action—that is to say, a class personality assumed in the act of striking new roots for itself.

So the would-be suburbanite picked his plot and his house type and got his homeowners' loan, and made a down payment. He moved his belongings to a row of Cape Cod or "ranch-type" or "split-level" houses. His wife furnished it to look like the layouts in *House Beautiful* and she shopped in supermarkets, highway stores, and shopping centers where she could park and get everything at once. She filled the house with the latest kitchen appliances, and there was a TV set in the living room. There were rows of middle-priced sedans and hard-top convertibles lining the block which were as interchangeable and standardized as the houses, deep-freezes, TV sets, magazines, processed foods, and permanent waves that a community survey would reveal. Husband and wife wore casual clothes which gave them a sense of release from the "rat race" of competitive dressing, while giving them also a leisure-class "country" feeling. They did without domestic help, except for an occasional baby-sitter or cleaning woman; they mowed and manicured their own lawns, cooked their own meals, and with the aid of self-help manuals they did for themselves on a variety of chores where outside expert help was too costly. The husband was in the city most of the day, and an intensive father from the time he came home from work until the children went to bed. It was calculated that in a lifetime, as a commuter, he traveled a half million miles (twenty times around the world) between home and office. But the reason he endured perpetual motion was that he might occupy that secure spot in the center of his tornado—in this case, the middle-class status of suburbanite.

As a way of life it defied all the traditional claptrap about American individualism. It was largely standardized and to a surprising degree collectivized. The intensive study of suburbia included in William H. Whyte, Jr.'s *The Organization Man* depicts brilliantly the emerging way of life today which may become the dominant way of life tomorrow. The suburbanites found new roots for their lives in a new sense of neighborhood which was closer than anything in previous American experience except college dormitories or fraternities or the communal settlements of the early nineteenth century. The neighbors in the same apartment court dropped in on one another with casual intimacy, rarely bothering to knock. Not only did the doors within houses tend to disappear (for economy, and to give a sense of space) but the outside doors ceased to have much function, and picture windows took their place. Newcomers were expected to become "outgoing" and to "join the gang"; introversion was frowned upon, and the society of ex-introverts was like the society of ex-sinners. There was intensive "joining" in club work and community participation, including greatly increased church membership, and there were daily morning get-togethers of the women in *Kaffeeklatsches*. There was little chance for the contemplative life. Privacy became "clandestine," in the sense that those who sought it did so apologetically. "Keeping up with the Joneses" was considered a form of exhibitionism; instead of "conspicuous consumption" the rule became "inconspicuous consumption," so that no one would embarrass anyone else. There were car pools for shuttling children to school and back; there was almost communal use of bicycles, books, and baby toys; there was an enforced intimacy, so that everyone's life was known to everyone, and no one had to face his problems alone. In Whyte's phrase, the suburbanites were "imprisoned in brotherhood."

This kind of living has some elements of the co-operativeness-in-crisis of the American frontier, some elements of Army life, and some of Socialist collectivism. The thinkers who celebrate the mystique of the organic community as against the atomistic individual may shudder a bit when they study the American "package suburb" as the flowering of the community impulse under conditions of American standardization. What made the standardization even bleaker was the uniformity of age, income, and class outlook. In their early stages these suburbs tended to comprise mainly young married couples (there were no bachelors and few chances for unmarried girls), with an average income of between $6,000 and $7,000, with children below ten (the childless couple was an anomaly, as were old people), and with a strikingly similar class outlook that was at once tolerant, mobile, hardworking, ambitious, and hopeful for the future.

But it would be a mistake to call it an entirely one-class society, except in the sense that so much of the new America is middle class. The big suburban "development" was not nearly as selective as the earlier and smaller suburbs had been. It had to appeal to a mass market, and so it accepted Catholics and Jews as well as Protestants (while drawing the line at the Negro), clerical and technical as well as professional groups, blue collar as well as white collar—taking all of them into the same neighborhood. The common denominators were income, age, and reliability. It was a democracy of a kind, on a broader spectrum of inclusion than was true of the "residential" and "restricted" neighborhoods in the cities and the earlier suburbs. Yet its exclusion of Negroes, mainly for fear that they would cheapen real-estate values, showed how limited a democratic dream it still was, and how the same dependence on the market that released it from some of the fetters of prejudice kept it fettered in others.

Suburban society was deeply involved with the mobile elements of the American class system. As a man moved from production line to foreman to shop superintendent or from salesman to division manager to sales manager, he would also move from one type of suburb to another. As the family income went up by stages the family moved from court apartment to ranch house and learned new ways of behavior, new standards of tastes, and met new circles of friends to keep pace with its rise. To some extent even the "lower-class" family could find its suburban niche—that of the plumber or carpenter, for example, which could live in the middle-class neighborhood to which the family income admitted it, even though the occupational level was that of the worker. But these gradations were roughly inside the broad limits of the middle class, and there was little of the sense of class crossing, class transcendence or class betrayal that one found in a less homogeneous society. The extremes of income were in the central city, not in the metropolitan rings.

I don't mean that Suburbia, U.S.A., is a conformist society. Its outer aspects are standardized and its ways of life tend to be uniform; yet this is different from conformism. The social intimacy that prevails in the suburb is partly a quest for roots, partly (as I have said) a flight from the temporariness and the loneliness of American life. To some extent it is also an effort to mitigate the bleakness of spending one's life within the confines of the same corporate "organization" and in pursuit of the same technical or sales proficiency. The chance to be intimate with people of different faiths and backgrounds, to share with them the experience of building a new community, and to take part in group action is an appealing one to those who have absorbed the cultural ideals and stereotypes of America. It would not be easy to impose conformity from without upon the suburbanites; but the conformity that comes from mutual accessibility and a yearning for group "belongingness" needs no outside pressures because the impulses from within are leveling ones. There were some observers who feared that this was the kind of society which the "organization man" would ultimately create in the image of his corporate ideal—a one-neighborhood, one-gang, one-class, one-perspective society.

There was substance to the fears. When Erich Fromm, among other writers, singled out the herd aspect of suburbia for attack he was adding a new facet to his escape-from-freedom thesis. But when, in his *Sane Society,* he added a vision of the way out which was strikingly similar to the Fourierist communities of the nineteenth century, he ignored the fact that it is precisely in the suburb where you would find a kind of new Fourierism. The defect of individualism is isolation, the defect of community living is standardization and conformism.

Meanwhile few of the suburbanites had such fears or reflections. Instead they had a stir of excitement in them because they had a widening of horizons and an accession of experience. What G. M. Trevelyan said of the English middle class in the eighteenth century might apply equally to this segment of the new American middle class in the mid-1950s: "Meanwhile the hour was theirs and it was golden."

But the golden hour was streaked with dross and was bound in time to pass. A one-class community like the new suburb was a community without a labor supply, and hence without an industrial base. The balanced community is not to be achieved without paying a price. The price is that of refusing to withdraw from the diversity and bustle of American life, but of embodying some of its noise and grime along with its energies. The parents in most American suburbs were certain they wanted only "the best" for their children in the way of schools, yet they were usually unwilling to subsidize that "best" by including taxable industries in their communities—even on the assumption that they could attract them if they tried. Often they rezoned the suburbs in order to keep out "undesirable" income groups and then wondered why their schools, thus cut off from a cross segment of an American life, proved to be aseptic and sterile. In the long run the suburb would have to turn by an inevitable tropism toward the centers of industrial life and find links with those centers.

There was also the question of the relation between the home and the job. The ideal of town planners was that a man would be able to walk to work and walk home after work. But when the reality of the suburb came, the journey to work was dependent on the automobile and became in most cases a traffic struggle every morning and evening. The newer trend involved a migration of a good deal of the commercial and industrial activities out of the central city into the suburban and metropolitan areas, so that large numbers of suburban dwellers ceased to be Central City commuters but found their jobs on the rim, closer to home. If these trends continued there was a good chance that the industrial and residential zones would be intermingled in the complex pattern, as was already true of the northern New Jersey area in the mid-1950s.

This meant a loose, sprawling cluster city, spreading out across the landscape, still depending on the automobile, but with job-home patterns now running both ways instead of only one. Unexpectedly it came closer to Frank Lloyd Wright's Broadacre City than to the comfortable and segregated "new towns" about which the English and American planners had dreamed. When I said earlier that the trend toward suburban America would continue I did not mean that the suburbs, growing in numbers and importance, would be self-contained, insulated entities. The phase of dispersal from the city was bound to be transformed into a phase of re-integration of the city and suburb in some pattern.

To take New York as an instance, it was clear that the five boroughs were reaching out across state barriers and forming—along with the suburbs in a larger industrial-residential complex—a vast cluster city. Its extent could scarcely be calculated because its boundaries spread out in an octopus pattern. In the 1950s, it had reached fifteen million people, perhaps more; by 1975 it would have passed twenty million people—larger than many sovereign countries. The migration to the suburbs changed the character of the central city too, leaving it an "underdeveloped area" which needed rebuilding and renewal, and leaving it also an area of steep class contrasts, with a diminishing middle class to mediate the abrupt differences between the rich town-house families and the low-income groups, often Negro and polyglot.

But neither the city nor the suburbs could survive by themselves: I have described what the new suburban way of life meant and the functions it filled; the city continued to serve its own constellation of functions, in industry and finance, in fashions, in recreation and the arts, in intellectual stir. Together the city-suburb complex would have to discover some new form of a cluster community government, which would require creativeness if it was to hurdle all the obstacles of law, habit, and convention. Yet whatever happened to the cluster community as a whole, the suburb was destined to be a permanent part of it, not as a hinterland to the city but as an equal among equals.

All this was being accomplished by Americans at considerable social and aesthetic costs. The cluster city, filling in the interstices that had once existed between cities, was consuming open space voraciously. There was often the kind of ugliness in the landscape that made a British writer, watching the same thing happening on his own countryside, call it a "subtopia." Yet here as elsewhere the Americans were accomplishing a transformation in their way of living which, despite its improvised quality, was an exciting response to their new needs and conditions of life. They were doing it in their own way. They did not follow the British lead of the "new towns" approach, although a number of the cities that were being planned for government and industrial workers around the centers of atomic experiment and power were "new towns." Nor did they follow the earlier American architectural dream of a landscape dotted with "Greenbelts." To the extent that a balanced community was emerging—which was doubtful—it represented a balance not within the central city nor within the new suburb, but between the larger frame of the cluster city.

It looked as if Americans were achieving this only through a chance combination of pressures and changes. If there was an internal logic in the improvisation it was the logic to be found in the rest of the American pattern.

Chapter TWO

THE PASSING OF THE

OLD ELITES

Introduction

A. The Old Elites

B. Forces of Change

TRADITIONALLY, the most familiar images associated with urban politics have been the machine and the boss. For well over half a century, the figure of the city boss dominated the political life of our major urban centers. The character of machines varied somewhat from city to city, but typically they were sustained by the votes of the many poor, often recent immigrants who received in return a variety of social services, patronage, and petty gratifications. To pay for those services the machine siphoned money from the public treasury or extracted tribute from those who desired favors. Among those who benefited from and condoned these practices were the economically powerful who profited from city contracts and assorted forms of political protections. The urban political machine was a political oligarchy which drew its sustenance from the economic extremes. The middle class was excluded and left shocked and impotent as it viewed the excess of corruption and machine influence.

A whole generation of journalists referred to as the "Muckrakers" dedicated itself to exposing the political machines. But while the big city machines were portrayed in headlines, less well publicized hierarchical political systems were developing in many smaller urban places. After the new cities passed through the democratic frontier phase, a second period, which might be termed the period of "indigenous capitalism," appeared. Some local entrepreneurs, through luck or ingenuity, gained wealth and with it came political power. These "indigenous capitalists" often became involved in local government through their interest in low property tax rates and the discouragement of labor union organizers.

Today, in most of our small cities and towns, only the vestiges remain of these old family systems. The wealthy and powerful elite who lived on the hill remain only as a stereotype in many of our popular novels or as local lore reported in the community studies of the sociologist.

The machine and the small city economic elites lost control, but not all at once. There were various factors contributing to their demise, but the events associated with the New Deal and World War II were probably the most significant. The New Deal radically re-oriented the content of local government by nationalizing labor and welfare policies. As a result, a whole new set of expectations and motivations for local government were developed. During the same period, the nationalization of American industries was accelerated, and the mines and mills of the old indigenous capitalists were absorbed into national organizations. The political outlook of the new branch manager varied drastically from that of the local owner-operator who was his predecessor. Lastly, there were drastic changes taking place in the character of our national population. The post-war generation was not only further removed in time from the ethnic environment of its parents, but also spatially removed, as Americans began living a more nomadic existence. The young college graduate employed by the big organization which insisted on frequent moves across the country typified the post-World War II generation. All of these forces generally foredoomed the older system of political control. Whether there are now newer forms of political elites arising to take the place of the old is a question which will be reserved for later treatment.

The readings which follow are divided into two parts. Gosnell and the Lynds wrote in the early thirties. They describe the old elites and their sources of power. The two excerpts from Gosnell are concerned with the relationship of the machine to the "little man" and to the economically powerful. The Lynds are concerned with the political-economic control group which typified the period of "indigenous capitalism." These writers foresaw very perceptibly the seeds of destruction of these systems.

The second set of readings deals with some of the forces which ushered out the old system and are creating a new one. The passage by William Foote Whyte, from a book subtitled *The Social Structure of an Italian Slum,* traces the changing patterns of politics in an eastern city where the defeat of an old ward has dramatized the change. Lubell continues the theme of the changing political values and geography of the new urban generation. Norton Long considers the new industrial executive and his role in local government. Finally, Morton Grodzins reminds us that as the Negro is filling our core cities, metropolitan politics is being profoundly changed. Current urban politics, therefore, is not simply the reincarnation of the ethnic politics which predominated a generation ago.

A. THE OLD ELITES

2. *Machine Politics*

HAROLD GOSNELL

(The central question of the book *Machine Politics* is why Chicago was so impervious to the New Deal reforms. None of the ethos or political values which characterized the national Democratic administration had permeated the Chicago Democratic party and government. The answer which Gosnell gave is "The Machine.")

In order to investigate the relief and friendly activities of the party organizations in Chicago, . . . nine hundred precinct captains interviewed were classified by date of interview and type of benevolent activity. . . .

Reprinted from *Machine Politics: Chicago Model* (Chicago: University of Chicago Press, 1937), pp. 70–74, 183–84, 191–93, by permission of the author and the publisher. Author's footnotes omitted. Harold Gosnell is a professor of political science at American University.

As in Boston, New York, and Philadelphia, so in Chicago the precinct captains were ready to distribute material goods to those of their constituents who were in need. One half of the precinct committeemen interviewed in 1928 said that they handed out food. These party workers were found in the depreciated residential areas of the city, where even in the prosperous twenties employment was irregular. At the beginning of the depression some of the ward organizations in the poorer sections of the city made valiant efforts to maintain soup kitchens. For a while some of the Italian committeemen bulldozed grocers and butchers into making contributions to Al Capone's famous free-lunch center. In return the merchants' short-weight scales were overlooked by the city scaler. As the economic crisis continued, it became impossible for the political organizations to continue elaborate food-dispensing facilities. In 1936 more of the precinct captains handed out food than in 1928; but they did it, for the most part, in emergency cases. One boss of a slum ward shrewdly remarked that he did not believe in giving food because it was finished off in fifteen minutes and then where was he. Instead he took the six dollars and bought the "kids" outfits, and the parents were always grateful.

A smaller proportion of the party officials distributed coal in 1936 than in 1928. One ward committeeman maintained a coal yard in a blighted area at the beginning of the depression, but he found that he could not continue this part of his business. The demands for free coal were so overwhelming and difficulties in making collections were so great that he had to close his retail business. Coal was distributed by party workers when there was some temporary breakdown in the regular administration of relief.

Since the public welfare agencies did not follow a very consistent policy with reference to the payment of rents, the precinct captains in the most depressed areas were able to provide temporary shelter from time to time for those who were homeless or who were about to be evicted. The depression apparently had no effect upon the proportion of party workers giving this type of aid. However, there is no question that the relation of the party organizations to those who were unable to pay rent had changed. In the boom days of the twenties one prominent politician who was a heavy owner of real estate in a working-class area was accustomed to a lenient policy of collections for those who voted right. After a few of the lean years of the early thirties, this party boss was compelled to bring five hundred eviction suits all at the same time. After the Democrats came to power in the various local governments, some of the Democratic precinct captains became more active than Republicans in preventing or postponing evictions. Some of the minor parties used the plight of those who had been evicted as a means of gaining an entree into districts where they had never before made any headway. If the regular relief agencies had not begun to pay rent, there might have been more serious eviction riots than occurred in the early thirties.

The practice of distributing Christmas or Passover baskets has continued during the depression period, although to a lessened extent because of the depleted state of the Republican ward treasuries. Democratic ward organizations which were formerly not concerned with this custom have taken it up in recent years. In fact, every ward in the city now has some families which are in a receptive mood for party charity around the holiday season. The Democrats have recently organized their Christmas giving on a grand scale. Teachers of the public and private schools are urged to sell tickets to a championship high-school football game, the proceeds of which are used for the mayor's Christmas fund, which is administered by the ward organizations.

In the foreign-born neighborhoods there are frequently many families in which the relations between the parents and children are strained. The new generation tends to discard the old-world cultural patterns, and the parents have many discipline problems. In an Italian settlement a precinct captain said that one part of his work was the solving of the problem of the "dago kids" who cut school and hung out all night with bad gangs. On the day that I saw him he said that he had placed such a child in a boarding school for a working mother. This same unit official said that he regarded it as very bad policy to interfere in domestic disputes. His comments on this subject were spicy but not printable. One-quarter to one-third of the precinct captains interviewed in 1936 said that they gave advice on domestic and family matters when asked. This was a slightly smaller ratio than was obtained in 1928.

Since the political parties in the United States have very limited financial resources of their own, it is necessary for them to rely upon the governmental agencies to supply most of the needs of their constituents who are in want. They act as brokers for the various governmental services filling the gaps left by the red tape provisions of the bureaucrats. Party workers refer their voters to the proper authorities and try to claim as much credit for themselves as possible.

During a period of large-scale unemployment, precinct committeemen try to function as job brokers. All the different governmental offices —federal, state, county, sanitary district, city, school, and park—the principal public utility concerns, and various private companies are approached for jobs. . . .

What is the balance sheet of machine politics in an urban center such as Chicago during a period of economic crisis? On the credit side of the ledger should be placed the success of the bosses in softening class conflicts. By granting petty favors to various nationalistic and local groups, by taking advantage of the subsidies offered by the national government, by keeping the attention of the voters distracted by factional quarrels and sham disputes, the party machines have kept minor party movements from gaining any headway. From the standpoint of the business leaders, this function of parties has been very useful. Some of the submerged groups may not be so appreciative, but the fact remains that during the years 1930–36 the city was comparatively free from violent labor disputes, hunger riots, and class warfare. The decentralized, chaotic, and inadequate character of the governmental organization of the city has discouraged far-reaching demands upon local authorities.

During the depression the machine has also acted as a kind of buffer for the various governmental agencies which have had to deal with the distressed. Eviction cases, emergency hunger cases, and emergency clothing shortages were sometimes cared for in first instance by the ward and precinct committeemen. The relief activities of the party workers were not systematic and, of course, were not disinterested, but they were devoid of red tape. Ward heelers asked no embarrassing questions, and they supplied at once any material aid they could. The demands of the period were such that the party organizations could not hope to meet more than a minute fraction of them, but they did leave the impression that they knew the ropes of the relief game.

The stability of the machine was reassuring to various groups that no upsetting innovations would be tried in local government. Ward leaders in particular showed an amazingly low turnover, considering the stresses and strains that accompanied the economic crisis. Business men, journalists, underworld leaders, bankers, and labor chiefs knew that they could count upon the local machine to do business in the old way in spite of the changes that had taken place in the role of the national government. Inefficiency in local government could be tolerated if it meant resistance to the extension of the local public services. The largest industrialists, newspaper proprietors, bankers, and gambling kings did not want a state income tax, a modern tax-collection system, or an expansion of municipal services and budgets. Party bosses were a bulwark against such changes. Those citizens who might have benefited from such modifications of the role of local government were indifferent, deficient in promotional skills, misled by the press, and disillusioned by the failure of reform waves to leave many permanent traces. . . .

If democracy is to survive in troublesome times like the present, it will have to have a firmer foundation than the cohesive power of

public plunder. Too often the methods employed by party machines
to finance their various activities have given rise to the charge that our
democracy is a demagogic plutocracy. As long as the parties rely upon
contributions from business men who are seeking special favors, criminal elements which are seeking protection against interference on the
part of the law-enforcing authorities, and office-holders who regard their
loyalty to the party above that to the state, cynicism regarding the electoral process will be widespread.

The power of money in American municipal politics could be regulated to a much greater extent than it is at present. The floodlight of
publicity, before and after elections, regarding the sources of campaign
funds and election expenditures, has weakened boss rule in a number
of states and cities. In addition, the regulation of certain types of expenditures, such as the hiring of party workers and watchers on election
day, has reduced the size of the machine vote where it has been tried.
Many of the states have inadequate corrupt-practices acts, and Illinois
is one of the states which has no law regulating the use of money in
elections.

Legal regulations are necessary in the fight against the spoilsmen,
but they are not sufficient. The American constitutional system is such
that it has tended to inculcate a legalistic mode of thinking about social
problems. We have had a naïve faith in the power of legislation—constitutional, statutory, and local—to change our habits and keep us good.
The colossal failure of the "noble experiment" with the constitutional
prohibition of the manufacture, sale, and transportation of alcoholic
beverages has, to some extent, shattered this faith. Laws which run contrary to the mores of an important element of the population can only
be enforced at a social cost which is prohibitive. On the other hand,
a legal device designed to purify politics is workable only if someone
is concerned with seeing that it does work. If machine candidates are
elected to the important appointing offices, they will find methods for
circumventing the civil service laws. Even the most perfectly drafted
election law can be manipulated by unscrupulous politicians who are
not carefully watched. The best that positive law can do is to create
a legal framework which makes the perversion of public office for private
profit risky and which facilitates the expression of civic points of view.

If the struggle against the party machine is to be successful, more
democratic methods for financing political campaigns must be devised,
local parties dedicated to the ideal of voluntary precinct work must be
organized, and the citizens must be educated to demand services of the
government rather than special favors from the politicians. That all of

these things are possible to achieve in the present generation has been demonstrated by a number of cities, American and European. The will to achieve has been lacking in some places—high places as well as low places.

Looking at the problem of urban democracy in the United States from a long-run point of view, the picture does not appear as gloomy in all aspects as Thomas Jefferson painted it one hundred and fifty years ago. In the past seventy-five years or so, machine voters have been recruited for the most part from the ranks of the unadjusted foreign-born groups, the unassimilated migrants from rural areas, the transient workers, and other such elements. The sinews of campaign warfare came from the robber-barons of American industry, particularly the real estate and the utility magnates. With the cutting-off of immigration, the slowing-up of the migration from the farms to the cities, the declining of the birth-rate of the newer immigrant groups, the maturation of the industrial revolution in the country, the growing socialization of the policies of the government, particularly the national government, the machines will have fewer and fewer persons to draw upon as the years go by. That section of the electorate which reads no daily newspapers, which depends upon petty handouts from politicians, and which is deficient in formal civic training will grow less and less. It may be that at the end of the next seventy-five years the problem of building up civic morale in the great metropolitan centers will not seem so hopeless as Jefferson thought it was or as some who live in the twentieth century now think it is.

3. *The X Family: A Pattern of Business-Class Control*

ROBERT S. LYND AND HELEN MERRELL LYND

(The objective of the second Middletown study was essentially the same as that of Gosnell. The Lynds wanted to assess the impact of the Great Depression on the way decisions were made in Middletown. They found the situation unchanged, protected by the "thick blubber of custom." The community re-

Reprinted from *Middletown in Transition* by Robert S. Lynd and Helen Merrell Lynd, copyright 1937 by Harcourt, Brace and Company, Inc., pp. 74–75, 75–80, 81–90. Footnotes in original text omitted. Robert Lynd is a professor of sociology at Columbia University.

mained essentially under the control of a business elite. The following passage describes the activities of the X family, the most prominent among this elite. In the remainder of the book, the Lynds point out that the power of the X family did not rest simply upon economic sanctions, but also upon the values which were pervasive in a capitalist society.)

Since *Middletown* was published, some local people have criticized it for underplaying the role of the X family in the city's life. This group of wealthy families, along with four or five others, was not characterized as an "upper class" in 1925, because "these families are not a group apart but are merged in the life of the mass of the businessfolk." Whether or not the earlier study was entirely right in so largely grouping them with the rest of the business class, certainly no local prompting was necessary in 1935 to call attention to their overshadowing position. For, after ten years' absence from the city, one thing struck the returning observer again and again: the increasingly large public benefactions and the increasing pervasiveness of the power of this wealthy family of manufacturers, whose local position since 1925 is becoming hereditary with the emergence of a second generation of sons. Since the ramifying power of this family stems from the economic life of the city, it is appropriate to discuss it here immediately following the city's activities in getting a living.

In and out of the picture of Middletown in 1925 wove the influence of this family of brothers who had come to the city with the gas boom, begun with modest capital and become millionaires, and had ever since held an unostentatious but increasingly influential place in the city's life. The boys had been born on a farm in Ohio, whence the family had migrated during the Civil War by wagon to another farm in western New York State. After receiving a common-school education, the five boys scattered to make their way in the world—one as a farm hand and timber cutter, one to become a doctor, others to develop a small business manufacturing fishing kits. When the latter plant was destroyed by fire, the brothers turned to the glass business. Their original Middletown plant began in 1887 on a $7,000 investment in a plant without foundations perched upon log piers. Now the plant is said to be the largest plant in the world manufacturing fruit jars. All five brothers subsequently lived in Middletown, one of them as a practicing physician and the other four engaged in the management of their glass plant and its extensive subsidiaries. . . .

Half a dozen other family names in Middletown are associated with the city's industrial development, but none of them so competely symbolizes the city's achievements. Of the original five brothers, four remained in 1924; and when shortly thereafter another died, the entire business of the city stopped during his funeral. Two of the brothers remain today, both men in their seventies, alert, capable, democratic, Christian gentlemen, trained in the school of rugged individualism, patrons of art, education, religion, and of a long list of philanthropies; men who have never spared themselves in business or civic affairs; high exemplars of the successful, responsible manipulators of the American formulas of business enterprise. In their conscientious and utterly un-hypocritical combination of high profits, great philanthropy, and a low wage scale, they embody the hard headed *ethos* of Protestant capitalism with its identification of Christianity with the doctrine of the goodness to all concerned of unrestricted business enterprise. In their modesty and personal rectitude, combined with their rise from comparative poverty to great wealth, they fit perfectly the American success dream.

Every American city has its successful businessmen, but the American success story has been kaleidoscopic in recent years. Local giants, the boys who have grown up with the town and made good, have shrunk in stature as rapid technological changes, the heavy capital demands of nation-wide distribution, and shifts in the strategic centers for low-cost production in a national market have undercut their earlier advantages of location, priority in the field, or energy; and as Eastern capital has forced them out or bought them out and reduced them to the status of salaried men, or retired them outright in favor of imported managements. One can classify American small manufacturing cities into two groups: those in which the industrial pioneers or their sons still dominate the local business scene, and those in which "new blood" has taken over the leadership; and it is likely that a census would show today a numerical predominance of the second group among cities containing major industries.

Middletown is, therefore, probably a minority city in this respect. The two remaining X brothers, reenforced by the active entry into the family business of four of the sons and two of the sons-in-law of the family, not only still own and control completely their wide business interests, but have become, amidst the local havoc of the depression, far more locally influential than ever before. It so happens that their industry, the making of glass fruit jars, is one that thrived on the depression; the great plant was not only kept busy, often employing night shifts throughout the lean years, but it returned profits reported to have been among the largest in their forty-five years of business. As the general level of the surrounding ground fell away in the depression, their preeminence increased. Their financial liquidity has been such that, with their public spirit, they have been able to cushion the local impact of the depression at a number of points; and a by-product of their strength in the midst of general weakness has been a marked increase in their banking and personal penetration into a number of areas of the city's business life. Both because of their generous help and this resulting increase in control, and because of a very human awe in the presence of a prestidigitator who can make money out of a business depression, the power and prestige of the X family among the business class in Middletown has grown decidedly with the depression. The fact that a local citizen could, late in 1934, characterize as "the one big point about this town" the fact "that the X's dominate the whole town, *are* the town, in fact" suggests the reason for the separate treatment of the family in this chapter.

Middletown has, therefore, at present what amounts to a reigning royal family. The power of this family has become so great as to differentiate the city today somewhat from cities with a more diffuse type of control. If, however, one views the Middletown pattern as simply concentrating and personalizing the type of control which control of capital gives to the business group in our culture, the Middletown situation may be viewed as epitomizing the American business-class control system. It may even foreshadow a pattern which may become increasingly prevalent in the future as the American propertied class strives to preserve its controls.

The business class in Middletown runs the city. The nucleus of business-class control is the X family. What the web of X wires looked like in 1935 may be seen from the following necessarily incomplete pattern of activities lying more or less on the surface of the city's life:

Getting a Living

(*a*) *Banking.* Middletown had five banks in 1925. When one spoke of "the banks" one meant the two leading banks and the affiliated trust company of one of them, in all three of which the X family had an interest. The remaining two small banks have gone under in the depression. On February 27, 1933, on the eve of the nation-wide bank "holiday," the local press carried the front-page announcement: "X Brothers Guarantee Sufficient Cash to Meet Needs of 3 [Middletown] Banks," followed by a statement from the X brothers that "We have first-hand knowledge that these three [Middletown] banks are in good condition." A fortnight later, when Middletown's banks reopened after the national bank holiday, there remained only one bank, with its affiliated trust company; Middletown had escaped the banking crisis, thanks to the X family, and the community had avoided a serious loss in the case of one major bank through a "merger."

On the board of directors of the one remaining bank are three members of the X family, with one of them as chairman; while on the board of the trust company are the X member who is chairman of the bank's board, one of the sons, and a son-in-law. In addition to the members of the X family, seven of the remaining eleven members of the board of the trust company are also members of the board of the bank. Middletown's credit facilities are therefore very centrally controlled. In addition, one son is a director in one of the city's building-and-loan associations and two other sons are directors in a small "Morris Plan" loan company.

The ramifications of this banking control of the community's credit resources are wide and subtle. Only the insiders know its details, but one picks up constantly the remark in conversation that "The banks now control the Jones plant"—and the Smith plant and the Brown plant. There is probably some measure of truth in the statement by a businessman, who in the earlier study had always proved a reliable source of information, that "If you don't join up with the inner ring, you can't work with them and you can't work against them, and you won't get the credit to run your business if they are not for you." Another member of the business class commented: "It's a one-bank town now. People don't dare complain about the way the Community Fund and other local affairs are run because all of these things stem straight back to the people who control our local credit resources."

Remarks like these must not be taken too literally and sweepingly, and it would be grossly unfair to read into the situation personal malevolence, least of all on the part of the X's at the center of the local control group. This inner financial group is simply the hub of a wheel engaged in running a city.

(b) *Legal Talent.* Middletown's best law firms are retained in one or another of the interests of the X family. This renders understandable the comment of a local paper during the depression that "Lawyers and banks get along here. They maintain a happy relationship here as compared with their conflict in other cities." The personal attorney of a leading member of the X family is city attorney.

(c) *Industry.* The X family has not followed a policy of deliberately seeking financial control of other industries in the city. While they have an interest, direct or indirect, in some of the city's industrial plants other than their glass plant, paper-board plant, and the city's interconnecting trunk railways (which they own entirely), their power in Middletown industry is otherwise largely banking power and the command-

ing power of prestige and example. No secretary of the Chamber of
Commerce could hold his position against X opposition. The statement
was repeatedly heard in 1925 and was again heard in 1935 that the X
influence had at one time blocked the entry of a Ford plant into Middletown in order to avoid the competition of the higher Ford wage
scale. The company's well-known stand in opposition to any considerable organization of local labor, . . . has been the keystone of local opposition to unionization. As a local professional man remarked: "The X's
have a long record of pressures against any assertion of claims by Middletown labor. Their philosophy is 'Keep 'em down—benevolently, but
firmly.' " Businessmen quote the X's alleged threat to move their plant
out of Middletown as evidence of the danger to the city of union
activity. . . .

(d) *Retailing.* During the depression Middletown's largest department store failed. Since it occupied a building owned by the X family,
the most conspicuous retail building in the city, the family has reopened
it as the "X Store." And, like all X activities, it is a far better store than
it was ten years ago under the former management, and a decided asset
to the city. The family is reported to have an active interest in at least
one other retail business, the leading furniture store in which one of
the X brothers is a director, while its indirect banking controls in the
retail field are particularly pervasive. Two dairies, run as playthings
by younger members of the X family, squeezed the local milk market
by pressing X milk into use in local institutions supported in part by
X charity, and in 1934 a large independent dealer capitulated and sold
out his business to the X's and became the manager for them. This kind
of move, again, represents a specific gain to Middletown, as some of
the city's milk is bad while the X milk is very superior. The output of
a brewery in a neighboring city, in which the X family has a large interest as an outlet for its glass bottles, is said to be heavily pushed
against all rivals in the local market.

Making a Home

Since 1925 the X family has literally moved the residential heart
of the city. An outstanding change in these ten years is the development
of the northwest section of the city, the section where the X's live and
the section most remote from local industrial plants, into the outstanding residential section. This shift has been carefully engineered by members of the X family. As a result, the aristocratic old East End, the fine
residential section in the pre-motor period when it was an asset to live

"close in" and even in the early 1920's, runs a lame second to the two new X subdivisions in the West End to which the ambitious matrons of the city are removing their families. Here the family has erected the most fashionable apartment building in town; here too it has recently located one of the two socially correct riding clubs (the other is on one of its farms a few miles out of town); and here the city has its first distinguished modern residential section, giving the city the air of what the local newspapers like to call "big-city stuff."

The X residential development in the West End is related to two other major developments engineered by the X's in that section, adjoining the new subdivisions: the purchase and transformation by the X's of the haggard old normal school into a cluster of beautiful buildings now bearing the name "X State Teachers College," with an associated handsome new laboratory grade and high school that is the envy of the rest of the school system; and the location, adjoining the college, of the new million-and-a-half-dollar hospital, an outright gift to the city by the X family. These combined developments give a distinction to Middletown's West End which no section of the city, grimy with soft coal smoke, had in 1925.

And yet, as one watches this flowering forth of the city under the guiding hand of the X family, one must bear in mind the comment of a local man that "The X's are about the only people I know of who have managed to augment their fortune by the art of philanthropy." After five preceding private normal schools had failed on the weedy property in Middletown's Normal City subdivision, the X brothers bought in the property in a receivership sale in 1917. They arranged with the State to donate the property to the State on condition that a strong State Normal School be built out of the moribund institution. In 1922 the X family gave a quarter of a million dollars to the school toward its new building program. Meanwhile, through the early 1920's when the normal school was quickening into life, the X real-estate agents were quietly buying up parcel after parcel of residential property in the then socially nondescript Normal School section of town. These houses have subsequently been removed or improved and these extensive operations must have involved a tidy profit to the X family as promoters, offsetting their benevolences to the hospital and college.

Training the Young

A member of the X family is president of Middletown's school board, and a prominent X attorney is school attorney. Middletown feels comfortable with a member of this family at the head of its schools.

An editorial comment in June, 1936, says: "There is still a feeling among women's organizations that there should be one woman on the [school] board, but that it is not likely to come about until a year hence, if then, or ever. Mr. X's term will expire a year hence *and there is no likelihood of replacing him if he still wants the job. . . .*" (Italics ours.)

The local college, though a State institution, is said to be X controlled both in its larger policies and in occasional small details. From both faculty and students, very guardedly in the former case and more openly in the latter, one heard of the pressure from the X's against radicalism in the college. One of the X's is reported to have been personally responsible for withdrawing certain books such as Bertrand Russell's *Marriage and Morals* and Dos Passos' *1919* from the shelves. The list of outside speakers invited by the student body is said to be scrutinized by the family. And it is freely reported that students with radical ideas find it difficult to get recommendations for jobs after graduation.

It is not intended here to suggest that X State Teachers College is under deliberate repressive control. Its student body contains the most politically liberal force in the city. What is here suggested is that the college, though a State institution, is so closely watched by the X family and is so dependent upon their power and influence that it tends to follow officially their intellectual and political emphases. This does not, however, mean that all liberal teaching is stifled.

The family's authority in local educational matters is enhanced by the fact that it has also given $1,000,000 to the State University. One brother is president of the University's board of trustees.

Spending Leisure

Both the Y.M.C.A. and the Y.W.C.A. buildings are X philanthropies. The former is reported by the local press to be "the largest and best-equipped Y.M.C.A. building of any town of less than 100,000 population in the United States." The Y.M.C.A. summer camp, a show place in the state, is an outright X gift bearing the name of a member of the family. To it three to four hundred local boys go for a week or two of vacation, some of them on free vacations paid for by the X's. It is characteristic of Middletown and of the X family that free trips to camp are used as rewards for excellence in the Y.M.C.A.-sponsored Bible classes in the schools. While the site for the Y.W.C.A. camp, new since 1925, was donated by a local civic club, it also is heavily X-subsidized.

The local Boy Scout camp is spoken of in the press as the "X Scout Camp."

Personnel and policies in the case of both "Y's" are closely controlled by members of the X family. When a new Y.W.C.A. secretary was needed in 1935, the choice lay directly with one of the X women, who set about looking for "a girl unspoiled by 'Y.W.' training and point of view." Among Middletown's requirements in a "Y.W." secretary are that she shall "reach our industrial girls" but shall not import into town any of the liberal economic thinking of the progressive group in the national offices in New York.

Among the family's other contributions to the leisure-time activities of the city are the extensive gymnasium at the college, where large local gatherings are held, and the college Arts Building—with its handsome auditorium for public lectures and recitals and galleries housing loan exhibitions of paintings and etchings by old masters and moderns from the family's art treasures. As noted in Chapter VII, under this X sponsorship, the artistic center of the city has shifted to the college. The two riding clubs, out of which have sprung during the depression the present great vogue of riding and the annual horse show attracting entries from all over the Middle West, are recent X projects. The Masons carry on their ancient mystery in a huge Temple, thrusting up above the city's skyline, made possible by X money. Among other things for which the city can thank X philanthropy are the donation of the ground and the equipping of the spacious local airport; the rejuvenation of the local county fair on property owned by the family; the donation of an entire city block containing an old mansion as headquarters for the American Legion; an important contribution toward a community drive to build a large field house and athletic field for high-school sports; a city golf course; assistance in the building of a new armory; and the equipping of a children's recreation center affiliated with a South Side church near the X factory. One of the brothers was for years city park commissioner, and the development of the city's park system as well as of the new riverside boulevard is in no small degree traceable to him.

Religion

A number of local churches, including working-class churches, have been helped in their building programs by X generosity. The X family, particularly the older generation, believes in the goodness of

religion and in steady churchgoing. The influence of the older generation is, on the whole, theologically conservative. It would be unfair
to say that their aid to local churches—from contributions to building
programs to playground equipment—is given in order to influence
these churches' teachings. Their gifts are undoubtedly prompted by
a desire to make Middletown a better place in which to live, and to
them as people of long religious tradition the church is an important
community civilizing agency. But, though not so intended, their philanthropy here as elsewhere operates as part of the local business-class
control system. All of business-class Middletown, including its ministers,
hesitates to come out in the open against X causes or X points of view.
One stubborn "liberal" minister is reported to have been "broken" by
the family ten years ago. It is significant that a responsible and informed
local citizen expressed the belief that the minister in the prominent
church attended by most of the family was "acting under orders" when
he flayed from his pulpit incipient political radicalism in X State Teachers College. The significance of this remark lies not in the allegation
that the minister did so act "under orders," which is extremely unlikely,
but in the realization by at least certain perspicacious citizens that
subtle psychological influences operate in such matters. Ministers express themselves very carefully about the X's. One of them, who must
obviously remain completely anonymous, remarked guardedly to the
investigator: "If the X's would only plow some of their big profits back
into the community by increasing by even two or three dollars a week
their low wage scale of fifteen to seventeen dollars a week, instead of
giving so much to philanthropy, they would make Middletown a lot
more Christian place in which to live."

Government

. . . Middletown is a Republican stronghold. The business leaders tend
to be solidly Republican, and in this the X family sets them a conspicuous model. A member of the family is Republican National Committeeman for the state; the family contributes heavily to Republican
campaign funds and to the Liberty League; and they pull a consistently
heavy oar financially and personally for the G.O.P. ticket, national, state,
and local.

In the face of this established situation, a small sensation was
created among Middletown Democrats when, after the turning of the
state and nation to the Democratic party in 1932, one of the abler mem-

bers of the second generation of *X*'s suddenly bobbed up as an influential local Democratic leader and head of the (Democratic) Governor's Commission on Unemployment. The Democratic weekly paper commented in the summer of 1935:

> *Young* X *has done pretty well for a new Democrat who voted the traditional* X *Republican ticket as late as the last general primary. He has laid himself up a job on the school board, as a Democrat, controls the Democratic mayor and county chairman, is the final word in hiring hands in relief work in ten counties, and the acknowledged boss of the Democratic party hereabouts.*

This paper, the erratic personal organ of an old-time swashbuckling editor who was mayor from 1930 through 1934, and the one paper in town that deals baldly with messy local affairs, headlined this situation with characteristic colorfulness:

Democratic Party Here Now a Possession of the Mighty X *Kin: Ruthless in Business and Piratical Forays in Realms of Finance, They Play Both Political Parties on Theory That Heads We Win, Tails You Lose; [and again, in a later issue:] Smooth-running Politics Makes New-fledged Democrat President of School Board; Strides Past D—— and Keeps G——, Republican, as School Attorney over Weak Protest of the Mayor; Young* X *Tells the Democrats Where to Get Off, but His Millions and Influential Family Surround Him With Groveling Servitors.*

The present mayor, a Democrat who was reelected in the fall of 1935, after having served as mayor fifteen years earlier, is now sometimes spoken of as "*X*-controlled." He is said by a political friend to attribute his earlier prison sentence to the opposition of local financial powers, including the *X*'s whom he had antagonized, but now to have remarked that he has "learned his lesson."

It is difficult to get the local values straight in this whole complex of local politics. Undoubtedly, the headlines quoted above exaggerate the situation, and undoubtedly we are not dealing here with the thing popularly called "boss rule." The present mayor is not a mere "tool" of anybody—including the *X*'s and the business group, whose will he has opposed in his efforts to end the relief commissary—but is a well-meaning man, with mellow emotions, a living to make, and, as a local paper remarked, "an inability to say 'no' to his many friends." An acute local observer, whose business involves the close following of such things, submits the following written statement regarding the relations of the X family and the mayor, as of July, 1936:

While there is no apparent working agreement between the mayor and the X's, they are much closer than when he previously was mayor. This arrangement probably came about through [one of the X son's] close connection with the state Democratic administration. [This X son] was an undercover supporter of the mayor in the 1934 campaign, although it is understood that the X family made contributions to both sides. After the election, the mayor named B—— as his city attorney. B—— is a really high type of man and has long served as personal attorney to [one of the X's]. This appointment also brought the X's and the mayor nearer together. Through [this city attorney] and [the son of the X family interested in politics] there have been no great lasting differences between the mayor and the X families, although there have been some rather sharp disagreements in which the mayor did not bow to the wishes of the X's. [The city attorney] usually has supported the mayor in these matters.

On their part, the X family does not seek to exploit Middletown politically in the sense familiar to students of American municipal administration, nor need one read skulduggery, as one local commentator suggested, into the refund of a $52,000 income-tax overpayment by the Hoover administration in December, 1932, to the one of the X's who is a Republican National Committeeman and a heavy contributor to Republican campaign funds. It seems more probable that we are simply confronted here by a situation of conflict between two ostensibly separate but actually interdependent sets of cultural institutions: on the one hand, a set of lagging political institutions fallen into disrepute because of the meager calibre of the men who find it financially worthwhile in this culture to run for municipal office and because of the patent waste and graft incident to their operation; and, on the other hand, a set of economic institutions more ably manned by the best abilities in the male population, somewhat more efficient, and more central to the concern of an industrial community. The operators of the economic institutions do not want to bother with the political institutions; but, on the other hand, they do not want too much interference with their central economic concerns from the political institutions. They, therefore, bother to inject just enough control over the confusion of local politics to insure a tolerable tax rate, support for "sound" municipal cooperation in maintaining an open-shop town, control over the numerically dominant working class, and similar broad policies calculated to enable their central business of money-making to go forward

without too much interference. And all of this is done by men like the
X's with a strong sense of their actions being "in the public interest."

Caring for the Unable

The strong arm of X philanthropies supports all Middletown charities. Year after year the deficit at the close of the Community Fund
drive has been anonymously met on the last day and Middletown has
gone "over the top." Y.M.C.A. and Y.W.C.A. deficits are quietly met.
Company memberships in the latter enable groups of employees to
swim and play basketball. An "X Foundation" handles many of these
gifts and varied things such as seeing that curable tubercular cases are
hospitalized. If funds are needed for seed for community gardens in
the depression, a member of the X family provides the funds. A school
principal in a working-class district adjacent to the X factory is approached and an arrangement made whereby he is given funds from
time to time for incidental welfare aid in his district, and the principal
and his family are sent up to the lakes for a three-week summer vacation. Middletown even has a $17,000 animal pound erected in 1930 by
one of the X's. The editorial comment in one of the papers in 1934 sums
up the pervasiveness of the X's in local good works: "As often has been
the case in a civic emergency, the X brothers and their families again
have come to the community's rescue, this time by providing," etc. X
members are scattered throughout the boards of local charitable institutions and their quiet insistence has been influential in bringing about
a centralized administration and some degree of coordination of Federal and local relief in the depression. As noted above, the new million-
and-a-half-dollar X Memorial Hospital is an outright gift by the family
to the city. Some years ago the family contributed heavily toward the
establishment of a hospital for crippled children in the state capital.

Getting Information (the Press)

The X family has held for some years a powerful stock interest,
loosely described locally as "controlling," in Middletown's morning
paper. This paper is sometimes spoken of locally as "the X paper."
The family also has an interest in a leading daily in the state capital.

In connection with the dissemination of information, one other
point deserves note. A local labor man pointed out in 1935 that the
X's now control, through their connection with the school board, Ma-

sonic Temple, and college, all the large meeting halls in Middletown. Such "control" is at present incidental and inconsequential. This type of situation can, however, assume real significance if, for instance, a labor or radical movement should become marked in Middletown.

B. FORCES OF CHANGE

4. The Defeat of a "Boss"

WILLIAM FOOTE WHYTE

When Boss Joseph Maloney lost his campaign for alderman in 1939, his Cleveland Club lost its last hold upon Cornerville, the South Side, and Welport. The power of the organization had been wasting away for years, and when the final collapse came, there was nothing that Maloney could do except look back upon the happier days from the 1890's through the 1920's, when the Cleveland Club, under its founder, Matt Kelliher, had dominated Ward 4. He told me the story of the club in this way:

We had a captain in every precinct. He was a man who knew everybody in his precinct and could tell how just about all of them would vote. We had quite a variety of precincts. Over beyond —— Street was a pretty high-class precinct. You had to have an educated man in charge there. Then we had another precinct where most of the freight handlers lived. That was a different kind of job.

When people wanted help from the organization, they would come right up here to the office [of the club]. Matt would be in here every morning from nine to eleven, and if you couldn't see him then, you could find him in the ward almost any other time. If a man came in to ask Matt for a job, Matt would listen to him and then tell him he'd see what he could do; he should come back in a couple of days. That would give Matt time to get in touch with the precinct captain and find out all about the man. If he didn't vote in the last election, he was out. Matt

Reprinted from *Street Corner Society, The Social Structure of an Italian Slum* (Chicago: University of Chicago Press, 1943), pp. 194–98 by permission of the author and the publisher. William Foote Whyte is a professor of sociology at Columbia University.

wouldn't do anything for him—that is, unless he could show that he was so sick he couldn't get to the polls. When Matt heard what kind of a fellow the man was, he could make up his mind about trying to do something for him.

When a man got a job through our influence, he would keep on paying his dues, and around election time we would expect him to make some kind of contribution to support the campaign. We never accepted money to indorse any candidate. In that way we kept our independence. . . . When I first ran for representative—I didn't want to run; I was selected by the organization—I contributed $150 toward the expenses, and the organization paid the rest.

In those days we held political office in order to be of service to the people. Of course, if Kelliher thought the city was going to buy a certain piece of property, and he had a chance to get it first, all well and good. He was in the real estate business, and there was a lot of money in that business when the city was expanding. But, with him, service to the people always came first. He never took a cent for the favors he was able to do. Matt and I never sold our jobs or charged for a favor.

In those days we really controlled. We could tell within fifty votes how the ward would go in any election. One time we changed the ward from Democratic to Republican overnight. That was in the mayoralty contest of 1905. There was a meeting in the club till three in the morning right before the election. We printed the slate we were backing and circulated it around as much as we had time for. When the people came to the polls, the captain would ask them, "Do you have the slate?" If they didn't, he would give it to them, and they would go in and vote it. When the votes were counted, we had carried the ward for the Republicans just like we carried it for the Democrats. One time a fellow says to Matt, "I'm not going to vote the ticket this time." There were thirteen votes against us in his precinct, and Matt would have given anything to know who the other twelve were.

Maloney explained the breakdown of the organization in terms of the shifting population, the New Deal, and the rise of "the racket element":

Today everything has changed. We've got a floating population in the South Side now. People are moving out all the time. You can't expect a precinct captain to know everybody any more. It's only in Cornerville that people stay in the same place.

Then the Italians will always vote for one of their own. We recognized them when we didn't need to. They didn't have many votes, and we could have licked them every time, but we gave them Italian representa-

tives. We did it for the sake of the organization. But they wouldn't stick by us. The Italian people are very undependable. You can't trust them at all. They play a dirty game too. I estimate that now there are between eight hundred and a thousand repeaters in Cornerville every election. I've tried to stop that, but you can't do it. You can't tell one Italian from another.

In speaking of the disloyalty of the Italians, Maloney referred actually to a conflict of loyalties. From the time that the Italian immigrants got into street fights with their Irish predecessors, there was bitter feeling between the races. Since the Irish controlled the ward politically, the Italians, as long as they were in the minority, had to follow the Cleveland Club in order to gain any political benefits. In recent years Italians who had the political support of the club were looked upon by Cornerville people as disloyal—traitors to the cause of Italian unity. As the proportion of Italian votes in the ward grew steadily, it was to be expected that the Italians would break away from the Cleveland Club.

To Maloney's charge about "repeating" in Cornerville, which is exaggerated but not otherwise untrue, Cornerville people reply with charges that the Cleveland Club would have fallen years earlier if it had permitted honest elections. My own observations and the unanimous testimony of Cornerville people indicate that the club used repeaters whenever needed. Maloney freely admitted that many of his voters lived outside the ward. "A man has a constitutional right to choose his own domicile. As long as he isn't registered in two places, it's all right." He continued his story:

In the old days it was different. The New Deal has changed politics altogether. With home relief and the W.P.A., the politician isn't needed any more in a district like this. Years ago a man out of work would come to us to see what we could do for him. Now he goes on home relief and then he can get on the W.P.A. That's all he wants. This relief is a terrible racket.

I asked whether a man did not need political backing to get on the W.P.A., and Maloney said it could be accomplished without such aid. I took this question up with Carrie Ravello, the wife of the state senator, and she gave me this answer:

That's right. If you're qualified, you can get on without going to a politician. But it will be four weeks before you get certified, and I can push things through so that you get on in a week. And I can see that you get a better job—if you're qualified. If you want to be a supervisor on a contracting job, I can't tell them, "Make Billy Whyte a supervisor," because you're not qualified for that job. You don't have the experience. I can only do something for you if you're qualified.

The corner boys corroborated some of these statements but added that many unqualified men with strong political backing had been able to get good W.P.A. jobs.

There were many politicians in Eastern City. The important question is: Whose political support was important in dealing with the W.P.A.? I asked Mrs. Ravello how she was able to help her constituents in this field. She explained:

I know Dave Collins. He is the state administrator, head of all the projects in the state. I can go right into his office. He knows my connections with [United States] Senator Corcoran.

I asked how Collins had attained his position.

He was appointed six months ago by the regional administrator. The regional administrator appointed him because he had the support of Senator Corcoran. Billy, I don't care what you say, these days it isn't what you know, it's who you know that counts.

She added that the most important connection one could have for the W.P.A. was the one with Senator Corcoran. Next in importance were connections with Representatives in Congress.

There were important changes in the federal administration of relief after the early days of the New Deal. In the beginning there was a tremendous demand for jobs, and there was no recognized means of distributing them except through the usual political channels. Paul Ferrante, the state senator's secretary, told me that the Ravellos obtained a number of work-assignment slips from a high state official so that, whenever they wished to place a man on a project, they had simply to fill out a slip. As the federal relief setup developed and became established on a permanent basis, the powers of local politicians in dealing with relief were progressively curtailed.

This does not mean that relief was taken out of politics. It means that the pressure had to come from higher up in the political hierarchy. As Carrie Ravello pointed out, she was able to deal effectively with the W.P.A. administration because of her connection with United States Senator Corcoran. If she had not such connections, she could have accomplished very little. This was substantiated by the stories of many other Cornerville people. They did not speak of going to see Senator Corcoran. From the view of the corner boys, his position was so high as to be out of sight. They did speak of soliciting the aid of Congressman Branagan. The congressman had several secretaries, one of whom was a young Italian who lived in the ward. Through him many Cornerville people were able to get W.P.A. work assignments.

There was no state boss to whom Senator Corcoran was responsible. On a smaller scale, Branagan had a similar standing. He had his own organization, and, since he represented several wards in Congress, he was not subject to any one politician in any one of the wards. There was no longer a ward boss in the Matt Kelliher sense in any of these wards. This did not mean that Corcoran and Branagan were independent of all other politicians. They had to perform services for and make informal alliances with other politicians in order to perpetuate their power. The important point is that they dealt with other politicians in their own right and were not subject to dictation from anyone in the areas they represented. With the immense power of federal patronage in their hands, they had achieved such a commanding position that other politicians had to come to them in order to secure their constituents a share in the benefits of the New Deal. With only his own organization behind him, the ward politician had scant power, as this story of Joseph Maloney indicates. He had to subordinate himself to his congressman or United States senator in order to meet the demands of his constituents.

Thus it appears that the New Deal helped to bring about a political reorganization whereby the localized organizations of ward bosses were to a great extent supplanted by a more centralized political organization headed by the United States senator with the congressman next in line, and the ward politicians assuming more subordinate positions.

5. The Old Tenement Trail

SAMUEL LUBELL

Possibly because it lacked the excitement of the Indian wars or because it still is so close to us, the saga of this twentieth-century odyssey of

Reprinted from *The Future of American Politics* (New York: Harper and Brothers, copyright 1951, 1952), pp. 62–63, 64–67, 75–78, 80 by permission of the publisher. Samuel Lubell is a political commentator.

America's urban masses has gone unsung. Yet the parallels between the old western frontier and the new urban frontier are striking.

To Frederick Jackson Turner, who made American historians frontier-conscious, the ever-receding frontier was the zone of most rapid and effective Americanization. At the outer edge, "where civilization and savagery met," was where "men of all races were melted down and fused into a new race." Each new zone of frontier settlement was a "beginning all over again" which took Americans ever further away from dependence on Europe's economy and ways.

That holds equally true for the new frontier. For the urban masses each advance into a new neighborhood has also been a "beginning over again," which took them ever further from their European origins in the case of the immigrants, or, with Negroes, from the Plantation South. There has been much pooh-poohing of social climbing, without appreciation of the fact that it is a vital part of the Americanization process. The move to a "nicer" neighborhood would often be celebrated by a shortening or Anglicizing of names. Items of alien garb would be dropped; foreign accents would lighten. There would be more American food in the grocery stores, less orthodoxy in worship, more intermarriage with other ethnic elements and—as an ironical index of Americanization—more divorce.

The role of the railroads in opening up the Western lands has been duplicated first, by the subway and streetcars and, currently, by the automobile, in making ever newer housing accessible. The role of the pioneer woman was repeated in the immigrant mother who, with the sieve of drudgery, rescued the savings which enabled the family to climb to higher rental reaches. The immigrant mother was also the guardian of respectability on the urban frontier.

Like the Old West, the ever-changing urban frontier has been more "a form of society" than a geographical area. And as the story of America's social evolution could be read page by page in the successive frontier zones through which the pioneer pushed, so the march of the urban masses can be charted by tracing the neighborhoods through which these groups have climbed. . . .

This . . . process of social exploration can be repeated with any of the former minority elements and in all of our larger cities. By going up and down the ladder of neighborhoods through which these different elements have climbed, one can see the progress they have made and the setbacks they have suffered—their clashes and reconciliations with other ethnic elements, and their assimilation into American society generally.

Do you wonder how the manners and habits of Negroes alter when they reach the middle class? In the North Bronx, around Gunhill Road, can be found a group of Negroes, mainly white collar and professional people, who have bought homes in recent years. As if feeling themselves on trial, they are as unlike the Harlem stereotype as imaginable in their habits. Their tastes in clothes and furnishings are sober. They pay cash at the neighborhood stores. At nearby Evander Childs High School their children rate tops scholastically. "Their drive to get an education is terrific," observes Dr. Hyman Alprin, Evander's principal. Oddly, every Negro child in the school takes Latin, as if seeking some mark of culture.

Or, one can follow the trek of the Irish in Boston, from the hilly streets of Charlestown out to Cambridge, on to Arlington and Newton; or of the Czechs in Chicago from South Lawndale, to Cicero and Berwyn. In Detroit the "up-town" upsurge has been eastward toward Grosse Pointe; in Milwaukee it has been northward along Lake Michigan and westward towards Granville.

If land hunger was the propelling force behind the agrarian frontier, the drive behind the urban frontier has been the hunger for social status. The changed nature of present-day political issues is largely a reflection of this contrast between the earlier agrarian frontier and its urban counterpart.

As the pioneers moved westward the obstacles they had to overcome were primarily physical and natural—breaking the sod in the semiarid plains, clearing the wilderness, driving railroad spikes across an untracked continent. Along the urban frontier the obstacles have been primarily man-made. The mountain barriers which have to be scaled are those of rents and restrictive covenants. Unemployment is the drought which could wither one's labors. The swiftly flowing rivers which have to be forded and bridged are those of class and social distinction, none the less treacherous because they are intangible.

The politics of westward expansion were bound to be sectional, since some parts of the country unavoidably lagged behind others and the newer settlements were often indebted, colonial offshoots of the older creditor areas. In contrast, the urban migration was bound to quicken class and social conflict, mirroring the uneven progress toward acceptance by different social groups.

In today's perspective, the Republican-dominated era can be said to have centered around one enormous historical fact: the spanning of the continent and the creation of a nation-wide economy. In the perspective of the future, we may look back upon today's Democratic era as an adventure in social unification, in the creation of the kind of nation-wide social structure which an industrialized civilization requires.

In any case, the reappearance of the frontier in a new urban form has been one of the most important political forces of our time. It explains the divisions between the old and new middle class. It generates the explosive force behind the civil rights issue. . . . It also has been transforming the big-city political machines, dooming the old-style political boss.

For the Democratic machines the spoils of office over the last twenty years have been fat indeed. Yet the reigns of the bosses have been growing progressively shorter. Fewer and fewer are dying with their patronage boots on. Usually this is credited to the fact that a beneficent federal government has replaced the political clubhouse in dispensing relief and other favors. Of equal, if not greater, significance has been the simultaneous coming-of-age of most of the old underdog elements.

As its large families have grown to voting age and as it has developed its own leadership, each minority group has been demanding an ever-increasing share of political recognition. Today, the plight of the Irish Democratic bosses, who managed most of the big-city machines, is not unlike that of the wearied rulers of the British Empire, who are everywhere on the defensive before the rising "nationality" elements they once ruled.

Tammany Hall, once as Irish as St. Patrick, fell to the Italo-Americans in 1947. A year earlier the Kelly-Nash dynasty in Chicago was superseded by Jacob Arvey, a Jew. In 1949, a coalition of dissident Irish, Italo-Americans and Polish-Americans terminated the thirty-two year, "I Am the Law" role of Frank Hague in Jersey City.

Currently, the most dramatic illustration of this trend is the rise of the Italo-Americans. In 1948 eight Italo-Americans were elected to Congress, twice as many as in any previous year. Two of these congressmen were from Newark, which in 1949 named an Italo-American mayor. Hoboken, Passaic and Paterson are among the other larger New Jersey cities which have elected Italo-American mayors since the war's end. Compared with 1936 more than twice as many Italian names are answering the legislative roll calls in Pennsylvania, New Jersey, New York, Connecticut, Rhode Island and Massachusetts—the six states with the heaviest Italo-American concentrations.

The intensifying Irish-Italian feud which has accompanied this rise wracks not only the Democratic party but also the Catholic Church whose hierarchy in this country is mainly Irish. It rocks gangland, too.

The struggle between James Pendergast and Charles Binaggio in Kansas City ended in violent murder. Of the gangsters cited by name in the Kefauver Crime Report, almost one half are clearly Italian.

That does not mean that Italians are peculiarly susceptible to criminal activity. The battle to control the nation's rackets now being pressed by Italo-American racketeers is part of the same "coming of age" process which is reflected in the growing frequency of Italian names on big league baseball and college football teams. Until 1929 not a single Italian name was listed on Walter Camp's annual all-star football team. Since then there has been hardly a year in which there wasn't at least one Italian name on the all-star list. . . .

What is often described as "The March of the Masses" is usually thought of as a radical, even insurrectionary development. The very phrase murmurs suggestions of mob rule and political lynching. Yet, with the Italo-Americans . . . their political upthrust was sparked not by hard times but by boom times. Their leadership came not from the most oppressed and discontented, but from those with the strongest middle-class drive.

The same pattern holds for other minority elements as well. None were stirred to political uprising when their grievances were heaviest. It was as they emerged from the social cellar and got their first whiffs of the fresher, middle-class air that their political spirits quickened. The key to the political progress of any minority element in this country would seem to lie in just this success in developing its own middle class. Sheer numbers alone are not sufficient for political power—witness the ineffectiveness so far of the Mexican-Americans in the Southwest. To be effective, numbers must be supported by economic, educational and social progress.

The climbing masses can hardly be described as a conservative force. But are they as radical as they appear? Since their emergence stirs class conflict, it is easy to view their rise as confirming Karl Marx's dire prophecies of class warfare. Actually we are witnessing an almost complete refutation of the Marxian thesis. Our class struggle, if it can be called that, arises not from the impoverishment of the masses but from their progress. It is evidence not of the failure of the American dream but of its successes.

Despite all the talk of monopolistic control of American economic life and the supposed end of opportunities, even the most downtrodden elements have been able to climb. And if the urban masses are challenging the *status quo*, their challenge, essentially, is a demand for acceptance into our predominantly middle-class society.

The trends of our times seem to be strengthening this middle-class bias of American politics. Not so long ago political appointees were more often graduates of saloons and street gangs than of universities. Old-timers in the Bronx can remember an amusing pair of local Irish judges who not only knew no law but couldn't even read. One of these judges, after hearing a case, would take down a thick lawbook, pore over it learnedly and announce, "This is a fine point of law, I will reserve decision."

At lunchtime he would hotfoot it to a higher court, get coached on the law, return and announce his verdict.

The second judge, equally unlettered, kept making a spectacle of himself until he decided to imitate his colleague. After hearing one case, he reached up to the nearby shelf, took down a fat volume and thumbed through it. Making quite a show of learned deliberation, he announced, "An exceedingly fine point of law is involved. I think I'll reserve decision." The spectators burst into laughter. The book the judge had consulted so learnedly was the telephone directory.

Today college training or its equivalent is required for an increasing proportion of appointments. To register its political strength a minority group has to have its own lawyers or leaders with equivalent training. In turn, the broader the middle-class base developed by any upclimbing element, the more clamorous become its demands for political recognition.

Patronage is peculiarly important for minority groups, involving much more than the mere spoils of office. Each first appointment given a member of any underdog element is a boost in that element's struggle for social acceptance. It means that another barrier to their advance has been lifted, another shut door has swung open. Whenever Roosevelt nominated a Negro to a white collar post in the federal government, for example, he transmitted a vicarious thrill to every young Negro who thought instinctively, "Maybe there's a place up there for me or my child."

The opening of these new opportunities, in turn, stimulates the political consciousness of the group, encouraging its leaders to eye the next highest post on the patronage ladder.

In most northern cities, the Democrats have actually developed a ladderlike succession of posts, through which the political progress of various minority elements is recognized. Just as one can judge how far any minority has climbed economically from its position on the residential ladder, so one can measure its effective political power by its place on the patronage ladder.

The earliest stirrings of any group usually are appeased by an appointment as assistant district attorney, which entails little more than that some members of the group be educated as lawyers. A county judgeship, on the other hand, requires a candidate who has succeeded in a lower post, a large enough vote to withstand the competing claims of other minority blocs, and the economic backing to finance a campaign. Similarly, with elected posts, the solid vote of an ethnic element may win an aldermanic district or a seat in the legislature or even in Congress. But no minority group can be said to have arrived politically until its members can appeal beyond their own ethnic boundaries, to win a county-wide or city-wide election.

This system of succession obstructs as well as advances minority progress. By compelling each element to serve its apprenticeship in lower posts, the machine bosses have been able to slow and temper the rise of the underdog elements. Largely through this system of seniority and by playing off one ethnic element against the others the Irish have been able to cling to a much larger representation among office holders than their voting strength would warrant.

The emphasis on hyphenated candidates, or what has come to be known as "League of Nations" politics, is often condemned as "un-American." Yet it is really an integral part of the Americanization process, serving as a means through which minority elements are assimilated into the structure of government. This was true during the Republican era, when the sons of the Norwegian, Swedish and German immigrants banded together to wrest greater recognition from the Yankee bosses who then controlled the Republican party. It holds equally true to-day. . . .

To sum up, despite the revolutionary changes it brought, the Roosevelt Revolution appears to have strengthened rather than weakened the traditional middle-class basis of American politics. The drive behind the climbing urban masses remains the essentially conservative hunger for middle-class social standing. The leadership of most of the former minority elements is mainly a middle-class leadership. The political apprenticeship each rising element has to serve also makes these elements more dependent on their ability to create a middle-class economic base, from which the resources can be drawn to climb still higher on the ladder.

The fact that both major parties are now actively competing for the vote of the various minority elements holds out the further promise that, in time, the cultural differences which now divide the big-city Democratic following from the Republicans will be steadily blurred.

6. The Corporation, Its Satellites and the Local Community

NORTON E. LONG

The corporation has profoundly changed the role structure of the local community. Increasingly, it replaces the old families as owner and operator of the most profitable local business. In all except the largest communities, a growing number of enterprises are branch plants run by bureaucratic birds of passage with career lines stretching onward and upward to the magic haven of the head office. The libraries, hospitals, and museums that bear the names of leading local families stand out as monuments of a civic past. The charities of the leading local citizen have been replaced by the corporation's committee on solicitations, whose federal-tax-induced beneficence has replaced the older order. In the lesser communities, the officers charged with the duty of corporate almoner are frequently limited to Community Chest and Red Cross, requiring higher approval for any departures from defined head-office policies on company benefactions.

Branch plant managers in their proconsular role are worlds apart from the leading citizen-owners of the past. As Schulze has pointed out in his study of Ypsilanti, their role as economic dominants does not give them the grip on local social institutions possessed by their predecessors.[1] A recent study of a smaller southern community supports the view that branch plant managers are too sensitive to home-office approval to risk rocking the public-relations boat by decisive action. The phenomenon of absentee ownership, on which Veblen lavished his irony, has developed into the practice of absentee management by non-owners. That this lack of ownership interest has made absentee management by corporate headquarters staffs any less responsible, from the point of view of the local community, is doubtful. In fact the professionalization of corporate managements and their public visibility and newspaper accountability seems to have given them a thinness of skin quite uncharacteristic of the earlier race of absentee owners.

Reprinted from *The Corporation in Modern Society*, Edward S. Mason, ed. (Cambridge: Harvard University Press, 1959), pp. 203–8, 210–15, 216–17 by permission of the author and the publisher. Copyright 1959 by the President and Fellows of Harvard University. Norton Long is a professor of political science and Director of Education of the Transportation Center at Northwestern University.

While the local catastrophe pictured by John Barlow Martin in the mine disaster of Centralia Number 5 is a phenomenon of absentee management as well as absentee ownership, it is likely that absentee corporate managers were far more sensitive to newspaper criticism and public opinion than absentee owners.[2] This criticism, flowing along the wires of the press services from the local community, can come to haunt them at their distant executive suites and jar their security and cloud their careers. The mine disaster of Centralia, with its tragedy of well-nigh classic Greek proportions of foredestined doom for the men in the pits, appealing to remote political, business, and union hierarchs to save their lives, dramatizes the general problem of remote control over vital decisions in the local community. In this case absentee corporate control of the mine was paralleled by, and even largely determined absentee political and union control of decisions that could have saved miners' lives. In the Centralia case there was almost the ideal type of the local community so eviscerated of vital decision-making power that it lacked even the elemental capacity of self-preservation.

Yet absentee corporate control is far different from market control, and, while corporate centralization may not be quite the grave-digger of capitalism that Schumpeter warned us it was, it seems inexorably to socialize a kind of responsibility that approaches the political. The management decision made in New York to close a mill in the Piedmont of North Carolina may provoke repercussions in Washington, labor troubles elsewhere, and an unfavorable piece of publicity in the St. Louis *Post Dispatch*. The size of the giant corporation, which at first sight seems to give self-evident verification to the ascriptions of managerial omnipotence given currency in Marxian, Veblenite, and the C. Wright Mills schools of thought, creates a vulnerability both to external pressure and to internal political weakness. As John Gunther in his *Inside U. S. A.* remarked of the automotive titans of Detroit, they resemble Japanese wrestlers, enormous but flabby, easily set quivering by a public-relations panic. A Harvard professor of government in the troubled days of the thirties was asked by a leading public-relations impresario what to do about a client's employees who had welded shut the doors of the plant in the course of a sit-down strike. The professor somewhat callously suggested the use of an acetylene torch. The gentleman from Madison Avenue, in horrified tones, said that this would never do, it would violate the God-the-Father governmental image.

In a short thirty years we have passed from a corporate order whose managerial style derived from the so-called "robber barons," the divine-right Baers, and the public-be-damned Vanderbilts, to the business-school-trained, public-relations-conscious professional of the highly specialized complex corporate bureaucracy of today. While the latter-day manager may not be as other-directed as Riesman and William H. Whyte, Jr., suggest as a nonowner and a professional manager, he has a concern for harmony and the avoidance of trouble that sets him apart from his predecessors. His attitude toward striking employees can never quite have the same sense of outraged feudal lordship confronted with a servile revolt that envenoms the Kohler strike. Nor as a non-owner can he have quite the same view of the corporation as his property to do with as he pleased, by God, as seemed so right and fitting to the self-made Calvinists of American industry's heroic stage.

The company town had an attraction for the older industrialist of the past. The names Lowell, Lawrence, Hershey, Pullman, Kohler sound like so many industrial duchies. The conflict in Marquand's *Sincerely, Willis Wade* illustrates the familiar owner with sentimental and patriarchal concern for employees and local community and the business-school managerialist. A Harcourt finds it hard to close the Harcourt Mills. For Willis Wade it is but a business transaction, albeit one to be treated with finesse, a degree of humanity, and a great deal of public-relations concern. All over the country, the paternalistic company town with mill-supported public service is giving way to a new philosophy that shuns the responsibility and the doubtful glory of conspicuous community dominance. Few corporations today regard it as desirable to have a major portion of the local labor force dependant on their payroll. When business decisions have too visible an effect, management must weigh public relations in the scales with economics, frequently to the disadvantage of the latter. Birch in his study of Glossop, the seat of the Dukes of Norfolk, points out how the Dukes built a branch railroad for the local community, a benefaction it could never expect from the corporations of the present.[3] The modern corporation has found the price of community dominance an inconvenient conspicuousness, that in a day when distant publics are potent, seriously limits corporate freedom of action.

If the corporation no longer views the company town with favor, the same cannot be said of its feelings toward the suburban satellite that enjoys access to a central city labor force but immunity from central city taxes and welfare problems. The literature of corporate location policy, at least latterly, pays homage to the principle of paying the corporate way for its employees' schools and other services. However, the suburb with nothing but the plant and lots zoned for five acres produces a congenial neighborly environment that has its temptations. The move from high-rise, narrow-bay structures to the single story wide-bay modern plant and the tremendous demand for parking space have played a dominant part in the suburbanization of industry. River Rouge, Aliquippa, and other industry suburbs antedate this more recent technologically induced development. Reputedly, the explanation of them resides in company desire to control the local police, avoid central city taxes, and escape responsibility for the relief of their periodically unemployed hands. In one case, anxiety over company control of suburban police is given as a major reason for one of the early failures to secure metropolitan government in the Pittsburgh area.

The strikes that ushered in the great labor-organizing drive of the thirties strained and tested the allegiance of all segments of the local community. The Mohawk Valley Formula, as described by R. R. R. Brooks, successfully pursued, lined up all respectable elements in the community on the side of law and order and against the strikers.[4] Almost as crucial in determining the outcome of the strike as the role of police and militia was the shutting off of credit by the local merchants. In case of a showdown between strikers and mill, whatever their private sentiments, sooner or later the stores and the landlords were bound to side with management.

Perhaps the most important change in the local scene is the growing evidence that this one-sided line-up has shown a dramatic shift. Peter Rossi's studies of Zanesville, Ohio, and Gary, Indiana, show that not only do the local merchants continue to give credit to the strikers, but the whole community, including the police, tends to side with them.[5] While this phenomenon may not be wholly chargeable to the development of absentee corporate control and branch plant management, it seems vitally related to it.

Rossi's data and evidence from other sources point to the effect of the branch plant system on local susceptibilities. Economic dominants who are not, and do not become, part of the local social structure may be as foreign within local communities in the United States as the United Fruit Company in Latin America. The upward-mobile branch plant executive and his associated corporate birds of passage may be as alien as the white plantation manager in the tropics. The phenomenon of colonial nationalism is not irrelevant to the politics and attitudes of local communities in the United States. Southern resentment against "Yankee imperialism" is an old story, but the development of absentee corporate control has given a visibility to alien power in the local community that the impersonality of the market tended to hide. The passing of the regime of the old families has created a gap between positions in the economic and social tables of organization. . . .

The modern large corporation executive likes to think of himself as a professional. Ideally, if not typically, he is the product of a business school. The business schools, *Business Week, Fortune, The Wall Street Journal,* and other media have appointed themselves the task of turning business managers into unimpassioned bureaucrats who worship along with the city manager at the altar of administrative science. In practice this has meant that corporate executives are rather vulnerable to the intellectual fashions that sweep the business schools and the media from which they derive their ideas as to what is currently modish in top-drawer management thinking. This is especially the case with respect to those matters that are remote from the segment of reality that comes under their corporate competence. A St. Louis insurance executive will inveigh against the jurisdictional mess of his metropolitan area in a staff-ghosted speech that repeats uncomprehendingly the clichés of current municipal reform. This activity is good corporate citizenship, the more so as the executive hasn't the foggiest idea as to how the changes he advocates will help his company, though doubtless in all honesty he thinks they will. It is difficult for the corporation executive to avoid a kind of ritualistic do-gooding when he embarks on the unfamiliar role of city father.

Where issues hit home to the corporate profit and loss account, there is a reasonably realistic calculus of appropriate action. At least the executive confronted with choices as to taxes, off-street parking, highways, and other governmental activities that seem to affect his business directly has a basis for rational action. This action may be as shortsighted, as when downtown stores seek to route an expressway through their basements, but at least the calculus is in principle rational rather than magical.

Top positions in the large corporation form a major segment of the prestige structure of the local community. Occupants of these positions are a natural target for the pressgangs seeking to man the local civic-committee structures. The executive finds the civic committee both a burden and an opportunity. Some activities, such as the Community Chest and the Red Cross, are built into company work loads and are even expected parts of a man's job. Moving up in them is part of a man's career. Good marks in them are functional to a man's favorable evaluation by his superiors. A smashing success in a fund drive may be a more visible mark of personal achievement than any company activity makes possible. In many quarters good corporate citizenship is regarded as a major public-relations value. Top management must personify, if not, as Maitland quipped of the British monarch, parsonify the institution. A president of a lesser corporation will candidly avow that his board of directors thought it not a bad thing for him to serve on a committee that might yield first-name acquaintance with the president of a large insurance company.

Such committees are usually safe vehicles for mixing with the prestigious members of the business community and securing pleasant and even useful publicity as a public-spirited leading citizen who represents the kind of corporation that has a "soul." Corporate executives discussing their roles in publicized civic committees point out that their service impresses and pleases their employees.

There is, however, a modicum of danger in the civic committee or even the assignment to a usually merely honorific post on a public board. Top-level civic committees are in the ordinary run merely required to lend their names to ceremonial occasions, the civic luncheon with its press release, the legitimatizing of some civic staff proposal, or, in the more arduous case, joining a plane-load of their peers in a flight to Washington or New York to plead the cause of the Chamber of Commerce in the wooing of a building. The unpleasant side of this otherwise merely time-consuming and occasionally profitable involvement is the frustration and loss of face when the publicized civic ceremonial fails. Usually failure is hidden from view by a change in the newspaper spotlight or obscurity as to just what the ritual is supposed to accomplish in particular. However from time to time newspapers, politicians, and public turn on the corporate elite as the savages beat their idols when they fail to bring rain. The expectation that the top corporate hierarchy should display some kind of effective leadership is fitful but real. The places of the leading families have to be filled or a kind of lubberland emerges. For a variety of reasons, the politicians cannot in the main attain the prestige of members of the corporate hierarchy. Where, however, the corporate elite fails to replace the old families in the top positions of the social structure, a situation results in which the rest of the local society is inclined to regard the management of the corporation as an alien force—almost, as was stated before, as the colonial representative of a foreign imperialism.

The process of suburbanization has placed many corporate managers, in even quite large head-office cities, in positions not unlike those of branch plant managers in smaller communities. The executive tends to be neither an active citizen in his suburban dormitory, nor more than a chamber-of-commerce ceremonial citizen of the central city where his office lies. The suburban politico and small businessman is likely to look on him as a resident alien and a spokesman for the big-town chamber of commerce, rather than for the local interests. In the central city, lack of residence and vote has a crippling effect on a more than ceremonial or checkwriting role. Beyond these disabilities a major, and often neglected, one is that of the corporate executive's preoccupation with his business. Amazingly enough he is busy, and this simple fact accounts for a good deal of his difficulty in competing with others of lesser status who are full-time professionals. The tired and overworked executive is wheedled and wheeled into place by civic and other staffs to provide the needed trappings of legitimacy to their own activities. The very scarcity value of prestige insures that a small group of top executives must stumble from one civic committee to another, without time for preparation and with exhausting demands on the limited time they can rob from their business, their families, and the daily toll of commuting.

Since prestige can only inhere in a few at the top—to spread the load would pack the "House of Lords" and fatally cheapen the titles —the few must pay the penalty of being both overworked and used. Their ceremonial roles are too numerous to be self-directed. Their conspicuousness, the fatal result of corporate status, makes them vulnerable to public demands for their services. These services they can only refuse at the cost of seeming callously aloof from the folk belief in their duties as work givers and civic problem solvers. They must touch for the king's evil whether they will or no. At best they can avoid being had by the numerous band of public and private courtiers who seek to further their own ends through the manipulation of their prestige.

The alienation of the corporate hierarchy from other segments of the local community is the progressive result of the trend toward corporate centralization and the branch plant. Even when top management resides in the headquarters city there is a tendency for it to regard its responsibilities as so national in character as to inhibit conspicuous local citizenship activities. Uncharitably viewed, this might appear a mere rationalization to escape a burdensome chore. However, in many cases the dilemma is sincere enough and Rousseau's caustic remark about the philosophers, that they loved the world in general in order to escape having to love anyone in particular, does not apply. The contrast between top managers whose status is derived from family and inherited wealth—the Rockefellers, the Fords, and the Mellons—and the non-familied is striking. For the man of family and inherited position, conspicuous local leadership has an appearance of legitimacy and appropriateness of role that seems lacking in the other case. In a real sense, a Rockefeller twice removed from the robber baron may be as much an acceptable gentry image as an earlier gentry several times removed from its robber-baron predecessors. The security with which some familied men of wealth have been able to appeal for the suffrages of the public at large is in marked contrast to the anxiety and almost

wallflower-like withdrawal of their associates in the corporate heir-
archy from a dance whose steps are beyond them and whose necessary
contacts repel them.

In an earlier day the utilities, requiring public franchises and deeply
dependent on municipal politics, were in the thick of it. The relationships described by Lincoln Steffens were close and the major figures
in the companies were in intimate and sometimes sordid contact with
the world of politics. The satiation of businesses with the fruits of successful political activity led to a withdrawal from overt and intense participation in the field of local politics. The activity of tending the local political fences became a specialized department in the corporate hierarchy
and was no longer a main concern of top management. The position in
the hierarchy of the man responsible for taking care of the corporation's
local political problems became downgraded and with the intensified
disesteem of politics and politicians, especially at the local level, his
post suffered from the bad odor of its clientele. The courts and a successful lobby with the state legislature permitted a growing neglect if
not contempt for local politics. Suburbanization meant a physical unconcern for all but company-related local services, and the politics of
top management's suburban residence represents scarcely anything
more momentous than the politics of the country club. Thus the
replacement of robber baron, resident owners, and leading families
by a withdrawn managerial elite has left vacant positions in the local
structure.

The managerial elite has been neither willing nor able to fill these
positions except in a ritualistic fashion that seems transparently the
product of company public relations rather than a personal community
commitment and identification. The socially perceived public responsibilities of the manager's positions in the local economic hierarchy have
differed increasingly from their own perception of their role as representatives of the company in the local banana plantation (apologies to
Keynes). While their economic position has made the managers seem
to be the appropriate and duty-bound incumbent of top local civic
statuses, their lack of family legitimacy and enduring local residence
identification in the community makes them more the representatives
of a foreign power than the rightful chiefs of the local tribe. This alien
allegiance on the part of the corporate segment of the local structure is
productive of public disaffection from the corporation and a sense of
anxiety and alienation in the corporate hierarchy. . . .

The reintegration of economic dominants into the local social structure is one of the main problems of our local civic life. This is a problem
not only for the corporation and its alien caste of career bureaucrats; it is

also to an acute degree a problem of labor. The president of a large corporation in a relaxed moment will admit that heads of a national union aren't such bad fellows; they too abominate wildcat strikes. But that Mulligan who leads the local wildcat strike, he's trying to prove something: his local power to the national union. Local autonomy in capital and labor is difficult to reconcile with effective centralized control. And local territorial loyalties provide a fertile field for those who would stir up resistance to the remote control of outsiders with no local legitimization for their power.

Clearly there are wide ranges of corporations and communities with differences ranging from the twenty-thousand-acre corporate ranch with Mexican peons, through the automobile company with a tough union facing a tough management, to the multi-million-dollar insurance company with its docile world of secretaries and file clerks headed by the million-a-year salesmen.

What the corporation is doing to the local community is an abstraction as dangerous as any Weberian ideal type of construction. Yet as an intuitive impression from a broad but scattered collection of data, there seems reason to suspect that the conflict between the corporation as an institutionalized center of loyalties and the local territorial community is real and important. It seems clear also that the vacuum created in the local social structure by the decline of the old owning families and resident economic dominants has upset the informal structure of political power. Whether the public-relations and educational onslaught on the problem of corporate political decline will succeed seems dubious. Reestablishing a valued legitimate elite structure in the local community is a major and possibly insoluble task. In the divided loyalty between corporation and local community, can one or other be more than synthetic? It would be reassuring to be able to say that a system of centralized corporations and unions is compatible with the reality of vigorous local self-government.

Notes

1. Robert O. Schulze, "The Role of Economic Dominants in Community Power Structure," *American Sociological Review*, vol. 23 (February 1958).

2. John Barlow Martin, "The Blast in Centralia No. 5, A Mine Disaster No One Stopped," *Harpers Magazine*, 196: 193–220 (March 1948).

3. Anthony Harold Birch, *Small Town Politics: A Study of Political Life in Glossop* (New York, 1959).

4. R. R. R. Brooks, *When Labor Organizes* (New Haven, 1937).

5. Peter Rossi, "The Impact of Party Organization in an Industrial Setting," to be published in a forthcoming volume entitled "Community Political Systems," edited by M. Janowitz and H. Eulau, Chicago.

7. The Great Schism of Population

MORTON GRODZINS

Almost nothing is being done today to meet what is likely to be the nation's most pressing social problem tomorrow. The problem can be simply stated in all its bleakness: many central cities of the great metropolitan areas of the United States are fast becoming lower class, largely Negro slums.

Some 95 million people, more than half the population of the United States, now live in what the Bureau of the Census defines as a standard metropolitan area: a central city of at least 50 thousand population with its ring of satellite communities "essentially metropolitan in character and socially and economically integrated with the central city." Fewer than one-third of the nation's population lived within these areas in 1900; slightly more than half resided there in 1950; and it is estimated that 70 per cent of the nation's total population will be metropolitan area dwellers by 1975.

The fourteen largest metropolitan areas, those with populations of over one million, contain more than half of the total metropolitan population and almost one-third of the nation's. These areas attract the largest number of Negro in-migrants from the South, and in them, generally, Negroes constitute a larger proportion of the total population. The consequences of the urban-suburban racial and class bifurcation, therefore, are most acute in these largest metropolitan areas. Some smaller metropolitan areas face the same problems in less acute form while others, because of their small number of Negroes, do not face them at all.

For several decades the Negro population of the great cities has been increasing more rapidly than the white population. The great changes come in time of full employment, and the explosive growth, as measured by the decennial censuses, took place between 1940 and 1950. In that decade, the total population of the fourteen largest metropolitan areas increased by 19 per cent, the total Negro percentage gain (65.1 per cent) being more than four times greater than the white increase (15.6 per cent). Negroes increased proportionately more rapidly in both central

Reprinted from *The Metropolitan Area as a Racial Problem* (Pittsburgh: University of Pittsburgh Press, 1958), pp. 1–3, 7–11, 12–15 by permission of the author and the publisher. Morton Grodzins is a professor of political science at the University of Chicago.

cities and suburbs, but the significant growth differential was inside the great cities. Whites increased by 3.7 per cent, Negroes 67.8 per cent. . . . The Negro population at least doubled in four central cities while whites in five cities decreased in number.

As late as 1950 non-whites constituted only a minor fraction of the total population in most of the central cities of the fourteen largest metropolitan areas. Washington, D.C., with non-whites totalling 35.4 per cent of total population, and Baltimore (23.8 per cent) had the largest group of non-whites in proportion to total population. In addition to these, only three other cities had 1950 Negro populations in excess of 15 per cent; three had less than 10 per cent.

Continued Negro migration, the comparatively greater rate of natural increase among non-whites, and the exodus of whites to the suburbs will dramatically raise the proportion of non-whites in central cities. The few special censuses that have been made since 1950 indicate this trend. In Los Angeles non-whites moved up from 6.5 per cent of the population in 1940, to 11 per cent in 1950, to 14 per cent in 1956. In Chicago, according to a careful unofficial estimate by Otis Dudley Duncan and Beverly Duncan of the University of Chicago, Negroes now comprise 19 per cent of the total, compared with 8 per cent in 1940. The city is expected to be one-third Negro by 1970. An official census in New York City showed that non-whites in the nation's largest city increased by 41 per cent from 1950 to 1957, while the white population decreased by 6 per cent. Non-whites made up 13 per cent of New York's population in 1957, as compared with 6 per cent in 1940 and 10 per cent in 1950. (Only a tiny fraction of New York's Puerto Rican population is enumerated as being "non-white.") New York City officials have forecast that in 1970 Negroes and Puerto Ricans together will constitute 45 per cent of the population of Manhattan and nearly one-third of the entire city. Washington, D.C. may already have an actual Negro majority.

Estimates of future population trends must take into account some reurbanization of white suburbanites as the proportion of older people increases and the suburbs become less attractive to those whose children have grown up and left home. Even making allowances for shifts of this sort, all evidence makes it highly probable that within 30 years Negroes will constitute from 25 to 50 per cent of the total population in at least 10 of the 14 largest central cities. . . .

The sheer cost of suburban housing excludes Negroes from many suburban areas. Furthermore, the social satisfactions of slum or near-slum existence for a homogeneous population have been insufficiently studied, and it is undoubtedly true that many Negro urban dwellers would not easily exchange life in all-Negro big-city neighborhoods for interracial suburban homes, even if moderately priced. The crucial fact, however, is that Negroes do not have any free choice in the matter. They are excluded from surburbia by a wide variety of devices.

Social antagonisms of suburban communities are themselves effective. Where it is plainly understood that Negroes are not wanted, Negro suburbanization is for all practical purposes impossible. In addition, suburban communities use their control of zoning, subdivision, and building regulations to achieve exclusion. Minimum lot sizes are increased to two or more acres; requirements for expensive street improvements are made—and then waived only in favor of "desirable" developments; large-scale building operations are defined as "business" for zoning purposes, thus excluding the possibility of low or moderate income suburban building; the suburb itself purchases all vacant land parcels that are large enough for subdivision and resells only to favored purchasers; builders are required to obtain certificates from the school board that educational accommodation will be adequate for the new residences; ordinances regulating "look alike" features or requiring certain building materials make home building expensive.

Where legal barriers of this sort are not sufficient to maintain a "white only" policy, land use controls are used informally—and of course illegally—to exclude Negroes. A Philadelphia builder recently told an interviewer that he would very much like to sell suburban houses to Negroes, but that it was impossible because it would ruin him economically. "If I sold just one suburban home to a Negro, the local building inspectors would have me moving pipes three-eighths of an inch every afternoon in every one of the places I was building; and moving a pipe three-eights of an inch is mighty expensive if you have to do it in concrete."

These practices are combined with social and economic pressures upon white owners of older homes and upon real estate brokers. Mortgage bankers habitually discriminate against the Negro buyer in the white neighborhood, and not always for purely economic reasons. Where all else fails, suburban residents have often turned to violence to prevent Negro occupancy. The total suburban facade is relatively impenetrable.

Suburban restrictions are everywhere aimed at Negroes as a racial group and not simply against people of low or moderate income. When such restrictions are applied uniformly, they of course also affect whites. But even this has an indirect effect upon the Negro concentrates within the cities. If middle- and lower-class whites who live next door to the slums were able to move to the suburbs, their places would quickly be taken by the slum-dwellers, especially those Negroes whose presence in the slums is due less to income than to the prejudice which excludes them from more desirable places. By raising the price of housing in the suburbs, land use regulations reduce the movement of the white middle and lower classes out of the city. And this in turn holds the slum-dweller in the slums and, accordingly, the Negro in the ghetto.

Consequences of Population Distribution

Some of the consequences of the urban-suburban racial and class schism are already apparent, and others can be reasonably predicted.

Within the cities the first result is a spreading of slums. There is no free market for Negro housing. The Negro population always increases faster than the living space available to it. New areas that open up to Negro residence become grossly overcrowded by conversion of one-family houses to multiple dwellings and by squeezing two or more Negro families into apartments previously occupied by a single white one. Though complete statistical evidence is lacking, it is likely that Negroes pay substantially more rent for such accommodations than do whites, and the higher rent itself produces higher densities. Housing occupied by Negroes is more crowded, more dilapidated, and more lacking in amenities such as private baths than housing occupied by whites with equivalent incomes.

Income factors account in part for the condition of life of the Negro community. Negroes are heavily over-represented in low income jobs: in the menial services, in unskilled and semi-skilled factory labor, and in "dirty work" generally. In this respect they are not unlike some earlier immigrants to the city; the Irish and the Poles, for example, also settled mainly in the slums.

Like previous newcomers to the city tasting the freedom of urban life for the first time, a significant portion of the Negro group does not possess the stable patterns of thought and action that characterize the "better" older inhabitants. And, as with all immigrant groups, old community patterns of control do not operate well in the new environment. Family disorganization among urban Negroes is high as measured by such indices as broken marriages, families headed by females, and unrelated individuals living in the same household. The development of social stabilization pivoted on family and community ties takes place against great odds. How does a mother keep her teen-age son off the streets if an entire family must eat, sleep, and live in a single room? What utility can be found in sobriety among a society of drinkers and in a block of taverns? What opportunity for quiet amidst the din of a tightly packed, restless neighborhood?

The conditions of urban life, rather than socializing new Negro residents to "desirable" life patterns, frequently have the opposite effect. They encourage rowdiness, casual and competitive sexuality, and a readiness for combat. The result is that the neighborhoods acquired by Negro residents eventually spiral downward. Disease and crime rates are high. Family stability is further prejudiced. Filth accumulates. The slum spreads outward.

These very conditions of life in the predominantly Negro neighborhoods lead the larger population to resist the expansion of Negro residential areas. The racial attribute—skin color—is added to the social attributes of lower class behavior. And while Negroes, like other urban immigrants, can readily lose undesirable social attributes, they cannot lose their color. They therefore do not have the mobility of other immigrant groups. They are racially blocked, whatever their social *bona fides*.

The Negro "black belts" of the great American cities as a consequence are by no means homogeneous. The very concentration of population within them plus the visible badge of color give them a spurious air of likeness. They contain, in fact, wide ranges of every social attribute: from illiteracy to high learning, from filth to hospital-like hygienic standards, from poverty to riches, from political backwardness to sophistication. Though the casual observer of the "black belt" neighborhoods sees only slums, the fact is that in every such area there are sub-areas, frequently on the periphery of the high-density mass, that are anything but slums. These are usually neighborhoods of newest acquisition, inhabited by the well-to-do of the Negro community. Density is low, lawns and gardens are well-tended, church attendance is high, neatness and cleanliness are apparent, parental standards of propriety for children higher than for comparable white groups.

Negro neighborhoods in the shadows of white luxury apartments are not unknown; but the more usual pattern is for low-income non-Negroes to occupy a buffer zone between all-Negro and the better white neighborhoods. Some of these are themselves new migrants to the city: Southerners and Japanese-Americans in Chicago, Puerto Ricans in New York, for example. Others are old residents on the lower ends of the income scale, people who, like the Negroes themselves, do not find success in life, or life itself, easy.

With the exodus of middle and upper classes to the suburbs, lower-income groups constitute a larger and larger fraction of the population of the central cities. Members of these groups generally exhibit a greater degree of intolerance and racial prejudice than do other whites. And the increasing juxtaposing of the Negro and the low-income non-Negro populations produces increased interracial tensions. Shirley Star of the National Opinion Research Center has shown that the greatest white animosity towards Negroes is found on the edge of the expanding Negro residential areas where whites fear their block or neighborhood will soon be "invaded." In these lower class and lower-middle class transitional areas, violence is incipient. Individual differences within the minority group are ignored. A young white resident of such an area in Chicago recently beat a Negro to death with a hammer. "I just wanted to get one of them," he explained, "which one didn't matter."

The total situation produces Negro communities in which people live their whole lives without, or with minimum, contact with the other race. With a Negro population numbering in the hundreds of thousands, and with this population densely concentrated, one can live, eat, shop, work, play, and die in a completely Negro community. The social isolation of the northern urban Negro is, for very large numbers, more complete than it ever was for the Negro rural resident in the South. . . .

Population shifts bring with them major economic consequences. Of first importance is the further decline of a large segment of business activity and associated property values, in the central cities. For reasons only remotely related—or unrelated—to the Negro-white population distribution, the economic feasibility of decentralized retail shopping has already been demonstrated. Suburban shopping centers have captured a large segment of the market in clothing, furniture, and other consumption goods; almost everywhere the "downtown" shops of the central cities have lost ground, absolutely and proportionally, to the peripheral developments. Retail sales in the central business district of Chicago decreased by 5 per cent between 1948 and 1954, while sales in the metropolitan area outside the city increased by 53 per cent. The relative sales loss of downtown areas has been even greater in other central cities.

Further developments can be foreseen. The downtown stores, with non-white and low-income customers more and more predominant in their clientele, will tend to concentrate on cheaper merchandise. " 'Borax' for downtown, Herman Miller for the suburb," is already a slogan of the furniture business. The decline of the central-city department store will be accompanied by a general deterioration of the downtown area. There are some striking exceptions, most notably in mid-town Manhattan. But in most cities—Chicago, Boston, Los Angeles are good examples—the main streets are becoming infested with sucker joints for tourists: all night jewelry auctions, bargain linens and cheap neckties, hamburger stands and jazz dives. The slums, in other words, are spreading to the central business districts.

A further, though more problematic, development is that the offices of the large corporations will join the flight from the city, taking along with them their servicing businesses: banks, law offices, advertising agencies, and others. The rapid development of closed circuit television, facsimile reproduction, and other technical aids relieves these businesses of the necessity of clustering at a central point. Their exodus from the city is already underway. New highways will make it easier in many places to get from one suburb to another than from suburb to downtown; and the losses of giving up central headquarters can be amortized over a number of years, frequently at considerable tax savings. Even the downtown hotel is likely to give way to the suburban motel except for convention purposes, an incidental further boost to the honkey-tonk development within the downtown business areas.

The rule seems to be a simple one: retail trade, the white collar shops, and the service industries will follow population. (Once their exodus is well underway, they also lead population.) The same general rule at least partially applies for manufacturing: the greatest suburbanization of manufacturing has taken place in those metropolitan areas where there has also been the most marked suburbanization of population, and some evidence indicates that manufacturing precedes population, rather than vice versa. Though the central cities have lost some manufacturing to both suburban and non-metropolitan areas, they have nevertheless maintained the preponderant share of the nation's total manufacturing enterprise. As Kitagawa and Bogue have shown, "the over-all spatial distribution [of manufacturing] in the United States has changed comparatively little in the past 50 years." The relative immobility of heavy industry has the result of fixing the laboring and semi-skilled groups, including large numbers of Negroes, within the central cities.

Even a conservative view must anticipate the exodus of a large segment of retail and other non-manufacturing businesses from downtown centers. Abandonment of these centers will lead to a host of municipal problems, not least of which is the loss of a substantial tax base. These economic developments are at once a step towards, and a consequence of, the city-suburban bifurcation of races that promises to transform many central cities into lower class ethnic islands. Successful attempts by central cities to encourage the establishment of new manufacturing plants as a means of rebuilding their tax base will of course hasten this process. . . .

Whatever the melancholy resemblance between older segregation patterns of the rural South and newer ones of the urban North, one important fact is different: the Negroes of the North possess the suffrage. How will they use it if they become the majority group—or at least the largest single group—in some of the great cities of the nation?

The most likely political development is the organization of Negroes for ends conceived narrowly to the advantage of the Negro community. Such a political effort might aim to destroy zoning and building restrictions for the immediate purpose of enlarging opportunities for desperately needed Negro housing against stubborn social pressures. If successful, the outcome might merely extend the Negro ghetto and cause a further departure of white populations to the suburbs. Yet the short-run political appeal of this action cannot be denied.

What the Negroes seek for themselves in Chicago in 1975 or 1985 might not be any more selfishly conceived than what Irish-dominated city councils in Boston and New York have sought in the past. In one essential field, Negro leadership may be more advantageous to the whole population: lacking devotion to the parochial schools, it would not be mean in the support of public schools. The rub lies in the very visiblity of Negro domination. Even on the assumption of Negro leaders and followers demonstrating wisdom and forebearance, what would be the consequence in one or more major cities of the city councils becoming predominantly Negro? What will be the situation in a state legislature when the largest group of big-city representatives are Negroes?

At the very least, cities politically dominated by Negroes will find it more difficult to bring about the urban-suburban cooperation so badly needed in so many fields. They will find greatly exacerbated what is already keenly felt in a majority of states: the conflict between the great urban center and the rural "downstate" or "upstate" areas. Similar unfortunate effects will follow in the national Congress, once a number of large cities are largely represented by Negro congressmen. The pitting of whites against Negroes, and of white policies against Negro policies, does not await actual Negro urban domination. The cry has already been raised in state legislatures. The conflict can only grow more acute as race and class become increasingly coterminous with local government boundaries.

In the long run, it is highly unlikely that the white population will allow Negroes to become dominant in the cities without resistance. The cultural and economic stakes are too high. One countermeasure will surely present itself to the suburbanites: to annex the suburbs, with their predominantly white populations, to the cities. This will be a historic reversal of the traditional suburban antipathy to annexation. But in the perception of suburbanites it will be justified: they will be annexing the city to the suburbs.

The use of annexation to curb Negro political powers is already underway. It was an explicit argument used by political leaders favoring an annexation to Nashville in 1952. And other recent annexations, largely confined to the South, have taken place at least partially to deny Negroes political powers they would otherwise achieve.

Other actions to the same end can be expected, especially the gerrymandering of Negro populations so as to deny them equitable representation in legislative bodies of city, state, and nation. Tuskegee, Alabama, was gerrymandered in 1957 to exclude all but a handful of Negro voters from city elections, and steps are currently under way to divide Macon County among five neighboring counties. Negroes have long lived within the city, and the county has for many years been preponderantly Negro, but only recently have the Negroes exercised their franchise in any numbers. In the border city of Cincinnati, fear of growing Negro political power was an important reason for the 1957 action that repealed proportional representation and subsequently defeated the reform City Charter Committee. During the campaign over proportional representation, whispering campaigns urged defeat of the system in order to prevent Theodore M. Berry, Negro vice-mayor, from becoming mayor, as well as to prevent Negroes from moving into white neighborhoods. The total political picture of continued racial bifurcation forecasts a new round of political repression aimed at Negroes. For this one, they will be better armed—[with respect to] effective numbers, economic strength, political sophistication, and allies in the white population.

Chapter THREE

COMMUNITY, POLITICAL

PARTICIPATION,

AND DEMOCRACY

Introduction

LOCAL SELF-GOVERNMENT has been from the very outset of our country one of the articles of our democratic tenets. The actual institution, as exemplified by the New England town meeting, was well established even before the founding of the nation. Subsequent political writings endeavored to articulate a rationale in terms of our democratic system. The claims for local self-government rest essentially on two separate grounds. First, it is argued that local decisions can best be made by the affected citizens in the local community, whereas the central government cannot be sufficiently sensitive to the various particular local conditions to maintain responsive policies. The second argument makes a much bolder claim, stating that local government provides a training ground for citizens and leaders, thereby making national democracy possible. Local self-government, offering the best opportunity for direct participation, is the very foundation upon which the whole democratic system rests.

Throughout the nineteenth century this view remained virtually unchallenged by democratic theorists. It was forcefully stated by early writers such as Jefferson and remained an important part of the political theory of such a recent writer as John Dewey. Prominent foreign political observers of the American scene, including Alexis de Tocqueville, James Bryce and John Stuart Mill, repeated essentially this same thesis, stressing both arguments on behalf of local self-government.

With the growth of large cities in the United States and the continued spread of urbanism, conditions have developed which present some troublesome problems for this view. To what extent is the theory of local self-government predicated on a society in which cities remained small, discrete, and easily defined units where face-to-face confrontations between the citizens were possible in the course of political deliberation? Secondly, we have experienced periods in which basically undemocratic local units of government, like those described by the Lynds and Gosnell, were prevalent. At the same time, national government retained its essentially responsive character despite these local difficulties. If, in fact, local democracy is truly the foundation of national democracy, how was this possible?

The readings in this chapter raise questions about the nineteenth-century assumptions in light of contemporary experience. Their criticism is less concerned with the desirability of local self-government than with the question of whether the theory of local self-government must be predicated on the nineteenth-century type of community life. Specifically, does local democracy require primary relationships and personal acquaintanceships among the citizens? Where these conditions do exist, do they, in fact, provide the proper training for democratic citizenship? If the older type of local political community has disappeared, what are the implications for the traditional theory of local self-government?

For a participation theory of local democracy, the basic question becomes: How large should a city be? This is a very old question in political philosophy; classical Greek political thought supported the view that cities should be small in size. Plato set the ideal at 5,000, for in such a city it was possible for every citizen to at least know someone who knew the leaders. Only in such a situation could the necessary set of stable political relationships rest firmly on the knowledge personally acquired by the citizens. On the other hand, the "mass" cities of Persia were pictured as places where "no one knew anyone," and here was the home of despotism.

Aristotle in the *Politics* refused to concur with the specific Platonic restrictions for size of the ideal city though he recognized the desirability of limits. He deferred the decision to the statesman in the particular city. Considerations such as economy and defense might dictate different ideals for different places at different points in time. Thus, while he saw the desirability of "primary" relationships, he also recognized that the city had many functions. Similarly, today, where the small city or suburb may offer an ideal "political" arrangement by providing the "primary" political relationships, they also have functions (i.e., industrial, commercial) unrelated to this ideal. It is, therefore, well to keep in mind Aristotle's point in the discussion of the ideal size of community—the choice cannot be made solely on the ground of abstractly conceived political institutions.

The first reading is an argument *for* the small community made by De Tocqueville. His assertion that there must be institutions between the citizen and his national government to avoid the perils of a mass society has a distinctly modern tone. For De Tocqueville, local government (and voluntary associations) provided the buffer against the tyranny of the national majority.

The article by Scott Greer builds on the assumptions of Aristotle. America is committed to an industrial society where large urban centers are institutions of specialization providing the foundation of industrial development. Given this kind of urban society, what, he asks, are the possibilities for popular participation?

Other modern critics indict the Platonic ideal as well as the democratic model described by De Tocqueville. It is their contention that the small community, even where it survives, is basically at variance with democracy in the context of modern industrial society. In their description of a village in New York, Vidich and Bensman argue that so few decisions are made locally that continued belief in local self-government is basically a self-deception which has undesirable effects on the individuals within the community, as well as on social institutions generally. In the passage excerpted, we see a description of village politics and the character of the democratic processes regarding the decisions which are made locally. Robert Wood, whose focus is on the partial re-creation of the small environment in the suburb, goes further in raising questions about whether or not the ideal of the small communities was ever desirable.

Lest it be supposed that the nineteenth-century view of local government no longer has defenders or that there are no communities which give some credence to this view, we have included selections by William H. Whyte, Jr. and Morris Janowitz. Whyte describes life in a packaged, rental suburb filled with transients. In this most unpromising soil, he finds evidence that De Tocqueville returning today might discover support for his view that opportunity for participation is the most significant feature of local self-government. Janowitz observes that even in a major urban center, such as Chicago, institutions exist which preserve a sense of community and provide some political protections for the interests of the local citizens.

The questions raised in this chapter are so basic to all considerations regarding urban government that the discussion of them cannot be wholly confined to any one chapter in this book. In this chapter the questions are particularly germane to the later chapters on metropolitanism, the civic reform movement, and patterns of power and influence. The question of whether or not local democracy provides a wellspring of support for national democracy must be considered in each of these various contexts.

It is necessary to bear in mind that mankind is, for the first time in his history, living in an urbanized society. This is a condition which the previous writers from Plato to De Tocqueville could only dimly foresee. Large cities have always existed, and obviously those who stressed the need for primary political relations looked outside of the large city for their models. This was no less true for De Tocqueville than it was for Plato. It is no longer possible for us to think in these terms. At best we can, as Whyte and Lerner indicate, look to suburbia. But even this area is obviously not the old independent, stable community. Those who wish to stress the importance of citizen participation in local self-government, must reconcile their desires with the emerging facts of urban existence.

8. Political Consequences of Decentralized Administration

ALEXIS DE TOCQUEVILLE

It is not undesignedly that I begin this subject with the Township. The village or township is the only association which is so perfectly natural, that, wherever a number of men are collected, it seems to constitute itself.

The town or tithing, then, exists in all nations, whatever their laws and customs may be: it is man who makes monarchies and establishes republics, but the township seems to come directly from the hand of God. But although the existence of the township is coeval with that of man, its

Reprinted from *Democracy in America*, Henry Reeve, trans.; Francis Bowen, ed. (Boston: John Allyn Publishing Co., 1876), pp. 74–76, 107–8, 112–17, 120–22. Author's and editor's footnotes omitted. De Tocqueville (1805–1859) visited the United States during the presidency of Andrew Jackson.

freedom is an infrequent and fragile thing. A nation can always establish great political assemblies, because it habitually contains a certain number of individuals fitted by their talents, if not by their habits, for the direction of affairs. The township, on the contrary, is composed of coarser materials, which are less easily fashioned by the legislator. The difficulty of establishing its independence rather augments than diminishes with the increasing intelligence of the people. A highly civilized community can hardly tolerate a local independence, is disgusted at its numerous blunders, and is apt to despair of success before the experiment is completed. Again, the immunities of townships, which have been obtained with so much difficulty, are least of all protected against the encroachments of the supreme power. They are unable to struggle, single-handed, against a strong and enterprising government, and they cannot defend themselves with success unless they are identified with the customs of the nation and supported by public opinion. Thus, until the independence of townships is amalgamated with the manners of a people, it is easily destroyed; and it is only after a long existence in the laws that it can be thus amalgamated. Municipal freedom is not the fruit of human efforts; it is rarely created by others; but is, as it were, secretly self-produced in the midst of a semi-barbarous state of society. The constant action of the laws and the national habits, peculiar circumstances, and, above all, time, may consolidate it; but there is certainly no nation on the continent of Europe which has experienced its advantages. Yet municipal institutions constitute the strength of free nations. Town-meetings are to liberty what primary schools are to science; they bring it within the people's reach, they teach men how to use and how to enjoy it. A nation may establish a free government, but without municipal institutions, it cannot have the spirit of liberty. Transient passions, the interests of an hour, or the chance of circumstances, may create the external forms of independence; but the despotic tendency which has been driven into the interior of the social system, will, sooner or later, reappear on the surface. . . .

Centralization is a word in general and daily use, without any precise meaning being attached to it. Nevertheless, there exist two distinct kinds of centralization, which it is necessary to discriminate with accuracy.

Certain interests are common to all parts of a nation, such as the enactment of its general laws, and the maintenance of its foreign relations. Other interests are peculiar to certain parts of the nation; such, for instance, as the business of the several townships. When the power which directs the former or general interests is concentrated in one place or in the same persons, it constitutes a centralized government. To concentrate in like manner into one place of direction of the latter or local interests constitutes what may be termed a centralized administration. . . .

The partisans of centralization in Europe are wont to maintain that the government can administer the affairs of each locality better than the citizens could do it for themselves: this may be true, when the central power is enlightened, and the local authorities are ignorant; when it is alert, and they are slow; when it is accustomed to act, and they to obey. Indeed, it is evident that this double tendency must augment with the increase of centralization, and that the readiness of the one and the incapacity of the others must become more and more prominent. But I deny that it is so, when the people are as enlightened, as awake to their interests, and as accustomed to reflect on them, as the Americans are. I am persuaded, on the contrary, that, in this case, the collective strength of the citizens will always conduce more efficaciously to the public welfare than the authority of the government. I know it is difficult to point out with certainty the means of arousing a sleeping population, and of giving it passions and knowledge which it does not possess; it is, I am well aware, an arduous task to persuade men to busy themselves about their own affairs. It would frequently be easier to interest them in the punctilios of court etiquette, than in the repairs of their common dwelling. But whenever a central administration affects completely to supersede the persons most interested, I believe that it is either misled, or desirous to mislead. However enlightened and skilful a central power may be, it cannot of itself embrace all the details of the life of a great nation. Such vigilance exceeds the powers of man. And when it attempts unaided to create and set in motion so many complicated springs, it must submit to a very imperfect result, or exhaust itself in bootless efforts.

Centralization easily succeeds, indeed, in subjecting the external actions of men to a certain uniformity, which we come at last to love for its own sake, independently of the objects to which it is applied, like those devotees who worship the statue and forget the deity it represents. Centralization imparts without difficulty an admirable regularity to the routine of business; provides skilfully for the details of the social police; represses small disorders and petty misdemeanors; maintains society in a *status quo* alike secure from improvement and decline; and perpetuates a drowsy regularity in the conduct of affairs, which the heads of the administration are wont to call good order and public tranquillity; in short, it excels in prevention, but not in action. Its force deserts it, when society is to be profoundly moved, or accelerated in its course; and if once the co-operation of private citizens is necessary to the furtherance of its measures, the secret of its impotance is disclosed. Even whilst the centralized power, in its despair, invokes the assistance of the citizens, it says to them: "You shall act just as I please, as much as I please, and in the direction which I please. You are to take charge of the details, without aspiring to guide the system; you are to work in darkness; and afterwards you may judge my work by its results." These are not the conditions on which the alliance of the human will is to be obtained; it must be free in its gait, and responsible for its acts, or (such is the constitution of man) the citizen had rather remain a passive spectator, than a dependent actor, in schemes with which he is unacquainted.

It is undeniable, that the want of those uniform regulations which control the conduct of every inhabitant of France, is not unfrequently felt in the United States. Gross instances of social indifference and neglect are to be met with; and from time to time, disgraceful blemishes are seen, in complete contrast with the surrounding civilization. Useful undertakings, which cannot succeed without perpetual attention and rigorous exactitude, are frequently abandoned; for in America, as well as in other countries, the people proceed by sudden impulses and momentary exertions. The European, accustomed to find a functionary always at hand to interfere with all he undertakes, reconciles himself with difficulty to the complex mechanism of the administration of the townships. In general, it may be affirmed that the lesser details of the police, which render life easy and comfortable, are neglected in America, but that the essential guaranties of man in society are as strong there as elsewhere. In America, the power which conducts the administration is far less regular, less enlightened, and less skilful, but a hundred-fold greater, than in Europe. In no country in the world, do the citizens make such exertions for the common weal. I know of no people who have established schools so numerous and efficacious, places of public worship better suited to the wants of the inhabitants, or roads kept in better repair. Uniformity or permanence of design, the minute arrangement of details, and the perfection of administrative system, must not be sought for in the United States: what we find there is, the presence of a power which, if it is somewhat wild, is at least robust, and an existence checkered with accidents, indeed, but full of animation and effort.

Granting, for an instant, that the villages and counties of the United States would be more usefully governed by a central authority, which they had never seen, than by functionaries taken from among them, —admitting, for the sake of argument, that there would be more security in America, and the resources of society would be better employed there, if the whole administration centered in a single arm,—still the *political* advantages which the Americans derive from their decentralized system would induce me to prefer it to the contrary plan. It profits me but little, after all, that a vigilant authority always protects the tranquillity of my pleasures, and constantly averts all dangers from my path, without my care or concern, if this same authority is the absolute master of my liberty and my life, and if it so monopolizes movement and life, that when it languishes everything languishes around it, that when it sleeps everything must sleep, and that when it dies the state itself must perish.

There are countries in Europe, where the natives consider themselves as a kind of settlers, indifferent to the fate of the spot which they inhabit. The greatest changes are effected there without their concurrence, and (unless chance may have apprised them of the event) without their knowledge; nay, more, the condition of his village, the police of his street, the repairs of the church or the parsonage, do not concern him; for he looks upon all these things as unconnected with himself, and as the property of a powerful stranger whom he calls the government. He has only a life-interest in these possessions, without the spirit of ownership or any ideas of improvement. This want of interest in his own affairs goes so far, that if his own safety or that of his children is at last endangered, instead of trying to avert the peril, he will fold his arms, and wait till the whole nation comes to his aid. This man, who has so completely sacrificed his own free will, does not, more than any other person, love obedience; he cowers, it is true, before the pettiest officer; but he braves the law with the spirit of a conquered foe, as soon as its superior force is withdrawn: he perpetually oscillates between servitude and license. . . .

I believe that provincial institutions are useful to all nations, but nowhere do they appear to me to be more necessary than amongst a democratic people. In an aristocracy, order can always be maintained in the midst of liberty; and as the rulers have a great deal to lose, order is to them a matter of great interest. In like manner, an aristocracy protects the people from the excesses of despotism, because it always possesses an organized power ready to resist a despot. But a democracy without provincial institutions has no security against these evils. How can a populace, unaccustomed to freedom in small concerns, learn to use it temperately in great affairs? What resistance can be offered to tyranny in a country where each individual is weak, and where the citizens are not united by any common interest? Those who dread the license of the mob, and those who fear absolute power, ought alike to desire the gradual development of provincial liberties.

I am also convinced, that democratic nations are most likely to fall beneath the yoke of a centralized administration, for several reasons, amongst which is the following.

The constant tendency of these nations is to concentrate all the strength of the government in the hands of the only power which directly represents the people; because, beyond the people, nothing is to be perceived but a mass of equal individuals. But when the same power already has all the attributes of government, it can scarcely refrain from penetrating into the details of the administration, and an opportunity of doing so is sure to present itself in the long run, as was the case in France. In the French Revolution, there were two impulses in opposite directions, which must never be confounded; the one was favorable to liberty, the other to despotism. Under the ancient monarchy, the king was the sole author of the laws; and below the power of the sovereign, certain vestiges of provincial institutions, half destroyed, were still distinguishable. These provincial institutions were incoherent, ill-arranged, and frequently absurd; in the hands of the aristocracy, they had sometimes been converted into instruments of oppression. The Revolution declared itself the enemy at once of royalty and of provincial institutions; it confounded in indiscriminate hatred all that had preceded it,—despotic power and the checks to its abuses; and its tendency was at once to republicanize and to centralize. This double character of the French Revolution is a fact which has been adroitly handled by the friends of absolute power. Can they be accused of laboring in the cause of despotism, when they are defending that centralized administration which was one of the great innovations of the Revolution? In this manner, popularity may be united with hostility to the rights of the people, and the secret slave of tyranny may be the professed lover of freedom.

I have visited the two nations in which the system of provincial liberty has been most perfectly established, and I have listened to the opinions of different parties in those countries. In America, I met with men who secretly aspired to destroy the democratic institutions of the Union; in England, I found others who openly attacked the aristocracy; but I found no one who did not regard provincial independence as a great good. In both countries, I heard a thousand different causes assigned for the evils of the state; but the local system was never mentioned amongst them. I heard citizens attribute the power and prosperity of their country to a multitude of reasons; but they *all* placed the advantages of local institutions in the foremost rank.

Am I to suppose that when men, who are naturally so divided on religious opinions and on political theories, agree on one point, (and that one which they can best judge, as it is one of which they have daily experience) they are all in error? The only nations which deny the utility of provincial liberties are those which have fewest of them; in other words, those only censure the institution who do not know it. . . .

I have already pointed out the distinction between a centralized government and a centralized administration. The former exists in America, but the latter is nearly unknown there. If the directing power of the American communities had both these instruments of government at its disposal, and united the habit of executing its commands to the right of commanding it; if, after having established the general principles of government, it descended to the details of their application; and if, having regulated the great interests of the country, it could descend to the circle of individual interests, freedom would soon be banished from the New World.

But in the United States, the majority, which so frequently displays the tastes and the propensities of a despot, is still destitute of the most perfect instruments of tyranny.

In the American republics, the central government has never as yet busied itself but with a small number of objects, sufficiently prominent to attract its attention. The secondary affairs of society have never been regulated by its authority; and nothing has hitherto betrayed its desire of even interfering in them. The majority is become more and more absolute, but has not increased the prerogatives of the central government; those great prerogatives have been confined to a certain sphere; and, although the despotism of the majority may be galling upon one point, it cannot be said to extend to all. However the predominant party in the nation may be carried away by its passions, however ardent it may be in the pursuit of its projects, it cannot oblige all the citizens to comply with its desires in the same manner, and at the same time, throughout the country. When the central government which represents that majority has issued a decree, it must intrust the execution of its will to agents, over whom it frequently has no control, and whom it cannot perpetually direct. The townships, municipal bodies, and counties form so many concealed breakwaters, which check or part the tide of popular determination. If an oppressive law were passed, liberty would still be protected by the mode of executing that law; the majority cannot descend to the details and what may be called the puerilities of administrative tyranny. It does not even imagine that it can do so, for it has not a full consciousness of its authority. It knows only the extent of its natural powers, but is unacquainted with the art of increasing them.

9. *Individual Participation in a Mass Society*

SCOTT GREER

The participation of the individual in his community is of importance on two grounds. Theoretically, an understanding of such behavior aids in the clarification and extension of our picture of modern society as a system. And, from a normative point of view, the nature and degree of such participation sets the limits and indicates the possibilities of social control in a nonhierarchical society. The dissolution of traditional orders, reflected in our fluid class structure and the uncertain basis for legitimacy, presents a major problem for modern society. Further, if we assume that the solvents destroying these older forms of order emanate from the process of rational transformation and increase in scale in the society, we may be confident that the problems experienced in America and the West are potentially universal problems.

The general ideology identifying the problem and indicating its solution is for Westerners some variation of the democratic dogma. We assume that for the hierarchical order of the past we may substitute an order based on individual option, control through the consent of the governed. In making such normative decisions, however, we are also making certain empirical assumptions about the nature of modern society. We assume the existence, at some level, of subcommittees, in which the individual has interest, influence, and concerning which he has some realistic information. Such subcommittees are the necessary condition for individual participation in the vast totality of society (though they are not sufficient conditions), and whoever says "democracy" is, in effect, positing such groups.

However, the western societies in which modern democratic political systems were first devised have changed radically since their democratic birth. America, approximately five per cent urban at the time of the Revolution, is today over sixty per cent urban and this predominantly urban, centralized society differs radically from the nation assumed by the framers of the democratic constitutions. While the rural population and the smaller cities still have their importance, the social structure of the large urban complex is crucial for the study of social

Reprinted from *Approaches to the Study of Politics*, Roland Young, ed. (Evanston, Illinois: Northwestern University Press, 1958), pp. 329–42 by permission of the publisher. Copyright 1958 by Northwestern University Press. Scott Greer is a professor of sociology and political science at Northwestern University.

participation and democratic process in contemporary society. It is upon individual participation in very large cities that this paper is focused.

Many current interpretations of the large city sharply contradict the empirical assumptions implied in the democratic dogma. The analyses of Louis Wirth[1] and Georg Simmel[2] emphasize these aspects of the city: (a) its heterogeneity (b) its impersonality (c) its anonymity and (d) the consequent social fragmentation of the individuals who make up the urban world. Such views are congruent with the long-run trends envisaged by Durkheim,[3] Tonnies,[4] Park,[6] and others—trends from a simple homogeneous society possessing an automatic *consensus universalis* and resulting solidarity towards a complex, heterogeneous society, in which order results from functional interdependence of differentiated groups, and solidarity within groups leads to dynamic relations between them. In this view (there are important differences between these theorists, but in major respect they are similar) the primary-group structure of society is in a process of rapid dissolution. Kinship groups, neighborhood groups, the church, and the local community are losing their importance. Their strength in controlling individual behavior is shifted to formal, secondary groups, which organize work, religion and politics. Even play is controlled by the large commercial organization.

From such a position, the theorist who wishes to emphasize the viability of democratic structure and process must, like MacIver,[7] accept the formal organization as the effective subcommunity—one which is capable of performing the function of organizing individuals in meaningful wholes which may then participate in the control of the larger society. The "Associational Society" is seen as the alternative to the hierarchical society of the past, based upon primary communities and hereditary strata.

These formulations concerning urban social structure are largely the result of keen observation and analysis, rather than large scale empirical studies. Their influence is largely due to two facts: (a) they are based upon observations available at random in any large city, and (b) they fill, neatly, a gap in the theoretical system of sociology. However, in the past decade, and even more in the last few years, a substantial body of work has been accumulated dealing with the specific area of participation in the urban community. It is possible, on the basis of this work, to sketch a tentative description of the modes of participation which occur among urbanites—a snapshot of the organizational topography of the modern city. Such a description serves as a test of earlier assumptions and the basis for new interpretation.

The Disenchantment of the City: Empirical Research

The studies to be summarized are focused upon participation in formal organizations—Kommarovsky,[8]—the local area as community—Janowitz,[9]—the urban neighborhood—Foley,[10]—and these together with other areas of participation—Axelrod,[11] Bell,[12, 13] Greer.[14, 15] The urban complexes included are: New York (Kommarovsky), Chicago (Janowitz), Los Angeles (Greer), San Francisco (Bell), Detroit (Axelrod) and Rochester (Foley). The net is thus spread wide, and the results are remarkably consistent—so much so that the discussion of findings will emphasize common trends, rather than variations. The following loci of participation will be discussed: kinship, the neighborhood, the local area, formal organizations, friends, work associates, and the mass media.

Some Empirical Findings

A) *Kinship.* One of the most striking results of this research is the extreme importance of kin relations for the urban residents. The results, in Detroit, Los Angeles, and San Francisco, all indicate the same fact: kin relations, as measured by visiting patterns, are the most important social relations for all types of urban populations. Half of the urbanites visit their kin at least once a week, and large majorities visit them at least once a month. Even the extended family is important; one-third of the Los Angeles sample visited uncles, cousins, and the like at least monthly. The conjugal family is of basic importance; the urbanite, in any local area, is apt to spend most of his evenings in the bosom of his family; this is true even in Hollywood, and extremely so in the suburbs.

B) *The neighborhood.* There is much more differentiation here— the range is from a substantial number of people who are intense neighbors to a substantial number who hardly neighbor at all. The degree of neighboring varies by local area, and within the city there is a wide range, but the average urban resident has some informal neighboring relationships.

C) *The local area.* Much like their neighboring behavior, urban residents indicate wide variation in their degree of "local community" identification and participation. Janowitz found a majority of his Chicago samples to be identified with their local area as their "true home," and in Los Angeles this was true of some areas, but varied considerably between areas.

D) *Formal organizations.* Although a majority of urban residents belong to churches, a minority which varies around forty per cent attend as frequently as once a month. Aside from church participation, most urban individuals belong to one organization or none. Low socio-economic rank individuals, and middle-rank individuals, usually belong to one organization at most, and it is usually work-connected for men, child- and church-connected for women. Only in the upper socio-economic levels is the "joiner" to be found with any frequency. When attendance at organizations is studied, some twenty per cent of the memberships are usually "paper" memberships.

E) Friendship. Informal participation in friendship relations, with individual friends or friendship circles, is an extremely frequent occurrence. Friendship, outside any organizational context, is a near-universal in the city. The urbanite is seldom isolated from this type of primary group.

F) Work associates as friends. Here one of the important hypotheses of urban theory is in question. As the primary community and neighborhood decline, friendship was expected to be more closely related to work organization. However, studies by Axelrod, Bell, and Greer all indicate that work associates are a minor proportion of the individual's primary relations when he is away from the job. Only in the upper socio-economic levels (where friendship is frequently instrumental for economic ends) is there a change. Work relations are usually insulated from free primary-group participation of the urban-dweller.

G) Mass entertainment. Cultural participation in organized entertainment is relatively unimportant for urban adults. Most of the Los Angeles samples attended fewer than three events a month. One-third attended no event, one-third one or two, and a few attended as many as ten or more. Most attendance was at movies, but the real importance of the mass entertainment media was in the home—television and radio are extremely important, but it is in the context of family participation.

In summary, the urbanite's individual "path" through social structure crosses these six areas of possible involvement and participation. According to one theory of urban society, his involvement should be increasingly intense with respect to formal organizations, work associates as friends, and mass entertainment; it should be correspondingly weak with respect to kin, neighbors, the local community, and primary groups other than these. The studies cited indicate no such clear-cut development. Instead, the usual individual's involvement in formal organizations and work-based friendship is weak; the mass media are most important in a family context; participation with kin and friendship circles is powerful, and with neighbors and the local community's groups it varies immensely by area.

The picture that emerges is of a society in which the conjugal family is extremely powerful among all types of population. This small, primary group structure is the basic area of involvement; at the other pole is work, a massive absorber of time, but an activity which is rarely related to the family through "outside" friendship with on-the-job associates. Instead, the family-friendship group is relatively free-floating, within the world of large scale secondary associations. The family is usually identified, although weakly, with the local community; it "neighbors," but strictly "within bounds." By and large, the conjugal family group keeps itself to itself; outside is the world—formal organizations, work, and the communities.

Such a picture is remarkably similar to that which Oeser and Hammond[16] present, from their studies in Melbourne, Australia. Melbourne, like the American cities studied, is a mushrooming metropolitan complex in a highly urbanized society. Its people are largely "middle rank" economically, neither poor nor wealthy. Its social order centers around the single family dwelling unit, the conjugal family, selected kinfolk, the job, and the mass media—the latter largely consumed in the home. Neither in Melbourne nor in American cities do we find much participation, by most people, in formal organizations or the community. The family retires to its domain, to work in the garden, listen to radio or television, care for children, and read.

A Typology of Urban Populations

Such findings as these are important in two respects: first, in their sharp departures from what would be considered the conventional picture of metropolitan life, and, second, in their consistency. The agreement between the various American studies, and between these and the Australian study, leads us to suspect that such participation patterns are a result of powerful trends in modern Western society. In explaining the average, and variations from it, it is useful to base a description upon social trends.

The Shevky-Bell typology of urban subpopulations[17,18] is one such method of describing and accounting for the varieties of urban areas. Based upon Colin Clark's studies of economic history,[19] and on analysis of the long-term changes in the nature of production, the organization of work, and the composition of the total society, the typology posits three dimensions along which urban subpopulations vary. These are: social rank (economic and occupational status), segregation (the proportion of segregated ethnic populations in a community), and urbanization. The latter refers to variations in life-styles; it ranges from the family-centered, home-centered life at the low-urbanization pole to an opposite pole where one finds many single individuals and couples without children. In this kind of subarea, among the highly urbanized populations, many women work outside the home, most people live in multiple dwelling units, and the market is of great importance as a center of cultural life.

Studies have indicated that the urbanization of an area is closely associated with the importance of the local area as a "social fact," as a community. And this, in turn, is associated with political participation.

The results of the Los Angeles study of four census-tract populations at middle social rank, without segregated populations, but varying from very highly-urban to very low-urban areas, were summarized as follows:

> In general, our findings indicate a growing importance of the local area as a social fact, as we go from the highly urbanized areas . . . to the low-urban areas. Neighboring, organizational location in the area, the residences of the members of organizations in the area, the location and composition of church congregations, all vary with urbanization and increase as urbanization decreases. Readership of the local community press also increases, as does the ability to name local leaders and intention to remain in the area indefinitely.
>
> Thus the studies of the small community, with its local organizational structure and stratification system, may apply in the low-urban areas; they are not likely to fit in the highly-urban area. We may think of the urbanization dimension as having, at the low pole, communities much like those studied by W. Lloyd Warner, August Hollingshead, and others. At the highly urbanized pole, we encounter the big city population of the stereotype, organized not in community terms, but in terms of the corporation, politics, the mass media, and the popular culture. But predominantly, the highly urban populations associate in small, informal groups, with friends and kinfolk.[15]

A comparison was made between the political attitudes and behavior of the very highly-urbanized population and the very low-urban population studied in Los Angeles. The latter were more involved in their local community (they could name more local leaders), had a more consistent voting record, were more certain of the social class position of their "community" (middle-class) and of their political preferences. This data is reinforced by that of Janowitz, who found that, among his Chicago sample:

> Family cohesion and primary group contacts seemed more relevant for predisposing an individual toward acceptance of the community's controlling institutions and associations.[9]

Janowitz took community newspaper readership and identification with the local community as indexes of community participation.

Regardless of the respondents' political affiliations, relative confidence in the effectiveness and honesty of local politics—projective measures of personal political competence—tended to be associated with high community newspaper readership.[9]

We may summarize the findings in this manner: (*a*) urban subpopulations may be arranged in a meaningful typology, based upon their place in arrays derived from indexes of social rank, segregation, and urbanization. (*b*) As the type of area varies, participation patterns vary. As urbanization declines, there is an increase in neighboring and participation in the local community in all its forms. (*c*) This participation is associated with more political involvement and a higher degree of political competence.

The picture of participation in the metropolis must be qualified in these ways: the highly-urbanized populations are atypical—they are an extreme of a continuum. Their behavior deviates from the stereotype of the atomistic man in their great involvement in the family and their intensive participation in primary groups. However, the majority of the population in a great urban complex does not lie in the highly-urbanized segments; instead, it is of middle to low urbanization, and middle social rank. At the extremely low-urban pole, the local area becomes a definite community—it is a social fact, as well as a geographical fact.

The galaxy of local residential areas which make up a great city may be seen as differing in their level of living (social rank) and their style of living (urbanization). At each level of social rank there are vast differences between areas of high and low urbanization. In general, the highly urban areas lie within the central city, and the low-urban areas lie towards the suburbs. One may keep in mind the image of the urban apartment house districts, on the one hand, and the tract developments and suburbs on the other. As one moves towards the latter, community participation in the local area increases, and political behavior in general changes.

However, even as few urban subareas approach the anonymity and fragmentation of the stereotype, fewer still approach the kind of subcommunity envisaged in the democratic ideology. Although more respondents can name local leaders in the suburbs than in the highly-urbanized areas, less than forty per cent can do so anywhere. And the percentage who cannot even name one city-wide leader is considerable. With this qualification in mind, the differences between the polar extremes are sharp and suggestive. What is the meaning of this great variation in "normal life style"—what accounts for it, and what are its consequences?

Community—and Modern Urban Society

The word *community* is an ambiguous one, with many theoretical meanings and varying empirical referents. Two core meanings, however, stand out in the theoretical and empirical uses of the term. In one, community connotes certain modes of relationship, in which the individual shares values, is understood and identifies with the aggregate. In the other meaning community indicates a spatially-defined social unit having functional significance, reflecting the interdependence of individuals and groups. In the first sense, the modern metropolis is not a community; in the second, it must be by definition.

Rather than choose one meaning, it is preferable to indicate the empirical interrelation of the two aspects. For it is likely that, when we refer to community, we have in the back of our mind the picture of the *primary community*—preliterate society, feudal holding, or peasant village. Such communities fulfilled both definitions: they were extremely significant functionally, providing all or most of the conditions for individual and group life, and they had a high degree of consensus and communion. Such is manifestly not the case with the urban community today, and the reasons lie deep in the nature of modern society.

The chief difference between societies based upon primary communities and urban societies is one of scale—modern urban society is the result of a vast increase in scale. Wilson and Wilson[20] have studied this process in Central Africa, tracing its nature and its effects upon three small village cultures. They noted the autonomy of the societies at the early stage—each small group had its own means of subsistence and order, and each was independent of the other. The process of increase in scale was one of increasing commitments to widespread social groups and dwindling dependence upon immediate associates. The wealthy Central African farmer, for example, became free of local economic coercion by the village head man at the same time he became dependent upon the international ground-nuts market. Thus, if one conceives of social organization as a network of mutually-sustaining activities, based upon necessary functions, one may say that the radius of this network was short in the primary community of village society; with the increase of scale, there is a lengthening of these radii of functional interdependence.

Such extension of interdependence is not necessarily the result of rational undertaking, nor are the results all functional. However, once such interdependence exists, the human need for predictability (and the demand for predictability in ongoing organized groups) tends to result in a flow of communication and a mutual ordering of behavior. To paraphrase Freud, "Where interdependence is, there shall organization be."

The process may be traced in the development of modern industry—Florence.[21] The need for a predictable source of supplies results in "vertical integration"; the need for a predictable market results in monopoly, oligopoly, and cartels; the need for predictable work-flow results in bureaucracy, and indirectly in some form of labor organization. The organization of one function acts as a catalyst producing further organization; thus industrial cartels produce national labor unions, and unions in turn force the further integration of management groups.

Returning now to the concept of the primary community, we note that in such communities the radii of many functional interdependencies were short, coinciding with the same aggregate of persons. The result was, for the individual, a complete dependence upon this community leaving him few choices; for the community, it was autonomy from outside groups. There was a coincidence of many organizational networks, based upon functional interdependence for various social products in the same small aggregate. The result was an extreme density of interaction. When such density of interaction occurs, a secondary function results: the social process. This may be defined as communication as an end in itself; it is identical with many meanings of *communion,* and it is the basis for that aspect of association which we call the primary group.

Interdependence based upon the need for the various social products (protection, economic production and consumption, etc.) and upon the need for the social process, or communion, thus creates an extremely strong social group coterminous with the spatially-defined collective. Such a group satisfies both the meanings of community advanced earlier: it is both a mode of relationships and a spatially-defined social unit having functional significance. In such a society the village is, to a large degree, one primary group. (For a more extended presentation of this theory, see Greer.[22])

The process of increase in scale, however, results in both the lengthening of the radii of interdependence (spatially and socially) and the disjunction of the different radii, representing the organizations fufilling different functions. Not only is the small local area no longer autonomous —the boundaries of the organizations upon which it is dependent no longer coincide. Work, government, education, religion—each is a congeries of organizations which include parts of the local area's population in their various spans, while this area is thrown with many others into various society-wide networks.

In this sense of the word, America has never been to any large degree a society based upon primary community for Western society was already large in scale and rapidly expanding when America became a colony; the very nature of colonialism insured dependence upon the imperial and international markets. There are, however, degrees and it is likely that, until the twentieth century, community existed in a widespread fashion in open-country neighborhoods, villages, and the country town. Such community, less complete than in the peasant village to be sure, was infinitely stronger than that to be found in any part of the modern metropolis. Scattered data from the novels celebrating the "revolt from the village," the criticisms by intellectuals like Thorstein Veblen, and studies of contemporary backwoods settlements in the Hispanola country and the southern Appalachians indicate that spatial isolation produced a marked degree of community.

Such community disappears under urban conditions; it has no hold over the individual, for its functions are preempted by large specialized organizations in the interest of rational control, while the individual is highly mobile and is isolated in the local area only when he chooses to be. As the functional bases for intense interaction disappear, communion goes with them.

As this occurs, the small conjugal family becomes increasingly important for the individual and, indirectly, for the total society. The reason is partly one of default; as the primary community leaves the spatially defined group, the conjugal family remains and is today probably the strongest basis for communion available to most people in the large city. At the same time, in a society of increasing scale, the family is relatively free from community norms (where there is little interaction there can be neither surveillance nor sanctions), and great individuation of family patterns is possible. With the surplus of freedom, of leisure, and of money, the individual can choose between family and nonfamily living—and the family can choose between community-oriented and noncommunity local areas to live in.

Thus the variations in urbanization, and in local community participation, found in the various studies cited can be understood as part of the large-scale process which (a) destroys the primary community, (b) releases its individual components for duty in large, segmental organizations, and (c) releases much time, expenditure, and behavior from community-enforced norms. The large scale society is, in this sense, one of emerging freedoms.

Implications for Political Control

The results of this brief excursus may now be compared with the empirical assumptions underlying democratic political structures. Much of that ideal pattern relies upon the belief in stable subcommunities, viable wholes through which the individual may clarify in social discourse and affect through social action the objects of his grievances and desires. Such a group requires sufficient communication and involvement to result in the ordering of individual behavior. It must then be important to a large part of its constituency. Our ideal example from the past is the New England township, and its image still has an overweening importance in our thinking. It is something of an archetype.

The local area today, however, particularly in the metropolis, no longer represents such a community. Instead of a primary community it is necessarily what Janowitz calls a "community of limited liability." The individual's investment is always small, and if he "loses" he can cut his losses by getting out—the community cannot hold him. Even among the most community-oriented, "small town" areas, those at the low-urbanization pole within the city, there is great variation in the importance of the area to the individual. The local merchants have more of a stake than the home-owning residents with children, and these are more invested than the couple without children who rent an apartment. However, even the most deeply involved can withdraw from the local community, and satisfy all needs elsewhere—and the withdrawal need not be physical.

The reasons may be restated: by community in the double sense we mean a spatially defined aggregate which is a powerful social group. Such groups exist only where there is functional interdependence (as the local community in the suburbs is most functional for the merchants, least so for the childless couple who rent). Only where such functional interdependence occurs is participation strong: constraint is, in this sense, the key to community.

If this is true, then it follows that primary communities are not possible in modern society save in a very few areas—in such survivals as the backwoods communities noted earlier, and in such institutional aggregates as the prison, the monastery, and the army. However, aside from such atypical collectives, there are other groups in which the individual must interact continuously and for a large share of his waking life. One such is the work organization.

The functional interdependence, the flow of communication, and the consequent ordering of behavior at the place of work bulk large in the individual's life. Some theorists, of whom Mayo[23] is the best known, imply that a primary community of work is therefore possible. Certainly economic production, a share in the surplus, and status in the general society are basic functional supports of such primary communities as the peasant village. However in a most cursory inspection of modern industry, several factors appear which make such a strong work community very unlikely. These include freedom of labor, the conflicting functions of the work organization, and their results in the labor union on one hand and the hierarchical organization of industry on the other.

Free labor, which is functional for the total economic system, allows the individual to leave a given work group and join another. His needs may be served as well or better—and likewise the functional demands of industry; however, his relations with others in the group are conditioned by this freedom. Even work is a commitment of limited liability.

Equally important is the hierarchical organization of work in our society. The "scalar principle" is undoubtedly necessary in large organized groups; still the net effect is that the most important social group outside the family is ordered in a way which contradicts the assumptions of democratic process. Further, the common interest of workers and management is so channeled, through the unstable division of the product into profits and wages, as to create a well-structured division of interest as well. This schism between the leaders of work and their followers drastically reduces the common ground of values, and the unions have arisen in response.

Finally, the division of labor at present is so great as to weaken the common conscience of the different levels of workmen. Durkheim postulated a solidarity, a group *élan,* based upon teamwork; however, to the routine worker his job is frequently merely the payment of a pound of flesh (Oeser and Hammond).[24] A large proportion of most work organizations is made up of routine workers, and their lack of control over their work, their competition with management for economic rewards, their organized voice, the union, and their ability to leave the job, all represent limiting conditions. It is difficult to see how strong communities could arise within such market-oriented organizations.

Thus the major institutional order of work is unable to supply the basis for primary community; the local area is functionally weak; the kinship system is important chiefly at the level of the small conjugal family. The remaining possible structure for individual participation is the formal voluntary organization. A brief review of the findings cited earlier, however, indicates that such organizations are relatively unimportant "at the grass roots." They are arenas for intensive participation to only a small minority of their members, and many individuals have no formal organizational membership at all.

One possible exception is the labor union. Here is an organization whose functional importance is great indeed for its members. Unlike industry, it is an organization based upon the assumptions of the democratic ideology: participation in decision-making is quite easy. Finally, it is an organizational type which is extremely widespread—it is probably the most important single kind of formal organization outside the churches. What of union participation?

Many studies indicate that the average attendance of members at a local union's routine meetings is extremely low—from less than one per cent to perhaps 20 per cent.[25,27] Most of those who attend are the same group, over and over, and these, together with the paid professional staff, have undue influence upon the organization. For the average member, on the other hand, the union is almost an aspect of government. He pays his dues, and, as in the national elections, frequently does not vote. His leaders, with the best will in the world, far overreach their responsibility —for there is nobody else to take responsibility. Most often the leaders "run the locals" (with some restraint from the small cadres of actives) and the members act as a "plebiscitary body" in Herberg's phrase.[26] Far from constituting a "real community" for the workers, the union is simply another service organization. It can mobilize the members to strike, but not to participate in the organization's routine functioning where the basic grounds for strikes are considered and argued out.

In summary, it is apparent that in a society with a democratic political structure and ideology democratic processes are relatively rare. Shared decision-making, control through consent, is most common in the conjugal family and friendship groups, but it is hardly transmitted through them to larger entities. The other areas where individual participation is possible, local community and formal organization, engage only a minority in more than token participation, and the organizations of work—most important of all in many respects—are structurally unfit for democratic processes. The following picture of participation in urban society results.

There is a plethora of formal organizations, labor unions, business and professional groups, churches and church-related groups, parent-teacher's associations, and the like. They exert pressure and they influence the political party—another formal organization. However, the leadership in such organizations is largely professionalized and bureaucratized, and such leaders become, in effect, oligarchs. At the same time the members participate in an erratic manner, and frequently "stay away in droves" from the meetings. The organization is a holding company for the members' interests; they exercise an occasional veto right in the plebiscites.

The local area is either not a community in any sense, as in the highly urban areas of the city, or it is a community "of limited liability"; communication and participation are apt to be segmental here as in any formal organization that is extraterritorial. And many are utterly uninvolved, even in the strongest "communities."

Formal government is highly bureaucratized and, aside from votes in national elections and (very occasionally) in local elections, the individual participates very little. Most party "clubs" are made up of professionals, semiprofessionals, and a handful of "actives."

The organization of work is nondemocratic in its nature, and the individual's participation is largely a matter of conforming to directions and decisions made far above him in the hierarchy. This is of great importance, for with the rise of professional leadership in all formal organizations—from labor unions to churches, Boy Scouts, and even recreation in general—the most intense participation in all groups is apt to be that of the official, for whom the organization is his *job* in a job hierarchy.

Thus interpreting the participation of the average individual in democratic society is a somewhat bizarre experience: by and large he does not participate. Since this is true, it is difficult to make a case for the widespread importance of the democratic processes for most people, except in the home and friendship circle. The Democracy we inhabit is, instead, largely a democracy of substantive freedoms, or what Fromm[28] calls "freedom from." Produced by the struggles between various professionally directed interest groups, largely quite undemocratic in their control processes, freedom of choice for the individual is something of a by-product. It exists, perhaps, through the balance of "countervailing forces."

This freedom is, however, a considerable area of the average person's "life space." It is manifest in the urbanite's ability to choose his marital and family status, his local area and degree of community participation—his life style. He may privatize his nonworking world, and turn inward to his single family dwelling unit and his conjugal family (which he does); he may refuse to participate in many activities and yield only a token participation in others (and he does).

Though his commitments to the job and the family are constant and have a priority in time and energy, he exercises freedom of choice—in the market, the large sphere which Riesman[29] calls consumership. He also has a freedom in the symbol spheres which has never been widespread before in any society—the variety of media and of messages is overwhelming. (There are approximately 1,000 hours of television available each week to the Los Angeleno.) His relative wealth, literacy, and privacy allow an exploration of meaning never possible before. In his homelife he experiments with leisure—the hobby industries, the do-it-yourself industries, the flood of specialized publications and programs bear testimony to the increasing use the urbanite makes of this choice. He is part of the *nouveaux riche* of leisure.

His rise is a measure of the leveling of the hierarchical orders; their remnants remain in the relatively higher rates of participation and leadership for the "upper ranks" in most of the formal organizations. Most people, however, are the equivalents and descendants of the illiterates of a hundred years ago. They have neither the vested interest nor the tradition of responsible participation—and they have a great freedom from forced participation in work. They exercise it in fashioning the typical life-patterns adumbrated, in avoiding organizations, politely giving lip-service to the neighbors and local leaders, avoiding work associates off the job, orienting themselves towards evening, week ends, and vacations, which they spend *en famille* looking at television, gossiping and eating with friends and kin, and cultivating the garden.

The bureaucratic leadership and the plebiscitary membership, the community of limited liability, and the privatized citizen are not images many of us hold of a proper democratic society. Perhaps it cannot last—perhaps power is accumulating too rapidly and in too few centers. On the other hand, the picture is less frightening than that of the atomistic man adrift in mass society, *anomic* and destructive. Furthermore, the picture of participation in the primary community is a rather strenuous one. Perhaps a revision downwards, toward effective "limited community" participation, and effective "plebiscites" might result in an adequate check upon the formal leadership groups—enough to represent a modest achievement of democratic participation and control through consent.

Notes

1. Louis Wirth, "Urbanism as a Way of Life," *The American Journal of Sociology,* XLIV (July, 1938), 1–24.

2. Kurt Wolff, trans. and ed., *The Sociology of George Simel* (Glencoe, 1950).

3. George Simpson, trans., *Emile Durkheim on the Division of Labor in Society* (New York, 1933).

4. C. P. Loomis, trans. and ed., *Fundamental Concepts of Sociology* (Ferdinand Tonnies, *Gemeinschaft und Gesellschaft*) (New York, 1940). . . .

6. Robert E. Park, *Human Communities* (Glencoe, 1952).

7. Robert M. McIver and Charles H. Page, *Society: An Introductory Analysis* (New York, 1949).

8. Mirra Kommarovsky, "The Voluntary Associations of Urban Dwellers," *American Sociological Review,* XI (Dec., 1946), 868–896.

9. Morris Janowitz, *The Community Press in an Urban Setting* (Glencoe, 1952).

10. Donald E. Foley, "Neighbors or Urbanites? The Study of a Rochester District," *The University of Rochester's Studies of Metropolitan Rochester* (Rochester, 1952).

11. Morris Axelrod, "Urban Structure and Social Participation," *American Sociological Review,* XXI (Feb., 1956), 13–18.

12. Wendell Bell, "Urban Neighborhood Types and Participation in Formal Organizations," *American Sociological Review,* XXI (Feb., 1956), 25–34.

13. Wendell Bell (with the assistance of Maryanne Force and Marion Boat), "People of the City," (processed) Stanford University Research Facility, Stanford, California (1954).

14. Scott Greer, "Urbanism Reconsidered: A Comparative Study of Local Areas in a Metropolis," *American Sociological Review,* XXI (Feb., 1956), 19–25.

15. Scott Greer and Ella Kube, "Urban Worlds: A Comparative Study of Four Los Angeles Areas," (processed) Laboratory in Urban Culture, Occidental College (1955).

16. O. A. Oeser and S. B. Hammond, eds., *Social Structure and Personality in a City* (New York, 1954).

17. Eshref Shevky and Marilyn Williams, *The Social Areas of Los Angeles* (Berkeley and Los Angeles, 1948).

18. Eshref Shevky and Wendell Bell, *Social Area Analysis* (Stanford, 1955).

19. Colin Clark, *The Conditions of Economic Progress* (London, 1940).

20. Godfrey Wilson and Monica Wilson, *The Analysis of Social Change* (London, 1945).

21. P. Sargant Florence, *The Logic of British and American Industry* (London, 1953).

22. Scott Greer, *Social Organization* (New York, 1955).

23. Elton Mayo, *Human Problems of an Industrial Civilization* (New York, 1933).

24. Oeser and Hammond, op. cit., Part V, "The Workers: Social Hierarchies."

25. Scott Greer, "The Participation of Ethnic Minorities in the Labor Unions of Los Angeles County," (unpublished Ph. D. dissertation), Department of Anthropology and Sociology, University of California at Los Angeles (1952).

26. Will Herberg, "Bureaucracy and Democracy in Trade Unions," *Antioch Review*, III (Sept., 1943), 405–417.

27. Seymour Martin Lipset, "The Political Process in Trade-Unions: A Theoretical Statement," in *Freedom and Control in Modern Society* (New York, 1954).

28. Erich Fromm, *Escape from Freedom* (New York, 1941).

29. David Riesman (in collaboration with Reuel Denny and Nathan Glazer), *The Lonely Crowd, a Study of the Changing American Character* (New Haven, 1950).

10. *Village Politics*

ARTHUR J. VIDICH AND JOSEPH BENSMAN

(In other sections of their study the authors show that the vast majority of important decisions affecting this small village's life were made outside of the community. They endeavor to show throughout how this has a profound influence, not only on the political process, but also on the complete social structure and the personalities and personal values of individual citizens.)

The elected officials of village government (three trustees, a mayor and a clerk) are with but few exceptions local businessmen, primarily

Reprinted from *Small Town in Mass Society* (Princeton: Princeton University Press, 1958), pp. 114–21, 121–23, 124, 125–26 by permission of the authors and the publisher. Authors' footnotes omitted. Arthur Vidich is a professor of sociology and anthropology at the University of Connecticut. Joseph Bensman is a lecturer in social science at Brooklyn College and a manager of consumer research.

owners and operators of retail stores. However, not all businessmen qualify for public office and not all officials are businessmen. As a primary qualification for election an individual must have been a resident of the community for at least ten years; preferably and most frequently he has been a lifelong resident of the village. Hence his personal "character" and his ideology are well known to the community at large. To be selected as a candidate for public office he must subscribe to a low-tax, low-expenditure ideology and be relatively unsophisticated in the techniques of political analysis and public administration. These qualifications tend to reside in the business community.

When a village official is regarded as especially competent in the affairs of government, he is usually "coopted" or promoted to a position in the "invisible government," where his talents can be utilized to better advantage and where he has a greater opportunity to exercise power (the cases of Howard Jones, who was mayor for fifteen years, and Flint, the village counsel, both of whom as noted below hold key positions in machine politics).

If an official is not a shopkeeper, he must possess, in addition to the above, the qualifications of economic vulnerability or a kinship connection with one of the dominant figures of machine politics. Examples of such cases include a janitor, a relative of Howard Jones engaged in insurance selling; a school superintendent whose professional functions have largely been superseded by school consolidations; and a recent mayor who is a part-time school-bus driver, part-time chiropractor, part-time strawberry grower. When board members are not directly engaged in small business, their life circumstances are such that they are easily able to reflect the ideology of the businessmen and fulfill the qualification of political and administrative incompetence.

Trustees are almost completely unfamiliar with the routine procedures for conducting village business. Legal terminology and the formal vocabulary of the government form, so central to the conduct of their business, are alien to their manner of speech and their way of thinking. More important, however, their life activity, circumscribed within business or some other specialization, leaves them unprepared to comprehend village-state relations and prevents their acquiring a perspective broad enough to encompass the range of political sentiment represented in the community. Hence, in calculating potential reactions to their actions, they think in personal rather than interest-group terms. They are not, then, able to assess their relationship to a constituency, and this lack of skill leads to the indecision which results in incompetence. What is more, the picture of their performance which emerges to the public level is generally regarded as reflecting a do-nothing, incompetent governing agency.

The incompetence of the board members is an open and widespread subject of public discussion among all groups in the community, and elected board members themselves are quick to admit to the outside observer that they "don't know much" about village government.

It thus happens that the incompetent, the economically vulnerable and the appropriately kinship-connected individuals are elected with a regularized consistency, as described below, to a village board on which they find they have nothing to do because, in their own perspective, the routine affairs of government are automatic. Meetings are routinized to fixed times and places and the ceremonies in which they participate are reduced to a pattern of talking which consumes time and accomplishes nothing.

The ceremony of talking while accomplishing nothing reflects the dominant psychology of those groups in the village which exist behind the scenes and control the processes and purposes of government. This group is composed of the small businessman who subscribes to the ideology of low taxes and low expenditures.

The Low-Tax Ideology and Business Dominance

The businessman exhibits the phenomenon of a psychology of scarcity. His private business operations are based on non-expansion and cost-cutting principles. Capital investment for the purpose of business expansion does not occur. Instead, the village businessman uses obsolete equipment and merchandizing methods. His business practices are based on the careful and jealous guardianship of a limited and local market. The primary appeal to the market is personal loyalty. Under these circumstances the businessman is concerned with minimizing the costs of operation and with accumulating savings. In his business as well as his private life he emphasizes the virtues of thrift, savings and the minimization of consumption. The virtues which he emphasizes result in accumulated savings which are partly hoarded as cash and partly invested in local real property. When this psychology of scarcity on the part of the businessman is translated into government operations, a premium is placed upon low government expenditures and low taxes.

In concrete personal terms, low expenditures mean low taxes and low taxes mean low fixed costs in business operations and the greater chance to accumulate as savings what might otherwise be "eaten up" in taxes. In the village board no expenditure is approved without a careful prior consideration of its consequences for the tax rate.

Hardly a meeting of the village board passes without some action being justified on the basis of the low tax principle—services are curtailed to avoid a tax raise, purchases of new equipment are postponed in order to avoid expenditures, the trustees complain to each other if street lights are not turned off at sunrise, payrolls are delayed near the end of the fiscal year when funds are short and new taxes have not been collected in order to save interest on a bank loan, state funds and services are accepted and sought "to save the taxpayer's money." It is habitual practice prior to the expenditure of any funds first to investigate whether the object for which the expenditures are being contemplated can be secured without cost by formal request to outside agencies, by informal deals with representatives of outside agencies or from private individuals or groups. Board members display a unanimity of agreement in this most cardinal of principles and apply it as a prior condition to any action except adjournment and accepting the minutes.

The understanding of the successful dominance of the low-tax, low-expenditure principle becomes clearer when placed in the context of the broader interests of businessmen. Businessmen as a group possess the greatest interest of ownership in the real property of the village. In addition to owning their business establishments, businessmen invest savings in local real property. Almost every businessman owns some residential property and those who have had long and successful careers in business may own as many as five, ten or fifteen homes. Their practice of capital investment in multiple properties provides the link to their adherence to the low-tax, low-expenditure ideology.

As noted, not all members of the board are engaged in retail trade, nor do all possess extensive investments in real property. However, all members of the board adhere to the low-tax ideology. The selection of candidates for public office is based on a prior knowledge of the willingness of the candidate to accept the ideology. In recruiting candidates, all other qualifications for office—incompetence, vulnerability, kinship connections—take a secondary place to this cardinal principle of government. On the village board itself, saving (purchasing secondhand equipment), short-cut measures to prevent expenditures (borrowing equipment and facilities from other agencies and individuals) are virtuous acts. The honored and esteemed member of the board in the eyes of other board members is the one who is quick to see the possibilities of "saving money" or who can think of a way of doing it the "cheap way." Indeed, this is one of the important areas of competition between board members. Hence it happens that even those board members without a direct economic interest voice, sometimes most frequently, the low-tax, low-expenditure ideology. Through these processes the business psychology comes to dominate the philosophy of government of the village board.

Machine Politics and the Selection of Officials

The effective membership of the local Republican committee consists of three individuals. The chairman of the Republican committee and the dominating but relatively invisible figure of local politics is Howard Jones, one-time mayor and owner of a feed mill and farm supply business, a farm implement and repair business, a building supplies business, several warehouses and half a dozen homes.

In addition to Jones, the committee consists of Sam Lee, town clerk and editor of the local paper, and John Flint, a local lawyer with a local clientele. Flint is legal counsel to the village board and as such sits in attendance at its monthly meetings and possesses the only technical competence available to the board.

It is justifiable to assume that nomination by the Republican committee is tantamount to successful election in the manner of Southern politics. The Democratic party does not offer a slate of candidates for village offices. Hence, the Republican nominating process is crucial. Individuals possessing the qualifications mentioned above are easy to find. It is more difficult to find a qualified person willing to stand for election, not because such persons are not flattered by being considered but rather because they do not want to appear to be eager "to seek public office." The potential candidate is coaxed to run, finally accedes and is elected to office.

The process of nominating candidates is conducted by Jones, Lee and Flint in an approximation of the following manner: Flint, with the assistance of one or two others, draws up a list of three or four possible candidates; he "consults" with Jones, who may make additions or deletions; together they arrange the names in the sequence in which the potential nominees will be approached to be asked to accept the nomination. Before the committee approaches a potential candidate, the list is shown to one or two more people. The persons whose names are on the list are then approached and one individual finally accepts without knowing how many before him have refused. Some days later Flint, who is politically antagonistic to Lee, tells Lee the name of the person who has accepted the nomination. Lee and Flint then make arrangements for a party caucus, setting and making public the day of the meeting. Lee and Flint and a handful of other individuals whom they have encouraged to attend appear for the caucus on the appointed day, but altogether they do not usually constitute a legally required quorum. Then, as Flint has noted, "Most of the time we have to go out and pick somebody off the street to get a quorum. Sometimes we even have a few Democrats voting in there." In any case, the result is uniformly the same: the party candidate is formally nominated in his absence and in the absence of Jones, who may not know the exact name of the nominee until he reads the newspaper. This nominating process results in the selection of candidates whose social characteristics conform to the requirements for success in village government.

In the past fifteen or twenty years, the years of our knowledge, no nominee, incumbent or new, of the party committee has been opposed by the party caucus. In the past twenty years no Republican candidate has been opposed by a Democratic candidate. Historically, nomination by the Republican caucus is equal to election. Trustees tend to succeed themselves unless they voluntarily retire, resign, move or die.

The election of one trustee occurs every year and the election of the mayor and clerk occurs every three years. Elections are held on the first Tuesday of April between the hours of 12:00 noon and 4:00 p.m. (thus excluding from voting those third of the employed individuals who work in surrounding cities) or, as sometimes occurs, between 2:00 and 6:00 p.m. and do not coincide with township, state or national elections. Between 15 and 35 individuals out of a potential electorate of 350–450 vote in a village election. In the certainty of a small vote, the board customarily contracts to print only 50 ballots. Village election day makes no dent on the routine affairs of the community. . . .

Those who vote are the candidate and those who nominated him and their wives. Lee and Flint make sure that at least 15 people vote. The party maintains a poll watcher who is familiar with the voting habits of those who vote and, should unexpected citizens appear to vote (as indicated in the newspaper clipping above), a party representative, who is on hand, hastily recruits counter-balancing voters. In this manner the inner-machine of the party assures the election of its candidates.

Public Interests and Political Paralysis

The village board and the Republican committee do not represent all the community views. There exist other groups who would be interested in "desirable" social expenditures, who lament the do-nothing attitude of the village board, and who would be interested in a revision of assessment evaluations. Residents of Back Street, as well as residents of several other streets, constitute an interest group who want paved roads and street lights. More recent migrants from cities (particularly professionals and industrial workers) would like recreational facilities and swimming instruction for their children and a community building as a center for social activities. The village as a whole is interested in snow removal and a garbage and trash removal service. The entire community is interested in better fire protection (replacement of obsolete equipment) and increased water pressure in kitchen spigots. Individual businessmen and home owners have grieved to the board for a reassessment of their property "to bring it in line with other assessments." A large but unorganized group of individuals is interested in bringing industry to the community. No action was taken on any of these measures in the years preceding and during the field work of the study.

These desires for improvement, change and increased expenditures are held by individuals who have no stake in or control over the village board and who are beyond the purview of party politics—they do not vote and only when they have a special cause or a special complaint or request do they attend meetings of the village board. Their efforts to secure the action they desire remain at the level of private complaining or of occasional attendance at a board meeting as individuals who represent themselves or a specialized organization with a specialized request. The most frequent complaint of local citizens, including board members themselves, concerns alleged inequities in the assessment structure of taxable property. In the entire history of the community, assessments have not been reviewed and great differences exist in assessments of equivalent properties.

In a specific case where an aggrieved property owner presented his grievances because his property was overassessed, all board members agreed that his grievance was justified. His property was assessed at the same amount or at more than much more valuable properties. The ensuing discussion brought out no more than that there were widespread discrepancies in the tax rolls and that a great many other grievances would be equally justified.

Village assessments are automatically copied from the township tax rolls which have never been reviewed or revised. The village board, however, has the jurisdiction to review and revalue village property, but changes in village assessments would involve recopying township tax rolls since the village assessors do not assess property but merely copy town assessments and for purposes of state subsidies, town and village assessments of village property have to be the same. Moreover, revaluation of one property would set a precedent for the reappraisal of others. On the basis of the time, effort and complexities involved, the matter was dropped, though no formal decision to do this was made.

The paralysis of the board in not being able to cope with this and other problems reflects an underlying paralysis of organized political action in the village at large, except for individual efforts among those groups which desire action. The groups and the individuals who want political action lack the tradition, the specialization and the organization to make their views felt. The complexity of organizing political support; the necessity for historical, legal and technical knowledge in defining an issue clearly; the lack of knowledge of procedure; the lack of time—all

these factors lead to inaction and a complaining but dissatisfied acceptance of the "business as usual" ideology of the village board. . . .

The Consequences of Political Paralysis

Reliance on Experts

In the village board the dominating and relatively publicly visible
figure is the counsel, Flint, who is not an elected member of the board
at all. Due to the legal and procedural complexities of conducting the
routine business of the village and the necessity of correctly filling and
filing the many documents which legalize and support the official actions
taken by the board, no action is possible without the assistance of the
legal counsel. Moreover, the counsel is the only individual competent to
conduct a correspondence with state and other agencies with which the
village must do business and he himself insists on following exact legal
forms even when only local matters are involved. Meetings of the board
do not ordinarily begin until the counsel has arrived. . . .

The legal counsel acts and is regarded as a source of information and
as an authority not only on legal questions but also on general matters
of procedure, precedent and history. When he speaks he is listened to
with attention and his suggestions and recommendations are ordinarily
accepted without question. . . .

The Social Basis of Unanimity

The dominating influence of Flint on the board does not deny the
possibility of conflict among the members. Beneath the public unanimity
of the board, there exist small but important differences of interest between board members. For one, who lives on a street without lights,
there exists a potential impulse to secure street lighting in needed places.
Another who is superintendent of the fire district is more inclined than
the others to spend money on fire equipment. The clerk who owns no
business property and is not a voting member of the board would be
favorably disposed to a reassessment program. The mayor tends to be
more "economy-minded" than some of the trustees. Each participant on
the board has a pet interest which serves as a potential basis for conflict.
Yet this conflict is never openly apparent and the principle of unanimity
of decision is never broken. When board business touches on issues of
potential conflict, each board member brings up for subliminal assessment the position of other members on the issue in question—i.e., who

would be apt to oppose the measure and with what intensity—and avoids further mention of the topic.

Since the board member has neither skill nor knowledge nor a constituency to support him, he lacks confidence in his own opinion and his own cause. Instead of pushing an idea, he retreats to more familiar territory, the espousal of "economy-mindedness" on which he knows all members agree. When an issue comes up on which the positions of all board members are not known—when some new problem presents itself, for instance—a long process of discussion, during which board members frequently contradict themselves, ensues. This discussion, which appears so strange to the outsider, takes place for the purpose of finding a common ground on which all can agree and in which no opinion stands out. In this way no member irrevocably commits himself on an issue and, hence, does not alienate himself from the other members of the board with whom he must deal from month to month and in his daily living on a "friendly" basis. These dynamics explain the lengthy and poorly directed discussion which occupies the time of the board and provide a partial explanation for the phenomenon of unanimity.

In addition, however, there is always the danger that, should an issue come into the open, conflicting parties will appeal to outside individuals or groups or to the more important figures in the machine. Public sentiment could easily be mobilized around the issues of assessments, street lighting and snow removal. There is the ever-present possibility that an issue can be taken directly to the leaders of the machine since the link between the board and the machine is intimate.

As a consequence of these dynamics, in any situation which suggests that differences of opinion exist, action is postponed or delayed to a subsequent meeting or indefinitely. Between meetings, interested parties are consulted, board members meet and talk informally and some type of "understanding" is reached before the next meeting. If the item at issue is small (where to place a street light), several important individuals in the neighborhood are talked to, and opinion is sounded in other neighborhoods which do not have street lights. If the issue is large (such as a several thousand dollar bank loan, to repair a broken water main—the issue being how good a job is to be done), Howard Jones is consulted directly. In many cases this activity between meetings settles the issue so that it comes up for perfunctory approval at a subsequent meeting; or, if a *modus vivendi* cannot be worked out, nothing further is heard of the issue.

In the ordinary conduct of business in this manner, potential issues and conflicts never become visible at a public level. Undisciplined appeals to outside groups which would threaten the monopoly of power of the controlling group do not occur. The board, especially the trustees who alone possess the voting privilege, openly state that they do not want "to stir up trouble." Since the board members themselves carry responsibility for their actions, they do not take action until the appropriate individuals are consulted and until it is apparent that responsibility is diffused into unanimity. There is the continuous effort to seek the formula by which unanimity can be achieved. Until unanimity is reached, there is a tacit agreement to discuss the proposal and to postpone the decision until the time comes when either by wearing down, time limitations or accident a formula is found. The formula itself takes many forms. Typically it is indefinite postponement. Frequently it is arrived at by "doing what we did last year or ten years ago." Sometimes it is reached by taking "the 'only' legal course open to us according to the law of the state." In no instance is a formula based on a recognition of conflicting interests which require balancing.

Dependence on Extra-Legal Bodies

As a consequence of this structure of decision making, the village board is not usually in a position to act when pressing action is required. When special problems arise which require non-traditional solutions or quick decisions and quick action, extra-legal bodies take over the functions of village government and meet the problem by extra-legal, quasi-legal or private means . . . problems which have arisen in the recent past may be cited to illustrate the manner in which community action is organized to meet problems requiring special action. . . .

In the past seven years, the various committees of the Community Club have concerned themselves with such board functions as the following:

   a. Established a state-supported youth recreation program
   b. Annual testing of swimming water
   c. Repairing and maintaining dam
   d. Petitioned the county board of supervisors to repair a road "over which much business comes to Springdale"
   e. Called in a representative of the state traffic bureau to explain state traffic policies with respect to Springdale and "complained" to him of inadequate traffic signals and facilities in Springdale
   f. Annual setting up of a community Christmas tree
   g. Agitated to secure street safety signs for school children
   h. Established an industry committee in an effort to attract industry to Springdale

i. Initiated a park development program on property recently deeded to the village
j. Established an annual clean-up day
k. Heard all manner of specific complaints from individuals and organizations on problems related to traffic, road signs, safety, roads, public transportation (bus service), rural mail service, inadequate garbage and snow removal facilities, and so forth
l. Has under consideration the acquisition of a community building.

However, in spite of its extra-legal functioning in the political sphere, the Community Club is not a political body. Political issues are treated as discreet items of business in general meetings without being placed in the context of an overall political program. The functions which the Community Club has co-opted from the village board have been those functions which the board has been eager and willing to give up, those which are regarded as a nuisance or as expensive. The political activities of the Community Club represent political agitation for a specific point or a specific issue or the redress of a specific wrong. Since responsibility is diffused into committees, no central direction is given to an overall political program.

These extra-legal bodies tend to draw into their fold supporters who are not active in village politics. Support for specific issues is usually limited to those with a specialized interest and their interest is sustained only until the specific issue is resolved or crushed. However, if such extra-legal bodies, particularly the Community Club, gather sufficient support in the community as to appear to disturb the routinized equilibria of local politics . . . the leaders of both visible and invisible government become interested in the activity and the official governing agency reflects this interest in action . . . . The invisible government becomes interested in an issue in order to control the activities of extra-legal bodies. The machine may take a direct interest in an issue and openly act as an extra-legal body; it may take over control of other extra-legal bodies for appropriate periods of time; it may influence the organization of extra-legal bodies, as was the case of the Community Club. Hence, it is through these extra-legal temporary groupings and organizations that a certain amount of community action occurs in spite of the fact that village government has abdicated most of its functions.

Political Ceremonies and Political Participation

The pattern of village politics can be summarized in terms of an analysis of the meaning of the political ceremony. The political ceremony consists of the endless and indecisive talk which occurs in formal meetings of the village board. The formal meeting itself is a social ritual in which discussion serves the purpose of avoiding decision making. The postponement and avoidance of decisions has a number of social functions.

The ritual of talking, in the first instance, serves the primary purpose of achieving public unanimity within the board. No board member states his case or argues on issues in irrevocable terms. Rather by continuous exploration of alternatives, blunting of the issues and searching for neutral statements, a point is reached where all the individual perspectives of the board members are merged into one perspective and unanimity is achieved. When such a condition of unanimity is achieved, the issue can be resolved in such a way that no aggrieved board member has need or grounds to appeal to the community at large for support. Hence, no new or outside pressure groups can be brought in to bear on local politics and to threaten monopoly of power of the village board and its controllers. Unanimity thus makes it difficult for outside groups to find an issue which would threaten the *status quo*.

The same process of endless talk stretching out from meeting to meeting and from year to year means that somehow the issues get lost even when unanimity is not achieved. After indefinite delay in dealing with an issue, the issue itself loses its salience and becomes irrelevant, and no action is required. In such cases unanimity is unnecessary because the issue over which potential conflict might arise has lost its importance with the passage of time.

In other cases the ritual of talk, postponement and unanimity works itself out in such a way that the necessary action gets accomplished without a decision being reached. This occurs in cases involving action relating to the requirements set by higher governmental agencies. In its postponement of decision making, the village board surrenders the legal prerogatives established within the framework of the village charter and state law. In not taking action where it has the option to do so, the village board allows mandatory alternatives to village action to become operative. Hence the state highway commission, the state traffic bureau and other state agencies actually determine village affairs.

In the various alternative cases described above, then, either a minimum of action is taken or only that action which does not threaten the *status quo*. This is understandable in terms of the patterns of political control in the village. The dominant political group is composed of small businessmen and property owners. Avoidance of action on their part represents an avoidance of expenditures and thus, in turn, results in the maintenance of low real-estate taxes.

The avoidance of splits, issues and controversies on the board

results in the exclusion from political participation of "outsiders" because the processes of unanimity destroy those issues which might be
capitalized upon by dissident groups.

Moreover, politics without genuine issues, as a further result, is
"dull" (nothing happens) and in terms of open issues there is nothing
for which it is worth exercising the ballot. As a result, politics, though
discussed incessantly by all, is only an amusing spectacle concerning
personalities. Only a handful of individuals vote in village elections,
those who have a direct interest—largely village and party officials and
their families. Thus, between 15 and 35 voters control village elections
and they do so by being interested in them. For other voters, the village
board ceremony of continuously talking without accomplishment, while
having the effect of producing disgust in those who are interested in political action, has the effect of producing disinterest and apathy among
all groups in the community except on those occasions when politics
may be viewed as a spectacle—i.e., when a newspaper editorial accuses
the trustees of graft when they raise their own salaries. It is a consequence of this apathy that such a small number of voters determines the
outcome of an election. . . .

When it is not possible to divert pressures for change and innovation, when extra-legal bodies gain sufficient support for an issue, and
when delay and postponement have not resolved the issue, the members of the board and the party machinery feel a threat to their political
existence. The advocates of change (usually members of the professional
and industrial class who are interested in social improvements) become
the bearers of an issue which can arouse the community, bring out
community-wide interest in the issue and the elections and, thus,
threaten the *status quo*. In such an emergency, and only as a last-resort
measure, the village board will consent to act. In acting it takes over
the issue advocated by outsiders, and gets the action accomplished
with the assistance of the machine. Once this happens the board becomes the sponsor and executor of the program and remains in control
of the decisive areas of decision making. The issue as an issue disappears
and the opposition to the board dissolves into its previous state of disorganization and is eliminated as a threat. Village government is then
able to continue (and acts) as if nothing has happened. By election
time there is no issue to dramatize politics and to threaten the control
through apathy which the local machine has over elections.

As a further result of these dynamics all opposition groups in the
village are, and can only be, organized around a single issue at any
one time. All such groups in the past have been temporary and the

machine has survived, even though in the process a number of local programs have been accomplished which otherwise might never have happened.

It is in this, perhaps minimal, way that outside interest groups are represented and that to some degree a democratic process is carried out. For, no matter what their own interests may be and no matter how reluctantly they aquiesce, the village board and the political machine, in order to maintain political control, must find some method of accommodating these pressures which, if avoided, would result in their loss of control. The reluctant acceptance of these issues and the programs which they entail constitute the foundations of democracy in the rural village.

11. A Re-examination of Local Democracy

ROBERT C. WOOD

Testimonials—the conclusions of important philosophers—are one way to defend the small community; logical argument is another. To buttress the case in the modern world, the insights and judgments of every age can be put together into a simple, apparently commonsense chain of reasoning that runs essentially like this: Small towns offer certain indigenous qualities which, taken collectively, create a milieu in which the American aims of equality and liberty are best secured. They promise the development of individual initiative, operate as a bulwark against concentrated political power, provide the most effective union of the collective and private disposition of mankind that we can hope to find. Destroy these qualities, embrace completely the gargantuan world in which we live, and the traditional goals of American society are also in peril.

But what specifically do the qualities of small town life contribute to a harmonious relation of man to man and to good government? In the logic of the faith, each characteristic has its own beneficial effect which can be recognized and defended. Whether found in the small town of other centuries or in the modern suburb, propinquity, interdependence, common beliefs and backgrounds, some measure of leisure time are

Reprinted from *Suburbia: Its People and Their Politics* (Boston: Houghton Mifflin Company, 1959), pp. 266–89 by permission of the author and the publisher. Author's footnotes abridged. Robert Wood is a professor of political science at Massachusetts Institute of Technology.

thought to encourage political activity which almost guarantees effective democratic government. And when their separate contributions are added together, the case for the small locality seems sturdy indeed.

Propinquity, for example, apparently provides the familiarity and experience, the intimacy of personal relations that Plato and Aristotle stressed so heavily and that helps ensure the sense of integration so sought after today. In a small town, individual identity is never a problem; people can know whomever it is important to know. There are fewer secrets and fewer idols than in the large cities; flaws and strengths of character are quickly recognized; the good are separated from the bad. In the small government, the public program and the official who carries it out are known, judged, understood directly; they can be experienced, they are visible. Life does not impose impossible demands on rationality and character; community organization is attuned to the reality of human nature. The situation is of manageable proportions, and, because the boundaries are fixed, it can stay within manageable proportions.

To the concreteness of life that propinquity provides, the condition of interdependence is thought to add a healthy motive of good will. Men want to cooperate in the small town; they cannot tolerate the troublemaker, for his existence threatens the existence of all. Since they are bound together in their common fortunes, the solutions to communal problems affects directly each man's personal future. Since total resources are limited, all members are encouraged to pull together, to be good neighbors. Sickness, adversity, natural disaster visited on one member are known to all, and since all recognize that an act of God may come again, the urge to help is reinforced by the knowledge that everyone "is in the same boat."

The bonds of fellowship that propinquity and interdependence encourage seem further strengthened by the common goals and common values inherent in the equality of a small town. The locality may be, relatively speaking, better off or less fortunate than its neighbors, or than similar communities elsewhere, but its very size fixes limits on the extremes within its own social order. There can be, it is argued, only a few who live on the Hill, if there is only one hill in town; only a few who are socially unacceptable if there is only one shanty town. Opposing values, different ambitions, sharply divergent beliefs are rarities in such a situation.

Even where differences in wealth and position exist, the variation seems acceptable. The successful succeed not through any mystique, but by working harder or being more excellent in the pursuits in which the majority are engaged. In these circumstances it is difficult to infect recognition of ability with envy and spite, for the means of accomplishment are open to all. Sharp dealings, to be countenanced, must be the established rules of the game, part of the mores of the entire community. A vast common ground of shared beliefs and customs makes cooperation comfortable and intimacy pleasurable.

Under these conditions, so the rationale runs, each member is likely to participate fully and freely in public affairs. A citizen speaks his piece in the small town first of all because what goes on is vital to his own ambitions. It concerns property, education, and the provision of utilities basic to existence. Wars, diplomacy, the fluctuations of the national economy, these matters are both difficult for the average man to understand and difficult for him to influence, but the land use of his neighborhood, the proper recording of his property, zoning, water rights, the protection of his person, the education of his children, the construction of a new highway at the right place and at the right time, affect his everyday life. Whether or not they are provided, how they are provided, the use made of the limited resources to which the citizen contributes directly and not by the accounting sleight-of-hand of the withholding tax, are matters he understands and cares deeply about.

And even if a small town resident did not care, if his stake were slight and his status low in the narrow scale of the social order, he would still participate in public affairs, for that participation expresses, asserts, and guarantees his political equality. Only the eccentric, the hermit, the deviate, remains aloof; the proof of citizenship is by association with your neighbor, and a man establishes himself when he stands up and is counted.

In such a context, the defenders of the small town insist, leadership partakes of special qualities, at once removed from the patrician and the rabble-rouser. A leader in the small community supposedly can be neither, for in an equal society he can neither assume that his fellows are inferior nor can he raise the standard of the underdog and cannily set slave against master. The leader expresses the sense of the community and he helps formulate and crystallize it. But he can never "deliver" the majority opinion and he cannot be above it. Bounded by the conditions of equality and participation, known intimately by his fellows, the leader cannot rely on oratory or adulation, nor can he exhibit only driving ambition. Typically, he operates almost invisibly, knotting together one personal association with another until he has secured sufficient respect and support to put his measures through.

The respect may be misplaced; the leader may simply have cultivated a familiarity which his neighbors mistake for fellowship. On the other hand, he may have a genuine, lively interest in the work which must be done, and a willingness to accept responsibility. But, regardless of motives, his leadership is never flamboyant. Small town leadership is in town moderator style, unassuming, calm, equitable and knowledgeable, without frills or airs. Accessibility is the key condition, whether the leader operates as a petty tyrant or a devoted trustee to the community spirit, and being accessible, his success depends on his own sensitivity to the moods and aspirations of his fellows.

Finally, it is argued, the activities of the small community are likely to take place in an atmosphere of leisure, in the sense that vocation does not consume all time and all attention. There is a limit to the number of things that must be done, and a limit to the number of events that demand attention. Each day or each week may bring a major problem to the fore, but it is likely that the problem is the only one for that period. The question of *choosing* the event is rarely an issue, for in the small town there is usually but one church social, one fire, one scandal, one television program, one public emergency at a time, and men shift attention successively from one event to another and are not—indeed cannot be—confused by competing spectacles.

So advocates of the ideology point out that there is time for reflection, for contemplation, for second thoughts, for deliberation, for the cooling of emotions, for rational appraisals, which permit a sense of direction and rational decisions. To many, this quality of time is the most precious blessing the small community can offer. More than propinquity, equality, the opportunity for active participation and passive leadership, the slower rhythm ensures the manageability of the small community. It encourages the expression of the communal nature of man in an orderly, regular fashion; it removes the tensions of self-seeking and provides the requisites for sensible common action.

The elaboration and description of these qualities, collectively and individually, is the reasoned argument that supports the authority of the philosopher and the instinct of the laymen who defend the small government. Its appeal seems universal, because the traits seem common to all men of all times. Good will, neighborliness, courage, fair play, tolerance, patience, open-minded inquiry—since Plato, these are the human qualities that are to be idealized. And they can exist, if one follows the logic, only in small settings. They are not, in Arthur Morgan's words, "the fruits of civilization, but rather its roots." Since they can apparently be found only on a small scale, great civilization paradoxically can be constructed only from small societies where government and neighborhood commingle and political and social reality become one.

It is little wonder that men wax sentimental when they write of the grassroots, speak of "plain citizens and humble leaders," and find poetry in the Town Meeting. The spirit of communion affects each quality observed, and reason confirms instinct in approving the Miniature. Individuality tempered by neighborliness, equality used to promote cooperation, community which tolerates eccentricity—this would seem to represent the best of America.

Probing the Lines

A faith so long established, so closely reasoned and so universally acclaimed has the aspect of a phalanx on the battlefield of philosophy. Yet the very unanimity of opinion is suspicious, for the two broad schools of thought that collectively supply the arguments for the small community have contradictory basic assumptions and seek widely divergent ends. Given this fact, evidently one of them is mistaken when it embraces the faith. Either the men who view society and politics as principally corporate affairs with collective goals beyond those of the individuals err when they applaud the ideology, or those who regard the state as a contrivance serving only private purposes are deceived. If the desirability of the Miniature is the issue, one question to ask is which philosophy was right and which wrong when it sided with the small town?

The most accurate answer to this question is that both of the philosophical camps we have been describing deluded themselves. The ultimate aim of those who see man essentially as a social animal is to create a body politic of such dimensions that the richness and variety of human experience can be encompassed. Their vision is a mosaic of intricate design, in which each individual makes his contribution to a purpose higher than his own aims, and the grandeur of that vision is used to justify the gradations in rank and status, the obligations of duty and discipline, the array of mutual responsibilities and social controls that are required to produce the splendid work of art.

But the small community, in and of itself, never realizes that end—it never comprehends the variety of life; at best, it can serve only as an intermediate grouping within the greater whole. In Greece, the golden age was not associated with the city-state; it arrived with the Athenian Empire. The medieval city had meaning only within the Kingdom of God; Burke's parish was but a connection between the family and the commonwealth. In short, civilization has never existed within village boundaries, and the small community is nothing more than a segment in the larger pattern, expressive of only one element in the universe, and by itself quite meaningless.

Yet if corporate philosophers can use the small community only as a stepping stone for its greater purpose, the advocates of individualism have even greater difficulty in fitting it into their scheme of values. Particularly, the American version of the ideology, with its emphasis on equality as a means for liberating the individual, errs grievously when it embraces the small community. Participation in communal affairs is a simple matter in the small towns, but this expression of equality does not lead necessarily to freedom in the personal sense. More often than not, the common standard of the small community, its proudly displayed principle of equality, its suspicion of "social airs," operates in a profoundly anti-individualistic way. In Louis Hartz's words, "The man who is as good as his neighbors is in a tough spot when he confronts all his neighbors combined."

Precisely because the small town represents the most radical application of the democratic theory, it raises the greatest problem for individualism. Here is the extreme expression of popular sovereignty against which Madison strove: popular control unchecked by a notion of minority rights; a principle derived from natural rights which destroys natural rights, with all the ethical and impersonal inconsistencies and deficiencies that Robert Dahl has detailed.[1] Here is no conscious agreement freely developed through debate and discussion but rather passive acquiescence, an irrational expression of uniformity of attitude and outlook, a certainty of the rightness of the majority which amounts to compulsion.

It may be true, as Dahl suggests, that theoretically the respective roles of majority and minority are never neatly balanced in the search for freedom, but certainly, in the small communities, the scale is weighed heavily in favor of the majority. "You have to go on living with people," Sherwood Anderson reflects, "day after day, week after week. You can't just ignore your brother-in-law, forget him as you might in a city. Tomorrow you will meet him in the street. You will be meeting him in the stores and in the post-office. Better make it up, start over again." Equality of this kind liberates only when the individual is part of the majority. When he dissents, equality is as likely to display as intolerant a disdain for private opinion as does an autocratic state.

When the lines are probed far enough the small community stands as representative of the worst of both philosophies: the requirement that man subordinate his individual aims to that of the group, without the group possessing any quality of greatness; the prescription that a man begins on the basis of equality with his neighbor, with no guarantee that he can go forward on his own. The respectable values that both interpretations hold out as perennially valid, the insights into human nature that they contribute, are lost. What is left over are the dregs of their speculation, the flaws of their grand analysis, the unacceptable portions of their doctrine. Order without purpose; equality without liberty; these become the hallmarks of the ideology.

The essence of this residue can be summed up in a single concept: fraternity. Grassroots life is "the test of man's ability to adjust himself. It tells the story of his skill in living with others." This is the heart of the small town, the reason it is acclaimed and the reason why it may be defective. It is not surprising that the descriptions of "democracy at work," town meeting style, become invariably anecdotal: instance after instance of informality, good will, the triumph of personality over procedure, the potency of the wisecrack at the proper time, the decision tailored to the person involved, the horseback judgment overriding the expert opinion. In the rosy glow of the fellowship which propinquity and equality produce, the pattern dissolves into a series of character sketches, each actor classified and typed, each reading his lines in the comfortable assurance that the script has been agreed upon by all.

Quite certainly, fraternity is a persistent inclination of mankind; it fills some needs of human nature. It promises security in a group of like persuasion; it bolsters faltering egoes, it banishes an awful sense of loneliness, it fosters togetherness and belongingness. To the degree that these qualities reinforce the individual, soothe nerves, banish discord, promote harmony, they are doubtless useful. Lodges, clubs, fraternities have their function, for when a man is free to choose his associates the choice can be both a bulwark against the world and an expression of himself. No one doubts the beneficial values of neighborhood, where the lessons of getting along with the outsiders are first learned in the company of friends, where a knowledge of the common traits of human nature is gained, and where the drift of affairs is, above all, predictable. In these circumstances, the uses of fraternity are sometimes admirable.

At other times, however, fraternity may be less than admirable, with overtones of exclusiveness, narrowness, provinciality and clannishness. Privacy cannot be countenanced in a brotherhood; personal ambitions bow necessarily to group aims; unanimity becomes essential, for how else can a fraternity survive? When the fraternal order is the only order of life, it seems unsatisfactory as a way of organizing society-at-large or establishing a government. When neighborhoods are equipped with political boundary lines, when the fraternal club becomes not an informal part of life but instead its formal expression, when individual purposes can be achieved only through the fraternal process, then the less attractive elements of conformity—compulsion and suspicion—come to the fore.

Yet the concept of fraternity as *the* way of life is, of course, the inescapable implication of grassroots autonomy: an ideal of a self-contained whole to which all members belong and from which none can exit without a violent wrench, a vision of a government which "institutionalizes the neighborliness of the village." But this neighborliness is no universal brotherhood with a higher purpose of a greater civilization, nor is it a voluntary brotherhood, where the common bonds of every man are freely recognized and freely defined. The fraternity of the small community is a union without ambition and without competition. It may be comfortable; it may be forgiving; but it cannot promise the excellence that civilization itself or the individual alone can possibly achieve. "It is," in Sherwood Anderson's words, "a case of love," justified because "Life can never be intimate enough."

Checklist of Operative Democracy: (1) The Rule of Law

The conflict between democracy and fraternity can be set forth in abstract terms; it can also be documented specifically. Once the spirit of the small community is equated with the spirit of fraternity, the violence the suburban image wreaks upon other operative ideals of American society becomes clear in three important ways. A nation committed essentially to the concept of contractual relations as the legitimate method to order human associations has embraced a doctrine of personal relations. A nation that has constructed sophisticated and highly complex restrictions on popular participation in the actual operation of government has accepted the doctrine of direct democracy in its most extreme form. A nation that establishes individuality as the prime goal for its society has deprived itself on the local level of the means to secure that end.

The inconsistency most immediately apparent is between the concept of fraternity and the theory of contractual relations. American life is built on the Lockian proposition of "the reality of atomistic social freedom," a view of the state as an association of free men and an insistence that there be a clear distinction between society and government.[2] The classical expression of this view of legitimate government has always been constitutionalism—the application of systematic regularized restraints on the political power, the guarantee that certain aspects of living are beyond the reach of organized community power, that the government is both something less than, and different from, society.

As Carl Friedrich describes the constitutional process, it rests fundamentally on law—on rules that organize a government, limit the exercise of its authority, and provide the means by which the community and its political organization are distinguished.[3] Government, restrained in action by a bill of rights, by the separation or geographical division of powers, by judicial review, remains apart from the community it governs, and the supreme power of the community comes into play only when the political process fails to function.

There is, of course, no place for such a systematic distinction between the social and political spheres within the meaning of fraternity. Although men are bound together in the American small town not as a hierachy but as a brotherhood, their bonds remain tightly drawn. They are simply members of a large family, and intimacy and intercourse are so inevitable that public and private affairs are difficult to separate. The proud boast so often repeated that "the town meeting *is* the town" is true, and the entire community is the government, not on the rare occasions of catastrophe but whenever public affairs are carried out.

One result, of course, is the special environment in which local government tries to carry out its duties. A public agency operates not so much according to law or under the collective supervision of the community assembled formally as its governing body; instead, it functions under the constant, haphazard, and sometimes suffocating scrutiny of whichever members of the town decide to busy themselves with the agency's affairs. The outstanding example is the public school, for here the line between public function and social institution becomes almost impossible to draw. Lane Lancaster captured the blending of the professional obligations and personal characteristics of the small town teacher in a memorable passage when he wrote: "Not only does the teacher live under the constant espionage of her charges, but she is seldom free from the feeling of utter dependence upon the community which controls her 'job.'⁴ From the moment she arrives in the community her goings and comings become matters of general interest and in every real sense her life ceases to be her own. Where she shall 'board and room,' do her banking, attend church, seek diversion and recreation, the charities she supports, the books she reads, where she will make her personal purchases, the choice of her associates and her clothes, the use of her weekends— all these are matters for gossip in the village which has 'hired' her and which exacts a rigid conformity to the lowest common denominator of village mores."

More serious, perhaps, is the intrusion government can make upon society under these circumstances. The concept of constitutionalism, of law, of impersonal relations between the individual and the group, becomes difficult to maintain. The notion of systematic, regularized restraints filters down from higher levels of government; statutes, regulations, Robert's rules of order become the departure point for public action. But the most significant feature of small town politics is the frequency with which legal and procedural requirements are overlooked and ignored. They are always to be adjusted according to the "common sense, down-to-earth judgment" of the participants, to take account of unique conditions and provincial peculiarities. Tickets can be fixed, favors granted, contracts awarded, not because these irregularities will remain hidden but because they are acceptable on the basis of personal esteem. The successful town moderator is the one who moderates between the rules of the game and the disposition of the meeting. Government indistinguishable from society, when no country gentry is permitted, no lord of the manor allowed, is personalized government. Men come to take on, as Granville Hicks notes, a profound cynicism toward the law. "Every predatory pioneer instinct goes into operation when the average native is confronted with his government—town, state or federal. Governmental bodies apparently exist to be cheated and regulations were made to be evaded."[5]

Personalized government can be both effective and beneficial. It can adjust abstract legal generalizations to the actual state of affairs, make regulations tolerable, and bring them into line with informal mores and customs. But it can also be offensive, as were the personalized duchies which Huey Long created out of the Louisiana parishes, the tight dominions of courthouse gangs, the one-man sovereigns of the rural county whose rule was no less arbitrary because it was accepted.

It is no accident that the folk hero of local America is the law-enforcement agent who interprets the law according to his own lights. The archetype of the Western sheriff substitutes his concept of justice for the statute book; he does his duty, as in *High Noon*, and then grinds his badge underfoot; he operates as often as a vigilante outside the law as within it. And he is applauded, approved, even today, because his concept of justice seems so direct, without frills, legalism, or delays. In short, his law ignored the processes of restraint and orderly procedure on which order is built.

So in the small community, power depends on personal qualities, on the "fit" of the individual to his neighbor, whether or not the official and the citizen are on good terms. Tocqueville identified this grassroots tendency precisely when he wrote, "In general, the American functionaries are far more independent than the French civil officers within the sphere which is prescribed to them. Sometimes, even, they are allowed by the popular authority to exceed those bounds; and as they are protected by the opinion, and backed by the cooperation, of the majority, they venture upon such manifestations of their power as astonish a European. By this means, habits are formed in the heart of a free country which may someday prove fatal to its liberties."[6]

Grassroots government may or may not be good government then;

it is difficult to say. It depends on whether the town is good or not. The smaller the town, the more justice is a matter of personal opinion in the community itself, rarely formalized, rarely examined, rarely permanently established, depending on the sentiment of the moment. It is little wonder that the local justice of the peace is the laughingstock of the legal profession. Even if he knows his duties, how can he possibly impartially administer justice in an atmosphere of overwhelming intimacy?

In this way personalized government, the only form acceptable to fraternity, moves counter to the tradition of law and constitutionalism, confident that familiarity makes it possible to rule by direct knowledge of the neighborhood in place of abstract principle. In such a context, the notion of contractual relations is replaced by the reality of personal relations, who belongs and who does not. The individual depends on the sanction of the group and remains uncertain of his rights and prerogatives. In the end, he has no fixed standard to indicate how he stands in the face and the eyes of his neighbors.

Checklist of Operative Democracy: (2) The Role of Controversy

An innate tendency toward personalized government is one way in which the small community goes against the grain of the broader American creed. An undiluted acceptance of the principle of direct democracy is another. Woven into the institutions and procedures of the nation and the states is an array of formal and informal provisions designed to limit direct popular participation in government, to check and to balance it. Partly, of course, these strictures arose as necessities for managing a popular government over a wide expanse of territory. Partly, they result from prejudices of the founding fathers, long since abandoned. But in good measure, these complicated arrangements are the product of considered judgment and experience as to how a popularly supported government can work effectively. They are rooted in both a realistic view of human nature and a thoughtful appraisal of the limits of popular sovereignty if left to function on its own.

The fundamental premise of American democratic politics, as of Western politics generally, is that men view the public good in different ways, from different perspectives. Factions and parties are regarded as part of the political process, however regretfully men may have accepted their existence and hesitated to sanction their operation. Given this recognition of conflicting opinions and judgments, it has followed, in the logic of constitutional government, that a public policy is hammered out in an arena of discussion and debate until some acceptable compromise develops. It follows also that in order to make the discussion meaningful and reasonably effective, "opposition," in V. O. Key's words, "should be institutionalized"; in short, that it be expected in the normal course of affairs.

In a sense, this expectation of disagreement provides the saving grace of humility to stand against the inherent arrogance of a belief in popular sovereignty and righteousness. The normal democratic political process becomes not a gilt-edge guarantee of responsible, able government, but instead, as Dahl explains, "one in which there is a high probability that an active and legitimate group in the population can make itself heard effectively at some crucial state in the process of decision."[7] A pair of competing party hierarchies, a polyarchal political structure in which many minorities participate, a pattern of interest groups and pressure politics appear as the most effective ways in which modern democracies can operate.

By these standards, the small community is singularly ill-equipped to construct a working democratic process. Its spirit of fraternity proceeds on an assumption quite contrary to disagreement and opposition: it expects essential unanimity. This unanimity is not just an agreement on fundamentals, a consensus about profound beliefs; it is a characteristic supposedly operative on every major public problem. The ideal of the town-meeting citizen is a man capable of divining the public good as a thing apart from his personal attitudes, prejudices, and beliefs. It is a notion of public discussion that has all the aspects of a conference, not a debate. Provide the facts, set forth the problem, and all right-thinking men will arrive at the same decision; or, in the rationale of suburban nonpartisanship today, "there is no Republican or Democratic way to pave a street, all the citizens want is 'good' government."

It is no accident that Madison, perhaps the most realistic of the early American statesmen, after his statement on the inevitability of divisions within the body politic, looked sourly on the direct democracy of the small town. To him, "The smaller the society, the fewer probably will be the distinct parties and interests composing it; the fewer the distinct parties and interests the more frequently will a majority be found of the same party; and the smaller the number of individuals composing a majority, and the smaller the compass within which they are placed, the more easily will they concert and execute their plans of expression." Madison saw clearly that the grassroots ideology had no expectation of serious divisions within its constituency and consequently made no effective provision for the protection of the minority. Instead, it embraced the principle of popular sovereignty to its limits, certain that the majority would always be right.

It is not the possible deprivation of the theoretical natural rights of a minority that is the central issue, however. It is doubtful whether a convincing case for natural rights, demonstrably defined by God, can be established in modern times. In any event, the popular sovereignty of small town and suburb will seldom produce persecution, or even the conditions of oppression that Madison hypothesized. The personalized aspect of local government, rather than its majority principle, is more likely to be the villain in this respect.

What is significant, however, in the direct democracy of the idealized small town is its ineffectiveness in providing a practical operating popular government. The highly optimistic conviction that reason will prevail fails to provide contrasting poles of opinion for meaningful discussion, and most of all, for effective opposition. Here is no spectacle of competing minorities, of parties appealing to the voters while always sensitive to the strategy of the opposition, of organizations sophisticated in political strategy, of seasoned leaders, of professional politicians ready to play the broker between the governed and the governing. Here is only the annual town meeting, the occasional popular referendum, the mass of citizens face to face with the complex public problem, expected to operate always at the peak of civic virtue. It is quite natural that Carl Friedrich, for all his sympathetic concern and respect for the grassroots tradition, could warn of the danger of the manipulation of mass psychology, and point out that too strong a dose of direct democracy destroys the balance of constitutional government. An excessive reliance on direct popular action can lead, as the discussion of suburban politics has suggested, to no popular action at all with the citizen baffled and perplexed and the expert and the small clique in charge.

Tested against the working standards of modern democratic theory, the small town version, with its reliance on citizens instead of institutions, thus operates under major handicaps. To begin with, its very scale makes it unlikely that a reasonable variety of attitudes and opinions will be brought to bear on a problem and that the process of discussion will provide information, knowledge and understanding. A minority that is hopelessly outnumbered can be forgiven for declining to make its case with vigor and completeness. In this way the prime function of minority rights —to provide an opportunity to persuade, to enlighten, to require the majority to defend its position more adequately, to amend and qualify— often goes by default. Sensible men hesitate to stick their necks out when the prospects of success are dim.

Even given a determined minority, however, the opportunity for that minority to organize itself and to operate as a going concern runs into severe institutional handicaps in an atmosphere of nonpartisanship and direct participation. The town meeting is not an effective arena for continuing debate or persuasive argument; it may "ventilate grievances" but it rarely settles them. A dissenter may make a noise, but he rarely can make the kind of noise Dahl defines as an effective voice: one that officials not only listen to "but expect to suffer [from] in some significant way if they do not placate the group, its leaders or its most vociferous members."[8] No wonder Lancaster discovered "New England querulousness institutionalized in the Town Meeting." An opposition, despairing of being effective and accustomed to unrelieved defeat, has a right to be peevish. Rousseau's judgment was even more succinct: "So perfect a government does not suit human beings."

Checklist of Operative Democracy: (3) The Quest for Freedom

The final defect in the grassroots model, and its most fundamental one when judged by operative democratic standards, is the limitations it places on individual development, or, more directly, on freedom. The most obvious of these restrictions applies to the isolated minority and arises out of the internal contradiction in the notion of equality when applied in too intimate circumstances. This limitation, as we have seen, is the fatal inconsistency in the liberal philosophical argument for the small democratic unit, the theoretical flaw in the doctrine of majority rule that has never been erased.

Yet, even if the individual in a small town belongs to the majority, believes in its values, and plays the part of a favored son, a second limitation comes to bear. Unless one believes "the local is the ultimate universal, and as near an absolute as exists,"[9] unless the outside world is only an endless repetition of experiences found within the village, then small size diminishes the prospects for individualism. Individualism can only be defined as the special way a man responds to an elemental and recurrent cycle of experiences—birth, courtship, marriage, family and death; spring, summer, fall, and winter. A spectacle arises of man inexorably facing the rhythm of nature, testing himself against a fixed number of temptations and a fixed number of challenges.

Ideologically, Americans have, of course, never accepted this view of individualism, in spite of the fact that in the context of the small town it is a true one. Opportunity, limitless, boundless, unfettered, has been the key concept—the notion that one could never tell what one would become, what experiences and what adventures one might have. The almost moral obligation of an individual to rise, to get up in the world, has been a fixed constant in our faith. "Energy, self-reliance, and independence, a strong conviction that a man's fate should depend upon his own character and conduct, are qualities without which no nation can be great."[10]

This type of individualism has had its crass side, of course, in the roughshod climb of an Horatio Alger scrambling for undreamed-of heights. And it has its idealistically optimistic side, the dream of perfectibility, as each generation moves another step along the road of progress. Its essence remains, however, a conviction that on his own initiative, a man selects from a number of alternatives instead of simply reacting to one; that growth is unlimited, and that as the number of alternatives expands, freedom expands as well.

The spirit of fraternity directly contradicts this American concept. It cannot rise above the commonness of experience. In place of a promise of progress, of many rainbows and many pots of gold, there is only the routine of the provincial life: the work week, the Saturday night revelry, the schooldays, the church service, the hours spent on the bench on the courthouse square. The village never stirs itself; it is moved only by exits and entrances from the outside world. And so, in place of incentive, of growth, of development, are the characteristics of parochialism: somnolence, lethargy and resignation, "the buried life," "cornpone opinions," the "mill-bound world." Or, as R. A. Woods has described it, "The country village is made up of those who are out of the fight because they never tried. Life runs in a narrow circuit; there is little to stir the blood or stimulate the imagination."[11]

Of course, under modern circumstances, the issue of individuality is cast in a different context. When suburbia becomes the carrier of the grassroots image, there is no physical isolation between the town and the city, and the variety among suburbs presents a spectacle of many ways of living. Thus Edward C. Banfield and Morton Grodzins see the existence of suburbs in the metropolitan area as enhancing the prospects for individuality when defined as a choice among alternatives. They liken the small town suburbanite to a consumer faced with an array of cultural islands, each representing a special brand of homogeneity The individual can live in the area that best represents the social status he desires, and "spheres of free choice for individuals and community groups" are maintained. "Wide options, including the option to be exclusive and expensive, prevail," and, in modern suburbia, "the consumer is in a position to know what combination of goods and services—trees and sidewalks as against food and clothing, for example—will give him the greatest satisfaction."[12]

Two comments are in order about the individualism fostered by the modern suburb. First, though a system which ensures "that the widest possible range of choice will be open to the consumer" is clearly within the American tradition, it is doubtful that it represents the best of that tradition. As the ideal of equality can result in conformity, so the ideal of personal enterprise can border on selfishness. The analogy of the "consumer" used by Banfield and Grodzins is revealing, for the individuality the modern suburb offers is of the laissez-faire variety. The man who chooses his community in the metropolitan free market in the same way in which he buys his car has embraced the theory of contractual relations in its most extreme form. Self-interest, unmitigated even by the notion of obligations freely entered into, because the definition of freedom, and issues of equity and humanitarianism are muted. The sense of responsibility of free men to one another and the recognition of common purposes that constitute a persuasive part of the American creed are lost, and the spectacle ensues of a simple scramble to the top for the best market baskets of local government services.

A second observation to make about the streamlined suburban version of the small town is that the rampant individualism it espouses by no means dampens the spirit of fraternity. Paradoxically, an attempt to rediscover fraternity becomes the overriding goal of suburban free choice. Freedom is sought in order to return to some facsimile of the elemental world; men struggle to succeed for the purpose of residing in a community peopled exclusively by their own kind. The growing homogeneity of these cultural islands, and the restrictive practices that bar the unsuitable, become little more than a reassertion of the fraternal spirit.

In this context, modern observers sometimes speak approvingly of the reappearance of clusters of suburban small towns as a means "for the effective management of conflict, especially of conflict arising from the growing cleavages of race and class." Yet, even the desire to "manage" conflict, to promote harmony by the ghetto system of society, remains basically a fraternal drive—and an anti-individualistic one. An individual exercises options among a series of fraternities but once he makes his choice, he reenters a world where individuality is suspect. Discussion, debate, disagreement thus have no role either in building a community on the basis of recognizing common interests, or in the expression and articulation of individuality. A man is freed to follow his immediate desires but forfeits his individuality by the very process.

Meanwhile, the carefully preserved boundary lines, the meticulously drawn building regulations, the informally applied restrictive practices, ensure that the fraternal spirit predominates; that harmony, once natural in the small town, is now contrived; that conflict, out of which understanding and individual growth conceivably could come, is carefully avoided. Unless one reconciles himself to a series of moves as his values grow and change, freedom of choice is exercised only once or twice. As an everyday proposition, it becomes unworkable.

Notes

1. For a systematic analysis of the Jacksonian concept of democracy, see Robert A. Dahl, *A Preface to Democratic Theory* (Chicago: University of Chicago Press, 1956) Chapter 2.

2. The "atomistic" assumptions of the American tradition are detailed in Louis Hartz, *The Liberal Tradition in America* (New York: Harcourt, Brace, 1955) Chapter 1.

3. For a systematic analysis of constitutionalism, see Carl J. Friedrich, *Constitutional Government and Democracy,* revised edition (Boston: Ginn & Co., 1950) Chapter 1.

4. Lane W. Lancaster, *Government in Rural America,* Second edition, (New York: Van Nostrand, 1952) p. 295.

5. Granville Hicks, *Small Town* (New York: Macmillan, 1946) p. 132.

6. Alexis De Tocqueville, *Democracy in America* (Reeve translation, Colonial Press Revised Edition, New York, 1900), p. 266.

7. Robert Dahl, *A Preface to Democratic Theory,* p. 145.

8. *Ibid.,* p. 145.

9. John Dewey, *The Public and Its Problems* (New York: Henry Holt, 1927) pp. 212–13.

10. Alexis de Tocqueville, *Democracy in America,* p. 336.

11. Robert A. Woods, *Neighborhood in Nation-Building, The Running Comment of Thirty Years at South End House* (Boston: Houghton Mifflin, 1923) p. 73.

12. Edward C. Banfield and Morton Grodzins, *Government and Housing in Metropolitan Areas* (New York: McGraw Hill, 1958) Chapter I, p. 15 and Chapter II, pp. 28–30.

12. The New Roots

WILLIAM H. WHYTE, JR.

To find where the mobility of organization life is leading, the new package suburbs may be the best place of all to look. For they are not merely great conglomerations of mass housing. They are a new social institution, and while the variations in them are many, wherever one goes—the courts of Park Forest, the patios of Park Merced in San Francisco, Philadelphia's Drexelbrook, the new Levittown, Pennsylvania—there is an unmistakable similarity in the way of life.

It is a communal way of life, and the residents are well aware of it. They are of many minds how to describe it. Sometimes they lean to analogies like the frontier, or the early colonial settlements. Other times they are a little more wry; "sorority house with kids," a projection of dormitory life into adulthood, or, slightly better, a lay version of Army post life. But no matter how sharp the coinages—"a womb with a view," "a Russia, only with money"—it is a way of life they find suited to their wants, their needs, and their times. They are not unwitting pawns; educated to be more aware of social trends than their forebears, they discuss their situations with considerable sophistication; at times, the way they

Reprinted from *The Organization Man* by William H. Whyte, Jr. Copyright © 1956 by William H. Whyte, Jr. By permission of Simon and Schuster, Inc. Mr. Whyte was an editor of *Fortune* at the time this study was made.

casually toss out words like "permissive" and "kid-centered," it almost seems as if everyone was his own resident sociologist.

In part, these communities are a product of the great expansion of the middle class, for the new suburbs have become a mecca for thousands of young people moving up and out of city wards. It is not these people, however, who are dominant. In his wanderings, the organization man has found in the new suburbs an ideal way station. He is the one who is most quick to move out, but as soon as he does another replaces him, and then another. It is he who sets the tone, and if he is as uncertain as any in keeping up with the Joneses, it is because he *is* the Joneses.

Park Forest, the community I studied most intensively, has its unique features, but its most salient characteristic is that it is virtually a controlled sample of organization people. As elsewhere, there are other kinds of people too, and for many a newcomer from the city such communities are an education in middle-class values. What might be called the modal man, however, is a twenty-five-to-thirty-five-year-old white-collar organization man with a wife, a salary between $6,000 and $7,000, one child, and another on the way.

If one wishes to study the next generation of organization men, a pretty good form chart is the record of how the younger ones handle their problems when they are away from their elders. Because they are jammed into such propinquity with one another in their new suburbia, everything they do carries a certain degree of exaggeration: the schools are a little more modern than elsewhere, the politics a little more intense, and most certainly the social life is a lot more social. Abnormal? Or the portent of a new normality? The values of Park Forest, one gets the feeling, are harbingers of the way it's going to be.[1]

This kind of suburbia is a natural phenomenon. They bear a resemblance to such utopian ventures as the Oneida community or the Fourier settlements, but where earlier utopias were an expression of revolt and idealism, the new suburbs are a response to social and economic realities. Park Forest, for example, was set up, quite simply, to make money, lots and lots of it. Looking at the real-estate situation right after the war, a group of Chicago businessmen saw that there was a huge population of young veterans, but little available housing suitable for young people with (1) children, (2) expectations of transfer, (3) a taste for good living, (4) not too much money. Why not, the group figured, build an entire new community from scratch for these people? The group, incorporated as American Community Builders, bought up 2,400 acres in the cornland thirty miles south of Chicago and brought in a remarkable man, former Federal Public Housing Commissioner Philip Klutznick, as president.

The plan was to build clusters of rental garden apartments (rent for two-bedroom duplex: $92) around a central shopping center, and then, as time went on, build ranch-type houses for sale ($11,995) on the periphery of the area. The housing would be merchandised at bargain rates. The real money would come from the waterworks and the company's cut (ranging up to 10 per cent) of every dollar spent in the shopping center. In effect, the developers were building a city to provide a sort of captive market—a constantly replenished, nonsatiable reservoir of 30,000 people, many of whom would ever be poised at the stage when families just begin to lay up possessions.

When the doors were thrown open in 1948 the rental courts were islands in a sea of mud, but the young people came streaming out of Chicago. The first wave of colonists was heavy with academic and professional people—the place, it appeared, had an extraordinary affinity for Ph.D.s. Since Chicago is one of the great business-training grounds of the U.S., however, another kind of affinity proved even stronger: poised at the nexus of America's junior-executive migration, Park Forest quickly became a haven for the organization man. Out came trainees for the big corporations, research chemists with the AEC, captains and majors with the Fifth Army, airline pilots, FBI men—in total, a cross section of almost every kind of organization man in America. . . .[2]

In much of the current writing about the need for belongingness, it is implied that participation is a kind of unity and that differences in what people are participating about are only differences in degree. Park Forest proves that it is not this simple; that there is a profound antithesis between different kinds of participation. But Park Forest indicates this, let me now point out, not because it is a failure, but because it is a success. Precisely because it comes so much closer to providing so full a spectrum of participation than other communities, the dilemmas of participation are more apparent there.

In the huge new life-insurance housing developments there is often a good bit of social activity—the "patio" at Park Merced, for example, functions very much like Park Forest's courts in this respect. There is little real civic or political activity, however. The developments are not political entities but parts of established communities, and the old residents do not solicit the help of the newcomers, nor are the newcomers particularly interested in giving it. Within the development itself, furthermore, issues remain latent. With what can be called semi-benevolent paternalism, the developers have attended to almost all of the community's physical problems, including even the cutting of grass (done at Park Merced by a corps of uniformed attendants). The developers provide room for hobby shops and the like, but they are not at all anxious to stimulate too active a sense of community. As one landlord confided to me, some originally innocuous group might easily become the nucleus of a tenants' organization and there would be no telling what would happen then.

Going up the scale of participation, there are quite a few new communities in which the developers do encourage social activities. Drexelbrook is an outstanding prototype. Here the paternalism is fully benevolent; builder Dan Kelly, a genial promoter who loves parties himself, runs his development on a bread-and-circuses principle. Unifying the 1,223 garden apartment units is the Drexelbrook Swimming and Tennis Club—a handsome affair with veranda terrace, swimming pools, and clubrooms which is made available at bargain rates. There is a full-time recreation director and in summer a corps of young girls to shepherd the children so mothers can take off for some shopping or the theater. Parties abound: "hunt balls" on Washington's Birthday, celebrity parties, "splash" parties (all you can eat for a dollar).

When residents want to start a social activity on their own, Kelly is usually glad to lend a hand. Several years ago, for example, a group of wives were sitting around wondering what they could get up. Somebody suggested maybe a garden club. They called up Kelly and he told them to count on him. As soon as they got things going he provided free busses for the club's first trip to the Philadelphia flower show and stimulated them in every way he could. The garden club now absorbs more of the wives' excess energies than any other activity. Another tradition partially subsidized by Kelly is the annual Christmas decoration contest. During December each court vies with the others to win the prize for the best Christmas displays, and they do such a striking job that over 10,000 people drive out each year to see the sight.

But it remains a development, more than a community. Understandably, no group has turned into a protest group against the developer; there have been mutterings about paternalism, but they have never coalesced into any active movement. As for the politics of the township of which Drexelbrook is a part, there occasionally is some ferment about matters which touch the immediate interests of the residents, like schoolbus arrangements, but other than this, residents don't take much interest. Besides, they don't have the time.

Statistically, the people at Park Forest are much the same as those of the Park Merceds or the Drexelbrooks. What makes their community so much more expressive than the demi-utopias lies in two factors: (1) it is a town in its own right, a real town with real problems;[3] (2) it has had a socially conscious developer.

From the beginning Klutznick decided that the affairs of the town would be turned over to the citizenry. This would put the tenants in the curious position of being able to tax the landlord, but Klutznick, a practical visionary, reasoned that this would be best for all—and for commercial reasons as well as idealistic ones. The more people get involved in running the place, he figured, the more they take root and thus the more stable would be the community—and the investment.

What happened was a severe wrench for Klutznick. Like many extremely dynamic men, he is not patient with what he feels is misguided opposition, and in no time he had plenty of it. Park Foresters fell to organizing their community, and what unified them more than anything else was the developer. Instinctively, they were against what he was for, and while they talked darkly of feudal barony and serfs, they certainly didn't act like serfs. No matter what the issue—the developer's rule against dogs, school appropriations—they reacted with the vigor of all those who feel they must do battle against tyranny. When Klutznick, in a moment of anger, expelled an activist tenant they organized a mass march on Klutznick's office complete with sound truck and placards. Even when Klutznick came bearing gifts they were contentious. "Father Klutznick, father of the village, eh!" I heard one tenant exclaim after a particularly handsome gift of land to the community was made by Klutznick. "He won't get away with it!"

But the autonomy was good for all concerned. For the tenants the result was a rich diet of issues on which to cut their teeth, and for the developers a disciplining force that helped them resist the temptation to cut corners. Klutznick, who can reflect that it will be a hell of a day when Americans come to love the landlord, became more philosophical about it all. Heavy as the cross may have appeared, he is a formidable debater, and few things were so stimulating to him as a public tussle with the equally vigorous young lawyer who was the village president.

But the pot had to simmer down. Democracy, Klutznick once remarked, meant the day when he could drive around Park Forest in his Cadillac Sixty Special without anyone's saying, "Look at that lousy bastard Phil Klutznick driving a Cadillac." That day has long since arrived. Patently, Park Forest works superbly, and even those for whom tilting with the landlord is reflex hold that while Klutznick has an immensely shrewd eye for the dollar, he has proved himself a wise and fundamentally idealistic partner. The new era of good feeling has by no means dulled the citizenry's reflexes, but lately some have confessed that they did wish there were more iniquities to get excited about. Writing in a vein unthinkable before, a local columnist, Al Engelhard, has asked for a substitute ogre: "Of itself, harmony between tenant and landlord is a salutary thing, testifying to the tenant's intelligence and the landlord's good will. But the price has been high. Apathy has been the child of Peace, Indifference the spawn of Concord. . . . Since he is a man of many parts, I have hope that Phil Klutznick, alert to the disservice he has done us by becoming a sweet and lovable old bug, is even now pondering some issue which will redynamize us. We need a common enemy we can magnify into a monster, whisper about, conspire about, hang in effigy."

. . . Because the emergency pressures have vanished, the emergency spirit has too, and many pioneers see this as a flight from virtue. Several, indeed, actually moved away they were so disappointed. Many of those who remain are similarly disillusioned to find that without the stimulus of necessity most people can take issues or leave them alone, and you will be assured that it's disgraceful how few turn up for meetings.

The rather high quotient of idealism generated there is immensely valuable; without it there would not be the *esprit*, the agitation that so animate the community. All the idealism does, however, tend to make some residents discontented with anything less than the complete Welfare Community. Thus aroused, they measure the very achievements against perfection—and the result is a sense of paradise lost that bedevils many of them. "We moved here because we decided this would be a brave new world," says one resident, without conscious irony. "But so many compromises have been made. We're disgusted." Now they say it's just like any other place.

It isn't, of course. Apathy is a relative matter, and to newcomers from outside the amount of participation is still a phenomenon. Since the issues are now those of a "maturing" community rather than one a-borning, there has of necessity been some change in the way of meeting them—symptomatically, the able young chemist who is the new village president is known as a noncontroversialist. But the *élan* is still there, and if Park Foresters are a little more good humored about their new furors these days, they can still burn over them. For an idea of the flavor, I append a sampling of recent headlines in the Park Forest *Reporter:*

ACB, TRUSTEES CLASH ON BLDGS
TEMPORARY SCHOOLS WRANGLE CONTINUES
DEVELOPER OBJECTS TO NEW REGULATIONS

TRUSTEES REFUSE APPROVAL OF ACB'S AREA TO UTILITY PLANS

LIQUOR LICENSE HASSLE CONTINUES AT SECOND PUBLIC HEARING

TRUSTEES PONDER ACB PARK AND SEWER OFFER

CAT ORDINANCE AROUSES FUROR

AREA 11 PLAT OKAYED BY VILLAGE IN SHORT AND PEACEFUL MEETING

I would not maintain that this activity fully compensates for the old kind of roots. The participation, as I have remarked, is often participation for the sake of it, and sometimes one is tempted to apply H. G. Wells's description of the town of Bromstead—"a dull, useless boiling up of human activities, an immense clustering of futilities." But this would miss an important point. In a community where there are real issues— schools to be built, segregation problems—its residents are immersed in the main stream of life, not insulated. If they appear stimulated over and above the call of community necessity, this itself is evidence of how very much they seek ties more meaningful than those of bridge and canasta and bowling.

For no one is this quest more important than the organization man. One of the dangers in the transient life is that these young people, be- cause they must move about so frequently, will more and more identify their total destiny with one particular organization. For society as well as for themselves, the organization transients need to multiply their alle- giances—to the church, to community, and the like. These additional allegiances provoke no great ideological conflicts with the office, cer- tainly, but they do turn the executive away from complete preoccupation with one encompassing organization. Places like Park Forest do not solve this problem—The Organization will still come first—but they do amel- iorate it.

This becomes evident when you talk to organization transients who have made their pause in more conventional environments. As might be expected, those who are in the cities have the least chance for participa- tion, but the traditional small towns are not much better, and transients who have spent a tour in them speak feelingly of rebuffs and cold shoulders. "We just play around with company people," says a resident of one elm-shaded town. "The regular people here are pleasant enough, I suppose, but they don't want our help in anything that really counts— except when they come around to solicit money for the hospital." Such transients may make common cause with one another; in many a ranch- type block on the new outskirts of old towns the Du Pont engineers and the GE men and other fellow transients turn inwardly to one another and create something of the *Gemütlichkeit* of life at a Drexelbrook or a Park Merced. But it doesn't mean much. The activity is at a superficial level and the residents know it. One may dispute how much deeper is the activity of a Park Forest. The fact remains, however, that its people do feel an importance there they do not elsewhere.

The ability to chew on real problems is functional in another respect too. On a purely utilitarian level it provides young transients a leadership training it would take them years to get otherwise—and one of their few opportunities to acquire a sense of capital. "We are a young group without mature leadership," explains a rising young banker, "so we are forced to take on responsibilities that older people usually assume. For the last two years I have been chairman of the board of the church, a job held by a fifty-five or sixty-year-old man in most communities. This gives me a training valuable in business. The church is a corporation with a $50,000 budget, and we've had to think about a $100,000 capital loan. How else could people our age get a chance to deal with that much capital? We're forced ahead of our time."

Many feel that community work is viewed with high approval by their companies—a fact that Park Forest leaders do not forget to mention in proselyting the laggard. Both of the two contenders for the village presidency in a recent election, they point out, worked in the research department of the same oil company, and it is a reasonable conclusion that the company does not view such activity with displeasure

Compared to lawyers, academic, and professional people, the young businessman is not markedly a civic joiner. There is evidence that those who are, however, are more likely to be "comers." A few of the civically active may have seized on the activity as compensation for a blocked career, but on the whole the active would appear to be more likely to get ahead than their less active brothers.

Undeniably, places like Park Forest do tend to spoil one. While most of the people who move to package communities move out of a simple economic necessity, after exposure to such an environment some people find a warmth and support in it that makes the prospect of other environments seem unduly cold to them—it is somewhat unsettling, for example, to hear the way some residents of the new suburbs refer to "the outside." Frequently, alumni of package communities go considerably out of their way to seek out a similar community when the next move comes up, even when they are making quite enough for a more fashionable spot.

On balance, however, the training of a Park Forest stimulates them more than it coddles them. The test is what happens to Park Foresters when they leave. Those who haven't left like to tell stories of how "lonely" ex-residents have become in other places, and there is the strong imputation that it very well served them right for leaving. But most are not homesick. Thanks to the "bringing out," transients are all the better fitted for the moves ahead of them. If they are annoyed at the disinterest they find in a traditional town, it is because they want to be active, and know how to, and the disinterest serves more often to challenge than inhibit them. We looked up ex-Park Foresters now living in other kinds of communities and found that most were more active in the community than their contemporaries. "I learned at Park Forest how to take the initiative," goes a typical explanation. "It certainly stood me in good stead. I found out when I got here that most of the people really didn't know one another, and I just naturally started getting them together." The majority of alumni confess they wouldn't want to go through Park Forest again, but they look back with fondness on Park Forest. "It all got pretty hectic at times," one recalls, "but one thing's sure—we were *living*."

Notes

1. These chapters are based on research I did for a *Fortune* study in 1953, and on subsequent research in 1955 and 1956. Originally, I had started to study Drexelbrook, Pennsylvania, but in late 1952, after visiting several other suburbs, I decided to use them for reference and comparison and concentrate on Park Forest, for it was the largest one that was a political as well as a social unit. Work commenced in December 1952 and continued over a six-month period until June 1953. During this period additional research was done at Drexelbrook, Levittown, Pennsylvania, and several developments in California. In 1955 I returned to Park Forest, after a deep breath, to check up on what had happened in the intervening time, and in January and February 1956 did further research at Levittown, Pa.

2. The cross section has remained constant. Old settlers at Park Forest like to tell you that they are being replaced by an "element" less worthy, but though the population has been greater each year (about 25,000 in mid-1956), there has been little change in basic characteristics. Median educational level for *all* adults remains about 2.5 years of college—the highest of any Illinois community. As far as occupation is concerned, a check of move-ins to the rental area in 1955 shows no change, save a few less university people. Here is a random sampling of newcomers in 1955: research chemist, Sinclair Oil Co.; salesman, Swift & Co.; major, Fifth Army; investigator, FBI; purchasing agent, Ford Motor Co.; industrial psychologist, Swift & Co.; space salesman, *Business Week* magazine; underwriter, Prudential Life; salesman, Du Pont Co.; buyer, Carson, Pirie Scott store; trainee, Burroughs Adding Machine Co.; lieutenant colonel, Fifth Army; research engineer, Continental Can Co.; engineer, Western Electric; sales trainee, Atlas Box Co.; engineer, General Electric; pilot, American Airlines; public-relations assistant, Acme Steel Co.; teacher, Rich High School; labor-relations assistant, Ford Motor Co.; writer, Time, Inc.; accountant, Gulf Oil Co.; copywriter, Chicago advertising agency.

3. The experience of Levittown, Pennsylvania, demonstrates the importance of political unification. It straddles four townships, and quite possibly always will. There was a chance early for Levittown being incorporated as a town in its own right, but the civic leadership was inept and the move failed. Since then there has been less community-wide spirit, and many who otherwise would have been active have withdrawn from participation. There is plenty of local activity in the "sections," but it does not stir banked passions.

13. Social Organization of a Local Community in a Metropolis

MORRIS JANOWITZ

(The following passage is from a book on the role of weekly community newspapers in the social structures of neighborhoods in Chicago. However, for our purposes, the subject is not the community press, but the political implications of Janowitz's findings with respect to social organization.)

The urban community press, in the light of the findings of this study, has a wide audience and a discernible impact. As such, its significance as an approach to the local community is more than a research assumption. The contents of the community press, the social attributes of its readers, and the social role of its publishers when viewed as elements of a communications system make possible inferences about social cohesion in the urban metropolis. In such a process of synthesis, the interpretative conclusions are likely to outrun the data at hand and become rather speculative because of the complexity of the task of understanding the urban community.

The analysis of the community press if it reveals nothing else indicates that significant proportions of the residents of the urban metropolis are not "rootless" individuals. Countertrends to large-scale organization continually develop which modify the impact of technological impersonalization and make possible the gratification of individual needs in the local community. This is a crude statement. Ultimately, the task at hand is to emerge with a theoretical "model" of the local community. Such a "model" will present a meaningful analysis of the complexities of the local community and point the way toward constructive support of those mechanisms and institutions which maintain social cohesion.

In moving toward such a "model" or generalized description of the local urban community, three basic social dimensions of analysis are required, similar to those relevant for analyzing most social systems; (a) the motivational involvements and gratifications (or non-gratifications) connected with community residence, (b) the social organization

Reprinted from *The Community Press in an Urban Setting* (Glencoe, Illinois: The Free Press, 1952), pp. 207–8, 212–17, 218–22, 223–25 by permission of the author and the publisher. Author's footnotes omitted. Morris Janowitz is a professor of sociology at the University of Michigan.

of the local community, and (c) the resultant patterns and mechanisms of social control on the local community level. . . .

The Social Organization of the Local Community

The analysis of the community press as a communications system reveals immediately some of the complexities of the process by which the individual and his primary-group affiliations are integrated into the large-scale organization of the urban metropolis. It reveals that despite the growth of mass communications and large-scale organization most individuals are not living in a "mass society" in which they are directly linked to the major agencies of concentrated social and political power. Rather, the growth of large-scale organization has been accompanied by a proliferation of intermediate haphazard-like social arrangements and communication patterns. The local urban community appears to be a complex of social interactions which tends to identify a local elite and local institutionalized patterns for controlling social change. The community press is but one institution that stands intermediate between the individual and the major institutions of the metropolis; and the publisher is but one of the members of this intermediate elite.

In power terms, the scope of this elite and the significance of its actions are obviously limited by the character of the decision-making process that finds a context on the local level. This local elite is composed of business, political, religious, voluntary association, and professional community leaders. At first glance it might appear that they constitute a network of individuals whose significance arises out of their hierarchical position midway between top metropolitan leadership and the bulk of the population whose consensus is required for collective action. In this view, interpersonal connections among community elite within a given community or group of communities do not loom significantly and the local elites are considered merely as agents rather than effective leaders.

This view of local leadership is conditioned by the lack of clear-cut correspondence between the geographical limits of the community and the geographical limits of the leaders' social influence. But this is an erroneous view of community leadership. The pattern of group leadership that emerges around the community press and its operations highlights a clear-cut pattern of interpersonal contact among local leaders within the community. The various institutions and associations which penetrate into the local community have no manifest geographical homogeneity or unity. Nevertheless, the lateral interactions of the local leadership within the geographical limits of the local community have a definite pattern which contributes to the self-consciousness and power of these local leaders. This process can be understood better only through prolonged participant observation which social scientists seldom undertake.

Moreover, community leadership does seem strikingly associated with residential stability. It is worthwhile noting the degree to which community leaders display residential stability (twenty years or over at the same address), again in contradistinction to the view of the urban community has a "rootless" mass. Beyond this simple fact, the social personality and the social techniques of local leaders remain to be investigated. The level of community management that this study probed uncovered again and again the effort at adjudication of conflict by emphasis on areas of common agreement and the postponement of disagreement. The role of the community newspaper in the political life of the community with its curious non-partisanship reflects this approach and makes it more difficult to uncover the realities of political conflict.

Today, local community organization is perhaps most threatened in precisely those areas where the socially articulate leaders of the community are in the process of departure or are unable to replace themselves. The development of social absenteeism, as the process can be called, need not be viewed as inevitable, for it does get altered, slowed or temporarily stopped.

The removal of leadership with strong community identifications through the process of social absenteeism can develop to the point where ultimately profound changes in local politics take place with most unfortunate implications. In a city such as Chicago, social absenteeism in certain traditional Democratic wards, located near the center of the city, with lower-class constituencies has fundamentally weakened the Democratic party organization. The ward organizations have been weakened to the point where the wards have suddenly turned Republican. This shift hardly represents the normal and desirable workings of the two-party system. These wards have not turned to traditional Republicanism for the working class elements of these depressed local communities are not expressing a political allegiance to the platform of the national Republican party. They have been forced and intimidated into support of a Republican machine so completely weakened through absenteeism that it fell easy prey to the underworld and a new kind of hoodlumism in politics.

Social absenteeism expresses itself in a variegated set of problems in the local community less dramatic than the collapse of traditional political institutions of the most depressed areas. Social absenteeism affects the public educational and social welfare system and even the religious institutions, although religious hierarchies are more aware of the need to act to offset these effects.

Because of the wide variety of functions which gravitate to a community publisher, he operates as a limited counterforce to social absenteeism. In those areas where social absenteeism is less of a problem, the publisher's role seems to be one of galvanizing the local leaders to collective action. Community publishers are self-conscious men because of the kinds of life experiences which have led them into their enterprises and which they have had in operating their enterprises. The peculiar skills of the publisher and the role he plays in seeking to adjust conflicting interests sensitizes him to the evolving trends in the local community. Economic interests, of course, condition his outlook. Nevertheless, he is less reluctant to accept the inevitability of adverse changes and more prone to press for desired change than the members of the business community. His promotional background and in part his quasi-intellectual outlook are here at work.

In particular, no group is more sensitive to the political and economic inequalities inherent in the present trends toward suburbanization than the urban community newspaper publishers. The divergence between the long established political boundaries and the changing patterns of population in a metropolitan area such as Chicago seems to increase continuously. Throughout the research, specific problems of social action took meaning in this overriding political context. The metropolis is an outgrowth of a machine technology which made possible large concentrations of population. While the distribution of commerce and transportation conditioned the form and location of the residential community, political boundaries seemed to coordinate, or discoordinate, social adaptations to these movements. The outmoded character for the legal limits of the urban metropolis is a striking case of a basically discoordinating element of local social organization.

It is not within the power of the community press to have a central role in altering these administrative and political trends. Yet if politicians in the near future seek to deal with this fundamental issue, either through boundary changes, new forms of political representation or new taxation basis, the community press—both in Chicago and throughout the entire country—constitutes an important resource for clarification and action.

Social Control at the Local Community Level

Social control at all levels involves the clash between individual motives and effective social organization. The code of ethics for operating a community newspaper is a skeleton of the social attitudes and group pressures that are operative in most collective actions at the local community level. . . .

The range of collective action which involves the community newspaper—from blood bank campaigns to support for police action—grows out of the leadership position and contacts of the publisher. But, in addition to collective action, social control involves the quest for respectability and morality. The ideology of the community newspaper, and of many other community institutions, seeks to present appropriate symbols of respectability and morality to those who have such motives. Yet for that substantial minority who seek anonymity, avoidance of community involvement and its consequent controls requires little effort.

Local social controls assume particular meaning when a link between these controls and the norms of the larger society can be established. The decisions made in the local community are of limited consequence for the "big" political issues of the moment; yet the motivational commitment toward the local community is certain to bear some relationship to the individual's orientation to the "politics" of the larger community.

In this context, a final hypothesis is presented. Individuals who display high local identifications are people who are likely to display higher political competence than those who have low or no local identification. This hypothesis is presented in its most general form; a minority who are "over-identified" in the local community might display low political competence, while on the other end of the continuum a minority with low community identification might display high political competence derived from ideological considerations. But leaving aside these sub-groups, should political competence correlate with community newspaper readership some light might be thrown on compatibility of local autonomy and local identification and the requirements of the larger political process.

Those portions of the readership survey which dealt with local community affairs included indirect questions on the individual's contacts and estimates of his local precinct captain, alderman and ward organization. Specific questions involved the problems of the local community and the capabilities of the political offices and officers to deal with these concrete issues. These questions were not designed to determine whether the respondent was a "Democrat," a "Republican" or an "Independent," but rather to probe his trust in and reliance on politics. They produced a flow of material revealing underlying attitudes toward the political process and made possible inferences about self-conceptions of competence in this area. For example, the following respondent leaves no doubt about his own low competence in politics:

"I think it's all the bunk. I'm a Democrat. I been a Democrat for years. If Truman runs again I don't think I'll vote for him. I don't think the little persons can do anything. The politicians may start out all right but they end up the same—corrupt. They can't help it. You need someone to rule. Everyone can't be for himself."

Regardless of the respondents' political affiliation, relative confidence in the effectiveness and honesty of local politics—projective measures of personal political competence—tended to be associated with high community newspaper readership. However, in the case of the political parties the association was larger and more statistically significant than for precinct captains.

These conclusions point to the ambiguities of the social roots of political agreement in the urban local community. Social scientists and reformers are frequently preoccupied with the political type whose competence is operative without a sense of specific local community identification. Indispensable as such individuals are for politics, it is likely that in the near future such individuals alone cannot maintain or strengthen the basis of democratic organization in a metropolis such as Chicago. To the contrary, further weakening of local community identifications is inextricably bound up with the growth of even greater anti-democratic potential among the rank and file residents than now besets the urban community.

An issue of social and political control which had mobilized a great deal of local community interest is that of federally supported public housing. This study was initiated before the outbreak of the hostilities in Korea, in a period in which a great deal of attention was being expended on the problems of developing new communities and the redeveloping of old ones. Since this was a period of full employment, it was understandable that urban development and redevelopment would be a fundamental concern. Conceptions of local autonomy and local community, which have so long been the basis of democratic organization, were subjected to a searching criticism on a very pragmatic basis.

Each community newspaper has implicit rules as to the role it intends to play in fashioning the real estate composition of its local community. This, of course, depends on whether the newspaper is confronted realistically with the urban development and redevelopment problems in its own area, or whether it deals with the problem in terms of principle. In general, the community press in the Chicago area has been in opposition to federally supported public housing including some in a most outspoken fashion. Moreover, because of parochialism the local community and its community newspaper, it was felt by certain critics, were likely, in fact certain to have created undemocratic standards for residence, particularly with respect to ethnic composition.

This issue can be considered a key to understanding the "manipulative" aspects of community journalism, for underneath the issue is the fear of altering the ethnic and racial composition of the community. Systematic attitude data is not available on public housing, but there is enough data on ethnic and racial attitudes in metropolitan areas to indicate that often the community press reflects rather than molds attitudes in its opposition to unsegregated public housing.

Therefore, for these same critics of the community press, democratic objectives frequently implied the elimination of local community autonomy if urban redevelopment and residential mobility were to be guaranteed. To justify such an attack on a traditional preconception of the democratic process, they frequently argued that in effect the local community no longer exists or could never possibly exist in an urban community. In this view, much is made of the "artificial" attempts to stimulate local autonomy in a world in which local autonomy has been rendered meaningless.

But a solution to the dilemma between local autonomy and freedom of residential mobility is not possible by denying the power of the local orientations that persist in the metropolitan community—the mass of evidence to which this study contributes is too great to be denied. Although the elimination of segregation is a basic and fundamental democratic value its achievement through the destruction of local autonomy would be undesirable. The destruction of all local community autonomy and all sense of local identification would seem to lead the individual as indicated previously to a sense of personal incompetence which can only result in an even greater anti-democratic potential than is present today.

The Community of "Limited Liability"

The findings of this study call into question theoretical formulations which see the local community merely in the time perspective of a historical shift from "gemeinschaft" (simple—intimate) social forms to "gesellschaft" (complex—indirect) social forms.

The analysis of the collapse or survival of postulated earlier and simpler social arrangements in the urban community eliminates much significant data on how community social controls operate. This observation has become increasingly evident to social scientists who are interested in the workings of power and voluntary association in the local community. The large-scale organization of the urban community hardly eliminates the necessity of theoretical analysis of the networks of intimate and cohesive social relations which supply the basis of collective action on the local community level. In a fundamental sense, the contemporary balance and interrelations between "gemeinschaft" and "gesellschaft" social forms in the local community are as relevant as estimates of long-term trends. (All too frequently, these estimates of the long-term trends in gemeinschaft merely focus on the formal aspects of social organization.)

Recent theoretical reorientations have sought to free the concepts and definitions of the sociology of the urban community from the limitations linked to the bias of implied value premises. The disrepute in which the concept "disorganization" has fallen in certain types of sociological writings is reflective of this issue.

It seems appropriate to point out that the generalized description of the urban residential community implied by this research is a community of "limited liability." Our community is clearly not one of completely bureaucratized and impersonalized attachments. In varying degrees, the local community resident has a current psychological and social investment in his local community. In varying degrees, use of local facilities is accompanied by community orientations. The extent and character of these attachments are in good measure linked to the individual resident's predispositions and acts. Raising a family and, to a lesser extent, length of residence and local social contacts predispose him to an acceptance of local community institutions and social controls. In the process, purely "rational" and "instrumental" relations are modified. In this regard, individuals vary in the extreme; some are more capable (or have more need) than others of developing these orientations.

But, in all cases, these attachments are limited in the amount of social and psychological investment they represent. Thus, the notion of a community of "limited liability" emerges. (The term is viewed as similar in many aspects to the individual's commitment of "limited liability" in economic affairs.) The individual, responding to the general cultural norms, is likely to demand more from his community than he will invest. But more significantly, his relation to the community is such—his investment is such—that when the community fails to serve his needs, he will withdraw. Withdrawal implies either departure from the local community or merely lack of involvement. Withdrawal to some extent takes place with individual aging. More often it accompanies changes in the ethnic or social composition of the community. For some the withdrawal is slight since the original investment was slight or non-existent. Finally the point of withdrawal may vary from community to community, from class to class, from ethnic group to ethnic group; but for each individual there is a point at which he cuts off his losses. Seldom is the investment so great that the individual is permanently committed to a community that cannot cater to his needs.

Thus, in summary, the dimensions of the local community point towards emerging social change in the largest metropolitan districts. Motives for community orientation center around the family with its gravitational pull toward the community and to a lesser extent around other primary group contacts. Within a specific local community, significant aspects of social organization operate without respect to socioeconomic status, although deviations (both higher or lower) from the status norms of the community tend to some degree to interfere with community cohesion. Local leadership functions in a social milieu of apparent rationalistic interpersonal contacts but these contacts are surrounded by a network of purely personalistic relations. Local leadership also involves a heavy emphasis on non-partisanship, which is in effect an emphasis on the perpetuation of the status quo. Compromise is the general theme except when fundamental values in the community are impinged by external threats.

The resulting balance of social control at the local community level is one which leaves relatively untouched only a minority of residents, heavily involves another perhaps smaller group in the community, and creates varying degrees of involvement for the bulk of the residents. Many of these elements are indicative of socially adaptive mechanisms seeking and struggling to modify the impact of industrialism and large-scale organization on the local community. This perspective eliminates the necessity of overemphasizing the impersonalized aspects of urban personality and thereby the character of social manipulation in the local community can be seen in its proper limits.

Chapter FOUR

METROPOLITANISM

Introduction
A. As an Administrative Problem
B. As a Political and Administrative Problem
C. As a Political and Intergovernmental Problem

THE TERM "METROPOLITAN PROBLEM" has recently received a certain notoriety and popular recognition. This "problem" basically refers to the effects of the startling increase in contiguous and overlapping units of urban government. The dramatic shifts in population that have been occurring are documented in the reports of the 1960 Census, and the pattern that is revealed is one of an America of sprawling urbanism. But the situation we are now facing has been long in the making and has been recognized by some for a number of years. The essay by H. G. Wells prepared for the Fabian Society in 1903 indicates just this.

While Wells considers the subject as an administrative problem, in the contemporary American context it takes on various colorations. It remains an administrative problem in the sense that an administrative device needs to be developed to insure cooperation among existing local units, or which has sufficient geographic jurisdiction to comprehend the problems. However, it is more than an administrative problem, for any alteration in the existing arrangement promises to reward some interests and impinge on others. Thus, it is also a political problem.

Solutions to the "problem" also involve questions of basic political values, such as those introduced in the previous chapter. Consolidation of local units raises anew the question of how big a community should be. All of the proposed "metropolitan solutions" in the form of new structural arrangements raise questions about the role of the citizen, the effects of centralized decisions, and the responsiveness and responsibility of officials under various alternative plans.

Finally, the metropolitan "problem" is not simply one involving re-arrangement of the units of local government. State and federal governments are inextricably involved, as the policies of the higher levels of governments have profound influence on all local policies today. Furthermore, the legal framework for new formal arrangements in the metropolitan areas must be approved by the states and, in the case of compacts, by the federal government.

As can be seen, the "metropolitan problem" is not one problem but many. The authors whom we have excerpted below were chosen to show these various facets. As each author has the same situation in mind, there is inevitably some overlapping in the facts which they review. As the selections are selected to present different conceptions of the problem, there are also certain areas of disagreement.

As previously noted, the first selection by H. G. Wells states the case for governmental reorganization based on the administrative values of efficiency and economy. Writing in a similar vein, Otis Dudley Duncan poses the question: "How big should a city be?" However, he finds efficiency a waivering standard in formulating his answer.

Some writers claim that we are being oversold on the need for structural change. In a volume which examines the possibilities which metropolitan government offered for the solution to urban housing problems, Edward Banfield and Morton Grodzins stress the fact that we have not sufficiently exploited the resources available to us under existing governmental arrangements. Robert Wood partially concurs, agreeing that justifications for metropolitan integration resting upon efficiency and economy may be overstatements. However, he argues, in terms consistent with his selection included in the previous chapter, that some system of comprehensive metropolitan planning and control is necessary to achieve democratic goals.

Many metropolitan analysts have stressed the role of state and federal governments in solving our metropolitan problems. Some claim that the states are in the most strategic position to act. But state legislatures, largely as a result of legislative apportionment, are often less than sympathetic with urban problems. In his article "How Long Will New York Wait?" Adolf Berle, Jr., emphasizes the clash of upstate-downstate politics and offers some additional illustrations of the character of metropolitan problems in our largest population center. Gordon Baker details the extent of urban underrepresentation in state legislatures.

The first systematic review of the alternative solutions for achieving coordination or integration in metropolitan areas was made in 1942 by Victor Jones in his book, *Metropolitan Government.* The major alternatives included annexation, consolidation, city-county consolidation, special districts, federation, and state or federal intervention. Jane Jacobs, in an article also entitled "Metropolitan Government," reviews our national experience in the fifteen years subsequent to Jones's book. She states a thesis concerning the essential needs and the alternatives which may be realistically entertained today.

A. AS AN ADMINISTRATIVE PROBLEM

14. *Administrative Areas*

H. G. WELLS

The areas within which we shape our public activities at present, derive, I hold, from the needs and conditions of a past order of things. They have been patched and repaired enormously, but they still preserve the essential conceptions of a vanished organization. They have been patched and repaired first to meet this urgent specific necessity and then that, and never with any comprehensive anticipation of coming needs, and at last they have become absolutely impossible. They are like fifteenth-century houses which have been continuously occupied by a succession of enterprising but short-sighted and close-fisted owners, and which have now been, with the very slightest use of lath-and-plaster partitions and geyser hot-water apparatus, converted into modern residential flats. These local government areas of today represent for the most part what were once distinct, distinctly organized, and individualized communities, complete minor economic systems, and they preserve

Reprinted from *Mankind in the Making* (Leipzig: Bernard Tauchnitz, 1903), vol. II, Appendix I, pp. 213–38, copyright edition. This essay was first delivered before the Fabian Society shortly after Wells's election to membership.

a tradition of what was once administrative convenience and economy. Today, I submit, they do not represent communities at all, and they become more wasteful and more inconvenient with every fresh change in economic necessity.

This is a double change. Let me first of all say a word in justification for my first assertion that existing areas do not represent communities, and then pass to a necessary consequence or so of this fact. I submit that before the railways, that is to say in the days in which the current conception of local government areas arose, the villages, and still more the boroughs, and even the counties, were practically complete minor economic systems. The wealth of the locality was, roughly speaking, local; rich people resided in contact with their property, other people lived in contact with their work, and it was a legitimate assumption that a radius of a mile or so, or of a few miles, circumscribed most of the practical interests of all the inhabitants of a locality. You got rich and poor in visible relationships; you got landlord and tenant, you got master and workman all together. But now, through a revolution in the methods of locomotion, and chiefly through the making of railways, this is no longer true. You can still see the villages and towns separated by spaces of fields and physically distinct; but it is no longer the case that all who dwell in these old limits are essentially local inhabitants and mutually interdependent as once they would have been. A large proportion of our population today, a large and an increasing proportion, has no localized interests at all as an eighteenth-century person would have understood locality.

Take for example Guildford, or Folkestone, and you will find that possibly even more than half the wealth in the place is non-local wealth— wealth, that is, having no relation to the local production of wealth— and that a large majority of the more educated, intelligent and active inhabitants derive their income, spend their energies, and find their absorbing interests outside the locality. They may rent or own houses, but they have no reality of participation and little illusion of participation in any local life. You will find in both towns a considerable number of hotels, inns, and refreshment places which, although they are regulated by local magistrates upon a basis of one license to so many inhabitants, derive only a small fraction of their profits from the custom of the inhabitants. You find too in Folkestone, as in most seaside places, a great number of secondary schools, drawing scarcely a pupil from the neighborhood. And on the other hand you will find labour in both towns, coming in by a morning train and going out at night. And neither of these instances is an extreme type. As you come in towards London you will find the proportion of what I would call non-local inhabitants increasing until in Brixton, Hoxton, or West Ham you will find the really localized people a mere thread in the mass of the population. Probably you find the thinnest sham of a community in the London boroughs, where a clerk or a working man will shift his sticks from one borough to another and move on to a third without ever discovering what he has done. It is not that all these people do not belong to a community, but that they belong to a larger community of a new type which your administrators have failed to discover, and which your working theory of local government ignores. This is a question I have already written about with some completeness in a book published a year or so ago, and called *Anticipations*, and in that book you will find a more lengthy exposition than I can give here and now of the nature of this expansion. But the gist of the argument is that the distribution of population, the method of aggregation in a community, is determined almost entirely by the available means of locomotion. The maximum size of any community of regular daily intercourse is determined by the length of something that I may best suggest to your mind by the phrase—the average possible suburban journey in an hour. A town, for example, in which the only method of progression is on foot along crowded ways, will be denser in population and smaller in area than one with wide streets and wheeled traffic, and that again will be denser and compacter than one with numerous tubes, trams, and light railways. Every improvement in locomotion forces the suburban ring of houses outward, and relieves the pressure of the centre. Now, this principle of expanding communities holds not only in regard to towns, but also on the agricultural countryside. There, also, facilities for the more rapid collection of produce mean finally the expansion and coalescence of what were previously economic unities.

Now, if, while this expansion of the real communities goes on, you keep to the old boundary lines, you will find an increasing proportion of your population straddling those lines. You will find that many people who once slept and worked and reared their children and worshipped and bought all in one area, are now, as it were, *delocalized;* they have overflowed their containing locality, and they live in one area, they work in another, and they go to shop in a third. And the only way in which you can localize them again is to expand your areas to their new scale.

This is a change in human conditions that has been a very distinctive event in the history of the past century, and it is still in progress. But I think there is excellent reason for supposing that for practical purposes this change, made by the railway and the motor, this development of local locomotion, will reach a definite limit in the next hundred years. We are witnessing the completion of a great development that has altered the average possible suburban journey in an hour from one of four or five miles to one of thirty miles, and I doubt very much whether, when every tendency of expansion has been reckoned with, this average hour journey will ever get much beyond sixty or seventy miles an hour. A radius of four or five miles marked the maximum size of the old community. A radius of a hundred miles will certainly mark the maximum of the new community. And so it is no effectual answer to my general argument to say that a revision of administrative areas always has been and always will be a public necessity. To a certain extent that always has been and always will be true, but on a scale in no way comparable to the scale on which it is true today, because of these particular inventions. This need in its greatness is a peculiar feature of the present time, and a peculiar problem of the present time. The municipal areas that were convenient in the Babylonian, ancient Egyptian, or Roman empires were no larger and no smaller than those that served the purpose of seventeenth-century Europe, and I believe it is highly probable—I think the odds are in favour of the belief—that the most convenient administrative areas of the year 2000 will be no larger and no smaller than those for many subsequent centuries. We are, in this respect, in the full flow of a great and permanent transition. And the social and political aspects of the change is this steadily increasing proportion of people—more especially in our suburban areas—who are, so far as our old divisions go, *delocalized*. They represent, in fact, a community of a new sort, the great new modern community, which is seeking to establish itself in the room of the dwindling, little, highly localized communities of the past.

Now what are the practical consequences of this large and increasing non-local element in your local government areas? First, there is this. The non-local people do not follow, have neither the time, nor the freedom, nor the stimulus of sufficient interests to follow, local politics. They are a sort of Outlanders. Local politics remain therefore more and more in the hands of the dwindling section of people whose interests really are circumscribed by the locality. These are usually the small local tradesmen, the local building trade, sometimes a doctor and always a solicitor; and the most energetic and active and capable of these, and the one with the keenest eye to business, is usually the solicitor. Whatever you put into the hands of local authority—education, lighting, communications—you necessarily put into the hands of a group of this sort. Here and there, of course, there may be variations; an organized labour vote may send in a representative, or some gentleman of leisure and philanthropic tastes, like Mr. Bernard Shaw, may confer distinction upon local deliberations, but that will not alter the general state of affairs. The state of affairs you must expect as the general rule, is local control by petty local interests, a state of affairs that will certainly intensify in the years to come, unless some revision of areas can be contrived that will overtake the amplifying interests of the delocalized section of the population.

Let me point out what is probably the result of a dim recognition of this fact by the non-local population, and that is the extreme jealousy of rates and municipal trading by the less localized paying classes in the community. That is a question we socialists, believing as we do, all of us at least in the abstract theory of municipalization, must particularly consider. The easy exasperation of the £1000-a-year man at the rates and his extreme patience under Imperial taxation is incomprehensible, unless you recognize this fact of his delocalization. Then at once it becomes clear. He penetrates the pretences of the system to a certain extent; and he is infuriated by the fact of taxation without representation, tempered by a mysteriously ineffective voting paper left at his door. I myself, as one of the delocalized class, will confess he has my sympathy. And those who believe in the idea of the ultimate municipalization of most large industries, will continue to find in this non-localized class, working especially through the medium of Parliament, a persistent and effective obstruction to all such projects, unless such a rectification of areas can be contrived as will overtake the delocalization and the diffusion of interests that has been and is still going on. I will confess that it seems to me that this opposition between the localized and the non-localized classes in the future, or to be more correct, the opposition between the man whose ideas and life lie in a small area, and the man whose ideas and life lie in a great area, is likely to give us that dividing line in politics for which so many people are looking today. For this question of areas has its Imperial as well as its local side. You have already seen the Liberal party split upon the Transvaal question; you yourselves have—I am told—experienced some slight parallel tendency to fission, and it is interesting to note that this was, after all, only another aspect of this great question of areas, which I would now discuss in relation to municipal trading. The small communities are fighting for existence and their dear little ways, the synthetic great communities are fighting to come into existence, and to absorb the small communities. And curiously enough at our last meeting you heard Mr. Belloc, with delightful wit and subtlety, expounding the very antithesis of the conceptions I am presenting tonight. Mr. Belloc—who has evidently never read his Malthus—dreams of a beautiful little village community of peasant proprietors, each sticking like a barnacle to his own little bit of property, beautifully healthy and simple and illiterate and Roman Catholic and *local,* local over the ears. I am afraid the stars in their courses fight against such pink and golden dreams. Every tramway, every new twopenny tube, every light railway, every improvement in your omnibus services, in your telephonic services, in your organization of credit, increases the proportion of your delocalized class, and sucks the ebbing life from your own communities into the veins of the new.

Well, you may say, no doubt this is right so far as it goes; existing local government areas do not represent real communities, but still these local government devices are of service for cutting up and distributing administrative work. But that is exactly what they are not. They are worse when you consider them in regard to function, than when you consider them in regard to representation. Since our conceptions of what constitutes a local administrative area were developed there has arisen the problem of water supply and of organized sewage, of railways, tramways, and communications generally, and of lighting and telephonic intercourse; there hangs over us, though the average local authority has no eyes to see it, the necessity of adapting our roads to accommodate an increasing new traffic of soft-tyred mechanical vehicles, and it is not improbable that heating by wholesale, either by gas or electricity, will presently be also possible and desirable. For all these things we need wide views, wide minds and wide areas, and still more do we want wide views for the business of education that is now also coming into the sphere of local administration.

It happens that I have had an object-lesson in this matter of local government; and indeed it is my object-lesson that has led to this paper tonight. I live upon the boundary line of the Sandgate Urban District Board, a minute authority with a boundary line that appears to have been determined originally about 1850 by mapping out the wanderings of an intoxicated excursionist, and which—the only word is interdigitates—with the borough of Folkestone, the Urban District of Cheriton, and the borough of Hythe. Each of these bodies is by way of being a tramway authority, each is at liberty to secure powers to set up generating stations and supply electricity, each is a water authority, and each does its own little drainage, and the possibilities of friction and litigation are endless. The four places constitute an urban area greatly in need of organized intercommunication, but the four authorities have never been able to agree upon a scheme; and now Folkestone is concerning itself with the project of a little internal tramway system all of its very own. Sandgate has succumbed to the spell of the South Eastern Railway Company, and has come into line with a project that will necessitate a change of cars at the Folkstone boundary. Folkestone has conceded its electrical supply to a company; but Sandgate, on this issue, stands out gallantly for municipal trading, and proposes to lay down a plant and set up a generating station all by itself to supply a population of sixteen hundred people, mostly indigent. In the meanwhile, Sandgate refuses its inhabitants the elementary convenience of the electric light, and when, quite inadvert-

ently, I connected across the convolutions of the boundary with the Folkestone supply, my life was darkened by the threat of impossible litigation.
But if Folkestone repudiates municipal enterprise in the matter of lighting, I gather it does not do so in the matter of telephones; and there has
been talk of a neat little Folkestone telephonic system competing against
the National Telephone Company, a compact little conversazione of perhaps a hundred people, rate sustained. And how is the non-local inhabitant to come into these things? The intelligent non-local inhabitant can
only save his two or three pounds of contribution to this folly or that by
putting in twenty or thirty pounds' worth of work in local politics. He has
no local connections, no local influence, he hasn't a chance against the
plumber. When the house I occupy was built, it was a mere interposition
of Providence that the drain did not go southward into a Folkestone sewer instead of northward into Sandgate. Heaven knows what would have
happened if it had! I and my neighbours are by a special concession permitted to have water from the Folkestone source. By incessant vigilance
we do, I believe, usually succeed in deducting the Folkestone water rate
from the Sandgate general rate which covers water, but the wear and tear
is enormous. However, these are details, dear to my heart, but the merest
marginal comments to my argument. The essential fact is the impracti-
cable silliness of these little divisions, the waste of men, the waste of nervous energy, the waste of administrative energy they involve. I am convinced that in the case of almost any public service in the Folkestone
district with our present boundaries, the administrative waste will more
than equal the profit of a private company with parliamentary powers
overriding our local authorities; that if it is simply a choice between these
little bodies and a company (of the common type even), then in lighting,
locomotion, and indeed in almost any general public service, I would say,
"give me the company." With companies one may hope to deal later; they
will not stand in the way of developing saner areas, but an obstinate little
authority clutching everything in its hands, and led by a clerk naturally
interested in litigation and who is also something of an expert in political
organization, will be an altogether harder thing to supersede.

This difficulty in greater or lesser degree is everywhere. In the case of
poor law administration in particular, and also in the case of elementary
education, the whole country displays what is another aspect of this same
general phenomenon of delocalization; the withdrawal of all the
wealthier people from the areas that are specializing as industrial
centres, and which have a rising population of poor workers, to areas that
are specializing as residential, and which have, if anything, a falling
population of poor labourers. In a place like West Ham or Tottenham you
find starved schools and an abundant delocalized industrial population, and, by way of contrast, at Guildford or Farnham for example, you

will find enormously rich delocalized people, belonging to the same great community as these workers, who pay only the most trivial poor rate and school rate for the benefit of their few immediate neighbours, and escape altogether from the burthens of West Ham. By treating these places as separate communities you commit a cruel injustice on the poor. So far as these things go, to claim convenience for the existing areas is absurd. And it is becoming more and more evident that with tramways, with lighting, with electric heating and force supply, and with the supply of water to great populations, there is an enormous advantage in large generating stations and large areas; that these things must be handled in areas of hundreds of square miles to be efficiently done.

In the case of secondary and higher education one discovers an equal stress and incompatibility. At present, I must point out, even the boundaries of the projected educational authority for London are absurdly narrow. For example, in Folkestone, as in every town upon the south coast, there are dozens of secondary schools that are purely London schools, and filled with London boys and girls, and there are endless great schools like Tonbridge and Charterhouse outside the London area that are also London schools. If you get, for example, a vigorous and efficient educational authority for London, and you raise a fine educational system in the London area, you will find it incomplete in an almost vital particular. You will give the prosperous middle class and the upper class of London the alternative of good teaching and bad air, or of what very probably, under tolerant local authorities, will be relatively bad teaching and open air and exercise out of London. You will have to tax this influential class of people for the magnificent schools they in many cases will be unable to use. As a consequence, you will find again all the difficulties of their opposition, practically the same difficulties that arise so naturally in the way of municipal trading. I would suggest that it would be not only logical but politic, for the London Educational Authority, and not the local authority, to control every secondary school wherever it happened to be, which in an average of years drew more than half its attendance from the London area. That, however, by the way. The point more material to my argument here is that the educational organization of the London area, the Thames valley, and the southern counties are inseparable; that the question of local locomotion is rapidly becoming impossible upon any smaller basis than such an area; that roads, light railways, drainage, water, are all clamouring now to be dealt with on the big scale; and that the more you cut this great area up, the more you leave it in the hands of the localized men, the more you sin against efficiency and the light.

I hope that you will consider this first part of my case proved. And now I pass on to the more debatable question—the nature of the new divisions that are to replace the old. I would suggest that this is a matter only to be answered in detail by an exhaustive analysis of the distribution of population in relation to economic standing, but I may perhaps just indicate roughly what at a first glance I imagine would be one suitable local government area. Let me remind you that some years ago the Conservative party, in an outbreak of intelligence, did in a sort of transitory way see something of what I have been trying to express tonight, and created the London County Council—only to quarrel with it and hate it and fear it ever since. Well, my proposal would be to make a much greater area even than London County, and try to include in it the whole system of what I might call the London-centred population. I believe if you were to take the whole valley of the Thames and its tributaries and draw a line along its boundary watershed, and then include with that Sussex and Surrey, and the east coast counties up to the Wash, you would overtake and anticipate the delocalizing process almost completely. You would have what has become, or is becoming very rapidly, a new urban region, a complete community of the new type, rich and poor and all sorts and aspects of economic life together. I would suggest that watersheds make excellent boundaries. Let me remind you that railways, tramways, drain-pipes, water-pipes, and high roads have this in common—they will not climb over a watershed if they can possibly avoid doing so, and that population and schools and poor tend always to distribute themselves in accordance with these other things. You get the minimum of possible overlap—such overlap as the spreading out of the great midland city to meet London must some day cause—in this way. I would suggest that for the regulation of sanitation, education, communications, industrial control, and poor relief, and for the taxation for these purposes, this area should be one, governed by one body, elected by local constituencies that would make its activities independent of imperial politics. I propose that this body should replace your country councils, boards of guardians, urban and rural district councils, and all the rest of them altogether; that you should elect it, perhaps triennially, once for all. For any purpose of a more local sort, local water-supply systems, local tramway systems—the tramways between Brighton and Shoreham, for example—this body might delegate its powers to subordinate committees, consisting, it has been suggested to me by Mrs. Sidney Webb, of the members for the local constituencies concerned, together with another member or so to safeguard the general interests, or perhaps with an appointed expert or so in addition. These committees would submit their detailed schemes for the approval of committees appointed by the general body, and they would be controllable by that body. However, there is no need for detailed scheming here and now. Let us keep to the main idea.

I submit that such a mammoth municipality as this will be on the one hand, an enormously more efficient substitute for your present little local government bodies, and on the other hand, will be able to take over a considerable proportion of the detailed work and a considerable proportion of the detailed machinery, of your overworked and too extensive central machinery, your local government board, education department, and board of trade. It will be great enough and fine enough to revive the dying sentiment of local patriotism, and it will be a body that will appeal to the ambition of the most energetic and capable men in the community. They will be picked men, to a much greater extent than are your guardians, your urban district councillors and town councillors and so on, at present, because there will be perhaps a hundred or a couple of hundred of them in the place of many thousands. And I venture to think that in such a body you may confidently hope to find a collective intelligence that may be pitted against any trust or board of directors the world is likely to produce.

I suggest this body as a sort of concrete sample of the thing I have in mind. I am quite open to hear and accept the most far-reaching modification of this scheme; it is *the idea of the scale* that I wish particularly to enforce. Municipalize on this scale, I would say, and I am with you altogether. Here is something distinctly and clearly subserving that making of mankind upon which all sane social and political proposals must ultimately base themselves. But to put more power, and still more power in the hands of these petty little administrative bodies that we have to-day, is, I submit, folly and darkness. If the existing areas are to remain the same, then, on the whole, my vote is against municipal trading, and on the whole, with regard to light, to tramways and communications, to telephones, and indeed to nearly all such public services, I would prefer to see these things in the hands of companies, and I would stipulate only for the maximum publicity for their accounts and the fullest provision for detailed regulation through the Board of Trade.

15. The Optimum Size of Cities

OTIS DUDLEY DUNCAN

What is the best size for a city?—The question can only be answered intelligently (if, indeed, there is an answer) by assuming a general view-

Reprinted from *Cities and Society,* Paul K. Hatt and Albert J. Reiss, eds. (Glencoe, Illinois: The Free Press, 1957 revised edition), pp. 759–72 by permission of the publisher. Otis Duncan is a professor of sociology at the University of Chicago.

point from which criteria of good, better, and best can be derived; working out an explicit set of such criteria; and examining the empirical validity of the criteria.

This procedure will be illustrated here by (1) assuming the viewpoint of the theorist of city planning interested in setting general standards for the planning of cities; (2) abstracting from the literature of city planning theory a list of specific criteria which have been offered therein for determining optimum city-size; and (3) examining each of the criteria on the list from the standpoint of observable relationships between city-size and the empirical variables involved in the criteria. The logical justification for this approach rests on the truism that any criterion of optimum population involves, implicitly or explicitly, two elements: first, the normative element, which places a positive or negative valuation on a particular situation; and second, a factual element which has the force of a statement of empirical relationships between variation in city-size variation in the situation in question.

Suppose a criterion of optimum city-size is that a city's size should be that which is most favorable to the health of its population. This criterion takes health as a positive value, and ill health as a negative one. Beyond this, it implicitly posits some significant correlation between city-size and health; for if there were no such correlation, there would obviously be no "most favorable" size, i.e., no optimum.

The establishing by scientific inquiry of a dependable relationship like that implied by a given criterion may be termed a process of empirical *validation* of the criterion. Normative issues are not involved here: —the value once assumed, validation of a criterion of optimum city-size is a purely empirical procedure, which, to be sure, may be carried out more or less adequately, depending on quality of data, soundness of method, and the like.

Clearly, examining optimum city-size from the viewpoint of the city planning theorist provides only one illustration of the proposed procedure for validating the concept of optimum city-size. It is, however, not a trivial illustration. There is good reason to suppose that the list of criteria furnished by the planning literature includes many criteria which would also be forthcoming under alternative viewpoints. There is the further point that planning standards based on the notion of optimum city-size have historically played an important role in the development of the theory and practice of planning. Some writers on city planning—notably those influenced by Ebenezer Howard[1]—have gone so far as to insist that realistic planning presumes some initial consensus as to the desirable size of the urban units planned for;[2] while others have urged that control of city-size is among the most important means of achieving the ends of city planning.[3] Though these may be extreme positions, they are influential ones, as is instanced by the planning efforts got under way in Britain after World War II.[4] Both enthusiasts for and opponents of such positions would do well to subject to searching scrutiny the underlying concept of optimum city-size. Thought and discussion on this question have been jolted by the recent bold proposals for meeting the threat of atomic war by dispersing the urban population. The idea that cities should be small enough to have a low probability of atomic destruction is, of course, a criterion of optimum size, and the discussion of this idea has raised anew the question of size considerations in city planning.[5]

General population theory discusses optimum population in terms of an economic criterion applicable, abstractly, to a closed economy.[6] This formulation has little application to the present problem, since cities are intrinsically "open" economies. Though some writers have sought to justify city optima on economic grounds, the economist himself has by and large remained neutral on the question of optimum city-size.[7] The general trend of discussion is in line with Firey's view that in this area explicit recognition should be given to a variety of interests, all having just claims as criteria of optimum population, and not all mediated in any obvious manner by purely economic factors.[8] The criteria considered in this paper are those which appear in discussions of optimum city-size in the literature of city planning and allied disciplines.[9] The classification of these criteria is the writer's and has merit only for reasons of its convenience. It will be obvious that, at least in the aggregate, planners have been hopeful of attaining far-reaching transformations and ameliorations of the urban way of life through control of city-size. The realism of such hopes is closely bound up with the validity of the concept of optimum city-size.

While the data on which this paper is based are to be summarized rather sketchily, most of them are from published sources; and in any case, there is elsewhere available to the specialist a complete and critical exposition of detailed empirical and methodological problems.[10]

Empirical Observations

1. Physical Plan of the City

The theorist of optimum city-size frequently demands that cities be small enough to enable ready access to the country-side and a reasonably moderate journey to work. The desirable area of a city is in question here, along with the bearing of area on transportation problems. According to a relationship between population size and area demonstrated for our cities as of 1940,[11] the average city of 10,000 will have a radius of one mile; the city of 100,000 a radius of 2.3 miles; and the city of a half-million 4.1 miles, on the idealized assumption of circular areas. For the average resident, accessibility to the various functional areas of the city varies inversely with its radius. With increasing city-size walking or cycling to work and play rapidly becomes out of the question, and automotive and mass transportation become indispensable. A 1942 survey showed that the average resident of cities over a half-million lived 4.8 miles from work, and required 24 minutes to get to his job. In these cities three-fifths traveled to work by mass transportation media, and three-tenths by auto. In the cities of 5,000–25,000 the median distance to work was but 0.8 of a mile, the journey to work requiring 9 minutes. Fewer than half utilized automotive and mass transportation. Respondents in large cities expressed somewhat more dissatisfaction than those in small cities over parking facilities and the distance their children had to travel to high schools.[12] Some form of local mass transportation is apparently required in cities over 15,000, since virtually all cities of this size have buses or street cars.[13] The automobile is a much less effective mode of transit in the large city: A fragmentary survey in 1942 indicated that in cities of 25,000–100,000 about four-fifths of vehicular passengers arriving in the central business district travelled by auto, as against only two-fifths in cities over a half-million; the remainder in each case arrived by some means of mass transportation.[14] Families in cities over 100,000 spend more than four times as much for non-automotive transportation as families in smaller cities.[15]

Although the statistical data are not adequate for a thorough cost analysis of transportation, the unequivocal indication is that the advantages of time, expenditure, and convenience all lie with the moderate sized or small city.

2. Health

One of the most frequently mentioned criteria of optimum city-size concerns the environmental and institutional aspects of the city-dweller's health. It can readily be shown that the ratio of physicians to population increases with increasing city-size, at least up to the million mark, with even more marked differences between large and small cities in the ratios of medical specialists to population than holds for general practitioners. Of the eleven numerically most important types of medical specialists, eight are regularly found only in cities over 50,000 population (as indicated by a ratio of one such physician per city).[16] Ninety-five per cent of the cities over 10,000 have general hospitals, as compared to three-fourths the cities of 5,000–10,000 and two-fifths the cities of 2,500–5,000; and the

model size of these hospitals varies directly with city-size.[17] Nine-tenths
of the births to residents of cities over 10,000 now occur in hospitals, as
compared to three-fourths in the case of cities below 10,000; and over
half the large city deaths occur in hospital beds as compared to one-third
in the smaller centers.[18] Health services and facilities are, therefore,
clearly more accessible to large city residents than to small.

The actual health status of the populations of different sized cities is
perhaps most reliably, though indirectly, shown by mortality statistics. Infant mortality varies inversely with city-size, and in recent years the
smallest cities have had rates two-fifths larger than cities over the million
mark. The association with city-size is uniform, and the differentials by
city-size have increased, rather than diminished, with the nation-wide improvements in infant mortality rates of the past three decades.[19] Likewise,
the larger cities experience an advantage with regard to maternal mortality, though here the differences are smaller—perhaps of the order of ten
per cent—and have diminished considerably in recent years.[20] For combined sexes in the total white population, the life expectancy at practically all ages was higher in 1940 for residents of cities of 10,000–100,000
than for residents of cities larger or smaller than this. The superior lon-
gevity in this city-size group is a function of age, increasing to age 35
and being most marked in the age range 36–65. However, at best these
cities experience only a three per cent superiority over larger cities, and a
much narrower margin over smaller cities.[21] Further, there are important
variations by population subgroups. In the West and the North, life expectancies of both races are higher in the smaller cities, but the reverse
is true in the South. In general, the advantage of the smaller cities increases with advancing age, amounting to as much as 5 to 15 per cent at
the old ages in the North and West.[22] Among the important causes of
death, large cities have the highest death rates from cancer, heart disease,
tuberculosis, diabetes, stomach ulcers (white population), and suicide.
Small cities have higher rates for pneumonia and influenza, appendicitis,
intracranial lesions, nephritis, and hernia and intestinal obstruction.[23]
Recalling the higher infant and maternal mortality of the small cities, and
the fact that their life expectancies are relatively greater at advanced
than at early ages, there is, therefore, some indication that the principal
health advantages of the large cities are in regard to the immediate
accessibility of superior services for the treatment of acute diseases and
childbirth; whereas the populations of these large urban centers are more
vulnerable to the long-term, accumulative environmental hazards eventu-
ating in chronic and psychosomatic disorders. This picture is, of course,
much different nowadays from that of a few decades ago before the con-

trol of epidemic infectious diseases. Recent advances in public health have presumably benefited the large cities more than the small. It is impossible to make a categorical generalization about the relative advantages of large and small cities with regard to health; but the probability is that the magnitudes of the historical differences in the health of populations in cities of different sizes are diminishing, on the whole.

TABLE 1

City-Size:	100,000 and Over	25,000– 100,000	10,000– 25,000	2,500– 10,000
Per cent of cities with psychiatric clinics, 1947	83	25	4	1
Per cent of births occurring in hospitals, 1943	92	88	84	74
Infant deaths per 1,000 births, 1948	29	31	33	36
Life expectancy, 1940:				
— At birth (sexes combined)	64.3	64.0		62.5
— At age 45 (sexes combined)	26.0	26.7		26.6
Age-adjusted death rates per 100,000 population, 1940:				
—From heart and circulatory diseases	354	309		295
—From pneumonia and influenza	64	67		77

3. Public Safety

It is sometimes stated that small cities are safer places in which to live than large cities. This assertion may be checked against the statistics of crime, auto accident deaths, and fire losses.

Most of the 24 offense categories used in *Uniform Crime Reports* show a tendency for crime rates, as measured by crimes known to police, or by persons charged, to increase with city-size. The relationship is not always of a simple character, but in general cities over 50,000 have higher rates than cities under 50,000, though the very largest cities by no means have the highest rates in all or most of these categories.[24] Lacking data to measure directly the cost of crime, it may be observed that per capita expenditures for city police forces increase directly with city-size, differences among city-size groups being of the order of three or four to one, comparing cities over a half million to cities below 10,000.[25] A similar comparison for per capita size of police force gives a ratio of roughly two to one.[26] These ratios of differential effort and expenditure are greater than the ratios of differential incidence in most categories of crime. Therefore, it may be generalized that the large city not only experiences a greater relative amount of crime, but also pays proportionately more heavily for it.

Statistics of automobile accident death rates are none too reliably compiled, and consequently exhibit certain illogical irregularities over the years. In general, occurrence rates based on population are lower for cities between 10,000 and 50,000 than for larger cities, for the recent years for which data are relatively complete. Occurrence rates based on numbers of registered vehicles give a somewhat clearer picture. Again cities of 10,000–50,000 have the lower rates, with the rates increasing regularly with city-size in the statistics of recent years. Although it is not entirely clear in what size group of cities there is the greatest personal risk of dying in an auto accident, it is obvious that the larger the city, the more lethal an instrument the automobile becomes. And it seems fairly clear that the cities below 50,000 enjoy the greatest safety from auto accidents, by perhaps ten per cent as measured by population based rates, and by a much larger margin in relation to the number of automobiles owned by residents.[27]

TABLE 2

City-Size Group	Average Annual Auto Accident Deaths per 100,000 Vehicles, 1942–46	Per Capita Police Expenditure, 1942	Average Annual Criminal Offensive Rate per 100,000 Population, 1940–1947		
			Murder	Robbery	Rape
1,000,000+	68	$6.71	5	73	14 (1,000,000+ – 250,000)
500,000—	54	5.80	8 (500,000 – 250,000)	74 (500,000 – 250,000)	
250,000—	50	3.80			
100,000—	46	3.57	7	56	
50,000—	40	3.37	6	40	11
25,000—	35	2.89	4	29	9
10,000—	35	2.34	4	23	7 / 8
5,000—		2.06	4 (5,000 – 2,500)	22 (5,000 – 2,500)	8 (5,000 – 2,500)
2,500—		1.64			

In regard to fire hazards, the results vary according to the statistical measure chosen. Per capita fire loss, in dollars, shows little systematic association with city-size, except for the possibility that within a given city-size group, there is greater variation in the scale of losses by individual cities among the smaller cities. This would indicate a greater vulnerability of the small city to losses from an occasional large fire.[28] Fire loss expressed as a percentage of total real property value is larger in the cities of 30,000–50,000 than in the cities over 1,000,000, the differences being greater when measured by the size group mean than when measured by the size group median—again indicating a skewing toward extreme values among smaller cities.[29] The annual number of fires per capita is related inversely to city-size, with fires being relatively one-third more frequent in cities 25,000–50,000 than in cities 500,000 and over.[30] On the other hand, the loss per building fire is more than fifty per cent greater in the larger of these two city-size groups.[31] There are only slight differences by city-size in regard to per capita size of fire departments, but the cities over a half-million spend 15 per cent more for them in relation to their population, than do the cities of 10,000–25,000.[32] While there is no unequivocal measure of fire hazard and of fire-fighting efficiency, the suggestion is that among all sizes of city larger than 25,000 the differences in fire losses are rather due to inherent fire hazards than to differences in the mobilization of resources for fire protection. While the choice among the above quoted indices is somewhat subjective, perhaps a fair case could be made for the greater safety of the small or medium sized city, on the average.

In most persons' minds, no doubt, the preeminent question about a city's public safety nowadays is its potential destruction by the Bomb in a future war. Fortunately, there are no statistics on the relative vulnerability of cities of different sizes to A-bombs; we have to rely on statements of authorities and certain *a priori* considerations. The question is not, of course, one of the destructive power of the Bomb in a direct hit, but rather of the probability of a city's suffering such a hit. It has been argued that the small city is safer, first because it is a smaller target, more difficult to locate and hit directly; second, because it is likely to be a less attractive target; and third, because the potential enemy's A-bomb supply may be limited, thus diminishing the probability of an A-bomb attack on any given small city. From considerations such as these, the National Security Resources Board urges that "further urban concentrations of more than 50,000 people . . . be avoided."[33]

4. *Municipal Efficiency*

It is a plausible hypothesis that the efficiency with which municipal services can be rendered should increase with increasing city-size to a point of diminishing returns, with an optimum size somewhere between the extremes. However, it is virtually impossible to get data to test this hypothesis. The existing data on municipal expenditures show, in general, a direct relationship between city-size and per capita costs in most of the 14 categories of expenditure: The larger cities spend more for high-ways, sanitation, public welfare, correction, schools, etc., than small.[34] However, these data reflect the separately varying factors of unit costs, amount, and quality of services. Hence they show little about municipal efficiency. From previously cited data, it may be seen that despite their greater expenditures, the large cities apparently enjoy no better situation than small with regard to crime and traffic control, fire protection, or health. This would argue that either these services are rendered less effi-ciently in large cities, or—what is more probable—that the initial problems of large cities are intrinsically more difficult. On the other hand, as will appear later, the higher levels of expenditure for schools, libraries, and recreation apparently reflect greater amounts and/or qualities of these services. Whether the increment of service is commensurate with the in-crement of cost cannot be accurately judged.

In only one area of municipal service can some tentative optimum population be established—the provision of residential electric service. Unit costs decline with increasing city-size up to the million mark, with cities between a half and one million getting electricity the cheapest.[35] Except for this one observation—which can by no means be immediately generalized—optimum city-size from the standpoint of municipal effi-ciency is still *terra incognita*.

5. *Education and Communications*

A variety of measures of city school systems may be cited. Larger cities have longer school years—one week longer in cities over 100,000 as compared to those below 10,000. But the difference is smaller in regard to average per pupil school days attended. The average annual salary of teachers increases markedly with city size, quite overshadowing any cost-of-living differentials. Likewise, per pupil expenditures of large city schools exceed those of small city schools, and a greater proportion of the total school budget goes directly into costs of instruction. Large cities are much more frequently able to provide such special services as sum-mer schools and night schools. On the other hand, the pupil/teacher ra-tio is greater in large cities, though the difference between large and small cities is only of the order of ten per cent.[36]

Facilities for advanced education are considerably limited by city-size. If we somewhat arbitrarily estimate the "population base" for a facility as that city-size at which 50 per cent of cities have the facility, the population base for a college or university is around 100,000, about the same for a junior college, and about 25,000 for a business college.[37] Accredited professional schools in such fields as business, engineering, law, medicine, and social work require larger population bases, of the order of 500,000.[38]

Despite the demonstrably superior educational facilities of large cities, their populations are at but slightly higher levels of educational status than those of small cities. As between cities of 250,000 and over and those below 25,000 superiorities of 0.2–0.3 in median school years completed are typical for ages below 18, but the slight observed differences amongst the adult populations are not all in this same direction.[39]

With regard to agencies of public enlightenment other than schools, estimates of population bases have been made as just indicated. For an art museum the population base is 100,000, with a somewhat higher figure for science and historical museums. The population base for a public library is 2,500, for a daily newspaper 5,000, for a radio station 10,000, for an FM station 50,000, and for television 50,000. Current trends suggest a raising of the required population base in the future for newspapers, and a lowering for libraries, FM, and television.[40]

TABLE 3

City-Size Group	School Expenditures Per Pupil, 1937–38	Median School Years Completed, Native White Males, 18–44, 1940	Per Cent of Cities with—		
			College or University, 1940	Art Museum, 1938	AM Radio Station, 1946
250,000+	} $120	11.0	100	86	100
100,000—			56	53	89
50,000—	99*	} 11.2†	43	25	72
10,000—	85*		19	4	39
2,500—	75	11.1†	6	1	5

* The dividing line between these two groups is 30,000, rather than 50,000.
† The dividing line between these two groups is 25,000, rather than 10,000.

A more detailed analysis of libraries shows that they generally meet desirable minimum professional standards only in cities as large as 50,000-75,000.[41] Although libraries in large cities have larger book stocks and spend more money per capita, their service to the population is less as measured by per capita book circulation. For a sample of 103 cities in 1943 there was a negative correlation of —.64 between city-size and per capita circulation. Holding constant percent of population registered as borrowers, book stock in volumes per capita, branch libraries per capita, and per capita expenditures, the correlation remained at —.51.[42] Another writer has demonstrated a negative correlation between city-size and per capita museum attendance.[43] Apparently for those facilities which do not operate by mass distribution, the superior facilities of the large city are purchased at the price of diminished community participation.

6. Public Recreation

An accepted professional standard for park acreage is one acre per 100 population. This standard is attained by one-fifth the cities between 50,000 and 250,000, by practically no city above that size, and by somewhat lesser percentages of the smaller cities. Parks in large cities have a much wider variety of recreation facilities, special use areas and buildings, and spend larger per capita amounts for operation and maintenance. On the other hand, the accessibility of parks, as indicated by the number of parks per capita is much greater in the small cities. In those cities reporting parks there are four for every 10,000 persons in the city of 25,000–50,000 as compared to 1 in the city over 1,000,000.[44] The optimum population for parks, on any equilibrium of these four variables, is clearly in the middle size range of cities.

The population base for zoos (estimated as before) is 100,000;[45] approximately the same figure holds for symphony orchestras.[46] Resident grand opera is found in only three or four of the country's largest cities, and the population base for opera of any sort is apparently above a quarter million.[47] On the other hand, motion picture theaters are found in every city, and even cities as small as 10,000–25,000 have variety and choice of cinematic offerings, with an average of three movies each.[48]

TABLE 4

City-Size Group	At Least One Park Acre Per 100 Population, 1940	Per Cent of Cities with— Park Expenditure of at Least $1.00 Per Capita, 1940	Zoo, 1940	Symphony Orchestra, 1946
1,000,000+	0	80	100	100
500,000—	0	100	100	89
250,000—	9	58	76	78
100,000—	20	42	57	55
50,000—	21	42	32	18
25,000—	17	27	15	5
10,000—	15	14	8	0
5,000—	14	13	2	0
2,500—	12	7	1	0

7. Retail Facilities

The oft mentioned values of the large city as a shopping center cannot be denied. However, in many standard lines of merchandise this advantage is slight, the real superiority of the large city being in style and specialty trade. It is worth observing that in no more than three of the 65 kinds of retail outlet listed by the census is a population base of over 50,000 apparently required.[49] Another study suggests that for some lines of specialty goods, stores in the largest cities apparently have no more "drawing power" for non-resident trade than those in cities of 100,000.[50] The optimum city population for adequate retail outlets, even for specialized trade, may therefore be no higher than 50,000 to 100,000.

8. Churches and Associations

Criteria of optimum city-size involving the organized group life are ordinarily not precisely stated. Rather there is usually some general reference to the desirability of a certain degree of variety and diversity of groups, preferably without too much loss of community consensus and cohesion. The following data will doubtless seem somewhat tangential to this formulation.

There are only 20 religious denominations in the United States (1936) which have as many as 1,000 urban local churches. These cover three-fourths of all local churches and nine-tenths of all memberships in urban areas. Perhaps 20 could therefore be regarded as a generous estimate of the minimum desirable number of denominations. From census data on number of denominations per city, it is estimated that 30,000 is the population base for this degree of denominational variety.[51]

There are no comparative statistics on the variety of voluntary associations present in cities of different sizes, and only fragmentary data on certain national organizations. From these, the estimated population bases for certain kinds of organization are as follows: Rotary Club, 5,000; Elks lodge, 10,000; Lions Club, 15,000; Boy Scout Council, 25,000; YMCA, 25,000; YWCA, 25,000.[52] The population base for any two or more of these would be somewhat higher, but in all probability most organizations of these types are well represented in cities no larger than 25,000–50,000.

9. Family Life

Advocates of small cities and decentralization often stress the greater strength of the family institution in small cities. Statistical support for this position may be found in the data on marriage and fertility. Of the native white population 18-64, only three-fifths are married in cities over a quarter million as against over two-thirds in cities 2,500–25,000.[53]

In 1940 no city-size group in the urban white population had a fertility level up to the permanent replacement quota. The cities of 2,500–10,000 were reproducing at 15 per cent below replacement, whereas cities over 1,000,000 were 35 per cent below.[54] In previous census periods the persistent inverse association of city-size and effective fertility has also been marked.

Another important aspect of family living—housing—has been minutely described by the 1940 census. The principal differentials by city-size are as follows. Home ownership is more frequent in small cities; rentals increase with increasing city-size; and owner-occupied units are less frequently mortgaged in small cities. Thus both ownership and rental are easier propositions in the smaller centers. Dwelling units in large cities are better equipped with regard to private bath, running water, central heating, flush-toilet, mechanical refrigeration, and gas or electric cooking. They are also in better repair, being somewhat newer on the average. In small cities a majority of dwelling units are in single family structures, whereas the reverse is true of large cities. However, there is somewhat more room overcrowding in small cities, as measured by the standard of more than one and one-half persons per room.[55] In sum, not all the advantages in regard to good housing lie with any one size group of cities.

TABLE 5

Housing Characteristics, 1940	Cities of—			
	250,000 and Over	50,000– 250,000	10,000– 50,000	2,500– 10,000
Home ownership	29%	38%	45%	49%
Average rent, tenent units	$32	$25	$23	$18
Single family units	33%	51%	61%	71%
Room overcrowding	5%	6%	6%	7%
Units needing major repairs	8%	11%	14%	17%
Units without running water	3%	6%	8%	15%

10. Miscellaneous Psychological and Social Characteristics of Urban Life

There remains a residual category of attributes, desirable and undesirable, which are sometimes mentioned as criteria of optimum city-size. Such epithets as provincialism, friendliness, community participation, standardization, anonymity, strain, spontaneity, and the like are perhaps applied with more heat than light in the absence of precise specification and reliable measurement of such urban traits.

One writer claims to find evidence of greater "social contentment" in cities below 25,000 in the fact that survey respondents there voice fewer complaints on certain questions about neighborhood and community characteristics.[56] Another attempt to get at some of the more intangible traits of cities through an analysis of student community reports[57] must be deemed methodologically unsound.

There is but one trait of this miscellany for which some approximate measurements can be made. This is the status of the city as a center of innovation and cultural diffusion. Rose's data indicate a positive correlation between city-size and cultural innovation.[58] Bowers has shown that amateur radio followed a diffusion cycle from large to small cities.[59] Data assembled for the present study indicate that commercial broadcasting, FM, and television follow a similar pattern. Another kind of measurement is the per capita incidence of persons in certain eminence groups. Inventors, artists, and persons in *Who's Who* are present in great numbers, relative to population, in large cities than in small.[60]

Discussion

The above summary of a considerable mass of data leads to the following comments: The optimum size of cities is quite different from the standpoint of certain criteria from what it is on the basis of others. It is found that even an apparently unitary criterion—e.g. health—may give conflicting indications of the optimum. There is no immediately obvious way in which these various optima may be objectively equilibrated, compromised, weighted, or balanced to yield an unequivocal figure for *the* optimum population for a city. Any numerical choice of a figure for the optimum population is involved in subjective value preferences and impressionistic weighting systems. Most theorists proposing a size or size range as the optimum adopt this procedure, or the alternative one of confining attention to a few of the many criteria of optimum city-size that have been proposed in the literature. Thus if the preeminent interest is in the planning of cities for safety in atomic war, some population, say 25,000 or 50,000, will be taken as a maximum desirable city-size. Some other interests will be compatible with this choice, e.g. those of physical plan, health, and public safety. Attention to the remaining criteria which indicate larger sizes is then shifted to a consideration of the sacrifices involved in limiting city-size. Data such as those cited in this paper furnish the starting point for such a consideration, assuming the relationship between city-size and urban characteristics to be those of the present time. The degree to which city and national planning could mitigate these sacrifices is a question which is still open, scientifically speaking, though there is no dearth of assertion on the subject.

The problem of optimum city-size originates in the realm of values and, ideally, eventuates in action. Only the middle term of the translation of values into action is open to scientific procedures, for the choice of values and the decision to act are intrinsically beyond the scope of science. Nevertheless, both valuation and action should profit from an occasional summing up of the evidence and its implications. This paper has reported an initial effort of that kind.

Notes

1. Howard's *Garden Cities of To-Morrow* first appeared at the turn of the century, it was reissued in 1946 (London: Faber and Faber, Ltd.).

2. F. J. Osborn, *Transport, Town Development and Territorial Planning of Industry*, No. 20, The New Fabian Research Bureau (London: Victor Gollancz, Ltd., 1934), p. 20.

3. Lewis Mumford, *The Culture of Cities* (New York: Harcourt Brace, 1938), p. 488.

4. Ministry of Town and Country Planning, New Towns Committee, *Final Report*, Cmd. 6876 (London: H. M. Stationery Office, 1946).

5. William F. Ogburn, "Sociology and the Atom," *American Journal of Sociology*, LI (January, 1946), 267–275; Tracy B. Augur, "The Dispersal of Cities as a Defense Measure," *Bulletin of the Atomic Scientists*, IV (May, 1948), 131–134.

6. Manuel Gottlieb, "The Theory of Optimum Population for a Closed Economy," *Journal of Political Economy*, LIII (December, 1945), 289–318.

7. Paul Samuelson, "The Business Cycle and Urban Redevelopment," *The Problem of the Cities and Towns*, ed. Guy Greer (Report of the Conference on Urbanism, Harvard University, March 5–6, 1942).

8. Walter Firey, "The Optimum Rural-Urban Population Balance," *Rural Sociology*, XII (June, 1947), 116–127.

9. The following are representative: National Council of Social Service, *The Size and Social Structure of a Town* (London: George Allen & Unwin, Ltd., 1943); William F. Ogburn, *op. cit.*; F. J. Osborn, *op. cit.*; *Report of the Royal Commission on the Distribution of the Industrial Population*, Cmd. 6153 (London: H. M. Stationery Office, 1940); Thomas Sharp, *Town Planning*, rev. ed. (Harmondsworth, Middlesex: Penguin Books, 1945); Raymond Unwin, "The Town and the Best Size for Good Social Life," *Town Theory and Practice*, ed. C. B. Purdon (London: Benn Brothers, Ltd., 1921).

10. Otis Dudley Duncan, "An Examination of the Problem of Optimum City-Size, microfilm (Chicago: University of Chicago Libraries, 1949). See also the following compilations of data on differential characteristics of cities by size: Fenton Keyes, "The Correlation of Social Phenomena with Community Size," Ph.D. dissertation, Department of Sociology, Yale University, 1942; *The Municipal Year Book* (Chicago: The International City Managers' Association, annual); William F. Ogburn, *Social Characteristics of Cities* (Chicago: The International City Managers' Association, 1937); U.S. Bureau of the Census, *Cities Supplement, Statistical Abstract of the United States* (Washington: Government Printing Office, 1944).

11. John Q. Stewart, "Suggested Principles of 'Social Physics,'" *Science*, CVI (August 29, 1947), 179–180.

12. Melville C. Branch, Jr., *Urban Planning and Public Opinion* (Princeton: Princeton University Bureau of Urban Research, 1942).

13. "Suburbs' Growth Expands Use of Cars," *Automobile Facts*, III (March, 1944), 1, 3.

14. Kendrick Lee, "Local Transportation," *Editorial Research Reports*, I, No. 118 (May 15, 1942), 311–325.

15. National Resources Planning Board, *Family Expenditures in the United States Statistical Tables and Appendices* (Washington: Government Printing Office, 1941), Tables 1, 196, 198, 200, and 202.

16. R. G. Leland, *Distribution of Physicians in the United States* (Chicago: Bureau of Medical Economics, American Medical Association, rev. ed., 1936).

17. Commission on Hospital Care, *Hospital Care in the United States* (New York: The Commonwealth Fund, 1947), Table 14.

18. U.S. Bureau of the Census, *Vital Statistics—Special Reports*, vol. 22, no. 1, 1945; and vol. 10, no. 51, 1941.

19. U.S. Bureau of the Census, *Vital Statistics of the United States* (Washington: Government Printing Office, annual).

20. *Ibid.*

21. Life tables computed from data in U.S. Bureau of the Census, *Vital Statistics Rates in the United States, 1900–1940* (Washington: Government Printing Office, 1943).

22. U.S. Bureau of the Census, *Vital Statistics—Special Reports*, vol. 23, no. 15, 1947, Table IV.

23. U.S. Bureau of the Census, *Vital Statistics—Special Reports*, vol. 23, no. 1, 1945.

24. Federal Bureau of Investigation, *Uniform Crime Reports* (Washington: Government Printing Office, semiannual).

25. U.S. Bureau of the Census, *City Finances: 1942*, Vol. III; and *Finances of Cities Having Populations Less Than 25,000: 1942* (Washington: Government Printing Office, 1944).

26. *Uniform Crime Reports, op. cit.*

27. National Safety Council, *Accident Facts*, Annual editions of 1933–1947.

28. *The Municipal Year Book, op. cit.*, editions of 1940 and 1945.

29. Mabel L. Walker, *Municipal Expenditures* (Baltimore: The Johns Hopkins Press, 1930), Table II.

30. *The Municipal Year Book, op. cit.*, annual editions of 1941–1945.

31. *Ibid.*

32. *The Municipal Year Book, 1945, op. cit.*

33. *National Security Factors in Industrial Location*, NSRB Doc. 66 (Washington: National Security Resources Board, rev., July 22, 1948), p. 4.

34. *City Finances: 1942, op. cit.; Finances of Cities Having Populations Less Than 25,000: 1942, op. cit.*

35. *Cities Supplement, Statistical Abstract of the United States, op. cit.*, Table 4.

36. U.S. Office of Education, "Statistics of City School Systems 1937–1938," *Biennial Survey of Education in the United States*, Bull. No. 2, 1940 (Washington: Government Printing Office, 1940), Ch. III; and "Statistics of City School Systems 1939–1940 and 1941–1942," *Biennial Surveys of Education in the United States 1938–1940 and 1940–1942* (Washington: Government Printing Office, 1944), Vol. II, Ch. VII.

37. Clarence Stephen Marsh, ed., *American Universities and Colleges* (Washington: American Council on Education, 4th ed., 1940); *Directory of Private Business Schools in the United States* (Washington: War Emergency Council of Private Business Schools, 1943); *Directory of Junior Colleges, 1941* (Washington: American Association of Junior Colleges, 1941).

38. U.S. Office of Education, *Education Directory 1941, Part III, Colleges and Universities,* Bulletin 1941, No. 1 (Washington: Government Printing Office, 1941).

39. U.S. Bureau of the Census, *Sixteenth Census of the United States: 1940. Population. Education, Educational Attainment of Children by Rental Value of Home* (Washington: Government Printing Office, 1945), Table III; and *Educational Attainment by Economic Characteristics and Marital Status* (Washington: Government Printing Office, 1947), Table 17.

40. Laurence Vail Coleman, *The Museum in America* (Washington: The American Association of Museums, 1939), Vol. III; *The American Library Directory, 1939* (New York: R. R. Bowker Co., 1939); *Directory, Newspapers and Periodicals, 1946* (Philadelphia: N. W. Ayer & Son, 1946); "Directory of Broadcasting Stations of the United States," *Broadcasting, 1946 Yearbook Number,* pp. 71–190; Jack Alicoate, ed., *The 1947 Radio Annual* (New York: Radio Daily, 1947).

41. Lowell Martin, "The Optimum Size of the Public Library Unit," *Library Extension: Problems and Solutions,* ed. Carleton B. Joeckel (Chicago: University of Chicago Press, 1945), pp. 32–46.

42. Original data taken from "Public Library Statistics," *Bulletin, American Library Association,* XXXVIII (April, 1944), 154–167.

43. Paul Marshall Rea, *The Museum and the Community* (Lancaster: The Science Press, 1932).

44. National Recreation Association, *Municipal and County Parks in the United States, 1940* (New York: National Recreation Association, 1942).

45. *Ibid.*

46. "Symphony Orchestras in the United States and Canada," *The International Musician,* XLIV (June, 1946), 7–8.

47. *Pierre Key's Music Year Book, 1938* (New York: Pierre Key, 1938).

48. *Motion Picture Theatres in the United States: A Statistical Summary, 1948* (New York: Motion Picture Association of America, Inc., 1948).

49. Population base estimated as city-size where number of stores per city is 1.0, by graphic interpolation; U.S. Bureau of the Census, *Sixteenth Census of the United States: 1940. Census of Business: 1939. Retail Trade Analysis by City-Size Groups* (Washington: Government Printing Office, 1942), Table 12C.

50. John Adams Pfanner, Jr., *A Statistical Study of the Drawing Power of Cities for Retail Trade* (Studies in Business Administration, The Journal of Business of The University of Chicago, Vol. X, No. 3, April, 1940).

51. U.S. Bureau of the Census, *Religious Bodies: 1936, Vol. I. Summary and Detailed Tables* (Washington: Government Printing Office, 1941), Table 13.

52. Official Directory 1935–1936 (Chicago: Rotary International, 1935); Keyes, *op. cit.,* p. 162.

53. U.S. Bureau of the Census, *Educational Attainment by Economic Characteristics and Marital Status, op. cit.,* Table 37.

54. Warren S. Thompson, *The Growth of Metropolitan Districts in the United States: 1900–1940* (Washington: Government Printing Office, 1947); and special computations from 1940 Census data.

55. *Housing—Special Reports,* Series H-44, Nos. 1–7 (Washington: U.S. Bureau of the Census, 1944–1945).

56. Branch, *op. cit.,* p. 31.

57. Walter T. Watson, "Is Community Size an Index of Urbanization?" *The Southwestern Social Science Quarterly,* XVII (September, 1936), 150–160.

58. Edward Rose, "Innovations in American Culture," *Social Forces,* XXVI (March, 1948), 255–272.

59. Raymond V. Bowers, "The Direction of Intra-Societal Diffusion," *American Sociological Review,* II (December, 1937), 826–836.

60. Sample of inventors from U.S. Patent Office, *Index of Patents, 1940* (Washington: Government Printing Office, 1941); sample of artists from *Who's Who in American Art, Vol. III 1940–1941* (Washington: The American Federation of Arts, 1940); R. D. McKenzie, *The Metropolitan Community* (New York: McGraw-Hill Book Co., Inc., 1933), Table 48.

B. AS A POLITICAL AND ADMINISTRATIVE PROBLEM

16. The Limitations of Metropolitan Reorganization

EDWARD C. BANFIELD AND
MORTON GRODZINS

(The guiding question of the book from which this excerpt was taken was: Would metropolitan government aid in the solution of urban housing problems? The authors gave a negative answer. The following passage is taken from the concluding chapter in which the discussion turns to metropolitan government in general. No attempt has been made to edit out the occasional references to housing which refer specifically to earlier sections of the book.)

In many discussions of metropolitan organization, there is a strong bias toward simplicity, uniformity, and symmetry of structure. It is often taken for granted that the presence of a large number of independent local governments in a single area means waste and duplication. That there may be even administrative advantages in decentralization is often overlooked entirely. Beyond problems of efficiency and economy, issues of community independence, sociability, and status are involved. Technical considerations concerning optimum areas for given services must compete for priority with political issues concerning the best organization for the public control of public officials. Issues of philosophy intrude: when does self-government in one locality impede self-government in another? Values of local control compete with values of area efficiency. A consideration of what is desirable in the way of organization ought to take into account the full range of problems. Intangibles—for example, the suburbanite's satisfaction in remaining apart from the central city— should be accorded some value. If a careful accounting is made with all relevant factors taken into consideration, the present "Balkanization" of government in the metropolitan areas may not be as undesirable as it is

Reprinted from *Government and Housing in Metropolitan Areas* (New York: McGraw-Hill Book Company, Inc., 1958), pp. 155–66 by permission of the authors and the publisher. Authors' footnotes omitted. Edward Banfield is a professor of political science at Harvard University. Morton Grodzins is a professor of political science at the University of Chicago.

often made to appear. At any rate, arguments in favor of metropolitan integration on the grounds of administrative efficiency must compete with other arguments that favor independence and separateness.

When the needed distinction is made between "problems which exist in metropolitan areas" and "problems which exist by virtue of the inadequacies of governmental structure in the metropolitan areas," the latter are relatively few. Transportation is probably the most common and the most pressing of the real metropolitan-area problems. Other common and important problems are air-pollution control and civil defense, and in some areas, water supply and waste disposal. Opinion, rather than technical considerations, may add other functions to this list. Even the few named do not require the same jurisdiction, a fact which makes it extremely difficult to say what the boundaries of an all-purpose general government should be. Moreover, there is no reason in technology why most of these functions cannot be carried on effectively by metropolitan governments which do not have general jurisdiction, or by several governments acting collaboratively.

Deep and persistent political conflicts divide the populations of most metropolitan areas. The conflict between the central city and the suburban ring—which also is a conflict between lower-classes and middle-classes and between Negroes and whites—in most places rules out any immediate possibility of "one local government for one local area." The sharpness of these conflicts makes it doubtful in some places whether metropolitan-area government would be immediately desirable even if it were possible. Though the argument for larger areas in the long run is a persuasive one, it is hard to say whether short-run conflicts are better managed if the parties to them are members of the same or of different political communities. But this question is not a practical one under present circumstances. The fact is that sweeping programs of governmental integration will be politically impossible in most metropolitan areas for a long time to come. . . .

If the twin questions of what is desirable and what is possible in metropolitan organization are considered in all their complexity, it will be apparent that no single scheme of reform will be applicable everywhere. Every metropolitan area presents a special case, and only detailed consideration of the intricacies and idiosyncrasies of a specific local situation can produce a "plan" that is both desirable and feasible. Recommendations found in reports like this one have their uses, but they are no substitute for the arduous process of local study, discussion, negotiation, and compromise.

The considerations outlined above lead to a "model" for action: a description in general terms of the means by which housing may be improved through changes in the structure of government in a "typical"—and therefore nonexistent—metropolitan area. The aim of the plan is to meet genuine area-wide housing needs with area-wide solutions while maintaining personal and community discretion. In the light of political and social obstacles to sweeping plans of governmental integration, the model places emphasis upon collaboration and the exchange of contractual services among independent governmental units. From the start, this creates a *de facto* local confederation; in the long run it looks forward to a scheme of local federalism.

The impulse for governmental reorganization affecting housing may come for reasons only indirectly related to housing: as a consequence of new transportation needs, or civil defense, or flood control, for example. Furthermore, the persons responsible for initiating structural change may be variously situated. They may be leaders of civic groups, powerful businessmen, members of a state commission, or state legislators. Whatever the immediate causes of reorganization and whoever the initiators, success of any plan will depend crucially upon the mayor of the central city. Even where others play the leading role, the mayor's acquiescence is mandatory. Where the central-city mayor opposes reorganization, it will fail. Where he supports it fully, chances for success are at their best. The central-city mayor is therefore the leading figure in the model.

What gives the central-city mayor his central role? The core city has more at stake in truly metropolitan matters than do the other governments. The biggest of the local governments, it is more likely to have the resources—financial, technical, and political—to initiate and carry on effective action. Moreover the mayor of the central city has a constituency large enough and diverse enough in its interests to permit him to view matters in metropolitan scale. A portion of this constituency, including heavy investors in downtown business districts, may demand rather than merely permit this course of action.

The mayor and his associates are therefore able to play the part of regional statesmen. That is to say, they can think in terms of the whole metropolitan area and when necessary can sacrifice the short-run special interests of the central city to its less immediate, but no less real, interest in the welfare of the area as a whole.

It is not unreasonable to expect statesmanship of this kind from the mayors of central cities. No doubt, in many cases nothing of the sort is to be expected. But in others—New York, Chicago, Philadelphia, Milwaukee, Denver, and St. Louis come to mind especially—action along these lines has already been taking place with encouraging results.

As the center and energizing force of metropolitan organization, the mayor of the central city will seek actively to bring the other units of government into the necessary cooperative relations. He will not do this merely by preaching or persuasion. The proposed model does not assume that the lesser officials of the metropolitan area will also be statesmen (though it does not rule out that possibility). In many cases the mayors of suburban towns or the county commissioners will be unwilling to co-operate in matters which offer no disadvantages to their jurisdictions. This unwillingness is not due solely to the lesser stature of the small-town official, although this may be a contributing factor. The decisive consideration is that the official elected by a relatively small and homogeneous constituency does not have the independence which would allow him to forego an immediate point for a more remote one, or to find support from one important constituency group when damned by another.

The mayor of the central city will not be without ability to impress others with the importance of cooperation. The merchants, bankers, real estate brokers, and other businessmen of the central cities suffer badly —in higher taxes, in lower income, and in difficulties of getting and keeping personnel—when property values decline in the core cities. Many of these leaders are influential residents of the suburbs, and often their interests, both economic and social, spill over the central-city boundary lines. Their civic groups are most often organized on a wider-than-single-city basis and have considerable influence in the affairs of many local governments. With the requisite leadership from the mayor, these citizens and their voluntary organizations may be mobilized to support areawide collaborative activities. (An effort to enlist them in grandiose programs of governmental integration is far less likely to succeed; these are the very people to whom, in their role as family heads and homeowners, suburban independence is most important.) To utilize already existing voluntary groups is to maximize the effectiveness of such a citizen effort.

The governor's office can also be expected to help. Many governors in the past, in the words of Mayor Zeidler of Milwaukee, have been "not only indifferent to the problems of the central cities but also hostile to them." But, to a rapidly increasing extent, the populations of states are metropolitan-area populations. In almost every state, the governor has especially close ties to the rural areas—to "upstate" and "downstate"— but his electoral base is more and more bringing him into the orbit of metropolitan interests. And as those interests are mobilized and made effective by the central-city mayor, the governor's cooperation can be assured. Downstate opposition need not always be anticipated. The possible economies in state expenditures that may accompany collaborative action of local governments in metropolitan areas may, on the contrary, produce downstate support. A combination of rural and suburban opposition will be fatal to the governor's cooperation with the central-city mayor; but if suburban cooperation is achieved, the governor's will follow.

If he is to play his role on the metropolitan scene with full effect, the governor must have at his command more substantial staff aides than he has at present, and the state legislature must supply him with requisite programmatic tools. (In a later conclusion these are set forth in some detail.) One important device available to him is the state grant-in-aid. State aid for such functions as sewage disposal, storm drainage, and water supply—and for housing and urban renewal as well—can be made contingent upon appropriate administrative collaboration at the metropolitan level. No such state requirements will appear spontaneously. They require political encouragement; and they have little chance of being passed without prior agreement of city and suburban leaders. The economies and program advances made possible by collaborative action are patent arguments for both the initial agreements and the state legislation itself. In short, with vigorous leadership from political leaders of the central cities, state aid can be used to promote an emerging federalism of the multiple governments in the metropolitan areas.

The mayor cannot hope for success in metropolitan arrangements by mobilizing citizen support or by lobbying at the state house. These are important adjuncts, not his principal weapons. In the main, he must rely upon direct negotiations with officials of other local governments. His bargaining position is good because he has power to give or withhold benefits which the smaller places want. Most of the local governments on the periphery of the central city need something from it. They want water and sewer lines extended. They want rapid transport to places of work. They want to use city parks and playgrounds. They want planning assistance.

If the mayor accommodates the suburbs overgenerously, he will not advance the cause of metropolitan collaboration. Once the petitioners get what they want, they are likely to be more indifferent to the needs of the central city than ever before. The mayor will do most for metropolitan organization if he drives a hard bargain. The suburb may have water from the central city at a fair price—but only if it first agrees to subdivision regulations consistent with the requirements of metropolitan development. The suburb may have its policemen trained in the central city and it may use the central city's crime laboratory—but only after it agrees to a plan for exchanging information about fugitives. The central city will agree to help support a planning staff—but only on the understanding that some of the planners will work on a metropolitan highway system while others do zoning chores for the suburbs.

Here again there is nothing new. Many central cities have brought an element of order into metropolitan relations in just such ways. The compact between Denver and its suburbs is a case in point. Salt Lake City is in an excellent position to bring about the orderly development of the entire county through bargaining with the smaller communities, because it controls the water supply. Grand Rapids has established uniform subdivision regulations on its peripheries by negotiating an agreement with suburbs concerning water, sewer, and other services.

Specialists in public administration frequently object to the creation of special-function districts because they further complicate the already complicated structure of metropolitan government. This is not a weighty objection if such special governments are utilized only for genuine area-wide problems. As noted previously, there are not many functions that really require a metropolitan jurisdiction. A more relevant objection to special-district governments, as they are usually constituted, is that they remove needed bargaining power from the mayors of the central cities. And this, even if special districts are few in number, becomes a towering obstacle to general intercommunity collaboration over a wide range of problems. A suburb that has its water supplied by an independent agency can cease to cooperate without penalty in other functions. The solution for this difficulty is apparent: when special-function governments are established, they should be governed not by separate, independent boards but by the regular political heads of the governments concerned. The mayor of the largest city on such a board will find his effectiveness augmented in fostering general area-wide collaboration; where independent boards are established, this effectiveness is diminished.

In the absence of metropolitan government, metropolitan planning has an important, but not decisive, role. . . . In the proposed model, there is not a single plan for an entire metropolitan region; rather, there are several. The mayor's office must obviously contain a planning staff; so must the governor's. Other planning groups will exist in the special-function districts. The important point is not to leave planning in limbo. It must be attached to the arms of action—all of them. In the long run, this may mean that the most decisive planning comes from the largest general-purpose government. But it may also develop as an adjunct to a special-purpose government for handling water, sewers, or transportation. The latter development will produce unified planning over a broad range of problems if political control runs, as has been suggested, to the offices of general government in the area concerned

The mayor's bargaining for specific area-wide programs should be geared to his larger purpose of achieving a more comprehensive regional organization. Where more than one local cooperative arrangement exists between two or more communities, efforts should be made to combine them into a single contract and to use common administrative machinery. As William Rafsky, Philadelphia Development Coordinator, has written,

"Thus cumbersome and overlapping devices are avoided, and the concept of broad regional cooperation is advanced." More than this, the steady accretion of cooperative programs, fitted together through the normal push and haul of political bargaining, provides an organic method of constructing, through time, a new form of metropolitan federalism. Special staffs from the core cities, augmented by representatives of other communities, should be assigned to cultivate this development, performing, at least initially, planning and professional services for suburban areas for which no return is expected. Simultaneously—or as a second step—central cities can make available on a cost basis to small municipalities and other local units such services as those governments cannot easily provide for themselves—for example, a comprehensive plan for a suburban village; central purchasing services for a school district; or an application for Federal aid on behalf of a county. Here, as elsewhere, the advantages of collaboration are best demonstrated by collaborative action, and the central city mayor must display initiative and resourcefulness in matters of small importance if he is to make progress toward his larger goals. It bears repeating that he will find substantial political support for such efforts.

These suggestions obviously do not add up to a "solution" to the metropolitan-organization problem. There is no solution in any absolute or final sense. There is, however, the possibility of moving step by step from where metropolitan organization now is to where it ought to be. The advantage of the proposed model is that it can accomplish some things immediately while simultaneously traveling toward a more comprehensive regional organization. In both the short and long run, the model takes account of the importance of community discretion and local freedoms. It recognizes that some joint programs will appear unpalatable at times to some communities, and that joint voluntary action adversely affecting the interests of any given community will not be achieved through simple exhortation or come about easily as one in a series of contractual relationships. It recommends that such difficulties be met through the usual political processes of bargaining and compromise within a large framework of intent: that of sharing joint functions through some sort of local federalism. The program can only succeed if it has energetic leadership from central-city mayors and other political leaders. With such leadership it can find support from the governors, from business and social groups, and from professional planners and administrators. The advances that are to be made through this scheme of development may be slow; but they have the positive virtue of respecting local options and the negative one of avoiding the complete failure that may follow insistence upon politically unattainable "ideal" programs.

17. The New Metropolis

ROBERT C. WOOD

. . . Growth and change in almost every aspect of American life form the backdrop of the studies of metropolitan regions and provide a concomitance of forces from which an analyst must choose. Innovations in transportation and communication, changes in housing construction and residential finance, mutations in the pattern of industrial development, almost instinctive aspirations for space and separate family accommodations, all play their part. So do the rising birth rate, the tradition of restlessness, nourished and intensified by the depression and the wars, the surging "upward mobility" within the middle class, prosperity and the family ethic.

From this concomitance, most of us who discuss the "metropolitan dilemma" and who call for radical reorganization of metropolitan government have traditionally selected three forces as being of major importance. The first is the pattern of population growth and distribution within the typical SMA, in particular the disproportionate increase in suburban residential population traceable for at least thirty years. The second is the slow diffusion of industry and large commercial activities throughout the area which has been taking place as new enterprises build their factories and shopping centers in fringe areas and old ones desert the central city to join them. The third is also diffusive in character, although less tangible: the gradual spread of the cultural ethos of the metropolis to enfold formerly independent communities and to blanket the hinterlands with a common set of mores and values. To most of us, each of these trends, taken alone, appears to have negative consequences for the fragmented pattern of government in metropolitan areas, and taken together, they seem to point positively in the direction of a common conclusion.

The now familiar negative aspects of suburban population growth are primarily three. The first concerns the costs of metropolitan governments. The journey to work, which the separation of residence and place of sustenance imposes, appears both to burden unfairly the central city and to impose crushing demands on the suburbs. The core is required to handle the cost of servicing a daytime population thirty to fifty percent in excess of its permanent number; the suburbs have unnecessarily large cap-

Reprinted from "The New Metropolis: Metropolitan Government 1975," *American Political Science Review*, vol. 52 (March 1958), pp. 108–22 by permission of the author and the publisher. Author's footnotes omitted. Robert Wood is professor of political science at Massachusetts Institute of Technology.

ital budgets since, in the welter of jurisdictions, economies of scale and size cannot be realized. Duplication and overlapping of facilities between surburbs and the core city and among suburbs result.

The population shift and the journey-to-work pattern which ensues appear to have a second negative effect. They seem to lead to a deterioration in the political process. The sturdy burgher class deserts the city, but the rigor of the commuting schedule makes its effective participation in suburban affairs unlikely. Big city politics is seen as becoming increasingly a struggle between the very rich and the very poor; suburban governments are held to be controlled by the old residents, merchants, and real-estate dealers, with only an occasional high-minded foray by the League of Women Voters. Most metropolitan inhabitants have their feet in at least two political jurisdictions; they are half-citizens, disfranchised either in law or in fact.

Third, what politics remains is likely to be bifurcated. As the suburban exodus goes on, we are told that the fringe and the central city are drifting farther and farther apart, the former increasingly Republican, the latter Democratic, so that the metropolitan areas are likely to be split into two warring camps. Prospects for mutual cooperation and understanding diminish, the metropolitan situation becomes cast in a rigid mold, and the opportunity for responsible consideration of regional problems diminishes.

These implications of suburban growth per se seem dismal enough, but the second force of industrial diffusion adds a further difficulty. It appears to compound the metropolitan fiscal problem by making impossible an orderly matching of resources to requirements, by taking away revenues from the jurisdictions which need them most. Again, the plight of the central city is highlighted. Its tax base, already weakened by a large proportion of tax-exempt property devoted to educational and cultural purposes, is weakened further by the departure of business. Slums and blighted areas take the place of busy commercial districts, renewal efforts become more difficult, and welfare and public safety costs increase. Meanwhile in the outer ring some suburbs receive windfalls from new industry, but adjoining ones are saddled with the expenses of the workers living in cracker-box houses and putting four children per family through school. Because population and economic location patterns do not coincide, the traditional inequities and inadequacies of the American local tax structure are further intensified.

As the metropolis extends its cultural influence, a third set of "negative" consequences ensues. Discrete local communities disappear; friendships become scattered randomly throughout the area; associations made in the course of work are different from those developed in residential neighborhoods. Only the ties of kinship and the stultifying communications of mass-media remain to bind men together. This development is thought to have two untoward effects: first, as men wander aimlessly in the lonely crowd, the capacity of existing units of government to function vigorously and effectively is impaired for they no longer engender civic consciousness and a sense of belonging. Second, without regional institutions, no loyalty to a higher order is possible. All that remains is a weak notion of metropolitan patriotism, a New Yorker's superficial pride in being part of the Big Show. So regional problems find no vehicle for their solution and the capacity to look ahead, to plan rationally, to awake a regional consciousness is lost.

In a positive sense and in a broad way observers believe these trends are interrelated and that they lead to a common conclusion so far as political analysis is concerned. The separation of home and place of work, the rise of "nuclear centers of dominance" in the metropolitan economic system, the spread of metropolitan culture, taken together seem to signify that a metropolitan community has come—or is coming—into being. We have been imprecise about what the word "community" means. . . . But generally, we have assumed that if an aggregate of people in a given area achieve economic autarchy, if social intercourse extends over the area, and if common mores and customs exist, the basic foundations for a genuine community are present. The three factors we have studied seem to indicate that fairly self-sufficient metropolitan economic systems have developed, that social interaction now takes place across the entire area, and that a growing consensus about values is at hand. The prerequisites for the metropolitan community appear imbedded then in the trends we emphasize today.

Given this positive interpretation, the common conclusion is that for a single community, there should be a rationally constructed set of political institutions. The metropolitan dilemma is defined as the existence of many governments within a common economic and social framework. The metropolitan solution has been seen in variations on the theme "one community—one government" by any one of the half dozen ingenious political inventions. Running through all these recommendations is the premise that if somehow present units of government are brought together, if they can share resources and administrative responsibilities, the negative consequences of the forces now at work will be avoided and their impact guided into useful channels. If such reorganization is not forthcoming, we have generally believed these areas face governmental crises of substantial proportions. To drift with the tide is to court political, financial, and administrative disaster for urban government in the United States.

The facts on which the case for metropolitan government depends are quite real, and we have not misread the figures. Yet nothing demonstrates the complexity of analysis so well as the results of our reliance on three trends, and three trends alone. Despite our predictions, disaster has not struck: urban government has continued to function, not well perhaps, but at least well enough to forestall catastrophe. Traffic continues to circulate; streets and sewers are built; water is provided; schools keep their doors open; and law and order generally prevail. Nor does this tolerable state of affairs result from an eager citizenry's acceptance of our counsel: we know only too well that our proposals for genuine reform have been largely ignored.

It may be, of course, that the breaking point has simply not been reached. There is certainly little sign that the tide of suburban growth is ebbing, or that industrial diffusion is slowing down, or that the representatives of the new American character are remorseful now that their values have been so cruelly exposed. If we are to look forward to 1975, we have good reason for believing that these trends will continue until the "linear city" is in being on both our coasts and probably in regions in between. Yet conditions were already serious enough in the nineteen-twenties to prompt investigation and to set loose prophecies of doom. Developments have continued unabated, and it is a fair question, given the technological changes of recent years and the stubborn public reluctance to listen to our counsel, to ask if we have discovered the whole story.

If we dip back into the arrays of factors and forces at work in metropolitan regions, other trends appear, and the more they are studied, the more important they appear. In effect, when other trends, formerly left unexplored, are reviewed, they seem to operate as countervailing forces that modify the trends on which we have concentrated our attention. At times they abate the consequences our basic factors imply; at times, they change the relationships we have assumed existed. And, at least in one important respect, they present a completely different picture of the SMA than we have been accustomed to portraying.

For example, while it is true that the disproportionate growth in suburban population has accelerated since World War II, that growth has been accompanied by an extraordinary period of prosperity. As the dominant feature of our economy for the past 15 years, inflation has swollen the cost of government, but it also swelled, although belatedly, the revenue. Urban governments have managed spectacular increases in their tax returns in the past few years, and we are told by no less authority than the President's Commission on Intergovernmental Relations that the potential of the property tax is by no means realized. Moreover, the rising level of incomes has an economic consequence quite apart from any particular tax structure: once basic necessities of life are satisfied, higher tax burdens, however imposed, are more tolerable, and borrowings become easier, so long as the market is not surfeited. Thus communities may be forced to a general reassessment of property values, or they may skate on fiscal thin ice, but they need not undertake a general structural reorganization. Metropolitan governments may be forced to pay the excessive costs which the fragmented pattern requires, but they have been able to do so without encountering municipal bankruptcy.

Nor should other forces which bolster the capacity of metropolitan governments to sustain themselves be overlooked. While no major structural reform has been accomplished, state and federal grants-in-aid have helped support critical services and new municipal tax sources have been discovered and utilized. The plight of the central city has been to some extent relieved by grants and shared taxes, and by state assumption of important responsibilities. The commuter has either directly by earnings taxes or indirectly through his payments to state and federal governments contributed some of his share to the core municipality. The special district has been used more and more frequently to sidestep statutory debt limits, to tap new revenue sources, and to scale jurisdictional barriers in important functional fields. And some suburbs have been content to forego services, to get along with amateur governments, and to ignore the welfare state in order to remain autonomous.

In less easily explicable ways, the deterioration of the urban political process seems to have been checked. Healthy signs of reinvigorated, capable political leadership have appeared in many of our large cities. Newcomers in suburbia have won important political battles, over schools and public improvements. Even the prophecy that the suburbs are irrevocably Republican and the central city irrevocably Democratic seems suspect in the light of the most recent election returns. The party battleground is more complex than previously supposed.

While the apparently obvious consequences of disproportionate suburban growth have been modified, other developments have affected the revenue side of the picture. Metropolitan areas as a whole have continued to hold their own in relative economic importance, and industry has continued to move out to the fringe. Yet, by concentrating on the pattern of industrial diffusion alone, we have overlooked even more important economic changes which sharply modify the "mismatched supply and demand" thesis.

The first of these is the shift in consumer demands. As output and income per worker have grown, and per capita consumption has risen, a relative decline has occurred in the consumption of agricultural products and a relative increase in the demand for "services." Employment has expanded dramatically in the fields of trade, amusement, research, education, medical care—the white collar category in general. Since these are the fields where real output per man has not increased very rapidly, the proportion of the labor force thus absorbed expands more rapidly than the absolute decrease in other categories would imply.

Second, the structure of manufacturing activities has changed. Not only have industry classifications included a larger number of truly white collar workers—management, advertising, special repair and maintenance staffs—but manufacturing processes and products have become increasingly specialized. An increasing number of specialists offer intermediate processes and products to a number of different industries, and their facilities provide the small manufacturer with "external economies" which allow him to compete effectively with larger firms. There are an increasing number of "unstandardized" final products, too, as firms depart from offering a few stable lines and present their customers with an array of choices.

Together with the decline in the pull of raw material sources as a locational factor, the relative increase in transportation costs, and the growing size of metropolitan markets, these changes in demand and in the structure of manufacturing help explain the continued growth of urban areas as entities. More important for our purposes, they move in the direction of counter-balancing the consequences of the industrial diffusion trend within metropolitan regions.

The rise in the importance of "services" in the urban economy means a broadening of the non-residential tax base exclusive of industrial plants. Offices, salesrooms, medical buildings, trade establishments of all sorts and sizes, while not as advantageous to municipalities in their cost-revenue ratios as manufacturing plants, still return more in taxes than they demand in public services. As the white collar occupations grow in importance, the facilities in which they work become part of the resource base, and as they are scattered through the region in general they provide additional sources for revenue quite apart from those supplied by factories. If only industrial location trends are studied, this growing number of service establishments is overlooked and important increments to the resource base omitted.

The changes within the structure of manufacturing also make an exclusive reliance on the industrial location trends undependable, particularly since, quite frequently, only larger firms are singled out for attention. The increasing specialization which characterizes more and more modern manufacturing means that the processes in any given industry from receipt of raw material to delivery of finished goods may be dispersed throughout a region. Large plants and service facilities may drift toward the suburbs in search of cheaper space, but this does not necessarily mean that former locations in the central city or inner ring remain deserted.

On the contrary, many small firms frequently find a location within the central city attractive, for here are available all the specialists in the intermediate stages of production whose services can be contracted for to permit competition with the larger plants. Other "external economies" arise: fractional use of transportation facilities at less-than-carload or truckload lots, urban public services—police and fire protection, water and sewage facilities—which might not exist in the suburbs, rented space, a larger labor market, and so on. The appearance of unstandardized end products also enhances the central city's position, for purchases usually depend on visual inspections, and when styles and grades of material are important, inventories have to be kept within strict limits. These conditions make the core attractive as a "seed-bed" for industrial development, and take up the slack as larger firms depart.

Moreover, for all firms, large and small, the central city offers certain unstandardized inputs which are best provided in a central location. Advertising agencies, law firms, banks, home offices, some types of salesrooms, are activities which require proximity with their competitors, both because of the irregular schedule in which they may be used, and because "knowledge of the industry," gossip of the trade, face-to-face confrontation are prerequisites for doing business. Here again the central city offers advantages which few suburbs can yet supply.

When the changes in the manufacturing structure are considered, neither the central city nor the suburbs seem in such desperate straits as are often described. As industrial diffusion goes on, and available land is taken up, more suburbs will receive "windfalls." More will actively search them out as well, for changes in plant architecture and the elimination of unfavorable site conditions, smoke, smells, water pollution, mean that many suburbs formerly hostile to development, will become enamoured of "light industry." Those who do not want, or will not find, industry will have their resources bolstered by service establishments following the market or by special facilities within an industry which can be separated from the parent plant.

Meanwhile, the central city is likely to find alternative economic activities, plants of small firms, business offices of large ones, and the cluster of professional and semi-professional services on which both depend. Moreover, the overriding necessity of these economic activities to maintain their central location makes their response to tax changes highly inelastic. Existing levies can be increased, or even new taxes on earnings and income imposed, and these special groups will still "stay put." Together with continued prosperity and a rise in real income, this inelasticity helps explain the recent successes in discovering new revenue sources. It further reduces the "certain" consequences of financial crises, which population and industrial trends have been thought to portend, to the status of mere possibilities, less likely than alternative courses of development.

Not only are our demographic and economic series suspect, but the less tangible hypothesis of "metropolitan dominance" comes in for critical scrutiny also. Without questioning the accuracy of the measures of newspaper circulation, postal delivery areas, telephone exchanges and journey-to-work patterns which imply the existence of a metropolitan "community," contradictory trends can be established. It is possible to submit that each region is an economic entity, that it has a circulatory and communication system of its own, and still argue that a scatteration of society has accompanied the scatteration of government; that metropolitan growth promotes a "huge mosaic of massed segregation of size, class, and ethnic groups" a "crazy quilt of discontinuities."

Admittedly, as indicated earlier, when we speculate about community, we are talking about a nebulous term. The models used for the study of community are many; the essential elements of community life are still uncertain and their relative importance unweighed. Yet it is significant that when authorities speak of the break-up of local communities in the metropolitan area, and the onrush of metropolitan dominance, their departure point is almost always the primary community, preliterate society, savage village or feudal holding where economic autarchy, social isolation and consensus of values were most complete. Such a community, if it ever existed at all, never existed in the United States. Our archetype has been the New England town or the hamlet of the Old Northwest, both quite different in their organization of space and their feeling for community affairs, but both relatively sophisticated types, having substantial economic and social intercourse with the outside world, numbering speculators and entrepreneurs among their inhabitants, and displaying mature political systems. While their differences were many, the common elements of these communities were the qualities of propinquity, homogeneity, interdependence, and equality, which produced our ideal local government—grassroots democracy.

If these qualities are taken as the essentials of smalltown life, then modern suburbs may be on the way to finding a substitute for economic self-sufficiency and social isolation to promote a sense of community consciousness. They may be using their political boundaries to differentiate the character of their residents from their neighbors and using governmental powers—zoning, residential covenants, taxation, selective industrial developments—to promote conscious segregation. From the variety of classes, occupations, income levels, races and creeds which the region contains, a municipality may isolate the particular variant it prefers and concentrate on one type of the metropolitan man. In a sense it may even produce a "purer" type of community than the American archetype, because it has a wider range of choice and it need not reproduce all the parts of a self-contained economic system. It can simply extract the particular functions it chooses to support, and achieve a social homogeneity never before possible.

Moreover, growth itself may aid and abet the process of strengthening community bonds in subareas of metropolitan regions. To the extent that a feeling of fellowship waxes strong in the early stages of community growth, that "political democracy evolves most quickly while the process of organization and the solving of basic problems are still critical," many suburbs may resemble earlier American towns in their political and social processes. At any rate, provocative comparisons have been made between group and individual characteristics in modern housing developments—the acknowledgment of equality and the recognition of interdependence in Levittown and Park Forest— and frontier towns of old.

A thesis that small communities are reappearing in the metropolitan areas, that the high-water mark of the process of communal disintegration has passed, is conjectural. But so is the rationale for the new metropolitan man, unattached and unrooted, and some interesting statistics support the first hypothesis. For one thing, the existence of fragmented governments do break up the area into manageable proportions—more suburbanites live in towns between 10,000 and 25,000 than in towns of any other size. For another, modern suburbs have captured that portion of the middle class most oriented, in terms of education, occupation, income and family status, toward being responsible members of their locality. Third, subareas in metropolitan regions are displaying a tremendous variety in their economic functions, social rank and ethnic and occupational order. Most important of all, this variety does not seem to be random in nature, but the result of conscious coalescing according to a pattern of spatial homogeneity. In brief, each suburb may be gathering its chosen few to its bosom, and not just in the broad terms which Burgess and Hoyt have outlined. More specifically, a clustering according to occupations seems to be taking place, in which different occupations, representing different status points in the social spectrum, put space between each other; and the wider the social differences, the further apart the members of disparate occupations live within the metropolitan area. Tracing this development in the Chicago metropolitan area, Otis and Beverly Duncan found a consistent pattern of residential segregation among occupations and a preference for neighbors with closely related occupations.

If this process of natural neighborhoods goes on in an area in which each neighborhood is equipped with a local government, then instinctive feelings of community are enhanced by the fact of legal and political power. A cultural *sui generis* results, and the existence of separate political institutions, separate powers to be exercised, individual elections to be held, reinforces the bonds which make the neighborhood. Within the region as a whole, we may be witnessing a popular attempt to dissect the metropolitan giant into small pieces, and to cap each with legal authority and some degree of civic consciousness.

To the extent that this is true, the notion of one metropolitan community may be misleading, and the characterization of modern culture as new may be overdrawn. Economically the region may be one, but it may be powerless to bid for the loyalties of its residents against the claims of the smaller neighborhoods. Its inhabitants may be conformists, gregarious, adjusted, seeking approval from their peer groups, participating eagerly in every form of social endeavor; but these qualities may not signify a new dominant culture. Instead, they may mark a return to the smalltown life De Tocqueville found, an expression of protest against the stratified, pecuniary structure of the Victorian city, a desire to re-create again the ". . . opportunity for companionship and friendship, for easy access to local services, and for certain forms of security . . .," a new vision of open-country culture to stand against the metropolis.

There are not enough reliable data over a long enough period of time to weigh the relative pulls of metropolitan dominance and grassroots renaissance. But there are enough data to allow us to be sceptical of the one community hypothesis, particularly when the history of public resistance to metropolitan reform is on our side. At least it seems clear that local loyalties are by no means abandoned, and that, if by some political sleight-of-hand, a metropolitan government is created, it may not find the instinctive springs of support and popular understanding which is supposed to be anxiously waiting for the creation of regional institutions.

So far this analysis has undertaken only to expand the frame of reference in which metropolitan politics and government is usually considered, to bring other factors and forces under review, and to qualify conclusions derived from a limited review of empirical facts. The results of the inquiry certainly do not unveil the metropolitan future, nor do they indicate what steps should be taken. Our findings to date have been tentative and negative. Seriously adverse financial or political effects may not be arising from suburban growth. There may be no shortage of resources for the central city or the inner ring. There may not be one community to bring into maturity. In short, there may not be the metropolitan crisis which so many of us have expected for so long, either now or in the future.

This does not mean that there are no metropolitan problems, nor that there is no case for reform. Problems there are aplenty: ugly implications of the growing segregation of classes, races, and occupations in suburban ghettoes; marginal costs and wastes and inefficiencies in government finance and organization to be eliminated, the overriding issue as to whether we will realize the potential, in politics, in land use, in social intercourse, in the amenities of existence which metropolitan regions promise. We may not face catastrophe, but this is no reason for countenancing one-hour commuting schedules, for permitting blight, for condoning the repellent sprawl of cheap commercial developments, inadequate parks, congested schools, mediocre administration, traffic jams, smog, pollution, and the hundred and one irritations which surround us. Even if we can exist in the present metropolis, the fact of survival does not excuse a failure to plan the future with more care, to avoid the mistakes we have made in the past and to bestow a more worthwhile legacy.

Yet while these are real problems and genuine issues, they are not categorical necessities. They are fundamentally questions of value and of judgment, of what we should and should not do, and of how much. In short they are issues for political science to tackle in its traditional way, and no trend is clear enough to give us the easy answer "we have to do it one way." Alternatives are before us; choice remains, and the burden of responsibility is off the shoulders of the economist and the sociologist and back again on ours.

Within this normative framework, the alternatives are several and, in this analysis, only a brief summary of their implications can be undertaken. But those which seem most important are three—greenbelts, grassroots or gargantua—and they are genuine alternatives. Quite frequently, we have tended to think of metropolitan planning, federation and consolidation as related steps to the single goal of achieving political institutions suitable to the metropolitan community. In practice, we have frequently chosen between them on grounds of political expediency. Yet, these reforms do not move in the same direction; they lead us down quite different paths and, in a certain sense, a choice among them can be "extrapolated" too. In a reasoned way we can explore the implications which a certain set of values have for the future, judged by the bench-mark of constitutional democracy. When this is done, though the task of metropolitan reform is complicated, its objectives are clarified. The discussion proceeds on the basis of a comparison of the values involved, in place of an excitable response to "inexorable" trends.

So far as the greenbelts alternative is concerned, the vision of order, balance, and beauty has timeless appeal for political philosophy as it has for the profession of planning. There are overtones of Plato and Aristotle, "an organic sense of structural differences," a corporate whole, in the concept, and there is the tough-minded insistence of Patrick Geddes, Ebenezer Howard, and Lewis Mumford that the vision is practical. When technology promises so much in terms of the capacity to shape nature to man's purposes, when the age of abundance is actuality, it seems reprehensible to permit the shapeless metropolitan sprawl. With such little effort, balanced communities could come into being, rational transportation systems provided, land set aside for recreational and cultural purposes, and the way cleared for Jefferson's common man to find "life" values in place of monetary values. The promise of individual dignity is combined with the aesthetics of a pastoral scene from which insects are banished and in which running water is supplied, and the metropolitan region becomes a true commingling of the best of rural and urban virtues.

There is of course a serpent in the garden of greenbelts as there was a crucial flaw in the Greek polis. Who defines the shape and substance of beauty, who determines the balance of each community, who arbitrates good taste, who decides the values of life? The advocates of greenbelts have always answered with injured innocence "the people," but they have been peculiarly reluctant to specify the means by which the people decide. They have, in modern times, reluctantly admitted that planning is properly a staff function; but when the chips are down, they have been scornful of the politician who curries votes, and indignant at his intrusion. The planners who have gained the most notoriety are those who have been the most ready to ignore the role of the elected official, to be contemptuous of the slow process of popular deliberations, and to hold themselves aloof from the electoral process. In short, while one implication of the greenbelt philosophy is harmony, another is in twentieth century socialism, American municipal style.

Until the defenders of this alternative are much more specific as to the ways and means they can suggest to reconcile their values with the public's in a liberal tradition, we are rightly suspicious of their plans.

In contrast, the grassroots alternative clearly avoids the danger of professional controls imposed from above, and of an excessive commitment to communal order and balance. If we retain our belief in the efficacy of small communities and small governments which spring spontaneously into being, there is actually very little action called for at all. Given the accuracy of the economic and social statistics reviewed earlier, the likelihood of suburban governments disappearing or of crises forcing an expansion of public authority does not appear great. We can drift with the tide, fairly confident that the course of events will produce the best possible arrangement for the metropolitan complex.

This wedding of an ancient image in American political folklore to favorable modern trends makes the second approach both attractive and plausible. First the existence of all shapes and sizes of communities within the region offers an individual a freedom of choice as to where and how he wishes to live. Second, the continued segregation of occupations, classes, and races fits in well with modern doctrine on how to "manage" social conflict. Let each man find his own, abstain from social contact with antagonistic elements, abjure political disagreement and debate by joining a constituency which shares his values, and his tensions, anxieties, and uncertainties are relieved. The virtues of small-town life come to the fore, and the elemental qualities of neighborliness, friendship, and civic spirit are revived.

Yet even though the grassroots thesis has ample precedent in our history, underneath it lurk some assumptions which seem unpalatable. The individual who chooses his community in the metropolitan free-market in the same way in which he buys his car is essentially a laissez-faire man. He pursues his own self-interest to the maximum, and depends on a natural order of events to provide for the common good. Local governments become truly a bundle of services, to be purchased by those who can afford them without regard to more general social consequences. Those with resources insulate themselves from those without them, and issues of equity and humanitarianism become muted. The garden city planners may place too much reliance on the social nature of man, but grassroots advocates reach toward the opposite extreme of unfettered individualism.

Further, given the general American consensus on values, our basic commitment to democracy and capitalism, the management of social conflict is not likely to be our most pressing public problem. The pressures for conformity, the profoundly anti-individualistic element which punishes the deviate so swiftly in our society, the absence of variety, are more serious issues. Encouraging a scatteration of communities and governments in the metropolitan area does not solve this problem; it intensifies it. The individual may be free to choose his community, but once this selection is made, it is difficult for him to change his values if he wishes to stay in his own home town. The small community is friendly and comfortable and it promises fraternity, but it is also intolerant, inquisitive, barren of privacy. It is at least an open question whether this creation of political boundaries around disparate groups and classes is an appropriate development in a democracy, or whether it truly frees the individual in the manner its advocates intend. Perhaps variety, disagreement, discussion, and debate are to be encouraged rather than avoided.

To the extent this proposition is true, there is something to be said for the third alternative—of gargantua—the creation of a single metropolitan government or at least the establishment of a regional superstructure which points in that direction. If genuine metropolitan political institutions and processes are provided, the excessive marginal costs which overlapping and duplication bring about are reduced, a genuine arena exists for debate about meaningful issues which affect the area as a whole, and there is an opportunity to realize the metropolitan potential which is at our disposal.

In this scheme, decisions about the regional destiny are not the exclusive province of professional value-makers; they lie with the constituency as a whole. Freedom of choice remains for the individual, for the entire variety of spectacles and experiences which a metropolis offers is open to him. But, in a political sense, this freedom is accompanied by responsibility. A man cannot escape his neighbor by retreating to an exclusive suburb; he has to face him, to persuade or be persuaded. Political parties cannot rest secure in the knowledge that they have preponderant majorities in particular jurisdictions; they compete in a region with so many diverse temperaments and outlooks, as almost to guarantee a close two-party fight. Harmony does not appear automatically, it is painfully put together by compromise, by adjustments, by trial and error.

A plea for gargantua is not an attack against neighborhoods, against the importance of "moral integration" or against the need for fellowship and companionship. It is simply a plea against confusing these socially desirable qualities with the prerequisites of good government, against equipping neighborhoods with political prerogatives. We do not have, in the philosophical sense, a conservative tradition in the United States which emphasizes communal purpose and morality or gradations in social status. We have instead a liberal tradition, however confused in its definition of individualism and beset with contradictions; and the essence of that tradition is a distinction between society and government, a preference for legal contractural relationships in public affairs in place of personal ones. Solutions which either in the name of the public good or paradoxically in the name of rampant individualism emphasize communal bonds excessively, seek harmony instinctive or contrived, and discourage variety, are alien to the highest purpose of that tradition. Men have always found privacy, civility, and urbanity, the marks of civilization, in great cities even though they have often paid the price of anonymity and loneliness. They are most likely to find the same qualities there today.

In the end, the case for metropolitan reform, the drive for larger governments and for one community is as strong as ever. It is not a case built on necessity, on the threat of impending disaster, or on the consequences of modern technology. It is a case dependent on value judgments and philosophical disputation. But it is a strong case and perhaps a more appealing and persuasive one once its norms have been frankly admitted, and pretensions of scientific objectivity left behind. Metropolitan reform may not have been right so far as its analysis of empirical data is concerned, but it has always been righteous in the best sense of the word, and it remains righteous today.

C. AS A POLITICAL AND INTERGOVERNMENTAL PROBLEM

18. How Long Will New York Wait?

ADOLF A. BERLE, JR.

New York City is the extreme illustration of how the swirling growth of twentieth-century population, economics, and techniques has ex-

Reprinted from *The Reporter*, XIII (September 8, 1955), pp. 14–18 by permission of the author and the publisher. Adolf Berle is an economist, public official, and free lance commentator on political and social trends.

posed our time-honored institutions of local government in metropolitan areas to a strain they cannot stand. Strikingly similar situations
are to be found in our own country and abroad. Conceivably they
can be met for a while by repeated postponement, patching up, and
political makeshift; ultimately an enduring solution of the problem
involving a recasting of the institutions of regional administration seems
inevitable.

Historically, the City of New York was built around a port. The
island of Manhattan was a great dock in a noble harbor. Water was
then the universal carrier; Long Island Sound and the Hudson River were
natural canals. Railroads and the Hudson-Mohawk gateway to the
West, greatest of the Allegheny crossings, quadrupled New York's importance. Sea and land lines met there, and the city grew. Finance
came with trade; the Erie Canal was opened; a metropolis started its
growth. Successive immigrant waves of Irish, Germans, and Italians
landed there and stayed. Jewish migration after the Russian pogroms
of fifty years ago, flight from a Europe torn by the First World War,
an influx of Negroes from the South and Puerto Ricans from the An-
tilles, coupled with the unforeseen population increase of recent years,
kept the city moving farther and farther beyond its historic lines.

The power of a metropolis kept drawing in people and activities
that in turn multiplied both its attractions and its power. Families came
to New York from Europe and sought refuge and work. Young men came
from Boston and Keokuk to make their fortunes in an imperial city.
The gasoline revolution added motorcars and trucks to railways and
shipping. The web of the city spread until it became the nucleus of
ten per cent of the population of the United States. Still a port, the
city was now a world financial center, a world transport center, and
a market for American and foreign products of all kinds. Even more,
it was the platform from which music, drama, art, fashion, books, and
ideas of all sorts were launched and attained recognition.

Increasingly city lines, city administrators, city economics, and
city institutions lost much of their relevance. City Hall was more a
badly organized management center for a huge set of public services
of growing complexity than a government. Formally New York is a
city governed from a beautiful Italian Renaissance building on the
lower tip of Manhattan and from five branch offices—the five Borough
Halls which have limited authority over local streets and public services. But half of the people in the metropolitan area are outside the
city's jurisdiction anyway. Scarsdale, Jersey City, Hempstead, Summit,
Mount Kisco, Montclair, and Massapequa are all in it. Their residents
are working New Yorkers; but as residents and homemakers they have

no responsibility and little relation to the metropolis. Basically New York lives upon, serves, and is served by sea traffic from the ends of the earth, by railroad traffic from north, south, and west; by automobile and truck traffic from everywhere, funneling into, shuttling through, and passing out of a complex which is at once market, sales office, banking medium factory, school, and power center, whose life is drawn from an immense area.

The New Deal and the Cities

The great depression of the 1930's forced the Roosevelt revolution, and the Federal government picked up a group of unfilled functions that the states could not handle. It discharged them by creating a national system of planned finance, a national system of welfare, a national system of electric-power distribution, and the rudiments of a national system of stabilization of industry and agriculture. Washington occupied most of the no man's land between the states and the Federal government.

But the cities? No one picked up the unfilled functions there. The struggle of the cities to survive, and of their adjacent regions to have services they needed, inevitably was intensified. The old city could not re-establish itself as a fully self-contained, self-ruling unit. Yet it had to go through the motions of administering itself as if it were one.

So it happens that in this very year 1955, out of its income base New York City's Welfare Department and charitable institutions must support its indigent and unfortunate to the tune of $222 million a year, in a time of peak prosperity, and each newcomer in New York can claim a share immediately. New York City can get back a large part of this sum from state or Federal government. But the city has no rebate or refund when it comes to paying the vastly expensive costs of medical care (the city hospitals alone cost $120 million a year), sanitation, and policing. The direct cost of relief to each working family of New York is estimated at a hundred dollars a year (before discounting state subsidies). In Westchester, relief averages out to less than five dollars a year per wage-earning family (likewise before discounting subsidies).

Government installations (of Federal, state, and independent Authorities) occupy some $1,300 billion worth of municipal real estate which the city cannot tax but must service. The seven hundred thousand suburbanites as well as city dwellers who use New York's subways twice daily cost the city an average of seven cents each ride, since the city alone pays the enormous debt service on the transit installations and their fare covers only operating costs.

City revenues, like city boundaries and even forms of city government, are survivals from an earlier day. Modern taxation must relate less to "values" than to current productivity and income. National and state governments consequently finance themselves chiefly through income taxes of one form or another. When productivity grows, income and revenue rise, as do government expenditures. The surge of productivity in the United States has kept peacetime national and state income and expenditure in rough balance—almost, though not quite. Cities like New York, however, do not have unlimited tax powers and are debarred from a share of modern tax revenues.

They can levy real-estate taxes—and sales taxes too, if the state government authorizes; and they have a few other sources. New York has a combination income-and-sales tax in the form of a business gross-receipts tax, invented by the writer at Mayor LaGuardia's instance in 1934. But the city's chief revenue base is still ad valorem taxes on real estate and the essentially regressive sales tax. Both are economically limited. If sales taxes are increased, business goes somewhere else—that is one reason why "shopping centers" and department-store branches are mushrooming outside New York City now. Real estate values cannot go up more than just so much while there is rent control—as there is in New York City. In consequence, the city with a budget now of a billion and three-quarters (more than the budget of any state government) must seek additional revenue. It needs, at a rough estimate, three-quarters of a billion dollars of capital funds merely to put its schools, hospitals, streets, transit, and other facilities on a modern basis. Mexico City is more modernly run today than New York.

New Institutions

Specific institutions had to emerge to bridge the historical boundaries. They came.

The port of New York is a geographical expression paying no respect at all to political boundaries. Part of it is in the State of New Jersey, and the Hudson waterway carries ocean traffic at least as far as Haverstraw. In 1921 a treaty was ratified between the States of New York and New Jersey establishing the Port of New York Authority, designed to coordinate policies so that the port could operate more or less as a whole. The Authority operates and collects tolls upon the Holland and Lincoln Tunnels and the George Washington Bridge crossing the Hudson to the

Jersey side; these are its great revenue-producing facilities. It finances its operations by issuing bonds secured by these and other revenues. Because trucks and busses use these entrances, it created busline terminals. Because airline terminals as such do not pay, the city turned over LaGuardia and Idlewild airports to it. As it continues to take over functions remote from its original purpose, "Port of New York Authority" is almost a misnomer.

A quiet separate Authority—the Triborough Bridge and Tunnel Authority—operates other entrances into Manhattan under the East River from the Long Island side. Since Long Island is in the State of New York, a treaty was not necessary though a state statute was. The Triborough Bridge, first despised by bankers, financed itself by revenue bonds with the help of the deceased Reconstruction Finance Corporation. It paid off. Presently the Queens Midtown Tunnel was turned over to it; still later it built the great tunnel from the Battery to Brooklyn, giving truck access to Long Island.

Fiorello LaGuardia dreamed of a tunnel under Manhattan connecting a Port Authority tunnel with the Queens Midtown Tunnel, so that millions in Long Island could connect swiftly with the Jersey mainland. The Triborough Bridge Authority, under the dominance of that amazing if somewhat arbitrary builder, Robert Moses, wanted the city to finance the tunnel across Manhattan, or, if not the city, the Port Authority. The city did not have the money, nor did the Port Authority, so the Triborough Long Island entrances now dump bridge and tunnel traffic into Manhattan.

A mass of cars and trucks and busses must find its way across to Port Authority bridges or tunnels, or northward out of the city, and thence via the New Jersey or the emerging New York toll-road systems to points south or west. The city is in the middle here: Some of this traffic stops in New York, but in part the streets of New York must provide a main transportation artery between out-of-city population areas.

Schools had a somewhat similar history. Emerging from days when each village ran its own school, the New York City school system presently found itself involved in the growth of state-wide standards. New Yorkers, justifiably thinking that city government is always political, sometimes dishonest, and frequently inefficient, gave support to making education a New York State responsibility and so it is. Eventually by statute the New York City school administration emerged as a kind of empire, connected with the city government only because its two boards —the Department of Education (which runs the lower schools) and the Board of Higher Education (which runs the municipal colleges and universities)—are appointed by the elected mayor. Standards are made by the state administration in Albany. No one believes (they are right) that the Board of Estimate or the City Council would be equipped to furnish educational standards and supervision.

The list of greater and less specific institutions, big and little, created to handle specific problems could be carried to interminable length. The New York Department of Water Supply delivers water to almost every faucet in the five boroughs; to do this it operates a four-hundred-mile system of aqueducts in Nassau County and through Westchester, Putnam, and Rockland Counties all the way to the headwaters of the Delaware River. The Transit Authority, a separate entity, runs the subways. It will have to pick up the Hudson & Manhattan Transit tunnels to Jersey City and not inconceivably may inherit the Long Island Railroad some day. And so forth.

What Is a 'City'?

So emerges the central problem: What is a "city government" today? Is there a "city"? What is "government" in these terms? What kind of institutions correspond to reality? The same question is being asked by nations, as NATO lays down requirements of defense. Jean Monnet's Coal and Steel Community overrides European national boundaries for purposes of modern economics, as every national radio smashes historical borders.

In anger or despair the city turns to the state. Where else can a harrassed Mayor of New York turn for assistance or redress—if not to Albany with hat in hand? New York City provided an estimated $710 million of New York State's $1,185 million in revenues in 1954, or sixty per cent of the total. A certain amount of this it got back by complicated formulas for welfare, road, and school aid, as did every other local government in the state. But in this transaction it found itself short-changed at every turn of the penny. Upstate, which includes suburbia, with less than half the state's population, got back $355 million from the general kitty; New York City got back $260 million. Upstate New York received state aid for its colleges and universities; New York City's universities were supported out of local taxes alone. Upstate schools received an average of $200 in state subsidy for each of their pupils, while the city got only $120 per child. A host of minor inequities could be added: Every other county in the state receives twenty-five percent of the automobile-registration fees collected in its area, but the five counties that make up Greater New York are lumped together as one unit. In a recent year the state paid $126 million to local communities in highway and road-building programs, but the city got only $11 million, or nine per cent.

The Secessionists

The reason why such figures irritate New York rather than excite it is simple and has its roots in deep reality. The only possible way to know how much or how little New York is mulcted by upstate would be to haul out of the museum of ideas the oldest in New York's history—the oft-repeated solution that New York City be made an independent and sovereign state of the Union. If this could be done, say the zealots, the revenues of the city would leap immediately by about $400 million a year without the addition of a single new tax not already imposed by the state and spent elsewhere; and with these sums, the city could really get to work on its problems.

Yet this idea is chimerical because neither Congress nor New York State would permit such an amputation, and it is doubtful whether a majority of New Yorkers themselves would vote for it. New York, like all our troubled cities, is hedged in between the constitutional frames of the state and the nation, and there seems to be no way out—so far.

Continuing invention of specific solutions for specific problems inevitably entails problems begotten by the solutions. Each new board, Authority, or government group rapidly becomes a center of power of its own. The Triborough Bridge Authority, for example, has the toll revenue from motor traffic coming from Long Island into Manhattan, from which it has accumulated a tidy surplus of $18 million or so. (Meanwhile, of course, the Long Island Railroad, serving the same traffic, went into bankruptcy, from which it is barely emerging.) Robert Moses decided that the city needed a Coliseum or convention hall—as indeed it does —and Moses is a pragmatist who believes in doing what you can do as and how you can do it. So the Triborough Bridge Authority is developing Columbus Circle and lifting a substantial area of Manhattan from depressing mediocrity into twentieth-century functionalism. So also the Port Authority is developing its tunnel head near 42nd street with bus terminals; some day it may do the same thing for helicopters. Whether the city needs a Coliseum or a bus terminal more than it needs hospital facilities, or a bus terminal more than it needs new schools, is a theoretical problem that remains unsolved; the Authorities can do these jobs, and cannot build hospitals or schools, The New York City Planning Commission, conceived as a co-ordinator, has never developed power, and for practical purposes can only contribute mildly toward co-ordination.

Something New Must Come

Short-changed by the state, without influence on the independent Authorities, without hope of substantial relief from the Federal government, New York, like other big American cities, will probably jog along in this fashion for some years until there is an explosion. How the explosion will come is unforeseeable. Maybe because General Motors can make automobiles faster than anyone can make roads, New York streets will be choked to impassibility. Perhaps because some major need is left scandalously unfilled in spite of the congeries of Authorities. Improbably because an atom bomb is dropped on New York. More likely, the change will be forced by growing financial strain. New public works and new services become increasingly essential, but cities cannot indefinitely increase old taxes or float additional bonds. More and better-paid teachers and more and better policemen will be needed—are needed now; and more services for health, for children and the aged. But revenues are not available. Eventually national politics must legitimately enter the situation when the crisis point arrives to make a solution imperative.

Needed: a New Point Four

It is too much to hope that the existing and foreseeable strains will be met by long-range economic planning. Such planning in the case of New York would require joint action of the city government and the governments of the States of New York and New Jersey and, in the not too distant future, Connecticut, concurred in by the self-administrating Authorities. Even if all these agencies worked together, probably they could not act without some help from the Federal government. Low-rent housing already is met by cities chiefly with Federal assistance. (Fiorello LaGuardia once observed wistfully that the two things that were most needed were beyond the power of the city government: It could not perform miracles and it could not print money. God wouldn't let it do the first; the United States Government would not let it do the second.) It is hardly conceivable that Federal credit facilities will not be needed when the time comes.

The past generation has been an age of extraordinary advances on every social front in America—on the farm, in civil rights, in science. Almost all these great advances have been brought about or fostered by Federal funds and Federal intervention on the unspoken assumption that when one portion of the nation gets stuck, the rest of the nation must lend a hand to get things rolling again. What has happened lately is not so much that the city has deteriorated but that the rest of the nation has rolled so swiftly on to higher standards that the city has become a backward area. Many other ways of life have outstripped the city way of life in attractiveness, except for those who live at the bottom or at the very top of the economic scale.

When the plight of our cities is faced up to at last, a fundamental attack on the whole problem of government in densely populated areas seems inescapable. Before this attack can take place, some basic ideas must be made clear. There are human values that can only be preserved by thinking in terms of small areas, the neighborly associations, homes and their qualities, contact between parents and schools. Even a New Yorker thinks not of the city or of his borough but of Gramercy Park or Brooklyn Heights, of West End Avenue or Kew Gardens, of his nearby school, his precinct police station, his familiar grocery. These are qualities of the village. For the rest, the city is a vast blur operated by political machines, a mayor—and other elected officials whose very names he hardly knows.

The actually powerful and functioning permanent officials, such as budget administrators, city and borough engineers, permanent administrators of housing, docks, hospitals, and finance, are almost wholly unknown. For practical purposes, New York City is governed by its budget director, Abraham D. Beame, supported by department engineers, administrators, and so on. City Hall is a sort of facade, designed to entertain; too often the elected officials find it easier to leave things just that way.

The Village and the Area

Analysis of the problem makes certain factors clear. Some economic functions have to be taken care of on an area basis: services and communications, water, transit, and main highways permitting entrance, exit, and access to the city and its parts, along with regulation of traffic and steady flow of supplies. These are as necessary to the suburbanite as to the inhabitant of Greenwich Village or Flushing. Nevertheless the centralized Authority, ramming its highways through, can wipe out the villages of human contact; the lively human centers even today fight a rear-guard action against the centralized blur that offers them services but destroys them at the same time. The more centralized complex that is the "city government" itself rises or falls on a tide of national communications, national economic and credit policies. The toll-road system now in rapid evolution is the twentieth-century equivalent of last century's railroad net. It is rapidly reaching the point of national rather than local significance. Its geography and rates can put a city's business on the map or force it to go elsewhere.

It follows, therefore, that somehow a system of government must be found that can do three things. It must liberate and protect the village for the things only a village can do. It must hold together the historical collectivity of the city for the things it can do. And it must set up some sort of entirely new overriding representative body to connect the sprawling population mass with its various parts and with the vaster population of outlying territory. In combination, the resulting system must operate intricate essential services, huge in scope, finance, and impact. It may not even be political in the old sense; its problems will be ninety per cent technical.

This is not theory. We shall, if the Twentieth Century Fund estimates are right, have a population of nearly 180 million by 1960 and perhaps 200 million by 1970. The New York complex, city and suburban, will be at least twenty million. In twenty-five years there is likely to be a continuous population mass from approximately New Haven straight down the Atlantic seaboard to Wilmington, Delaware, or perhaps still farther south. (The "New York area" is now almost a continuous settlement from Bridgeport to Trenton, with only a few shrinking unoccupied intervals.) The governmental structure built on historic townships, counties, and cities can carry the load only about so far. Eventually the whole problem must be met.

The King's Peace

Lest this be taken as mere speculation, let it be remembered that government has evolved just like this in ages past. When peace and order in England was preserved only by local lordlings, the feudal system broke down. An unknown genius, remembering that the king could preserve peace around his own property and castles, conceived the brilliant device of taking over as royal property the principal roads of the realm. Thereupon the king could enforce the king's peace on the king's highways; and so a national system of order, courts, police, and justice emerged in Britain. Our modern problem is to find an organizing principle that can do today what the king did then.

The riddle is not insoluble. Two decades ago Franklin Roosevelt called into being the Tennessee Valley Authority to meet the regional problem of stagnation in the Tennessee Valley—which covered several states. He hung it on the peg of Federal government power over navigable waterways. Once organized, under the genius of David Lilienthal it invoked co-operation of the governments of several states and cities. The TVA built itself into a semi-autonomous regional institution that met a problem of regional underdevelopment.

New York, New Jersey, and Connecticut wrestle with the problem of overdevelopment, and there are many pegs on which they, with the Federal government, could construct an institution. The Hudson and Long Island Sound are navigable waters; truck traffic is interstate commerce; the Holland and Lincoln Tunnels are interstate thoroughfares; states have power to make treaties with Federal approval. There is government power enough to discharge the functions that are regional or national in character as distinct from those which concern only New York City, Jersey City, Hoboken, and the commuting towns. Federal financing should be available; have not Federal guarantees of mortgages and public-housing aid already rebuilt the eastern shore of Manhattan?

Village units within and without New York City could likewise be strengthened; Gilbert Chesterton's fantasy of the armies of Bayswater held at bay by the forces of Notting Hill in modern London could come to pass here by assigning certain responsibilities to Greenwich Village or Brooklyn Heights. It should become a solid personal advantage to live within the jurisdiction of the "New York Area Authority" and at the same time be a resident of Morningside or Kew Gardens.

The area institution could be dramatized and given focus—though it might not have the luck of TVA, whose enemies dramatized it in violent attack. If Jean Monnet and Robert Schuman could create the Coal and Steel Community of Europe, and Foreign Offices can send ambassadors to it, America should be able to create area community governments endowed with enough democratic self-rule to stand up alongside the governments of the states and of the nation.

We struggle today for order in the economic fabric, and the problem of the cities is not dissimilar. Functions still have to be apportioned. Centralized and representative institutions of technical capacity must necessarily deal with regional services. More localized institutions are still needed to deal with over-all area responsibilities. Tiny tenacious groupings are still needed to defend hearth, home, and a modicum of beauty and aesthetics. Political invention and construction must be accomplished in each case. The day of Authorities jerry-rigged to deal with a particular tunnel or development may be almost over. The riddle of twentieth-century area government is demanding solution. Cities like New York will not allow its solution to be postponed for long.

19. Rural Versus Urban Political Power

GORDON E. BAKER

What is the extent of rural advantage throughout the nation, and what is its degree of intensity? Answers to these questions can be furnished in large part by data revealed in Table 1. . . . For this purpose the principal urban areas in each state have been studied from the standpoint of the relation which their population bears to their representative strength in each house of the legislature. While this method cannot divulge a complete picture in any state, it can provide a concise and graphic outline of the way in which representative patterns affect urban political power. In nearly all states, of course, the total urban population is considerably greater than the percentage listed for the selected areas. However, for statistical purposes there are numerous advantages in using only the larger cities in most states. Smaller municipalities are often located in larger districts with substantial rural populations, thus complicating an estimate of legislative strength. Moreover, the most populous urban areas in each state generally receive the main brunt of the discriminatory patterns.

. . . In order to focus more clearly on the extent and degree of urban underrepresentation, the forty-eight states listed in Table 1 are grouped into five separate categories. In group V are the only two states that provide an unmistakable pattern of representative equality for urban citizens. Group IV contains seven states whose urban districts are only moderately underrepresented. In group III the situation is slightly more serious. Group II includes the bulk of states, twenty-two in number, where distortions from democratic theory can be considered substantial. Finally, group I is reserved for eight states where the situation seems especially severe.

Of the few states allowing urban populations a proportionate voice in the legislature, Massachusetts comes closest to the ideal of "one man, one vote." Districts for both houses follow a relatively equal population pattern with amazing consistency. Representation is based upon the distribution of legal voters instead of population, though the results would be much the same on either standard. The latest reapportionment in Massachusetts occurred in 1947 and 1948 following the state's decennial

Reprinted from *Rural versus Urban Political Power* (New York: Random House, 1955), pp. 15–19 by permission of the author and the publisher. Gordon Baker is a professor of political science at the University of California.

census of voters held in 1945. The districting arrangements have not, however, escaped the charge of being an unusually effective partisan

TABLE 1
REPRESENTATION OF PRINCIPAL URBAN AREAS*

States	Selected urban areas	Per cent of state population	Per cent of lower house	Per cent of senate
	GROUP I—SEVERE			
Georgia	6 largest urban counties	32	9	7
Florida	9 most urban counties	60	23	24
Delaware	Wilmington urbanized area	59	23	24
Maryland	Baltimore & 3 largest urban counties	67	44	31
Connecticut	10 largest cities	46	7	46[a]
Rhode Island	10 largest cities	77	67	34
New Jersey	8 largest urban counties	75	73	38
California	4 largest urban counties	59	59	10
	GROUP II			
New York	New York City	53	43	43
Kansas	3 largest urban counties	26	7	8
Alabama	3 largest urban counties	30	13	9
Iowa	5 largest urban counties	24	10	10
Oklahoma	2 largest urban counties	26	12	6
Texas	4 largest urban counties	29	19	13
Minnesota	2 largest urban counties	35	23	22
New Mexico	largest urban county	21	11	3
Tennessee	4 largest urban counties	38	22	20
Arizona	2 largest urban counties	62	62	7
Nevada	2 largest urban counties	62	40	12
Michigan	Wayne County	38	35	21
Missouri	St. Louis & 2 largest urban counties	45	25	41
Illinois	Chicago	42	39	31
Ohio	8 largest urban counties	54	39	54
South Carolina	3 largest urban counties	22	22	7
Vermont	entire urban population	36	6	36[a]
Idaho	4 largest urban counties	28	19	9
North Dakota	4 largest cities	17	12	10
Montana	5 largest urban counties	37	32	9
North Carolina	4 largest counties	22	16	16[a]
Mississippi	2 largest urban counties	10	4	4

TABLE 1 CONTINUED

States	Selected urban areas	Per cent of state population	Per cent of lower house	Per cent of senate
	GROUP III			
Utah	3 largest urban counties	64	48	48
Indiana	6 largest urban counties	46	32	34
Washington	3 largest urban counties	52	44	48
Colorado	Denver city	31	26	23
Oregon	largest urban county	31	27	23
Nebraska	2 largest urban counties	30		23
Kentucky	3 largest urban counties	23	17	18
Louisiana	3 largest urban parishes	34	26	26
Maine	8 largest cities	27	19	27*
	GROUP IV—MODERATE			
Pennsylvania	2 largest urban counties	34	32	28
Virginia	8 largest cities & 4 largest urban counties	34	28	33
West Virginia	3 largest urban counties	21	19	12
Wyoming	5 most urban counties	48	41	33
South Dakota	6 largest urban counties	30	28	23
Arkansas	3 largest urban counties	16	12	14
New Hampshire	3 largest cities	27	25	29
	GROUP V—EQUAL REPRESENTATION			
Wisconsin	3 largest urban counties	33	32	33
Massachusetts	All cities over 50,000 population	50	50	50*

Figures are rounded to nearest percentage
  * Based on 1950 census figures; calculations made on the basis of 1954–1955 representation.
  * Approximate

gerrymander. Boundary lines are so drawn that the Republican Party has apparently benefited considerably in a close two-party state. However, the equitable weight given all urban areas is still a unique accomplishment.

Wisconsin's legislature, which had not been reapportioned for some thirty years, can finally claim—beginning in 1954—one of the most representative lawmaking bodies in the nation. While several distortions in district populations are made inevitable by constitutional restrictions against breaking county lines, most districts fall reasonably close to an ideal average. The few inequalities do not work to the disadvantage of urban areas. Reapportionment brought about substantial gains for both smaller and larger urban counties. The Milwaukee and Madison regions especially benefited from the change.

In a few states where Table 1 indicates an underrepresentation of urban districts the situation is less disadvantageous to city population than the figures might indicate. Wherever numerous delegates are elected at large from a county that contains rural as well as urban population, the city often tends to dominate the elections because of its favorable position. This means that while the delegation may be underrepresented on the basis of a total percentage, the city viewpoint receives adequate support. Wyoming, West Virginia, South Dakota, and Arkansas are four rural states where larger districts as such are underrepresented; but the situation cannot correctly be considered as one of inadequate urban power. At-large elections help modify the degree of urban underrepresentation in Indiana and Utah as well.

As might be expected, the largest city within most states is the primary target of discriminatory representation. New York, Chicago, Los Angeles, St. Louis, Detroit, Baltimore, Atlanta, Birmingham, and Providence are all well-publicized examples. The list could be extended to include most principal cities. Notable exceptions to the rule are Boston, Milwaukee, New Orleans, Richmond, and Norfolk—all of which receive representation approximately equivalent to population. Moderately below strength are Philadelphia and Pittsburgh. It is interesting—and unusual—that underrepresentation in Virginia and Louisiana, while not extensive, is confined to medium-sized cities rather than to the principal ones.

In addition to cities proper, fast-growing suburban areas are often among the most severely underrepresented constituencies. As once-sparsely-settled districts increase in population many-fold, additional inequalities arise. For example, Baltimore city was originally the principal victim of Maryland's apportionment pattern. While the city's strength in the legislature is still far from adequate, even less proportionate weight is now held by suburban Baltimore County and the two flourishing counties that house many commuters from Washington, D.C. The most underrepresented areas in Pennsylvania prior to a reapportionment in 1953 were the suburbs surrounding Philadelphia. It is significant that political equality went long unnoticed by some state legislatures until growing suburban areas began to feel the pinch of inadequate representation. This is doubtless due to the fact that political sentiment in suburbia is generally conservative and often quite compatible with rural views on how the state should be governed. This would seem to be the main explanation behind the 1954 movement to amend the Illinois constitution in respect to representation. So long as Chicago proper was the primary victim of the situation, the rural-dominated legislature saw no need to obey constitutional provisions for reapportionment according to population. By 1954 the city as a whole was still underrepresented, but far less than nearby suburban territory. Politically, the city is Democratic, while both suburban Cook County and downstate Illinois are largely Republican. In 1953 a Republican governor managed to persuade a Republican legislature to propose a constitutional amendment for a "balanced" area-population scheme of representation. Ratified by the electorate in 1954, the new basis of apportionment resulted in moderate gains in one house and moderate losses in the other for the city of Chicago. But suburban Cook County increased its representation enormously, gaining five times as much weight as formerly in one house and six times as much in the other. The total effect of the amendment was to leave the city under-represented, while giving suburban Cook County legislative strength proportionate to its population. Downstate areas lost some strength, but remained overrepresented in the senate.

20. Metropolitan Government

JANE JACOBS

In spite of a potent grass-roots-and-town-meeting folklore, the U.S. has become a nation of metropoli; very peculiar metropoli with problems that are something new—at least in degree—under the sun. Sprawling over municipal lines, township lines, school district lines, county lines, even state lines, our 174 metropolitan areas are a weird melange of 16,210 separate units of government. The Chicago metropolitan area, one of the prize examples of fragmentation, has about a thousand contiguous or overlapping local government units. But the problem is similar everywhere: how does the metropolitan area (which lacks governmental entity) contend with urgent and massive problems of a metropolitan nature, armed with a cross-purpose jackstraw heap of local sovereignties representing genuinely clashing interests?

The metropolitan problems—monstrous traffic, missing or bankrupt transit, incompatible land uses, unbalanced land uses with their sequel of unbalanced tax structures, transformation of old core cities into racial

Reprinted from *Architectural Forum*, CVII (August 1957), pp. 124–27, 204–5 by permission of the publisher. Copyright 1957 by Time Inc. Jane Jacobs is a publicist.

and economic ghettos, pollution of air and water, and a host of others —are not new in kind. But they have become abruptly massive and urgent during the past ten years because we have had a phenomenal growth of metropolitan population and this has coincided with the phenomenal scatteration made possible by the automobile. These problems will become still more massive as the present metropolitan area populations of about 96 million increase by an estimated 54 million in the next 18 years.

Cumulatively, the number, size, and complexity of the metropolitan problems add up to a metropolitan crisis. . . . Looked at another way, they also add up to one of the greatest adventures in inventive self-government that any people has ever had a chance at.

Governmentally, we have never really come to full grips with the fact of cities, and this is a root of our trouble. Our governmental structure is based on static units of territory, rather than on dynamic units of populations. Our states, divided into their revealingly named *counties*, are an organizational heritage from feudal territorial war lords who fitted the city into their scheme of things as a special, chartered "exception." It is still an "exception" theoretically, although the ancient legal form of the city and its physical reality began to part company half a century ago, when the early suburbanites hop-skipped along the railroad lines out in the county.

But it would be folly to jump to the conclusion that the states, and the cities' positions within them, represent a troublesome archaism necessarily. The American political genius has consisted in the ability to take the instruments at hand and evolve them to new purposes as needed. It is quite possible that the salvation of our fragmented metropoli will be found in the existing states, rather than in the creation of new layers of "supercity" metropolitan government, an idea now intellectually fashionable.

In any event, the first thing to understand about metropolitan government is that it is going to be dealt with not by abstract logic or elegance of structure, but in a combination of approaches by trial, error and immense experimentation in a context of expediency and conflicting interests. Whatever we arrive at, we shall feel our way there.

The Approaches

In broad terms, there are three possible approaches to metropolitan government and one impossible approach.

The possible approaches are: 1) much greater extension and evolution of present *ad hoc* devices such as special districts, authorities, compacts, contracts, and taxation ingenuities; 2) greater dependence on the federal government for the required money and hence for the required decisions and authority; and 3) federation of governmental units within metropolitan areas; such a joint government might be a council, or it might be a decentralized agency of the state, and the local units would surrender sovereignty over certain problems.

The impossible approach is consolidation of municipalities within metropolitan areas, making the metropolitan area one big city, at least within state lines. It is well to deal with this idea first and at some length because it shows, in sharpest relief, many of the limitations and complexities that apply to the other approaches too.

Consolidation: Impossible

Consolidation is impossible, first, as a pragmatic fact, because the citizenry of most of the units concerned strongly oppose it. Annexation, for example, has very lean pickings nowadays. . . . No cities other than Houston, Mobile, Dallas and El Paso annexed so much as 10 sq.mi. Among annexations by 348 other municipalities having a population of 10,000 or more, the average was ⅗ths of a sq.mi. And these figures, so pathetic against immense urban scatteration, are the best since the war.

The bigger the metropolis, as a rule, the more ardently its outliers will defend themselves against being "swallowed." This fear, while possibly selfish and shortsighted, is not imaginary, as one illustration of a common situation shows. In Philadelphia, the city government has had to contend with the problem of "the suburbs in the city," areas within the city of low density housing which the city needs to intersperse with higher density zoning because of population pressures and cost of services. Although the citizenry in the "suburbs" involved has been vociferous and politically active in its opposition, it has consistently been defeated because it is a minority voice in the city as a whole. Conflict of precisely this nature, in many different guises, is the hard core of the whole metropolitan government problem.

Political Scientist Edward C. Banfield comments: "The problem is not, as many seem to think, merely one of creating organization for effective planning and administration. It is also—and perhaps primarily—one of creating or of maintaining organization for the effective management of conflict, especially of conflict arising from the growing cleavage of race and class. These needs may be incompatible to some extent. . . . Indeed it may be that area-wide planning and administration would of necessity heighten conflicts by raising questions which can only be settled by bitter struggle. Conflict is not something to be avoided at all costs. It may be well, nevertheless, to consider whether there are not decisive advantages in organizational arrangements . . . which, although handicapping or entirely frustrating some important undertakings, nevertheless serve to insulate opposed interests and to protect them from each other."

Aside from being politically impossible—and in the Banfield view perhaps politically undesirable—consolidation may also be illusory as a planning solution for the following reasons, which have their influence on all schemes of metropolitan government. It presupposes more or less neat and manageable arrangements of core cities surrounded by satellites. The map . . . shows, however, that there are now 18 growing "urban regions" where two or more standard metropolitan areas overlap or adjoin. Where we had wheel or star-shaped urban structures, we are now getting amorphous masses. In even the largest of these regions, the core-city-satellite concept still does have validity for many purposes, especially the journey to work, but it has little validity in solving other problems, such as general traffic, air pollution, water supply. The logical "jurisdictions" of such problems do not even necessarily coincide with each other, nor is the territory involved today likely to be the same in 20 years or even five years.

Then there is the entire problem of size, workable size for a specific governmental function. The problem of the school district too small for efficiency, or of the suburb with its tax base and child population wildly out of whack, is well known. On the other hand, the huge New York City Board of Education, with more than 900,000 children to provide for, tries hard to plan but also has poor success with it, probably because it is just too big. Decisions on sites and buildings, for instance, are necessarily made so remotely from the "communities" intimately involved, and with such an absence of natural give-and-take and explanation, that the result is a system of ukases from above, countered by frenzied pressures from below, with planning lost in the shuffle. Execution of planning, generally, suffers many defeats by dealing in units of great size, as well as by being confined in units too small. In a unit of very large population, departments and bureaus, each an empire in miniature, require increasing layers of coordinators and mayoral assistants constantly engaged in attempting, often vainly, to pull things together.

Size also involves the entire problem of local responsibility and the principle, probably inseparable from vigorous self-government, that any division of government should be kept as close to the people as function permits.

In short, consolidation does not answer the situation: if the metropolitan problems themselves are a fearsome snarl, the problems entailed in going at them make a fearful snarl too.

Ad Hoc Devices

How much promise is there in such *ad hoc* devices as special districts, authorities, compacts, contracts, and taxation ingenuities? (This we have called the first of the "possible" approaches.) A great deal of invention is now being spent on unraveling the metropolitan snarl one knot at a time. For instance, "special districts" created to deal with problems that cross governmental lines, are by far the most rapidly growing category of governmental unit. Since 1942, 6,124 new special districts have been created. California, with 330 municipalities (and 1,841 school districts) has 1,652 special districts. Illinois has 1,785. Not all special districts are metropoltian, but most are. Their ancestor was the Boston metropolitan sewage district created in 1889. Many are authorities with independent borrowing power, modeled after the Port of New York Authority which was created in 1921.

Among dozens of other inventions, for attacking this facet or that of fiscal or physical disability, are ungraduated city income taxes (applying to suburbanites too), county home rule (for metropolitan areas within a county), state taboos on new incorporations in the sphere of a core city, and planning powers for the core city extending a few miles beyond its boundaries.

One of the strangest inventions is the Lakewood Plan, named for a Los Angeles suburb of 75,000, which in 1954 incorporated and contracted with Los Angeles County for almost all its services. This scheme, hugely popular, has triggered 11 incorporations in the county since, and detailed price lists have been worked out for buying services, such as $3.63 for each health call; $7 a day for women in jail, $3.50 for men; $73,000 per year for one around-the-clock police patrol car. These communities even contract with the county for technical services in tax assessment and collection, planning and zoning and civil service administration. They have made headway in solving the problem of duplicated governmental overhead and inefficiency, but these communities still retain their autonomy, set their own policy—notably zoning—a point to keep in mind.

Looking at current devices as a pattern, two rather alarming motifs stand out. The first is the effect of the "special district" approach. "The great disadvantage of special districts and authorities lies in the cumulative effect of their use," comments Political Scientist Victor Jones. "One special district may be of no import, but ultimately their use will lead to functional disintegration. This is a problem of politics, of control as well as of administration, and will force us to reorder our values or start all over again to build a community from functional fragments."

The second motif is the apparent inability of any of the inventions to come to grips with land planning policy. Many existing arrangements do pretty well with things that flow and fly: with water supply, sewage, smoke control, pest control and, to a degree, even with traffic and transit. If things that fly and flow were all that need be considered, we might expect the metropolitan problems to come under reasonable control in time, with existing devices.

The Fixed Anarchy

But something very fixed is involved: the land. And land planning remains in complete anarchy. This anarchy touches everything. It is the road . . . which in the city is zoned to serve as a fast-moving arterial feeder, but at the city line becomes a stop-and-go roadtown. It is Suburb A zoning for heavy industry against the residential district of Suburb B. It is School District C, divided so swiftly into builders' developments that, before anyone realizes, it has no way of getting money to support the schools it needs. It is the suddenly vanished open land that had given the city relief and recreation. It is the new bridge approach, tearing out the heart of an old community or cutting off school from students. It is the ever greater segregation of low income and minority populations in the core city, daily increasing the cleavages and conflicts with which Banfield is so concerned. It is an ever longer journey to work. It is shopping centers, whose inpouring of traffic and lack of buffer territory cast blight.

Anarchy in land planning makes new metropolitan problems faster than they can be solved. And it is the untouchable among metropolitan problems. Perhaps the best example of dealing with it thus far is in Nashville, and there only the negative step can be taken of county veto on proposed zoning changes. Even Miami and its environs, which have just voted in a form of federated metropolitan government for Dade County, have left zoning and planning to local municipal control. Schemes like the Lakewood Plan, referred to above, are devised mainly to keep land policy thoroughly local because land planning policy also involves who your neighbor shall be, or in what way you can make money from your holdings and how much.

Regional or metropolitan planning in the land area is always set up as a voluntary or advisory arrangement because everyone recognizes that anything else would be politically impossible. But, as Planning Director Henry Fagin of the Regional Plan Association in New York points out, the advisory regional planning board with no metropolitan governing officials to give advice to is a "floating" body, by definition politically irresponsible—and it acts politically irresponsible. "It does not need to come to grips with the real conflicts, as effective decision makers do," says Fagin. "Too often the 'lesson' it teaches is that planning is futile or undesirable." At best, Fagin thinks, the floating planning board can indicate realistically what it thinks is going to happen anyway, which is useful information. This is mainly the role played by those regional advisory boards, such as Detroit's, which have managed to earn respect.

Law Professor Charles M. Haar, analyzing the statutes by which 22 states authorize regional planning activity, notes how boldly they prescribe research, studies and the drafting of a master plan, and how vague they leave the question of what is to be done with it. "Even the process of preparation is not drawn up so as to elicit public support nor to be illuminating either to the general citizenry or to the planning staffs and boards. Certainly the procedures for adoption are not devised with the thought of . . . having the final acceptance of the plan, which after all sets basic goals that affect the lives of the citizens in many intimate ways, a matter of public concern. Without such clarification, there is small hope for a reconciliation of divergent interests, without which planning becomes simply a pleasant intellectual hobby." He notes that 90 major planning surveys have been made of metropolitan areas, of which only three can lay any possible claim to having had any effect. But hope springs eternal. In June, Chicago civic groups finally succeeded in getting a metropolitan planning commission past the legislature. It will be advisory—because nothing else is politically possible.

Federal Solutions?

This missing link—lack of means for adopting genuinely effective metropolitan land planning policy—is important to keep in mind when considering the second "possible approach" toward metropolitan government: the use of federal cooperation, aid and authority. The main point in this approach is that the federal government has highly effective ways of getting tax money out of localities and, in returning it as expenditure, can use the powers of decision that accompany powers of money disbursal. The hope that federal means will succeed, where the means available to cities and states cannot, is implied in current bills for establishment of a cabinet rank Department of Urban Affairs and proposals for a White House conference on urban problems.

The federal government does already have an enormous influence on metropolitan land planning. For instance, Federal Housing Administration and Public Housing Administration policies, between them, have probably had more to do with the progressive ghettoizing of core cities, the class segregation of the suburbs and the form of metropolitan scatteration, than any other factors. These results have not been deliberate however; the two agencies have been unable to formulate policies that take cognizance of each other, let alone take cognizance of the metropolitan situation as a whole. The great federal highway program now getting started will influence metropolitan land use for good or ill more than all the metropolitan land planning ventures of our time put together, but there is no sign that this is understood by those who wrote the legislation or those who will administer it. . . . While these great forces blunder about blindly, doing "planning" on true metropolitan area scale, the Urban Renewal Administration applies its little poultices and encourages municipalities to produce plans—on a municipal scale.

Most proposals for a Department of Urban Affairs recognize this unhappy situation; they list among the Department's proposed functions investigation of the impact of federal programs on cities and coordination of such programs.

Is such coordination actually possible? With all its money and authority, can the federal government succeed in producing rationality where the cities and states have not? First, there is the difficulty of federal programs coordinating among themselves. "No community ever approaches its government problem *in toto*, for it never exists that way historically," notes Sociologist Albert J. Reiss Jr. This is spectacularly true of the federal government, as witness the current misidentification of urban rebuilding with the depression-fighting theory out of which it was born, or the inability of the HHFA coordinator to coordinate the historically separate FHA and PHA.

Second, there is the difficulty of coordinating federal programs with the local situation. "Planning by its nature looks to the coordination and integration of governmental functions," points out Lawyer Jerome J. Shestack. "There is an over-all and continuing aspect to planning that requires involvement of all the community resources." At the most optimistic, even assuming that the federal government could miraculously coordinate its own parts with respect to their impacts on the metropolis, it is impossible to imagine Washington filling a planning role satisfactory for the metropolitan area. "All of the community resources" means many with which the federal government cannot possibly be concerned or be aware of. On the contrary, if and when we do get effective metropolitan governments, one of their most pressing tasks will certainly be to bend, educate and influence federal aid and controls as they apply to specific metropolitan areas.

The Federated City

Most students of metropolitan government are now agreed that the most logical aim is the third "possible approach": some form of federation of governmental units within a metropolitan area, with the units surrendering some of their sovereignty to a metropolitan government.

This is by no means a "simple" approach. There is nothing simple about such relationships, as the entire history of our federal-state partnership attests. The only metropolitan federation in operation thus far in North America—the federation of Toronto and 12 suburban satellites (all in one county, with some planning powers overlapping two other counties)—is a little too simple, in fact. So much power resides in the metropolitan council, and especially in its chairman, that, for US consumption, it embodies many of the objections that apply to consolidation.

The nearest approach in the US is the Miami plan (again involving one core city and its satellites in one county) which the voters have just accepted. The Miami scheme does not provide for unified planning as such, but it does give unified powers over slum clearance, traffic and parking and drainage, for instance—activities which in practice determine many great questions of land planning policy.

Powers of this type are probably the great opportunity for achieving metropolitan government. For they are the handle, several authorities believe, by which we can best grasp hold of reasonably unified planning and administration.

Jones suggests, for example, that the way out of the impasse of having single-minded authorities or special districts is to form their governing boards from elected officials of the municipalities and counties concerned, as the San Francisco Bay Area Air Pollution Control Board is organized. The next step would be for the *same* local officials to serve on new special boards as they are created. This collection of boards with the same elected officials on them could evolve into a metropolitan district with many general powers of government, an integrated view of the many different but related problems and, eventually, a popularly elected chief executive.

Haar suggests that the state is the logical instrument of federation —or at least federated planning—because its role is already so large in many matters affecting metropolitan and regional development: flood control, highways, schools, for example. The state judiciaries, he argues, are already "plunged into the vacuum of [planning] power," with inter-community disputes about land use increasingly thrust on them.

Fagin suggests that a practical first step would be to abandon the idea of the floating regional planning board, but by no means abandon metropolitan and regional planning. Instead the regional planning staff should be attached *as a working instrument* to a regional agency which has decision-making powers over key aspects of regional and metropolitan development. This could be a federated metropolitan council or it could be a regional agency of the state. To govern properly, many states have already decentralized the administration of parks, roads and health, into districts. Such districts could be redrawn and pulled together to permit them to deal with their functions on a metropolitan level. To them could be added powers over pollution or over transit, over almost anything which the states now delegate to special districts or authorities. The point would be that these powers would be exercised consciously in the context of a broad area plan, and that the plan, for its part, would be formed in the context of genuine decision making.

Like Jones, Fagin thinks the agency of federation should be composed of elected local officials, but Fagin would add elected officials of the state, including some from the areas involved. After experimentation with the process of delegating some powers of the state "downward" to a region, and some of the powers of the local communities "upward," the scheme might be regularized. The states, long the declining stars of our national firmament, might well become more important in their role as senior partners in state-city federations than in their role as junior partners in the nation-state federation.

This or any other federated scheme would work, Fagin thinks, only if the metropolitan or regional body were firmly confined, probably by a "constitution type" statute, to matters of regional import. This would not preclude a joint underwriting of certain minimum standards throughout the area, with option by the communities to better the standards locally, a concept already familiar in many types of state aid. It would preclude centralization of all real decision making and the degeneration of local units into janitorial government. For example, how the suburb of Bronx-ville, N.Y. wants to zone the commercial district around its railroad station, or what internal street pattern a builder chooses to put in his housing development, would be of no regional import. But whether New York puts public housing or port facilities on its waterfront, or where a parkway runs and what borders it, likely would be. Litigation would draw the effective lines between what is regional and what is local—a process already under way as Haar has shown, but with no planning framework or theory at present to assist the judges.

There are several persuasive reasons for the state to take over the new function of metropolitan government. Metropolitan areas are dynamic, not fixed, and a state regional body (even one made up of local officials) could have a matching flexibility of jurisdiction, difficult to build into a distinctly new layer of supercity government. Where metropolitan areas cross state lines, state governments are the logical units for making pacts and setting up joint bodies or programs. Most important, the states have a strong and well-understood tradition of popular government and of give-and-take with localities, something that has to be worked into, slowly and chancily, with new managerial layers of government.

There is a further reason, little noted yet, but vital. In California, where the future seems to happen faster than anywhere else, two of the "Lakewood Plan" incorporations in Los Angeles county happen to be rural dairy-farm districts which incorporated to protect themselves from urban encroachment. Agricultural conservation is going to become deeply enmeshed, in many places, with the metropolitan problem. . . . Thus the very "rural mindedness" of the state legislatures, long a burden to the development of the cities, could be a valuable pressure on the metropoli of the future. Certainly no scheme of federation which overlooks the problem of agricultural conservation—or is set up to deal with it strictly from an urban viewpoint—will be suited to making planning policy for our monstrously growing metropoli.

If the problems of achieving metropolitan government seem formidable, and even the thinking about means to achieve it maddeningly tentative, it is well to remember that nobody has been trying very long. Most planners and many theorists were unaware of the metropolitan government idea until Jones' *Metropolitan Government* was published in 1942. Most government officials have learned of the idea only within the past three or four years. Some have not yet grasped its importance to them. Predecessors of current state governors showed no public awareness of the concept. . . . It is, in fact, encouraging that the era of experiment and of investigation (much of it with foundation money, as in Cleveland and St. Louis) should have begun so quickly and should be enlisting so many lively and practical minds.

And for those who despair that it can ever be worked out with neatness and certitude, it is well to remember Architect Henry Churchill's wise words: "Within the broadest possible framework of the general good, disorder must be allowed for, lest the people perish. Any form of initiative is disordering of the status quo and so needs encouragement, not suppression, if democracy is to retain vitality."

Chapter FIVE

GOVERNMENTAL STRUCTURE

AND FORMS OF ELECTIONS:

AN ASSESSMENT OF THE

MUNICIPAL REFORM MOVEMENT

IN THE DECADES around the turn of the century the reputation of municipal government in this country was at low ebb. There were widespread allegations of corruption, inefficiency, and ineptitude in city governments throughout the nation. The symbols of ill repute were the "city boss" and the "machine." The character of the boss system which drew political support from the immigrating masses and graft from city business is so familiar that it need not be reviewed here. (Some attention has been given to it earlier in the reading from Gosnell in Chapter Two.)

The low esteem in which city government was held was diagnosed by civic reformers as the natural result of a structure of government which encouraged the recruitment of those who were prone to corruption. In most American cities, the reformers argued, the governmental arrangements had originally been designed for a rural setting where face-to-face political relationships were the rule. In a more complex urban environment these forms of government created a civic burden for the citizen which made it impossible for him to hold his government responsible. At the same time these governments were so ill equipped to handle the difficult tasks accompanying urbanization that they were easily captured by the boss who at the very minimum brought some degree of order from administrative chaos, albeit at a stiff price.

In response to these conditions, a national movement of municipal reform was founded. It drew its support primarily from middle-class citizens, many of whom were businessmen and professionals. The leading organization which grew out of these efforts was the National Municipal League (which publishes the *National Civic Review*). The watchwords of reform were efficiency, economy, and democracy. The reformers were moralists who assumed that the structure of government could be manipulated to bring the "good" people (the majority) back into control. Under the reformed structures those trained to govern in the spirit of scientific management would be placed in charge. Efficiency was viewed as maximizing the potential of the resources available. The reformers, true to a Calvinist heritage, deplored waste. The democratic element of the reform program was closely related to the administrative ideas. A government could be democratic only when it was so efficiently organized that the citizen would have no difficulty in determining who was responsible for any particular action. The specific program of the reform movement was spelled out in a series of legal changes for election laws, charter provisions, and legislative-executive arrangements. The model for efficiency measures was often the private business corporation.

A primary objective was to find a new form of government to replace the old weak-mayor system. During the first decade of this century many reformers thought the answer was found in the commission plan, but by the second decade the council-manager plan, accompanied by nonpartisan elections, had emerged as the "best form." Today the council-manager plan is still the form recommended by the National Municipal League. It is also the most popular in terms of new adoptions. The hallmark of the manager plan is professionalization, an objective of the reform movement from its outset. As most city jobs are of a technical nature—building streets and sewers, fighting fires, and catching thieves—the tasks were to be performed by trained technicians. The manager plan created the capstone to this idea by placing a professional general administrator over all the other professionals. Thus the idea of a civil service rather than a patronage personnel system was part and parcel of the manager plan.

A number of political changes accompanied the manager plan which were designed to safeguard the new professional staff. Nonpartisan elections were advocated for councils. The objective was to divorce local politics from partisan politics. It was felt that this would decrease the pressure for patronage, entice "public-minded" persons to run for office regardless of party interests, and insulate local elections from the "coat-tail" influences of the national campaigns. In addition, after a brief flirtation with proportional representation, at-large elections were advocated. This was to break up the old wards which produced the "brokerage" councilmen interested only in benefits for the neighborhood and have them replaced with persons attuned to the needs of an entire city.

At this late date the question is no longer whether the council-manager plan has been successful. It has certainly proved itself to be a popular arrangement for thousands of American cities. Few would dispute that it is in general a quite efficient arrangement for managing municipal affairs. Major criticisms of the plan have centered on its political rather than its administrative characteristics. A number of critics have raised questions about the plan, claiming that matters appropriately in the arena of politics and policy-making are treated as technical problems. Therefore, in keeping with the general theme of this book, it is to these questions that we address ourselves.

In the first section of this chapter, the reader is introduced to the theory and application of municipal reform. The first selection is by one of the foremost popularizers of the city-manager system, the short ballot principle, municipal nonpartisanship, and a number of other highly specific devices. A man whose writings show robust faith in the ability of the majority, Mr. Childs has spent a lifetime seeking ways in which to make the citizen's role more viable. The next selection is from a monumental study of the council-manager plan carried out on its twenty-fifth anniversary. Over fifty cities were studied, and from one of the case studies we have excerpted a story of one city's experience with the plan.

This study by Stone, Price, and Stone provides perhaps the most thoroughly documented defense of the council-manager plan. From the concluding chapter of their study, we have excerpted sections dealing with the manager's role in policy-making. This serves as an introduction to the section reassessing the impact of the municipal reform movement. Stone, Price, and Stone (and for that matter the City Manager Code of Ethics) recognize that the manager is more than an administrator. He may also have to become a community leader. Indeed they introduce the intriguing argument that local democracy is enhanced by the council-manager plan, for among other things it makes local government more effective and deserving of citizen respect.

Some advocates of the plan have argued that the division of tasks between the council and the manager is defined by the difference between policy and administration. Karl Bosworth reminds us that this is hardly the case, that the manager is also very much a policy leader. (Stone, Price, and Stone say "community leader." Is there a difference?) However, he also raises a more serious question when he asserts that the nonpartisan, council-manager plan obfuscates the choices which are open to the citizen. This same theme is picked up by Adrian and Wood who reiterate the danger that political questions may be masked by merely calling them nonpolitical.

While the council-manager plan is the fastest growing form of city government and each year witnesses increased municipal adoption of nonpartisan and at-large election forms, other structures and forms not only continue to exist, but also have their defenders. Arthur Bromage points out how, given proper leadership, the "outmoded" weak-mayor system can be made to operate in a medium sized city. There are strong arguments that the reform devices are not appropriate for conditions in large cities. It is argued that civic action in a major city requires the mobilization of political power, which neither a professional manager nor a leaderless council can normally supply. Meyerson and Banfield stress the roll of the political party in setting an over-all policy responsive to the electorate. Freedgood argues for the strong mayor as the only hope of such cities (as did Banfield and Grodzins in an earlier reading). Sayre describes the general-manager idea as a means of strengthening the political executive. An administrative reply by Sommers, a city manager, follows. He poses the question whether such a politically sensitive position can be professionalized.

We begin the chapter with Richard Childs, a reformer who celebrates the great accomplishments in municipal government he has seen in his lifetime. The chapter ends with a statement by James Reichley, a much younger man who views the accomplishments of the reform movement with greater restraint. An eyewitness to events in Philadelphia, he asks whether the victory can truly be permanent. His criticism, at its root, is that civic reform attempts to be nonpolitical toward subjects which by their nature discourage neutrality.

A. THE PRINCIPLES OF MUNICIPAL REFORM

21. The Faith of a Civic Reformer

RICHARD S. CHILDS

> The preachers who tell corrupt cities that the people are steeped in sin are the descendants of those who used to associate sin and plagues.
> —*National Municipal Review*, 1936

The people—pronounced by the orators "pee-pul"! Or "the plain people," who, we are to understand, have certain supernatural virtues not possessed by "the people"! It is in some minds lèse-majesté to allege that there are limitations to the people in either morals or learning. Rounded periods are out of fashion on every other subject, but rhetorical vaporings still enshroud "this great people." And if you should have the temerity to opine that most of the people vote for a state treasurer blindly without adequate knowledge of his qualifications, editors (after having looked up the name of the state treasurer themselves to be sure of it) will explode in paragraphs of scorn—"Doesn't he trust our people?" In the same editorials, after exalting the virtue of the people, they may proceed to deplore their wanton "apathy."

Apathy is assigned as the reason for every failure of the democratic process. Tie upon the backs of the people a triple burden of duties and if they do not carry it well, if they do not do the tasks which writers of state constitutions and city charters assigned to them, bewail their "apathy"!

But we see in the United States some clear phenomena that upset the notion that the people are always to blame when things go wrong. The

Reprinted from *Civic Victories, The Story of an Unfinished Revolution* (New York: Harper and Brothers, 1952), pp. 3–6 by permission of the author and the publisher. Mr. Childs, a businessman, became active in civic reform early in the century. He was, with Woodrow Wilson, the founder of the Short Ballot movement. He was also an early exponent of the city-manager plan and many other structural reforms. Throughout his long career, Mr. Childs has been very active in the National Municipal League.

government of New York City has been over a period of some years markedly better than that of Chicago in the view of both informed New Yorkers and Chicagoans. Must we then assume that there is some great moral difference between the two populaces? Isn't it a fact that they are indistinguishable in any candid light?

The people of Dayton have had good government for thirty-eight years unbroken through twenty biennial elections, but if its population moved to Chicago, would those people be distinguishable?

Cincinnati in the 1920's was commonly described as our worst-governed city; after 1926 it began calling itself the best governed and is still plausibly doing so. The governmental mechanism changed, but Cincinnatians remained the same people before and after!

Kansas City has had good government for twelve years—ever since it got rid of the 60,000 phantom voters who used to pervert its elections under Boss Pendergast—but. . . the government of Jackson County, of which that city's population is 80 per cent, continues backward, inefficient, and suspect under a government of antique design.

If such differences of performance are not to be found attributable to long-run differences in the morality or civic energy of those constituencies, they must be due to differences in the mechanism.

So let us admit that the people are men and women, not demigods; men and women, not moral delinquents! If we thus concede to the people the merits and faults possessed by men and women, we can proceed calmly to consider them as the great underlying base of our government-by-elected-officers, with certain familiar and, so far as we are concerned, unalterable characteristics to be reckoned with as we erect the political superstructure.

Think of the people as you would of a brook when building a water mill! You would waste no time in deploring its lazy tendency to slip downward through every crevice in your dam; you would admit the fact and build a tight dam. You would not plan to have the water flow uphill, knowing that you would inevitably be disappointed. If your mill finally failed to work, you would still not blame the water but only the mill, and would strive to adapt its gearing to the force of the stream. Yet you would have just as much right to sit by the motionless mill and curse the characteristics of water (which consistently fails to fulfill your man-made requirements) as has the Charter Revision Committee to devise a city charter that imposes requirements on the people which ample experience demonstrates that the people will not fulfill, and to curse the people for apathy when they fail to live up to these arbitrary man-made duties.

So let us consider the people in the same candid scientific spirit in which we would consider the millstream, ascribing to them no unnatural virtues, no powers that have not been revealed in practice, no halo! Consider them as a phenomenon of nature, which in a given set of circumstances will actually do this and rarely do that.

In the past we have approached the people as a pagan approached the waterfall—to worship and peer around for nymphs. We must today approach the people as the mill builder approaches the waterfall—open-eyed, unafraid, expecting no miracle, measuring its capacity, making allowance for its variations, and irreverently gauging its limitations in order that our mill shall not exceed them.

In considering the people thus we need not become cynics. A cat may look at a queen and a student of the American political panorama may apply a steel tape to the people and develop a discriminating admiration.

Human nature being what it has always been through the ages, the problem is: Given the American people, as they actually are, how may a government be organized among them which will be impelled promptly and anxiously to learn their desire and perform it?

This does not mean merely that the government will obey on those occasions when the people in a paroxysm proclaim from press, pulpit, and mass meeting that a certain thing must be done (though even that would be substantial gain in some American communities). It means that the government will be so sensitive to the currents of public opinion that it will even anticipate the popular wish.

There is nothing fanciful in such an ideal. Commerce is no less sensitive than that. Every taste of the public in food, art, and comfort is catered to without any conscious public inquiry for such satisfaction. . . .

22. Janesville, Wisconsin—A Case Study

HAROLD A. STONE, DON K. PRICE, AND KATHRYN H. STONE

Janesville's civic leaders, with visions of commercial progress and political reform, were determined as early as 1910 to do something about their municipal government. Dissatisfied with the aldermanic form, which

Reprinted from City Manager Government in Nine Cities (Chicago: Public Administration Service, 1940), pp. 5–15 by permission of the publisher. Don Price is Dean of the Graduate School of Public Administration, Harvard University. Harold and Kathryn Stone were employed by the Committee on Public Administration of the Social Science Research Council at the time this and the following writing were done.

was operated on a basis of partisan politics and ward representation, they turned to the commission form, then the best advertised plan, as a means of salvation. After one defeat, they established the commission plan in 1912, and the mayor and a large board of aldermen, with their two-year terms, were replaced by a three-man commission: a mayor elected for six years and two commissioners with overlapping four-year terms, all elected at large.

The businessmen and civic leaders who supported the commission plan, among them men as prominent as George S. Parker of the Parker Pen Company, were, of course, too busy to take part in the street-corner politics by which the ward leaders had controlled the municipality. They hoped to abolish "politics" by the simple expedient of abolishing the board of aldermen and letting the administrative officials work without interference from the politicians. They made the man who had been city treasurer for eighteen years mayor and the city clerk a commissioner.

The *Janesville Gazette* was fully in sympathy with them. It was so enthusiastic in the matter that it called the speeches of those who wished to abandon the commission plan "such as one would expect to hear from a Lenine (sic) or a Trotsky," and said that any advocate of aldermanic government must be either "a knave or a fool."

But in spite of this reputable support, commission government lasted only six years. The city voted for a return to aldermanic government in 1918, and remained under that form until 1923.

Aldermanic Government

The men who dominated the aldermanic government, both before 1912 and after 1918, and who fought the commission plan, were those who later opposed the establishment of city manager government. These men were the political leaders of the workingmen's neighborhoods west of Rock River. The strongest political leader, who has dominated the old Fifth Ward since 1905, was J. J. Dulin, a railway conductor. With him on the council in 1919 were three small contractors, a carpenter, a dairyman, a former sheriff, a machinist, a railway switchman, and a dye-house worker. The mayor was Thomas E. Welsh, tobacco dealer, Exalted Ruler of the Elks, Grand Knight of the Knights of Columbus, and member of at least a half-dozen lodges. "I favor a new deal" had been his campaign promise in 1918. Messrs. Dulin and Welsh, with a few associates, remained in control until 1923.

The principal characteristic of these men was that they enjoyed handling the public relations of the city in street-corner gatherings, saloons, and the other centers of the social life of the less prosperous and less enterprising half of Janesville. They relished the sense of power and prominence that they could not get from their business or social life, and some of them took a deep interest in the procedure and conferences through which the petty administrative work of the city was handled. It is said that Mayor Welsh ruined his own business by attending to the city's. There was no distinction in their minds between political and administrative functions. They looked after their wards and the administrative departments alike.

There is no evidence of dishonesty in the aldermen's handling of municipal affairs, although the civic and social leaders of the community were always suspicious of paving contracts and purchases. There was no systematic machine patronage, and the "shake-down" was unknown. Even in 1918, when they returned to office after being out for six years, they started their administration by retaining all the incumbent officials. The principal effect of politics on administration was in the regulation of the saloons, and later the pool-halls; they were the centers of social and political life of some of the aldermen's friends.

The waste that unquestionably existed was a result of the handling of important work intermittently by mediocre individuals through a cumbersome and involved procedure. The city clerk-comptroller, the treasurer, and the attorney were elected; the street commissioner and the city engineer were appointed by the council; the fire and police commission, the water board, and the board of health were appointed by the mayor. The mayor had little power; the council committees and the independent boards were in control of administration.

The council's procedure was involved and painfully slow. Individual bills, even those of less than a dollar, were put on record in the minutes of the council twice before final approval. Each matter under discussion was referred by resolution to some administrative official, board, or committee chairman for action, or perhaps for consideration and report. Petty matters called for debate, discussion, and formal resolution; the minutes record that "Alderman Dulin moved that the chairman of the police committee see that the traffic policeman on the corner of Main and Milwaukee Streets be equipped with a traffic policeman's whistle," and that the motion was duly carried. Long squabbles over salary scales, with protests and petitions from employees and their friends pouring in, were matters of course as fiscal plans were debated. With all this attention to detail, there was no one who had enough power and foresight to carry out any long-term program of public works or service.

In this maze of procedure, those aldermen were most influential who looked most carefully to the welfare of their wards, and who knew most thoroughly the intricate rules of the game. By virtue of long experience and hard work, Mr. Dulin became chairman of the highway, purchasing, and license committees, and was recognized as political boss of the city.

Because the mayor, who by law was the executive head of the govern-ment, was not a full-time official, it fell to the elected clerk to accomplish what little coordination was possible in the absence of actual authority. His work was severely restricted by the delegation of petty administrative details to individual aldermen or committees and the necessity of running for office.

The aldermanic leaders made some effort to fall in line with the movement toward business progress that was prevalent at the time, al-though they had denounced the preceding commission government as the tool of the Commercial Club, the predecessor of the Chamber of Com-merce. Mayor Welsh was elected on a reluctant promise of more streets and municipal progress. He acquiesced in the abandonment of partisan elections when the aldermanic form returned. He supported a school-bond proposition that was a burning issue of 1919; the Chamber of Com-merce had proclaimed that the General Motors and Samson Tractor companies intended to expand their local factories only if more schools were built. His administration employed John Nolen, a nationally known city planner, to make a plan for Janesville. Thus Mr. Welsh won a majority in the fashionable Third Ward and the temporary support of the influential *Janesville Gazette.*

But the business leaders of the city remained unsatisfied. J. K. Jensen, chairman of the industrial development committee of the Chamber of Commerce, and A. J. Gibbons, a furniture manufacturer, were elected as aldermen from the Third Ward in 1923, and the *Gazette* editorially hailed the representation of businessmen "with large interests" in city affairs.

Those dissatisfied with the aldermanic form of government in 1922 belonged substantially to the same groups that had disliked it in 1912: the business and professional men, and the Protestant church groups that wanted more strict regulation of public morals. But since 1912 they had added a powerful supporting block of votes, those of the organized women's groups of the city. The women of the city, only recently en-franchised, fell in line with the spirit of business and municipal progress. The women voted by more than four to one for the school-bond issue of 1919, which men's votes supported by less than two to one. A League of Women Voters was organized and soon became an influential force.

The Charter Campaign

The movement for city manager government was led by sub-stantially the same groups, and by some of the same individuals, who had

been prominent in working for commission government ten years earlier.
A. J. Gibbons, one of the businessmen on the council, and William H.
Dougherty, who had been city attorney under the commission, were
among those who participated in both reform campaigns.

The city manager movement began in Janesville when the two business leaders who had won places in the council, disgusted with their associates and their methods of administration, talked over methods of reform with two or three other individuals of influence. Stephen Bolles, the
new editor of the *Gazette*, brought from other cities an acquaintance
with municipal government and its latest variations. News came from
Kenosha of the inauguration there of C. M. Osborn as city manager, and
he was asked to describe the manager plan to leading citizens of Janesville. Gaylord Cummin, formerly city manager of Jackson, Michigan, was
brought from the Institute for Public Service in New York to provide
ammunition for the campaign that the reformers planned. Carefully dis-
guising his purpose, he interviewed city officials and gathered information. His denunciatory but uncritical findings were published in a series of
articles spread in large type over the front page of the *Gazette*, which
summarized the municipality's troubles as a "general 'Don't Care' attitude
of the department heads coupled with ignorance and peanut politics."

The essential features of the city manager plan, in the minds of its
leading proponents, were election at large and a small number of councilmen with overlapping terms to serve without pay. (The aldermen had
received a small salary.) These provisions, it was felt, would break the
power of those who had maintained influence in local politics by working
for their individual neighborhoods.

The *Gazette* led the campaign for the manager plan. For three
months before the election, a paragraph in its masthead demanded managerial government for Janesville. A series of editorials attacked aldermanic government, and demanded the manager plan. Emphasis in the
news columns on the petty faults of the city government provided further
campaign publicity.

The personal work of electioneering was handled, however, by a
group of women's organizations. The League of Women Voters, the
Women's History Club, and the Philomathian Literary Club joined to set
up the Women's Committee for City Management. This organization
brought Walter J. Millard of the National Municipal League to explain to
them the theory of city manager government, and sent to the University
of Wisconsin for educational material. An extensive newspaper advertising campaign was carried on over its signature. A special appeal was
made to the workingman, pointing out that organized labor in other cities
was in favor of city manager government.

The women's participation led to charges that the city manager movement was a blue-law movement, which embarrassed the campaigners considerably in the lower income neighborhoods. The women's work was effective, however, for it split the working-class and the Catholic vote.

The opposition was organized by a "Citizens' Committee," which was supported by Mr. Dulin and all other members of the council except Messrs. Jensen and Gibbons, both of the Third Ward. The old political leaders managed to hold the Fourth and Fifth Wards, the neighborhoods of workingmen on the west side of the river, by about two to one. But the upper-class neighborhoods, especially in the two most well-to-do wards, voted even more heavily in favor of the city manager plan, as embodied in the optional provisions of the state law, and thus carried it by 3,098 to 2,387 votes.

No one considered that the fight was over then. The Citizens' Personal Campaign Committee was formed to support the candidates chosen by those who had put city manager government into effect. Its secretary was the man who had been city clerk under the commission government. A nominating committee chose six men and one woman (a leader in Catholic women's work) and the choices were ratified in a Sunday afternoon mass meeting at the Y.M.C.A. Five incumbent aldermen were on an opposition ticket of seven supported by the People's Independent Voters' League, an organization (said the *Gazette*) that Mrs. Dulin set up in order to make Mayor Welsh city manager. This organization held its meeting in St. Patrick's School, the parochial school.

The adoption of the city manager plan, the *Gazette* proclaimed, had been a "repudiation of the Mayor of Janesville, clear, clean, and unmistakable . . . a repudiation of J. J. Dulin and his kind of government. . . . The people of Janesville face a conspiracy," it warned, in the effort of Mr. Dulin to retain power. The "conspiracy," if it deserved the name, was foiled by the election of the entire ticket of the Citizens' Personal Campaign Committee.

City Manager Government

Since the election of the first ticket of supporters of the manager plan, the council has been controlled by members nominated and elected by the business and professional men who are generally considered to be the civic leaders of Janesville—the men who established the manager plan and their successors. Four successive organizations, each of the first three of which lasted only one campaign, have been formed by this group to keep representatives of the civic leadership of the city in control of the council. The group that has worked together through these years is a nameless and unorganized one—merely a few influential men motivated by a common purpose. Among them at present are the editor of the newspaper, the president of a local bank, a Republican national committeeman, a lawyer who was city attorney under commission government and later worked with General Motors Corporation, a president of the Kiwanis Club, and the lawyer who was city attorney from 1918 to 1931. In working for a community purpose rather than for individual privilege, their objective has been twofold: First, to keep the people of Janesville loyal to those business and professional men who are their civic leaders, thus preventing them from being led by ward politicians or labor organizers; second, to keep up their support of the city manager and the city manager plan.

Since Janesville councilmen are elected for two-year overlapping terms, there is an election each spring. Sixteen elections have been held since the manager plan went into effect. The strength and unity of the local civic leadership, and the popularity of the city manager and his government are shown by the fact that in seven elections, five of them consecutive (from 1928 through 1932), there was no opposition whatever to the candidates chosen by the civic leadership; in two other elections the opposition was insignificant; in three others it was scattered and unorganized; and in only four elections have organized opposition tickets appeared.

The men who have been nominated and elected to the council by this group have been professional men and business proprietors or executives, several of them from the city's largest industries. Almost without exception they have been members of the "socially acceptable" classes. From 1923 to 1936 the civic leaders' group elected a woman to the council, first Mrs. Emma Manning, then Mrs. Addie Fitzgerald, each a president of the Catholic Women's Club. Both were helpful in attracting the support of Catholic women's organizations, including, of course, many of the workingmen's wives. Except for them, the council has been predominantly Protestant. The political support of the women's organizations of the city, several of which carry on social work as agencies of the municipality, has been extremely helpful to the administration leaders.

The first three opposition tickets (1923, 1925, 1926) were led by men connected with the previous forms of government, dissatisfied with the way in which civic leaders had taken their political careers away from them, or with the new policies in municipal affairs. The only successful one was in 1925, when an opposition ticket was elected, winning every ward and polling about twice as many votes as the "Business and

Harmony," or incumbents', ticket. By winning all of the four places that fell vacant that year, the opposition gained a bare majority on the council. This election and the events immediately after are of considerable significance in Janesville's political history.

There were two types of issues responsible for the repudiation of the incumbents in 1925. The first was the extensive paving program which the government had undertaken, and the way in which it was handled. Ervin J. Sartell, who had served as city clerk from 1920 until 1924, was one of the four opposition candidates. He denounced the fact that property owners were being forced to pay through special assessments for the paving of intersections, formerly paid for by the city out of the general fund. He also claimed that the manager was charging too much against the special assessment fund for engineering and inspection services furnished by city employees, and accordingly demanded a considerable rebate on the assessments. These charges were probably not understood by one-tenth of those with whom they carried weight, but they were effective because the paving program, undertaken without much preparatory discussion by the council, was disliked by a great many people who objected to paying special assessments for public improvements.

The second, and more understandable, issue was a veiled dissatisfaction with the new manager form of government. The opposition candidates swore fidelity to the manager plan in speaking before the League of Women Voters but advocated reducing the manager's salary. This salary issue has been for fifteen years the most obvious one on which to appeal to the workingman's vote of Janesville, where it is hard to convince any man on hourly wages that his public servant is worth seven or eight thousand dollars a year.

On the ticket with Mr. Sartell was another man with political experience under the old regime, Henry C. Klein. He had been in the city fire department for twenty-nine years and, after serving as fire chief for several years, had retired on a pension in 1919 and opened a battery shop. He then ran twice for the office of mayor, and lost both races to Mayor Welsh. W. E. Evenson, a travelling salesman, and Robert R. Conway, a bank cashier, completed the ticket. Mr. Conway was secretary of the Elks Club, and Mr. Sartell had held the same position. This was the organization of which Mayor Welsh had been Exalted Ruler, and of which Mr. Traxler, the city manager, became a member soon after the election of Messrs. Conway and Sartell. Mr. Conway was more moderate than his associates on the council. He refused to vote with them for more than a 20 per cent rebate of paving assessments, accepting that figure as a compromise. He refused to vote to cut the manager's salary from $7,200 to $4,500, and forced his associates to agree to a salary of $5,000.

While the salary-cut ordinance was going through its three readings, it was made a vital issue in local politics. The *Gazette* and the administration minority charged that it was an underhanded blow at the manager plan and a means of getting rid of the manager. Two unofficial straw votes were conducted by the council, and the difference in their results indicated the cleavage in local sentiment. In one, the ballots were sent to the large taxpayers of the city, to be returned with signatures. In this vote, the count was ninety-three to nine against the salary cut. In the other, secret ballots were sent to names chosen at random from the poll lists, and the vote was seventy-five to fifty-eight in favor of the salary cut.

Then, on the third reading of the ordinance, Mr. Conway yielded to overwhelming social pressure and changed his vote, providing a bare majority against the salary cut. He explained his action by saying that the manager had told him that he would resign if the ordinance were passed. This was the crisis in the history of manager government in Janesville, and whether the manager was bluffing or not the city will probably never know.

When an opposition ticket was beaten in 1926, the threat from the old-fashioned ward leaders against the control of the council by the city's civic leaders was ended. (Messrs. Klein and Evenson were accepted by the civic leaders' forces in spite of Mr. Klein's attitude of belligerent independence, and they still serve on the council.) Then for six years there was no threat to the incumbents, who virtually coopted members as individuals retired.

A few scattered candidates offered opposition in 1933 that was insignificant but for one fact: at the very bottom of the list, with only 508 votes, was the secretary of the Central Labor Union. Two years then passed with uncontested elections, and in 1936 Janesville's civic leaders awoke at the end of a campaign to discover that the face of municipal politics had changed: Waldo Luchsinger, the organizer and first president of the local United Automobile Workers, a C.I.O. union, was elected to the council with Frank Britt, a labor sympathizer, and Henry Klein, who was a large enough property owner to be accepted as safe by the administration, and cantankerous enough to win the votes of labor. Two incumbents were defeated: Mrs. Fitzgerald, who had been her ticket's appeal for the votes of the Catholic women, and Frank Fitzpatrick, the Chevrolet plant manager, the last of General Motors' three representatives on the council. Mr. Fitzpatrick, who lost to Janesville's first C.I.O. candidate, had been considered responsible for a "speed up" system that the Chevrolet plant workers detested.

Civic leaders had been caught unprepared in this election, but they were ready the next spring. The Public Relations League, an organization formed by business and professional people of the town to settle the General Motors strike, was continued as an organization to elect civic leaders and to defeat the bid of labor and labor sympathizers to control the council. It was successful in 1937 and again in 1938, when the Non-Partisan Labor League entered a ticket that showed how the old ward-politician opposition had become transformed into a labor opposition. The Labor League renominated Mr. Luchsinger, and put on the ticket with him Mark Egbert, vice-president of the U.A.W. local, and J. J. Dulin, the old aldermanic leader, who had retained his neighborhood following.

The Public Relations League was willing in 1938 to endorse Mr. Klein, in spite of his obstructive tactics in council meetings. He delights in conspicuous independence, and enjoys the prestige and ceremony of public meetings. Throughout his councilmanic career, his battery shop has been the meeting-place for all those with grievances against the administration, and he has championed their causes constantly, vociferously, and inconsistently. Mr. Luchsinger, on the other hand, had proved to be a discriminating and sensible councilman, whose attitude was that labor had no particular grievance or desire to change municipal policy, but was merely determined to have its proper representation. But Mr. Luchsinger's affiliation with the C.I.O. was too much for the Public Relations League, originally a strike-settling agency, to swallow. The influence of General Motors' representatives blocked the attempt of the moderates to endorse him, and Clayton Orcutt, personnel manager of the Fisher Body plant, was nominated—and was the only Public Relations League candidate who lost, while Mr. Luchsinger alone among the Labor League candidates was elected.

This election made the Public Relations League leaders rejoice over election at large. J. J. Dulin carried his ward, but was defeated by the other voting districts in the councilmanic election at large. In the simultaneous election of county supervisors, each of whom is elected by a ward. Labor League candidates won in six of the city's fourteen wards—wards Nine to Fourteen, on the south and west sides of the city, the former strongholds of the ward leaders. Every contested municipal election in Janesville's history since 1910 has shown this general clevage between the two sides of the river—the two social spheres of the city.

These two parts of Janesville have divided, throughout the city's experience with city manager government, on three general issues. One has arisen now and then since 1923: how much money is an expert administrator worth to a municipality? On this question, the business and professional classes have favored a relatively high salary for the manager, the working classes, a relatively low one.

A second issue was important from 1923 through 1926: how far should Janesville go toward adopting, and paying for, new municipal works and services—streets, storm sewers, parks, health service, and the like? During these years it was in general the business and professional groups that demanded, and the workingmen's groups or their ward leaders that opposed this kind of civic progress; the well-to-do wanted an extension of municipal functions in order to put Janesville on the map as a progressive city, and demanded expert administration as a means to that end, while the poor resented paying taxes to gratify needs that they had never known, and disliked the corollary encroachment of professional administration on the amateur politics that had been their means of self-expression. This issue was settled a decade ago, as the small taxpayers came to think of paved streets and municipal golf courses as their natural rights.

Since Janesville's era of uncontested elections ended with the depression, a third issue has arisen: how much influence in local affairs shall organized labor share with the business and civic leaders who think of themselves as the natural rulers of Janesville? This issue has not been settled.*

B. EVALUATIONS OF MUNICIPAL REFORM

23. The Council-Manager Plan

HAROLD A. STONE, DON K. PRICE, AND KATHRYN H. STONE

The leading advocates of the city manager plan in nearly every city had a general purpose in common: to have the city government devote its energies more effectively toward getting work done for the community and toward wasting less of its money and effort on incidental or factional purposes. To achieve their purpose, they proposed three ideas—the three principal political ideas that characterized the city

* Over twenty years after this study was published, Janesville voted to abandon the manager plan and return to mayor-council government. But that is another story, and one which is atypical for the many cities which have experienced council-manager government.

Reprinted from *City Manager Government in the United States* (Chicago: Public Administration Service, 1940), pp. 236–56 by permission of the publisher.

manager movement. Each of these ideas was reflected or embodied in one of the three fundamental principles of the city manager form of government.

First, there was the idea that most capable and public-spirited citizens should serve on the governing body as representatives of the city at large, to determine policies for the benefit of the community as a whole, rather than for any party, faction, or neighborhood. This idea was embodied in the nonpartisan ballot and in the system of election at large of a small council.

Second, there was the idea that municipal administration should be delegated to a thoroughly competent, trained executive, who should get and hold his job on his executive ability alone and should be given a status and salary comparable to that of an executive in charge of a private corporation. This idea was embodied in the concentration of administrative authority in the city manager.

Third, there was the idea that the voters should hold only the councilmen politically responsible and should give the city manager a status of permanence and neutrality in political controversy. This idea was embodied in the unification of powers in the council as a body comprising the only elected officials in the city government.

No matter how many different immediate objectives characterized the campaigns for city manager government, the city manager movement was motivated by these ideas. In cities that were accustomed to partisan patronage, the advocates of the city manager plan expressed them in terms of a crusading appeal for the elimination of partisan influence in municipal administration and for an increase in the influence of technical experts. In other cities there was no such public appeal; members of the governing body simply decided to get a city manager in order to get their job done better. In other words, the objectives of the city manager movement were pretty much the same in all these cities, although its advocates had to adapt their tactics to different local conditions. . . .

The cities in which the possibilities of the new form of government were not fully realized were those in which the ideas of the city manager movement came into conflict with traditional political ideas. In such cities some of these ideas that contributed to the reaction against the city manager movement were held by leading advocates of the city manager plan. This reaction, which developed several years after the establishment of the plan in most of the so-called Machine-Ridden and Faction-Ridden cities . . . was by no means caused entirely by the selfish material interests of professional politicians. The reaction was instigated by such politicians in some cities, but not in all of them. Nevertheless, in all cities in these two groups the success of the reaction depended on popular support, which could be organized only where the reaction was in harmony with popular political ideas—ideas which the reader, according to his point of view, many call either ideals or prejudices.

Improvement in Political Leadership

The adoption of the city manager plan brought about improvements in the political leadership of municipalities in two ways. First, it broadened the possibilities of municipal politics. Second, it heightened the prestige of the councilmanic office and thus led men of greater ability and reputation to be willing to serve as councilmen.

The first type of improvement came about in all groups of cities. In a municipal organization that included no administrators of ability and performed none but the minimum routine functions, the political leader at best was a dignified but negative participant; at worst he was a grafter. An effective organization under an expert manager, on the other hand, broadened the political leader's scope; he could promote more positive municipal policies because their effective execution had become a possibility.

This contrast is stated in extreme terms, but the general improvement in administrative machinery under the city manager plan certainly changed the function of the political leader to some extent in nearly every community, no matter what its former political tradition. In Lynchburg the councilmen gave less time to detailed supervision of public works and to parliamentary red tape and were considering city planning and cooperation with the state municipal league; in Austin they forgot the old neighborhood factionalism and promoted housing projects in Mexican districts; in Rochester they paid less attention to patronage and more to transportation facilities and to the industrial development of the city.

In the increase in the prestige of the councilmanic office and in the improvement in the ability and the reputation of councilmen the changes were less uniform. Some cities that adopted the manager plan had long been accustomed to electing the community leaders of the greatest prestige and public spirit to their governing bodies, and the change in the form of government did not affect this habit. In these cities, a councilmanic election was not a contest between factions that were interested either in patronage or in special policies. It was an expression by the community of confidence in its leaders, who served for the prestige of the office and from a sense of civic responsibility rather than from a desire to further the interest of any group. But no one group—economic, religious, or political—maintained a monopoly on municipal affairs. Voters, in choosing councilmen, thought more of the general prestige of candidates in the community than of their membership in any faction. Councilmen, as a result, tended to think more of the community as a whole and less of factional interests in making their decisions. . . .

Assumptions Underlying the Theory of Group Representation

The whole idea of group representation depends upon certain assumptions that are not truly applicable to city government and overlooks what is usually the most important issue of municipal politics. It assumes that the policy determined by the council will depend more on what groups or factions the councilmen belong to than on how much public spirit and intelligence the councilmen have. A councilman elected by the votes of a neighborhood of underprivileged citizens, according to this theory, should be more active in promoting that neighborhood's welfare than a councilman elected at large or by some other group of voters. In the cities covered by this survey, however, real changes in municipal policy were rarely brought about by competition among self-interested political groups. The most conspicuous changes were not made by representatives acting on mandates from a group of their constituents that stood to benefit by the new policies; on the contrary, they were made by leaders of the community as a whole, acting out of public spirit on the proposals of a trained administrator. For example, there were the inaugurations of the comprehensive health, recreation, and welfare programs in Dayton, in Austin, and in Janesville. These programs were established on the recommendations of city managers by councilmen, most of whom were well-to-do and important businessmen, in the face of bitter political attacks from the traditional political leaders of the lower-income neighborhoods, the very neighborhoods that needed the new programs most.

The idea that various groups ought to have representatives on the council to look after their interests overlooks what is usually the most important issue of municipal politics. In many cities the greatest issue, and the greatest conflict of interests, was between those who supported a system of partisan patronage and those who demanded impartial administration. The interests of any social or economic group may often be more greatly affected by the quality of administration of noncontroversial municipal policies than by the decision—one way or the other—of the controversial issues. The competition of municipal political factions did little in these cities to bring about democratic control of policies. On the other hand, it did a great deal to destroy the prestige of local government and to subordinate its fundamental purpose of community services to factional interests. The idea of group or neighborhood representation was one of the great handicaps to the election of public-spirited representatives for the city as a whole under the city manager plan.

Improvement in the Prestige of Administration

Municipal administration in many of these cities, regardless of the nature of their politics, had a low reputation before the adoption of the city manager plan. In some cities those who administered the government were not concerned primarily with the services that it was rendering but with doing favors for their friends or furthering the interests of their political factions; the purpose of administration was obscured by patronage and campaign activity. In other cities, those in which there was no patronage or political favoritism, there was an assumption that municipal affairs had to be managed according to less strict and efficient standards than other institutions in the community and that a public official had to restrict himself to routine work to avoid getting into political controversy.

By concentrating administrative authority in a single official appointed for an indefinite term, the city manager plan made possible an improvement in the reputation, the purpose, and the continuity of municipal administration. This possibility was achieved most thoroughly in the cities that had maintained a high level of political leadership. The new chief executive, the city manager, was generally expected to devote himself to administrative interests, to improve the efficiency of the administration, and to propose new techniques for getting the work done. By general agreement among the political leaders he was given a status of prestige, permanence, and political neutrality. This status enabled him to act as a community leader and to be highly influential in questions of policy; so long as the council could have the last word on any proposal that he might make, it wanted him to take the initiative.

In these cities—described . . . as Community-Governed cities—the local tradition had generally kept politics out of the administration and had provided for virtually permanent administrative tenure. The change that the city manager plan brought about was to make it possible for an administrative officer to take the initiative in proposing new municipal policies. The city manager, unlike previously appointed officials, could be a leader in the community.

The Manager as Community Leader

A clear distinction must be made between the terms, "community leadership" and "political leadership." Community leadership covers such activities as taking part in the work of service clubs, charitable organizations, churches, and civic affairs in general. It includes explaining the work of the city government, and proposing new policies for it, to the members of the council and the general public, either in private conversation or by public speaking. It includes negotiation with private citizens and community organizations in order to get them to support particular aspects of the work of the city government. With the approval of the council community leadership may include speaking in a campaign for a referendum on a bond issue, if the question at stake is not identified with factional interests or a factional disagreement.

On the other hand, it does not include participation in any campaign for the election or the recall of councilmen, and it does not include promoting any policy by offering special favors or threatening political opposition or punishment. Most certainly it excludes an appeal by the manager to the voters over the heads of the councilmen.

It is generally impossible for a city manager to escape being a leader in matters of policy, for it is an essential part of his administrative job to make recommendations. The most important municipal policy is embodied in the budget, and the city manager, of course, must prepare and propose the budget. The city manager's recommendation on an important policy, even if he makes it in an executive session of the council, is usually a matter of common knowledge.

Some managers in these Community-Governed cities deferred to the councilmen by refraining from speaking in public and made their proposals before committees of the council and before small groups of private citizens. But others proposed policies freely, and with the council's consent spoke in favor of those policies before civic organizations and at public meetings. They did not, of course, take part in councilmanic campaigns and their leadership did not involve them in political controversy; it heightened the influence of administrative considerations without endangering the managers' tenure of office.

In other words, the city manager applied his expert point of view to controversial issues without unnecessarily offending those who disliked his proposals. He was careful to give the general impression that his recommendations were always controlled by his expert knowledge and professional interest, never by selfish considerations or political friendships. He never suggested that candidates should be elected to the council or defeated for their views on his recommendations, nor did he ask a councilman to support his proposals for personal or factional reasons. Furthermore, he maintained the support of the councilmen and avoided offending councilmanic candidates by making it clear that he was willing to administer any policy that the council might determine.

The change in the status of administration that he brought about was not so much to make it nonpolitical—it had generally been that —but to make it a positive and vital force. Previous administrative officials—when there had been any—had tended to look on every municipal action as a matter to decide according to its legal or clerical or parliamentary aspects. The city manager was more concerned with getting things done. . . .

Primary Importance of the Council

The council is . . . of primary importance in the operation of the city manager plan. It is responsible for administration as well as for policies, for the city manager can do nothing unless the council will delegate adequate authority to him. Actually the council delegates to the city manager authority over the functions that are his according to law or charter; he exercises his authority by grace, not by right.

Despite these apparently obvious facts, the advocates of the city manager plan, in those cities where its adoption involved a sharp change in political practices, put faith in the city manager, in the form of government, and especially in those charter provisions that prohibited the council from interfering with the city manager in his execution of specific powers and duties. Instead of recognizing the principle of unification of powers in the council and of making it clear to the voters that the council was to be wholly responsible for the administration of the city manager, the advocates of the city manager plan promised that the new charter would of itself bring about reforms by guaranteeing certain powers to the city manager. No reformers were more ineffective than those who tried to organize public opinion to protect city managers against interference by councilmen. When a majority of the council wanted good administration, it usually protected the city manager against a minority; when a majority wanted to interfere, it usually found a city manager who would cooperate with its interference.

The effort to bring about political reform by putting great emphasis

on the city manager and his powers under the charter was an effort
to apply the theory of checks and balances to the city manager plan
rather than to accept the principle of unification in the council of
powers and political responsibility. This effort was a handicap to the
city manager plan in three ways: it made the city manager more vulnerable to political attack, and it permitted community leaders to
deceive themselves into thinking that the city manager could take care
of the government without their participation in politics, and it opened
the system to attack as undemocratic. . . .

A proper relationship between the council and the city manager
is essential to good politics and good administration. Such a relationship depends, not on conformity with a charter, but on a free delegation of administrative authority regardless of legal provisions. A council
that wished to have city manager government did not, in some cities,
even have to have a charter; it could delegate powers formally by ordinance and informally by agreement with the city manager. If it had
a charter that assigned incomplete authority to the city manager, it
could make it work by giving the city manager more authority than
the charter definition of his powers called for. If it had a good charter,
it had to go beyond its provisions and give the city manager support
in a number of ways that the charter could not define, in order to
carry out its intent.

In all the talk about the concentration of administrative authority
in the city manager the other essential principle of the city manager
plan was nearly ignored: the unification of powers, which implies
the concentration of political responsibility, even for administration,
in the council. When the voters complied with this principle, chose
councilmen for their leadership and character, and expected them to
make independent decisions on questions of policy, the councilmen
were apt to delegate administrative authority to the city manager. The
council, and the council alone, had to be held politically responsible
by the voters if a city was to build up a tradition that the administration must not be the football of politics.

When the voters made a habit of choosing councilmen primarily
either to get rid of a particular city manager or to keep him in office,
either to diminish the manager's authority or to support it, they made
administration a political issue. Whenever the voters elected councilmen primarily to keep a competent professional city manager in office,
they kept politics out of the administration, an accomplishment which
in some cities was a remarkable one; on the other hand, they failed to

keep the administration out of politics, because they made the city manager the symbol of controversy and because they made administrative continuity dependent on the outcome of political campaigns.

"The city manager plan," as one of the early city managers said, "is broader than any charter; it is more simple than any charter can be made." The extent of its success in each city depended upon the community's acceptance of its general purpose and of its fundamental political ideas—the purpose that the city government should devote its energies more effectively to getting its work done and the ideas that it would do so if the city elected its best leaders to the council on a nonpartisan basis, if the council delegated administrative authority to a city manager, and if all concerned respected the distinction between politics and administration.

24. The Manager is a Politician

KARL A. BOSWORTH

Upper governmental bureaucrats everywhere live under the imperative of thinking of the continued justification of the activities of their bureaucracies. What are the possible ways of modifying programs and methods? How appealing to whom are the alternatives? What are the dangers to be avoided? Are the achievements impressive? Is there a firm and possibly growing body of public awareness, satisfaction, and support? These and similar considerations haunt the thoughts of the prudent governmental officer. What he does with these thoughts may depend upon the form of government and political system within which the officer works.

Council-manager government, by placing the manager directly in public view, accentuates public interest in how this kind of bureaucrat operates as a political leader. Not only is he inevitably in public view, but the range of his operations is broad, and the fate of his community may be determined in part by the public goals his thoughts lead him to set for his government. Recent awareness of the broad roles in policy leadership admitted by some city managers has raised the question as to whether council-manager government is developing now as an acceptable political system. In other words, given this bent, is it still a

Reprinted from *Public Administration Review*, XVIII (Summer 1958), pp. 216–22 by permission of the author and the publisher. Author's footnotes revised. Mr. Bosworth is a professor of political science at the University of Connecticut.

popular government or is there a danger that an undemocratic political system is being contrived?

It is the view here that the relatively recent willingness of city managers to admit generally that they are community leaders does not reflect a marked change in their role. City managers, abetted particularly by the International City Managers' Association, have been concerned about the image of themselves presented to the public. The role of the manager has been, after all, in the process of being structured; and the fortunes of the managers and the Association depended upon public acceptance of a described role.

The description of the role as it affects policy leadership has varied from time to time and place to place. Looking at three "styles" of city managers as these roles have been described will, I think, point up the relatively minor nature of the recent changes. One should not think of these "styles" as a historical series. Although some case might be made for a historical trend, the emphasis here is on the presence of policy initiating elements in all the styles of manager that have been described.[1]

The Administrator Manager

One stylized view of the city manager has so sought to emphasize his role in internal administration as to leave no room for policy initiative. In this view, he just carries out administrative duties such as hiring, setting up the tasks, reviewing the work, and looking for ways of getting more production from the same input or the same production from less input. Of course he also makes up the budget, and therein, if nowhere else, he is in politics.

A manager could, and a few have tried to, provide a council with budget estimates in which there was no firm proposal but rather a pricing of amounts of programs with supplementary programs priced in a fashion so that the council could buy as much or as little as it chooses. But the firm, balanced budget is the rule, and in such a proposal the manager says to the tax-saver that the city "needs" stated amounts for various programs and to the spender that the city "can get by" on the stated totals. The saver must find some program from which he can make deductions, if he would tinker with the proposal, while the spender has either to do the same or to propose the raising of taxes. Even if a manager has had budgetary guidance from the council, he cannot ordinarily escape some public responsibility for his proposed budget: "He didn't include anything new for us," or "They got nearly everything they wanted." Whether such statements emanate from employees or from others interested in programs, they are the essence of politics.

Let us not depreciate the manager's role as an internal administrator, for that is one of the plan's principal justifications. However, even in this role the administrator-manager is likely to set goals whose achievement may impress people with the desirability of the plan and the ability of the manager; good politics, in other words. Short run goals may include the rewriting of some of the city's contracts for services or insurance with a view toward savings or improved service or coverage. These can be matters of policy as well as administration, and if one of the changes proves to be controversial, this is politics. A longer run goal may be the transformation of a mediocre department into a technically proficient one—a change, if accomplished, resulting in changes in the quality of the services and almost unavoidably in the quality and kinds of service. The effective city policy has changed whether the change has been noticed or not.

It is difficult not to imagine our administrator hearing of state legislation which compels or allows the city council to make some new decision and transmitting this information to the council, along with administrative advice and the news about other cities initiating a service locally unknown; but these items may, if desired, be saved for the next "style" of city manager.

The Policy Researcher and Manager

The manager may have learned that all policy issues have their administrative aspects, and that he, as administrative expert, should advise the council on the ramifications of their proposals, including the budgetary consequences. It is likely, further, that in comparison with council members, the manager is highly informed about municipal affairs and about sources of municipal information and how to mine these sources. The council will insist that the manager enlighten their deliberations.

In this role, the manager who is also a policy researcher will contrive to know about what is coming up in a council meeting from sources other than his desk so that he can be somewhat prepared with relevant information. He will further seek to school the council to refer to him for study and report nearly all issues which anyone wants seriously to consider. Councilmen, impressed with the manager's expertise and concerned with their own responsibilities, fall readily into the pattern of asking his assistance.

It should be noted that these policy proposals may come from anywhere: councilmen, other individuals and organizations in the community, or the manager. It has long been accepted that managers should bring overt policy ideas to the council. This was implicit in the manager's presumed expertise in municipal affairs. He had had more opportunity than the council to learn about alternative and supplementary municipal services or regulations, and he could be expected to give attention to the channels of current municipal information.

The standard role of managers, in fact, goes well beyond the passive or reactive patterns suggested above. The manager has been expected, like any good mayor, to study the problems, programs, and facilities of *his* city and to make proposals to the council on these matters. Any perusal of the several editions of *The Technique of Municipal Administration,* including chapters devoted to administrative research, planning, and particularly programing, shows that the International City Managers' Association has been hoping for a strong measure of city-statesmanship in its managers. The current word is that it is one of the responsibilities of the manager to see that issues of the maintenance, discontinuance, and initiation of program elements be systematically reviewed by the legislative body. It is, of course, official dogma that the manager be in a position to participate in long-term planning as well as the planning of programs for current operations.

The researcher-manager acknowledges all the while that he is the council's man. He works for the council. He studies the proposals they refer to him and reports to the council. He initiates policy studies for presentation to the council. He advises the council; warns it and even argues with its members. Others may read or listen, but the role is structured in relation to the representative body. He is aware of the community, but he works for the council. They hired him; he works for them; they are responsible for the decisions.

Although our manager is the council's man, he gives attention to public relations. He seeks to have the city avoid offending the public unnecessarily. He wants all elements of the administration to present an appearance of courtesy, consideration, and effective operation. He seeks through news channels and reports to get city accomplishments told to the public. Many managers also seek ways to get some communication from the public. Systems for handling complaints aid the manager in gauging public expectations as well as in reviewing operations. And managers everywhere explain to publics the council-manager form of government, an inevitably self-referring form of communication.

It may be important to note two models of this researcher-manager style, differentiated by their policy presentations. One seeks to emphasize factual materials, stating alternative policies and predicting the consequences of following each. He seeks to avoid making recommendations. The other model, perhaps at the council's insistence, or perhaps by personal inclination, presents his policy proposals as recommendations, with reasoned factual support but a minimum of "confusing alternatives." This could be an important enough difference to merit thinking of the recommender as a separate style of manager. However, the manager with facts and alternatives does make recommendations—as in his budget. And he will surely weigh the values of his council and community in considering alternatives to present to the council. Interest in economy of time and of effort in explanation will lead even the cautious manager to pre-judge a great many policy issues for council.

The Community Leader and Manager

Throughout the history of the movement, some city managers have ventured into overt community leadership in the settlement of public problems. Through the same period, some students and proponents of the plan have feared that the role of active policy leadership would bring discredit to the form of government. Although the argument has never terminated, the common doctrine has described the manager in clear and continuous subordination to council, expressing his activist political inclinations upon and through council. A minor variation would include the mayor as an alternate in the intermediate role.

In the last ten years, however, there have been numbers of instances in which managers have admitted or proclaimed the broader role for themselves, and there is now a common doctrine of valid, if limited, manager initiative in policy formation. Different ones would draw the limitations variously, so the picture of this manager is less precise.

Even the latest edition of *The Technique of Municipal Administration* states that "The city manager is free to act as a community leader in the great majority of municipal policies which do not involve political controversies."[2] The 1958 edition also gives what may be the key to the newly described role:

"A manager can often serve effectively as a community leader without heading a committee or taking direct leadership in civic programs. By searching out and discovering the many real leaders existing in the community, interesting them in new improvements for the community, and keeping them supplied with new ideas and encouraging them to work together, he can achieve far more than by direct leadership of his own."[3]

Managers are thus expected to study the informal power structures of their communities and to use the persons in these channels of influence in so far as they will cooperate to achieve the managers' goals. This may be simply a more candid expression of what experienced managers have commonly done or it may emerge from a more sophisticated perception of the distribution of influence. In any case, relevant power may rest elsewhere than in the council and the managers are seeking to use it.

What are other characteristics of this style of manager? He accepts without question the role of city emissary to state and federal government organs, including legislative committees, to state and national professional and civic associations, and to other municipal governments. To some he will express the city's point of view and with others he may negotiate for his city.

He will pay particular attention to all organized groups in his community, partially as a means of making the acquaintance of the natural leaders of these groups. "It is the manager's job to provide facts, offer counsel, encourage and tactfully to guide community groups in the planning of worth while improvements."[4] The telephone numbers of the executive directors of associations presuming to speak for the interests of commerce, health, welfare, education, industry, religion, labor, good government, and real estate, among others, ought to be readily at hand. These executives may include most of his cohorts outside his administrative team, for they and the manager may have adjacent goals as well as similar methods of operation.

He may seek to participate in the meetings of boards and commissions of his own government and, whenever possible, the meetings of boards of special districts covering his city. "Personal contacts by the manager with various county officials open the door for unannounced leadership."[5]

When he has acquired acceptance in the community power structure, his opportunities for influence will broaden and he is likely to be consulted by groups making plans for any segment of the community. "In this concept a manager can and should deal with political parties on much the same basis as other interest groups. By avoiding any sign of preference or of dealing in personalities, a constructive influence can be had."[6]

What are the limits to this role? In one sense, the question is unanswerable, for managerial leadership "is a function of the instant, the setting, and the personalities."[7] In another sense, the community-leading manager is limited by his sense of appropriate behavior for his role as servant of the public. In yet another sense, although conscious of his power, the manager must remember that this power is a result of the

tolerance for him of the present city council and any council membership which may soon be elected. Any Tuesday night could be the last,
particularly the meeting following election of a new council. No one
suggests that managers should depart from their traditional watchful
obliviousness to these elections, although a few will admit that they
seek to develop possible candidates for the council among board and
commission membership.

Are There Serious Risks?

The city managers in any of these styles are not simply master mechanics of bureaucratic routine. Even our administrator-manager had better be able to sense the public pulse at budget time. And he may have
more difficulty predicting public satisfaction with his planned administrative achievements than does the community leader who feels free to try
his ideas on his local acquaintances. City managers, whichever role they
wish to follow, must seek to be among the best politicians in town,
for their work deals with the satisfaction of the wants of people who
have the privilege of discussing and voting about this work.

There are risks to popular government in council-manager cities.
A manager could convince his council and significant elements in the
community that only by his nonpartisan, objective mind can the city
problems of first, second, and third importance be identified and only
through his skilled, impartial analysis can the correct solutions be found.
The special risk here is that the values the manager uses in making these
decisions will reflect those of some limited group within the city rather
than values representative of his city.

There are risks that the administrative mind will successfully insist
that matters decided shall stay decided; that some newly proposed facility cannot be considered because it is not in the six-year capital outlay
plan; or that any undesired change in operation cannot be considered
because "we have a policy on that." Managers cannot be blamed for
hoping that complex issues may be considered fully, decided upon, and
that the decision stick. But it should not be the manager's discretion
which determines when decisions shall be reconsidered.

There are risks that a city's effective policies may be determined
increasingly through processes of negotiation between the city and other
governments, and with banks, utilities, development and other corporations, professional and business groups, and unions. If the manager is
an uninstructed ambassador in these negotiations, his negotiating premises partially may foreclose later consideration by his governing body

of alternative policies to those on which negotiation has been concluded.

These are real risks, but the risks of concentrated political leadership are not limited to council-manager cities. We are thus thrown back to the question of whether the values of managers will represent those of their communities and whether the local political and representative system will enforce some correspondence between popular wishes and governmental performance.

With regard to the political systems in council-manager cities, it may well be time to give thought to both informal and formal arrangements. If only stooges for some manager-supporting power combine are elected to the council, or if the system has made the ardent practice of political leadership unprofitable for all save the manager, or if the political system is incapable of expressing either discontent or contentment, or if a competing point of view to the government position cannot gain intelligent expression, it is time to be inventive. Perhaps there is need for a tax benefits association, with research staff, publicists, and publications, as well as a taxpayers' association. Perhaps it needs to be recognized that local parties are not going to develop and that charter groups are commonly going to confuse the public about the manager plan by asking the voter for support of the plan or the manager rather than support of a program of current policies. Perhaps thought needs to be given to findings suggesting that the nonpartisan election does not readily permit the registration of protest and perhaps permits no clear indication of assent. Perhaps it can be remembered that our national political parties are federations of state and local parties, that political parties have demonstrated a capacity to express ideals with some contrast, and that not only "nice people" but most of the talented ones who are aspirants for elective office are now accustomed to working in parties. Although we have had enough of faith in gimmicks, perhaps it is time to think of some system which will assure the representation of both parties on the council—where this is feasible—rather than no parties. If we want a political system which will diffuse the public attention now placed on the manager as political leader, perhaps we should ask the parties for assistance in providing public discussion from some variety of points of view. In any case, care needs to be given to the selection of a governing body. It may decide to govern; or in the absence of a manager it may have to govern for a time.

Governments depend greatly upon the values held by their important bureaucrats, and democratic governments depend on the capacity of these bureaucrats to sense the values of the communities the governments serve. There appears to be a basis for some belief that government employment, including the manager profession, attracts individuals whose values seem realizable in service to the public, in contrast to more dramatic or more pecuniarily promising roles. Helping to achieve public goals, to "do some good," is appealing. A stronger than usual ethical sense may be present. The training of these people is likely to be highly inculcating and reinforcing of values of personal integrity, fair play, just dealing, and appreciation for the rights and views of others.

The leadership of the International City Managers' Association has used its literature and conferences to seek to maintain in managers values consistent with their roles in democratic government. The injunctions to walk uprightly before men, compassionately before the weak, and humbly before the council stand out in the tracts. The personal moral tragedies among managers must be relatively few, judging from the small publicity of such events.

The problems with regard to the values of managers are in part concerned with their own values and in part concerned with those of the community. A risk is that as the manager becomes an upper-income citizen he will have preferences like an upper-income citizen, that he may learn to think like those with whom he lunches, or to think that no good idea could come from a source that has seemed not to appreciate him. These risks are probably no greater, however, in the administrative leader manager than in the other styles, for the leader in his varied community contacts must sometimes listen. The manager's staff and department heads may also be correctives for his preferences.

City manager dogma used to include the notion that the plan of government was appropriate only for those cities that wanted this form of government—cities whose people were willing to sacrifice some of the fun of political controversy and patronage for the benefits of a skilled management. Without exploring in detail the boundaries set by such criteria, it may be possible to suggest that cities in which there are very strong and deep disagreements over values test, perhaps beyond reasonable expectation, the possibility of any career general executive representing in his decisions the preferences of the community. Similarly, in communities where the relevant local government values shift, as a result of population mobility or new problems, or where the electoral system results in frequent changes in the value components of the community being represented, the capacity of any manager to sense and move with the changing dominant values of his community may be tested beyond his or the council's endurance. Can a particular manager shift back and forth in his preference system as the majority on the council shifts from labor to conservative inclinations? Probably in situations such as these one should not expect the manager to stand exposed and alone.

These calculations undoubtedly leave most of the suburbs, many independent cities, and some central cities appropriate grounds for the manager plan. And where managers are used, let us think of them as officers of general administrative direction *and* political leadership, for that is what they are.

Notes

1. Any attempt to think about the roles of managers must depend heavily upon the work of Harold A. Stone, Don K. Price, and Kathryn H. Stone (and others) done in the late 'thirties and, especially, their book, *City Manager Government in the United States* (Public Administration Service, 1940). They seemed to weigh more heavily than one would today the formal responsibility of the council, and they seemed to have had a clearer distinction between policy and administration than can be mustered today, but one cannot much project their insights.

2. Institute for Training in Municipal Administration, (4th ed., International City Managers' Association, 1958), p. 31. In a book of biblical character coming from many hands one should not expect all statements to agree with that quoted.

3. *Ibid.*, p. 32.

4. "Leadership Functions of the Manager," 37 *Public Management* (March 1955), pp. 50–54. This is a report prepared by a group of managers for discussion at the 40th Annual Conference of ICMA held December 5–8, 1954.

5. *Ibid.*, p. 52.

6. *Ibid.*, p. 54.

7. *Ibid.*, p. 53.

25. *Some General Characteristics of Nonpartisan*

Elections

CHARLES R. ADRIAN

Out of the middle-class businessman's "Efficiency and Economy Movement" that reached full strength in the second decade of the twentieth century came a series of innovations designed to place government "on a business basis" and to weaken the power of the political parties. The movement was inspired both by the example of the success of the corporate structure in trade and industry and by revulsion against the low standards of morality to be found in many sectors of political party

Reprinted from *American Political Science Review*, XLVI (September 1952), pp. 766–76 by permission of the author and the publisher. Author's footnotes abridged. Additional material added by the author. Mr. Adrian is a professor of political science and Director of the Institute for Community Development at Michigan State University.

activity around the turn of the century. The contemporary brand of politician had recently been exposed by the "muckrakers" and the prestige of the parties had reached a very low level.

Of the numerous ideas and mechanisms adopted as a result of the reform movement, one of the most unusual was that of election without party designation. Early in the twentieth century, under the theory that judges are neutral referees, not political officers, and that political activities should therefore be discouraged in the choosing of them, many communities initiated "nonpartisan" elections (the term that is usually applied) in the balloting for judicial posts. Next, using the argument that local officials should be businesslike administrators—there being no Republican way to pave a street and no Democratic way to lay a sewer— and that politics on the national scene have nothing in common with local problems, the movement spread to other offices. In a number of states various district, county, township, judicial, school, and city offices were made nonpartisan. And in 1913 largely as the result of a strange political accident, Minnesota not only made its county and municipal offices nonpartisan, but extended the principle to the election of the state legislature.

The principle lost much of its fascination for the public after the early years of the 'twenties, although it enjoyed some revival after Nebraska applied the method to the choice of its widely discussed unicameral legislature authorized in November, 1934. In recent years the nonpartisan plan has not spread further but the fact that nearly one-half of the nation's voters are called upon to make some of their electoral choices from a nonpartisan ballot makes its nature and consequences matters of continuing importance for study.

As a term, "nonpartisanship" is at best somewhat ambiguous, and to the poorly informed voter it may often be misleading. The expression cannot be said to denote the absence of adherence to factional groups or political interests. No matter how ephemeral the organizational structure, wherever men are elected to offices that require the making of *public policy* decisions, there are always persons and groups interested in getting certain candidates elected and in defeating others. All elections are partisan in the sense that people and groups take sides and struggle against one another for victory; and offices filled "without party designation" are partisan enough according to this meaning. As it is used in the United States, "nonpartisanship" actually describes a situation in which (1) public offices are filled without party designations being placed on the ballot and (2) the long ballot is used. (The Australian ballot, employed in many British Commonwealth elections, has no party designation, but the voter is ordinarily called upon to cast but a single vote for a single office and presumably can hardly avoid knowing the political affiliation of the two or three candidates for the seat.)

While nonpartisan elections have not been given close study by many scholars, the materials available indicate that the system has certain characteristics which reappear whenever the plan is used. The purpose of this study is to submit some tentative propositions which seem to be characteristic of nonpartisanship. These propositions are based upon available empirical evidence, and all require verification through additional research. Owing to space limitations little evidence is actually presented here; personal observations and studies of the state legislatures of Minnesota and Nebraska and of the city councils of Minneapolis and Detroit[1] have furnished most of the data suggesting the hypotheses.

Certain qualifications must be made in establishing a frame of reference. First, where comparisons with partisan situations are made, a general two-party system is presumed—not necessarily an "ideal" two-party system, but one in which members of one party may conceivably replace members of another party in office. In one-party situations, a quasi-nonpartisanship obtains that makes comparisons with nonpartisanship meaningless. In addition, where local, rather than general parties are found, it is probable that some of the characteristics postulated for nonpartisanship would be valid while others would not. Second, what might be called an impersonal type of politics is presumed. Where elections are held in constituencies small enough to have government by personality, it would be unsafe to say that the material below is applicable.

The following are offered as propositions:

1. *Nonpartisanship serves to weaken the political parties in those areas where it is in effect.* This is what its creators intended that it should do. They felt that the established political parties, closely tied up with the system of spoils and other Jacksonian precepts, were not to be trusted. Ideally, they wanted to see the principles of "sound business management" applied to government, not by professional politicians, but by established and successful business men of the community.

The removal of the party label from certain parts of the ballot has resulted in the weakening of political party organizations for several reasons. The reduction in the number of offices to be filled by the parties has weakened them by making active participation in their activities less attractive to the citizen: with fewer elective or appointive jobs available as rewards, there is less incentive for the individual to give his energies. There is not even the incentive of seeking to influence party members in the many areas where the parties are no longer effective in the determination of policy. Furthermore, the removal of some or all of the state and local offices from the party ballot has served to cut away the local roots of the party; weak local organizations in turn have made effective campaigning difficult by removing the ordinary citizen from regular and frequent contact with the parties.[2]

Altogether, in states where nonpartisanship applies to an important sector of the ballot, the party organizations have been weak. This remains true, for example, in California, Michigan, Minnesota, Nebraska, and North Dakota;[3] and further evidence of the debilitating effect of nonpartisanship upon the established parties is to be found in the attitudes of professional politicians. When the system was first proposed in Minnesota, Republican leaders in large measure stood in opposition to the elimination of the party label. While some Democrats at first believed that the party had nothing to lose in a situation in which it was already extremely weak, they later changed their minds, and leaders of all three of the state's major parties eventually took strong stands against the plan. In Michigan, Democrats at first supported the nonpartisanship movement, but subsequently regretted their action. Party leaders viewed nonpartisanship in the Nebraska legislature with apprehension.

2. *The voting public views participation in partisan and nonpartisan elections as two different kinds of activities, each independent of the other; and the nonpartisan office-holder is normally expected by the voting public to keep any party activity on his part separate from his role in nonpartisan office.*[4] This tendency toward segregation is commonly carried even further, with office-seekers usually following, one road or the other, but not both. The effect of this pattern upon Minnesota politics when the legislature of that state was removed from the party ballot is clearly described in the following quotation from the *Fergus Falls (Minn.) Daily Journal*.

The new law which requires county officers and members of the legislature to be elected as nonpartisans takes all of the vitality out of a party campaign. Heretofore it has been the county officers and legislative candidates who have paid most of the expenses and harrowed up the country for the benefit of state candidates. This year it is all different. Only two of the county offices have contests and as they are nonpartisan they are taking no part in the state campaign nor are they paving the way for the state contestants.

Here was a basic alteration in traditional campaign techniques. The local organizations had been the very heart of the political parties in Minnesota, but it now became necessary for the parties to establish regional campaign personnel separate from politicians on the local scene.

(The obverse situation obtained as well: party state central committees immediately chose virtually to ignore legislative and county contests.) With some exceptions, as indicated below, parallel sets of office-seekers, aides, and organizations had to be created, with very little intercourse between them. This was [predominantly] the case in all four of the areas observed for this article; an individual who wished to become active in politics had to choose one road or the other.

3. *Channels for recruitment of candidates for partisan offices are restricted by nonpartisanship.* It is unusual for a successful nonpartisan politician to move up into higher partisan ranks. Thus the fact that personnel for the two ballots are kept largely separate creates a problem for the parties, which ordinarily use local and legislative positions as the training ground for higher offices.

The problem has not been acute in Minnesota (though certainly it is present), because a workable, particularly competitive two-party system has in recent years provided impetus for recruitment of able personnel. But in Michigan where Detroit, most of its suburbs, and other cities have nonpartisan elections, the system appears to have had a definitely adverse effect upon the quality of party personnel. This is particularly true of the Democratic party, which draws most of its strength in the state from the city of Detroit, and the results are especially apparent in the consistently low overall quality of the Wayne county legislative delegation.

In exceptional circumstances an outstanding campaigner from nonpartisan ranks will receive overtures from one or both political parties, but even in these rare cases there are many obstacles to success. For example, Edward J. Jeffries, Jr., the greatest vote-getter ever to serve as mayor of Detroit, was wooed by both major parties as a gubernatorial candidate, and after having served four terms as mayor (the longest tenure in city's history), he filed for the Republican nomination for governor in 1946. He ran a poor fourth in a field of four. Some members of the Minnesota legislature have looked fondly toward the governor's chair, but party regulars understandably take a dim view of bringing in candidates "from outside the party," and success is rare. Since the overwhelming majority of the members of the Nebraska and Minnesota legislatures are inactive in the regular parties and so without chance for further advancement there, their services are not available for positions of higher party leadership. Similarly, almost no members of the Minneapolis or Detroit city councils have been active in party affairs, and the same, with only a few exceptions, may be said of the mayors of the two cities. These office-holders are not available to the political parties, or, at the very least, the parties do not wish to avail themselves of their services.

4. *Channels for recruitment of candidates for nonpartisan offices are restricted by nonpartisanship.* The securing of active political party members to fill nonpartisan positions is difficult. In Minneapolis, a party regular seeking a nonpartisan council or mayoralty seat is at a disadvantage and seldom makes good, especially in the case of the former. In Detroit, where nonpartisanship has become a refuge of conservatism, any attempt by an active party member to penetrate into the city's nonpartisan elections, and especially an effort to carry along "partisan politics," is greeted by powerful and effective blasts from the newspapers and from the Detroit Citizens' League. And status as active party members almost invariably places legislative candidates at a disadvantage in Minnesota and Nebraska.

Occasionally it is possible for an active party member to enter the nonpartisan lists and sometimes even to go on from there to higher positions within the party. Frank Murphy, the only mayor of Detroit to achieve national fame in the more than three decades since the city's present charter was adopted, was an active Democrat both before and after his tenure in the city hall. Murphy's election, however, was the result of a combination of unusual circumstances—including the recall in 1930 of the incumbent mayor, whose unethical behavior in office had temporarily weakened public confidence in some of the groups ordinarily most influential in choosing the chief executive, the extreme economic depression that affected Detroit even more than the rest of the nation and the very strong support given him by the *Detroit Times;* and Murphy made a strenuous effort to keep his partisan and nonpartisan political activities separate from one another.[5] A few other Detroit mayors have had loose party connections and one had served in Congress before becoming mayor, but that was in the earliest days of nonpartisanship in the city government.

Hubert H. Humphrey, an active Democrat, became mayor of Minneapolis in 1945, but on a largely nonparty campaign to "clean up" the city and with support from the Republican Cowles newspapers. Very active in partisan affairs while mayor, he moved on from that position to the United States Senate, while his successor, who had never been active in partisan activities, returned to the customary nonpartisan pattern. It is also to be remembered that James Michael Curley was for a time head of both the nonpartisan city government and the Democratic party in Boston, although his once vast support was always more of a personal than a party matter.

Certainly cases of party actives successful in obtaining nonpartisan offices are always exceptional. The usual picture finds nonpartisan mayors rising from nonpartisan councils and nonpartisan councilmen coming from political obscurity—successfully reaching the council usually only after several tries have afforded the chance for the public to become familiar with their names.

5. *Limited new channels for recruitment of candidates for nonpartisan offices are opened by nonpartisanship.* Proponents of nonpartisanship have always argued that the system encourages many able, successful, well-known citizens of the community to run for office who would never become candidates under the traditional method since they would be unwilling to become entangled in the ordinary processes of party politics. There is evidence in all nonpartisan jurisdictions to support this contention. To be sure, the candidate under any elective system (except, perhaps, in very small communities with a purely personal type of government) must have a yen, or at least a tolerance, for electioneering; but many persons who have established reputations as business or professional men would fear the condescending attitudes often taken by Americans toward candidates who engage in party activities. These individuals sometimes can be persuaded to hold a nonpartisan office in the council or legislature as a civic duty. Such persuasion appears to be effective from time to time and probably helps bring many capable persons into law-making bodies or mayoralty offices.

Nonpartisanship does not, however, *insure* the filling of available seats from among the community's successful. The individual who has never "made good" at anything else, who is a perennial office-seeker, and who depends for a livelihood upon scraps from the political table—the "political hack" of the vernacular—is a familiar figure around the Minneapolis council table and certainly is not unknown in the Detroit council or the Minnesota and Nebraska legislatures.

6. *Segregation of funds for financing nonpartisan and partisan election campaigns is nearly complete.* Nonpartisanship has produced parallel financing systems. In Michigan this separation of funds is required by law, but even in Minnesota, where rapport with the regular parties is close to being established, most individual candidates must shift for themselves. In that state, the Republicans, indirectly and *sub rosa,* give aid to certain needy candidates who agree to join the Conservative caucus in the legislature; but the Democratic Party has given no similar assistance, and the general practice in nonpartisan jurisdictions is for the individual candidate to seek out his own support. This is hardly surprising in light of the fact that political parties are almost never really rich and, needing money to support their own candidates, can scarcely be expected to give assistance to persons over whom they probably would exercise little or no control, granted election.

Individual financing has a tendency to confuse the voting public, leading many persons into believing that, while the political parties are beholden to those who pay their bills, nonpartisans are "independent." This naive belief is often encouraged in nonpartisan jurisdictions and results in a definitely undesirable development, for it means that the public is quite unaware of the nature of the commitments made by, or the type of support being given, a candidate. (The fact that state law may require the filing of a statement of campaign contributions does not fundamentally alter this situation.)

7. *Facilities for fund-raising by candidates for nonpartisan offices are restricted by nonpartisanship.* Under the traditional political system, the party carries on much of the financing burden as a staff function. If a candidate can secure organizational backing, he is free to carry on his campaign with little or no worry about the requisite funds: the party has machinery to care for this problem. On the other hand, the nonpartisan candidate is an individual who, when he first enters politics, has no organized support or money-raising mechanism. When he knows that he must spend his own money, or that of friends, or persuade an important interest group to give him aid, the burden of campaigning is made so heavy that the likelihood of an individual's trying to gain a seat is decreased. When this situation is combined with the discouraging advantage held by the incumbent (discussed below), it is not surprising that relatively few persons run for nonpartisan offices and that those who do become candidates do not, and cannot, campaign extensively.

8. *Nonpartisanship encourages the avoidance of issues of policy in campaigns.* Since voting "for the man" and other frontier concepts have kept American political parties from exercising responsibility, the lack of definite platforms and the failure to carry out concrete campaign promises under nonpartisanship have not been as apparent as would otherwise be the case. The system does not make campaigning upon issues profitable, but discourages it even more than does the present party system. Seldom does a nonpartisan candidate take a firm, widely-publicized stand upon the important issues of the day, and this is especially true if he is running for a seat in a collegial body.[6] He prefers to take no stand at all, or an ambiguous one, or to discuss irrelevancies. He would rather try to be all things to all people, depending upon a well-known political name, or upon religious, ethnic, or other extraneous associations.[7] In fact, fence-straddling is much more tempting than under the conventional election system, since in the latter the presence of a party label suggests some sort of "position" to the electorate. And since under nonpartisanship the voter seldom can associate a candidate with a position, he comes, as a last resort in his confusion, to choose "name" candidates. This means that there is a premium upon personal publicity; that the individual with newspaper backing often has an inordinate ad-

vantage; and that the *incumbent* nearly always (unless he has somehow managed to develop notoriety) is in a very strong position simply because his name has appeared more or less regularly before the public during his years in office.

9. *Nonpartisanship tends to frustrate protest voting.* This is so because the electorate, when disgruntled, tends to vote on a party basis and, of course, cannot do so without party labels. American politics is characterized by an "in" party versus an "out" party. Even if there is little philosophical cohesion within each, there is at least the label to serve as a guide for the voter. Under ordinary circumstances, the voter will accept the "in" group; but in times of grave dissatisfaction he can turn to the "out" party for the hope of relief. In nonpartisan jurisdictions, this is impossible. In the first place, there is no collectively identifiable "in" or "out" group. Whether or not there is within a legislative body a majority clique, caucus, or set indebted to the same interest groups, its members are to the voter, who seeks to hold them accountable, merely a collection of individual names. In the second place, if the voter seeks to "turn the rascals out," he has no guide for doing so. He may, if interested enough, determine the incumbents' names, but he usually has no way of knowing whether the opposing candidates will follow a policy of reform, or whatever it is that the voter desires. In partisan politics, the "out" party under such circumstances would promise changes akin to what the voter wanted and could be held accountable for producing them after the election. But the non-incumbent nonpartisan candidate usually prefers the middle-of-the-road; even if he makes definite commitments, his eventual voting behavior can be known to the individual voter only with the greatest difficulty; and under no circumstances need he bear responsibility for the acts of the body to which he belongs.

Although violent changes have taken place in partisan legislative bodies, as in the early day of the great depression, no similar drastic changes can be found in nonpartisan bodies. In 1931 the Michigan House of Representatives was under Republican control by a majority of ninety-eight to two; in 1933 the Democrats organized the House with a fifty-five to forty-five majority. A similar result took place in the Senate, where in 1931 the Republicans held a majority of thirty-one to one; two years later the Democrats were in control with an advantage of seventeen to fifteen. Evidence of the effectiveness of protest voting was even more spectacular in the state of Washington. There, the Republicans held a majority in the 1931 House of Representatives of ninety to eight. In 1935 the relative positions had been completely reversed and the Democrats were in control, ninety-one to eight. Similarly, in the 1931 Washington Senate the Republicans were in charge, forty-one to one; four years later the Democrats held a majority of thirty-seven to nine. No such changes took place in the nonpartisan Minnesota legislature during the same period, despite drastic changes in the partisan state offices. In 1931 when the Farmer-Labor radical Floyd B. Olson was swept into the governorship, the House Liberals were too weak even to have a candidate for the speakership. In 1933, fifty-eight per cent of the House and fifty-five per cent of the Senate were made up of incumbent holdovers from the previous conservative era. Olson never held a working majority in either house, although he won three consecutive decisive victories for himself. The voters apparently did not know how to give him a legislative majority.

10. *Nonpartisanship produces a legislative body with a relatively high percentage of experienced members, making for conservatism.* This follows from the lack of provision for protest voting, the scarcity of campaigns based upon issues, and the resultant advantage given the incumbent as the voter casts about for a familiar name.

In Minnesota, nonpartisanship has produced a continuing trend toward a large number of holdovers from one legislature to the next.[8] In Nebraska, the trend has been striking and uninterrupted since the adoption of nonpartisanship[9] and in Detroit the incumbent's advantage has been one of the most definite characteristics of elections to the council. In the 1951 Detroit election, in fact, all nine incumbents were returned to office. An incumbent in that city is rarely defeated so long as he contests for a seat.

A study of ten non-southern states made a number of years ago indicated that Minnesota had a more experienced legislature than any except the most populous states, where the salary is outstanding (among state legislatures) and a high degree of political organization aids stability.[10] Unlike the situation in many state legislatures (as in the Michigan and Washington cases cited above), where first and second-term members must be called upon to shoulder committee chairmanships and other important positions, the Minnesota legislature has almost never had to place inexperienced persons in key positions. This is also true in the Nebraska legislature and in nonpartisan city councils.

The tendency to reëlect members of the policy-making body has helped to make nonpartisan organizations lean toward conservatism. As indicated above, traditional legislative bodies are often called upon to sacrifice experience for flexibility in the face of demands of the public. Sessions that result are often chaotic, but they are ordinarily productive and responsive. Under nonpartisanship, a much more conservative approach may be expected, and as a result there is a tendency for legislators to diverge from contemporary public thinking on issues.

In Detroit, and to a lesser extent in Minneapolis, the vacuum caused by the absence of party labels as a guide for the voter has been partly filled by newspaper activity. Since daily newspapers are for the most part conservative, especially on local affairs, and since they have a disproportionate advantage in nonpartisan elections by the dissemination of all-important publicity, the conservative tendency of nonpartisan bodies is enhanced. (In legislative constituencies of rural Nebraska and Minnesota, newspapers are of less influence than they are in metropolitan areas, probably because of the more personal nature of a rural campaign.)

11. *There is no collective responsibility in a nonpartisan body.* This follows from the fact that there is no unifying organization or symbol. Each individual stands alone, responsible to his constituents for his own acts only, and for them but vaguely, since nonpartisan campaigns do not ordinarily center upon definite issues. Individual political behavior is not tempered by the fact that a political party has "a past to honor and a future to protect," in the words of a former Minnesota governor.

Without collective responsibility and a well-knit internal organization, a legislative body is likely to be lacking in a collective, comprehensive program. This often results either in a great deal of wasted motion and ineffective floundering or in the leadership's passing to an individual outside the legislative body who is in the public eye—the governor or mayor. In Nebraska, the former appears to have resulted, while in Minnesota the governor has become the dominant policy-maker, taking away much of the potential legislative leadership. In Detroit, the mayor has completely overshadowed the council in policy leadership—aided, to be sure, by the fact that the city has a strong-mayor form of organization.

Without collective responsibility, no one, except possibly the governor, is answerable for the budget in Nebraska or Minnesota. The individual legislator can always, and frequently does, assert that he voted for those items of interest to his district, while disclaiming responsibility for the budget as a whole, or for the legislative pork barrel. From the beginning of legislative nonpartisanship in Minnesota, claims have been made that the system encourages excessive legislative expenditures and logrolling for this reason. The writer has heard similar charges voiced against the Minneapolis and even the Detroit councils, although the fact that the latter is elected at large probably mitigates the tendency there. The Nebraska legislature has been charged with being a "fraternity of tolerance" because of vote trading and pork barreling.[11] Nonpartisan legislatures could hardly be called unique in this respect, but the lack of a party answerable or padding of the budget surely places legislators in sore temptation.

It should be noted that although the Minnesota legislature is organized into two caucuses, "Liberal" and "Conservative" to which nearly all members nominally belong, these two groups do not bear collective responsibility for legislative actions. Caucus labels do not appear on the ballot, and the voter often finds it very difficult to discover the allegiance of a non-incumbent candidate, especially since membership is largely optional and often is not announced publicly until after election. Furthermore, caucuses do not directly parallel the two major parties and are not party adjuncts; caucus membership may be very nominal; and both caucuses are without effective methods of disciplining "members."

The twenty-six member Minneapolis city council is likewise divided into two caucuses, "Liberal" and "Progressive," but the same statements may be made about this structural arrangement as have been made concerning the Minnesota legislative caucuses. The Nebraska legislature, in a proper respecting of the spirit of nonpartisanship, does not have caucus organizations, while the Detroit and many other nonpartisan city councils are too small to have even a nominal bifurcation.

Notes

1. See Charles R. Adrian, "The Origin of Minnesota's Nonpartisan Legislature," *Minnesota History*, Vol. 32, pp. 155–63 (Winter, 1952); C. C. Young, *The Legislature of California: Its Membership, Procedure and Work* (San Francisco, 1943), pp. 129–130; and Maurice M. Ramsey, "Some Aspects of Non-Partisan Government in Detroit, 1918–1940," unpubl. Ph.D. thesis (Ann Arbor, 1944).

2. For an extreme example, see John W. Lederle, "Political Party Organization in Detroit, 1920–1934," unpubl. M.A. thesis (Ann Arbor, 1934) and also Arthur Pound, *Detroit, Dynamic City* (New York, 1940). It should be noted, however, that party organization in Michigan has never been very strong; see Arthur C. Millspaugh, *Party Organization and Machinery in Michigan Since 1890* (Baltimore, 1917).

3. The rigidity of structure in a city with a high degree of political organization may delay the weakening effect, especially where nonpartisanship is grafted onto a "machine-governed" city, as was the case in Boston and in the city council in Chicago. In recent years party organizations have been weakened in both cities. The degree to which this has been caused by the long-range effect of nonpartisanship as against possible other causes, including the decline of the factors that made the nineteenth-century political boss possible, this writer is not prepared to say. Recent developments in Boston, in particular, would appear to support the general hypotheses expressed in this paper.

4. This modification from the original is by the author and is based on his "Typology for Nonpartisan Elections," *Western Political Quarterly*, Vol. 12, pp. 449–458 (June, 1959).

5. Ramsey, *op. cit.*, pp. 58–59. To discourage direct party activities, Michigan law prohibits overt participation by parties in nonpartisan elections and forbids both party endorsements previous to election and the spending of party money on behalf of nonpartisan candidates. The law is so drawn as to be easily circumvented, but little evasion appears to take place. Minnesota, in contrast, has no such legal restrictions.

6. In the not untypical 1951 election for the Detroit council, perhaps two of the eighteen finalists in the run-off could be said to have campaigned energetically and clearly upon several major issues of the day. A few others made fairly definite positions known on one or two issues. Most candidates preferred ambiguity, generality, or silence upon these matters. One incumbent campaigned for "the perpetuation of our way of life," while another stood largely on the implicit platform that he had been an able shortstop on the Detroit Tigers' baseball club. A similar type of campaign regularly takes place in Minneapolis.

7. For a detailed description of a vicious use of extraneous associations in a municipal nonpartisan campaign, see Carl O. Smith and Stephen B. Sarasohn. "Hate Propaganda in Detroit," *Public Opinion Quarterly,* Vol. 10, pp. 24–52 (Spring, 1946).

8. In the six election for the House preceding the establishment of nonpartisanship, the percentage of holdovers averaged 36.8. In the six elections following, the holdovers averaged 50.9 per cent and the trend continued, reaching an all-time high of 77.9 per cent in the election of 1944. Senate elections followed a similar development.

9. In the six elections for the House preceding the establishment of nonpartisanship, the percentage of holdovers averaged 41.6; for the Senate, 46.9. In the six elections following, holdovers amounted to 56.2 per cent. The percentage followed an *uninterrupted* upward trend, reaching 62.7 per cent in the 1948 election. In each election since 1944, the percentage of holdovers has been higher than it ever was in *any* election under the partisan system. (Figures for 1950 are not available.)

10. See Charles S. Hyneman, "Tenure and Turnover of Legislative Personnel," *Annals,* Vol. 195 (Jan., 1938), pp. 21–31.

11. See Richard C. Spencer, "Nebraska Idea Fifteen Years Old," *National Municipal Review,* Vol. 39 (Feb., 1950), p. 86.

26. Nonpartisanship in Suburbia

ROBERT C. WOOD

(One rationale of nonpartisan local elections asserts that it is a design to encourage greater and more direct participation by citizens in shaping local policies through eliminating the political party as a middleman. The following excerpt is a discussion of this view.)

. . . Given a structure designed to encourage as much participation as possible, the citizen is expected to handle, on his own, the hot issues of the day. No barrier stands between him and his government: he takes pride in calling the police chief by his first name. As a consequence, the quality of the police force is the citizen's responsibility. Ideally, he is always in charge; and, ideally, he is committed to the tasks of constant surveillance of the public's business.

The reality of this energetic, civic-minded model citizen is frequently

Reprinted from *Suburbia: Its People and Their Politics* (Boston: Houghton Mifflin, 1958), pp. 161–66 by permission of the author and the publisher. Robert Wood is professor of political science at Massachusetts Institute of Technology.

questioned by observers. As the activities of suburban government grow more complex, the town meeting or the public sessions of the borough council are sometimes described as "government by wisecrack" and written off as mechanisms too cumbersome to make real decisions. It is pointed out that even the most earnest voter is not able to give sensible decisions about water mains, fire engines, school curricula, and zoning patterns. It is suggested that while his present political institutions may serve a useful purpose in creating a sense of community, they rarely serve as effective instruments of popular government.

This less romantic interpretation of the actual results of nonpartisanship suggests that it is not the citizen but the local bureaucrat who is most influential. As the citizen finds the substance of public affairs growing increasingly intricate he finds ways to whittle down the size of his civic job. This feat is accomplished by a redefinition of what falls within the province of popular decision-making and what does not. Because nonpartisanship is built on the assumption of a like-minded constituency, contemplating no fundamental disagreements, it is a short, logical step to classify a whole range of public activities as entirely nonpolitical.

Thus, by making budget preparation the province of the professional finance director, zoning decisions the responsibility of the professional planning director, and supervision of the local bureaucracy the duty of the professional city manager, the burden on the citizen is mercifully lightened. Street repair and traffic control, it is argued, are no longer matters of each resident filling in the potholes in the public ways adjacent to his own property and warning the teamster that the bridge down the road will not bear his wagon's weight. They are properly the province of the highway department and the traffic engineer. Issues of public health can no longer be decided by public debate, or even by general practitioners in medicine; their resolution requires the scientific investigation of public health specialists. It is not enough to maintain a jail for the unruly. Criminology and penology are complex subjects, and sentences and prison routines need to be guided by the latest findings on juvenile delinquency. A modern welfare program is not a matter of Thanksgiving baskets for the poor, but a complicated process of interview, determination of need, case investigations and evaluations in which many specialists may take part.

So, function by function, more and more public activities in suburbia are called administrative and professional, removed from the list of subjects to be discussed and decided by public action, and routinized in budgets too large for scrutiny, let alone understanding. Since the average citizen cannot in fairness be asked to comment upon building codes, methods of water treatment and the relative merits of various types of police equipment, no citizen should have to comment at all. The exercise of popular control is restricted to only the most important of local issues, carefully culled to ensure that the citizen will have the time, energy and capacity to deal with them, and the arena of popular debate is kept small.

But exactly what are the issues that remain? With so many of the activities of local government the special province of the expert, acceptable matters for debate, so far as the general suburban government is concerned, are usually reduced to three: honesty, the tax bill, and land development. The question of outright corruption and wrongdoing on the part of public officials, by its nature, arises only sporadically, and, in a nonparty suburb, usually as a result of the suspicions and energy of the local press. It is likely never to be a major problem, if only because of the growing professionalization of the administrative side of local government. Even when skulduggery is detected, the average citizen can be expected to be indignant but not especially useful in either investigating or punishing it. Public action can express itself only by locking the barn door after the horse is stolen.

Nor does the issue of taxes offer the public much more opportunity to make rational policy. A higher tax rate can call forth cries of anguish and protest, but without familiarity with the budget and adequate information about the relative priorities among the locality's public needs, citizen action is not likely to be effective, and it can quite easily be harmful. Organized legislatures on the state and national level, equipped with committees and featuring an opposition party primed for attack, have difficulty enough in establishing a reasonable budget process. Town meetings, city councils, and commissions run into more trouble; and the voter's role, in a nonpartisan atmosphere, is usually reduced to accepting or rejecting bond issues at election time. Conflicts between the professional administrators and the elected officers quite frequently arise, but the lay citizen rarely finds an effective channel for participation.

Roughly the same situation exists so far as the control of land use and zoning is concerned. In suburbia, most residents reserve their strong opinions for the topic of the community's future development. Home ownership is, after all, a distinguishing characteristic of the residential suburb, and the instinct to protect property values is strong and widespread. Yet once again the effectiveness of citizen action is questionable. Planning has become the preserve of the specialists, and if the planner goes unheeded, a vast range of alternatives faces any locality. Shall developments be permitted or excluded? Shall the design of residences be regulated, to make sure that ultra-modern or ultra-conservative homes are kept out? Shall architects be permitted to experiment with new-fangled construction materials and techniques? Is there to be a commercial sector or an industrial zone to relieve pressures on the tax rate, and if so, where and how big? What reservations are proper for recreational purposes? What attitude should be taken toward the location of the new express highway, other than the obvious position that it should not be allowed to come through the town?

Even assuming a collective, public, nonpartisan answer to these questions and a consensus about what the suburb wishes to become, stubborn technical problems of law and zoning remain. Private property rights still have sizable defenses, and the complicated procedures of zoning, regulations, appeals, and exceptions permit many modifications of any suburb's master plan. If the citizen were truly to fulfill his obligation with respect to land use, he would spend evening after evening listening to individual pleas for extending the building line in this instance or that, contructing a "nonconforming" garage, or putting a commercial building, by spot zoning, in an established residential area.

It is quite true that citizens of the metropolis as well as of more isolated cities face the same problem of understanding the technicalities of modern government and of controlling the burgeoning ranks of bureaucrats. Where nonpartisanship holds sway, all these municipalities may be in the same boat with the suburbs. Where party politics exist, however, even if predominantly one-party politics, there are professional politicians who make it their business to know developments and there are party organizations which, in the end, and, if the situation becomes too outrageous, may be held accountable.

Suburban municipalities, committed for the most part to part-time mayors and selectmen, resentful of open claims to political leadership, dependent upon the energy and zeal of the individual citizen, do not often possess this intervening layer of surveillance. Despite the classifiication of more and more problems as administrative, and the most energetic displays of public spirit, the average suburban citizen's capacity to deal effectively even with the issues which remain in his province grows more questionable. Nonpartisanship may faithfully preserve the image of Emerson's restless, prying conscious man, and the resort to professional expertness may limit the range of issues into which he is expected to inquire. More and more frequently, however, the reality of control seems to rest on the shoulders of relatively few, either elected officials or informal leaders, who stand between bureaucracy and the nonpartisan public.

C. ALTERNATIVES TO THE REFORM PROGRAM

27. "Weak Mayor" Government in Chicago

MARTIN MEYERSON AND
EDWARD C. BANFIELD

(This excerpt is taken from a case study of a decision involving the selection of sites for public housing in Chicago. While the specific issue was building-site selection, the whole future of public housing in Chicago was at stake. It was a particularly controversial issue because to white neighborhoods, public housing meant the entrance of Negroes. Most vacant land was in all white areas of the city, and these sites were generally favored by the public housing authority, the official unit for administering public housing. However, site locations had to be approved by the city council. Thus, a most complex set of pressures and cross pressures were focused on the council. While the final decision of the council did authorize the continuation of the public housing program, its site selections were bitterly criticized by many public-housing supporters.

The following selection is drawn from one of the concluding chapters of *Politics, Planning and the Public Interest* in which the authors reflect on the Chicago form of government in light of the decision made in this particular case.)

At the height of the site selection struggle, the editors of the *Sun-Times* pointed to it as evidence that the city government was in need of drastic reorganization.

"Chicago needs a city government which can govern," the editorial began. "Chicago needs a city government which will provide a just and workable balance between the local interests of its many neighborhoods and the general interests of the city as a whole. Chicago needs a city

Reprinted from *Politics, Planning and the Public Interest* (Glencoe, Illinois: The Free Press, 1955), pp. 285–300 by permission of the publisher. Documentation omitted. Martin Meyerson is the Director of the Joint Center for Urban Studies for Massachusetts Institute of Technology and Harvard University.

government which can plan, legislate, and administer public services for the common good of all of its two million citizens, rather than for the special interests of special groups."

With a city council consisting of 50 delegates from 50 localities, each elected by a small constituency, each owing nothing to the city at large, and with only the mayor elected by the citizens at large, it was inevitable, the editorial said, that local interests, narrow interests, sectional interests, factional interests should often prevail over the interest of the city as a whole. Chicago should have a council of 15 or 20 members. In order that local interests have fair representation, half of the council, perhaps, should be elected by districts. The rest of the members, together with the mayor, should be elected by and represent the city at large. "Such a city government," the editorial concluded, "would not always act wisely. But at least it could come to some decision on the vital problems of a vital metropolis. And when it acted unwisely, its members could be held responsible at the polls."

This view was widely accepted among students of municipal government in Chicago and elsewhere. Indeed, not many important cities still had governments like Chicago's. For many years the trend all over the country had been to reduce the number and powers of aldermen and to increase the powers of the executive. In several hundred cities (although not in any of the 20 largest) a small elected council hired a professional manager who administered the affairs of the city as unpolitically as if it were a business or a factory.

That Chicago's government was behind the times was unquestionable. But it was probably exaggerated to say, as the *Sun-Times* did, and as many liberals concerned with reform in Chicago did, that the struggle over public housing showed that the city could not act effectively because it was broken into 50 wards, each represented by an alderman. . . .

In Chicago, political power was highly decentralized *formally* but highly centralized *informally*. The city had what textbooks in municipal government called a "weak-mayor" form of government to be sure, but it also had a powerful mayor, or, if not a powerful mayor, a powerful leader of the Council. This paradox of a "weak" government that was strong was to be explained by the presence of the Democratic machine, an organization parallel to the city government but outside of it, in which power sufficient to run the city was centralized. The weakness of the city government was offset by the strength of the party.

The "Big Boys"* could get and keep power enough to run the city

---

* The "Big Boys" refers to the powerful, Democratic leadership clique on the city council.

only by giving the favors, protection, and patronage which were essential for the maintenance of the machine. It is quite possible, of course, that they preferred to operate the city government in this way. But whether they preferred it or not, the "spoils system" and even to some extent the alliance between crime and politics were the price that had to be paid to overcome the extreme decentralization of formal power. If overnight the bosses became model administrators—if they put all of the city jobs on the merit system, destroyed the syndicate, and put an end to petty grafting, then the city government would really be as weak and ineffective as the *Sun-Times* said. Indeed, under Kennelly the government of Chicago became both a great deal cleaner and a great deal weaker than it had been for many years.

The people of Chicago probably did not fully realize the price that was being paid to assemble power enough to govern the city. But although it had never calculated the costs in deliberate ways, the public, it seems safe to say, had some awareness both that these costs were there and that there were some benefits in return—in fact, the disadvantages of a formal centralization of power, although different in kind, might possibly be even greater.

As they actually worked (but not as they were formally designed to work), Chicago's governmental institutions achieved a high degree of centralization *and* a high degree of decentralization: they put a great deal of power over some matters in the hands of the city administration while leaving a great deal of power over other matters in the hands of the neighborhood and ward leaders. The politically active people in the wards had their way in all matters which were not of first importance to the city administration. The voter who stood well with his precinct captain (and most voters could) could expect prompt action if he complained that the street in front of his house needed repairs, if he wanted a change in the zoning law so that his son-in-law could go in the pants-pressing business, or if the traffic cop was too free with his tickets. Having power like this close at hand was of great importance to many people: street repairs, zoning changes, traffic tickets and the like were the main business of city government from the standpoint of most citizens. Government so close to many people and so responsive to them was "grassroots democracy," although perhaps not the kind that those who most use the term would recognize as such.

Most of the matters that were decided locally were of local interest. Whether a street was to be repaved, the zoning law for a block changed, and the traffic cop transferred were questions which had direct and clearly ascertainable consequences mainly for the locality. It was true that they might have even more important indirect consequences for the city as a whole (for example, an exception to the zoning law may set in motion a series of changes which cause the decay of the neighborhood and ultimately affect the ecology of the whole city) but these consequences were usually so obscure and so involved in detail that a central authority would rarely have staff or time to take them into account. Some matters were on the border between being of local and of city-wide interest or were of both local and city-wide interest. In these matters there would be friction because of overlapping jurisdictions of the local and central powerholders, but this was not a very strong argument for eliminating local autonomy altogether.

Whether an issue is to be regarded as primarily of local or primarily of city-wide interest may depend upon the observer's value premises and especially upon whether his model of the public interest is individualistic or unitary. One who takes what we call an organismic view of the view of the public interest subordinates all other interests to that of the social "organism." At the other extreme, the Utilitarian, granting that matters like housing have more than contingent or constructive importance to the whole population of the city, tries to compare utilities so as to arrive at the "greatest happiness."

Machine government (which, as its opponents have always recognized, depends for its existence upon ward organization and a formally weak executive) and its opposite, "honest and efficient administration in the public interest" (which implies a small council elected at large, often by proportional representation, and a strong mayor or city manager), are suitable to separate and distinct social and economic class interests.

Lower and lower-middle class people, especially members of ethnic minorities, have often favored machine government rather than its opposite, and not, we think, chiefly because, as Lord Bryce and many others have supposed, they have been ignorant of democratic traditions. Many of these people have found the ward and precinct organization an almost indispensable intermediary between them and the formal organs of government, especially the courts, and they have known that the machines, however corrupt they might be, are run by people of economic and ethnic origins similar to their own. The interests these people usually regard as most important are local, not city-wide, and their outlook is generally self- or family-regarding rather than community-regarding. Machine government seems to serve them best.

It is mainly upper and middle class people who have fought the machines and sought to establish a cleaner, more businesslike, and more respectable government. As a general rule people of these classes have little need of petty favors; many of them have business or other interests which are city-wide and which are facilitated by progressive, impartial, and low-cost administration; many of them act in representative rather than in personal roles (e.g., as officers of voluntary associations) and these roles are commonly community-regarding, and, of course, upper and middle class people, too, like to be ruled by their own kind.

In communities where middle and upper class people have an overwhelming preponderance of political power—despite their sizeable numbers, these groups, except for some businessmen, were typically bypassed by the Chicago machine—this model of local government, the apogee of which is the council-manager system, is likely to succeed very well. But where control is not firmly in the hands of the middle and upper classes or where there is an important ethnic or class minority—and therefore in all of the great polyglot metropolises of the United States—"honest, impartial, businesslike" government is not likely to be tolerated for long because it runs counter to the ends and to the class feeling of many citizens.

It was, we think, an advantage of the Chicago system of government that it conformed to the tastes and interests of the most numerous social group (no government which did not do this reasonably well could survive, of course, but foolish and costly and less successful attempts might have been made and might have persisted long enough to do great damage). But it was also an advantage of the Chicago system that, while keeping control over local matters within the voter's reach, it interposed the party between the voters and the most important city-wide (as well as state- and nation-wide) decisions. The heads of the machine could not ignore the voters on all issues, but they could ignore them on many issues and on almost any particular issue. The advantages of this were great. Chicago was not governed, as are some cities in which strong machines do not stand between the voter and the issue, by the pull and haul of a few irresponsible pressure groups which get the voter's ear at election time; instead, there were only two important political organizations, the Democratic and the Republican parties, both of which had to accept some responsibility for not one or a few interests but for all of the many conflicting interests that were important in the life of the city. And since they depended upon a highly disciplined organization built upon a system of material incentives, the leaders of the machine did not have to rely mainly upon ideological appeals to the voter. This meant that, although issues were often decided upon non-ideological grounds, they were not settled upon the basis of an anti-democratic ideology. The South Side of Chicago, it should be remembered, was Studs Lonigan's stamping ground, and Studs and his friends would have been happy to vote for a man like Senator McCarthy (who was a product of idealogical, not of machine, politics); instead, they voted for Governor Adlai Stevenson and Senator Paul Douglas because Jacob Arvey, the man who ran the Democratic machine, could afford on behalf of its liberal wing the luxury of some "high class" candidates.

In our opinion, believers in traditional democracy, both the conservatives and the liberals among them, in their criticism have neglected the advantages of effective machines in Chicago. The machines not only give the mass of the people, with their limited interest in politics (what some would call their "apathy") the kind of government they seem to want—or least object to—but they also insulate traditional democratic values and institutions from the forces which unscrupulous demagogues using mass communications media can so easily unloose in a society deeply divided by ethnic, economic and other conflicts. Naively to destroy the political machines and to undertake to govern the city in the way its "best elements" think is impartial, businesslike, and in the public interest is to run the risk of deepening the conflicts which already exist while at the same time discarding a social structure by which conflicts may be confined and managed.

If, as some of the reformers had suggested for years, the size of the Council were to be reduced to 15 or 20 members, half of them elected at large, and if the power of the machine were also reduced (as we suppose they intended), the result in our opinion would be to eliminate both the regulated local autonomy which many people so prize and the concentration of power in the hands of the city's leaders which makes effective city-wide action possible. Instead of making the government of the city stronger, such a change would make it weaker; while making it impossible to decide anything on a neighborhood basis, it would also make it impossible to decide anything centrally.

In order to centralize formally as much power as is now centralized informally, a governing body of not more than six persons, all elected for long, overlapping terms from a city-wide constituency and a mayor whose power is preponderant within the governing body might be required. Little short of such extreme centralization would yield power enough to govern the city in the absence of some kind—not necessarily the present kind—of a strong machine. The dangers of such a government we have already pointed to, but the more probable danger—the danger associated with a half-way proposal such as that proposed by the Sun-Times and the liberal reform groups—is of a government which would not have enough power, formal and informal, to enable it to rule effectively.

Since 1938, New York has had the kind of a governmental structure that students of municipal administration generally approve. New York, therefore, offers an instructive contrast to Chicago, the institutions of which are often taken as an example of the worst than can be found.

In New York, power is highly centralized both formally and informally. The city is governed by the Board of Estimate, a body consisting of the five borough presidents, the comptroller, the president of the almost vestigial City Council, and the mayor. The mayor has three votes in the Board and he is the chief administrative officer of the city: the major city departments are directly responsible to him. Within this formally-centralized structure, moreover, there has arisen a further, informal centralization. Since 1934, a gifted man named Robert Moses has come to be the undisputed head of what is virtually a parallel government of matters concerning public works and related activities. Moses' only salaried job is Park Commissioner, but he has managed to get formal or informal control of several key agencies and, by placing his engineers, architects and other followers in strategic positions and by rewarding his friends and punishing his enemies among the host of contractors, consultants, and politicians who depend in one way or another on the operations he controls, he has managed to build what Chicago politicians would call an "organization," albeit one which is generally supposed to be "clean." City administrations come and go, but Moses keeps his tight grip on countless committees, boards, authorities, and commissions, and Moses is an exceedingly highhanded man.

New York City has built a great deal of public housing and it has built it without graft. Unlike the Chicago ones, the New York projects are not racially segregated, but this is owing not so much to the centralization of municipal government in New York or to Moses as to the circumstance that the city has about 2,500,000 Jews, 600,000 Negroes, 250,000 Puerto Ricans, and 1,000,000 Italo-Americans. Moses himself has never been especially concerned about racial issues: indeed, he has been outspokenly contemptuous of "long-haired" efforts to achieve "social" objectives of any kind.

The Board of Estimate and Moses have had enough power between them to prevent the New York City Planning Commission from functioning effectively, and this although the Commission has extraordinary legal powers. The City Charter directs the Commission to prepare a master plan for city development and it provides that all proposals for capital improvements must either conform to the master plan, be approved by the City Planning Commission or be approved by a three-quarters vote of the Board of Estimate. Despite these requirements, the Commission, the budget of which is passed upon by the Board of Estimate, has never been given staff sufficient to prepare a comprehensive or master plan. As a basis for decisions regarding public housing, the work of the New York City Planning Commission was no more derived from a comprehensive plan than that of its counterpart in Chicago.

Ordinarily in New York it is possible to protest the location of a public housing project only *after* the decision has been virtually made. Such preliminary planning as is done is usually completed before a project proposal is submitted to the City Planning Commission and the Board of Estimate and the groundwork for the project's acceptance by the Board is laid in advance behind the scenes by the Moses organization. Thus the Citizens' Housing and Planning Council of New York is occupied not so much appealing for new projects as getting an opportunity to be heard before the Board of Estimate on projects already planned. Sometimes the Council is unable to get any information about a project until the planning is almost done. Recently, when the City Planning Commission held hearings on a housing and redevelopment plan, the proposal was criticized by the Council, the Citizens' Union, the New York Chapter of the American Institute of Planners, and the Metropolitan Committee on Planning. The areas selected for housing and redevelopment, the Citizens' Council said, "have been spotted without any consideration of their relationship to the larger areas of which they are a part, or to the existence of basic utilities, schools, transportation, and other facilities which are necessary for the proper development of entire areas in the city as a whole."

Judging from this, these sites were not particularly superior to the "bus-window" selections made by the Chicago aldermen. But the parallel between New York and Chicago is even closer. According to the Citizens' Housing and Planning Council, Moses in 1952 by-passed the Federal regulations requiring equitable provision of public housing for all minority groups. According to a Council spokesman, one of Moses' committees said that 20 per cent of the persons living on certain proposed public housing sites would find places in the new projects, whereas in fact, because of income and other requirements, only four per cent were eligible.

These indications are perhaps enough to suggest that, even if ample power is centralized in the hands of an able administrator (in this case of course, one opposed to planning), site selection for public housing may not be done much better, if indeed any better, than it was done in Chicago. But even if this was not the case—even if the public housing program in New York was all that Moses would claim—we do not think that it would necessarily follow that the New York way of making decisions is altogether preferable to the Chicago way. In even the biggest cities the local community remains an important agency of social control.

To be sure, in metropolitan areas it is not possible for the local community, as such, to take much part in deciding the "big" issues of the day; nevertheless, it is politically important, for identification with a local community or neighborhood seems to encourage some people to acquire the interests and skills that make for political competence. But this identification and this encouragement to political competence can only occur if some real power remains in the local community. If all power is in the hands of a hierarchy with a high-handed and "efficient" administrator like Moses at the top, then a local community leader like Stech, a truck driver who led a crusade against public housing in Chicago in order to get into politics, would not have a path to political action or power. However, unless there is real power—not merely the shadow of it—to be exercised locally, "grassroots democracy" is meaningless. Even in New York, of course, political and other organizations do offer local community leaders some scope; these opportunities, though, seem to be fewer and more limited there than in Chicago.

That the "Big Boys" had power enough to make decisions in the public interest did not mean that they would do so. The very fact that most of their power was held informally was an encouragement to *sub rosa* deals by which they might personally profit at the expense of the public interest; "insiders" who "knew the ropes" might have undue influence on them, perhaps even by bribery. Unquestionably there have been times when some leaders of the machine have taken bribes. (It was said that Samuel Insull was more responsible for the corruption of Chicago government than any one man.) In the case of the public housing issue, however, it seems that the "Big Boys" were not bribed or otherwise "captured" by the powerful interests which opposed public housing or, for that matter, by the Authority itself.

Our conjecture is that in the housing struggle the "Big Boys" were trying to do what they thought would be best for the party. What was best for the party, they probably thought, would also be best for the city as a whole.

This, of course, was a rather simple-minded view of the matter. The public on which the machine depended for maintenance—despite our stress on the machine's broad base—was by no means the whole public of Chicago: and so what might be very good for the machine might be very bad for large sectors of the public. Moreover, the leaders and mainstays of the machine all represented individual, neighborhood, and class interests and, except when some compelling necessity arose (in the case of public housing, conflict among local and special interests), it was to the interest of the machine to sacrifice the interest of the city as a whole to these special interests. Insofar as it coincided with it at all, the interest of the machine coincided with only one conception of the public interest among many possible ones and not, perhaps, with the one which was most appropriate. The machine took as the ultimately relevant data those ends, whatever they might be, the satisfaction of which would tend to make the party an effective vote-getting organization and those ends, whatever they might be, that the voters happened to have uppermost on election day. Organizational maintenance was best served by doing what was least likely to antagonize any group or faction within the party and by devoting attention to the economy of incentives which held the principal figures in the party together. Issues were secondary or even altogether unimportant. In order to win an election, it was not necessary to take a far-sighted and comprehensive view of the city's fundamental problems, to point out in clear terms the alternatives that were before it, or through leadership to resolve fundamental conflicts by appeals to reason and to the most comprehensive and morally significant ends. To win an election it was necessary to be stronger than the other party on election day. This did not mean that it was necessary to please the voter. It was only necessary to be in the eyes of the voter the lesser of two evils.

And yet, after these qualifications are made, there was an important element of truth in the politicians' belief that what was good for the party was in the public interest. The party was a mechanism through which a vast number of more or less conflicting interests arrived at terms on which they could work together, and over the long run the party could not survive and prosper if it deeply offended any large sector of its public. The Democratic machine, for example, could not survive if it outraged the Negroes or the whites in the conservation areas. The survival and prosperity of the machine depended upon its ability to find settlements which both sides would agree represented the public interest or something approaching it.

28. New Strength at City Hall

SEYMOUR FREEDGOOD

At the troubled core of the big city stands City Hall, a block-square, granite citadel heavily encrusted with myth. It was a half-century ago that Lincoln Steffens described the "shame of the cities"—the bosses, the

Originally published in *Fortune,* LVI (November 1957), reprinted in *The Exploding Metropolis* (Garden City, New York: Doubleday & Company, Inc., 1958), pp. 62–78, 84–86. Reprinted here by permission of the publisher. Seymour Freedgood is a publicist.

boodlers, the job sellers, and the hopeless inefficiency of the city's house-keeping. The image persists. Most people are aware that the machines have fallen on parlous times—but they're not sure that what's left is much better. The dramatic corruption may have gone but the belief that the big city's government is a mess remains. When people look for models of municipal efficiency, it is outward, to the hinterland, that they are apt to turn; here, where "grass roots" are more visible, are the slumless smaller cities and the towns with city managers, and it is to them that most of the accolades for municipal success are directed.

The emphasis is misplaced. Where the problems are the toughest—in the big, crowded, noisy city—government has virtually transformed it-self. Today the big city must rank as one of the most skillfully managed of American organizations—indeed, considering the problems it has to face, it is better managed than many U.S. corporations.

The suburbanization of the countryside has plunged America's big cities—specifically the twenty-three cities with population of 500,000 and over—into a time of crisis. Hemmed in by their hostile, booming suburbs, worried about the flight of their middle class, and hard pressed to main-tain essential services for their own populations, they need, if they are to hold their own, let alone grow, top-notch leadership.

They have it. Since the 1930's, and at an accelerating rate after the second world war, the electorate in city after city has put into office as competent, hard-driving, and skillful a chief executive as ever sat in the high-backed chair behind the broad mahogany desk. At the same time they have strengthened the power of the office.

This has not been a victory for "good government." To most people, good government is primarily honest and efficient administration, and they believe that the sure way for the city to get it is to tighten civil service, eliminate patronage, and accept all the other artifacts of "scien-tific" government, including the council-city-manager plan. But today's big-city mayor is not a good-government man, at least in these terms, and if he ever was, he got over it a long time ago. He is a tough-minded, soft-spoken politician who often outrages good-government people, or, as the politicians have called them, the Goo-Goos.

One of the biggest threats to his leadership, indeed, is too much "good government." The big problem at City Hall is no longer honesty, or even simple efficiency. The fight for these virtues is a continuous one, of course, and Lucifer is always lurking in the hall, but most big-city governments have become reasonably honest and efficient. Today, the big problem is not good housekeeping: it is whether the mayor can pro-vide the aggressive leadership and the positive programs without which no big city has a prayer. What is to get priority? Industrial redevelop-ment? More housing? (And for whom?) There is only so much money, and if hard policy decisions are not made, the city's energies will be diffused in programs "broad" but not bold.

The mayor is hemmed in. As he strives to exercise policy leadership, his power is challenged on all sides. In his own house the staff experts and the civil-service bureaucrats threaten to nibble him to death in their efforts to increase their own authority. Then there are the public "authorities." Some are single-purpose authorities—like the city housing authorities, and the sewer districts; some, like the Port of New York Authority, handle a whole range of functions. They are eminently useful institutions, but however efficient they may be, they are virtually laws unto themselves and they have severely limited the mayor's ability to rule in his own house and, more important, his ability to plan for long-range development.

The power struggle also goes on between the mayor and the state legislature, which has a controlling voice in the city's fiscal affairs, but whose membership is apportioned in favor of the rural areas. It is the rare mayor who need not make frequent trips to the state capital for additional funds, and the legislature is usually unsympathetic. Colorado's, for example, gives Denver a niggardly $2,300,000 a year in state aid for a school system of 90,000 children; right next to it, semi-rural Jefferson County, with 18,000 pupils, gets $2,400,000.

There is the continuing struggle between the mayor and the suburbs, whose people, the big city firmly believes, are welshing on their obligations to the city. The mayor must win the cooperation of his suburban counterparts if he is to do anything at all about the city's most pressing problems—e.g., the traffic mess—and the going is grim. No one is against "saving our cities," but in this seemingly antiseptic cause there are fierce conflicts of interests and the power struggle is getting more intense.

What Citizens Want: More

There has been a change in City Hall because there has been a change in the city itself. For the better part of a century, the core of big-city life was its immigrants—waves and waves of them, many illiterate, few English-speaking, all poor. Their grinding misery kept the machine in power at the hall. The machine fed on the immigrants, but it also helped them—with jobs, with welfare services and personal favors, with Christmas baskets and dippers of coal—and the immigrants, in turn, were generous with their votes. The 1924 Immigration Act put an end to this cycle. Reduced immigration gave the city time to absorb the earlier newcomers, reduce the language barriers, educate them and their children, and raise many of them into the middle class. This, along with federal social security and unemployment insurance, reduced the dependence of the big-city masses on the political machines. After World War II came the huge influx of southern Negroes and Puerto Ricans, but by this time the machine was beyond a real comeback.

A half-century's work by the National Municipal League, the Institute of Public Administration, and other government research groups was a big factor. They fought and in many places won the hard fight for the short ballot, which eliminates "blind" voting, and for better city charters, better budgeting, and more efficient management methods.

Better-qualified people came into government. During the unemployment of the 1930's governments could recruit talent they couldn't before. Most of the bright young men went off to Washington, but many of them went into city government too. Some now man its top administrative posts, and they have done much to raise civil-service standards.

Most important, the public began asking for more. It now demands as a natural right better-administered services—police and fire protection, water, sewerage, and all the rest—and it judges its public officials on how well they are able to satisfy this demand. It also demands services—psychiatric clinics, youth boards, air-pollution control—it never had before. City government, as a result, has been transformed into an enormous service machine, infinitely complicated to run.

The Management Men

To many an aspirant who wouldn't have thought of city politics a generation ago, the mayoralty is now eminently worth his mettle. This has been particularly true in cities where long-standing sloth and corruption had created the possibility of a dramatic reversal; in these places an able and ambitious man might well conclude that his opportunities for spectacular, visible achievement outran those of a governor or senator. But the new mayors are more than opportunists. They come from widely different social and economic backgrounds, and they differ as widely in temperament, but all share a sense of mission; while it also happens to be good politics, they feel deeply that they should make their decisions in terms of the community-wide interest rather than the interest of any one group.

The profile of today's big-city mayor—with one difference—is quite similar to that of the chief executive of a large corporation. Typically, the mayor is a college graduate, usually with a legal or business background, and is now in his late fifties. He puts in hard, grinding hours at his desk, sometimes six or seven days a week, and his wife suffers as much as his golf game. The difference is in salary: he usually makes $20,000 to $25,000. There is also a chauffeur-driven limousine and, in some cities, an expense allowance, ranging from $2,000 (Milwaukee) to $55,000 (Chicago).

"Public relations" take a big chunk of his time. He is aggressively press-conscious, holds frequent news conferences, often appears on TV-radio with his "Report to the People"; and from his office flows a flood of releases on civic improvements. About five nights a week there are civic receptions, banquets, policy meetings, and visits with neighborhood civic groups. In between he may serve as a labor negotiator, or a member of the Civil Defense Board.

The mayor is also seeing a lot more of the city's business leaders, whose interest in urban renewal is growing steadily. Despite the fact that His Honor is likely to be a Democrat, he gets along very well with the businessmen, though he is apt to feel that they have a lot to learn about political decision-making. A City Hall man recently summed up the feelings of his fellows: "These businessmen like everything to be nice and orderly—and nonpolitical. They're getting hot now on metropolitan planning. They think it's not political! Throw them into shifting situations where there are a lot of conflicts and no firm leadership and they're completely buffaloed. It's painful to watch them trying to operate. But once there's a firm program lined up and they've bought it, they're very effective."

Above all the mayor is a politician. True, he may have risen to office on the back of a reform movement. But he is not, as happened too often in the past, a "nonpolitical" civic leader who rallies the do-gooders, drives the rascals out of City Hall, serves for an undistinguished term or two, and then withdraws—or gets driven out—leaving the city to another cycle of corruption. Instead, he fits the qualifications of the mayors whom Lincoln Steffens called on the public to elect: "politicians working for the reform of the city with the methods of politics." His main interest is in government, not abstract virtue, and he knows that the art of government is politics.

DeLesseps Morrison of New Orleans is a notable example of a political leader who leaped into office on a reform ticket, then used the methods of politics to put his programs across. In the years since insurgents elected Mayor Morrison over opposition from the long-entrenched regulars who had run the town wide open, he has done more than demonstrate that hard-working and efficient management can change the face of a city. Morrison has consolidated the gains—in large part by his ability to turn the loose organization that first supported him into a thoroughly professional political organization, which regularly helps elect friendly councilmen. The Morrison organization, not surprisingly, is anathema to the old Democratic machine.

In Philadelphia, Richardson Dilworth and his predecessor, Mayor (now Senator) Joseph Clark, have followed the Morrison pattern up to a point. In 1952 Philadelphia civic groups wrested control of City Hall from a corrupt and contented Republican machine, and the Clark and Dilworth administrations have given the city vigorous and honest government ever since. Mayor Dilworth, in office since 1956, is making considerable headway with his programs; unlike Morrison, however, he has not yet chosen to organize his followers into a political organization that can regularly get out the vote on election day. The old-line Democrats and Republicans, as a result, have been increasingly successful in electing their own men to the council.

The new mayor, of course, does not need a dragon to fight. Indeed, some of today's best mayors are in cities that have enjoyed reasonably honest government for quite some time. Detroit's late aggressive Mayor Albert Cobo was one of these. He believed that government should be run like a business: during his eight years in office he overhauled the city's government, department by department, replacing the old, wasteful ways of doing things with machines and management systems that would do credit to any corporation.

St. Louis, Cincinnati, and Milwaukee, all with long traditions of honest government, have a remarkable trio of mayors: each wears a distinctively scholarly air, and is a pretty good politician to boot. St. Louis, once an ailing city, has found one of the ablest leaders in its history in an engineering professor, Raymond Tucker. Enthusiastically backed by the city's business leaders and the St. Louis press, Mayor Tucker has persuaded the voters to approve new taxes and public-improvement bond issues with which he has pulled the city out of the red and away from the blight. Milwaukee, a well-governed city since 1910, now has professorial, mild-mannered Frank P. Zeidler as its mayor. He too has stimulated a conservative, frugal citizenry into approving needed physical improvements. Cincinnati, under council-city-manager government since 1926, has Charles Taft, a top mayor who has given the city's urban-renewal and highway programs a powerful boost.

Bridging the Gap

The mayors of Pittsburgh and Chicago bridge the gap between the traditional machine-boss mayor and today's management-man mayor. Pittsburgh's David Lawrence and Chicago's Richard Daley are both powerful Democratic organization leaders as well as strong mayors: each has given his city increasingly good government—and a big push forward in meeting its problems—while at the same time maintaining his organization in viable if declining power. Of the two, Daley has been the bigger surprise. When he was elected many people believed he would sell City Hall to Cicero without a qualm. Instead, Daley went along to a remarkable extent in putting into effect reform legislation that tightened and improved the structure of Chicago's city government. Chicago, Senator Paul Douglas once observed, is a city with a Queen Anne front and a Mary Ann rear. That may still be the case with its government: it undoubtedly has much to do before its rear is as respectable as its front. But Daley, a man who has been known to do odd things with the queen's English, seems determined to close the gap. "We will go on," he once announced at a town-and-gown dinner of the city and the University of Chicago, "to a new high platitude of success."

The Strong Mayor

In his drive for more power, the big-city mayor is in direct conflict with a strong trend in municipal government. This is the council-city-manager plan, which is the fastest spreading form of government among cities of 25,000 to 100,000. To many do-gooders, it is the ideal form of government for the American city, big or small. Basically, it is government by a board of directors: an elected committee decides on city policies, and the hired manager and his experts carry them out.

The system has been most successful in smaller cities—e.g., Watertown, New York (population, 35,000), whose inhabitants are for the most part homogeneous and native born, where ethnic and economic tensions are low, and where the future holds no big threats. Cities like Watertown may thrive under such government; most big cities cannot.

Their electorates seem to sense this. When asked to vote on a new city charter, they have usually settled on one providing for a strong mayor rather than committee leadership. As a result, the trend to the strong chief executive, long evident in the federal government and the urban state capitals, is now running high in the cities. Of the twenty-three largest, fourteen have adopted some kind of "strong-mayor" charter, five still vest most power in the council, and four use the council-manager plan.

Philadelphia, which is symbolic of so much of the best and worst that can happen to a city, has indicated why the major cities are choosing the strong-mayor-council rather than the council-city-manager form of government. In 1949, civic dissatisfaction with the machine was picking up so much steam that Mayor Bernard Samuel consented to the appointment of a fifteen-man bipartisan commission to draft a charter for the better government of the city. After months of study, the commissioners arrived at these alternatives:

New York

Under the 1938 charter, drafted by a commission appointed by Mayor La Guardia, New York's mayors were given strong statutory powers, and the city council, then called the board of aldermen—and sometimes the Boodle Board or the Forty Thieves—was cut in both size and authority. The charter gave the mayor two prime tools of the strong chief executive: the right (1) to hire and fire his key department heads and (2) to make his operating budget, which the council may cut but not increase. He may also veto council ordinances, and a two-thirds vote is needed to override him. But the mayor's fiscal powers were shackled from another direction: the city's "upper house," the board of estimate, may do almost as it pleases with his budget and the mayor has no veto there.

Cincinnati

In 1924, civic reformers, now called the Charter party, swept out the corrupt administration of Boss Rud K. Hynica and adopted a package of related reforms—the city-manager plan with a nine-man council elected at large on a nonpartisan ballot by proportional representation. Under the plan, the council elects the mayor, who, with the council's approval, appoints the city manager and the city's boards and commissions. The manager, in turn, picks his department heads and is responsible for administration.

The Philadelphia commissioners, at least half sold on the beauties of the council-manager plan, decided to visit Cincinnati to take a firsthand look at a successful city-manager city. They spent a day in the city, and consulted closely with Charles Taft and other Cincinnati officials. Finally, the Philadelphians asked Taft if he would recommend the manager plan for a city of two million people—i.e., as large as Philadelphia. "No," he said flatly.

"When the Lord himself said he didn't want those ten commandments spread elsewhere," an ex-commissioner observes, "that was the death knell."

One reason the manager plan has worked admirably in Cincinnati is that the Charter party—which first sponsored the system—is a fairly well-organized political party, and it has been helped considerably at the polls by proportional representation. The Charterites, a fusion of independent Republicans and Democrats, have been able to beat off the regular Republican machine at election time and thus maintain a majority—or at least a strong minority—on the council. (The city, although technically nonpartisan in municipal elections, has local political parties, and the voters generally know who the parties' candidates are.)

In other cities, however, the council-manager form of government revealed a significant flaw: it failed to produce political leadership on which responsibility for the city government could be pinned. The very large cities, with all their complex needs and challenges, require an elected chief executive to serve as the center of political leadership and responsibility, and to provide policy guidance and planning.

The new Philadelphia charter, overwhelmingly approved in 1951, incorporated the elements of New York's "strong mayor" plan with the significant omission of the board of estimate and with some very important additions. Most notably, the mayor's office was strengthened by permitting him to appoint a managing director, who, with the mayor's approval, appoints most of the city's department heads and is responsible to the mayor for over-all administration. The idea was to relieve the chief executive of routine administrative chores, and thus give him more time for the important job of hammering out policy. . . .

Child of the State

The big test of the mayor as policy leader is whether he can provide the city with vigorous programs of development and expansion—if possible, within an organized plan. The problem is awesome, and much of it boils down to money—money for capital development, and money to meet the rising costs of city services, including services to suburbanites who don't want to pay for them. The city's own tax revenues are rarely enough to pay for all its needs, and to raise taxes much higher would simply drive more people to the suburbs. For a solution of his money problem, the mayor must rely on governments other than his own. He must look to the encircling suburban governments, and to the state legislature. When he looks, he may be excused for blanching.

The arena in which the big-city mayor wages this fiscal struggle is the state legislature, and the struggle can be rough. The city, as a municipal corporation, is the child of the state, and the state legislature or constitution usually limits its power to levy taxes or borrow money. City dwellers, moreover, pay a wide variety of state taxes, but the big city, as likely as not, gets a disproportionate share of the return. Pennsylvania, for example, pays every nonsectarian hospital $8 a day for care of indigent patients—except Philadelphia's city-owned General Hospital. The revenue loss to the city is almost $2,500,000 a year.

Low on the Totem Pole

Chicago's Daley has summed up the consistent lament of most big-city mayors: "I think there's too much local money going to the state capitals and Washington. It's ridiculous for us to be sending them money and asking for it back. I don't think the cities should have to go hat in hand when they need money for improvements. We're going to have to clarify the role of the locality in relation to state and national governments. The cities and metropolitan areas are the important areas of the country today, but they're still on the low part of the totem pole."

Chicago isn't starving for money: its maximum property-tax rate is not set by law, and Daley recently won an additional privilege—although at a price. He got a bill through the state legislature giving him a ½ per cent sales tax, which the state collects and returns to the city, minus 6 per cent for its bother. A number of other cities, among them New York, Los Angeles, and New Orleans, are in fairly good financial shape, in part because they have been authorized by the state to levy special taxes in addition to the basic property tax. They and others—among them Pittsburgh and Dallas—have also been helped by their building booms, expanding the property-tax base. But some of the rest are in trouble, and the trouble can be bad. Boston, perhaps, is in the worst shape of all. It has had a legacy of inefficient government; both its population and its property-tax base are shrinking, and the state government, itself strapped for funds, won't help the city with its problems.

29. The General Manager Idea for Large Cities

WALLACE S. SAYRE

A new managerial idea is taking hold in the large cities of the United States. This idea is that the administration of large city governments requires general managerial direction and that this requirement

Reprinted from *Public Administration Review*, XIV (Autumn 1954), pp. 253–58 by permission of the author and the publisher. Documentation omitted. Wallace S. Sayre is a professor of political science at Columbia University.

can best be met by establishing under the mayor a general manager who will, in greater or less degree, be the city government's second in administrative command. The general manager plan thus builds upon the strong-mayor tradition as the most widespread form of city government in the United States. By marrying the manager idea with the idea of the elected chief executive, the general manager plan preserves the office of mayor as the center of political leadership and responsibility. In large cities this center is widely regarded as indispensable to effective government.

The general manager plan may be regarded either as a competitor of the council manager idea or as a more mature form of the manager idea, reflecting the judgment in the larger cities that the council manager plan represents an unnecessary surrender of the values of leadership and accountability found in the institution of the elected chief executive. The general manager or mayor manager plan, its proponents emphasize, captures the advantages of the council manager plan without the risks of abandoning the elected chief executive. An effective manager, they believe, is no less likely to be chosen by a mayor than by a city council.

The council manager plan has not found acceptance in the large cities of the United States. Cincinnati, the largest city using the plan, has a population of a half million. Of the seventeen other cities having a population of a half million or more, only one city—Cleveland—has ever adopted the plan, and it was abandoned there more than twenty years ago. In the last decade (perhaps even longer), no large city has given serious consideration to the adoption of the council manager plan.

The literature of the council manager movement does not provide an answer to the question: why has the plan failed to find support in large cities? In fact, the literature does not tell us much about the ecology of the council manager plan in adoptions and operations. Why, for example, are half of all the council manager cities to be found in six states (California, Florida, Maine, Michigan, Texas, and Virginia)? Does the council manager plan find acceptance primarily in particular social, economic, and political environments? Does it, for example, find greatest acceptance and operate most successfully in one-party or in "nonpartisan" constituencies? Is the affinity between the council manager plan and small and middle-sized cities the result of the plan's suitability for the management of the particular governmental problems to be found in cities of such size? Is the council manager plan particularly attractive to cities which are growing rapidly in size or to those which are declining in population and resources? To these and other questions about the council manager plan we do not yet have the answers.

The Large Cities Turn Toward the Mayor Manager Plan

Eight large cities (Boston, Los Angeles, Louisville, Newark, New Orleans, New York City, Philadelphia, and San Francisco) have now established some kind of general managerial assistance for the mayor. In two others (Chicago and Detroit) proposals for such general managerial arrangements have been made.

This new managerial trend in large cities has not resulted from an organized effort by municipal reformers with a symmetrical design for the improvement of city government. In fact, this new form of the manager idea in city government has not yet acquired a distinctive label. Some observers call it the mayor manager plan, to emphasize its contrast with the council manager plan; others call it the mayor administrator plan; and still others name it the general manager plan.

The general manager idea for cities began its governmental history in San Francisco in 1932, when charter revision movement established the office of chief administrative officer. This office represented a compromise solution between those who urged a council manager form and those who supported the retention of the strong mayor form. The plan was not widely noticed, but it has prevailed to the general satisfaction of the electorate. In 1938 New York City's new charter established the office of deputy mayor, an office which developed more as a center of legislative and political assistance to the mayor than as a center of managerial aid. In 1941, Lent D. Upson proposed a general manager under the mayor for the city of Detroit, but the proposal was not accepted. In 1948, Louisville began a related experiment with the appointment of a city consultant-administrator who serves as general managerial assistant to the mayor. In 1951, Los Angeles established a city administrative officer. In the same year, Philadelphia's new charter took a long step forward in developing the general manager idea by establishing the office of managing director with substantial powers. In 1953, New Orleans adopted a new charter which established the office of chief administrative officer, with powers similar to but greater than those of Philadelphia's managing director. In the same year, Boston established a director of administrative services and Newark adopted a new charter which established the office of business administrator under the mayor, the option under the New Jersey statutes closest to the general manager idea. In 1954, New York City established the office of city administrator, with Luther Gulick the first incumbent. And in September, 1954, the staff report to the Chicago Charter Revision Commission recommended the adoption of the general manager plan for that city.

Thus the experiment begun in San Francisco over twenty years ago has captured civic interest and has led to official action in an impressive portion of the large cities. Why has this happened? Several explanations may be suggested:

1. The council manager plan had proved to be unacceptable in large city environments, but the values of the managerial idea were still sought in some more attractive structural form.

2. The office of mayor—an elected chief executive who is the center of energy and of public leadership and the focus of responsibility for policy and performance—had become too important an asset in large cities to be exchanged for the speculative values of legislative supremacy and a city manager as represented in the council manager plan.

3. The mayor manager plan fits comfortably and easily into the American political system: it preserves the elected chief executive; it keeps the mayoralty as the focus of the party battle; it emphasizes the values of integration, hierarchy, and professional management, all made familiar doctrine by a half-century of administrative reorganizations in national, state, and municipal governments and by the doctrine of the council manager movement itself.

Emerging Elements of the General Manager Idea

The idea of a general manager serving under the mayor has not been a pre-packaged solution developed as finished doctrine by municipal reformers. Rather, its evolution has been experimental, each application being worked out in relation to local experience and governmental conditions, and varying with the boldness or caution of local leadership. There are several discernible trends in the successive adoptions, however. These can be briefly stated as follows:

1. The general manager is increasingly made more clearly the managerial agent of the mayor, "The mayor's man." In San Francisco in 1932 the manager was made virtually irremovable, but under 1953–54 provisions in New Orleans and New York City the manager holds office at the pleasure of the mayor.

2. As the manager is made more responsible to the mayor, he tends to be given more power—to approach more nearly the status of second in administrative command. In New Orleans and Philadelphia, the cities which represent the most full-bodied application of the general

manager idea, the manager is given, for example, the power to appoint and remove the heads of most of the city departments with the approval of the mayor.

3. There is a continued ambivalence in deciding whether the general manager's authority and responsibility should center upon the "staff" or upon the "line" agencies and activities of the city government.

In almost every instance the manager is given primary responsibility for administrative planning and for other organization and methods work. In Los Angeles and New Orleans he has responsibility for budget preparation and execution; in Philadelphia and New York these activities are not under the manager's jurisdiction. In no city does the manager directly supervise the personnel agency. In New Orleans, New York, and Philadelphia the "line" agencies are the manager's major responsibility. The two extremes are represented by Los Angeles, where the manager's responsibilities are focused upon the management functions (except personnel), and by Philadelphia, where the manager's powers are centered upon the "line" agencies.

4. There is some tendency to create a new and smaller cabinet institution under the mayor, consisting of the general manager and the heads of the "staff" agencies. This is particularly the case in Philadelphia and New York. The heads of the "line" agencies, when they function as a cabinet (as they do in Philadelphia), do so in a meeting presided over by the manager.

Variations in the Office and Powers of the General Manager in Five Large Cities

The variety as well as the trends in the development of the general manager idea in the large cities of the United States may perhaps best be seen through a more specific description of the office and the powers conferred upon it in Los Angeles, New Orleans, New York City, Philadelphia, and San Francisco.

Title

In San Francisco and New Orleans the manager is called chief administrative officer; in Los Angeles, city administrative officer; in Philadelphia, managing director; in New York, city administrator.

Appointment

In every instance, the manager is appointed by the mayor. Only in Los Angeles is council approval required.

Term

In San Francisco, Los Angeles, New Orleans, and New York, no term is specified. In Philadelphia the term of the manager is four years, corresponding to the term of the mayor appointing him.

Removal

In New Orleans and New York the mayor may remove the manager. In Los Angeles, the mayor may remove the manager, but the approval of the council is required. In Philadelphia the mayor must prefer charges; the manager may appeal his removal to the Civil Service Commission which may award him compensation but may not restore him. In San Francisco the mayor may not remove; the manager is subject to recall in an election, or the legislative body may remove him by a two-thirds vote. In Los Angeles and New Orleans the council may also remove the manager—in Los Angeles by a two-thirds vote and in New Orleans by a majority vote of all members.

Powers of the Manager

The powers of the managers may be described in three categories: (1) the power to appoint and remove heads of city agencies; (2) the power to supervise city administrative operations; (3) the power to provide general advice and assistance to the mayor.

1. To *appoint and remove heads of agencies:* In Philadelphia, New Orleans, and San Francisco, the managers appoint and remove the heads of specified city departments and agencies. In San Francisco the manager does not need the mayor's approval for such appointments or removals; in Philadelphia and New Orleans the mayor's approval is required. In New Orleans the manager's power to appoint and remove extends to the heads of all but two city departments (law and civil service); in Philadelphia it includes all but finance, law, and personnel. In neither of these two cities does the power to appoint and remove include members of boards or commissions. In San Francisco, the power extends to departments specified by name in the charter; such departments constitute about half of the city agencies.

In neither Los Angeles nor New York does the manager have the power to appoint or remove heads of departments.

2. To *supervise city administrative operations:* In San Francisco the power of the manager to supervise is confined to the departments specifically assigned to him by the charter. In Los Angeles the manager's opportunities for supervision flow solely from his role as city budget officer. In Philadelphia the manager's power to supervise is largely

confined to the departments whose heads he appoints, but some more general supervision flows from his powers to perform the administrative analysis function in all city agencies.

In New Orleans the manager has more general supervisory authority. He supervises not only his own subordinate agencies (which include most of the city agencies), but he also gives "general oversight" to law, civil service, and the City Planning Commission (which are outside his appointing and removal authority), prescribes standards of administrative practice to be followed by all agencies and boards, prepares and supervises the operating and capital budgets, surveys the organization and procedures of all agencies and boards, and may require reports from any or all of them.

In New York City the city administrator, although lacking any power to appoint or remove, has a broad supervisory assignment. Under the direction of the mayor, he "shall supervise and coordinate the work of all agencies under the jurisdiction of the mayor" except law, investigation, budget, the construction coordinator, and boards, commissions (which include personnel), and authorities. He may convene heads of agencies singly or collectively, procure information and reports, require the keeping of management records, conduct work studies, and establish management standards for most, if not all, city agencies.

3. *The power to provide general advice and assistance to the mayor:* In Philadelphia and New York the manager is under a special obligation to serve as general management adviser to the mayor. In Philadelphia the managing director is required to report periodically to the mayor concerning the affairs of the city government (not merely the affairs of his own departments), and he is authorized to make recommendations on matters concerning the affairs of the whole city government. In New York the city administrator is required to "prepare annual and all such other reports as the mayor shall require," and to "analyze and report to the mayor concerning impending policy decisions affecting the management of the city and the agencies." He is also directed to "maintain liaison with civic and community groups on matters of governmental management."

In both Philadelphia and New York the manager derives special status from cabinet arrangements, established by the charter in Philadelphia and by the mayor's action in New York. In each city there is a small top-level cabinet group meeting weekly with the mayor, in which the manager plays a central role.

The managers in the other three cities have no explicit responsibility to serve as the general adviser to the mayor on management matters. In these cities, the manager's role in this respect is implicit, if it exists at all. In San Francisco it would seem difficult to join such a role with that of an almost autonomous manager. In New Orleans it would seem to be a logical and natural development. In Los Angeles, it would appear to be a more confined but possible development.

The Future Course of the Mayor Manager Plan

The invention and recent growth of the general manager idea in large cities is a product of many influences. Some of these influences would seem to be of reasonably permanent rather than transient character. The larger cities of the United States have developed complex administrative establishments which require strengthened central managerial leadership, direction, and coordination. These cities have also, almost without exception, developed an increasing reliance upon the elected chief executive—a mayor with extensive powers to appoint, to remove, and to direct the heads of administrative agencies—as the main institution of governmental leadership and accountability. The electoral contest for this office has become the primary instrument of popular control of the city government and the main occasion for public education and participation in city affairs. The office of mayor in large cities has, in addition, become more important as a prize in the party battle, its possession one of the significant keys to state and even national party power. It would seem unlikely that any large city would abandon such a governmental and political asset.

But if the institution of the "strong" mayor in large cities has come to stay, then it would also seem that such mayors, no less than the President, need managerial help. The mayor manager idea is a response to this felt need in the large cities. In this sense, the mayor manager plan is in the mainstream of the administrative doctrine heralded by the President's Committee on Administrative Management in 1937, and reaffirmed by the Hoover Commission's later studies of the national government. The central idea of these studies, and dozens of their counterparts in the states, has been to strengthen the position of the elected chief executive in his political and administrative leadership.

The mayor manager plan is likely to dominate the course of large city administrative reorganizations for the next several years. The council manager plan is not likely to break into the large city league, because this plan does not represent an accommodation to either the political or the managerial requirements of the large cities. The emergence of the mayor manager plan has breached the monopolistic claim of the council manager plan to the managerial virtues by presenting the new and strong competition of an alternative manager plan.

Not only is the mayor manager plan likely to hold its own and to extend its scope to most of the largest cities, but it is also probable that it will become an attractive solution for many (perhaps most) of the one hundred and five cities with 100,000 population or more. In contrast with the council manager plan, the mayor manager plan is elastic in its formal arrangements, and it can thus respond more easily to local priorities, customs, and personalities. To the strong mayor cities, it offers an evolutionary transition, buttressing rather than discarding the values which have been built up around the leadership of the elected chief executive. To these cities, the mayor manager plan offers the same managerial gains as does the council manager plan, but at much less risk. The strategic and tactical advantages of such an offer in the political world can hardly be exaggerated.

The mayor manager plan will, as it evolves toward its own institutionalization, be confronted with dilemmas which can now be only partially anticipated. The plan may ultimately acquire its own protective guild of practitioners and advocates, transforming it into an inelastic plan unresponsive to the changing needs of the cities. It may be drowned in a few dramatic "failures."

The mayor manager idea will probably encounter its severest test in the effort to give the manager sufficient power to provide him with adequate leverage to infuse the values of professional management into the administration of a large city government. Philadelphia and New Orleans have made the clearest and strongest effort to insure this result. The Devereux Josephs Commission, in the most complete formulation of the mayor manager plan (*Four Steps to Better Government of New York City*, 1953–54), proposed still greater strength for the manager while making him also more clearly the mayor's administrative agent. The range of variation in managerial power is wide among the cities using the mayor manager idea. The trend in official action and civic opinion—particularly on the manager's appointing power—is not conclusive, but it seems to run toward the grant of greater managerial leverage.

The mayor manager plan will also encounter, perhaps early in its development, the politics-administration dilemma which increasingly bedevils the council manager plan in operation. Can the general manager be at once both a professional administrator and the mayor's second in administrative command? That is, can he be (with the mayor) the effective maker and protagonist of policy proposals which are certain to be controversial without sacrificing his professional managerial status? This dilemma plagues the council manager plan even more deeply (because council manager doctrine emphasizes council monopoly over policy while practice underscores the necessity for policy leadership by the manager), but this fact provides merely an advantage rather than a solution for the mayor manager advocates. The trend in mayor manager cities is not yet clear, but the general manager in a large city seems at this stage no more likely to become a career manager in that city than has the city manager in his.

Some observers profess to see in the mayor manager plan merely a compromise step toward the council manager plan. The reverse would seem to be the more likely development, if any such transference is to occur. The essential ingredient of the mayor manager plan is the appointment and removal of the manager by the mayor as the elected chief executive. The distinctive contrasting feature of the council manager plan—the selection of the chief administrator by the city council—was not only something of an historical accident in the United States; it was also a striking anomaly in a country in which the most distinctive political institution is the elected chief executive as the keystone of political, governmental, and managerial progress. The mayor manager idea has the great and lasting value that it brings the reorganization of our city governments back into a familiar focus, consistent with our efforts in the national and state governments. In this respect it is an indigenous political idea.

30. A Reply

WILLIAM A. SOMMERS

Dr. Sayre ably presents some of the possible explanations for the city manager plan's halt near the water's edge of the bigger cities and he points to the growth of the strong mayor with an administrative assistant or general manager as the possible solution. He also gives city managers food for thought in some of his deftly stated criticisms of the council-

Reprinted from "Council Manager Government: A Review," *Western Political Quarterly*, XI (March 1958), pp. 144–47 by permission of the author and the publisher. Documentation omitted. Mr. Sommers is a practicing manager employed at present by Franklin Township in New Jersey.

manager plan. It is true that the latter has not cracked the population barrier in the 500,000 and over class of cities and there is little doubt that the overriding considerations in these oceans of governmental chaos are political and not administrative, as Dr. Sayre points out. Moreover, [he] lays bare a criticism of the city manager organization itself that has more wisdom than the Association cares, perhaps, to admit. The critique occurs when Sayre comments on the growth of the "general manager" idea, saying:

The mayor manager plan, will, as it evolves toward its own institutionalization, be confronted with dilemmas which can only now be partially anticipated. The plan may ultimately acquire its own protective guild of practitioners and advocates, transforming it into an inelastic plan unresponsive to the changing needs of the cities.

His reference to the International City Managers' Association in the "protective guild of practitioners" is unmistakable and, to some extent, justified. The danger has been pointed out by city managers themselves who feel that the Association may not rise above the level of a fact-gathering institution and a machine for making studies aimed at improving administrative efficiency. It has been stated by a past president of the Association in this way:

In the growth and development of the Association, we have set up procedures and professionalization beyond the standards which will be generally accepted by the local governments we serve. This is one mark of a professional group and is to be expected and desired but over-professionalization carries with it the very serious danger of leaving behind the people we serve.

The mayor-administrator idea which has made headway in the last few years is not an extension of the council-manager principle; rather, it is an attempt at compromise which tries to achieve both the political strength of the strong mayor and the administrative improvements which are closely associated with council-manager government. Perhaps the best argument for the plan arises when an existing strong mayor system, founded on political necessity arising out of its unwieldy size, is modified to provide for administrative improvement.

The greatest long-run advantage, however, of council-manager government over the "general manager" form lies in the demonstrated continuity of the former. While turnover in city managers is comparable to that in similar positions in public and private employment, the manager plan cannot be sustained if replacements are not available, who are disciplined in the principles of municipal administration and who subscribe to a common method of practice. The history of council-manager government shows that even with expected turnover of city managers most cities under the plan have preserved for them continuity of administration. The International City Managers' Association has been the key in developing standards and procedures and thus furnishing the thread of continuity to managerial practice.

But standards are only part of the story. The natural result of professional growth is to weave between members engaged in the same work a consistency in ethical responsibility. City managers adhere to an ethical standard which has evolved over the years. While there exists no real machinery for discipline among managers, the importance of professional standing and acknowledgment in the field has acted as a far more potent regulator of conduct than any board of discipline. Of course, sour apples are not unknown among city managers: however, the ideals of the profession have held up remarkably well. And with over fourteen hundred manager cities in operation there is an ample field from which replacements can be recruited while well-trained novices are becoming available in great numbers. Thus, a city, upon losing its present manager, can recruit from a field of trained and experienced people who have a common grounding in the principles of municipal operation and who subscribe to a general standard of conduct.

The council-manager plan has been freed of partisan shackles in its day-to-day operation. While the city manager does not shy away from the role of community leader nor completely ignore policy proposals, he has resisted the obvious temptation to dabble in the political, partisan conflicts which may engage the city council; and it is well understood that the city manager is not a political leader nor a partisan messenger boy for groups within the council or the community. The city manager, in other words, is not tied to the strings of a political mentor, be it mayor, council, or special interest group.

There is not enough experience in the operation of the general manager plan to assess the result as to administrative continuity, professional standards, and the separation from political identification and partisan struggles. However, the general manager setup does not bode well for such future developments. Being the appointee of the mayor, the administrator cannot long escape identification with the political success or failure ascribed to the mayor himself. And, in fact, it is difficult to see how his actions at the behest of the mayor cannot help but blend administrative fact with the political necessities of the mayor's own elective career. What professional reserve or reservoir of previous practice is to preserve the administrative sphere of operation from important political partisan inroads? These are merely conjectures on the future of the general manager plan but ones to be considered against the demonstrated accomplishments of the council-manager plan. They cannot be disregarded as easily as Dr. Sayre sometimes finds it necessary to do in pursuing his advocacy of the general manager plan.

Another of Dr. Sayre's sallies should not escape comment. It is contained in the last paragraph of his article:

The distinctive contrasting feature of the council-manager plan—the selection of the chief administrator by the city council—was not only something of an historical accident in the United States; it was also a striking anomaly in a country in which the most distinctive political institution is the elected chief executive as the keystone of political, governmental, and managerial progress. The mayor manager idea has the great and lasting value that brings the reorganization of our city governments back into a familiar focus, consistent with our efforts in the national and state governments. In this respect it is an indigenous political idea.

This is an interesting, albeit romantic notion, particularly regarding "an indigenous political idea." One has but to review the growth of American local government to see that the elected chief executive is not all of a solid piece. School district government, county and township organization afford little evidence of this "most distinctive political institution." The history of municipal government is so interwoven with executive boards and commissions that the figure of the chief executive is somewhat clouded in contrast to the clear picture given us by Dr. Sayre. In Peoria, for example, the strong mayor form was in continuous operation until the adoption of council-manager government in 1952. However, the functions of the library, the parks, the sanitary operation, playgrounds and recreation, health and tuberculosis control were all in the hands of semi-independent boards whose members were either elected or appointed and who in turn appointed a professional person to act as chief administrator. The mayor may have operated within a strong executive form but the functions over which he exercised direct administrative control were limited. And Peoria's case is not atypical. Boards, commissions, and appointed administrators are an integral part of local government in the United States, emphasizing the strong roots of the council-manager idea in our tradition. On the other hand, it is nice to have a practicing romanticist even in political theory.

31. The "Weak Mayor" System in a Small City

ARTHUR BROMAGE

(While Arthur Bromage personally favors the council-manager plan, in the following personal account he shows how some degree of coordination may be achieved under a system which structurally incorporates features frowned upon by many administrative reformers.)

When I was elected to the Ann Arbor council in 1949, my approach to municipal government stemmed from a systematic study of the "forms" and "principles" of public administration. The literature of such organizations as the National Municipal League emphasizes the values of the council-manager plan. It underscores also the importance of such reform trends as: the short ballot; small city councils; nonpartisan nomination and election; election at large, or by the Hare system of Proportional Representation; longer terms for councilmen. The literature of reform points to the desirability of separating policy and administrative management. This can be achieved by a council confined largely to policy and a manager charged primarily with administrative fulfillment of policy.

For years, the trends in municipal statistics have been to the council-manager plan and to such features as: the small council, election at large by nonpartisan ballots, and longer terms for councilmen. *The Municipal Year Book,* over recent decades, has reflected the movement to a new concept of American local democracy. This concept combines the small, representative council, possessing a unity of power, with professional management as exemplified by the growing numbers of trained managers. The latter, like interchangeable parts, are capable of serving in numerous cities under various councils.

With this background, I undertook four years of service as a councilman in a weak-mayor city. Ann Arbor was organized in the nineteenth-century American manner with a ward-elected, partisan council, fairly large, with numerous committees. It had direct committee-administrator relations. The mayor, with the consent of the council, appointed citizens to lay boards and commissions which had responsibility for departmental administration. Thus, both the mayor and council committees were con-

Reprinted from *Councilmen at Work* (Ann Arbor, Michigan: George Wahr Publishing Co., 1954), pp. 72–80 by permission of the author and the publisher Mr. Bromage is a professor of political science at the University of Michigan.

fronted, in dealing with the police chief and other line administrators, with a citizen lay group also possessed of authority over departments.

In the population range of 50,000, few American cities today present such an intricate, organizational system, so untouched by modern concepts of administrative management. Moreover, Ann Arbor's structure was supported by a political, representative process virtually unchanged from nineteenth-century norms: wards and partisanship; large council and short terms.

Assuming the objectivity of the laborer in the aldermanic vineyard, one might hope for a test of norms and principles in relation to practical experience. Either one might become convinced that the Ann Arbor system served its purpose well enough, or one might conclude that there is really something to be said for our modern trends in political organization and administrative management.

Summing Up

What are the deficiencies of the American weak-mayor system, particularly when it is so intricately organized as in Ann Arbor? Councilmen have the responsibility for political representation and public relations under any system. They must carry on with legislative policy-making and broad directional functions, such as the budget and capital improvements. These operations, in and of themselves, will keep any councilman busy.

In my experience, Ann Arbor's type of weak-mayor government added many burdens to these primary duties. Executive problems arose in connection with the confirmation of mayoral appointments and the making of appointments by council. Much administrative detail concerning everything from street lights to stop signs found its way into council deliberations and committee work. An old charter made for a series of proposed charter amendments. The most striking omission was that of a working executive or "common boss" for the department heads. In the absence of a common superior, they found direction from their lay boards, from council committees, and from the mayor. Problems got into a series of transfers from council to committees, to boards, and to administrators.

As an alderman, it was sometimes confusing as to where a particular problem had lodged in the mechanism, and whose responsibility it was to dislodge it. Matters which had been cleared by the park superintendent, the park board, and the health, park, lighting, and water committee of the council still had to be restudied by the budget committee if a contingent fund appropriation was involved. In the process the budget committee might and sometimes did reverse the preliminary decision.

Moreover, so many persons were involved in decision-making that responsibility was potentially obscured. Time was consumed by all. A small detail such as a fence around a park took as much time as consideration and reconsideration by different groups required. Problems were identified but it was a long process before they were brought into the sharp focus of decision-making. If it was sometimes difficult for an alderman to retain his interest and enthusiasm, what about the general public? Citizens, frustrated by the obscure turnings of these wheels within wheels, came direct to "their" councilmen to make certain that something was done. On occasion, they sat down with council committees and/or administrative boards to make sure that their views were known and would be followed. The system was open-ended, and citizens could normally gear into any phase of the operation, if they wished to push on decision-making. But, their ultimate resort was to councilmen who had to stand for reelection in their respective wards, or to committee chairmen.

Informal Coordination

American weak-mayor, strong-council government can be made to work by informal coordination. The price of informal coordination is paid in extra hours of effort by mayor, council, committees, administrative boards, and administrators. To compensate for a lack of integrated authority and responsibility, all must pull together through experimental and informal methods of cooperation. If informal techniques fail, chaos can result. The system must be carried by the unusual, personal persistence of the mayor, committee chairmen, lay members of administrative boards and administrators. Since policy-making, policy-forming, executive action, and administrative details are not clearly defined in terms of the responsible parties, anyone, anywhere in this disintegrated mechanism, may be involved in one or more of these activities at any time and within any group.

The committee system worked reasonably well on non-controversial and repetitive types of action, such as creating special assessment districts, awarding small contracts and passing technical ordinances or ordinance amendments. Most of the city's business did not create serious division in the council. Matters flowed from administrators to boards, committees, and council, itself, in an unending stream.

If 90 per cent of the business wasn't controversial, why go through this process? The answer was that weak-mayor, strong-council government had no alternative. The mayor might propose, but the council committees disposed. If the mayor, under a weak-mayor system, were to attempt a severance of committee interrelationships with administrators, he would be violating both the letter and the spirit. The elaborate series of checks meant, to those who liked limited government,—and the more limited the better,—that nothing would be done in a rash moment by one body of decision-makers. By the same token, some things didn't get done, or were done only after supreme human efforts.

The question of a hip roof for a new fire station will illustrate. The lay board of fire commissioners, together with the chief and an architect, reviewed the flat roof *vs.* the hip roof as a design. They gave council two preliminary sketches, and council by resolution voted for a flat roof. Next the fire commissioners proceeded, after further review, to request bids, using specifications calling for a hip roof. The Board of Public Works actually issued the call for bids. The public works committee of the council reminded the councilmen that bids had been called for, although the fire commission had ultimately decided on a hip roof, contrary to council resolution!

The "issue" was then referred to the traffic and safety committee of the council, and this group met with the fire commissioners and chief. They decided to wait for the presentation of bids. The low bid (with the hip roof) came in at $169,000, whereas the city's estimate had been $170,-000. Under these circumstances, the committee recommended that the city accept the low bid, hip roof to the contrary notwithstanding. The station is now built, and it has a hip roof. This demonstrates what can happen when informal methods of coordination prove inadequate and must be bolstered with extra hours of committee work.

The point is, that different structural systems can be made to work, provided councilmen and administrators are considered readily expendable. In Ann Arbor's weak-mayor system, only those individuals who could afford to give 300 to 500 hours per year could undertake to render comprehensive service as councilmen. They dealt, in an admixed pattern, with policy-making, policy-forming, legislation, directoral functions, executive problems, administrative details, and public relations. They had to cooperate with mayor, fellow councilmen, lay administrative board members, and administrators. They had to substitute at times for the missing link,—a common boss for the administrators. It was certainly a democratic system of a disintegrated type, but not always efficient in using representative and administrative talents and energies.

By extra effort councilmen could keep the system in balance and moving forward to new objectives. This was part of the price of informal coordination. Another aspect of price was that administrators were sometimes confused by the divergent and contending forces of council committees and administrative boards. Finally, citizens were put to extra effort to find out just where responsibility rested for policy and administrative action. In major issues, the departmental chief, lay administrative board, council committee, council and mayor, had ultimately to reach agreement. At a minimum this meant a meeting of minds of some 20 busy persons over an indefinite time span. A special council committee to deal with an inter-departmental problem, pulled more persons into the stream of programming and deciding. It is a question whether democracy must necessarily be that complicated. Yet, many of our American cities continue in this kind of weak-mayor, strong-council system, and we are not the only country where this kind of democracy and administration prevail.

Partisanship As A Coordinator

It would be most unrealistic to close these observations without reference to partisanship as a means of coordination. For decades, Ann Arbor has been governed by the Republican organization. During my four years on the council, the Democrats had not more than two and not less than one of the 14 seats on council. The Republicans held the mayorality and presidency of the common council. New ideas in public administration had to be sold to the dominant party group. Emphasis was placed on police, fire, public works, public health, parks and recreation; and on three utilities; water, sewage treatment and off-street parking. Policy was conditioned by the conservative philosophy of a majority of the members.

The Republican party did not hold a caucus before each council meeting. However, at least once a year there was an informal gathering of councilmen at the invitation of the mayor. These meetings included *all* councilmen and principal administrators, as well as members of administrative boards. Usually, the mayor had something interesting to say about program and policy, as he saw it, before the evening was over.

I can recall only one instance where the Republican councilmen as such were gathered together. This was in the basement of city hall one night in 1952, and it related to the party's stand on charter revision, a most fundamental issue. This session was by no means unanimous, and no attempt was made to bind the membership. Ultimately, council did submit the question of charter revision to the voters.

On certain policies, such as the parking-lot and carport system, the mayor exercised leadership. On other matters, the council president exerted initiative; on still others, old-time, influential council-committee chairmen fought for a policy. The councilmen were very independent in their judgments, and had to be "sold" on policy. None of them, as far as I could see, could be told what to do by anyone,—mayor, president, or committee chairman. Sometimes, the party split, as it did over the coordination of city and county health units. A party minority held out against this to the end, and voted NO on the final resolution. On the other hand, on the elimination of rent control, only one Republican voted with two Democrats in the minority.

My estimate of the situation was that coordinating party devices such as frequent caucuses were unnecessary. On the fundamentals of policy in taxation and services, the Republicans were basically united anyway. As a four-term council president was heard to say, the policy was to administer the city in the black. The "socialism," represented by a water utility, a sewage treatment plant surcharged on water rates, and an off-street parking system supported by the nickels from the street meters and lot and carport fees, was accepted. But, no public housing was built. The program of the party had many inarticulate, major premises that did not need to be discussed in caucus. Continued victories at the polls and long experience in governing made frequent party caucuses to discuss programs unnecessary. The party dominance was one of the binders which held a loose-jointed administrative structure together.

The role of the Democratic party was one of active opposition to the Republican majority. Each year, the Democrats mustered a slate of candidates for most or all of the wards. They continued to run candidates for council in wards which were traditionally and overwhelmingly Republican. Their leaders sought to attract support by emphasizing the needs for more recreational facilities and for better housing conditions. The energetic action of the Democrats as a minority in the balloting activated the Republicans to work hard at party organization and policy. One might very well conclude that it was partisan strife which produced party responsibility in government. Consequently, the responsibility of the major party was the primary source for coordination of basic policy-decisions.

Other Coordinating Devices

In addition to the party mechanism, various coordinating devices were at work at the council level and among the administrators. It has already been noted that the mayor took the leadership in the development of an off-street parking lot and carport system. The council president was active from time to time in the resolution of conflicts. He threw his influence at one time to support and carry a plan of city-county, coordinated public health administration.

The most significant integrating device was the budget committee of the common council. This committee received the budget prepared by the budget director, and went to work on the document. The committee held hearings with all the department heads, administrative board members, and sometimes with organized employees. Since fiscal management is very close to general management, the budget committee chairman was a prime integrator. It was the budget committee which finally decided for the addition of more policemen and firemen or against the inclusion of more public health nurses. Once the committee had whipped the budget into final shape it was presented to council and generally adopted without change. A few slight modifications might be made while the budget was passing through council, usually the result of an after thought by the budget committee before any council action. This committee not only set the fiscal policy for the year, but was also the gateway through which budgetary transfers had to pass during the ensuing fiscal period. It was a large committee composed of one councilman from each ward.

Two other committees were most influential as coordinators, the ordinance and public works committees. The ordinance committee exercised the same kind of control over legislative policy which the budget committee had over fiscal affairs. The decisions of the ordinance committee normally became the conclusions of the council on legislation. Matters were sometimes referred back to this committee for further study and modification, and occasional amendments were adopted on second reading. These exceptions only proved the rule of committee leadership. This was not remarkable, since the ordinance committee also was composed of one councilman from each ward, and chaired by an old-time member of the council.

The public works committee in all matters of buildings, streets, sewers, sidewalks, garbage collection and disposal, sewage treatment plant operation, and off-street parking system, exercised a similar kind of dominance. It, too, had membership from each ward. Its range of business was so broad that, like the ordinance committee, public works had to meet before each council session. While other council committees had their bright moments, in council, on policy from time to time, the triumvirate of budget, ordinance and public works was easily predominant. Council members who wanted to work and influence policy cherished assignments to budget, ordinance and public works committees.

During my terms on council, the departments of public works, parks, and water had administrative chiefs that had served the city for decades.

The most influential of these line department heads, in relation to over-all city policy, was, in my judgment, the city engineer. This followed from his long service, the range of functions entrusted to his department, and personal qualities. However, there was no established policy by which department heads met regularly with the mayor or council pres-ident to discuss coordination. Such meetings as were held were largely of a special problem-solving character, and usually included department heads, council-committee members and the council president. Some-times, if the issue was unusually acute, administrative board members were also brought into the group discussion.

It followed that management in Ann Arbor had to be found among a series of devices: the mayor, council president, prominent committee chairmen, budget, ordinance, and council committees, informal leader-ship structure among the administrators, and party responsibility. De-partmental management as distinct from general management was the responsibility of specific lay, administrative boards working with the departmental administrator. The latter was in close association with a council committee. Councilmen had to work at the problem of executive management alongside key administrators.

D. ASSESSMENTS

32. The Doubts of a Political Reporter

JAMES REICHLEY

(This selection is pieced together from Reichley's study of Philadelphia's politicians and civic reformers. Throughout the examination of his central subject, there are comments on the civic reformer and what is lacking in his approach to municipal politics. When placed together as they have been here, these observations seem to us to form a coherent essay on the limita-tions of reform politics.)

Reform, it has been said, is what we have in America in place of ideology. Political participation by those not professionally involved in

Reprinted from *The Art of Government* (New York: Fund for the Republic, 1959), pp. 107–16, 122–28 by permission of the publisher. Mr. Reichley is a pub-licist.

politics is built around periodic attacks on the alleged corruption in government. Unfortunately, these attacks in most areas turn out to be few and far between, and the reform doctrine does not supply the kind of motivation that would keep the greater part of the population politically activated during the long dry spells between uprisings. What is the reason for this failure of "reform" to produce permanent interest in politics, and is there any possibility that it will in the future perform a function of social integration as well as eliminate the abuses at which it is primarily aimed? To answer these questions it will first be necessary to examine the nature of the reform idea. . . .

This philosophy, in both its moral and its economic forms, seems to be oriented toward particular projects rather than toward any broad social image. It promises to perform certain worthwhile tasks of government, whether throwing the crooks out of City Hall or providing a more efficient means of circulating downtown traffic, instead of seeking to understand and to satisfy the fundamental needs of human beings. It takes the needs of human beings as given, and sets out to eliminate obstacles to the relief of these needs which it detects in the framework of society (like crooks) or which have been created by society's own rapid expansion (like street congestion). These objectives, even the moral ones, seem finally to be reducible to an economic view of the nature of man: Crooks are bad because they steal the taxpayers' money; traffic congestion is bad because it is strangling the economic life of the city; city planning is good because it provides an orderly means for the development of metropolitan commerce. . . .

The economic view, coupled with a prevailing individualism which insists that government must limit itself to removing the obstacles to fulfillment of the economic needs of the population rather than undertake to fulfill them itself, makes difficult if not impossible any sustained, large-scale political effort dedicated to the objective of "reform." The declared purpose of reform is the solution of this or that economic problem; when the problem is solved or when it has turned into a bore, the whole reason for the effort has collapsed. The possibility of "continuity" in the reform movement therefore becomes slim, and before very long it is "the same faces" of the organization politicians or ones very much like them that again begin to appear in the halls of government.

A little more than seventy years ago two young Philadelphia gentlemen, Mr. E. P. Allinson and Mr. B. Penrose, wrote a little book called *City Government in Philadelphia* in which, discussing the ultimate failure of a recent reform campaign in their city, they observed:

In its nature, however, the remedy was esoteric and revolutionary, and therefore necessarily ephemeral. It would not retain the spoils system and therefore attract the workers. Its candidates, when elected, often betrayed it and went over to the regulars, who, they foresaw, had more staying qualities. Its members became tired of the thankless task of spending time and money in what must be a continuous, unending battle. The people became restive, and refused their support to what jarred on their conservative ideas, and what they were pleased to call the dictation of an autocratic, self-constituted body. The cry was raised, "Who made thee a ruler and judge over us?"

Mr. B. Penrose, having learned his lesson, went on to become U. S. Senator Boies Penrose, the mighty and unidealistic boss of the Pennsylvania Republican machine.

On a fall afternoon in 1947, twenty-five years after Penrose had died, Richardson Dilworth, then campaigning for the first time for mayor of Philadelphia, told a rally of students on the campus of the University of Pennsylvania: "If I am elected, I will control the Democratic city organization because it will be completely dependent on me. The Democratic organization will be my organization, the organization of reform." The modern politician has stuck by the cause of reform with greater tenacity and firmer dedication than did the old Republican boss; all the same, he has not succeeded in turning his party into "the organization of reform." In the end, almost certainly, it will be the "regulars" who will have "more staying qualities," and the government of Philadelphia, institutionally improved and technologically modernized though it may be, will again slip away from the citizens who are its proper custodians and into the grip of a political machine strikingly similar to that from which Dilworth and his collaborators rescued it in 1951. . . .

If the motive for political participation is strictly an economic one, then it must take its place within the hierarchy of similar economic motives and concerns. Inevitably, the place that it enjoys there cannot be a very high one. It must rank behind the job which is the direct source of personal income; it must rank behind the nominally social activities that are really instruments for personal advancement; it must rank behind the numerous exercises for self-improvement which can be turned back into the direct economic struggle. Since man does not live by bread alone, it will also probably rank behind the explicitly non-economic activities of leisure time. Unable to gain a high priority among

economic motives, it is removed by its economic taint from competition
with the activities that are labeled "pleasure." If political activity is
really primarily motivated by economic concerns, as many reform politicians have seemed to assume, there is little hope that the greater portion of the population can ever be drawn for long stretches of time into
active politics. Luckily, this does not seem to be the case. . . .

Let us now suggest that the sense of frustration and the real failure
in fact belong together: that the reformers and the voters are frustrated
today not so much because a few crooks still loiter about in the corridors
of City Hall but because they have failed in extending the opportunity
for active political participation to the larger number of ordinary citizens. But why should these citizens feel frustrated over being denied
the opportunity for political participation when, as we have argued,
the economic motive for political activity is not a very intense one?

This returns us to the question of what the "boys" really mean when
they say they "love politics." We have admitted that the quest for status
is involved in this motivation, as no doubt it is with the urge that the
ordinary citizen may feel toward the political realm. But we have also
suggested that status hunger alone cannot explain the satisfactions the
"boys" seem to gain from their work, just as it does not explain the clear
emotional return experienced by a Joe Clark or a Richardson Dilworth
or a Thacher Longstreth. Let us look more closely at the concept, "love
politics." What, after all, is politics? Politics, we are told, is who gets
what, when, and how. Viewed in one light, no doubt. But if that is
politics, then what is economics? Is not economics also who gets what,
when, and how? Are politics and economics then identical? Hardly,
since there are clearly economic activities—like selling automobiles and
buying cucumbers—that are not political activities. Is politics, then, a
division within the general class of economics? One thinks not. The feeling of frustration associated with reform, for instance, seems to have
little economic basis, and neither does the feeling of camaraderie that
is so valued by the "boys." *Is not politics more truly defined, all things
considered, as the expression of the will of the individual within the
society of his fellows, or, more completely, the participation of human
beings in the activities of conserving, distributing, and improving the
values that are created by a civilized community?** In short, is not politics the "art of government"? And if this is true, is not the question of
why human beings should "love politics" similar to the question of why
men should love women? Is not the answer to both, that is that it is the na-

---

* Editor's italics.

ture of the beast? Is it not true, then, that political activity is a normal manifestation of human nature, and the real question is: Why should there be men who do *not* love politics?

With this question in mind, let us return for another look at the Protestant group whose mores have set the dominant pattern in the United States, and whose general lack of political interest has been used as an argument in favor of the theory that politics, insofar as it is not economic, is a "status-conferring" function. Let us suggest now that the general lack of political activity among members of the Protestant middle class is due not so much to the fact that they may be in a secure status position as to the effect of an unduly individualistic philosophy which over-emphasizes the private will at the expense of the social context in which it seeks to operate. If this is so, we would expect the political instinct to find expression among Protestants (and among other members of the middle class who have adopted their mores) in some non-political way.

We need not, of course, look very far. The flourishing American institution of service clubs is a perfect device for political behavior that is at the same time outside of real politics. The service clubs perform the subsidiary functions of managing charity, providing an outlet for gregarious impulses, and giving their members a chance to make valuable business contacts; but anyone who has observed their highly organized and extremely active hierarchies of administration, or participated in the parliamentary debates of their conventions and local meetings, must be struck by the fact that they are primarily instruments to enable their members to enjoy the sensations of government while incurring few of its responsibilities. The same can probably be said for many veteran and fraternal organizations and for many organizations of women in the United States. A great many members of the service clubs before whom I have talked agree that the tragedy of the service clubs is that they harness enormous political energies to the necessary but nonetheless secondary tasks of charity and community recreation while leaving the primary work of government to the frequently ill-equipped, ill-directed, and ill-manned party machines. We may submit this manifestation of political behavior growing up behind powerful ideological inhibitions as strong evidence for our contention that man is by his nature a political animal.[1]

What are the blocks that inhibit the attachment of natural political energies to the machinery of government in America today? There are several. Some of them reach far back into ideological history; others are of more recent origin. The magnetic pole around which most of them may be grouped is the philosophy of individualism associated (for somewhat different reasons) with both Protestantism and the Enlightenment. This philosophy, reenforced by the economic conditions of the New World, was a ruling passion with practically all of the Founding Fathers who managed the American Revolution and established the Republic. To some extent modifying and limiting the philosophy of individualism in the minds of some of the Founders was the ideology of nationalism, also being turned up by the European experience of that time. But these two, individualism and nationalism, were almost universally regarded as sufficient summaries of all the virtues that need be included in the good state. The institution of the political party, seeking to confine the liberties of the individual and at the same time detract from undivided loyalty toward the nation, appeared to be inimical to both, and was thoroughly denounced by Founders of all shades of political belief (with the possible exception of one Aaron Burr, whose advocacy unfortunately did nothing to improve the party system's good name). Willy-nilly, however, the party soon proved itself a functional necessity which was able to triumph over the sternest ideological disapproval. It became what it has ever since remained and what we have found it to be in our present study: the effective instrument for government in most parts of the United States. Success in this case, however, was not sufficient to remove the onus of a bad reputation, and party politics has remained in the popular mind as well as in the opinion of most intellectuals a necessary evil at best. This reputation was strengthened by some of the developments of the party system in American history.

The mention of only a few of these will recreate the sinister and disorderly atmosphere in which most Americans regard politics as being bathed: The rigid legal prohibitions enacted in many locales by the Protestant conscience, sometimes over populations who did not themselves share the same moral outlook, created wide areas of publicly tolerated but legally forbidden conduct, thus assuring the intrusion of lawless forces into politics . . . Succeeding waves of immigration to the United States inevitably divided the population into antagonistic ethnic groups; some of these antagonisms found expression in politics; and later generations wishing to escape the antagonisms found it prudent to avoid the party struggles in which they are preserved. . . Many of the political leaders themselves have preferred to maintain the parties as clubby little gangs among whom the swag of public wealth can safely be divided rather than turn them into unmanageable popular movements . . . Theories about the "insiders" or the "power elite" who actually run the country have done their share to persuade the populace that political participation does not have any real meaning . . . Warfare between economic classes accompanying industrialization, though less severe in the United States than in any other Western nation, has to some extent found expression in politics, and the large number of persons who have wished to remain neutral in this warfare (the class of small merchants, for instance) have avoided political involvement . . . The ideological unity of American life, as Louis Hartz has pointed out, has diminished the emotional intensity of our politics and made mobilization of popular feeling in political contests difficult.

The remarkable thing when we survey this list—and it could be added to—is that the party system in this country has worked at all. And yet it has worked. It has produced statesmen who compare favorably with the products of all other political systems during the past two hundred years; it has, with one major breakdown, successfully presided over the conquest of a continent, a revolution in the means of economic production, a half-dozen international wars, and an incredible bringing together under one sovereignty of all races and nations of mankind; it has, with all of its glaring shortcomings and injustices, extended the rights of democratic citizenship more broadly than any previous or contemporary political system in the history of the world. Balancing faults with virtues, the party system must receive surprisingly high marks. It has served both the individual and the nation well, and perhaps the time has come for it to be admitted with them to the court of ideological respectability. Some of the factors that have previously hindered its wider development—such as the ethnic antagonisms that have been channeled along party lines—seem to be weakening in our national life. Others may in time be eliminated through the processes of democratic experiment. In any case, the party system, unlike its collectivist and oligarchic competitors, is available to anyone who will use it. The party boss may appear a formidable figure, but he is only as strong as he is permitted to be by the failure of citizens to express their will through participation in organized politics.

Notes

1. This argument has encountered thoughtful criticism from some of the political scientists who have read this report. It is claimed, for example, that studies have shown that men active in service-club work tend to be active in politics as well, and therefore that the one cannot validly be said to take the place of the other. My own observations lead me to believe that those who are *most* active in service clubs do often eventually get into politics (with varying success), but that the great mass of club members, many of whom clearly enjoy the democratic rigmarole of club government, do not participate in politics except to vote and make an occasional contribution to their party. It is my understanding that the service clubs of Ohio were

enlisted to support the re-election drive of Senator Taft in 1950, and that they proved remarkably effective during that campaign. A more fundamental objection to the theory that service clubs provide an outlet for unused political drives is that it is one of the "drainage" theories that modern behavioral science has shown to be unprovable and unnecessary to a scientific understanding of human nature. My answer is that while I do not pretend to be able to "prove" the existence of a political instinct, I do not believe that its existence can be disproved either; and since its existence provides an explanation for many things—such as the popularity of service clubs— that cannot be well explained in any other way, and since, moreover, *the assumption of its existence provides a working basis from which to launch a program for the reinvigoration and reorganization of our admittedly deteriorating political life,* I shall continue to argue for its utility to any general theory of politics.

Chapter SIX

STRUCTURES OF POWER

AND INFLUENCE

Introduction

A. Power Structure Analysis

B. Alternative Models for Analysis

THE IMPORTANCE of formal structural arrangements largely dominated the thinking about urban government until the close of World

War II. A few students (as some of the readings in this volume illustrate) took a broader view of the political process, but such insight appeared to be the exception rather than the rule. As one critic described it, the field was "The Lost World of Municipal Government" where students and practitioners seemed unaware of modern findings in other social sciences or even in the fields of political science itself.

The traditional concentration on structure had two unfortunate by-products. One of these was that a set of administrative principles was enshrined as theology, and little attention was given to the way in which political pressures might distort the flow of decision-making. The organization chart, with its neat flow of power lines, was often viewed as if it were, in fact, reality.

The second unfortunate result of this emphasis was the assumption that the political scientist should be interested only in the formal governmental institutions and should remain unconcerned about the social, economic, and political environment in which government operated.

Many post-war studies of urban government mark a shift from these traditional approaches. More attention is now given to the political process, including analysis of all informal factors which influence policy decisions. Many of these newer approaches are the product of cross-fertilization between political science and sociology.

While recent studies have brought greater realism into the literature on local government, empirical studies still suffer from the lack of a model which adequately portrays the local political process. The older hierarchical models such as the machine (Gosnell) and indigenous economic elites (the Lynds and Warner) are no longer useful in the form in which they were originally presented because of the changes which have taken place in urban society in the last several decades. (Some of these changes have been described above in Chapters One and Two.) Of the models currently being employed, the most popular among sociologists, judged by their writings in the journals, is a revival of the economic elite idea stated in new terms. The leading proponent of this view has been Floyd Hunter with his model of the community power structure.

The first group of readings includes a selection from Hunter's study, *Community Power Structure,* and several other studies which depend on Hunter's method as their point of departure. It is exceedingly difficult to compress Hunter's analysis into proportions permissible under the format of this volume. However, there follows an edited version of his fourth chapter, which sets forth his technique of analysis and essential perception of the "community power structure." A fuller reading of his book, however, is desirable for those who wish to follow the large number of studies which have used, modified, or reacted to his model.

William H. Form uses the Hunter approach in a case study assessing the political power of labor in one community. It is also used by Robert Agger and Daniel Goldrich in tracing the effects of community power structure on political styles in two small Oregon communities. Solon Kimball and Marion Pearsall are concerned with the consequences of the existence of a power structure on the isolated and alienated "west end" of a small city.

The boldness of the power structure model has attracted some social scientists who have long been critical of both the structuralists with their stress on legal arrangements, and the idealists with their broad participation models based on De Tocquevillian conceptions. However, there have also been many dissenters who believe power structure analysis mistakenly discounts the power of formal political leaders or even the wider public by drawing the pattern of power too neatly. Reference to some of the specific criticisms is included in a footnote.

In the second section of this chapter, we have included four authors who address themselves to the same problems as did Hunter. Though they present alternative models for forms of analysis, they are not primarily concerned with a criticism of his model. The model of analysis presented by Norton E. Long is nearly an antithesis of Hunter's. In Long's terms, community actions and policies are often merely the result of individuals, each pursuing his own private goals and, in the process, cooperating and using each other with little over-all direction from a guiding elite or anyone else.

Peter H. Rossi does not set up a model; rather, he comments on the character of community decision-making based upon his experiences in studying a number of different decisions. Rossi particularly notes the effect of anticipated power resources on the decisions that are made. Employing the more traditional concepts of the political scientist, Robert H. Salisbury explains certain decisions in St. Louis by weaving together the effects of interest groups, party organizations, and governmental structure.

Finally, Robert A. Dahl directs his criticism more particularly toward the De Tocqueville model of universal participation. He hypothesizes that the number of persons who will avail themselves of formal opportunities to participate in decision-making will be relatively small in all forms of social organization, including local government. He analogizes from economics to politics, suggesting a *bargaining* model for local democracy. Mr. Dahl is concerned with improving methods for empirical analysis. But his hypothesis is also directed at a re-evaluation of the traditional participation theory of local democracy. Of course, not only Dahl's article but all the selections in this section have implications for a theory of local democracy.

A. POWER STRUCTURE ANALYSIS

33. Community Power Structure in a Southern Regional City

FLOYD HUNTER

(The following is an edited version of Chapter IV of Hunter's book. In this chapter, he sets forth his essential methodology regarding the determination of the community power structure. Stripped of nearly all illustrative material, this version is robbed of some of the supports which collateral examples may give to a thesis. However, the essentials of Hunter's approach are retained.)

One of the first tasks in making a theoretical analysis of the community is that of delimiting and defining it as a structure. The task of delimitation may take into account four basic elements, namely (1) personnel (members), (2) test(s) of admission and membership, (3) distinctive roles or functions of the members, and (4) norms regulating the conduct of the personnel. . . . We shall presently be concerned with all of the elements suggested here, and most particularly with the first three, but only in relation to a segment of the community—the power element. The fourth item, norms regulating conduct within the community of Regional City, presents problems with which the present study does not deal, except in a passing fashion. All of the norms of behavior of power personnel in Regional City are not known, but some specifications of men which may indicate norms will be outlined.

Reprinted from *Community Power Structure* (Chapel Hill: University of North Carolina Press, 1953), pp. 60–62, 82–83, 88–94, 112–13 by permission of the author and the publisher. Author's footnotes abridged. Floyd Hunter is a professor of social work at the University of North Carolina.

The personnel with which the current discussion is concerned represents but a minute fraction of the community in which it moves and functions. It does represent a definite group, however, and a very important one in Regional City. No pretense is made that the group to be discussed represents the totality of power leaders of the community, but it is felt that a representative case sample is presented, and that the men described come well within the range of the center of power in the community.

It will be recalled that the leaders selected for study were secured from lists of leading civic, professional, and fraternal organizations, governmental personnel, business leaders, and "society" and "wealth" personnel suggested by various sources. These lists of more than 175 persons were rated by "judges" who selected by mutual choice the top forty persons in the total listings. These forty were the object of study and investigation in Regional City. Some data were collected about the total number. Twenty-seven members of the group were interviewed on the basis of a prepared schedule plus additional questions as the investigation proceeded. Any figures used in the study will need to be tied fairly rigidly to the twenty-seven members on whom there are comparable data. . . . The fourteen under-structure professionals in civic and social work who were interviewed have also provided data which may be considered comparable.

The top leaders, the under-structure professionals, and the Negro community leaders represent community groups. They are identifiable groups. Since they are definitely groups, I shall rely to a considerable extent, in this portion of the discussion, upon George C. Homans for certain hypotheses he has put forward on group structure.[1]

The system of power groups which is being examined may not be called a closed system. The groups are links in a total pattern, which may offer suggestive clues to total power patterns in the operating system of Regional City. There are gaps in the power arc which investigation may not be able to close. Actually the discussion here is primarily concerned with the structuring of power on a policy-making level. Only a rudimentary "power pyramid" of Regional City will be presented. One may be content to do this because I doubt seriously that power forms a single pyramid with any nicety in a community the size of Regional City. There are *pyramids* of power in this community which seem more important to the present discussion than *a* pyramid. . . .

The validity of the question concerning who might be chosen to "decide" on a community project cannot be measured purely in terms of a pyramid-structuring. Its validity for this study lies in the fact that the question determined, in some degree, "how near the center" this group was that could "move things" in the affairs of the community. Each man interviewed was asked to add names of persons he considered as powerful as or more powerful than the men listed. Sixty-four names were added to the list. Thirty-seven of the additional names were mentioned but once by informants. Sixteen were mentioned twice; five, three times; five, four times; and one, five times. Eleven informants added names, but there was general agreement that the list was a fairly comprehensive one as it stood, with the exceptions mentioned.

The high consensus regarding the top leaders on the list of forty, plus the lack of any concerted opinion on additional individuals, would indicate that the men being interviewed represented at least a nucleus of a power grouping.

The question was also put to interviewees, "How many men would need to be involved in a major community project in Regional City 'to put it over'?" The answers to this question varied from, "You've got the men right here on this list—maybe ten of them," to "fifty or a hundred." One informant said, "Some of the men on this list would undoubtedly be in on getting the project started. After it got moving, perhaps six hundred men might be involved either directly or indirectly." This was the largest figure any informant gave. The informant elaborated on the answer by saying that a large fund-raising campaign was the thing he had in mind, and he illustrated the point by speaking of a fund drive for a hospital building program that had recently been completed in Regional City. He said that he could count the men on his hands who had "sparked" the drive, but hundreds of volunteers had been used from the civic associations and the general community to "put the drive over the top." He felt that any project for civic improvement would likely involve the same type of organization.

In the above illustration of structured action, the "men of independent decision" are a relatively small group. The "executors of policy" may run into the hundreds. This pattern of a relatively small decision-making group working through a larger under-structure is a reality, and if data were available, the total personnel involved in a major community project might possibly form a pyramid of power, but the constituency of the pyramid would change according to the project being acted upon.

In other words, the personnel of the pyramid would change depending upon what needs to be done at a particular time. Ten men might, for example, decide to bring a new industry into the community. Getting the industry physically established and operating might take the disciplined and coordinated action of a few more men or several hundred men, depending on the size of the project. Some of the same decision men in another instance might be involved in starting a program for some local governmental change, but another group of men would be involved in carrying out the decisions reached. Both projects are power orientated, but each requires different personnel in the execution. The men in the under-structure may have a multiplicity of individual roles within the totality of the community structure which can be set in motion by the men of decision.

As I became familiar with the list of forty names through the interviewing process, it became evident that certain men, even within the relatively narrow range of decision leaders with whom I was dealing, represented a top layer of personnel. Certain men were chosen more frequently than others, not only in relation to who should be chosen to decide on a project, as has already been indicated, but the same men interacted together on committees and were on the whole better known to each other than to those outside this group. Through analyzing the mutual choices made by those interviewed, it will be shown that there is an *esprit de corps* among certain top leaders, and some of them may be said to operate on a very high level of decision in the community; but this will not necessarily mean that one of the top leaders can be considered subordinate to any other in the community as a whole. On specific projects one leader may allow another to carry the ball, as a leader is said to do when he is "out front" on a project which interests him. On the next community-wide project another may carry the ball. Each may subordinate himself to another on a temporary basis, but such a structure of subordination is quite fluid, and it is voluntary. . . .

The question was also asked each person interviewed, "Indicate how many persons (in the list of forty) you have worked with on committees within the past five years?" The upper-limits group* indicated that they had worked with an average of twenty-nine persons on the list. The lower-limits group indicated that they had worked with an average of only twenty-one persons on the list. The professional under-structure of civil and social workers were asked the same question and indicated that they had worked with an average of only ten persons on the list. There is a definite drop, therefore, in the rate of interaction between each of the three groups and the group of forty leaders. Each group has access to the other, but those in the upper-limits group are in contact with other leaders more frequently, in committee work, at least. The under-structure professionals, with few exceptions, interact

* The "upper-limit" group consisted of twelve men among the forty who were involved in the greatest number of mutual choices in response to the question: "Who might decide best on a project?"

with persons immediately above them and with other professionals close to them in the power scale.

Another index used to discover the degree of relationship existing between the leaders interviewed and the total group of forty leaders was based upon a question which asked, on a six-point scale, how well known each person on the list of forty was to the interviewee. The scale read: "How well do you know each person (on the list of forty): (1) related——, (2) know socially——, (3) know well——, (4) know slightly——, (5) heard of him——, (6) not known——." By again utilizing the upper-limits and lower-limits groups of leaders, and through comparison of these two groups with the professional under-structure personnel, we see a definite differentiation between the groups. In order not to present too confusing an array of figures, we shall indicate only the average number of persons known well or better in each group.

The upper-limits group knew well or better an average of thirty-four persons in the list of forty. The lower-limits group of top leaders knew an average of 28.7 leaders well or better. The professional under-structure averaged only 7.3 persons for this same degree of acquaintance. Obviously the upper-structure is better acquainted with the total group of top leaders, in addition to having a higher rate of committee interaction with this same group. The professional persons who carry out the decisions of the policy-making group are definitely differentiated from the top leaders in rates of interaction and in degree of acquaintance with the top leaders.

Our rudimentary statistical conclusions on the degrees of relationship among the persons named were borne out in qualitative interviewing. Over and over, the same persons were named as influential and consequently able to "move things" in Regional City. The significance of a high degree of interaction is suggested by Homans' hypothesis, "The more nearly equal in social rank a number of men are, the more frequently they will interact with one another." Our findings bear out this hypothesis.

One other index was used to determine how closely integrated the upper-limits group was in relation to the lower-limits group. By ranking the leaders according to the number of leadership choices received from other leaders and analyzing how far up the scale or how far down the scale each went in making his choice, one finds a differentiating picture of the two groups. Members of the upper-limits group would go both up and down the scale from their own position in their choices, but not very far. They would go up an average of 5.4 places. They would go down an average of 4.9 places in their choices. These figures indicate a tendency to choose persons as leaders who are fairly close to the choosers in the scale.

The lower-limits personnel, on the other hand, tended almost entirely to choose men above them in rank. They would go up the scale an average of 13.1 places, and would go down only 0.6 places in their choices. It would seem from this evidence that the under group defers to the upper group, and that there is some solidarity in the upper echelons of policy-makers.

As shown earlier, power has been defined in terms of policy leadership, and the data given in the present chapter make a beginning at defining structural power relations. A group of men have been isolated who are among the most powerful in Regional City. It has been shown that they interact among themselves on community projects and select one another as leaders. Their relations with one another are not encompassed in a true pyramid of power, but some degree of ranking, even in the top-level policy leadership group, has been indicated. Let us now look at policy personnel patterns in another way.

In sizing up any individual one often asks, "What do you do for a living?" The reply to this question allows one rather quickly to rank another in a rough scale of social values. The men under discussion hold commercial, industrial, financial, and professional positions in Regional City that tend to classify them in the minds of any observer. . . .

Most of the leaders hold positions as presidents of companies, chairmen of boards, or professional positions of some prestige. Generally speaking, the companies represented in the listing are of major enterprise proportions. More than half the men may be said to be businessmen, if the term is used broadly. The major economic interests of the community are overwhelmingly represented in the listing. The pattern of business dominance of civic affairs in Regional City is a fact. No other institution is as dominant in community life as the economic institution, and this phenomenon will be dealt with at greater length under an appropriate heading. . . .

In the general social structure of community life social scientists are prone to look upon the institutions and formal associations as powerful forces, and it is easy to be in basic agreement with this view. Most institutions and associations are subordinate, however, to the interests of the policy-makers who operate in the economic sphere of community life in Regional City. The institutions of the family, church, state, education, and the like draw sustenance from economic institutional sources and are thereby subordinate to this particular institution more than any other. The associations stand in the same relationship to the economic interests as do the institutions. We see both the institutions and the formal associations playing a vital role in the execution of determined policy, but the formulation of policy often takes place outside these formalized groupings. Within the policy-forming groups the economic interests are dominant.

The economic institution in Regional City, in drawing around itself many of the other institutions in the community, provides from within itself much of the personnel which may be considered of primary influence in power relationships. A lengthy discussion on institutions per se is not proposed. Their existence as channels through which policy may be funneled up and down to broader groups of people than those represented by the top men of power is easily recognized. Some of the institutions would represent imperfect channels for power transmission, however. For example, the family as an institution is not a channel of itself for bringing about general community agreement on such a matter as the desirability of building a new bridge across Regional River. On the other hand, the church might represent a more potent force on this question. The preacher could preach a sermon on the matter in any given church, and the members could sign petitions, attend meetings at the behest of the church bureaucracy, and go through a whole series of activities motivated by the institution in question.

It may be noted here that none of the ministers of churches in Regional City were chosen as top leaders by the persons interviewed in the study. The idea was expressed several times by interviewees that some minister *ought* to be on the listing, but under the terms of power definitions used in the study they did not make "top billing." It is understood, however, that in order to get a project well under way it would be important to bring the churches in, but they are not, as institutions, considered crucial in the decision-making process. Their influence is crucial in restating settled policies from time to time and in interpreting new policies which have been formed or are in the process of formulation. Church leaders, however, whether they be prominent laymen or professional ministers, have relatively little influence with the larger economic interests.

One cannot, in Regional City at least, look to the organized institutions as policy-determining groupings, nor can one look to the formal associations which are part of these institutions. . . .

Neither the institutional, associational, nor economic groupings comprise the totality of the power scheme in Regional City. The difference between policy-making and policy-execution has been stressed and it has been shown that the various organizations in the community may be very important in carrying out policy decisions. Segments of structure including individuals and cliques, particularly those related to the upper decision-making groups, have been identified. One more organizational component must be analyzed before tying together the units of the community structure. This component is what may be termed a fluid committee structure.

The committee is a phenomenon which is inescapable in organized community life in American hamlets, villages, small cities, and great metropolitan centers. Almost every activity of any importance in our culture must be preceded by committee work, carried on by committee work, and finally posthumously evaluated by a committee. Regional City is no exception to the general rule. Day after day the hotel, club, and associational meeting rooms are packed with men going through the familiar motions of calling meetings to order and dismissing them. Committees may have short lives or they may go on for years. An example of the latter is the Committee of 101 previously discussed. Committees may be quite formally organized, utilizing parliamentary rules of order, or they may be loosely organized and informal in their procedures. They may be accompanied by food and drink or they may be devoid of such amenities. They may have serious or light purposes, and consequently solemn or gay occasions as the case may be. Withal, each is accompanied by a certain degree of ritual befitting the occasion. Men used to committee work are sharp to detect poorly conducted meetings. No meeting, for example, can be said to have amounted to much if at least one motion is not put, passed, or put down—that is, in the more formally organized meetings. Men trained in conducting meetings are in demand, and such a person may display rare skills in ordering a group as it goes about its business.

Meetings are often a substitute for group action. As one Regional City professional phrased it, "There are those who believe in salvation by luncheon!" There is great faith manifest in certain quarters of our society that if people can just be got together in a meeting all problems will be solved. And there is some justification for this faith, since so many matters of community business, as well as private transactions, are brought to successful conclusions in meetings.

Meetings have the functions of clarifying objectives of a group and of fixing and delegating responsibilities for action on any matter. They may in like manner hold action in abeyance. Decisions reached in meetings may be solemnly binding, or they may not be. Decisions arrived at in one meeting may be changed in the next meeting. Responsibilities may be shifted and membership changed according to the will of the group as a series of meetings proceeds. Rarely are committee meetings bound by "constitutional" prohibitions or heavy legalistic trappings which characterize so many associational and institutional gatherings. The outstanding characteristic of the ordinary committee meeting is its fluidity and

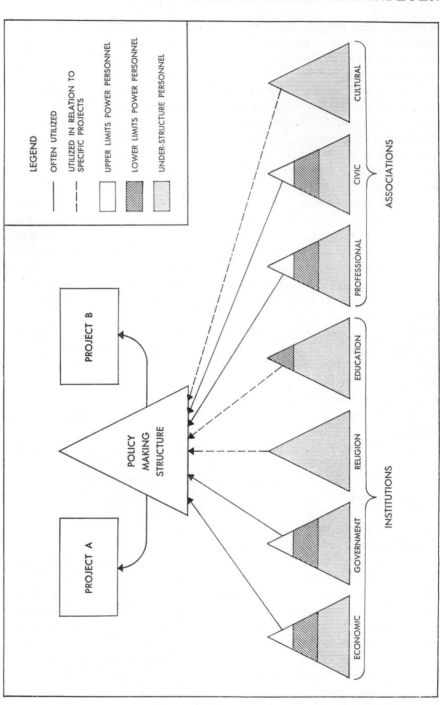

GENERALIZED PATTERN OF POLICY COMMITTEE FORMATION UTILIZING INSTITUTIONAL AND ASSOCIATIONAL STRUCTURES

its adaptability in adjusting to changing conditions, which are so essentially a part of our modern urban culture. The importance of the committee in power relations cannot be overstressed.

While it is important to stress the fluidity of committee structure, it must also be pointed out that there is a stable base of personnel who are seen time and again in a variety of committee meetings. There are men in any community who devote large portions of their waking hours to attendance at one meeting or another. Public-relations men in industry and associational secretaries are paid to devote considerable of their time to meeting attendance. It becomes commonplace among this latter personnel group to see one another at committee meetings, and such personnel become familiar with community leaders who operate on a similar level with them. There is a tendency to judge the importance of these meetings by who is in attendance.

Most of the top personnel of the power group are rarely seen at meetings attended by the associational under-structure personnel in Regional City. The exception to this general statement may be found in those instances in which a project is broad enough so that the "whole community needs to be brought in on the matter." Such meetings as bring in the under-structure personnel are usually relatively large affairs, rather than the smaller, more personal meetings which characterize policy-determination sessions. The interaction patterns of the two groups discussed here have shown a much higher rate of interaction among the top group than between the top and lower groups.

In matters of power decision the committee structure assumes keystone importance. The committee as a structure is a vital part of community power relationships in Regional City. Let us illustrate graphically in [the] figure the place of two hypothetical policy committees in relation to institutional, associational, and corporate groups.

Not all the institutions and associations in Regional City were identified as being related to the power leaders studied. For example, none of the leaders in a power relationship could be identified as representing the institution of the family or a cultural association. This does not mean that either of these groupings was unimportant for some of the top leaders, but in the specific power relations studied no identification could be made of persons within these groupings as such. Because of this, in [the] figure the cultural association is indicated as a pyramid grouping for under-structure power personnel only. No family institutional pyramid is shown. On the other hand, some of the institutions and associations could be identified with both upper-limits and lower-limits power personnel, and these pyramids show this by contrasting shaded portions for the two types of power leaders. We have also indicated in the figure that some institutions and associations are more frequently drawn upon for power personnel than others. The dotted lines represent those groups that are potential contributors to the policy-making structure. The cultural association group has been so designated, for example, since policy is formulated around some cultural activities which may have bearing on power relations. As an illustration, the status factor operating when a leader becomes a patron of the arts may have some relation to his general power position.

A few generalized remarks may be made concerning [the] figure, using a hypothetical example, after which it will be illustrated concretely how the structure worked in relation to a specific community project in Regional City.

If a project of major proportions were before the community for consideration—let us say a project aimed at building a new municipal auditorium—a policy committee would be formed. This may be called Project Committee A. Such a policy committee would more than likely grow out of a series of informal meetings, and it might be related to a project that has been on the discussion agenda of many associations for months or even years. But the time has arrived for action. Money must be raised through private subscription or taxation, a site selected, and contracts let. The time for a policy committee is propitious. The selection of the policy committee will fall largely to the men of power in the community. They will likely be businessmen in one or more of the larger business establishments. Mutual choices will be agreed upon for committee membership. In the early stages of policy formulation there will be a few men who make the basic decisions. As the project is trimmed, pared and shaped into manageable proportions there will be a recognition that the committee should be enlarged. Top-ranking organizational and institutional personnel will then be selected by the original members to augment their numbers, i.e., the committee will be expanded. The civic associations and the formalized institutions will next be drawn into certain phases of planning and initiation of the project on a community-wide basis. The newspapers will finally carry stories of the proposals, the ministers will preach sermons, and the associational members will hear speeches regarding plans. This rather simply is the process, familiar to many, that goes on in getting any community project under way.

Project B might be related to changing the tax structure of the community. Much the same organizational procedure will be repeated, but different associations may be drawn into the planning and execution stages. The policy-making personnel will tend to be much the same as in Project A and this is an important point in the present discussion.

There will be a hard core of policy leadership on Policy Committee B that was also present on Project Committee A. This relative stability of the top policy-making group is a pattern quite apparent in Regional City civic affairs. A similar pattern of stable committee membership exists in the under-structure of the associational and corporate bureaucracies in the community which interact in a chain of command with the top power leaders on given projects.

It must be stressed that the same policy leaders do not interact repeatedly with the same under-structure personnel in getting projects put over. The interaction is based entirely upon a given project that is under consideration at a given time. The under-structure personnel may be likened to a keyboard over which the top structure personnel play, and the particular keys struck may vary from project to project. The players remain the same or nearly so, however.

A variation in the pattern of structuring a top-decision committee may be found in those policy committees in which the decision is made by individuals who are not to be out front on the project. In other words, the men of policy may wish to remain anonymous in relation to the action phases of the program in question. In such cases, the policy group remains informally intact, and "second-rate" or "third-rate" men are advertised as the sponsors of the particular project. This pattern may occur when a project is somewhat questionable as to its success. The policy-forming group is just as real, however, as if it were named publicly. The men upon whom falls the burden of carrying the project into its action stages are well aware of the persons who chose them.

Projects that are not originated in the policy-determining group are often allowed to proceed with a tentative blessing of a few of the men of decision if their interests and dominant values are not threatened by the proposed activity. If such a project goes sour, the men of decision cannot be blamed. This is another variation of structure and represents a real behavorial pattern in civic affairs in Regional City. . . .

Two of the hypotheses of the study have been discussed in some measure in the preceding analysis. These hypotheses, restated, are as follows:

1. The exercise of power is limited and directed by the formulation and extension of social policy within a framework of socially sanctioned authority.

2. In a given power unit a smaller number of individuals will be found formulating and extending policy than those exercising power.

A corollary of the latter hypothesis was also touched upon: All policy-makers are men of power, but all men of power are not, per se, policy-makers.

The top group of the power hierarchy has been isolated and defined as comprised of policy-makers. These men are drawn largely from the businessmen's class in Regional City. They form cliques or crowds, as the term is more often used in the community, which formulate policy. Committees for formulation of policy are commonplace, and on community-wide issues policy is channeled by a "fluid committee structure" down to institutional, associational groupings through a lower-level bureaucracy which executes policy.

It has been pointed out that intra-community and extra-community policy matters are handled by essentially the same group of men in this city, but there is a differentiation of functional activity within this policy group. Some men operate on different levels of policy decision, particularly in matters concerning governmental action. Some structural weaknesses in the power structure have been touched upon but at no great length. Finally, it was found that the structure is held together by common interests, mutual obligations, money, habit, delegated responsibilities, and in some cases by coercion and force.

Notes

1. George C. Homans, *The Human Group* (New York: Harcourt, Brace and Company, 1950).

34. Organized Labor's Place in the Community Power Structure

WILLIAM H. FORM

It is a commonplace that organized labor has had little influence in community policy in the United States. Prior to the New Deal, community decisions were made largely by business and professional groups. Since

Reprinted from *Industrial and Labor Relations Review*, XII (July 1959), pp. 526–39 by permission of the author and the publisher. Author's footnotes abridged. William Form is a professor of sociology and anthropology at Michigan State University.

1932, when organized labor obtained legal support for collective bargaining, unions have gradually begun to challenge this domination of the city by already established groups. Thus, while labor's main political effort was made on state and national levels, it has also sought to challenge local patterns of control. The Political Action Committees of the CIO have become increasingly interested in local politics. During World War II the CIO created the Community Services Organization to broaden its area of community involvement. Although lagging somewhat, the AFL has also expanded its political and other activities in the community. As Cook has shown, unions are establishing liaison with all important institutions and demanding representation on all community-wide organizations in cities where labor is highly organized.[1] The full circle of challenges to the traditional power structure of the local community now appears complete: economic challenge, political challenge, and finally a challenge on all local institutional fronts.

Many scholars have observed, however, that labor unions still do not occupy a place in this power structure commensurate with their numbers or with their role in the economy. But precise documentation of this fact is generally lacking. Orme W. Phelps made one of the early systematic studies which documented the gross under-representation of labor union officials among (a) honorific biographical listings and (b) appointments to public offices, boards of foundations, university boards, and service clubs.[2] This study focused primarily on recognition of union officials at state and federal levels.

Other students have analyzed some aspects of organized labor's power in the local community. James McKee's pioneer study of Steelport (a city of 40,000)[3] showed that the CIO had indeed established *formal* political control of the community after 1945, but had not altered the basic strength of business in the community. Hart indicated that the UAW in Windsor (population 100,000) was disengaging itself from management-dominated organizations and was substituting union-sponsored activities to meet the social needs of the workers.[4] In Illini City, (population 70,000) Wray found that unions had not (despite increased bargaining strength) influenced the programs of local associations very much. The tendency there was to incorporate union representatives into business organizations such as the Chamber of Commerce. This retarded the elaboration of functions which unions might otherwise consider.[5] Walker indicated that in Steeltown (population 14,000) the unions traditionally used their strength to settle economic and grievance problems, but not political, welfare, educational, or other problems. Yet in a crisis situation unions had power resources which had been manifested earlier.[6] In

Jonesville, (population 10,000) unions failed to become a significant force in community life since they had not expanded their activities beyond the narrowest limits of collective bargaining.[7] Almost the same situation existed in Hunter's Regional City (population 331,000)[8] and in the satellite city of Cibola (population 20,000).[9]

The impression gained from all these studies is that despite labor's increased representation in many local agencies, it has not changed their goals and has not effectively challenged the power of other groups. Whether differences in the community power of unions are of significance can only be determined by studying over time localities containing important structural differences in size, industrial composition, degree of unionization, and related variables. For this reason it is urgent to make systematic benchmark studies of labor's power in communities with different structural bases. The main purpose of this study is to suggest a systematic profile for doing so.

Research Site and Study Design

Lansing, Michigan, is a city of 100,000 population and the capital of the state. Its main "industries" are automobile manufacturing, metal manufacturing, and government employment. Before World War I the auto plants were locally owned. Now most of the large plants (Oldsmobile, Fisher Body, Motor Wheel, Reo, John Bean) are absentee-owned. Most of the forges and auto parts plants, however, are still locally owned and employ about 40 percent of the industrial labor force. The city currently has a labor force of over 75,000, of whom about 20,000 are employed in automobile and metal manufacturing. About half of the labor force resides outside the city. About a third are organized, 20,000 into former CIO unions and 4,000 in former AFL unions. The UAW is the largest union in the city. Since World War II, the UAW has encouraged its locals to become involved in the entire institutional life of the city and to challenge the domination of business and industry.

Unlike many other middle-sized cities in the industrial east and mid-west, the proportions of foreign-born and Negro workers in Lansing are relatively small. Native-born workers constitute about 90 percent of the labor force. Over two-thirds of them are descendants of early New England migrants, later German immigrants, and more recent migrants from the rural South. Southern-born workers probably comprise 10 percent of the labor force and Negroes only 4 or 5 percent. The community has grown relatively slowly and has a remarkably stable labor force for an auto manufacturing center. Approximately seven-tenths of the manual workers own their own homes. With two exceptions the city has voted Republican in all national elections since its founding in 1859. A recent survey revealed that the residents liked the city because it is relatively small, conservative, and friendly. In short the city contains a large and conservative native-born working class many of whose members belong to the UAW, a dynamic and ideologically oriented union which is dedicated to contest management's influence in local, state, and national affairs. The present research task is to determine the degree of union penetration in various segments of the community power structure.

Five components of community power may be distinguished. First, the structure of community power is affected by changing power relations among the associations or institutions of the broader society of which institutions in a particular locale are but a part. Second, within any particular community a certain balance of power may have become more or less established and "institutionalized." Local institutions have worked out ways of living with each other when represented on established local agencies dealing in well-established ways with matters of joint and long-standing concern to the institutions represented. Third, there is the community power complex: the network of power arrangements which arise when organizations are activated to resolve specific inter-institutional and community-wide problems *not* normally resolved by the everyday functioning of local agencies. Fourth, community power structure consists of a group of "top influentials" who are commonly drawn into community issues, projects, or disputes which are not resolved by the permanent structures. Finally, community power structure may be said to contain also a group of "key influentials" who represent the top ten among the "top influentials."

The first component, the institutional power structure of the broader society, by definition, cannot be investigated empirically on the community level. Indeed, two assumptions were made: first, that economic associations initiate most of the change in American society and are, in this sense, the most powerful; and second, that within the economic complex, business and industry are dominant over other economic agencies including labor unions. It was assumed that these conditions existed in the research site. The third component of community power, the community power complex, is by definition observable only at times when special issues or projects are being considered. Hence only incidental references will be made to it. The following analysis will, therefore, deal largely with labor's penetration into some segments of: (a) the institutionalized power structure of the community, (b) the top influence structure, and (c) the key influence system.

Institutionalized Power Structure

The full range of institutional agencies typically found in middle-sized cities is found in Lansing. While limitation of space precludes a complete description of this component, a first approximation of labor's power may be obtained from the proportion of union members, or representatives sympathetic to unions, found on important policy-making boards and agencies in the community. These proportions may be compared with those representing other occupational groups in the following areas: economic bargaining, governmental and political agencies, private social welfare agencies, educational agencies, mass communication, and religion.

Limitations of representational analysis to measure power are obvious: (a) power may be concentrated in the hands of persons not found on boards of community-wide agencies, and private organizations may dominate community decision-making; (b) unions, business, professional, and other occupational associations may not have a consistent or cohesive ideology dealing with the community, thereby obscuring the meaning of organizational representation; (c) the use of a representative's occupation to predict his behavior in concrete community issues is hazardous; (d) important sources of power may be located outside the community. Despite these objections, gross differences in occupational and other types of representation are commonly found in different communities, and they provide important clues to differences in the structuring of community power. Certainly, historical changes in occupational representation point to other changes occurring in the community which need to be interpreted.

Economic Power

The relative economic strength of management and unions in the auto and related industries in Lansing is, in the main, a reflection of the pattern worked out between General Motors and the United Automobile Workers in Detroit. Locally owned manufacturing plants tend to accept this pattern in an effort to retain their labor force.[10] The list of gains which the UAW has wrested from GM since World War II are impressive and suggest a shift in power toward organized labor. No single, unambiguous index of change in bargaining power exists, but the increased bargaining strength of unions is reflected in their ability to obtain new kinds of economic gains (fringe benefits, for example), as well as wage increases which keep ahead of the rise in the cost of living and of the rise in distributed profits.

The UAW has achieved the following gains since World War II: (a) sizeable increases in basic wages, (b) cost-of-living clauses, (c) a share of the fruits of higher productivity, (d) supplementary unemployment benefits, (e) hospital and medical benefits, and (f) expanded pension, insurance, and related provisions. These concessions probably include a relative loss in GM's bargaining strength even though the company could easily afford them. More important, until 1956, locally owned enterprises generally met the "GM package," and for them this represented a relatively greater concession.

Our own empirical evidence tends to confirm that the local bargaining strength of management and unions is perceived as equal, perhaps slightly weighted toward the unions. Interview data from thirty influential businessmen in the city revealed that they perceived the unions as dominating collective bargaining. The top forty labor influentials interviewed estimated their bargaining power to equal that of management.

Power in Local Government

Lansing city government is allegedly nonpartisan, but it was not difficult to identify the party loyalty and union attitudes of candidates for office. Labor union officials were asked to identify the candidates whom they supported for mayor, council, and other elective offices for the period of 1948–1957, when labor was most active. The candidates were further identified by occupational background to ascertain whether occupational identity affected union support.

Table 1 shows that almost three-tenths of the 185 *candidates* received moderate support from organized labor. Only 4 percent, however, had all-out support. Actually, one-third of all *elected* city officials had moderate backing from organized labor, although only one union official was actually elected. Labor backing thus had only a slight effect on a candidate's chance of being elected. While almost seven-tenths of the labor-backed candidates were elected, so were almost six-tenths of those who did not have labor support.

Despite the fact that only 15 percent of all political candidates were in working-class occupations (manual and clerical nonsales), labor showed some occupational selectivity in the candidates it supported.

Table I indicates that, during the period 1948–1957, candidates who were union officials, managers, and employees of state government received more labor support than candidates who were proprietors and

TABLE 1

OCCUPATIONAL BACKGROUNDS OF CANDIDATES FOR MUNICIPAL ELECTIVE
OFFICES, BACKED AND NOT BACKED BY UNION OFFICIALS, 1948–1957

Occupational Levels	Candidates Elected		Candidates Defeated		All Candidates	
	Labor Backed	Other	Labor Backed	Other	Labor Backed	Other
Proprietors	17%	34%	11%	22%	15%	30%
Professionals	19	20	11	15	17	17
Gov't officials:						
State	17	1	5	—	13	—
City and County	22	16	—	7	15	12
Managers and officials	17	3	11	7	15	5
Supervisory	—	—	5	7	2	3
Sales and clerical	5	17*	17	31†	9	23
Manual workers	—	7	17	5	6	6
Union officials	3	—	22	—	9	—
Not ascertained	—	3	—	5	—	4
Totals	100	101	99	99	101	100
Number of cases	36	76	18	55	54	131

* All salesmen.
† One-half are salesmen.

salesmen. Taking all available data into account, it may be estimated that organized labor directly accounted for at most one-quarter of the city officials elected during that time. This proportion may well represent their degree of political power in this area.

These figures must be interpreted within the context of two trends. First, over the decade, 1948–1957, organized labor tended increasingly to back incumbents who had proved "not unfriendly" to labor, although they were not initially supported when they ran for office. Almost one-quarter of the incumbents fell into this category. While this technique may have stimulated incumbents to be friendly to labor's interests in order to obtain its backing, it reduced the direct political initiative of organized labor. Although the political strength of labor seems, therefore, to be increasing, no council has yet been elected the majority of whose members had explicit union support.

Finally in this area of labor's power in the community's government, note should be taken of the degree of influence which the community's own employees have on the behavior of the City Council. Prior to 1955, only a few skilled workers employed by the city were covered by collective bargaining agreements. At that time a successful organizing drive was launched which resulted in about three-quarters of all municipal employees (including the police) joining unions. Although these locals are not covered by collective bargaining agreements, their presence undoubtedly has some effect on the operations of the council and the municipal boards, difficult though it is to measure this effect precisely.

There are nineteen municipal boards in the city, whose members are selected by the mayor with the approval of the council. The president of the Lansing AFL-CIO Council publicly announced that it was union policy to get "working-class people" more adequately represented on municipal boards and commissions. The mayor answered the charge of bias by insisting that all people who work for a living are "working class," and that he did not intend to allow unions to dictate city policies.

Table 2 shows the occupational composition of almost four hundred members who served on municipal boards from 1945 to 1957. Those in

TABLE 2

OCCUPATIONAL COMPOSITION OF
MUNICIPAL COMMISSIONS, 1945–1957

	Number	Percent
Professional	50	13.4
Proprietors	112	30.0
Managers in business	54	14.5
Government "officials"	71	19.0
Clerical—sales	15	4.0
Clerical—office	12	3.2
Manual workers	31	8.3
Union officials	4	1.1
Not ascertained	24	6.4
Total	373	99.9

manual, protective, clerical,[11] and service occupations comprise about 13 percent of the total and meet the union definition of "working class." This figure is about the same as working-class *candidates* for elective municipal offices.

A closer inspection of the data reveals that no manual workers or union officials (who constituted 9.4 percent of commission membership, as may be seen from Table 2) were appointed to seven boards; less than the expected average of 9 percent served on six boards; and more than this average were appointed to six boards.[12] However, exactly half of all manual workers represented were firemen or policemen who were either trustees of the Police and Fire Retirement Board or members of the Traffic Commission. Excluding these, a liberal estimate of manual worker–union representation on city boards and commissions would be about 5 percent.

Clearly, proprietors and managers in business have overwhelmingly dominated the municipal boards and commissions. Real estate and insurance companies, typically heavy contributors to political campaigns, were especially heavily represented. Government employees contributed one-fifth of the total board members and professionals one-eighth. Over the decade, proprietors were slowly increasing their representation on these boards at the expense of professional and managerial employees. Increases in manual-union representation were almost imperceptible.

Political Parties and Education

Lansing has been traditionally Republican in state politics. On only three occasions has it elected a Democrat to the legislature. Certainly organized labor has virtually no influence in the local Republican party. While the local Democratic party would have no elective potential without the support of organized labor, the latter cannot "guarantee" the votes of union members. In a poll conducted among workers in the UAW in 1956, the party found that only 40 percent would support Democratic candidates for state and national offices. Labor is indirectly represented on the county executive committee by a labor lawyer, and unions have substantial representation in the over-all state and county Democratic committees. But no labor union official is a member of the county executive, finance, or advisory committee of the party, although they have been in the past. Local help in electing a Democratic governor and an occasional congressman, however, has given Lansing unions some political capital which they might otherwise not have.

In the area of education unions had little interest before 1947. With a change in local UAW leadership, labor began to concern itself with the operation of local educational agencies. There are now four educational areas in which labor is interested: school board elections, the joint industry-labor apprentice program, Business-Industry-Education Day, and the adult education program.

Since school board elections are considered more important than other areas, labor's success here may be evaluated first. Analysis of the occupational background of members of the Board of Education in Table 3 reveals that only two union members have been elected to the board since 1935, and only one-tenth of the candidates were manual

TABLE 3

Occupation of Candidates and
Elected Members of the Board of
Education, 1935–1959

Occupational level	Candidates		Total
	Defeated	Elected	
Professional	6	15	21
Government officials	5*	3†	8
Proprietors	4	24	28
Managers in business	3	3	6
Clerical workers	4	3	7
Skilled workers	2	2‡	4
Not ascertained	1	—	1
Totals	25	50	75

* Three professionals.
† Two professionals.
‡ Union officials.

or clerical workers. Almost half of the board members were proprietors or managers in business, and one-third were professional workers. Two-thirds of the proprietors were in wholesale and retail trade and the remainder were insurance or real estate brokers. Candidates who were managers from large industries were generally defeated because of insufficient local reputation.

In 1950 union officials decided to invest more time and energy in school board elections. They decided to back "liberal candidates sympathetic to labor," rather than run their own candidates. All three candidates meeting this requirement were elected, and since that time labor has assisted in electing an average of three board members out of the ten who are usually sympathetic to labor. Recent elections have been hotly contested. Significantly, the chances of a proprietor getting elected to the board have been nine out of ten, compared to seven out of ten for professionals, and four out of ten for managers, government officials, and others. A trend analysis of the school board elections showed an increasing competition for office, especially among the professionals. Over two-thirds of the candidates resided in census tracts ranked in the highest socioeconomic level, and less than one-fifth resided in or even adjacent to a working-class census tract. On the basis of occupation and residence alone, it appears that less than a fifth of the board members would be sensitive to the educational needs of the "working classes."

The Joint Apprentice Program Committee in the city school system supervises the job training and part-time schooling of those planning to enter the trades. Management and the unions have an equal representation on this committee. Although the participants agree that the program has been administered equitably and to the satisfaction of both labor and industry, it is clear that industry is in a dominant position because it can accept or reject candidates for the program, and because foremen are solely responsible for reports to the committee on the progress of apprentices.

The adult education program of the Board of Education was greatly expanded after World War II. In addition to offering the standard academic and technical courses, the board instituted courses "on demand." Almost all of the course requests from organized labor were met by the board and, in some cases it has paid instructors to teach courses of interest largely to union members. In addition, school administrators annually have a dinner with union officials to discuss problems of mutual concern. This is a far cry from the situation in 1937, when school administrators headed the Citizens' Committee against the UAW sitdown strikes.

Michigan has been in the vanguard of the Business-Industry-Education Day movement. Lansing educators and businessmen have enthusiastically participated in the program annually ever since the idea was suggested over a decade ago. Since organized labor has been denied participation, its officials condemn the event as an attempt by businessmen to win the loyalties of the teachers. Educational administrators have repeatedly offered to establish an independent Labor-Education Day, but union officials have pressed for participation in the present arrangement.

To summarize, the influence of labor in various educational agencies has been uneven. Influence has been substantial only where there has been no resistance to it, namely, in the adult education program, followed by the apprentice program, membership in the Board of Education, and Business-Industry-Education Day.

Welfare Agencies

Organized labor is attaching increasing importance to the activities of private welfare agencies in the community. Not only do union members even in normal times utilize the services of welfare agencies probably more heavily than other groups, but these agencies may be called upon to relieve the distress of union members during certain emergencies, such as prolonged strikes and unemployment. Business groups back private welfare efforts in order to minimize government spending and control in this area, and because welfare activities provide them with a highly legitimate status platform. In addition, business likes the idea of having some control over funds distributed to workers during prolonged unemployment.

Other groups in the community may not agree with labor that the Community Chest is an important arena of social power. Labor is sure that it is. The history of labor's share in the control of welfare associations rather accurately reflects its increasing collective bargaining power. Thus, in 1929, no union representative sat on the Community Chest Board of Directors, and an involuntary payroll deduction plan was in effect in most of the plants. In 1933, perhaps in an attempt to head off the UAW, representatives of company unions were placed on the Chest Board. In 1940 two regular union members were hired on the staff of the Community Services Council and union officers were made cochairmen of the Industry and Labor Section of the annual Community Chest Drive. At present, six of the thirty-six members of the Chest Board of Directors are union officials as is one member of the Community Services Council. One-third of the members of the Labor Participation Committee of the Community Chest are union representatives. In addition, union members are found in 21 of the 24 local agencies participating in the Community Services Council. Through such participation unions can obtain representation on the huge and important 152-member budget committee of the Community Chest.

Table 4 presents data on the occupational composition of the boards comprising the Community Services Council. Several findings are noteworthy. First, businessmen are not as highly represented on the boards as they are on the Community Chest Drive and other community agencies. Professional workers, who are often more sympathetic toward labor, are the dominant occupational category on these boards. Together with staff members of the agencies who are on the boards, they comprise over two-fifths of the members, compared to slightly under two-fifths for proprietors and managers. Labor union officials, manual and clerical workers make up about one-tenth of the total board membership. Organized labor is generally dissatisfied with its small representations on the boards of individual agencies in the Council, the Council itself, and the Community Chest Board. It has openly announced its intention to increase its representation on all welfare agencies.

Labor has far to go to equal the power of business groups in the welfare field. No labor representative is found in three of the twenty-four local welfare agencies. No labor official has ever been elected to the

TABLE 4

OCCUPATION OF THE BOARD MEMBERS OF
32 HEALTH AND WELFARE BOARDS
IN INGHAM COUNTY, MICHIGAN, 1953

Occupations	Men	Women*	Total
Employees of voluntary and public health and welfare agencies	6%	1%	6%
Professional workers	39	34	37
Proprietors and managers	34	27	32
Junior executives and supervisors	5	8	6
Governmental officials	3	5	2
Salaried workers	2	8	4
Manual workers	3	5	4
Labor union representatives	5	—	3
Not ascertained	3	12	6
Total	100	100	100
Number of cases	427	182	609

* Occupation of husbands or self, if single.

presidency of the Board of Directors of the Community Chest. No union member has ever been the general chairman of the annual fund drive. Labor has never sponsored the "progress" dinners held during the annual drives. Speakers for these dinners are typically businessmen and professionals. While the ability to attain such offices may represent prestige rather than power gains, management hesitates to relinquish these offices. The importance of such offices is illustrated by the fact that the president of the Board of Directors of the Community Chest has always been a top influential in the community. The hospital expansion drive and other community projects have usually been organized and led by influentials who have had the highest posts in the Council, Chest, and campaign committees.

How can labor's over-all position in the welfare arena be evaluated? The strongest card that organized labor holds is the threat to withhold contributions. Since labor is responsible for collecting about 40 percent of the funds, it can, by withholding support, limit local welfare efforts. Although this has been threatened, labor is reluctant to assume welfare burdens without outside support. In the Community Chest structure, labor has one-sixth of the seats on the strategic Board of Directors, one-third of the members of the Labor Participation Committee, and the cochairmanship of the important Labor and Industry Section of the annual drive organization. Considering also the influence of union members who are on the staff of the Chest and the support received from some professionals in and out of the Chest, labor could, in an extreme case, nearly match the power of the other combined groups.

Mass Communications and Religion

The only daily local newspaper, the television station, and radio stations in the city are strongly pro-business. During the past decade, however, the local daily, *The State Journal*, has steadily increased the amount of news about local union activities. The acquisition of a labor reporter who weekly or biweekly reports on the activities of local unions indicates some recognition of the influence of labor. In addition to the literature sent to union members from their Internationals, *The Lansing Labor News*, an independent weekly with a circulation of about 20,000, reaches all members of ex-CIO locals and some members of ex-AFL locals. In an interview study of the membership of a UAW local, nine-tenths of the respondents reported that they read the paper regularly. A content analysis of a sample of issues over a six-month period revealed that almost one-half of the paper was devoted to advertising and three-tenths to local labor news. Two-thirds of the local news consisted of reports about the activities of the locals and their individual members, and the remainder reported on local community activities. The high readability of local news and free want ads for union members serve to maintain reader interest.

An analysis of the positions on major elections, referenda, and city projects taken by the *State Journal* during the decade 1945 to 1955 re-vealed that they were almost overwhelmingly followed by the voters. In two referenda the *Labor News* took a position opposite to the *Journal's*, but lost. The *News* campaigned vigorously against an increase in bus fares and it opposed the floating by the city of a general obligation bond to build parking ramps. On a subsequent referendum on bus fares (taken during a bus strike) the *Journal's* stand to double the fares was endorsed by the voters. On the parking-ramp issue the real estate lobby flooded the *Journal* with paid advertising urging voters to reject the proposal, while the *News* espoused the same position editorially. In the outcome of the referenda on both issues, the position taken by the *Labor News* was victorious. However, the voting turnouts were comparatively small, less than half of a "good" turnout. While the *News* could not claim even minor responsibility for its apparent victories, it can be influential in lightly contested campaigns, especially when its position is endorsed by other economic interests in the community.

Religious leaders in the city have generally avoided open involvement in management-labor controversies. Both management and labor representatives, however, have included Protestant and Catholic clergy among the top forty influentials of the city. In the welfare sector especially, these clergymen have frequently sided with labor. In an effort to increase labor's rapprochement with the clergy, a permanent liaison organization between the two groups has been instituted. Clergymen themselves like to interpret their public roles vis-à-vis labor and management as neutral, and both sides seem to respect this definition. This abstention from issue commitment has the effect of leaving business domination of public communication channels unchallenged. High-status churches remain under strong business influence.

Community Influentials and Key Influentials

During 1957 and 1958 a panel of community influentials and a panel of labor influentials were interviewed. The former were derived from nominations of two "knowledgeables" in each of seven institutional sectors: mass communication, management, labor, welfare, education, government, and religion. They were asked to nominate persons whom they considered to have the greatest amount of influence and control over important community-wide projects and issues. Forty persons about whom there was the most consensus were selected as "community influentials." They were interviewed and asked, among other things, to choose from the list (or add the names of) the ten most influential people in the community. The ten who received the most votes were arbitrarily named the "key influentials."

Two labor officials appeared in the list of community influentials. A clergyman and an insurance agent on the list could sometimes be expected to be neutral or prolabor. The remaining seven professionals and 29 businessmen were Republican and generally expressed antiunion attitudes. Those sympathetic to labor thus comprised at most one-eighth of the community influentials.

Neither the union officials nor those sympathetic to labor qualified as *key influentials*. While the latter received on the average one-half of the votes they could theoretically receive as key influentials, those sympathetic to labor received about one-seventh, compared to one-fifth for the entire panel. The two union officials received one-tenth of the possible vote. A generous estimate of labor's strength among community influentials would be about one-fifth of the total strength.

A panel of "top forty" labor influentials in the community was selected from nominations submitted by knowledgeables in mass communication, industry, government, and professors in the Labor and Industrial Relations Center at the University. The top forty labor influentials were then interviewed and asked (among other things) to name the ten most influential persons in the community. Twenty percent of the names in this list were labor union officials, as contrasted to five percent of the names found in the general list of community influentials. Somewhat over three-fifths of the labor panel nominated union officials as *key influentials*. The two labor officials who were on the list of community influentials received about half of the vote which they could theoretically receive as key influentials from the labor panel. This may be compared to one-tenth of the votes they received from the community influentials themselves. Thus, labor's self-perception of its representation among both the community and key influentials was much greater than that acknowledged by other community influentials.

Conclusions

This case study of Lansing, Michigan, confirms the findings of McKee, Phelps, Cook, and others that organized labor's community power lags behind its economic power. Prior to 1937, when organized labor lacked strong bargaining in its relations with management, unions had virtually no power in community-wide agencies. Since that time labor has attained a position in collective bargaining of near equality with management. Labor's gains in community representation, though small, have been so significant that one must conclude that an equality of bargaining strength was the necessary condition for increasing community involvement. During the decade 1937 to 1947, labor sought to increase its influence in the community by using the same bargaining style which had been so effective in industrial relations disputes. However, the blunt accusations, the insistent demands, and the disregard of social niceties characteristic of class-conscious unionism were not acceptable in an arena dominated by business, and labor's advances were resisted.

Labor's change in style after World War II was more acceptable to middle- and upper-status groups in the city. The white shirt, soft spoken words, and a willingness to back "reasonable" leaders whatever their backgrounds became the new modus operandi. This approach not only enabled labor to increase its representation in community organizations, it also permitted two or three union officials to become community influentials.

An over-all appraisal of union power in various community segments from high to low would result in the following rank order: economic bargaining, welfare, education, political parties, elective municipal offices, city appointive boards, religion, and mass communication. In all these sectors labor is heavily outweighed in terms of representation and power by businessmen and professionals. In almost all of the boards studied, labor union members and manual workers constituted about 10 percent of the members. Greater variation was found in the proportions of businessmen and professionals on these boards. Labor developed most strength where it could guarantee financial support—as in segments of the Community Chest, the Board of Education, and the Democratic party. As an integral part of these structures, labor derived its power from an ability to withhold its much needed support.

Labor also appeared to have somewhat more influence in agencies in which professionals had greatest representation. This was not only due to the sympathy which some professionals had for organized labor but, perhaps more important, to the fact that businessmen had to share leadership with another high-status group which sometimes had different values. Labor obtained the least power in agencies where it was denied participation, and where it needed general and voluntary community support to make headway. Thus it had least representation on the city council, the municipal appointive boards, church boards, and mass communication agencies. In the separate agencies of welfare, education, mass communication, and government, labor's penetration was uneven.

Labor's representation and strength among community influentials tended to lag behind its representation and strength in local agencies, for influence cannot easily be usurped, but arises out of recognition and legitimation of power. Without control of municipal elective offices, labor's penetration into the community power structure will be limited. Success in this arena is circumscribed by at least three important factors. First, nonpartisanship makes it difficult to conduct partisan campaigns acceptable to middle-status groups. Second, the mass media of communication, which are conservative, are quick to stigmatize labor's political interest as partisan. Last, labor's drive for respectability in other community arenas decreases its community visibility to the rank and file. Never highly identified as a workingman and often politically apathetic and conservative, the Yankee worker presents an anomaly to union officials. The more respectable the latter become, the less visible they become, and the more difficult their task of involving the rank and file in community affairs.

Notes

1. See Alice H. Cook, *Labor's Role in Community Affairs,* (Ithaca: New York State School of Industrial and Labor Relations, Cornell University, 1955), Bulletin 32, pp. 4–15. Community participation by local unions may be stimulated by their need to continue to perform significant functions at a time when their traditional bargaining functions are being assumed by the International.

2. See "Community Recognition of Union Leaders," *Industrial and Labor Relations Review,* April 1954, pp. 419–433.

Population data in this and the other studies referred to apply to the year the studies were made.

3. McKee asserted that business maintained its strength for three reasons: (a) it continued to be concerned with state and national legislation (which are considered really as more important than municipal legislation), (b) its position in such local "master decisions" as taxation was never challenged, and (c) its prestige was so high that, in general, the tendency was to continue to accept business as the legitimate voice of the community. James McKee, "Organized Labor and Community Decision Making; A Study in the Sociology of Power," Ph.D. dissertation, University of Wisconsin, 1953; "Status and Power in the Industrial Community," *American Journal of Sociology,* January 1953, pp. 364–370.

4. C. M. M. Hart, "Industrial Relations Research and Social Theory," *Canadian Journal of Economics and Political Science,* February 1949, pp. 53–73.

5. Donald E. Wray, "The Community and Labor-Management Relations," *Labor-Management Relations in Illini City* (Champaign: Institute of Labor and Industrial Relations, 1953), pp. 7–145.

6. Charles R. Walker, *Steeltown* (New York: Harper & Brothers, 1950), pp. 42–45.

7. W. L. Warner and others, *Democracy in Jonesville* (New York: Harper & Brothers, 1949).

8. Floyd Hunter, *Community Power Structure* (Chapel Hill: University of North Carolina Press), 1954.

9. Robert O. Schulze and Leonard Blumberg, "The Determination of Local Power Elites," *The American Journal of Sociology,* November 1957, pp. 290–296.

10. Twenty managers of locally owned plants indicated that the 10 percent wage differential that existed between the large absentee-owned plants and their plants prior to World War II had virtually disappeared. In another study by the author and Sigmund Nosow of a sample of 580 manual workers in the community, two-fifths were employed in locally owned plants. See Nosow, *loc. cit.,* pp. 20–31.

11. About half of these worked for commissions and were not considered "working class."

12. Members were appointed for two-year terms. Following the agency is the number of members serving during 1945–1957. None of the following boards had working-class members or union officials: Children's Home, 6; Civil Defense Council,

7; Public Service Board, 9; Civic Center Commission, 10; State Board of Appeal, 16; Zoning Board of Appeal, 21; City Planning Commission, 42. The following boards had memberships of which less than 9 percent were manual workers and union officials (the numerators indicate the labor members and the denominators the total number of members): City Employees Retirement System Trustees, 1/29; Board of Water and Light, 2/38; Air Pollution Commission, 1/17; Board of Cemetery and Public Park Commissioners, 2/26; Transit Commission, 1/12; Municipal Parking Authority, 2/15. The following had more than the 9 percent average; Municipal Parking Authority, 2/15; Traffic Commission, 5/35; Board of Plumbing and Zoning Ordinance, 2/14; Board of Health, 1/9; Trustees of Board of Police and Fire Retirement, 5/32; Board of Electric Examiners, 3/8.

35. The West End Story: A Study in Political Impotence

SOLON T. KIMBALL
AND MARION PEARSALL

(In this selection the authors are concerned with persons on the other end of the political scale from Hunter's "top influencials." The authors, two sociologists, were present in this community to conduct a health survey which is referred to as the "Inventory.")

The "Community," with its prosperous stores around the square, its substantial houses on tree-lined avenues, its principal churches, its educational institutions, and its civic and social clubs, sets the cultural tone of Talladega and provides the most active leadership and participation in community affairs. Around the peripheries of the "community," however, are a number of separate, unrelated neighborhoods whose residents are not full participants in the life of Talladega, although they make up nearly half the white population. These are the areas of workers' homes that have grown up through the years of expanding industry from the 1890's to the present.

Some of the areas are distinct in that they are adjacent to and, at least originally, were owned by mills; their inhabitants are identified with particular industries. Others have grown more haphazardly as labor has been attracted from surrounding rural areas in the course of change from an agrarian to an industrial based economy. Ties to the community begin and practically end with occupational and trade identity with the town. The areas are under city government and educational

Reprinted from *Talladega Story* (University, Alabama: University of Alabama Press, 1954), pp. 163–72 by permission of the authors and the publisher. Solon T. Kimball is a professor of sociology at Columbia University. Marion Pearsall is a professor of sociology at the University of Kentucky.

systems. Beyond that, they remain socially and geographically isolated from the heart of the community.

Of all the peripheral neighborhoods, an area of several blocks in the northwest sector of town linked to the center of the city by one main artery most nearly forms a natural area. It is the only predominantly working class residential area that became incorporated at all into the activities of the Community Council. . . .

Persons in West End already knew about the Inventory through the newspapers. They had wondered if anyone would ask them to take part. They were afraid they would be overlooked in this project as in other "community" activities, and it was not part of their customary behavior to volunteer for anything in the "other side of town" where they might not be welcome. Now, however, the visit released a tide of pent-up complaints about conditions in West End—the need for sewers, paved streets and sidewalks. The residents obviously felt that Dr. Davis, whom they identified with the people who "run the town," had the power to get all these improvements for them. Dr. Davis and Dr. Kimball were both surprised and apprehensive over the enthusiasm which greeted them, but they made plans to explain the Inventory at a public meeting in West End.

The initial reaction in West End was the same as in other groups. The people already knew the health conditions that might be improved. It did not occur to them that people in other parts of town might not be aware of the needs. They seized upon the Health Inventory as a chance to get quickly what no amount of talk and complaining had hitherto secured for them. A whirlwind of enthusiasm produced an explosive meeting and subsequent petitioning of city officials that spelled doom for any hopes of immediate improvements and nearly put an end to any hopes of further integration of the neighborhood into Council activities.

The eventful meeting took place on a stormy midsummer evening in 1951 in one of the three small churches in West End. A lightning bolt had extinguished the lights so the first fifteen minutes of the meeting were conducted by flashlight. Oscar Hurst presided, as he was the man Dr. Davis had first approached. The meeting was attended by about twenty-five men of the neighborhood. Four women were also present and sat on the left side of the church with Dr. Davis and the Presbyterian minister, Dr. Crowe, who were representing the Community Council. Several members of the research team represented the University staff. Mayor Wallis Elliott was also present at the invitation of the Council, since it was known that the main discussion would center around problems that would eventually call for action by the City Commission.

The meeting started in orderly fashion with explanations about the Health Inventory from Council and University representatives. But they were unable to communicate to the group the full meaning of the Inventory. The background of West End residents was one in which a person proceeds directly from desire to fulfillment. Direct action was far more comprehensible than a long and cautious survey process which dealt in words, facts, figures, and more words. The sanitation issue was obviously too "hot" to be contained within the orderly framework of a health inventory. Formal order disappeared as conflicting values came to the surface. West End did not grasp the Council's values, nor was West End itself a united neighborhood with any simple set of attitudes about plumbing or anything else.

For the majority at the meeting, there was only one answer. Faced as they were with the daily inconvenience and olfactory awareness of pit privies, and having a desire to share in the material conveniences of American town life, they wanted immediate extension of city sewerage. They were more than willing to assume their share of the expense. Knowing that he voiced the majority opinion, Mr. Hurst spoke of the need for sanitary facilities and asked "our mayor" to explain the necessary procedure for presenting a request to the city for sewerage.

Mayor Elliott explained that they should appoint a committee of five to appear before the City Commission. They should present a petition for sewerage signed by three-fourths of the property owners of the area. He did not at this time explain some of the engineering difficulties that were involved in granting such a petition. Increased population had strained existing facilities to their limit and it would be impractical to add a new burden without altering the main system. As it turned out, these problems would not be faced by the City Commission for some time to come, at least not because of any action from citizens of West End.

There were immediate volunteers to serve on the necessary committee. This was the signal for the opposition to protest the whole scheme. Three men opposed any extension of sewerage into the area. Their objections were those of the small but (in an area like West End) powerful property owner who has worked hard to acquire a little rental property but feels he cannot afford to make improvements on that property.

The opposition, backed as they were by strong family relationships in West End and believing firmly in their individual rights, were not afraid to voice their sentiments. One had nine houses rented in the neighborhood; it would "break" him to connect them to the sewer system. Another told of the five houses he had built in a cotton patch years ago. The twenty-three dollars a week from them was his only income in his old age. Someone reminded him he could borrow money to pay for the sewerage, but he refused to consider going into debt in his declining years. He had more to say about those who would force the issue. He had just returned from the Florida Everglades where the Indians lived the way he would like to, all "to themselves, left alone by the government and the people." Futhermore, he did not like the way a certain "dried-up, squanty man" had been going around talking for this sewerage.

At this point, Mr. Hurst owned to being the "dried-up, squanty man" and let it be known that if the men cared to say anything more, they could step outside the church and "have it out." He spoke again about how badly West End needed sewerage. He illustrated with stories of worms crawling from the privies into the houses. He intimated that he could tell more if they were not in a church and if there were no ladies present.

After further heated comments from both sides, Dr. Crowe—ever the able moderator—arose and told the gathering that the greatest principle in existence was "co-operation." "Neighbors are wonderful," he said, "but you have to pay for good neighbors. There can be no community without give and take. It will cost you something to have good neighbors, but they are worth it."

To this there were fervent "amens"—meant at the time—but the excitement had just begun. Reports soon reached Council members that two petitions were circulating in West End, one for and the other against requesting the city to extend sewerage service to the neighborhood. Emotions counted far more than serious evaluation of the advantages and disadvantages of sewerage or even the expense involved. The issue itself was lost in a maze of personal antagonisms. . . .

The Commission postponed the meeting at which the petitioners were to appear. No formal notice was given, and only a few of the interested persons received word informally. They ceased their efforts, while others, with the liaison officer, continued to prepare a map of West End, showing the location of all property owners who favored extension of city sewerage to their property.

Meanwhile, in West End, sewerage had become a bitter issue setting neighbors against each other. Accusations and counter-accusations were made about the validity of signatures on the petitions. The "pro" forces in particular complained that the others had included renters as well as property owners. They also charged intimidation to the point that at least one owner had been frightened into withdrawing his signature. Another owner talked seriously of moving out of West End.

Finally, on the appointed day some from both committees appeared at City Hall for the meeting that was never held. One commissioner was in the hospital and another was out of town; but both sides suspected a deliberate plot and now talked amiably with each other as they transferred their anger to the political system. Members of the "pro" committee had further cause for irritation because the two who had their petition were not there.

Later events revealed that the absent committee members, learning of the change in meeting plans, had presented the petition earlier but had not notified the others. As turned in, the petition requesting the city to extend sewerage to West End had fifty-one signatures, representing eighty percent of the property owners. The opposing petition had only thirteen signatures. For a political system not committed to take any more action than necessary, especially for groups unable to bring much pressure to bear, the evidence of any dissension was excuse enough not to act. Months later one of the commissioners stated that the reason no action had been taken was that more persons opposed than favored the request, a convenient lapse of memory.

The elements contributing to the initial failure of the Inventory in West End are not all immediately clear. Two fundamentally important factors stand out. First, although the town tends to think of West End as a homogeneous area there was no real unity in the area, certainly no existing system for organized neighborhood action. Secondly, there was little basic framework for interaction between West End and the rest of the community. There were no well-worn paths of communication between West End and the town. . . .

The principal connection between West End and the city is through the political system. For citizens in West End the "they" who are credited with running the city are the politicians. Once an election is over, interaction between West End and the political system most commonly takes the form illustrated by the sewerage events, with about the same results.

The relation of West End to political office-seekers shows the essentially family-based nature of relationships in the neighborhood. Residents cannot be counted on to vote as a bloc, and there are no formal associations through which a politician may work. But there is a functioning informal system through which an individual may pledge the votes of his many kinsmen and perhaps a few unrelated friends.

For an office-seeker, the points of contact with West End are several small neighborhood grocery stores. Vote trading is done on the basis of money or in terms of personal favors rather than election issues. For this reason, a candidate does not have to make many promises about paving streets or providing sewerage. He is more certain to gain support by reducing a fine or assuring a job with the city for a son or nephew of the grocery store proprietor.

Money and favors may not assure election. At least one official in recent years has lost strength in the neighborhood by acting counter to values held by many in the neighborhood. While not united in any organizational way, the people do have in common certain strongly held attitudes about religion and what behavior is allowable around the churches. One of the West End churches was using a loudspeaker for some of its revival meetings, and the official sent police to stop them. The church people of the neighborhood felt this was an infringement of their right to hold services as long and as loud as their consciences dictated. They further raised the issue of the official allowing bay rum to be sold in the local groceries. Characteristically the complaint was that men were getting drunk and creating disturbances around the churches. Coincidence or not, the official in question lost a substantial number of votes in West End at the next election.

The pattern of West End voting as described by a person from the main part of town is close to the reality of the situation, and he notes some changes that are occurring:

Let them vote for their streets instead of voting for the man. Let them vote for the fellow who will pave their streets and put in their sewerage instead of voting because my brother's kin to somebody's sister-in-law. Time was when anybody could walk into West End and pick out a half dozen people to pass the liquor and greenbacks to and carry that section of town. Now, you've got to go and ask every one of them for his vote. They will take your liquor and your money right on, but they'll go ahead and vote like they please. You find a man who can deliver more than five votes down there and you've got a big shot.

With other activities as with voting, West End is not homogeneous, although the majority of the townspeople who are aware of West End at all are inclined to view it as a lower class neighborhood. The conventional picture of American social classes—upper, middle, and lower levels with further sub-divisions within each—is not, in itself, overly important to the functioning of Talladega. There is however, a sharp division of long standing between the working class and all other levels. This has its roots in the history of the region and a social system in which manual labor of any sort was looked down on.

When cotton mills first began operations in Talladega more than half a century ago, the workers formed a definite class. For the most part them came from the surrounding rural areas, moving from a low position in the agrarian social system into an equally subordinate position in industry. Their residential areas were, and still are, separate. The average town person and the mill worker rarely crossed each other's orbit. Presumably, the mill worker had his own life; but no one bothered to find out. The mill streets were so unattractive that people in the "community" avoided driving through them.

There have been many changes in the past forty-five or fifty years, but there are still few contacts outside the economic realm. Each group tends to think in stereotypes about the other. The town person, if he gives the matter any thought, believes that most members of the working class are satisfied with their living conditions. If they were not, they would move to better neighborhoods. This is part of the great American philosophy that anyone who wants to improve his condition can do so.

Judging the West End entirely from external appearances, as most non-residents do, gives an inaccurate and incomplete picture. Viewed from within, the neighborhood is not nearly so clear and simple. The unpaved streets alternately muddy or dusty, houses of generally poor frame construction, the pit privies much in evidence, all suggest a lower class neighborhood. A closer look, however, shows that a good number of the houses do not entirely conform to this idea. Their yards are neat and have flower gardens which show care and cultivation against considerable odds. A good many have vegetable gardens at the rear, and perhaps a chicken coop. Inside, the houses are comfortably furnished with all the modern conveniences except plumbing. All that remains of the "lower class" impression is the shabby exterior and the overcrowded appearance of too small rooms.

Families in the more cared-for houses own their own homes. They see West End as a place where they hope to raise children and grandchildren. They want to improve the neighborhood so it will be a place of which they can be proud. . . .

Among the property owners in West End, just as in other parts of town, there are two general attitudes toward change. On one side are those who spend their energies protecting what they already have, content with their present degree of security. On the other side are those who perhaps have as much but are willing to risk something to gain more. The two attitudes were represented in the alignment of forces for and against sewerage. In other parts of town the distinction between the two attitudes might not have been so apparent; but the working people in West End believe in direct, and at times violent, action. They are not used to the hours of devious discussion and the use of intricate lines of power that tend to mask the real feelings of groups in other parts of town.

There is a third element in West End that also affects the neighborhood. These are the "floaters." Whether they stay in Talladega one year or ten, they think of themselves as temporary residents and have no sense of allegiance to the community. They rent from week to week or month to month from owners who see no reason to make improvements for either the tenants' or the neighborhood's sake. These rental shacks are interspersed among the more permanent residences so that each block has one or two, making it difficult for other families to maintain a "respectable" neighborhood. . . .

The meeting and its consequences caused both the Council and the active supporters in the neighborhood to retreat. The residents of West End who had received what seemed to be a glowing opportunity withdrew again into their neighborhood shell, more convinced than ever that the city was not interested in their welfare. They had been "bitten" again as so often before. Each such episode increases apathy and increases resentment, making any further attempts at cooperation that much more difficult.

36. Community Power Structures and Partisanship

ROBERT E. AGGER AND DANIEL GOLDRICH

A comparative community study of local politics in two communities in the Far West in 1953–1954 affords an opportunity to examine the nature of, and relationships between, the political parties in the community, the informal Republican organization of Main Street, and the local power structure. None of the recently reported community power structure studies has focussed upon the question of whether there may be important relationships between the local power structure and partisan behavior.

Reprinted from *American Sociological Review*, XXIII (August 1958), pp. 383–92 by permission of the authors and the publisher. Authors' footnotes abridged. Robert Agger is professor of political science at the University of Oregon. Daniel Goldrich is professor of political science at Michigan State University.

Local elections are legally non-partisan in Valley City, a small retail trading center of about 2,000 adults, as well as in Boomtown, a rapidly growing industrial community of about 16,000 population. In each community self-identified Democrats outnumbered self-identified Republicans but the Republicans have been consistently more successful in state and national elections in Valley City than in Boomtown. In both communities the partisan atmosphere on Main Street was predominantly Republican, although much more so in Valley City than in Boomtown. These partisan differences afford an especially good opportunity to examine the possible relationships between party and power structure at the community level. The Republicanism of the business community on the Main Streets of small towns and cities (outside of the South) is a fact frequently noted in the political literature. That Main Street plays an active if not dominant role in the functioning of local power structures is a fact receiving empirical underpinning in recent investigations of community power structure. The connection between these two facts is the central concern of this analysis.

Assumptions to be Examined

A political scientist comments on the traditional Republicanism of Main Street as follows:

. . . Republicans number among their supporters by far the greater proportion of the business and professional groups who, without changing their way of life, engage in politics as a matter of course. . . . Republicans have a great many individual supporters who belong to . . . organizations (in the community) that function continually, and that without breaking step with their routine operation, can convert themselves into political organizations . . . Society is like a giant spider web of communications and contacts, and Republicans tend to be stationed at the centers of contacts and communications with the society at large. As spare-time politicians, such contact controllers and opinion leaders can easily bring to bear upon the political process their strong influences and political leadership. In brief, the normal structure provides an informal Republican party organization.[1]

This view of Main Street as "the natural organization" of the Republican party seems to rest on the following interlocking assumptions:

1. A positive and substantial relationship exists between socio-

economic status (SES) and Republican party identification.

2. A positive and substantial relationship is to be found between SES and participation in community organizations.

3. Therefore, Republicans dominate the organizational membership structure (OMS) in the community.[2]

4. Republican domination of the organizational membership structure creates or reinforces a Republican atmosphere on Main Street, if not throughout the community.

5. The Republican atmosphere on Main Street increases Republican electoral strength by weakening Democratic party loyalties.

The recent community power structure studies suggest (implicitly) a further elaboration of the foregoing assumptions which augments the view of Main Street as the natural organization of the Republican Party.

6. The dominants in the local power structure are or have been (or have as their agents) dominants in the organizational membership structure.

7. Therefore, Republicans dominate the local power structure (because Republicans dominate the organizational membership structure).

8. Republican domination of the local power structure in a legally non-partisan community either: (a) does not reinforce a Republican atmosphere throughout the community because the top leaders in a local power structure are, or are perceived to be, non-partisan; or (b) further reinforces a Republican atmosphere on Main Street, if not throughout the community.

Research Methods

The two major research methods for examining these assumptions in our two communities were a random sample survey in each community and participant observation. The survey in Valley City was approximately a ten per cent sample of the adults living outside the city limits and in the surrounding fringe areas (260 respondents). In Boomtown the survey was approximately a five per cent sample, with half of the respondents living within the city and half on the fringe (752 respondents).

Two techniques were used to identify top leaders: nominations by respondents in the samples of the most influential community policy-makers; the judgments of the participant observers. There was a considerable consensus between the two.

The Two Communities

The smaller community, Valley City, gives one the impression of stability. The population has remained comparatively stable, less than doubling in size from 1930 to 1950. Boomtown has been one of the fastest growing communities in the state. Its population has increased more than five times between 1930 and 1950. The major economic activity in Valley City is retail trade. In Boomtown about 35 per cent of the population is engaged in manufacturing, with almost 90 per cent of the manufacturing related to the lumber industry. Most of the industry is absentee-owned. In the Valley City sample, almost 20 per cent of the respondents were farmers as compared with less than one per cent of the sample in Boomtown. The percentage of the population deriving its principal income from wages or salaries was 84 per cent in Boomtown and 54 per cent in Valley City. Workers in Boomtown were the more heavily unionized.

Valley City is about fifteen miles from Big City on a major U.S. and state highway. Big City is a retail trading, university, and governmental center for the area. People living in the country between Big City and Valley City had begun to shop more extensively in Big City. Even Valley City residents were beginning to desert the home-town merchants, a trend of great concern to the latter. The seasonal fluctuations in the lumbering industry of the area added to the insecurities of the merchants of Main Street.

Boomtown is adjacent to and is the industrial hand-maiden of Big City. The major economic problem in Boomtown has been the depressed and unstable condition of the one major industry in the community—lumbering and associated activities.

Politics and Power Structures

During the period of the study the Democrats had almost no formal organization in Valley City. The one organized partisan activity during the national election period in 1952 was an informal dinner meeting arranged at the home of one of the few visible Democrats on Main Street. The Republicans in Valley City were organized and represented in the Republican councils of the county and state. There was a Republican state legislator from Valley City. Perhaps because of the absence of organized local opposition, organized Republican activity at election or other times did not seem to be very great. Even though registered Democrats outnumbered registered Republicans in the community, there was a general feeling that continued Republican domination was inevitable.

In contrast, in Boomtown, both parties were organized and active locally. Republican strength was centered on Main Street. Democratic organization, although weaker and more informal than that of the Republicans, included professional persons and some businessmen as well as labor union people. This differed dramatically from the situation in Valley City where it was extremely difficult to spot Democrats among the merchants and professional men on Main Street. There was not a single admitted Democrat in the officialdom of Valley City. In Boomtown Democrats held a few governmental offices.

Among the group of top leaders in Valley City, three men stood out as the most influential. All three at the time of the study had governmental positions. The senior leader of the community, the state legislator, was a wealthy automobile dealer as well as a large property owner. His son-in-law was the mayor, and the mayor's brother, the third most influential person, was a member of the school board. Associated closely with these three in an effective policy-making group which met regularly to discuss community affairs were seven or eight respected members of the business community. On all important policy questions one or more of these men was consulted. Almost all of these top leaders served actively in the highest positions in the civic organizations. A card-playing club afforded a regular meeting time and place for group discussion. In interviews, these men repeatedly expressed a sentiment for keeping Valley City small and stable in the image of Jeffersonian democracy. Big City was viewed as a horrible example of what might happen to Valley City if it ever became a "boomtown."

The local government officials, some of whom were top leaders, agreed that the role of local government should be that of passive housekeeper for the community. Rather than play a more active role in influencing the future urban or industrial growth of Valley City, the local government was following *status quo* policies. These included decisions not to annex new territory, not to extend city sewer and other services beyond the town limits, not to grant any tax or other concessions for new business or industry, and to retain a low tax rate with a minimum of expenditures for community improvements.

A few merchants openly expressed the view that the *status quo* policies of Valley City leaders were certain to lead to economic ruin. Some of these men tried to establish a Chamber of Commerce in order to set about the task of bringing more industry into the community. At the time of the study this effort had been thwarted through pressure brought to bear by the top leaders on the dissidents, pressure ranging from argument to social ostracism to economic boycott.

Local government in Boomtown was more dynamic and growth-oriented. In this rapidly growing city the need for providing more adequate services of all kinds was pressing. Local government was attempting to meet this need and to do something about the major problem of seasonal unemployment. New firms were encouraged to locate in Boomtown in order to diversify the economy.

Overshadowing these issues, however, was the matter of public versus private power in Boomtown. The period between the end of World War II and 1950 was marked by poor quality of service provided by the private utility company of the area. By the late 1940's a number of people, particularly young politicians, were demanding that Boomtown build a competing municipal utility system. After widespread discussion the voters gave resounding approval to such a proposition. But the establishment of the municipal utility did not end the controversy, which continued to color politics in Boomtown. Party identifications seem to have meant relatively little on this issue. Some Republicans took positions supporting the municipal utility without rejecting their party's national position in favor of private power. And some Democrats opposed the municipal utility. City Hall itself was not unified in favor of the municipal power system.

In this expansion era in Boomtown the political pie, as represented by local offices, had not yet been firmly divided nor had permanent accommodations been reached by contending groups. There was little of the sort of hierarchical power structure found in Valley City. There was much less consensus among Boomtowners than among the residents of Valley City about who were the most influential people—the popular view on this point corresponds to the findings of the research team. Boomtown had a polynucleated set of leadership groups at the top of the power structure. Around top leaders were numerous small and relatively impermanent cliques often containing both Republicans and Democrats.

Testing the Assumptions

Do the assumptions underlying the conception of Main Street as the natural organization of the Republican party apply to Valley City and Boomtown?

1. A positive and substantial relationship exists between socio-economic status (SES) and Republican party identification.

This assumption seems to be accepted generally and uncritically by
political sociologists. Empirical findings do substantiate the positive relationship, but few studies have specified its size. In our two communities
the relationship of the three indices of SES (education, income and
occupation) to Republicanism vary considerably. Some of these relationships are statistically significant and others are not (Table 1). Some differ-

TABLE 1

RELATIONSHIP OF SOCIAL-ECONOMIC STATUS (SES) TO PARTY IDENTIFICATION°

	Valley City				Boomtown			
	Reps.	Dems.	Totals		Reps.	Dems.	Totals	
	%	%	%	No.	%	%	%	No.
Education								
Grades 1–9	39	61	100	92	39	61	100	234
High School	44	57	100	95	32	68	100	314
College	56	44	100	39	62	38	100	90
Income								
Under $3,000	51	49	100	63	45	55	100	132
$3,000–$3,999	31	69	100	52	36	64	100	141
$4,000–$9,999	44	56	100	90	35	65	100	326
$10,000 and over	55	45	100	11	76	24	100	25
Occupation								
Business and Professional	53	47	100	38	45	55	100	100
Farmers	41	59	100	22	60	40	100	5
Skilled and semiskilled	34	66	100	38	34	66	100	174
Unskilled	48	52	100	21	32	68	100	78

The relationship between Republicanism and both education and income in
Boomtown is significant at the .001 level, using chi-square.
° All tables are based on data collected from the random samples.

ences are large and some are small.[3] In order to give the benefit of any
doubt to the assumptions discussed below, we consider that this initial
assumption is supported by the evidence although in need of revision.[4]

2. A positive and substantial relationship is to be found between
   SES and participation in community organizations.

There is a positive, statistically significant relationship between SES and participation in community organizations in both communities (Table 2).

TABLE 2

RELATIONSHIP OF ORGANIZATIONAL MEMBERSHIP (OMS) PARTICIPATION TO EDUCATIONAL LEVEL

	Valley City					Boomtown				
	High	Grades				High	Grades			
	College	School	1–9	Totals		College	School	1–9	Totals	
	%	%	%	%	No.	%	%	%	%	No.
High OMS	33	36	31	100	64	32	51	17	100	109
Medium OMS	14	44	42	100	100	12	49	39	100	288
Low OMS	7	45	48	100	62	9	49	42	100	241

The relationship between OMS participation and education is significant at the .01 level in Valley City, and at the .001 level in Boomtown.

3. Therefore, Republicans dominate the organizational membership structure in the community.

In both Valley City and Boomtown, Republicans do dominate the OMS. The critical question, however, is whether this assumption is supported *because* of the relationship between SES and Republicanism (assumption 1, above). An alternative explanation for the finding that Republicans dominate the OMS concerns the psychological inhibiting-facilitating functions of partisan self-identifications. Democratic party identification may function psychologically to repress participation by Democrats in community organizations dominated by Republicans. In order to test which of these hypotheses holds, education is held constant.

There are differences (although they are statistically insignificant) between levels of participation in the OMS of the college educated Democrats and Republicans in both communities (Table 3). Assumption 3 must be revised because it is not sufficient to account for the lower OMS scores of equally well-educated Democrats. The assumption may be rephrased as follows:

Republicans dominate the OMS partly because they are of higher SES than Democrats, and partly because the latter may be inhibited by their partisan self-identification from participating in the upper strata of the community's OMS.

4. Republican domination of the organizational membership structure creates or reinforces a Republican atmosphere on Main Street, if not throughout the community.

Our estimate of the partisan atmosphere on Main Street is based for the most part upon two types of evidence: first, the visibility of Repub-

TABLE 3

RELATIONSHIP OF ORGANIZATIONAL MEMBERSHIP (OMS) PARTICIPATION TO
PARTY IDENTIFICATION, BY EDUCATION LEVEL

		Valley City					Boomtown				
		High OMS	Me-dium OMS	Low OMS	Totals		High OMS	Me-dium OMS	Low OMS	Totals	
		%	%	%	%	No.	%	%	%	%	No.
College											
	Rep.	50	45	5	100	22	30	52	18	100	56
	Dem.	23	59	18	100	17	18	53	29	100	34
High School											
	Rep.	12	61	27	100	41	8	54	38	100	102
	Dem.	9	59	32	100	54	6	57	37	100	211
Grades 1–9											
	Rep.	5	64	31	100	36	2	58	40	100	92
	Dem.	5	61	34	100	56	1	54	45	100	142

licans as compared with Democrats on Main Street; and second, the assessment of the partisan content of informal discussion in organizational contexts.

Concerning visibility, the field workers shared the feeling that there was not a single Democrat on Valley City's Main Street, although the sample survey proved this impression to be incorrect. In Boomtown there were obviously some Democrats on Main Street but the research team again was surprised by the number of self-identified Democrats in the business community that turned up in the sample survey.

The Republican partisan atmosphere could probably be assessed more accurately by devising systematic sampling methods to measure the partisan content in the flow of discussion within the community organizations. Although we have used no such refined measure, participant observers independently agreed that the partisan discussion occurring in organizational settings was predominantly pro-Republican, although more so in Valley City than in Boomtown.

5. The Republican atmosphere on Main Street increases Republican electoral strength by weakening Democratic party loyalties.

Democratic party loyalties presumably may be weakened in one of three ways: by weakening or transforming Democratic party identifications; by inhibiting Democrats from accepting official positions in the local party organization; or by keeping Democrats inactive in informal party activities.

In Valley City, the Republican atmosphere did not seem to weaken or transform Democratic party identifications (50 per cent Democrats, 39 per cent Republicans and 11 per cent independents). In spite of the pervasive Republican climate on Main Street, 47 per cent of the business-men and white collar workers were self-identified Democrats (Table 1). There was no discernible increase in the number of self-identified independents, which, if it had been present, would possibly have been an indication of a first step in transition to a Republican orientation or an attempt to "pass" in a hostile partisan environment.[5]

No Democratic local party organization existed, nor were Democrats as active as Republicans in informal party activities, as judged by the research team. The Republican atmosphere, while not undermining Democratic party identifications, functioned to inhibit more overt partisan activity.

Like the Main Street merchants in Valley City, those in Boomtown also retained their Democratic self-identifications (Table 1.) The strong Republican atmosphere on Boomtown's Main Street, although less pervasive than that in Valley City, neither prevented some Democrats from participating in official positions in the local party organization nor inhibited their informal party activities.

6. The dominants in the local power structure are or have been (or have as their agents) dominants in the organizational membership structure.

Recent studies of community power structures have found two types of top leadership. In one type, the leaders, those who exercise maximum influence in important community policy-making, are the economic dominants. In the other, top leaders are from somewhat lower strata in the economic structure in the community. It has been suggested that this second situation occurs when major local industries are absentee-owned. In both types of power structures, however, the top leaders reportedly have had a background of high OMS activity.

In Valley City the economic dominants were among the top leaders. All such leaders were themselves active in the OMS, as well as having

agents who were high OMS people. In Boomtown the economic dominants and top leaders were for the most part two separate groups. Some
of these leaders achieved their positions through, and operated primarily
in, other than OMS channels. These persons were Democrats and the
channels were political and governmental.

7. Therefore, Republicans dominate the local power structure (because Republicans dominate the organizational membership structure).

This assumption holds for Valley City but not for Boomtown. Even
though Republicans dominated the OMS in Boomtown (Table 3), Democrats were among the top leaders.

In the local power structure, there exists a second level, consisting
of participants in the making of community policy who are not however
perceived as top leaders. This group participates, though not as extensively as the top leaders, in most of the policy-oriented discussion, advis-
ing and advocacy. Most of these "second-level" persons relate themselves
to top leaders by interacting or identifying with them. A composite index
of participation in community policy-making based in large part on discussion of community policy matters was used as the measure of participation in the local power structure.

Democrats and Republicans were about equal participants in Boomtown's power structure. Holding education constant, a small, statistically
insignificant relationship is found between Republicanism and high
participation among the college-educated (Table 4). This Republican
advantage is overcome, however, by the positive relationship between
Democratic party identification and high participation among the high
school-educated.

In Valley City there is a larger (though statistically insignificant)
relationship between Republicanism and participation in the power structure among the college-educated.

Our findings in reference to assumptions 6 and 7 suggest that in
Valley City the local power structure substantially overlaps the organizational membership structure for the top leaders and the "second-level"
participants. Highly educated Democrats participate less in both structures and there are no Democrats in the top leadership group. In Boomtown the two structures are not as overlapping. Democrats participate
less than Republicans in the OMS but equally in the power structure,
and Democrats are among the top leaders.

8. Republican domination of the local power structure in a legally
   non-partisan community either: (a) does not reinforce a Repub-

lican atmosphere throughout the community because the top leaders in a local power structure are, and are perceived to be, non-partisan; or (b) further reinforces a Republican atmosphere on Main Street, if not throughout the community.

Other studies of community power structures do not specifically discuss the partisan complexion or functions of the structures. Presumably

TABLE 4

RELATIONSHIP OF PARTICIPATION IN LOCAL POWER STRUCTURE TO PARTY IDENTIFICATION, BY EDUCATION LEVEL

		Valley City					Boomtown				
		Participation:					Participation:				
		High	Me-dium	Low	Totals		High	Me-dium	Low	Totals	
		%	%	%	%	No.	%	%	%	%	No.
College											
	Rep.	82	14	4	100	22	66	30	4	100	56
	Dem.	59	35	6	100	17	56	44	0	100	34
High School											
	Rep.	39	46	15	100	41	32	53	15	100	102
	Dem.	32	44	24	100	54	42	45	13	100	212
Grades 1–9											
	Rep.	14	61	25	100	36	22	53	25	100	92
	Dem.	16	55	29	100	56	23	51	26	100	142

top leaders are assumed to deal in non-partisan fashion with matters of community policy, especially where local government is technically non-partisan. On the other hand, even in a non-partisan setting, it is possible that a top leadership group consisting almost entirely of members of one party can enhance the prestige and status of that party and weaken the party loyalties of the opposition.

Assumption 8 does not apply to Boomtown because Republicans did not dominate the local power structure.

Valley City had non-partisan elections and the top leaders did not participate in community policy-making, at least publicly, as partisan Republicans. Republican domination of the local power structure did not reinforce the Republican atmosphere in the community. But this is not because the top leaders were perceived to be non-partisan (as suggested in 8, a). Democrats nominated Democrats as top leaders and Republicans nominated Republicans. This partisan difference in perceptions of top leaders was not due to differences in education or level of participation (Table 5).

TABLE 5

RELATIONSHIP OF TOP LEADER NOMINATIONS TO PARTY IDENTIFICATION, BY EDUCATION AND PARTICIPATION IN LOCAL POWER STRUCTURE

| | Valley City | | | | | Boomtown | | | | | |
| | Top 3 Leaders | Others | No One | Totals | | Top 2 Republicans | Top 2 Democrats | Others | No One | Totals | |
	%	%	%	%	No.	%	%	%	%	%	No.
Education Level											
College											
Rep.	77	18	5	100	22	16	5	36	43	100	56
Dem.	29	41	30	100	17	6	18	23	53	100	34
High School											
Rep.	44	37	19	100	41	14	15	25	46	100	102
Dem.	32	37	31	100	54	5	16	29	50	100	211
Grades 1–9											
Rep.	25	39	36	100	36	11	8	25	56	100	92
Dem.	38	32	30	100	56	6	9	25	60	100	142
Participation											
High											
Rep.	59	28	13	100	39	16	8	41	35	100	83
Dem.	39	36	25	100	36	7	21	39	33	100	136
Medium											
Rep.	41	41	18	100	44	13	12	22	53	100	120
Dem.	34	38	28	100	61	5	10	26	59	100	182
Low											
Rep.	19	25	56	100	16	5	5	20	70	100	40
Dem.	27	30	43	100	30	2	6	16	76	100	63

The relationship between Republicanism and nomination of the Top 3 Leaders among the college-educated in Valley City is significant at the .01 level.

Comparing the nominations of only the top two Republicans and the top two Democrats in Boomtown: the relationship between party identification of respondents and nomination of top leaders of the same party is significant among the college-educated at the .05 level (using the Fisher Exact Test), among the high school-educated at the .05 level, and among high participants at the .01 level.

The local power structure, then, in "non-partisan" Valley City, was perceived in a partisan frame of reference. A similar pattern of partisan perceptions was found in Boomtown (Table 5). Although the number of cases is very small, the data in Table 5 suggests that partisanship affects perceptions to the greatest extent among the highly educated and the highly participant. It is these people whom one might expect to be most sensitive to party affiliations of top leaders. Not only does their education make them more alert to political facts of life than their fellows, but their participation in the power structure affords them the opportunity to see through political myths of non-partisanship.

Assumption 8 must therefore be revised to read:

Republican domination of the local power structure in a legally non-partisan community does not reinforce a Republican atmosphere throughout the community because: (a) Democrats tend to perceive or identify themselves with top leaders who are Democrats, or (b) Democrats fail to perceive or identify themselves with Republican top leaders.

Summary

This comparative study of two towns in the West has led to qualifications in several assumptions about relationships among community social and political structures and partisanship. The Republican atmosphere on Main Street, especially in the community organizations, did not lead to conversion so much as it inhibited the expression of Democratic loyalties. Under certain conditions, as in Boomtown, this atmosphere does not even function to inhibit such expression. When Democrats hold important positions in the local power structure, as they did in Boomtown, channels exist for the activation of Democratic loyalties.

Control by the economic dominants in Valley City of the overlapping organizational membership and power structures discouraged Democratic activities in local politics. When economic dominants do not control the power structure, as they did not in Boomtown, opportunities exist for Democrats to move directly into top leader positions without a long apprenticeship in the Republican-dominated social structure.

The efficacy of the natural organization of the Republican party on Main Street therefore depends on the partisan complexion of the community power structure, which in turn depends upon the relationships among the local power, economic and social structures.

Notes

1. Alfred deGrazia, *The Western Public,* Stanford: Stanford University Press, 1954, p. 185.

2. Participation in community organizations is conceived as the organizational membership structure (the OMS). The OMS is the formally organized social structure in action. As the social structure has strata, so too does the OMS. John M. Foskett developed an index for position in the OMS based on membership and activity scores. Those with the highest scores are in the top stratum of the OMS; they tend to control organizational policy-making. Some of those in the top stratum, the dominants, in the OMS may not receive high scores because of membership in many organizations; rather, they may participate actively in two or three organizations. Cf. Roland J. Pellegrin and Charles H. Coates, "Absentee-owned Corporations and Community Power Structure," *American Journal of Sociology,* 61 (March, 1956), pp. 415–416, and Floyd Hunter, *Community Power Structure,* Chapel Hill: The University of North Carolina Press, 1953, pp. 85–87.

3. A difference which is statistically significant at the .001 level may be small and "essentially meaningless for sociology at present," while others may be statistically significant below the five per cent level in a small sample and "be of major theoretical importance." Hanan C. Selvin, "A Critique of Tests of Significance in Survey Research," *American Sociological Review,* 22 (October, 1957), p. 524.

4. Education is the index of SES most closely related to socio-political participation in both communities and is used as the central index throughout this analysis.

5. These functions of self-identification as an independent are discussed in Robert E. Agger, "Independents and Party Identifiers: Characteristics and Behavior in 1952," in Arthur Brodbeck and Eugene Burdick (editors), *American Voting Behavior,* Glencoe, Ill.: Free Press, 1959, pp. 308–29.

B. ALTERNATIVE MODELS FOR ANALYSIS

37. The Local Community as an Ecology of Games

NORTON E. LONG

The local community whether viewed as a polity, an economy, or a society presents itself as an order in which expectations are met and functions performed. In some cases, as in a new company-planned mining town, the order is the willed product of centralized control, but for the most part the order is the product of a history rather than the imposed effect of any central nervous system of the community. For historic reasons we readily conceive the massive task of feeding New York to be

Reprinted from *American Journal of Sociology,* LXIV (November 1958), pp. 251–61 by permission of the author and the publisher. Norton Long is professor of political science and Director of Education of the Transportation Center at Northwestern University.

achieved through the unplanned, historically developed cooperation of thousands of actors largely unconscious of their collaboration to this individually unsought end. The efficiency of this system is attested to by the extraordinary difficulties of the War Production Board and Service of Supply in accomplishing similar logistical objectives through an explicit system of orders and directives. Insofar as conscious rationality plays a role, it is a function of the parts rather than the whole. Particular structures working for their own ends within the whole may provide their members with goals, strategies, and roles that support rational action. The results of the interaction of the rational strivings after particular ends are in part collectively functional if unplanned. All this is the well-worn doctrine of Adam Smith, though one need accept no more of the doctrine of beneficence than that an unplanned economy can function.

While such a view is accepted for the economy, it is generally rejected for the polity. Without a sovereign, Leviathan is generally supposed to disintegrate and fall apart. Even if Locke's more hopeful view of the naturalness of the social order is taken, the polity seems more of a contrived artifact than the economy. Furthermore, there is both the hangover of Austinian sovereignty and the Greek view of ethical primacy to make political institutions seem different in kind and ultimately inclusive in purpose and for this reason to give them an over-all social directive end. To see political institutions as the same kind of thing as other institutions in society rather than as different, superior, and inclusive (both in the sense of being sovereign and ethically more significant) is a form of relativistic pluralism that is difficult to entertain. At the local level, however, it is easier to look at the municipal government, its departments, and the agencies of state and national government as so many institutions, resembling banks, newspapers, trade unions, chambers of commerce, churches, etc., occupying a territorial field and interacting with one another. This interaction can be conceptualized as a system without reducing the interacting institutions and individuals to membership in any single comprehensive group. It is psychologically tempting to envision the local territorial system as a group with a governing "they." This is certainly an existential possibility and one to be investigated. However, frequently, it seems likely, systems are confused with groups, and our primitive need to explain thunder with a theology or a demonology results in the hypostatizing of an angelic or demonic hierarchy. The executive committee of the bourgeosie and the power elite make the world more comfortable for modern social scientists as the Olympians did for the ancients. At least the latter-day hypothesis, being terrestrial, is in principle researchable, though in practice its metaphysical statement may render it equally immune to mundane inquiry.

Observation of certain local communities makes it appear that inclusive over-all organization for many general purposes is weak or nonexistent. Much of what occurs seems to just happen with accidental trends becoming cumulative over time and producing results intended by nobody. A great deal of the communities' activities consist of undirected co-operation of particular social structures, each seeking particular goals and, in doing so, meshing with others. While much of this might be explained in Adam Smith's terms, much of it could not be explained with a rational, atomistic model of calculating individuals. For certain purposes the individual is a useful way of looking at people; for many others the role-playing member of a particular group is more helpful. Here we deal with the essence of predictability in social affairs. If we know the game being played is baseball and that X is a third baseman, by knowing his position and the game being played we can tell more about X's activities on the field than we could if we examined X as a psychologist or a psychiatrist. If such were not the case, X would belong in the mental ward rather than in a ball park. The behavior of X is not some disembodied rationality but, rather, behavior within an organized group activity that has goals, norms strategies, and roles that give the very field and ground for rationality. Baseball structures the situation.

It is the contention of this paper that the structured group activities that coexist in a particular territorial system can be looked at as games. These games provide the players with a set of goals that give them a sense of success or failure. They provide them determinate roles and calculable strategies and tactics. In addition, they provide the players with an elite and general public that is in varying degrees able to tell the score. There is a good deal of evidence to be found in common parlance that many participants in contemporary group structures regard their occupations as at least analogous to games. And, at least in the American culture, and not only since Eisenhower, the conception of being on a "team" has been fairly widespread.

Unfortunately, the effectiveness of the term "game" for the purposes of this paper is vitiated by, first, the general sense that games are trivial occupations and, second, by the pre-emption of the term for the application of a calculus of probability to choice or decision in a determinate game situation. Far from regarding games as trivial, the writer's position would be that man is both a game-playing and a game-creating animal, that his capacity to create and play games and take them deadly seriously is of the essence, and that it is through games or activities analogous to game-playing that he achieves a satisfactory sense of significance and a meaningful role.

While the calculability of the game situation is important, of equal or greater importance is the capacity of the game to provide a sense of purpose and a role. The organizations of society and polity produce satisfactions with both their products and their processes. The two are not unrelated, but, while the production of the product may in the larger sense enable players and onlookers to keep score, the satisfaction in the process is the satisfaction of playing the game and the sense in which any activity can be grasped as a game.

Looked at this way, in the territorial system there is a political game, a banking game, a contracting game, a newspaper game, a civic organization game, an ecclesiastical game, and many others. Within each game there is a well-established set of goals whose achievement indicates success or failure for the participants, a set of socialized roles making participant behavior highly predictable, a set of strategies and tactics handed down through experience and occasionally subject to improvement and change, an elite public whose approbation is appreciated, and, finally, a general public which has some appreciation for the standing of the players. Within the game the players can be rational in the varying degrees that the structure permits. At the very least, they know how to behave, and they know the score.

Individuals may play in a number of games, but, for the most part, their major preoccupation is with one, and their sense of major achievement is through success in one. Transfer from one game to another is, of course, possible, and the simultaneous playing of roles in two or more games is an important manner of linking separate games.

Sharing a common territorial field and collaborating for different and particular ends in the achievement of over-all social functions, the players in one game make use of the players in another and are, in turn, made use of by them. Thus the banker makes use of the newspaperman, the politician, the contractor, the ecclesiastic, the labor leader, the civic leader—all to further his success in the banking game—but, reciprocally, he is used to further the others' success in the newspaper, political, contracting, ecclesiastical, labor, and civic games. Each is a piece in the chess game of the other, sometimes a willing piece, but, to the extent that the games are different, with a different end in view.

Thus a particular highway grid may be the result of a bureaucratic department of public works game in which are combined, though separate, a professional highway engineer game with its purposes and critical elite onlookers; a departmental bureaucracy; a set of contending politicians seeking to use the highways for political capital, patronage, and the like; a banking game concerned with bonds, taxes, and the effect of the highways on real estate, newspapermen interested in headlines, scoops, and the effect of highways on the papers' circulation; contractors eager to make money by building roads; ecclesiastics concerned with the effect of highways on their parishes and on the fortunes of the contractors who support their churchly ambitions; labor leaders interested in union contracts and their status as community influentials with a right to be consulted; and civic leaders who must justify the contributions of their bureaus of municipal research or chambers of commerce to the social activity. Each game is in play in the complicated pulling and hauling of siting and constructing the highway grid. A wide variety of purposes is subserved by the activity, and no single over-all directive authority controls it. However, the interrelation of the groups in constructing a highway has been developed over time, and there are general expectations as to the interaction. There are also generalized expectations as to how politicians, contractors, newspapermen, bankers, and the like will utilize the highway situation in playing their particular games. In fact, the knowledge that a banker will play like a banker and a newspaperman like a newspaperman is an important part of what makes the situation calculable and permits the players to estimate its possibilities for their own action in their particular game.

While it might seem that the engineers of the department of public works were the appropriate protagonists for the highway grid, as a general activity it presents opportunities and threats to a wide range of other players who see in the situation consequences and possibilities undreamed of by the engineers. Some general public expectation of the limits of the conduct of the players and of a desirable outcome does provide bounds to the scramble. This public expectation is, of course, made active through the interested solicitation of newspapers, politicians, civic leaders, and others who see in it material for accomplishing their particular purposes and whose structured roles in fact require the mobilization of broad publics. In a sense the group struggle that Arthur Bentley described in his *Process of Government* is a drama that local publics have been taught to view with a not uncritical taste. The instruction of this taste has been the vocation and business of some of the contending parties. The existence of some kind of over-all public puts general restraints on gamesmanship beyond the norms of the particular games. However, for the players these are to all intents as much a part of the "facts of life" of the game as the sun and the wind.

It is perhaps the existence of some kind of a general public, however rudimentary, that most clearly differentiates the local territorial system from a natural ecology. The five-acre woodlot in which the owls and the field mice, the oaks and the acorns, and other flora and fauna have evolved a balanced system has no public opinion, however rudimentary. The co-operation is an unconscious affair. For much of what goes on in

the local territorial system co-operation is equally unconscious and perhaps, but for the occasional social scientist, unnoticed. This unconscious
co-operation, however, like that of the five-acre woodlot, produces results. The ecology of games in the local territorial system accomplishes
unplanned but largely functional results. The games and their players
mesh in their particular pursuits to bring about over-all results; the
territorial system is fed and ordered. Its inhabitants are rational within
limited areas and, pursuing the ends of these areas, accomplish socially
functional ends.

While the historical development of largely unconscious co-operation between the special games in the territorial system gets certain
routine, over-all functions performed, the problem of novelty and breakdown must be dealt with. Here it would seem that, as in the natural
ecology, random adjustment and piecemeal innovation are the normal
methods of response. The need or cramp in the system presents itself to
the players of the games as an opportunity for them to exploit or a
menace to be overcome. Thus a transportation crisis in, say, the threatened abandonment of commuter trains by a railroad will bring forth the
players of a wide range of games who will see in the situation opportunity
for gain or loss in the outcome. While over-all considerations will appear
in the discussion, the frame of reference and the interpretation of the
event will be largely determined by the game the interested parties are
principally involved in. Thus a telephone executive who is president of
the local chamber of commerce will be playing a civic association, general
business game with concern for the principal dues-payers of the chamber
but with a constant awareness of how his handling of this crisis will
advance him in his particular league. The politicians, who might be expected to be protagonists of the general interest, may indeed be so, but
the sphere of their activity and the glasses through which they see the
problem will be determined in great part by the way they see the issue
affecting their political game. The generality of this game is to a great
extent that of the politician's calculus of votes and interests important to
his and his side's success. To be sure, some of what Walter Lippmann has
called "the public philosophy" affects both politicians and other game-
players. This indicates the existence of roles and norms of a larger, vaguer
game with a relevant audience that has some sense of cricket. This
potentially mobilizable audience is not utterly without importance, but it
provides no sure or adequate basis for support in the particular game that
the politician or anyone else is playing. Instead of a set of norms to
structure enduring role-playing, this audience provides a cross-pressure
for momentary aberrancy from gamesmanship or constitutes just another
hazard to be calculated in one's play.

In many cases the territorial system is impressive in the degree of intensity of its particular games, its banks, its newspapers, its downtown stores, its manufacturing companies, its contractors, its churches, its politicians, and its other differentiated, structured, goal-oriented activities. Games go on within the territory, occasionally extending beyond it, though centered in it. But, while the particular games show clarity of goals and intensity, few, if any, treat the territory as their proper object. The protagonists of things in particular are well organized and know what they are about; the protagonists of things in general are few, vague, and weak. Immense staff work will go into the development of a Lincoln Square project, but the twenty-two counties of metropolitan New York have few spokesmen for their over-all common interest and not enough staff work to give these spokesmen more substance than that required for a "do-gooding" newspaper editorial. The Port of New York Authority exhibits a disciplined self-interest and a vigorous drive along the lines of its developed historic role. However, the attitude of the Port Authority toward the general problems of the metropolitan area is scarcely different than that of any private corporation. It confines its corporate good citizenship to the contribution of funds for surveys and studies and avoids acceptance of broader responsibility. In fact, spokesmen for the Port vigorously reject the need for any superior level of structured representation of metropolitan interests. The common interest, if such there be, is to be realized through institutional interactions rather than through the self-conscious rationality of a determinate group charged with its formulation and attainment. Apart from the newspaper editorial, the occasional politician, and a few civic leaders the general business of the metropolitan area is scarcely anybody's business, and, except for a few, those who concern themselves with the general problems are pursuing hobbies and causes rather than their own business.

The lack of over-all institutions in the territorial system and the weakness of those that exist insure that co-ordination is largely ecological rather than a matter of conscious rational contriving. In the metropolitan area in most cases there are no over-all economic or social institutions. People are playing particular games, and their playgrounds are less or more than the metropolitan area. But even in a city where the municipal corporation provides an apparent over-all government, the appearance is deceptive. The politicians who hold the offices do not regard themselves as governors of the municipal territory but largely as mediators or players in a particular game that makes use of the other inhabitants. Their roles, as they conceive them, do not approach those of the directors of a TVA developing a territory. The ideology of local government is a highly limited affair in which the office-holders respond to demands and mediate conflicts. They play politics and politics is vastly different from government if the latter is conceived as the rational, responsible ordering of the community. In part, this is due to the general belief that little government is necessary or that government is a congery of services only different from others because it is paid for by taxes and provided for by civil servants. In part, the separation of economics from politics eviscerates the formal theory of government of most of the substance of social action. Intervention in the really important economic order is by way of piecemeal exception and in deviation from the supposed norm of the separation of politics and economics. This ideal of separation has blocked the development of a theory of significant government action and reduced the politician to the role of registerer of pressure rather than responsible governor of a local political economy. The politics of the community becomes a different affair from its government, and its government is so structured as to provide the effective actors in it neither a sense of general responsibility nor the roles calling for such behavior.

The community vaguely senses that there ought to be a government. This is evidenced in the nomination by newspapers and others of particular individuals as members of a top leadership, a "they" who are periodically called upon to solve community problems and meet community crises. Significantly, the "they" usually are made up of people holding private, not public office. The pluralism of the society has separated political, ecclesiastical, economic, and social hierarchies from one another so that the ancient union of lords spiritual and temporal is disrupted. In consequence, there is a marked distinction between the status of the holders of political office and the status of the "they" of the newspapers and the power elite of a C. Wright Mills or a Floyd Hunter. The politicians have the formal governmental office that might give them responsible governing roles. However, their lack of status makes it both absurd and presumptuous that they should take themselves so seriously. Who are they to act as lords of creation? Public expectation neither empowers nor demands that they should assume any such confident pose as top community leaders. The latter position is reserved for a rather varying group (in some communities well defined and clear-cut, in others vague and amorphous) of holders for the most part of positions of private power, economic, social, and ecclesiastical. This group, regarded as the top leadership of the community, and analogous to the top management of a corporation, provides both a sense that there are gods in the heavens whose will, if they exercise it, will take care of the community's problems and a set of demons whose misrule accounts for the evil in the world. The "they" fill an office left vacant by the dethronement of absolutism and aristocracy. Unlike the politicians in that "they" are only partially visible and of untested powers, the top leadership provides a convenient rationale for explaining what goes on or does not go on in the community. It is comforting to think that the executive committee of the bourgoisie is exploiting the community or that the beneficent social and economic leaders are wearying themselves and their digestions with civic luncheons in order to bring parking to a congested city.

Usually the question is raised as to whether *de facto* there is a set of informal power-holders running things. A related question is whether community folklore holds that there is, that there should be, and what these informal power-holders should do. Certainly, most newspapermen and other professional "inside dopesters" hold that there is a "they." In fact, these people operate largely as court chroniclers of the doings of the "they." The "they," because they are "they," are newsworthy and fit into a ready-made theory of social causation that is vulgarized widely. However, the same newspaperman who could knowingly open his "bird book" and give you a run-down on the local "Who's Who" would probably with equal and blasphemous candor tell you that "they" were not doing a thing about the city and that "they" were greatly to be blamed for sitting around talking instead of getting things done. Thus, as with most primitive tribes, the idols are both worshiped and beaten, at least verbally. Public and reporters alike are relieved to believe both that there is a "they" to make civic life explicable and also to be held responsible for what occurs. This belief in part creates the role of top leadership and demands that it somehow be filled. It seems likely that there is a social-psychological table of organization of a community that must be filled in order to remove anxieties. Gordon Childe has remarked that man seems to need as much to adjust to an unseen, socially created spiritual environment as to the matter-of-fact world of the senses.

The community needs to believe that there are spiritual fathers, bad or good, who can deal with the dark: in the Middle Ages the peasants combated a plague of locusts by a high Mass and a procession of the clergy who damned the grasshoppers with bell, book, and candle. The Hopi Indians do a rain dance to overcome a drought. The harassed citizens of the American city mobilize their influentials at a civic luncheon to perform the equivalent and exorcise slums, smog, or unemployment. We smile at the medievals and the Hopi, but our own practices may be equally magical. It is interesting to ask under what circumstances one resorts to DDT and irrigation and why. To some extent it is clear that the ancient and modern practice of civic magic ritual is functional—functional in the same sense as the medicinal placebo. Much of human illness is benign; if the sufferer will bide his time, it will pass. Much of civic ills also cure themselves if only people can be kept from tearing each other apart in the stress of their anxieties. The locusts and the drought will pass. They almost always have.

While ritual activities are tranquilizing anxieties, the process of experimentation and adaptation in the social ecology goes on. The piece-meal responses of the players and the games to the challenges presented by crises provide the social counterpart to the process of evolution and natural selection. However, unlike the random mutation of the animal kingdom, much of the behavior of the players responding within the perspectives of their games is self-conscious and rational, given their ends in view. It is from the over-all perspective of the unintended contribution of their actions to the forming of a new or the restoration of the old ecological balance of the social system that their actions appear almost as random and lacking in purposive plan as the adaptive behavior of the natural ecology.

Within the general area of unplanned, unconscious social process technological areas emerge that are so structured as to promote rational, goal-oriented behavior and meaningful experience rather than mere happenstance. In these areas group activity may result in cumulative knowledge and self-corrective behavior. Thus problem-solving in the field of public health and sanitation may be at a stage far removed from the older dependence on piecemeal adjustment and random functional innovation. In this sense there are areas in which society, as Julian Huxley suggests in his *The Meaning of Evolution,* has gone beyond evolution. However, these are as yet isolated areas in a world still swayed by magic and, for the most part, carried forward by the logic of unplanned, undirected historical process.

It is not surprising that the members of the "top leadership" of the territorial system should seem to be largely confined to ritual and ceremonial roles. "Top leadership" is usually conceived in terms of status position rather than specifiable roles in social action. The role of a top leader is ill defined and to a large degree unstructured. It is in most cases a secondary role derived from a primary role as corporation executive, wealthy man, powerful ecclesiastic, holder of high social position, and the like. The top-leadership role is derivative from the other and is in most cases a result rather than a cause of status. The primary job is bank president, or president of Standard Oil; as such, one is naturally picked, nominated, and recognized as a member of the top leadership. One seldom forgets that one's primary role, obligation, and source of rational conduct is in terms of one's business. In fact, while one is on the whole pleased at the recognition that membership in the top leadership implies—much as one's wife would be pleased to be included among the ten best-dressed women—he is somewhat concerned about just what the role requires in the expenditure of time and funds. Furthermore, one has a suspicion that he may not know how to dance and could make a fool of himself before known elite and unknown, more general publics. All things considered, however, it is probably a good thing for the business, the contacts are important, and the recognition will be helpful back home, in both senses. In any event, if one's committee service or whatever concrete activity "top leadership" implies proves wearing or unsatisfactory, or if it interferes with business, one can always withdraw.

A fair gauge of the significance of top-leadership roles is the time put into them by the players and the institutionalized support represented by staff. Again and again the interviewer is told that the president of such-and-such an organization is doing a terrific job and literally knocking himself out for such-and-such a program. On investigation a "terrific job" turns out to be a few telephone calls and possibly, three luncheons a month. The standard of "terrific job" obviously varies widely from what would be required in the business role.

In the matter of staffing, while the corporation, the church, and the government are often equipped in depth, the top-leadership job of port promotion may have little more than a secretary and an agile newspaper-man equipped to ghost-write speeches for the boss. While there are cases where people in top-leadership positions make use of staff from their own businesses and from the legal mill with which they do business, this seems largely confined to those top-leadership undertakings that have a direct connection with their business. In general, top-leadership roles seem to involve minor investments of time, staff, and money by territorial elites. The absence of staff and the emphasis on publicity limit the capacity of top leadership for sustained rational action.

Where top leaderships have become well staffed, the process seems as much or more the result of external pressures than of its own volition. Of all the functions of top leadership, that of welfare is best staffed. Much of this is the result of the pressure of the professional social worker to organize a concentration of economic and social power sufficient to permit him to do a job. It is true, of course, that the price of organizing top leadership and making it manageable by the social workers facilitated a reverse control of themselves—a control of whose galling nature Hunter gives evidence. An amusing sidelight on the organization of the "executive committee of the bourgeoisie" is the case of the Cleveland Fifty Club. This club, supposedly, is made up of the fifty most important men in Cleveland. Most middling and even upper executives long for the prestige recognition that membership confers. Reputedly, the Fifty Club was organized by Brooks Emery, while he was director of the Cleveland

Council on World Affairs, to facilitate the taxation of business to support that organization. The lead time required to get the august members of the Fifty Club together and their incohesiveness have severely limited its possibilities as a power elite. Members who have tried to turn it to such a purpose report fairly consistent failure.

The example of the Cleveland Fifty Club, while somewhat extreme, points to the need on the part of certain activities in the territorial system for a top leadership under whose auspices they can function. A wide variety of civic undertakings need to organize top prestige support both to finance and to legitimate their activities. The staff man of a bureau of municipal research or the Red Feather Agency cannot proceed on his own; he must have the legitimatizing sponsorship of top influentials. His task may be self-assigned, his perception of the problem and its solution may be his own, but he cannot gain acceptance without mobilizing the influentials. For the success of his game he must assist in creating the game of top leadership. The staff man in the civic field is the typical protagonist of things in general—a kind of entrepreneur of ideas. He fulfils the same role in his area as the stock promoter of the twenties or the Zeckendorfs of urban redevelopment. Lacking both status and a confining organizational basis, he has a socially valuable mobility between the specialized games and hierarchies in the territorial system. His success in the negotiation of a port authority not only provides a plus for his taxpayers federation or his world trade council but may provide a secure and lucrative job for himself.

Civic staff men, ranging from chamber of commerce personnel to college professors and newspapermen, are in varying degrees interchangeable and provide an important network of communication. The staff men in the civic agencies play similar roles to the Cohens and Corcorans in Washington. In each case a set of telephone numbers provides special information and an effective lower-echelon interaction. Consensus among interested professionals at the lower level can result in action programs from below that are bucked up to the prestige level of legitimitization. As the Cohens and Corcorans played perhaps the most general and inclusive game in the Washington bureaucracy, so their counterparts in the local territorial system are engaged in the most general action game in their area. Just as the Cohens and Corcorans had to mobilize an effective concentration of top brass to move a program into the action stage, so their counterparts have to mobilize concentrations of power sufficient for their purposes on the local scene.

In this connection it is interesting to note that foundation grants are being used to hire displaced New Deal bureaucrats and college professors in an attempt to organize the influentials of metropolitan areas into self-conscious governing groups. Professional chamber of commerce executives, immobilized by their orthodox ideology, are aghast to see their members study under the planners and heretics from the dogmas of free-enterprise fundamentalism. The attempt to transform the metropolitan appearance of disorder into a tidy territory is a built-in predisposition for the self-constituted staff of the embryonic top metropolitan management. The major disorder that has to be overcome before all others is the lack of order and organization among the "power elite." As in the case of the social workers, there is a thrust from below to organize a "power elite" as a necessary instrument to accomplish the purposes of civic staff men. This is in many ways nothing but a part of the general groping after a territorial government capable of dealing with a range of problems that the existing feudal disintegration of power cannot. The nomination of a top leadership by newspapers and public and the attempt to create such a leadership in fact by civic technicians are due to a recognition that there is a need for a leadership with the status, capacity, and role to attend to the general problems of the territory and give substance to a public philosophy. This involves major changes in the script of the top-leadership game and the self-image of its participants. In fact, the insecurity and the situational limitations of their positions in corporations or other institutions that provide the primary roles for top leaders make it difficult to give more substance to what has been a secondary role. Many members of present top leaderships are genuinely reluctant, fearful, and even morally shocked at their positions' becoming that of a recognized territorial government. While there is a general supposition that power is almost instinctively craved, there seems considerable evidence that at least in many of our territorial cultures responsibility is not. Machiavellian *virtu* is an even scarcer commodity among the merchant princes of the present than among their Renaissance predecessors. In addition, the educational systems of school and business do not provide top leaders with the inspiration or the know-how to do more than raise funds and man committees. Politics is frequently regarded with the same disgust as military service by the ancient educated Chinese.

It is possible to translate a check pretty directly into effective power in a chamber of commerce or a welfare agency. However, to translate economic power into more general social or political power, there must be an organized purchasable structure. Where such structures exist, they may be controlled or, as in the case of *condottieri*, gangsters, and politicians, their hire may be uncertain, and the hired force retains its independence. Where businessmen are unwilling or unable to organize their own political machines, they must pay those who do. Sometimes the paymaster rules; at other times he bargains with equals or superiors.

A major protagonist of things in general in the territorial system is the newspaper. Along with the welfare worker, museum director, civic technician, etc., the newspaper has an interest in terms of its broad reading public in agitating general issues and projects. As the chronicler of the great, both in its general news columns and in its special features devoted to society and business, it provides an organizing medium for elites in the territory and provides them with most of their information about things in general and not a little of inside tidbits about how individual elite members are doing. In a sense, the newspaper is the prime mover in setting the territorial agenda. It has a great part in determining what most people will be talking about, what most people will think the facts are, and what most people will regard as the way problems are to be dealt with. While the conventions of how a newspaper is to be run, and the compelling force of some events limit the complete freedom of a paper to select what events and what people its public will attend to, it has great leeway. However, the newspaper is a business and a specialized game even when its reporters are idealists and its publisher rejoices in the title "Mr. Cleveland." The paper does not accept the responsibility of a governing role in its territory. It is a power but only a partially responsible one. The span of attention of its audience and the conventions of what constitute a story give it a crusading role at most for particular projects. Nonetheless, to a large extent it sets the civic agenda.

The story is told of the mayor of a large eastern metropolis who, having visited the three capital cities of his constituents—Rome, Dublin, and Tel Aviv—had proceeded home via Paris and Le Havre. Since his staff had neglected to meet the boat before the press, he was badgered by reporters to say what he had learned on his trip. The unfortunate mayor could not say that he had been on a junket for a good time. Luckily, he remembered that in Paris they had been having an antinoise campaign. Off the hook at last, he told the press that he thought this campaign was a good thing. This gave the newsmen something to write about. The mayor hoped this was the end of it. But a major paper felt in need of a crusade to sponsor and began to harass the mayor about the start of the local antinoise campaign. Other newspapers took up the cry, and the mayor told his staff they were for it—there had to be an antinoise campaign. In short order, businessmen's committees, psychiatrists, and college professors were mobilized to press forward on a broad front the suppression of needless noise. In vindication of administrative rationality it appeared that an antinoise campaign was on a staff list of possibilities for the mayor's agenda but had been discarded by him as politically unfeasible.

The civic technicians and the newspapers have somewhat the same relationship as congressional committee staff and the press. Many members of congressional committee staffs complain bitterly that their professional consciences are seared by the insistent pressure to seek publicity. But they contend that their committee sponsors are only impressed with research that is newsworthy. Congressional committee members point out that committees that do not get publicity are likely to go out of business or funds. The civic agency head all too frequently communicates most effectively with his board through his success in getting newspaper publicity. Many a civic ghost-writer has found his top leader converted to the cause by reading the ghosted speech he delivered at the civic luncheon reported with photographs and editorials in the press. This is even the case where the story appears in the top leader's own paper. The need of the reporters for news and of the civic technicians for publicity brings the participants of these two games together. As in the case of the congressional committee, there is a tendency to equate accomplishment with publicity. For top influentials on civic boards the news clips are an important way of keeping score. This symbiotic relation of newsmen and civic staff helps explain the heavy emphasis on ritual luncheons, committees, and news releases. The nature of the newspapers to exercise a serious governing responsibility in their marvels and miracles puts a heavy pressure for the kind of story that the press likes to carry. It is not surprising that civic staff men should begin to equate accomplishment with their score measured in newspaper victories or that they should succumb to the temptation to impress their sponsors with publicity, salting it to their taste by flattering newspaper tributes to the sponsors themselves. Despite the built-in incapacity of newspapers to exercise a serious governing responsibility in their territories, they are for the most part the only institutions with a long-term general territorial interest. In default of a territorial political party or other institution that accepts responsibility for the formulation of a general civic agenda the newspaper is the one game that by virtue of its public and its conventions partly fills the vacuum.

A final game that does in a significant way integrate all the games in the territorial system is the social game. Success in each of the games can in varying degrees be cashed in for social acceptance. The custodians of the symbols of top social standing provide goals that in a sense give all the individual games some common denominator of achievement. While the holders of top social prestige do not necessarily hold either top political or economic power, they do provide meaningful goals for the rest. One of the most serious criticisms of a Yankee aristocracy made by a Catholic bishop was that, in losing faith in their own social values, they were undermining the faith in the whole system of final clubs. It would be a cruel joke if, just as the hard-working upwardly mobile had worked their way to entrance, the progeny of the founders lost interest. The decay of the Union League Club in *By Love Possessed* is a tragedy for more than its members. A common game shared even by the excluded spectators gave a purpose that was functional in its time and must be replaced—hopefully, by a better one. A major motivation for seeking membership in and playing the top-leadership game is the value of the status it confers as a counter in the social game.

Neither the civic leadership game nor the social game makes the territorial ecology over into a structured government. They do, however, provide important ways of linking the individual games and make possible cooperative action on projects. Finally, the social game, in Ruth Benedict's sense, in a general way patterns the culture of the territorial ecology and gives all the players a set of vaguely shared aspirations and common goals.

38. Theory, Research, and Practice in Community Organization

PETER H. ROSSI

The ideas presented here are based on the published literature in this field and data collected in half a dozen studies in communities well scattered over the northeastern third of the country.[1] The communities have ranged considerably in size and in their economic and social compositions, ranging from a neighborhood in Chicago at one extreme to a middle-sized Southern Ohio city at the other. Of course, they do not constitute any sort of fair sample of American communities.

Observations on Community Social Structure

When compared with the American community in the 19th century, the most striking characteristic of contemporary cities is the relative drop in the importance of local government, not only in comparison with state

From an address delivered at the Kellogg Center to members of the Institute for Community Development of Michigan State University, May 1959. Reprinted by permission of the author and publisher from Charles Adrian, ed., *Social Science and Community Action* (East Lansing, Mich.: Institute for Community Development, 1960), pp. 9–23. Peter Rossi is professor of sociology at the University of Chicago.

and federal governments, but also relative to the importance of local voluntary associations. To understand what is happening within a contemporary community an investigator cannot confine himself to the official table of organization for municipal government but must add to it a host of voluntary associations which act on behalf of the community and which together with the formal structure of local government form the basic organizational framework of the local community.

There is no doubt that this is the age of the "community project." Significant community enterprises are often initiated outside the frame work of local government, aided and abetted by a proliferation of civic associations and citizen committees.

In many communities the Mayor and City Council often appear to be dragging their heels while organized "prominent" citizens exhort the community to push towards progress. The voluntary associations, ranging from the more permanent varieties—the Community Chest, Chamber of Commerce, and service clubs—to the *ad hoc* Citizens' Committees, have taken over many of the functions of initiating social change and marshalling community support for such changes that are formally allocated to local government and to political parties. While it is true in many cases that these voluntary associations eventually must move local authorities, the initial spark and much of the task of mobilizing public opinion have been performed for the latter in advance.

My colleague Edward A. Banfield tells me that this is a peculiarly American pattern, not to be encountered in England or in other Western nations. In England particularly, local government agencies well staffed with experts, are the prime movers of social change in the community.

Another striking characteristic of the American community in comparison with the past is the status gap between the personnel of local government and the local elites of wealth, intellect and status. The local echelons of the party organizations and the elective offices of municipal, county and even state governments are manned by persons whose social positions are often many levels below the denizens of the Country Club, Rotary Club and the Chamber of Commerce. The city Fathers and the county commissioners are recruited, at best, from among local lawyers of somewhat uncertain income and miscellaneous clientele, and more likely from among small proprietors of professional politicians. Money, status and intellect seem in one place and political control in another. Such anomalies lead to the hypothesis that things are really not what they seem and that somewhere there are strings by means of which local government is guided from without.

How things "get done" has therefore become more and more problematical as the lack of articulation grows between the political elite and the industrial, commercial, and professional elites. It is hard to believe that the corner grocer elected mayor can govern in his own right in a community with branch factories of several national firms, a local elite of some wealth, and several large commercial establishments.

This apparent "mushiness" to the local community gives rise to problems common to both the community sociologist and the community organizer. It is hard to understand what makes a community "tick" and it is hard to grasp how to operate the machinery. It is difficult to understand why one community manages to be run with admirable attention to modernization while another apparently similar stagnates.

A. Power Structures

There is a great temptation to resort to a model of explanation which sees the ultimate source of innovation and social change in the local community in either a single individual or in a very small group of men. I do not deny that there is evidence that this explanation is warranted in some communities or that some data on all communities tends to support this viewpoint. However, I do wish to deny that this is always the case or even that it is the case more often than not.

The existence of power phenomena on the local scene cannot be denied. Citizens are not equal either in their interest and involvement in local affairs nor are decision makers equally sensitive to the opinions of every citizen. It is this inequality of status, wealth, leadership, and involvement which is at the base of power.

The important issues in this connection are two in number: first, what accounts for the differentials in effectiveness, and secondly, over what kinds of decision makers is power particularly effective?

In each of the several communities which we have studied, the same types of persons are encountered as those whose wishes or demands carried particular weight with decision makers. The set of effective power wielders would vary somewhat according to the decision maker involved and the issue under consideration. But, in each case it was possible to discern for that case some overall ranking of effectiveness along which prominent citizens could be ordered uni-dimensionally.

The way in which the content of an issue determined who would be effective in moving a decision suggests that it would be difficult to define a single overall pyramidal power structure. Yet, there is an overall pyramidal structure of power; not of *exercised* power, but of power *potential*. In other words, men and social positions could be ranked uni-dimensionally according to how much weight they could *possibly* carry, but not according to how much weight they *actually* throw around. This implies two things: First, the exercise of power is voluntary and some persons of considerable potential elect not to employ it. Secondly, power rarely is used in all the spheres of community life where it might be employed. In part, this is because partisans seem to "specialize" in some areas of community life and in part, some areas of community life are more immune to power.

What are the attributes of people or social positions who can wield effective influence? Listed below is a partial catalogue of bases of power:

1. Control over wealth and other resources: This is rarely sufficient by itself. Wealth needs to be turned into control over resources or institutions that can be used as sanctions—e.g., control over banks, land, mass media—or accompanied by a tradition of community activity and concern. Thus, in "Bay City", Massachusetts one wealthy family was very powerful because in the past as well as in the present it had made heavy contributions to the community by endowing hospitals, playgrounds, and the like, and was recognized as having a claim to be heard. Another family, equally wealthy, but without such a history, would have been resented if it had made the same demands on the community.

2. Control over mass media: Any newspaper publisher is *ipso facto* powerful whether or not his newspaper can wield a great deal of influence with the public. Thus in a Southern Ohio town, the newspaper has a poor reputation in the eyes of the public, yet the publisher plays an important role in the community decisions. The controllers of the mass media are in a strategic position because they can either give or withhold both attention and approval. These powers are exercised within limits, since a newspaper still must publish some news.

3. Control over solidary groups: Persons who are at the head of cohesive organized groups or who are reputed to have influence over large segments of the public can wield power by threatening to withhold support. Even when support by public opinion is not strictly necessary to the carrying out of a decision maker role, as in the case of a Chamber of Commerce campaign to get new industry into town, the threat of withholding public support may be an effective sanction.

4. Control over values: Those social positions, such as minister, priest, and certain of the professions, which are concerned primarily with the interpretation of cultural values wield power by virtue of their right to make value judgments. A minister's moral judgment counts more because this is his "speciality."

5. Control over prestigeful interaction: Control over entree into desirable social circles is an important sanction over the behavior of

decision makers. The transformation of a rough-and-tumble labor leader into a tractable and well-behaved member of the Community Chest in a large industrial city was accomplished by tempting him into the social circles of high level management.

In connection with this list, it is important to note that it may not be the *objective* facts which count so much as the *reputed* facts. Thus the managers of industrial establishments in a Southern Ohio city are ranked in power roughly according to the perceived size of each firm. However, size is rarely accurately seen but distorted to fit the rank order of power. Similarly, the Protestant Republican politicians in "Bay City," Massachusetts saw the Catholic priest as important leaders in the Democratic Party who through their control over their flocks prevented access to the Democratic masses. In point of fact, a majority of the priests in the community were Republican in their personal political convictions.

The manipulation of the appearance of power is, of course, one of the major techniques of the skillful would-be leaders. The source of power which is most easily manipulated in this sense is leadership in organized groups. Few of the organized groups on the local scene have the power to mobilize public opinion that they are reputed to have.

Who has power over whom? Perhaps the clearest distinction here is between the two areas of community life—local government and the voluntary community associations. For local government officials who are ultimately brought to the bar of public opinion on election day, the leaders of solidary groups normally on their side carry the most weight. In so far as wealth and the mass media are seen as potential influencers of public opinion, they too are powerful. Within the voluntary community associations which depend largely on the bounty of large contributors, wealth and its control play the major role.

Another distinction must be drawn according to types of issues. An issue which divides the community (or with potentially might divide the community) can be moved to a decision point only by solidary groups. I have in mind in this connection such issues as integration in public housing or public schools. Projects which can be achieved without striking deeply at the gains of one particular group are perhaps best moved by the elite of wealth and status. Thus the best way to get a Hospital Drive underway is to get together a committee of prominent citizens but the best way to get an FEP ordinance is to prove that some significant portion of the electorate is for it. This is what is meant by "non-political" policy issues.

While this portrait is probably true in a last-analysis, ultimate showdown sense, it should not be taken as the picture of day-to-day activities.

The potential for power is only intermittently exercised. By and large, a City Council goes its own way, the Mayor himself makes the major part of his own decisions, the Chamber is guided by its full-time secretary, and so on. Thus, decisions are made with the potential power structure in mind, but few issues are clear in their implications for the powerful.

A tremendous amount of energy is expended in connection with community projects in negotiating consent and support. The urban renewal of Hyde Park-Kenwood, for example, required thousands of hours of negotiation between and among politicians, University officials, community leaders, and downtown businessmen. From the viewpoint of an observer like myself, much of the negotiation at first glance appeared unnecessary and redundant. The key to the explanation of this activity lay in the profound uncertainty of the decision makers concerning the ability of individuals and groups to veto the plan. In particular, it was necessary to convince the mayor that no significant group opposed the plan and further that there were positive benefits to the mayor's career to be gained by going along with it. In part the process consisted of showing persons opposing you represented "only themselves" while your supporters represented wide-spread consensus among large segments of the population.

The practical significance of the view of community power structure presented here is on a general level. The community organizer bent on getting some change introduced into a community has a wider range of alternative tactics from among which to choose than would be the case were a single pyramidal model of community power structure a good fit to all communities. The problem of the community organizer becomes one of identifying which portions of the potential power structure it is possible to enlist and which would be most effective in moving the community toward a decision.

Two specific tactics are also implied in the power structure model. First, in order to enlist the aid of voluntary association sector of the local community, it is important to define the issue as non-controversial and the proposed change as a benefit to all groups or at least a detriment to no groups. (Additional reasons for employing this tactic will be given later on in this paper.) Secondly, it is important to appear to recruit mass support through the aid of reputedly solidary organizations if you want to move local government, and as a corollary it is important to move masses of resources if you want to move the voluntary organization sector.

Perhaps the most important task of the community organizer is the negotiation of consent and support from possible sources of opposition. The most successful community organizers whom I have encountered were extraordinarily skilled at this prime task and spent upward of half of their time at it.

B. *The Origination of Change*

There is no doubt that in the study of the local community, the topic that engages our attention more quickly than any other is the study of how social action—the deliberate and intended changes—comes about.

The first question we may raise in this connection is, from where do these changes originate? There are several sources to be encountered typically within a community. To begin with, a major source of innovations are those professionalized occupational roles centrally concerned with community institutions. Part of the job of certain occupations is to constantly propose changes in community institutions. Such professional roles as city managers, school superintendents, public health officers and the like carry within themselves the notion of constant improvement in the services involved.

For example, there is no doubt that the major source of change within school systems stems from the school administrators. School administration as taught within the three graduate schools of education with which I am acquainted is haunted by the dilemma that a superintendent's worth in the profession depends on how many changes he can introduce into his system, but his tenure in the community often depends on completely different criteria. School superintendents and other community professionals faced with similar dilemmas react to this conflict by an extraordinary mobility rate.

Another point of origin for social action lies in the competition among community leaders. Often enough local politics appears to be a wild search for issues, with issue after issue being offered up to the public. While few such attempts succeed in capturing public fancy sufficiently to develop into large scale controversies, this possibility is another spectre that haunts every community leader and public official. This anxiety is the ultimate source of the non-partisan citizens committee and the desire to "take politics out of" schools, highways, police protection and the like.

Finally, one must acknowledge the elusive but fairly important role played by general American value standards. The Cult of Civic Improvement has many devotees in the typical American community, to be found in greatest number within the Chamber of Commerce and the service clubs. The search for something to do in the way of improvement and amelioration and especially to provide symbols of Progress, preferably concrete, provides a constant stream of community "projects." Indeed, the demand for community projects is sufficient to provide a small industry replete with publications, training sessions, and the like to supply the demand. Certainly the existence of community service organizations like that at Southern Illinois or here at Michigan State is in part in response to this demand.

Hunter's study of Atlanta particularly shows how a group of restless and energetic businessmen spent some significant portion of their time organizing "projects" to improve their city. In the achievement of an urban renewal project around the University of Chicago, not the least expenditure of effort came from the high level businessmen closely connected with the University.

In this last connection, it is important not to take for granted the participation of high level businessmen in civic activities in the local community by a glib but unsophisticated interest explanation. If it is to the interest of business enterprises to expend funds and provide the time of business managers for community projects, the interest is far from specific to the usual business enterprise. Furthermore, it is precisely those enterprises whose fates are most closely linked with the local community —small commercial establishments—whose civic participation is weakest.

For an explanation of business participation in community projects, it is more useful to look to the social functions played by such participation within the business community. So much a part of community life, as lived in the middle and upper echelons of the business world, are community projects that the latter have taken on the function of providing a measure of the prestige positions of firms and business managers on the local scene. In proportion as a man and his firm play important roles in such projects, he and it are judged by their business peers as having both power and prestige. While often enough the public relations office of the firm rationalizes the expenditure of resources as an investment in community goodwill, the primary audience in fact turns out to be the rest of the business community while the general public remains virtually unaffected.

In a way, the Community Chest or the Hospital Drives are non-wasteful potlatches in which both firms and individuals validate their bids for prestige by the amounts of money they contribute. Conspicuous charity and good civic works in the middle 20th Century have replaced the conspicuous consumption and private piety of the late 19th Century, aided considerably by the contributions to charity provisions of our income tax laws.

It is characteristic of the charity and community project fields that those who foot the bill call the tune. These community organizations are not "democratic" ones, ultimately responsible to a constituency widely defined. Rather they are ruled by boards and committees who nominate and choose their own successors. Thus a structure of power is more clearly visible in this area of community life than in any other. The boards and committees heavily weighted with large contributors most closely approximate the pyramidal model of a power structure. In this area of community life, wealth and power go hand in hand. Participation in such activities becomes a way of cashing in the resources that one may control, transforming money into prestige. It is this tie-in between prestige and participation in the community affairs which makes it possible to recruit easily the higher ranks of the business and professional worlds to serve on the boards and committees of community organizations.

One consequence of this latent function of civic participation is that such civic participation tends to shy away from the controversial and to stick to things that no one possibly could disagree with. Favorite projects for the Chamber of Commerce in a Southern Ohio community included a club house for youth and rounding up votes for a school bond issue. Nobody in the business community would tackle fair employment laws or even fluoridation for fear that failure of the project would jeopardize the prestige position which participation validates. Similarly, businessmen joined in the fight for urban renewal in Hyde Park-Kenwood only when it was clear that there was no significant opposition to the plan and when it was clear that it would eventually go through. This pattern is one of the major sources for the businessman's aversion to politics.

The practical implications of this interpretation are considerable. For one thing, this provides a remarkable source of manpower for the citizen committees of community projects. Secondly, it underscores the necessity for making sure that a project is not going to be controversial if business community support is to be recruited. This gives rise to a new public relations art, that of coopting a sufficient portion of community leadership to take the potential sting out of any community project.

C. Citizen Participation

Citizen Participation is a social invention which is characteristic of American community life. The idea of ordinary citizens taking part in improving the commonwealth is very congenial to our conception of democracy in which superior wisdom is imputed to an enlightened citizenry. According to its proponents much good is credited to this social invention. A minimum claim is that when the ordinary citizens of a community get together, the final outcome is something that has an easier chance of widespread community acceptance. Some claim that better decisions result. Some extreme proponents have claimed all sorts of miracles: One psychiatrist has claimed that better mental health results in the community when participation really works.

Over the past year, my co-workers and I have been studying the effectiveness of citizen participation in the urban renewal planning of Hyde Park-Kenwood, the neighborhood immediately surrounding the University of Chicago. If ever citizen participation was to achieve its claims, this was the neighborhood in which success was most likely. The density of liberal, intellectual homeowners in the area probably exceeds that of any comparable urban place. In fact, this may be the only urban neighborhood in this country in which intellectuals occupy the highest prestige rank, a phenomenon which results in 85% of the faculty residing within one half mile of the University.

The area can be characterized as hyper-organized. The local citizens' organization, the Hyde Park-Kenwood Community Conference, has 4,000 members on its rolls. Block groups affiliated loosely with the Conference can claim an additional 4,000 persons, without counting overlapping membership. Thus approximately 40% of the families in the area are connected organizationally with the Conference. Of the non-members, "fellow travelers" account for an unknown but undoubtedly large proportion. The expertise that the Conference can call upon from its membership is nothing short of fabulous: prominent social scientists, city planners, geographers, real estate moguls, lawyers, all of first rank, are active members and participate heavily in the Conference's many committees. Thousands of man hours of work and thousands of dollars of foundation funds went into the stimulation and organization of citizen participation in the replanning of the area. Block groups met, considered plans drawn up by professional planners, made recommendations which were carried to the planners, new plans were communicated to the block groups and so on.

The achievements of the Conference must be judged considerable but only in some directions. A large number of minor changes were made in the plan surrounding such decisions as which house on a block was to be demolished to provide playground space around a public school. Undoubtedly, the level of anxiety in the neighborhood concerning the meaning of the plan to individual householders was lowered. Intense popular support for the final plan was mobilized. But the Conference was unable to have included in the plan provisions close to its central ideological goals, such as provisions for middle income housing, public housing, guarantees surrounding relocations of displaced residents and the like.

The lesson of the Conference and Hyde Park-Kenwood for the student of community organization was that citizen participation is a co-optation device which progressively committed the citizens to the plan while their right to dissent was being undercut. This occurred because a large group of citizens, no matter how well trained, working on a part time basis can only come to a firm consensus on *general* goals and hence are in an inferior bargaining position *vis à vis* a smaller but full time group of professionals. (There are, of course, other elements at work in this case which complicate the matter and into which we can not go in this short paper.)

The Hyde Park-Kenwood experience raises serious questions in my mind concerning the effectiveness of citizen participation for some of its goals. Grass roots groups like the Conference can only react to proposals made by professionals and despite the professional competence that might be involved in such an organization, its major function turns out to be that of giving the appearance of consent upwards and the appearance of participation downwards. While it is clear that the participation of citizens and their wholehearted involvement in the plan made it easier for the plan to be accepted, it can hardly be said to be a plan made by the citizens themselves.

The lesson for the community organizer is plain: the function of citizen participation is to support, not to create. The function of the professional is to create.

D. *Observations on Community Differences*

A perennial problem of the community researcher is the nagging fear that the community he has studied was somehow so atypical as to be completely idiosyncratic. While the obvious solution is to plan comparative community researches, few such researches have been carried out.

The major problem we wish to pose in this section is what are the differences between communities which might conceivably affect the ways in which decisions are made? Drawing again on field experiences, we will enumerate below some of the community variations which seem of some importance:

First of all, it is obvious that the formal structure of local government plays an important role. The legal structure of local government designates who is to have the power to make important decisions. Despite the wide variation in this country in the forms of local government, little is known of effects of such variations on the types of decision processes involved or on the outcome in terms of municipal services. It is true that there is a great deal of "folklore" knowledge on this score, but there is little in the way of systematic research.

For example, as far as voting behavior is concerned, we scarcely know anything about the effects of non-partisan electoral procedures. There was some evidence in our own study of "Bay City" that by de-emphasizing the organizational ties of candidates—not only to party but to other associations as well—non-partisan elections favor demagoguery in the same way as in the one-party South. In addition, by obscuring the cues used by voters, non-partisan elections appeared to favor the well organized minority (usually the middle class) against the relatively unorganized mass.

Perhaps the major differences among the communities we have studied concern the relative popularity of the two political parties. In heavily Democratic "Bay City," governmental institutions, with the exception of the school and library boards, are run by representatives of the newer immigrant groups, while the voluntary community associations are in the hands of the largely Protestant, Yankee Republican group. The separation between control over local government and power within the non-political areas of community life is almost complete. Two broad power structures have emerged centered around each of these sets of institutions. The prestige of political activity is low. In a large mid-Western industrial city, the same phenomenon is emerging at present. In both these communities how one gets things done politically is quite different from getting things done in other areas of community life.

In contrast, in a predominantly Republican Southern Ohio town, there is some continuity of membership between the voluntary associational life and political life. The members of the City Council are also members of the Chamber of Commerce and of Kiwanis and Rotary. Conflicts tend to center about battles between "ins" and "outs" rather than around the more enduring cleavages of class and ethnicity. The closer associational ties between the various decision makers tend to soften conflict and produce greater consensus. Making community decisions tends to become a somewhat informal activity contained within the dominant business community, as the personal ties between decision makers afford easy access to each other. At the same time, the homogeneity of the political and associational elites has made the numerically larger working class feel somewhat alienated from the community decision processes. The possibility of grass roots revolt in the town is quite real.

These considerations suggest that on a higher level of abstraction two crucial differences may exist among communities: the degree to which coincide the lines of cleavage along class, ethnicity, and political party lines; and the extent to which the associational life of the community forms an unbroken or a discontinuous web. Where cleavages coincide, as in "Bay City," conflict tends to become regularized and channelled in the same fashion on a wide variety of issues. It is possible to predict in advance how the various groups in the city will line up on a given issue, and also to specify what are the processes of accommodation that will probably be employed. Where the lines of cleavage do not coincide, conflict tends to be more sporadic.

Where associational life forms a continuous web knitting together the major groups within a community, conflict may become muted through the familiar cross-pressures mechanism. Thus in our Ohio community, cooptation is the most familiar way to minimize differences: the bond issue for the new high school was sponsored by a Citizens' Committee headed by a Catholic, a Jew, and a Protestant. The committee which headed the drive for money for an addition of the Catholic hospital was the same as that which subsequently headed a committee for the Methodist hospital. Almost every leader has ties of a personal or associational nature with every other and avoidance of open conflict is one way of preserving such ties.

One type of community where discontinuity in social life is highly likely to occur is the dormitory suburb. The symbiotic division of labor in the self-contained community helps to mitigate conflict, a factor which is not present in the suburb. We can therefore expect that conflict will be bitterer and longer lasting in a suburb than in a more self-contained community.

Certainly city size would be a crucial difference among communities although it is by no means entirely clear how size *per se* works. One can expect that the web of associational life would be less continuous in a large city than in a smaller one. Other mechanisms are undoubtedly at work, but perhaps the major differences between cities of different sizes stem from the accompanying differences in economic structure and population composition.

This last consideration is perhaps not the least. Variations in the structure of control over economic institutions may be expected to affect the nature of community life and the decision making process. One-industry towns may be so strongly controlled by the firm in question that independent and diverse bases of power may not exist, leading, perhaps, to a polarization between a small elite and a large mass. Towns with locally owned industries as compared with absentee-owned companies might show a richer community life—as Mills and Ullmer have claimed[3]—or shown a semi-feudal paternalistic pattern as was the case in the past of the Ohio city we have studied. Perhaps the firmest generalization possible is that the greater the diversification of the economic control the less likely the concentration of power and the more likely a "healthy competition" for leadership among different social positions in the community.

Notes

1. Published studies of community structure have been summarized in Peter H. Rossi, "Community Decision Making," *Administrative Science Quarterly*, Vol. 1, No. 4 (March 1957) pp. 415–43. Reprinted in Roland Young (ed.), *Approaches to the Study of Politics* (Evanston, Ill.: Northwestern University Press, 1958), pp. 363–82. Reports of my own studies are as follows:

"Industry and Community" (with James A. Davis), *Report #64*, National Opinion Research Center, University of Chicago, October 1957.

"The Impact of Party Organization in an Industrial Setting" (with Phillips Cutright), in *Community Political Systems: First International Yearbook in Political Behavior Research*, Morris Janowitz and Heinz Eulau (eds.), (Glencoe, Ill.: The Free Press, 1960).

Rebuilding the City: The Shaping of Public Interest in Urban Renewal Planning in Chicago (with Robert Dentler), (Glencoe, Ill.: The Free Press, 1960).

2. The ideas presented here have been influenced very much by James Coleman, *Community Conflict* (Glencoe, Ill.: The Free Press, 1957).

3. C. Wright Mills and Melville Ullmer, "Small Business and Civic Welfare," *The Report of the Smaller War Plants Corporation*, United States Senate Document No. 135 (Washington, D.C.: 1946).

39. St. Louis Politics: Relationships Among Interests, Parties, and Government Structure

ROBERT H. SALISBURY

Political scientists have been troubled in recent years by just what it is they mean when they talk about a political party. Whether the discussion concentrates on the American scene or includes comparative data from other countries, the ambiguity of party as an analytical tool remains. Particularly difficult and very largely untouched by specific empirical analysis are the relationships which connect core party organizations, the social and economic interest group configuration, and the formal governmental structure of a community. Whereas some political scientists have assumed the crucial importance of the formal structure in shaping the political life of the community, others have tended to regard structure as largely irrelevant and to argue instead that the only significant variables were embraced in interest group activity. This paper will offer a synopsis of the situation in one city, St. Louis, Missouri, in an effort to suggest the way in which the three factors mentioned are interrelated.

Reprinted from *Western Political Quarterly*, XIII (June 1960), pp. 498–507 by permission of the author and the publisher. Robert Salisbury is professor of political science at Washington University, St. Louis.

The burden of the argument here is that a somewhat peculiar bifurcated structure of local government plays a crucial role in shaping the
nature and scope of political conflict in the city. Two broad interest
groupings in St. Louis, each composed of rather loosely allied groups and
each pursuing different sets of goals in the political arena, are enabled
to live under the same party label by the fact that each grouping can
control one segment of the governmental structure and from that control
secure the portion of its goals most vital to it. Neither group gains complete satisfaction thereby, but the consequence is that the two groups
are not forced into the full range of sharp competition that a more centralized and monolithic structure might require.

The Interests

The constellation of social and economic interests which make up
the body politic of St. Louis is like in some ways and in some ways
unlike that of other major American cities. In common with other metropolitan centers, the St. Louis area has experienced rapid growth in the
post-World War II period, but unlike most other cities, this growth has
taken place almost entirely outside the city limits, which were fixed by
constitutional provision in 1876. The growth of the St. Louis area, further, has not kept pace with many other parts of the country, particularly
because the hinterland of the city has not grown much. Consequently,
St. Louis business leaders have been concerned to bring new industry to
the city, and this effort has spurred the desire, shared by other metropolises, to solve traffic and transit problems, to renovate and rehabilitate
slum areas, and to revive the downtown business district.

In common with many cities, St. Louis has experienced a great influx
of Negroes and "mountain whites" in recent years with a resulting increased demand for various types of municipal services. As elsewhere,
these "new immigrants" play the same role in relation to ward organizations of the party that nationality groups did in past decades. The tight
and inflexible boundaries of the city have, at the same time, meant that
St. Louis has lost upper income population to the suburbs. The combination of an increasingly lower income population and the desire to attract
new industry and therefore to keep tax rates at reasonable levels has left
the city in almost perpetual financial embarrassment in the postwar
period, an embarrassment alleviated only by the impression of an earnings tax of 1 per cent on all income.

If one looks at the major economic interests in the city, one can
begin with familiar categories, labor and business, and discover some

degree of conflict between these two groups. Yet no analysis can explain St. Louis politics satisfactorily by relying solely upon labor-management conflict. Labor, for example, is not monolithic. The largest unions are the Teamsters, the Building Trades, the Machinists, and the Auto Workers, while a number of smaller unions also play some role. These unions differ considerably in their local political significance. The Teamsters are the most active locally and the most controversial. They have a fairly fully articulated set of goals for St. Louis which includes general expansion of services for low income groups and which emphasizes heavily the betterment of race relations and equality for Negroes. The militance of the Teamsters, with its ideological flavor, is in contrast to the unphilosophical bread-and-butter concerns of the Building Trades which seek jobs and contracts and find that extensive political alliances are of great assistance in securing these goals. They are not really interested in most of the program of the Teamsters, and the Teamster leaders sometimes express contempt for the unconcern with policy exhibited by the "pork chop" unions. Nevertheless, each group finds that under present conditions their channels of action often bring them into working agreements with each other on political questions. The UAW and the Steelworkers differ from each of the two types of labor groups mentioned above, since they are largely unconcerned with local politics. Their union interests are not much affected by decisions in the local arena, and though their leaders sometimes go through political motions, neither these unions nor the management of the plants where they work are normally active on the St. Louis political scene.

The business community is likewise divided along a number of lines. Dominating the public view are the industrial, banking, and commercial leaders of locally controlled large businesses, the "downtown" business community. These are the men who need more industrial development in the city, these are the men who have significant stakes in the rehabilitation of the slums and the consequent revival of the core city, and these are the men who also form the social elite of the city. The interests of this configuration are articulated by the metropolitan daily press, and they are identified with "Progress" and "Good Government," while they are against the "Politicians." The bulk of the middle and upper-middle income residents of the city and the professional, religious, and educational leadership tend strongly to identify their interests with those of this business elite.

The small business community, on the other hand, does not. Composed of small downtown enterprises like parking lot operators and of neighborhood commercial establishments, this group is concerned with specific, individual treatment at the hands of governmental authority.

Specific tax measures, provision of stop signs, regulation of on- and off-street parking, zoning, and the like are their primary goals, and they very often line up with organized labor groups in political alliance against the "downtown" interests.

The social composition of the city is noteworthy in two main respects, the impact of the Negro influx and the ethnic make-up of the city. More than one-fourth of the city's population today is Negro, and Negroes are achieving increasing political power. Six wards of the city's twenty-eight are represented by Negroes, and significant influence is exerted in at least three others. Desegregation of swimming pools, schools, and, to some extent, of places of public accommodation has followed the rise of Negroes to influence. Until the New Deal and again during most of the 1940's the Negro community was predominantly Republican, but since 1949 Negro wards have produced overwhelming margins for any candidate bearing the Democratic label.

Nationality groups have not played as important a role in St. Louis politics as in many cities. St. Louis experienced a large German immigration and a significant Irish immigration during the mid-nineteenth century. For decades these two groups formed the backbone of the Republican and Democratic parties respectively. But the "late immigrants" from Eastern and Southern Europe largely by-passed St. Louis in favor of the heavy industrial centers. Thus the European "ethnics" in the city have had nearly a century to become assimilated, and today, except for one Italian ward, it is difficult to find many traces of genuine nationality identification. The heavily Catholic religious heritage of St. Louis remains, but national origin seems to have little meaning in St. Louis politics.

St. Louis thus displays two broad configurations of interests. On one side are the locally oriented labor unions, Negroes, neighborhood businessmen, and lower income people generally. This grouping focuses its attention primarily on the specific bread-and-butter issues of jobs, stop signs, spot zoning, and the like, and exhibits a sharp antipathy toward any suggestion of increased tax rates. Downtown business interests and the middle and upper-middle income residents, on the other hand, are primarily interested in broader policy questions—economic growth, urban renewal—and their approach to problems of fiscal solvency is more sympathetic to the needs for more tax revenue.

The Structure of Government

The structure of St. Louis government is *sui generis* in many respects. The city is governed under a charter adopted by the voters in

1914. Some important aspects of the city's business, however, are not under home rule control. The police department, for example, is controlled by a Board of Police Commissioners appointed by the governor, and a Board of Election Commissioners is similarly appointed. Originally, the device was adopted to enable a pro-Southern state administration to have police control in a Unionist city. Later it allowed a Democratic state administration to have patronage to dispense in a normally Republican city. The contemporary significance of this arrangement is quite different as will be noted later. In the city a moderately strong mayor administers nearly ten thousand employees of whom he can appoint some seventeen without regard to civil service requirements. An elected comptroller acts jointly with the mayor and the president of the Board of Aldermen, elected at large, to form the Board of Estimate and Apportionment which prepares the city budget, a budget which the Board of Aldermen may cut but not increase. The budget includes in its provisions many of the most vital policy decisions affecting the city, and the mayor is certainly the key figure in its preparation. The Board of Aldermen is composed of the president and twenty-eight representatives elected one each from the twenty-eight wards. The mayor and the members of the Board of Aldermen each serve four-year terms. The aldermen, of course, must pass all ordinances for the city, but even though a majority of the Board often opposes the mayor on policy issues, the latter clearly dominates the policy-making process.

Almost entirely separate from this portion of the city government are the so-called "county offices." St. Louis, like Baltimore, is not a part of any county. Nevertheless, under state law, the functions ordinarily performed by county officials must be performed in St. Louis by officials like sheriff, collector of revenue, license collector, recorder of deeds, magistrates, and others who are elected by the voters and are completely outside the control of the city administration or the city charter. These officials make few policy decisions of any importance, but taken together they provide nearly one thousand non-civil service jobs, and, as one of the few remaining sources of patronage in the city, they are prizes of great importance to those who are interested in patronage.

The Board of Education should also be mentioned here. It, too, is outside the budgetary control of the city. The Board is elected separately and its tax rate is determined through separate referendum elections. It, too, controls a substantial pool of patronage jobs in its building and maintenance departments, and patronage rather than educational policy is the major issues in Board of Education elections.

Thus the structure of St. Louis government contains two largely separate sets of offices. One is centered in the mayor's office and is the natural focus of attention for those interested in broad problems of

municipal policy. The other is based upon the county offices, Board of
Education, and Board of Aldermen and consists essentially of a patronage
pool and a means for securing individual favor with very little responsibility for policy.

The Party Situation

St. Louis has undergone two rather remarkable political meta-
morphoses during the past three decades. The first it shared with many
other metropolitan centers, the change from consistent Republicanism to
overwhelming Democracy as the New Deal coalition produced sizable
pluralities on the local level. The shift to the Democrats embraced practically all elements of the community, but perhaps the most notable
changes took place among the Negroes, and among many of the German
areas of the city. Silk stocking and delivery wards alike went Democratic during the thirties. But although the state and national Democratic
tickets continued to carry the city comfortably, during the next decade
from 1941 to 1949, the Republicans returned to power on the local scene.
We need not examine the reasons for this switch except to note that it
took in much of the city, especially Negroes, and it was backed by
much of downtown business and the metropolitan press. This Republican
swing carried the party into the mayor's office (by a two-to-one majority
in 1945), swept the Board of Aldermen nearly clean of Democrats, and
helped elect Republicans to Congress, although the Democrats hung on
to some local offices and Roosevelt won handily.

The period of Republican control ended in 1949, however, and since
that time the Democratic sweep of all offices at all levels, save only a
maximum of four aldermanic seats, has been complete. This time the
Negro wards shifted overwhelmingly to the Democrats and have shown
no sign of defecting despite that tendency in some other cities. The
upper income areas—smaller now than formerly—have shown remarkable
Democratic strength, largely undisturbed by the Eisenhower era. The
lower income sections of the city, which include the Negro areas, are
staunchly Democratic, to the extent that the Republicans are badly demoralized and have difficulty in finding either candidates or money to
make a serious race for any political office in the community.

Yet this cyclical variation in the fortunes of the two parties does not
conform to the configuration of interests in the community. As outlined
above, the city is broadly divided along some sort of quasi-class basis
into two groupings; labor, low income, small, neighborhood business,

and at least recently Negroes, against large downtown business, the forces of "Progress," with the daily papers as spokesmen and the so-called "newspaper wards" as sources of voting strength. This general division of the community interests has not changed greatly during the past decade except perhaps as the proportion of Negroes has increased while the old German Republicans have lost their ethnic identity. But these changes surely do not account for (a) the massive shifts in the strength of each party over a relatively short period of time, or (b) the absence of fairly sharp and relatively even competition between the two parties for local office. For this latter fact is perhaps most prominent; namely, that when one party has been dominant the other party is moribund. This is especially true of the Republicans since 1949. With a constellation of interests that normally might be expected to support Republican candidates, the latter lose by margins exceeding three-to-one.

Interest, Party, and Structure in St. Louis

We cannot here go into all the reasons for the variation in party fortunes and the recent lack of Republican success. But we do want to examine the forms of institutionalization of this division of interests in the community. If it has not taken the form of inter-party conflict, how has it been expressed? The answer is that two fairly distinct groupings have appeared *within* whichever party was dominant in a particular period, one representing the larger business groups the newspaper ward areas, and the forces of "Progress" generally, while the other is characterized by the "Politicians" who are spokesmen for a medley of lower income, labor, small business, and minority groups. Such a division was notable within the Republican ranks during the late 1940's. Such a division is quite obvious within the Democratic ranks today. *This division is not only one of conflict over economic and social interests in the community, it is also manifested in the formal structure of government.*

In both the Republican and the Democratic parties the intra-party division has followed essentially the same lines. On the one side, the downtown business groups and the other interests associated with them have found their representation in the office of mayor primarily, usually with co-operation from the comptroller and the president of the Board of Aldermen. All these officials are elected on a city-wide basis with substantial newspaper attention to their campaigns which tend to cost considerable sums of money for publicity. These three, forming the Board of Estimate and Apportionment, make the key fiscal decisions to the city, and, however hard they try, the Board of Aldermen can alter these decisions only at the margins. Moreover, the mayor, as mentioned before, is by all odds the most significant policy-making official in the city. It is policy, of course, with which the large business constellation is concerned—broad civic policy affecting the location of industry, general tax rates, availability of full city services, the social climate of the community necessary to attract technical personnel for their businesses, and the social climate of the community necessary to preserve the status of an old-line, social elite whose autonomy of local operation is being eroded by the nationalization of business and labor alike. It is this group which wants civic reform and civil service, which sponsors the many Citizens Committees to study local problems, and so on. The group is not reactionary or even particularly conservative in the usual meanings of those terms. Some of its leaders are liberal Democrats on the national scene, and many are outspoken defenders of equality for Negroes on all levels. Its co-operation with organized labor is never more than lukewarm, but again, on the national scene, the Teamsters and the Building Trades, the dominant labor groups locally, are not noted for their liberalism.

The other side is likewise focused on a set of public officials, the holders of the "county offices," supplemented by the dominant group on the Board of Aldermen. The county offices are filled in city-wide elections too, thus giving them the same formal constituency as the mayor and his associates. But these elections are not attended by wide publicity, they are held in conjunction with November general elections instead of the municipal elections in the spring, and the chief requisite of victory is a dependable vote delivered by an effective ward organization. The newspapers take little part in these elections and correspondingly have little influence on them. Instead they are dominated by the so-called "delivery wards" of the city generally, the lower income and Negro wards. Again this was true when the Republicans controlled these offices as well as now when the Democrats are supreme.

The complex of interests which supports these political leaders also finds it important to have influence with the aldermen. In the wards inhabited by lower income residents, aldermen are selected in the same way as the county office-holders; nomination dependent largely upon the support of the ward committeemen and election dependent upon an effective ward organization. Many county office-holders are also ward committeemen and the alliance between these elements of the core party organization is firm. By and large, this element of the party is not particularly concerned with broad social or economic policy as such. It is concerned rather with the immediate needs of effective ward organization, and these needs are not notably different today than they traditionally have been. Patronage remains the lifeblood of the organization and, of course, the county offices are sources of significant patronage in the city. Consequently, control of these offices is vital to the organization. For the same reason, control of the Board of Education is important. More than that, however, the county office element of the party is concerned with the needs of its electoral supporters as the latter interpret these needs. This means broadly *individual favor.* Jobs are crucial, but so also are specific contracts for building contractors, stop signs and parking regulations, assistance in getting into a public housing project, route location for a throughway, and so on. Assistance for individuals in need, the classic basis of urban political organization, remains the basis for this wing of the party, and such assistance is necessarily funneled through the particular set of offices which this wing seeks to control; jobs through the county offices and Board of Education, and individual attention from the Board of Aldermen achieved through a log-rolling system known locally as aldermanic courtesy. These are the concerns of Negroes, low income groups, the politically active elements of the local labor movement, and of many kinds of small businesses. Thus there is not much question of which element in the party these groups will support in a situation of conflict between the two party groups.

One interesting thing about this division, both of interests in the city and of offices, is that conflict between the two groupings is minimized. The group focused on the mayor is not interested in patronage, although from time to time its conception of good government requires that it advocate the further extension of civil service. By the same token, the county office group and many of its electoral supporters are profoundly indifferent to most matters of public policy. Aldermanic courtesy does create conflict, since the granting of individual favors—e.g., a stop sign in front of a confectionery—often runs counter to broader policy concerns—e.g., a master traffic plan. Nevertheless, there are many areas of policy and of patronage where each element of the party is content to let the other element control. Each group needs the other. The county office people need the financial support for their precinct workers which the mayor-led group contributes to the party. The mayoral group needs the support of the delivery wards to get many of its policy goals put into effect. This mutual need is sufficient at least to permit the two groups to share the same party label, and perhaps to require it.

But there is always latent and sometimes manifest conflict between the two groups. Issues like the distribution of the tax load, recognition of labor organizations among municipal employees, and particularly charter reform, which might threaten the existence of the patronage offices, all activate not only the office-holders within the party but, more importantly, bring into operation most of the interest groups in the community which ally with one or the other faction. On such questions the mayoral group is sharply opposed by the majority of the aldermen as well as by the dominant elements in the city committee of the party, the ward committeemen—county office forces. The tendency toward conflict is reinforced by the fact that each group tends to view the other as an unholy conspiracy aimed at destroying its opponents. As it happens in St. Louis this conflict often takes the geographical form of what is nearly a north-south split with the south side and west end supporting the mayoral faction while the north side is the heart of the county office group strength.

A word should be said about the rather special effect that the structure of the police department, headed by a Board appointed by the governor, has on the political scene. Two consequences are apparent. In the first place, influence with the police department follows from influence with the governor, and consequently, successful gubernatorial candidates are much sought after figures in St. Louis politics. Secondly, although the police department is run on the merit system, there is a substantial amount of patronage available in the form of assignments and promotions. This patronage is, of course, of more interest to the county office group than to the mayoral group and the former seeks it more assiduously. In this quest the county office group joins forces with the representatives from St. Louis to the state legislature in an alliance that is facilitated by the dependence of the state legislators upon ward committeeman endorsement in order to win office. The close liaison between the state delegation and the county office forces means that the county offices themselves, established by state statute, are safe, and that the desires of the city administration for new state legislation will often get a cool reception from a state delegation allied with the opposing faction of the party. When the St. Louis delegation to the legislature is not united in behalf of the city's demands, they have little chance of passage, and policy requests from the St. Louis administration are blocked most often not by rural opposition, as so often is alleged, but by the county office faction of the St. Louis party.

Perhaps there is no way to prove categorically that the formal structure of government is the crucial variable in determining the particular form which the interest conflict in St. Louis politics has taken. Certainly the total political process in the city is complex. Yet it can scarcely be doubted that if the county offices did not exist and their meager functions were performed by regular administrative agencies of the city, the contending interest groupings in the city would have to find other channels for the satisfaction of their needs. Without the county offices there would be no patronage and hence ward organizations would be weakened. In that event, those interest groups, notably labor, which now work through the ward organizations, would be forced to play an even more direct role in the political process than they do now. Without the county offices there would be only one really important office through which to exert political power, for whatever purposes, and that would be the office of mayor. The aldermen, without effective ward organizations, would need to turn more directly to the interest groups of their wards, and again the conflict between the two broad interest configurations of the city would become more open. If the office of mayor became the chief and virtually the only prize for the contending groups, then it would seem that at least two consequences would follow, given the interest group line-up as it now exists in St. Louis. First, the two groupings which now form factions within the party would divide into two separate parties. This process might be slow. It might be effected through the use of "Blue Ribbon" slates running against "politician" slates, or it might in time result in the revival of the Republican party. In any case, the conflict would be more open than it is now. Secondly, it would be more continuous and involve a broader range of issues. Whereas now there is a substantial area of autonomous operation left to each faction, if the mayor's office were the only prize, then victory and the battle to achieve victory would cover all the issues in which the two sets of interests are even potentially in conflict. Either one side would win or it would lose, and there would be none of the present partial victories for both sides, which, however frustrating they are sometimes, at least give some satisfactions and some basis for compromise and mediation to each group.

If the present alignment of interests were altered in any significant way, a development which the militant and volatile character of the Teamsters and the increasing numbers and self-consciousness of Negroes make possible, the significance either of the present structure or of any alternative arrangements would be altered too. Under the present conditions, however, this analysis seems to be valid and, indeed, is confirmed by each major political event in the city. Any discussion of the effects of a really different structure, of course, must be speculative, since the proposal to change the structure so as to abolish the county offices will be met with sharp resistance by those groups which utilize the offices to advantage.

If the data reviewed here permit one to offer a tentative statement about the relationships between interests, party, and structure, it would appear that the interest group system is, as the Bentleyans argue it must be, basic. At the same time, however, the governmental structure affects in crucial ways the manner in which these interests will be articulated into political parties, and in so doing it plays an important role in determining the scope and intensity of political conflict in the community. It seems doubtful whether one could say that a particular structural form would in every case bring about a particular party system or give a particular shape to the conflict, since the structure and the interest configuration interact in each case. If the interest groups of St. Louis were more amorphous and diffuse and not joined in any bimodal pattern, even the most centralized structure of strong mayor control could not be expected to produce sharply competing parties. On the other hand, the present, somewhat diffuse structure would not appreciably moderate the conflict if St. Louis were divided into rigid class groupings of a quasi-feudal nature. Perhaps the study of the relationships of interests, parties, and structure in other cities will permit comparative analysis of a manageable range of data, and in turn lead us to more confident generalizations about the problem.

40. The Problem of Participation

ROBERT A. DAHL

One of the most interesting developments of the past century is the full-blown contrast that has arisen between the assumptions of many of the older democratic theorists and what now appear to be the actual facts of political life. Yet if classical theory is demonstrably invalid in some crucial respects, it is not so clear how we are to go about constructing theoretical models to replace the older ones.

The data show something roughly like the following. Only about half of all Americans eligible to vote actually go to the polls in national elections. What is far more significant, probably not more than 20 or 25 per cent of all adult Americans engage in any kind of political activity beyond the act of voting itself. The picture for something like 75 to 80 per cent of the adult population is therefore one of almost total political inactivity. It is tempting here to infer that the inactive are also politically indifferent and apathetic; and what data exist do show, as one might expect, that the active are more interested and the less interested are more inactive. But in any case what is striking is the relatively small portion of the adult population engaged in any sort of significant political activity. Although

Reprinted from *Research Frontiers in Politics and Government*, Stephen K. Baily, ed. (Washington, D.C.: The Brookings Institution, 1955), pp. 50–55 by permission of the publisher. Robert Dahl is professor of political science at Yale University.

voting participation is lower in the United States than in any other major democracy, we have no reason to suppose that other forms of political participation are less here than in other countries. Moreover, it looks as if the data on participation in governmental decisions can be generalized to most social organizations, including the whole range of community organizations—from trade unions to the P.T.A. in your community. Thus I think we need to lay down as our basic hypothesis in examining the necessary and sufficient conditions for these different kinds of decision-making that: *The proportion of individuals who will avail themselves of formal opportunities to participate in decision-making, at least in the United States, will be relatively small in all forms of social organization.*

If this hypothesis is true, then it suggests certain conclusions—tentative though they may be—about democracy, hierarchy, and bargaining. As to democracy, the hypothesis calls attention to the crucial importance of competition among political leaders combined with the opportunity for ordinary citizens to switch their support from one set of leaders to another. If it is unreasonable to suppose that large numbers of citizens will bring their influence to bear upon the making of decisions, then for such control as we exert over our political leaders in democratic organizations, we must rely heavily on the competitiveness of leaders, that is, on their constant and unending rivalry in satisfying the demands of relatively small groups.

Second, the most we can reasonably expect in any social organization is not perfect competition, but a kind of monopolistic competition among political leaders. In the economy, it has been discovered that the problem of regulating a system of highly competitive entrepreneurs is one thing; but the regulation of monopolistic competitors is quite another. Much the same thing seems to be true in politics: Here our problem is not to guarantee perfect competition for office—which is impossible—but only to regulate, so far as may be possible, the great political oligopolies.

The third inference to be drawn from our basic hypothesis is that even if the dichotomy between majorities and minorities is highly useful for normative political theory, it is not a very useful dichotomy for empirical theory. For we almost never know whether a given decision really corresponds with the preference of a "majority." All we have to go on are the activities of quite small groups—"minorities" if you will—operating within a context of a relatively apathetic "majority."

Finally, I think we must conclude that the classic assumptions about the need for total citizen participation in democracy were, at the very least, inadequate. If one regards political equality in the making of decisions as a kind of limit to be achieved, then it is axiomatic that this limit could only be arrived at with the complete participation of every adult citizen. Nevertheless, what we call "democracy"—that is, a system of decision-making in which leaders are more or less responsive to the preferences of non-leaders—does seem to operate with a relatively low level of citizen participation. Hence it is inaccurate to say that one of the necessary conditions for "democracy" is extensive citizen participation. It would be more reasonable simply to insist that some minimal participation is required, even though we cannot specify with any precision what this minimum must be.

If we turn our attention now to hierarchy, we see that our basic hypothesis also has some important implications for that system of making decisions. Given our basic hypothesis, the essential problem here is this: How is it possible for the community to exert any significant degree of control over the hierarchies within its midst? It is hierarchies that carry on most of the essential tasks of the modern society: from military organizations and other government bureaucracies to business corporations and trade unions.

The extreme case, at least for Americans, is no doubt the business corporation. A generation ago, Messrs. Berle and Means pointed out that stockholders had little control over the decisions of the corporations they owned. It is significant that within the past year Mr. Berle has returned to this problem in another way.[1] For if the stockholders cannot control an organization, and if, as is clearly now the case, the business corporation is the key device for getting things done in our economy, how can we ensure that the decisions of a corporation somehow mesh with other values possessed by members of the American society? The economist will be quick to say that the price system allows adequate control; others will be equally quick to say that when the price system breaks down, government regulation can take over. The difficulty with the first answer, as Mr. Berle rightly points out, is that there are important areas of decision-making where the price system is relatively neutral, such as the employment of people who are Communists, or accused Communists, or suspected by someone of being disloyal or otherwise deviant in their behavior. Indeed, the price system may not even be neutral; consumers may actually use it to encourage and even force business corporations to indulge in vicious employment practices that run flagrantly counter to Anglo-Saxon traditions of justice.

As for the other solution, one ought not to underestimate the importance of a government bureaucracy acting as a check on a business bureaucracy. But it is more than doubtful whether this technique can be applied to all of the problems the solution of which is of importance to the rest of the community. The fact is, I think, that the moment we do not quite know our way out of this dilemma. It is perfectly clear that business corporations will exercise decisive influence on the second half of the twentieth century, at least within the United States, and therefore indirectly on the whole world. It is not at all clear how this influence will be controlled by the American society and used more or less within the limits set by the dominant values of the greater number of adults in the society.

Another form of hierarchy that is illuminated by our basic hypothesis is the trade union. Considered exclusively in terms of its formal constitution, the trade union is, of course, a "democratic" organization. Yet as even sympathetic students of the labor movement sometimes point out, the trade union contains within itself powerful forces propelling it toward oligarchy.[2] Our basic hypothesis is, among other factors, clearly at work. For trade union leaders to be highly responsive to their members would presuppose that the members participate actively in trade union politics; on the whole, however, they do not do so. Inevitably, then, power is lodged in the hands of the top leaders. Moreover, the trade union lacks many of the traditional institutional devices for ensuring competition among leaders; for example, there is—with only one exception, I think—no two-party system within any trade union in the United States. Thus the key prerequisites for a democratic order, competition among leaders and the opportunity for non-leaders to switch their support from one set of leaders to another, tend to be absent within a trade union.

To say so much is not to imply wickedness on the part of trade union leaders or trade union members. If our basic hypothesis is right, then low participation is simply a fact of all political life. I am not urging that trade unions should somehow be made more democratic; nor am I even sure that if they were, it would lead to healthier labor relations. But I think it is reasonable to expect that trade unions will tend to become bureaucratic and dominated by their top leaders. And, paradoxically, to the extent that the accomplishments of the labor movement minimize tensions in industrial society, the tendencies toward apathy among the trade union members, and therefore bureaucratization within the trade union might well be even more pronounced.

Our basic hypothesis also shows us, I think, the critical importance that bargaining plays in the political system. For if we cannot expect citizens always to check leaders by their participation in the decisions of an organization or a nation, then we are forced to rely heavily on checks exerted by other leaders inside and outside the particular system of decision-making.

But again, let us not lose sight of the essential point: Earlier assumptions about the amount of participation required for democracy seem to have been faulty, and more realistic assumptions give rise to questions about democracy, hierarchy, and bargaining that have not yet been answered.

Notes

1. A. A. Berle, *The Twentieth Century Capitalist Revolution* (1954).
2. A comprehensive survey of the factors leading to oligarchy in trade unions is S. M. Lipset, "The Political Process in Trade Unions: A Theoretical Statement," in *Freedom and Control in Modern Society*, ed. Morroe Berger and others (1954), pp. 82–124.

RESPONSIBILITY OF THE

MUNICIPAL BUREAUCRACY

ONE OF THE THORNY PROBLEMS for local government is that of defining the role of the permanent bureaucracy. The career officials are, by virtue of their position, situated centrally in the community decision-making process. Due to their familiarity with the affairs of the city they possess a kind of knowledge which the general public cannot have. As we have seen in the discussion of the council-manager plan in Chapter Five, there is a danger that the skills, knowledge, and strategic position of a career bureaucrat may, at times, obscure the political nature of the decisions which he is making. But the problem is present whether the bureaucracy is headed by an elected chief executive or a career chief executive supervised by an elected council.

Under any form of city government, the bureaucracy must not only carry out specific governmental tasks (line functions) but must also aid the executive in managing the over-all civic enterprise (staff functions). One of the traditional staff functions is that of aiding the chief executive in coordinating line departments. Coordination is formally achieved through a pyramidal hierarchy of responsibility. In larger cities especially, however, the annual budget is an alternative means. By controlling the budget proposals it is possible for the executive to enforce his policy on departments through granting or refusing to grant budget requests. In the first section of the chapter this operation is shown in two selections. The first reading by Sayre and Kaufman illustrates a classic case where coordination through direct supervision breaks down. As fire and police units endeavor to insulate themselves from formal lines of control, the budget bureau rather than the departmental chiefs becomes the coordinating arm of the executive. Lillian Ross gives a colorful description of the budget process in New York City, a view that emphasizes its policy-making features.

In addition to the carrying out of its administrative functions, the bureaucracy also aids the executive, whether appointed or elected, in the development of an agenda of policy proposals that he acts upon and can submit to the public as his record in office. The electorate, in general, judge municipal services by results and expect the proposals for improvements to come from the politician and public official. It is the incumbent executive who bears the responsibility for immediate action. He must develop and screen a set of proposals, gauging their acceptability for inclusion in the program upon which his reputation will rest.

Aiding the executive is his staff. In the smaller cities this consists only of the heads of the administrative departments. In larger cities, it also includes specialists whose skills touch the line activities of all departments such as finance, legal, and personnel officers. Norton Long, in an article directed to professional city planners, suggests that the coordination of all activities affecting the physical plant of the city into an over-all program or plan is such a staff function for planners. It is also a highly political one since the decisions are by nature controversial. To retreat from this role into the safety of simply carrying out established policy without any thought of initiating proposals, Long claims, would rob planners of the most effective contribution they can make to the public from their professional knowledge.

But the bureaucracy must not only be responsive to the public in anticipating public needs; it must also be sensitive to public sentiment. The problem of the expert in a democracy is that, given the dangers and inconveniences of the political process, he is tempted to bypass the process and simply prescribe what he feels is good for the public. Democratic principles require that public programs must be at least sold, and never prescribed. However, in the complexity of modern urban society, it is sometimes difficult even to establish meaningful contact with the municipal public. The last section of readings in this chapter explores this problem of responsiveness.

In a large city the bureaucracy may have difficulty finding its public. Mass urban conditions not only make public initiative complicated, but they also make it difficult for the bureaucracy to assess public desires. In a study which is concerned with government employees at the local, state, and federal level, Janowitz, Wright, and Delany describe the problems of achieving a responsive bureaucracy in a large city setting.

Charles Haar addresses himself to this same problem in a hypothetical case which could take place in a city of any size. Responsiveness is impeded here by the character of the particular activity, rather than the complexities in an urban environment. The activity is city-planning generally and master-planning specifically. While master plans and zoning ordinances have been used by urban governments for a number of decades, they still constitute a relatively new regulatory function. With more traditional urban regulatory powers such as in health, sanitation, fire prevention, and traffic controls, the rights and powers of citizens and officials have become well established in law and custom. Zoning ordinances and master plans are always authorized by law, but the novelty, the changing ideas of the emerging planning profession, the lack of familarity with planning concepts on the part of citizens, councilmen, and lay planning commissioners, and the conflicts of interests implicit in land use regulation all make it difficult to bridge the gap between community sentiments and recommendations of professional experts.

A. COORDINATION

41. Fire and Police: A Case Study in Coordination

WALLACE S. SAYRE AND HERBERT KAUFMAN

(In *Governing New York City*, Sayre and Kaufman challenge a number of widely held stereotypes, including what they call the

Reprinted from *Governing New York City* (New York: Russell Sage Foundation, 1960), pp. 428–31 by permission of the authors and the publisher. Wallace Sayre is professor of political science at Columbia University. Herbert Kaufman is professor of political science at Yale University.

"myth of wholesale public corruption." They write: "The city of New York can confidently ask: What other large American city is as democratically and as well governed?" For example they argue that because of their functions, police and fire departments are always subject to some graft, but the authors do not regard its extent as a major problem.

They are more concerned, however, with the lack of central direction that results from the diffusion of decision-making centers throughout the unwieldy municipal structure. They propose a strengthening of the mayor's office as the city's "symbol of unity," "the central focus of responsibility and accountability," and "the potential source of affirmative, innovating leadership."

The selection reprinted here deals with a problem of coordination, rather than one of corruption. The authors discuss the professionalism of fire and police organization, noting how it has led to a growing insulation of these departments from pressures outside themselves, including influence or intervention from the official policy-making units of the municipality.)

The organizations of policemen and firemen in New York City began in the early 1890's as "benevolent" associations, and their formative years extend down to 1914. They have never possessed the self-conscious "professional" aspirations so strong with the teachers, but they too have confronted the dilemma of "unionization." For the firemen, this question was answered affirmatively in 1918 by affiliation with the AFL. The police have been inhibited in such inclination by law and tradition, and their associations have continued to be divorced from the labor movement.

Police and fire personnel have avoided the pronounced fragmentation of the teachers in their organizational development. Each rank has its separate association in each department. These, however, are not only less numerous than the teachers' subdivisions, but there has been a further tendency toward unification provided by the tradition that the two largest associations (the Patrolmen's Benevolent Association for the police and the Uniformed Firemen's Association for the firemen) should take the lead for the others in the political contest. The Joint Council for all city police and fire organizations has also served to bridge the separate aims of the different organizations more effectively than has the Joint Committee for the teachers. But there are nonetheless some major separatist tendencies. The officer associations (inspectors, captains, lieutenants, battalion chiefs) frequently diverge from the rank-and-file groups in each department, especially in terms of immediate goals.

Each association prefers to live so far as possible a separate group life, and this leads to some constant differentiation of role for the leaders of each. There is the further fact that the fire organizations may look toward the labor movement for allies, while the police must find theirs elsewhere.

The leaders of the city's police and fire associations are experienced and strategically placed participants in the political contest. The police forces were, so to speak, born in politics, served a long apprenticeship as the indentured servants of the party organizations, and continue to exercise powers of the most intimate concern to party leaders. The fire forces, growing out of volunteer fire groups, were also initially intimately bound to the party organizations. Considering these origins, the leaders of the police and fire associations have placed a surprising distance between themselves and the party leaders. The party leaders continue to court them because of the sanctions which the police can impose and the privileges they can bestow in their discretion, and because of the strength in numbers, strategically distributed over the city, which both the police and the fire forces represent. Firemen, too, have their important acts of discretion (in inspection, for example), and they have leisure hours which, long ago at least, could be devoted to the party. But the main drive of the police and fire groups, as with almost all bureaucratic groups, is toward an autonomous, not a sub-ordinate or even a committed, relationship to the party organizations.

The leaders of the police and fire organizations as participants in the city's political process look first, as do the teachers, to Albany, where they enjoy some basic advantages. This tradition was firmly established before the "home rule" acts gave the city government power to do many things the associations wished, and their leaders have never been persuaded of the logic of abandoning Albany. To the state legislature they have gone for a variety of gains and protections: hours of work, pension rights, rates of pay, promotion procedures, relief from liability, and other elements of their personnel system. If they have not succeeded in securing a parallel to the Education Law, neither have they returned annually from Albany empty-handed. What they have gained gives them leverage; and the existence of the Albany channel of access is always an additional, alternative line.

The leaders of the police and fire associations focus their attention most continuously upon their own agencies—the top command of the Police and Fire Departments. Here their first aim has been to reduce, as drastically as they can, the access of outsiders to the decision-making process and to absorb the supervisory and executive ranks of the two departments into their own bureaucratic system. With the aid of the

state legislature, the approval of civil service reformers and the newspapers and other communication media, the indulgence of the Civil
Service Commission, and the gradual concessions of hard-pressed Mayors,
they have succeeded, perhaps even beyond their own expectations. The
two departments are now closed in the most exact sense. The police and
fire bureaucracies are supervised and directed by officers and officials
whom they recognize and regard as "their own," whose values and
capacities they understand and whose decisions they feel confident they
can anticipate, contain, or manipulate if the temptations of departmental
top leadership should lead to idiosyncrasy and disregard of accepted
routines of policy or practice. The virus of "new blood," that carrier of
new doctrines and new technology, is now limited to the newest recruits,
at the lowest rank, where its contagion can be slowed by the low
temperatures of long indoctrination before freedom of movement is
allowed. In the Police Department, the closed system now extends by
accepted custom up to and including the Commissioner, with only one
or two secondary posts of limited assignment open to outsiders. In the
Fire Department, the custom does not yet so regularly include the
Commissioner, but he is isolated from the uniformed staff and the trend
is evidently toward the absorption of his post into the bureaucracy.

   Police and Fire Commissioners and their "high brass" associates
have their occasional respective differences with the leaders of the police-
and fire associations, but the associations have nevertheless steadily
cemented their command over the terms and conditions of their personnel system. In pursuit of this goal, the leaders of the associations have
profited from the state constitutional guarantees of a competitive merit
system, the general provisions of the state Civil Service Law, plus some
special statutory provisions for the police and fire forces, and they have
exercised some of their most persuasive influence on the city's Personnel
Department and Civil Service Commission. Promotion to all ranks in
the Fire Department (including the position of Fire Chief, second in
command under the Commissioner) is by competitive examination
limited to members of the next lower rank, the examination being conducted by the city's Personnel Department, and seniority being usually
decisive in the rating. In the Police Department, competitive examinations
of like character control all promotions through the rank of Captain
(except for detectives) and all higher positions in the force must be filled
from the ranks of Captains. Dismissals in each force are inhibited by
special statutory safeguards. Each force has a special and separate
pension fund, each with a board on which the respective associations
are represented.

   As with the teachers' organizations, it is when they move toward

City Hall as participants in the city's political contest that the leaders of the police and fire bureaucracies encounter most resistance. And it is also primarily budget questions which bring them to the Mayor and the Board of Estimate: higher salaries, hours of work, pension contributions, retirement rights; whether the city should have more policemen and firemen, or higher paid men on shorter tours of duty. The leaders of the police and fire associations are usually better united on such issues than the teachers are, and they usually have the support of their Commissioners (although these officials will tend to urge additions to their manpower quotas more consistently than higher wages or shorter work weeks), but they encounter other competing agencies, bureaucracies, and interest groups pleading before a Mayor and a Board with limited budget resources. The "economy" interest groups are more tolerant with police and fire groups than they are with the teachers, but they tend also to prefer greater manpower over higher wages or fewer hours. The result is frequent frustration for the members of the associations, belligerent tactics by their leaders, delay and avoidance by officialdom. (A favored strategy of the 1920's and 1930's was to refer the issue to popular referendum by the voters of the city, the associations winning while the officials not only saved money by the delay but transferred the onus of the costs to "the people.")

The leaders of the police and fire associations have other business to transact at City Hall. Police graft and irregularities are an endemic and perennial phenomenon, and the fire forces, in their inspection and licensing duties, are periodically susceptible. The Commissioner of Investigation and his staff (not without some competition from the District Attorneys) are normally the instruments of exposure and sanctions. The leaders of the police and fire associations (themselves sometimes the subject of investigation) seek usually to avoid involvement; but they will often speak in defense of their members, referring eloquently to "a few rotten apples," or, if the net of investigation spreads wide, they are likely to charge that the inquiries are "vindictive," "fishing expeditions," or "lynching parties." Even Mayors are not always immune from such attacks by the leaders of the associations.

Police and fire association leaders are decreasingly tempted to form overt alliances with party leaders. Old associations and traditions are not easily dissolved, but the association members tend to view major commitments or concessions to party leaders as hazardous for their own association leaders and unfruitful for the rank-and-file members. Newer channels and modes of influence are more stable and more rewarding. Close alliance with party leaders is an adventure which most bureaucrats would prefer to confine to the lone wolf bureaucrat, or to the tactical necessities of the day, excluding such alliance from the agenda of their major associational strategy.

The leaders of the police and fire associations live a more beleaguered life as political contestants than do the leaders of the teachers' groups, but they do not need to envy many other city bureaucracies. They have influential access at Albany; they are usually viewed with tolerance by the newspapers (for which their members provide more drama and color than do other bureaucracies); the "economy" groups are more indulgent toward them; they have largely achieved their goals in their closed personnel systems; and they are more than ordinarily secure in their own "citadels," their own departments into which fewer and fewer outsiders (whether Mayors, other officials, party leaders, or interest groups) are allowed to intrude except on terms of deference and a willingness to subscribe to the established mores.

42. $1,031,961,754.73

LILLIAN ROSS

Along about last Thanksgiving, Mayor O'Dwyer gave a luncheon at Gracie Mansion to which he invited a few of his associates for an informal thrashing out of some of the municipal problems that weren't making it any easier for him to sleep nights. Afterward, while coffee and cigars were being served, he remembered something he had intended to mention and, turning to his Director of the Budget, Thomas J. Patterson, he asked him if he was all set to start drawing up the city's budget for the 1947–48 fiscal year. Patterson replied that he and his staff at the Bureau of the Budget were indeed all set. As a matter of fact, he said, he was just about to draft a form letter to the heads of all departments—the usual way of referring to the hundred and nine branches into which the municipality's complex structure is broken down for budget and administrative purposes—asking them to submit their annual requests for money. "Fine, Pat, fine," said the Mayor. "But take it easy on every penny. It's going to be a tough budget. We'll have the usual blather from people who think they're not getting enough and from people who think we're spending too much, but blather doesn't pay bills. We'll have to get along without a lot of things we need." He gave his Budget Director a friendly

Reprinted from *The New Yorker*, XXIII (July 12, 1947), pp. 27–36 by permission of the publisher. Copyright 1947 by the New Yorker Magazine, Inc. Lillian Ross is a publicist.

were out making on-the-scene studies of departmental needs. When the requests arrived, the examiners would go over them carefully, pruning as they saw fit, and then, after Patterson had approved the results, the Bureau would call in the department heads for separate hearings.

"We're here to help the Mayor figure out what he ought to spend," Patterson said. "The Comptroller is the one who tells him how much revenue he'll get to spend. He'll has *his* estimates ready next month— the conservative ones, that is. Comptrollers are always conservative in the beginning. We've got to have our figures ready for the Mayor by the middle of March. That's when a mayor always goes into what we call the annual budget retreat—right here, in a conference room next door. Takes about two weeks, all day every day." After the Mayor has approved the budget, Patterson told me, the Board of Estimate gets a crack at it, and then the City Council. "But they won't change it much," he said. "Actually, all the work on the budget is done right here. My examiners know more about the departments than the departments know themselves. You might say they help me piece this book together. Come back in a month or so, when we've got something good to show you." As I left, he was unwrapping a fresh stick of gum.

I stopped by to see Patterson again about the middle of February. This time, I found him standing before his desk looking agitated and chewing gum at an accelerated clip. "Can't spare a minute," he said, pommelling himself on the temples. "Got to go over estimates with eight examiners to-day. The Comptroller just sent us his revenue estimates, and now we've got to revise some of our figures downward. Hardly a month before the Mayor comes over for his retreat, and we've got to be ready for him. He'll want to know why we can't do without this and why we can't do without that. It was nerve-racking under LaGuardia and it's nerve-racking with this man." He sat down and sighed heavily. "It was *especially* nerve-racking under LaGuardia," he said. "Fiorello moved right into my offices for two weeks. I had to move out and sit with Miss Pray—that's my secretary. Fiorello never went out to lunch. Sent out for hot dogs, which he ate with mustard provided by us. We never got an appropriation for it, either. Tell you what. You talk to a few of my examiners. I'll get you some who've already gone over their estimates with me, and then you'll know what we're going to tell the Mayor."

He picked up his phone, asked for a Mr. Fitzpatrick, and told him to come in for a minute. Then he turned back to me. "One of our oldest and stingiest men," he said complacently. "You couldn't do better than talk to Fitzpatrick. Let me tell you, the departments asked for a total of eighty million dollars more than they got last budget. We'll give them ten or eleven. On top of that, though, there'll be about a hundred and twenty-five million of what we call mandatory, or inescapable, increases—for debt service, pensions, things like that." He shook his head gloomily. "Even the Public Administrator of Richmond County wants more. Remember I said he would? Well, he wants two thousand more. We *need* stingy examiners. Not that we're trying to deprive the departments or anything. Take Grant's Tomb, for instance. We're giving the Tomb seven thousand in this budget. That's two hundred and fifty dollars over last year. Well, our Grant's Tomb examiner is satisfied that they really need that extra two-fifty for repairs, new flags, keys, fuses, furniture polish, and uniforms—for the caretaker, I mean, not Grant."

The door opened and an elderly, white-haired man with a high stiff collar came into the office. "This is Mr. Fitzpatrick—Libraries, Museums, and Gardens," Patterson said. "Mr. Fitzpatrick will show you how the examiners work." Mr. Fitzpatrick nodded gravely and asked me to come with him. I followed him down a long corridor to his office, where he introduced me to two other examiners, named Walsh and McEneney, assigned, respectively, to the Police and Fire Departments. Both of them were working in their shirtsleeves at desks piled with papers. These, and two more desks that were unoccupied at the moment, pretty well filled the room. Mr. Fitzpatrick walked over to one of the vacant desks. "I work on several departments," he said stiffly. "Mr. Walsh and Mr. McEneney, they are concerned wholly with a single department each."

"Cops keep you busy," said Walsh, a stocky, square-jawed, middle-aged man with bright pink cheeks, who was smoking a cigar in a long holder.

McEneney, a dour, six-foot, sandy-haired man in his fifties, looked at him thoughtfully. "Firemen keep you busier," he said.

"We enjoy quite a bit of friendly rivalry," Mr. Fitzpatrick said as the other two returned to their work. He pulled a chair over beside his desk, arranged it precisely parallel to his, and bowed slightly in its direction. I sat down. "I think we'll run through the Botanical Garden first," he said, choosing his words carefully and speaking in a slightly querulous voice. "They were pretty good this year." From the top drawer of his desk he took a folder containing several sheets of paper covered with figures. "The Botanical people didn't exaggerate their circumstances very much," he went on. "They requested three hundred and fifty-three thousand two hundred and eighty dollars, and we're giving them within six thousand of that. And in the case of many items, I must say I didn't have to restrain them very much." He consulted his folder before continuing. "Let's see. They wanted a hundred and fifty for bamboo poles for plants to climb up on, forty-five for pot labels, a hundred and ten for fish-oil soap, seven hundred and fifty for cow manure, and three hundred and twenty-five for a motor scythe to work on rocky and rough ground a regular mowing machine can't operate on. All those sounded reasonable to me and I gave them exactly what they asked for. But they also wanted two hundred for two new typewriters, and I said no. I'm not very liberal on typewriters." I asked him what happened when a department and he disagreed on how much was needed, and he replied that some officials complained directly to Patterson. "But the Budget Director and I, we usually have a meeting of minds on the question," he added.

"Some Commissioners go crying to the Mayor," said Walsh, pushing his papers aside. "But not my Commissioner. Not Wallander. That I'll say for him." A band down in the street, twelve stories below, started to play "My Old Kentucky Home," and the music came clearly through the windows. "My cops are getting medals over at City Hall," Walsh said. "That's their band. Don't it play loud and nice?"

Mr. Fitzpatrick cleared his throat noisily, gave Walsh a cool look, and started to tell me why he was going to recommend increasing the salary of the lady in charge of the picture collection at the Public Library from $3,120 a year to $3,660, but before he got very far, his telephone rang. When he had hung up, he said I'd have to excuse him. The Budget Director wanted to go over his estimates on the Metropolitan Museum of Art with him. He put the folder carefully away in his desk, adjusted his collar, took another folder from a cabinet, bowed to me, and left.

"That's O.K.," Walsh said to me. "McEneney and I will tell you what goes on. But don't get me wrong. Fitz is all right. Nothing gets past him." Without turning around in his chair, he pointed behind him to a big green calendar on the wall. On it was printed, "Official Calendar, Police Department, City of New York, Arthur W. Wallander, Commissioner." "I've been taking care of cops these past fifteen years, so I guess I've got a right to it," Walsh said. "A four-bit calendar. We're giving the cops five hundred of them in the new budget. Cops got to have their own calendars, because it wouldn't look proper, now, to walk into a station house and see one put out by a beer company or something the butcher gave out for Christmas."

McEneney, who had been listening to all this with a skeptical look, remarked dryly, "Fire gets along all right with calendars from the butcher."

"The Mayor is more particular about cops," Walsh said. "They're asking for ninety-two million. We'll give them about ninety—maybe more. We're even giving the mounted cops two vans to carry horses in. Each van costs ninety-five hundred. Holds eight horses in stalls and eight mounted cops in a section of their own up front. For five years I've been saying no on those vans. Now the Budget Director's got himself convinced that the Mounted Division needs them. Horses get all tired out, he says, walking all the way from their barn in Queens to scenes of emergency, like I Am an American Day. I was overruled, but I still say horses can walk. They don't need taxis."

McEneney remarked that he didn't give money away that easily to the Fire Department. For one thing, he had turned down a request for $688,200 to pay the salaries of a hundred and forty-four additional lieutenants, and the Budget Director had backed him up. "Fire can get along without *any* new lieutenants," McEneney said. "They've already got a lot of lieutenants posted in theatres and night clubs. They say they've got to be there to reassure the public in case of conflagration. I say nonsense. I say theatre ushers can reassure the public. What Fire can do is inspect the theatres and night clubs, so that conflagrations won't break out. All those lieutenants can be released and go to work. Patterson agreed with me. Fire wants fifty-six million. We'll give them about fifty-three, maybe less."

A short, swarthy man came into the room. "Look who's here," Walsh said. "Carlo Montecalvo—Licenses, County Clerks, City Register, City Sheriff, Board of Elections, City Record. The stingiest examiner in the office."

"I'm the stingiest," McEneney said mildly.

Montecalvo pulled up a chair in front of McEneney's desk and straddled it. "Always fighting about who is the stingiest in getting up the good book," he said amiably.

I asked whether any of the department heads had been making much fuss over the allotments at their hearings with the Budget Director, and Walsh replied that, speaking for himself, the Police hearing had taken all of twenty minutes. The Police Commissioner had simply read a statement summarizing his requests. "He said he wanted two hundred and thirty-two new motorcycles and so forth," Walsh told me. "We're giving him fifty new motorcycles and so forth. But the Commissioner don't know it yet. I didn't want to start any discussion. You start a discussion and it goes on for days."

Montecalvo said he had had no trouble at all with Licenses. Among other things, he had allowed the Department five additional inspectors (twenty requested), one fluorescent desk lamp for the Commissioner's office (one requested), three wall clocks (five requested), and no typewriters with Gothic type (five requested). He had allotted twenty-six dollars for paper towels. "Licenses used roll towels before, but paper towels cost about the same," he said. "They got a right to change their tastes."

The Board of Elections and the City Sheriff, on the other hand, had not been so easy. "The Board is going to cost us two million two hundred and thirty-four thousand nine hundred and ninety dollars," Montecalvo said, rattling off the figure as easily as if he were telling me the price of a pair of shoes. "We got two election primaries for his budget—the primary next fall and the spring Presidential primary—and the cost of printing ballots is way up." He suddenly looked forlorn. "We had to give the Board three hundred thousand more than what we did a year ago," he said. The two other examiners shook their heads sympathetically. "I cut them down thirty-thousand, though," Montecalvo continued, brightening. "They wanted a lot of things I turned them down on. And if I can persuade the Budget Director that the canvas voting booths don't need a cleaning this year, I'll save another sixty-two hundred."

In the case of the City Sheriff, Montecalvo confessed, he had been overruled by the Budget Director on two or three counts. "I gave the Sheriff a new washing machine for the New York County Jail," he said. "The machine they got now, it's so old and dilapidated, even when it works it tears apart all the sheets and cooks' aprons they put in it. But then the Sheriff wanted a seven-hundred-and-fifty-dollar set of law reports, and I gave that a big zero, because I figured he could go on using the Bar Association's reports, just like he's been doing all along. But the boss didn't agree with me. Oh, well, I can take a rebuff the same as the next man."

"My Aunt Minnie," Walsh said, grinning at his two colleagues.

On my way out, I stopped in at Patterson's office to thank him for his help. He was there alone, going over Water Supply, Gas, and Electricity's requests, and I asked him what had become of Mr. Fitzpatrick. "Gone up to the Metropolitan Museum," he replied, adding that both he and Mr. Fitzpatrick had decided they needed more information about the duties of a $2,640-a-year steamfitter there. "Got to keep our noses to the grinding stone," he went on, chewing his gum furiously. "Got to have everything in order for the Mayor when he comes over for his retreat." I said I'd like to sit in on some part of the retreat, and he told me that to do so I'd have to get in touch with Louis Cohen, Assistant to the Mayor. "Cohen was over just the other day," Patterson said. "Encouraging us to get our estimates lower. So the Mayor can see our figures without seeing red, if you catch what I mean."

By the middle of March, Mayor O'Dwyer was ready for his retreat, and the Budget Bureau was ready for him. On the day the retreat began, I got in touch with Cohen, who said he'd try to get me in. There probably wouldn't be any vetoing of appropriations while I was there, he said, as differences of opinion on such controversial matters are usually kept confidential. "We don't want to hurt a department's feelings any more than necessary," Cohen explained. He added that he was going to be present at the retreat himself that afternoon and said he would take me along if I came down to his office at City Hall at one o'clock. When I arrived there, he was sitting at his desk, adroitly eating a cheese sandwich and talking into the telephone. He waved me to a chair and went on talking. Cohen is a careworn, cynical Democrat from the Bronx who started as an office boy in the Health Department in 1908 and worked his way up to Deputy Commissioner of Hospitals under Mayor Walker. He was elected a City Councilman during the LaGuardia regime and served as chairman of the Council's Finance Committee, in which capacity he found many pleasurable opportunities to hack away at the Fusion Mayor's budgets. "The Mayor can raise or lower the budget, and so can the Board of Estimate," Cohen once told me. "But the Council can only lower it. And that's what we always tried to do. LaGuardia was always claiming that he had cut his budget to the bone, and I'd always thunder at him, 'Send in the bone! We'll cut it!' "

Upon finishing his phone call, Cohen jammed his hat on his head and led the way outdoors. It was a warm day, the sun was shining, and a peanut vender in City Hall Park was doing a fine business with the lunch-hour crowds. The benches in the park were filled with men and women sitting with their coats open and their faces lifted to the sun. "Municipal Civil Service workers," said Cohen, with elaborate sympathy. "Look at them. They're so pale. They're just getting over twelve years of horror." He changed his tone abruptly. "Listen, you sure you know where the city gets its money?"

"Taxes?" I suggested.

"That's what they all think," he said, glancing at me pityingly. "But how about forty million from water rates, thirty million in federal aid, a hundred and forty million in state aid? A million here, a million there —licenses, market rentals, student fees, ferry tolls. They all bring in money. Remember that. Sure, there are taxes, too—the Comptroller estimates a hundred million from the sales tax, three million from the hotel-room tax. Whatever we need in addition to all such steady income we have to make up by taxing real estate. But, except for whatever's needed to service the city's debt for capital improvements, you can't tax real estate more than two per cent of the average assessed valuation for the last five years. That's the law, and that's one reason you've got to keep the budget down."

A patrolman was guarding the door to Patterson's conference room. He greeted Cohen, and just then two men, one in a Fire Department uniform, came out of the door, looking flushed and unhappy, and hurried away. Cohen identified them as the Fire Commissioner and his Chief and said that he suspected they had just heard the Mayor veto a number of their pet projects. Then he excused himself, explaining that he'd better go ahead and see if this was a good time for me to sit in. In a moment, he reappeared in the doorway and beckoned to me. I walked into a spacious room with a table running almost its entire length. The Mayor and Patterson were sitting side by side about halfway down it and there were eight or ten other men seated around it—budget examiners, Cohen said. The table was heaped with documents, and in front of the Mayor stood a tumbler holding seven or eight cellophane-wrapped cigars. O'Dwyer, I thought, looked heavier and more fatigued than he had when I had first met him, about a year before. He nodded as I took a chair on the opposite side of the table, and, helping himself to one of the cigars, put it in a holder and lit it. At that point, my old friend Mr. Montecalvo came into the room and advanced toward an empty chair at the table. "Boys, I know this man," Cohen said. "Montecalvo. Examiner of Licenses. He wouldn't give away the right time of day." Montecalvo grinned self-consciously as he sat down, and the Mayor looked at him approvingly. "Now," said Patterson, "the Department of Licenses is going to cost two hundred and seventy-two thousand one hundred and seventy-five dollars this year, Mr. Mayor. It's up forty-five thousand over last year, but it's eighty thousand less than the Department wanted. We gave them five new inspectors, for one thing."

"Have they increased the number of licenses to be inspected?" the Mayor asked, in such a low voice that I could hardly hear him. Montecalvo replied that inspection work was expected to increase considerably because it looked as if licenses were going to be issued to at least four new categories of business.

"This department brought in sixty thousand more than last year," Patterson said quickly. "And the inspectors, they're . . . That right, Montecalvo?"

"Yes, the inspectors are absolutely necessary," the examiner said. "In fact, I've been very miserly with Licenses, Mr. Mayor. The Commissioner asked for a lot more inspectors, but I told him he could use the Police Department for the rest."

"Now, is that sound?" the Mayor asked, studying his cigar holder. "Is it sound for the License Commissioner to be so short of his own men that he has to use the police?"

"Why, Mr. Mayor, he'd need a *thousand* new men if he didn't use the police," said Montecalvo.

"Didn't *you* have to help out with license inspections when you . . . ?" Patterson asked, looking at the Mayor in amazement.

The Mayor leaned far back in his chair. "Oh, that's right," he said. "Come to think of it, in the days when I was on the police force, you had to turn in a report on every hole in the street. You had a card with a list of things to look for on your tour of patrol, and if you failed to report an unlicensed junk wagon or something, and the sergeant came along and spotted it, you were subject to discipline. All right, Pat," he said, straightening up and tapping the ashes off his cigar. "Licenses looks all right to me. Believe me, friend," he said turning to me, "all the departments aren't as reasonable as this one." Then he nodded at Montecalvo, who left, looking flattered.

"Now, how about Debt Service, Pat?" the Mayor asked. "Debt Service—the mortgage on the home," he went on, while Patterson placed some papers in front of him. "Before we can move, before we can buy so much as a lead pencil, we've got to provide the money for Debt Service—amortization and interest payments on what the city owes. How much is it, Pat?"

Patterson said it came to $201,583,273.69 and was, as usual, the biggest item in the budget. "And how much does the city owe altogether?" the Mayor asked, as if he were leading the recital of a catechism, and Patterson chirped, "Two billion eight hundred and fifty-seven million twenty-three thousand nine hundred and ninety dollars and forty-eight cents."

After a properly respectful silence, Cohen grumbled that the city's indebtedness was the fault of earlier regimes and that nobody could do anything about it now. "It's like that time around 1870," he said, "when they went and issued two hundred and seventy-eight thousand dollars' worth of seven-per-cent non-callable bonds so they could lay some wooden planks on a street up in the West Farms section of the Bronx. The last of those aren't going to mature until March 1st, 2147. A hundred and ninety-eight thousand dollars' worth of them are still outstanding, and they're going to cost us nearly fourteen thousand in interest this year."

"You mean we still don't own the Bronx, Louie?" the Mayor demanded.

"Just two hundred years more and it'll be ours," Cohen assured him. "But for that matter, practically all the bonds the city has ever issued were non-callable because the bankers say they won't take any other kind. Why, only back in 1940, when the city took over the subways, it issued more than three hundred million dollars' worth of three-per-cent bonds that won't mature until 1980. Today we could borrow that money at two per cent or less, but we can't call those bonds in."

"Most of the subway equipment the city bought with that money has already been discarded," the Mayor said. "But we'll still be paying

for it for the next thirty-three years. How much is the interest on all the
city's non-callable bonds, Pat?" About a hundred and two million dollars
this year, Patterson told him. "I wish I know who thought up the idea
of non-callable bonds," the Mayor said. "I'd heave every plank in West
Farms at him. But I suppose most of the planks are worn out by this
time."

"All of them are," said Cohen.

On April 1st, Patterson sent me a copy of his twenty-one-and-a-half-
pound book printed (at a cost of $32,575.20) in advance of approval or
amendment by the Board of Estimate and the City Council on the assumption that whatever alterations were to come would involve nothing
more than changing some of the figures and then running another edition
off the presses. With it, he enclosed a copy of the Mayor's budget message
(three ounces) to the Board and the Council. I read the message first.
In it, the Mayor lamented that the budget did not provide for all the
services that he considered essential but declared that it was the best
he could do within the city's financial limitations. He noted that he had
pared $68,400,000 from the total requested by the various departments.
He did not mention horse vans, voting booths, typewriters with Gothic
type. The total sum he felt obliged to spend during the coming fiscal
year he said, was $1,029,120,314.73. (Upon reading the message, a con-
scientious representative of a taxpayers' organization sat right down and
figured out that at this rate the city would be spending $32.54 a second.)

I then read enough of Patterson's book to discover that the Mayor
had decided that the Police Department needed about half a million less
than Examiner Walsh thought it did and that the Fire Department
needed about a hundred thousand less than McEneney thought it did.

During the second week of April, public hearings were held at which
a hundred and sixty-seven of the 7,835,000 citizens of New York City
appeared before the Board of Estimate to argue for changes in the budget. They had their say for five fairly fruitless days—the longest series of
hearings on the subject in the city's history. The official steno-typist for
the Board, who has been recording budget hearings for the last nineteen
years and estimates that all told they have run to a total of at least forty
million words ("Maybe it's fifty million," he says. "All I know is I've got
a broken back"), took down 620,000 words during those five days.

On the morning of the first hearing, I went around to Patterson's
office beforehand to catch up on the latest developments. Patterson told
me that several days after the session of the retreat I had attended, the
Mayor and he had totted up totals and discovered that the budget was
something like twelve million dollars more than the revenue anticipated
by the Comptroller. So they had gone back over most of the large depart-

mental appropriations and after several hours of anguish had cut out those twelve million. "We had to cut a lot of items we still think are essential," Patterson said as we walked over to City Hall together. "The Mayor was very unhappy about it. Much as I hate to admit it, we even had to cut Education a million and a half—fuel, salaries for substitute teachers, and a hundred thousand dollars' worth of school supplies. We had to take away two inspectors from Licenses, too." I asked him how about the horse vans for the Police Department and he said Police would get only one van, instead of two. I asked him what had been done about the sixty-two hundred dollars the Board of Elections wanted to clean its voting booths. "Well," he said, "I thought we ought to clean them, but that looked like a good way to save a little. As a matter of fact, you know, Montecalvo was against it all along. Well, here we are, just in time for the start of the great debate."

The hearings were held in the Board's large, drafty chamber on the second floor of City Hall. The members of the Board are the Mayor (three votes), the Comptroller (three votes), the President of the City Council (three votes), and the five Borough Presidents (two votes each for Manhattan and Brooklyn, and one vote each for Queens, the Bronx, and Richmond). The Board members sat at a horseshoe-shaped mahogany table on a dais at one end of the room, facing the public, which occupied cream-colored pewlike benches. All Board members were provided with a copy of the 1,425-page book and a glass of water, and the Mayor with an ebony gavel, as well. Throughout the hearings, the Mayor nearly always had something to say in reply to those who had something to say to the Board. The majority of those who showed up turned out to be municipal employees pleading for higher pay. At one stage in the proceedings, a man named Max Weintraub, who described himself as a stenographer in the Magistrates' Court in East New York, told the Board that he and seventeen other court stenographers were getting a bad deal. True, they had received small raises last year and the year before, bringing them up to around $3,500, but prior to that they had received the same salary for thirteen years and now the new budget made no provision at all to increase their pay. Moreover, according to Mr. Weintraub, court stenographers were given little opportunity to get ahead in the world. "Firemen can become lieutenants, patrolmen can become sergeants, we can become nothing—so here we are," he said. "Max, I know you boys work hard," the Mayor replied. "I know because I was a magistrate and I remember you. Many a new magistrate you broke in, including myself." He then told Weintraub that the city was simply too poor to grant him a raise this year and asked him to give his regards to the boys at the court.

About a score of speakers asked the Board to cut the budget. The rest wanted the city to spend more money, and some of them offered their own pet ideas of how to raise it—by licensing bicycles, baby carriages, bookies, and crap-game operators; by charging fees for police protection of payroll messengers; by imposing special taxes on the rich; by raising the transit fare and the price of ashes sold by the Sanitation Department; and by *making* Governor Dewey give more money to the city. By the fifth day, the members of the Board looked exhausted. The Borough Presidents of Manhattan and Queens took to dozing intermittently, and the Borough President of Brooklyn took to winking benevolently at elderly ladies in the front pews. The Mayor began to make frequent references to the grievous effect of public service upon a man's health. "Believe me, I'd rather see the flowers as they grow instead of in some funeral parlor," he remarked at one point. A Department of Sanitation man got up to describe the difficulties of his work on cranes and derricks and asked the Mayor to turn to an item on page 762 of the budget. "Just tell me what's on the page," the Mayor said wearily, taking a sip of water. "If we go on like this much longer, I'll be wrecking my wrist." But the people who had come to be heard kept on speaking. A man from the Department of Welfare wanted subway passes for social workers, officers of Parent-Teacher Associations protested against the cut in the allotment for school supplies, and a physician spoke up for more generous treatment of hospital psychiatrists. And so it went. At seven-fifteen that evening, the Mayor recognized the only remaining occupant of the benches—Myra Barnes, a retired schoolteacher from Staten Island, who, it developed, had come to complain not about the budget but about the dumping of garbage in her borough. She talked on for twenty minutes, and when she had finished, the Mayor banged his gavel on the table and declared the hearing adjourned. As the members of the Board started to leave, a man dashed into the room, clamoring that he had waited days to speak and had just left the room for a moment to call his wife to say he'd be late getting home. The Mayor and his colleagues resignedly took their seats again, and the man introduced himself as a climber-pruner for the Parks Department. He felt that since the city had two and a half million trees waiting to be pruned, its pruners should be better paid. The Mayor thanked him, and the hearing was adjourned, finally and officially, at seven-forty-five.

Three days later, the members of the Board of Estimate met again, this time in a closed session at which the Comptroller, I subsequently learned, brought the good news that he had underestimated the city's revenues for the year by about $2,000,000. But any substantial increase of the budget over that figure, he warned, would mean exceeding the limit set on real-estate taxation. In less than an hour, the Board decided to boost the budget $2,841,440—all for the benefit of schools, child-care centers, hospitals, and charitable institutions—and the following day, at an open meeting, it approved its own decision in a matter of minutes. Nothing was said about the problems of climber-pruners, court stenographers, or the dumping of garbage on Staten Island.

I had a brief talk with Mr. Patterson after the Board had approved the budget. He seemed very happy. His face was flushed with excitement and his jaws champed with even more than their accustomed vigor. "Have you read the book yet?" he asked eagerly. I was able to tell him truthfully that I had examined a number of its pages. "It isn't like last year's book," he said. "Last year, the Mayor and the Board did it over three times and then stuck in *eight* million. They barely touched it this year. Less than three million."

Within a week after the Board of Estimate had completed its labors, the City Council received the budget and passed it on to its Finance Committee for study. The Committee is headed by Colonel Charles E. Keegan, a Bronx Democrat who served as Military Governor of Bavaria in 1945, and it has nine other members, six of whom are also Democrats, two Republicans, and one a Communist—a political balance intentionally like that of the twenty-three-member Council. On May 1st, the Finance Committee held a public hearing on the budget in the Council Chamber, a few doors from the Board of Estimate's meeting place. In the chamber are a gallery for the public, a dais for the presiding officer, and desks and chairs for the Councilmen, arranged in a semicircle. When I got there, the gallery was empty, but all the members of the Committee were present except the Communist, Benjamin J. Davis, Jr., who was out marching in the May Day Parade. On the floor with them were five persons who wanted to be heard. Four of them representing municipal workers' unions, asked that the budget be passed without cuts. The fifth, a spokesman for the Citizens Budget Commission, thought he saw how reductions totalling $5,687,676 could be made. He wanted to cut out the appropriations for the upkeep of airports leased by the city to the Port of New York Authority, for Station WNYC (which, he said, the city should lease to a private operator), and for a number of other things. The hearing lasted only thirty-five minutes. After it was over, I asked Colonel Keegan how long it would take the Council to act on the budget. "Well," he said, "we're licked if we can't find anything to whittle out before May 22nd. That's our deadline, but we might be able to do the job in two weeks." He promised to let me know when the Finance Committee had finished its studies and was ready to report to the Council.

Mr. Cohen, who had also attended this desultory session, walked downstairs with me from the Council Chamber. He was in a cheerful mood. "This is the time *I* always used to make trouble when I was a member of the Council," he said. "I got in LaGuardia's hair. I got in Patterson's hair. I was trouble." He went on to say that if the Council should decide to make any changes, the budget would have to go back to the Mayor, who has the power of veto. If the Mayor should exercise that power, it would take a three-fourths vote of the Council to overrule him. I asked him what would happen if the city should be obliged to spend beyond its means. "Well, it's happened often enough in the past," he said. "When it does, the city pays the extra by issuing notes against future budgets."

At the foot of the stairs, we met a pudgy, bald man in shirtsleeves who was smoking a pipe. Cohen introduced him to me as Councilman Hart of Brooklyn, I asked him whether he thought the City Council would cut the budget.

"What budget?" he asked.

"Why, you know, the city budget," said Cohen.

"Oh, *that*," said Councilman Hart, putting a hand on Cohen's shoulder. "Louie knows we wouldn't cut that. What the Council does about it is just a formality."

Shortly before lunchtime five days later, Colonel Keegan telephoned me to say that there was a change of plan and the Council was going to consider the budget that afternoon. Most of the Councilmen were already at their desks when I arrived, and I saw Councilman Hart among them, alternately puffing at his pipe and talking to Cohen. The gallery was filled with high-school boys and girls from a current-events class, many of whom were earnestly leaning over the rail to get a better view of the taxpayers' representatives in action. One of the Councilmen came over to me and said that action was being taken two weeks earlier than expected, because some of the city accountants who would have to compute the real-estate tax on the basis of the budget as finally approved had planned a fishing trip. (Before taking off with their rods and reels, the accountants produced a set of figures that called for a nineteen-point rise in the city-wide tax rate—from $2.70 to $2.89 on each $100 of assessed valuation.)

When Council President Vincent Impellitteri got the meeting under way, Colonel Keegan reported that the Finance Committee had no changes to recommend in the budget and advocated its adoption. This precipitated an hour-long session of arguments, motion-making, and general confusion, in the course of which Councilman Phillips, a Republican of Queens, moved that the $161,000 allotted to Station WNYC for salaries be deleted. At this, Democratic Majority Leader Sharkey of Brooklyn got up and said that he had been opposed to the operation of WNYC

under the LaGuardia administration but favored letting it run under
the present one because it was now furthering "the cultural development
of the people." Councilman Hart, who is also a Democrat, expressed
pleasure that WNYC was not being used any longer as "an instrument
of torture." The motion to deny funds for the station was defeated 20-3.
Councilman Goldberg, a Liberal of Brooklyn, moved to adjourn the
meeting, saying that more time was needed to study the budget. Councilman (or Colonel) Keegan moved to table his motion. Councilman Goldberg was ruled out of order and replied by shouting that a motion to
adjourn was always in order, "Likewise a motion to table!" Councilman
Keegan shouted back. Councilman Goldberg said a motion to adjourn
could not be tabled. His motion was tabled, 16–7.

When the Council got around to voting on the adoption of the Finance Committee's favorable report, Councilman Palestin of the Bronx,
another Liberal, voted against it, and a moment later, before the voting
was completed, stood up and said he wanted to change his vote and
would be glad to tell his colleagues why. He explained that he had voted
against adoption because the budget was so big and, he felt, was being
steamrollered through without giving the Councilmen sufficient time to
study it. He declared that the first he had heard of the budget was on
May 5th, and here it was only May 6th. He wound up by saying, "Now
that I have heard my own remarks, I think I will not change my mind
after all and will still vote against adopting the report." The report was
adopted, 16–7. Before a vote was taken on the budget itself, Councilman
Sharkey said that Councilmen Goldberg and Palestin had had twenty
days in which to study the document. "And if you had another twenty,
or two hundred, you still wouldn't open that book!" he shouted. I looked
at Budget Director Patterson, who was slouching in a chair across the
room from me. His jaw was still, and he was staring disconsolately first
at Goldberg and then at Palestin. The Council President finally halted
the wrangling by announcing that the vote on the budget would now
be taken. The budget was adopted, 23–0.

After the meeting was adjourned, I went over to Patterson and con-
gratulated him. "Thanks," he said, but he didn't look particularly happy.
"How do you like *that?*" he asked irritably. "Everybody here had a copy
of the book in front of him, and as far as I could see, not one of them
even opened . . . Say"—he grabbed my arm and smiled proudly—"do
you know that more than ninety-nine per cent of this budget stood as
we made it? Well, that's that for a while," he added, tenderly gathering
up a mess of papers and a copy of his book from underneath his chair.

Two days later, in his office, the Mayor signed a statement certifying
that $1,031,961,754.73 was the amount approved to keep the city running

during the next fiscal year. He did so at a two-minute ceremony attended only by Cohen and a meagre scattering of the press. The Mayor's large desk was bare except for the statement, two fountain pens in a stand, a clock, an ashtray, and, looming large far to his left, a copy of the budget. A moment after the Mayor had signed and a couple of photographers had taken his picture, a friend of his happened in and remarked, "It looks like a big book, Bill."

O'Dwyer grimaced. "It's *too* big, chum," he replied. "Don't think I like it. But it's a budget that makes the two ends meet. And all the blather in the world couldn't have made it one penny more or, believe me, one penny less."

B. SETTING THE AGENDA

43. *Planning and Politics*

NORTON E. LONG

Politics is still a dirty word despite attempts to clean it up. Its association with planning presents the same image of incongruity and bad taste as the ward boss arm in arm with the city manager. Like civil service, planning has reflected a civic virtue of weak constitution, requiring special protection from the rude hands of the unenlightened and the selfish. Like civil service, it has depended for its limited efficacy on a special brand of politics, the politics of a do-gooding elite, of middle-class respectability, of newspaper support, and of a widespread acceptance that planners have a special wisdom akin to that of Platonic philosopher kings. The politics of planning has consisted in the development of a civic New Year's resolution, the master plan, and a campaign by the press and civic elite for its adoption.

This work of art, the master plan, once adopted becomes holy writ to be defended by an amateur lay board of hopefully high civic prestige, spurred on and kept to the mark by a professional staff of planners. The battle is fought along the lines of piecemeal engagements as the facts of power, the pressures of economics, and the tastes of the populace force

Previously published as "Planning and Politics in Urban Development," *Journal of the American Institute of Planners*, XXV (November 1959), pp. 167–69 by permission of the author and the publisher. Norton Long is professor of political science and Director of Education of the Transportation Center at Northwestern University.

a patchwork desecration of the architects' pretty rendering of green and white lines and dots. Like the W.C.T.U., the proponents of planning find that it is one thing to achieve the noble experiment in law, another in the drinking habits of sinful men. In both cases bootlegging represents the recrudescence of rugged individualism. People want their prohibition and their liquor too. The same is true of planning.

Historically planning has been associated with the dogmas of municipal reform. It has been, willy-nilly, part and parcel of the congeries of nostrums and specifics that the National Municipal League and kindred earnest souls have thought efficacious for curing "the shame of the cities." The antipolitical bias of the reform movement deeply affected the view the older planners held of their function in the political vale of tears and, in turn, the view politicians held of planners. Mutual suspicion and distrust came naturally. Much of this has now changed. The time was when if one were to insist that it was as much the planner's business to face the facts of political feasibility as to face the facts of economics or topography, he would be regarded as an agent of the Devil if not the Tempter himself. Today, except among the elder statesmen, lip service at least is given to the relevance of the political facts of life. In some quarters it might even be accepted that the values provided by politics are legitimate primary considerations to be accepted as directives rather than treated as unfortunate limiting conditions. Practitioners of the arts of public personnel administration and administrative organization have been in a similar boat. The administrative organization expert has looked for the professional approval of his colleagues even though his plan died; in this he but follows a sound medical tradition. Purity from politics has a consequent sterility. However, the chaste have their own reward.

Currents toward Realism

The currents which have been eroding the dogmas of the economy and efficiency movement, the immaculate conception of a nonpolitical, businesslike municipal management where the one best way known to the experts would replace the wasteful wars of partisanship, have been eddying around the planners. Plans are policies and policies, in a democracy at any rate, spell politics. The question is not whether planning will reflect politics but whose politics will it reflect. What values and whose values will planners seek to implement? The politics of a municipal civil service commission usually reflects the alliance of organized employees, unions, leagues of women voters, civic groups, newspaper editorial writers who professionally oppose patronage-hungry politicians, and the like. The parallelogram of political forces working through the civil service commission determines its operation, and the 365-days-a-year bread-and-butter interest of municipal employees is likely to be the most enduring and influential pressure. The politics of planning as it stems from the organizational structures of planning agencies and the values and contacts of planners is likewise subject to a pressure-group analysis. It probably needs as does the other to be supplemented by an analysis of the relevant ideologies of the practitioners and the elite and general publics involved.

The changed way of looking at the world that comes from serving as a staff arm of the mayor, rather than as the forlorn defenders of an unappreciated activity way out in civic left field, is tremendous. Location of planners as staff to the mayor promises a major change in planning perspectives. This change will both compel political realism and enrich the end systems of planners by forcing them to understand the politicians' perspectives and incentives, and it will jeopardize the planners' capacity to take the long and detached view. Realism will not be an unmixed blessing, though it is essential to get a sufficient range of values into the planners' thinking.

For a time joining the fire brigade in hot-shot alley may lead to far greater dissipation of energy than any projectitis of the past. Planners, if they are worth their salt are generalists, useful Indians for an overburdened chief executive. Putting planning under the mayor will not put politics in planning—it has always been there. It will change the values that go into the politics and, hopefully, for the better.

Plans as Action Programs

The best thing that could happen to planning is that it be taken seriously instead of accepted as a kind of elegant drawing-room accomplishment which receives the same lip service as the other unloved civic virtues. When the greasy, grimy hands of politics are laid on planning because it means votes, the subject and its practitioners have come of age. This means planning has come to matter. The fearful would do well to join Ophelia in a nunnery.

Mayor Richard Lee of New Haven has proved to many a practical politician that there is gold in urban renewal and not just Washington gold. Mayor Daley of Chicago finds his planners' pictures of Chicago the best sort of election posters—ones that get published in the press, for

free. Housing and urban renewal have made planning attractive politics
for some, poison for others. Housing has meant an adventure into sociology, complete with all the headaches of race relations, poverty, and
slums. Growing concern with the decay of the central-city core, the location of industry, and the economic viability of the city has forced the
planner to become a horseback economist as well as a horseback sociologist. Concern for the problems of highways and transit, sewage, water,
pollution, the fiscal inequalities of governments and school districts has
forced the planner to become political scientist and consider how the
fractionated governments of the metropolitan area can be structured to
permit planning to take hold.

While the planner may feel most truly at home when he is at his
drawing board, he finds his major work as sociologist, economist, and
political scientist, or just plain politician. The congeries of problems
which call for planning in their solution run the gamut of the professions.
The planner, like the top public administrator becomes a generalist with
a vengeance. As such, his plans are in reality political programs. In the
broadest sense they represent political philosophies, ways of implement-
ing differing conceptions of the good life. No longer can the planner take
refuge in the neutrality of the objectivity of the personally uninvolved
scientist. His plans are action programs that are in no sense value-neutral
in the large. Hopefully, in important areas, consensus will be so general
that planning can proceed with a maximum of agreed value premises.
In many, clearly they will not. The planner is in the thick of the politics
of racial accommodation, the battle for central-city survival, and the re-
constituting of the metropolis.

The discovery by the politician of the value of planning as a means
of getting votes is a sign of returning health for local democracy. What
better issue for political debate than the plans of a city's future? The
Russian magic of the five-year plans can teach local democracy a needed
lesson. Targets for Boston, Chicago, or Cleveland, spelled out as planned
versions of a desirable future, can provide meaningful issues for political
debate and restore vitality to a shared civic life. Planned urban development has the promise of enlivening local communities and leading to the
creation of new and wider communities where a common civic future
can be endowed with challenge and appeal. The politics of metropolis
will be a battle to control the pictures in people's heads. In such a battle,
the planners will have a major role, not perhaps as philosopher kings,
but as generalists with special skills in a political process in which answers are created out of the situation and the values of the participants
in an endless human process of trial and error. That plans should be

policies, political programs critically, self-consciously, understood as such and debated as such, will be clear gain for local democracy. Parts of plans massively agreed upon may so enter our local constitutions as to provide firm foundations for solid growth. One element of consensus, as yet unattained but high on the civic agenda, is to create a civic order that is capable and desirous of planning as a prized means to desired ends. Critical, self-conscious, awareness of a wide range of relevant values including probable consequences proximate and remote is a goal of political rationality. Planning as the eyes and conscience of politics is a high aspiration of democratic theory.

C. RESPONSIVENESS

44. The Bureaucracy and Its Public

MORRIS JANOWITZ, DEIL WRIGHT, AND
WILLIAM DELANY

(Previous selections have dealt with the problem of government in the urbanized environment from the citizen's viewpoint. This selection is from a study of public administrators of three governmental agencies in the Detroit area: one Federal, one state, and one city. It views the problem of democratic responsibility to the community from the vantage point of the practicing urban official.

The state agency involved was the Michigan Employment Security Commission (MESC) with fourteen branch offices in the Detroit metropolitan area. The Federal agency was the United States Bureau of Old Age and Survivors Insurance (BOASI) with five field offices. The local agency, the Detroit

Reprinted from *Public Administration and the Public—Perspectives in a Metropolitan Community,* Michigan Governmental Studies No. 36 (Ann Arbor, Michigan: Institute of Public Administration, University of Michigan, 1958), pp. 85–90, 92–93, 95–100 by permission of the authors and the publisher. Authors' footnotes abridged. Professor Janowitz is a member of the Sociology Department at the University of Michigan, Professor Wright of the Political Science Department of the State University of Iowa, and Professor Delany of the Sociology Department of Cornell University.

Board of Education (Bd. of E.), had a complete administrative
staff which administered 275 separately located schools in the
city.)

Public officials have to communicate with different publics. They have
to communicate with key group and association leaders, for the strategic
political support of their agency depends upon these leaders. They have
also the task of day-to-day communication with the agency's clients and
with the citizenry at large. The patterns of communication between public officials and these publics, however, are fundamentally discontinuous and segmental. Each side has only a partial and all too fleeting
contact and image of the other. These segmental contacts create powerful limits to communications between public agencies and their different
publics. Additional limits to effective communication with these publics
arise from the hierarchical organization within an agency and the segmental contacts that operate between upper and lower level personnel.[1]

Community Barriers to Communication

The consequences of segmental contacts on effective communications
in the metropolitan community have long been a topic of concern to the
urban sociologist. These segmental contacts—group and individual—and
the impersonality that they imply are rooted in the structure of the metropolitan community. The size and density, the social stratification, and
the rapid rate of social change of the metropolitan community are crucial factors that create problems of communication for public administrators.

Size and Density

The size and density of the metropolitan community means that
each important government agency has multiple operating units. Managerial civil servants in each operating unit must of necessity have limited lateral contact and communications. To prevent friction between
operating units and to coordinate communications with organizational
leaders, the agency's higher administration has had to establish "proper"
channels. Managerial civil servants in these operating units tend to build
up "proprietary" rights to service, and to communicate with particular
firms, trade unions, newspapers, and radio stations and with clients in the
area of "their" branch office or school. Continually, the personnel of one
operating agency have to communicate with persons residing in the geographical district of another operating unit. The necessary rules for "clearing" with lateral operating units create communication barriers.

The size and density of the metropolitan community means, moreover, that the public official is likely to live in an area remote from the
location of his particular operating unit. Branch managers, principals,
and other key managerial officials of each operating unit, however, are
expected to know personally those in their service areas with whom their
agency deals—key organizational leaders, business and trade union representatives, and heads of voluntary associations.

Not only does the public official tend to live outside of the area, but
some of the group and organizational leaders with whom he has contact
live outside as well. Place of work and place of residence are indeed
separated in the modern metropolis so that contacts tend to become limited to official agency duties. One administrator, who directs the operation of fourteen branch offices in metropolitan Detroit, summarized the
problem and its implication when asked, "How much do the managers
of the Detroit offices participate in the affairs of the area served by their
office?"

*Well, in the outstate offices [i.e., those outside metropolitan Detroit]
the managers live in the communities which they are serving and participate actively in its affairs. The people they know in Lions or Chamber
of Commerce outside the office are also the employers and claimants in
the area they service. Thus, hardly anyone comes into one of the offices
who isn't acquainted with someone in the office. This makes the work
run a lot smoother. In Detroit, though, almost none of the managers actually live in the areas they service. For example, the manager at Mt.
Clemens lives in Detroit. An exception is Dearborn. There the manager
lives in the community and takes part in community activities. . . . But
the Royal Oak manager doesn't live in Royal Oak but in Detroit. Most of
the managers in Detroit are active in a number of civic and other organizations but the people they come to know socially are not usually those
who they deal with each day as claimants, employers or trade union
"Reps." As a result, from the point of view of the agency, such participation is not so important in Detroit. This makes dealing with the public
in Detroit offices a lot more formal and increases the difficulties of our
operations here.*

The manager of another MESC branch office underlined the same
observation. He was born and raised in Wyandotte, has most of his
intimate friends there, lives in Allen Park, and works in Detroit.

*Isn't that typical of the metropolitan dweller? I belong to the Ex-
change Club in Wyandotte and am very active in their Chamber of Commerce. But the friends I make there don't help my job here in Detroit at*

*all. In an outstate office, belonging to these groups would mean that I was
getting to know socially employers and others who come into the office.
... But even if I did belong to such groups here in downtown Detroit,
which I don't, it wouldn't help much. You see, the people who work here
in this area don't live here. They only work in the same area but live and
belong to groups all over the metropolitan area. . . . [Therefore] I
wouldn't say I know many of the management people well at all. Actually,
I know the businessmen in Wyandotte better in a social way than the
ones in my area here. Better, probably, than the manager of the office at
Wyandotte.*

Interestingly enough, our sample of metropolitan Detroit public employees was predominantly recruited from the local environs, was longer
resident locally than the rest of the metropolitan adult population, was
highly identified subjectively with Detroit, and, finally, participated more
extensively and intensively than the average middle class Detroiter in
a great variety of voluntary associations. They had, in short, all the social
characteristics that one would attribute to members of a civil service
capable of contributing to the integration of an urban metropolitan
community. Nevertheless, they were still part of the pattern of metropolitan life.

Social Stratification

The patterns of social stratification in the urban metropolitan community determine the social prestige of the managerial public servant,
influence his social access to groups and associational leaders, and thereby limit his communications potential. He is faced with a number of
prestige barriers in his social contact with his community counterparts.
Despite the rise in prestige of public employment, in the large metropolitan community such as Detroit the managerial civil servant has markedly
lower social status than top businessmen, international labor union officials, large employers, and ranking persons in the mass media to whom
he seeks access.

Repeatedly, members of our sample of managerial civil servants mentioned that noteworthy barriers to their contacts with business and management persons are the business "expense account," the expensive luncheon, the bar, and the golf club that often provide the setting for informal
work contacts in the metropolis. One manager of a federal field office
mentioned that a middle-sized firm employing one of his friends pays
$1,000 a year for memberships in the O ... Country Club for the com-
pany's executives and salesmen. He had found out that one large auto
manufacturer pays for forty employee memberships in that club alone.

Reflecting on his comparatively lower income and the utter heresy of "expense accounts" in government employment, he said:

A government employee can't maintain social contacts with business-men under such conditions. If you go along on golf games and such things and don't reciprocate invitations you're looked on as a "sponger." As a result, I stay away from all memberships and activities that my own budget won't handle. Today, for example, I was invited to a meeting of the E. . . . Club but refused. The lunch and especially the drinks you have to buy cost too much for me. I only go when I'm asked to address a meeting, then they usually pay for your lunch. . . .

With some emotion, he went on to talk about his contacts with the particular business and labor officials with whom he works in his service area:

I got to realize that I'm a field office manager. If you face reali-ties of life in a big city like Detroit you know that I have no dealings with really "big shots" in the big firms or union internationals. I couldn't mix with them if I wanted to because they all make at least five or six times my salary. . . . I don't belong to the real snooty clubs like the Detroit. . . . and the Detroit. . . . Even when it came to the E. . . . Club or the S. . . . Club, which are more my level and where I've already been invited, I can't afford it on the salary I make. Not that the dues are so steep. It's the lunches, the drinks, the tips and so on. . . .

Social status and lack of access to the metropolitan leadership serves to condition the civil servant's self-conceptions and limit his ability to make use of the mass media to project an image of government onto the public. This same federal official went on to say:

The things are a lot different here in a metropolitan area like Detroit than in a small town. I started out in this agency in a small town, as a man-ager in Smalltown, Ohio. In Smalltown, Ohio, I was known to everyone and knew all the "big shots" in the town. When I left, my name was on the front page of the paper. . . . Here, a field office manager gets to know people like those in charge of pension and retirement matters in the large firms. . . . but naturally, not the executives who run the companies. In Smalltown the manager is considered one of the representatives of the Federal Government in the community, as Mr. Social Security. In De-troit, he is just another government employee, a sort of "glorified clerk" . . . .

Social stratification not only creates barriers to communication with metropolitan leadership groups but also separates the managerial civil servant of middle class orientation from those of his clients who are of the lower class. It was obvious, especially where the operating unit was in a Negro or working class area, that the middle class standards of the managing official himself created barriers to informal communications with unemployment or social security claimants and even with the local leaders of Negro and labor groups. Again, these communication barriers associated with social stratification are probably not as great in small communities. . . .

Interpersonal Contacts

To deal with these fundamental barriers to effective communications, government agencies in the metropolitan community must develop solutions which rest on their organizational resources. First, direct "face-to-face" contact with agency clients and with key private group and association leaders form the basic core of the public information program in these three agencies. Second, officially and unofficially, the mass media and mass devices are enlisted both by agency personnel and by private groups associated with these agencies. The resources available for the public relations function to these government agencies are indeed limited in a business enterprise system, and especially at the metropolitan community level of administration.

In any mass service agency, public information and public relations becomes an ongoing task of the entire agency. It is by means of a continuous flow of face-to-face, telephone, and written messages that information is disseminated to the mass clientele and to the association leaders linked to the agency.

The extent to which agency officials selected for study in these three agencies are involved in client contact can be seen from the extremely low percentage which did not have some direct interpersonal contact with agency clients or with the general citizenry during an "average" week. In all, about 96 per cent of these public employees from the three agencies reported that they had some such contact. (The percentage with no such official contact was for the BOASI 4.5 per cent; for MESC, 7.5 per cent; and for the Detroit Public school systems, 1.7 per cent.) Moreover, the amount of contact and interaction was high. During the average week, the modal employee had between 100 and 150 contacts.

In each agency, beyond direct operational contacts with clients, there are managerial and administrative assignments which carry the main responsibility for maintaining contact with private groups and association leaders. We found a variety of association and group leaders who communicate directly with the personnel in our three agencies. These contacts with group and association leaders link the public agency to the community power structure and to the general citzenry. These elected or appointed leaders represent a range from trade unions, management associations, veterans, business and civic groups like Rotary and Kiwanis to church, neighborhood, and youth groups.

Contact with association leaders, while extensive, was less widespread among agency staff than contact with agency clientele. Sixty-five per cent of the sample public employees have some contact in an average week with association leaders as compared with 96 per cent who have some contact with clients. As was to be expected, lower level employees tended to communicate more with the agency's individual clients, while upper level administrators had more frequent and diverse contacts with association leaders. . . .

It is striking to note the extent to which the association leaders involved in these face-to-face contacts with public officials were paid job holders rather than volunteers or elected associational officers. Group representation has come to be a professionalized occupation. Thus, for example, in approaching a mass social welfare agency like the BOASI or MESC, large firms, labor unions, veterans associations, and even service clubs rely on professional personnel for government contact work. The technical problems in social welfare require contact work by skilled specialists. This is less the case in the educational field, although here as well there were numerous professional staff people representing special interest groups. Thus, a large number of the public contacts of the upper level managerial civil servant in the metropolitan community seemed to be with these newer organizational professionals.

Most of the 44 top managerial civil servants who were interviewed agreed that interpersonal contacts in operational units constituted the main public information and education work of their agency. The success of over-the-counter "public relations" depends on the time allowed for office interviews and the skills and knowledge of personnel. Effective "community relations" depends upon the personnel resources available for out-of-office contacts. Inadequate funds and personnel prevent the development of effectve office interviewing and community relations programs. In the operational units many of the top administrators interviewed were keenly aware of the problem and concerned to use their limited resources as effectively as possible. But the long-term trends in budget allocation have complicated their efforts and made them less and less effective.

In both the BOASI and MESC over the last decade increases in staff and administrative budget have not kept up with the growth of these programs. The school system is in a similar position. In fact, in the case of MESC the agency's staff has been decreasing in size without corresponding decreases in work load. Moreover, the quality of the interviewing skills of its branch offices is frequently diluted by hurriedly hired personnel demands due to large and sudden increases in work load from seasonal unemployment.

The pressure upon the staffs of most metropolitan branch offices of BOASI and MESC leads to a concern with expediting interviews and emphasis on the so-called "production" tasks. This means less time with each client and less effective interviews. In the words of one supervisor:

Due to understaffing of the office, it has been necessary to conduct so-called guided interviews, to hold down the necessary time. Interviews would be much more enjoyable for the public and interviewers alike if it wasn't necessary to cut to a minimum interviewing time. This is undoubtedly the biggest deterrent to good public relations in this office at the present time.

Concern with the pressure of office production tasks in turn reduces public contact and informational activities outside of the office.

To begin with, budget and classification officers, although aware of and sympathetic to the need for giving consideration to outside contact and information activities, do not take bold steps in this area. Such activities are not easily measured and legislative pressures are against their inclusion. Because of the work pressure of office routines, even the meager staff time allocated for outside activities often cannot be used. Our interviews showed that many managerial civil servants are not merely "production minded." However, when faced with the choice of organizing and supervising either internal office interviewing or outside information activities prescribed for their roles, the majority are forced realistically to the first alternative. In one of the agencies, an office manager study done by the agency itself had concluded that most managers were, in fact, neglecting minimal outside information and education activities.

Utilization of Mass Techniques

Public information activities based on mass media techniques have hardly become an acceptable part of public administration in the metropolitan community. In fact, the pressures against the use of funds and personnel is so great that part of the public information function of these agencies has been transferred to private voluntary associations.

The difficulties which confront a public agency in its effort to obtain mass communications specialists are apparent in these three agencies. No agency can develop a mass communication program without the use of technical specialists. At the time of our interviews, BOASI had no public information technician in the Detroit metropolitan area. In fact, in 1952 the Congress eliminated the appropriation for a regional public information officer program, which had allocated one officer for the Michigan-Ohio office.

MESC does have one public information specialist in Detroit, an experienced newspaperman and part-time publisher of his own weekly newspaper in a small town in the Detroit metropolitan area. He plans the information and education for the entire agency and carries out most of the activities of the agency involving the mass media. His tasks include preparing and distributing press releases and magazine articles, writing radio and TV scripts, preparing speeches, posters, and exhibits, and performing other tasks normally assigned to a public relations specialist. Recently the budget reallocations eliminated his one full-time clerical assistant and, as he put it, "my staff has been reduced by 50 per cent." The Detroit Board of Education has a public information officer and a small but, apparently, adequate staff.

Despite these personnel limitations all three agencies seem to make resourceful use of the mass media. No administrator interviewed complained that the total public service time on radio or TV was inadequate, although clearly he was accepting the realities of the situation. Reliance on the metropolitan press seemed to be much less extensive, especially by the BOASI and MESC. These administrators were especially aware of the potentialities of the urban community press in residential and suburban areas. The same held true of the ethnic press.

The other devices of mass communications on which an adequate information program would have to be built were limited: films, slides, printed pamphlets, posters, charts, and window displays. On occasion, government pamphlets have been reprinted by business and labor groups for special distribution to employees or members.

Pressure against the development of a public information program arises out of the traditional fear that such activities constitute lobbying and should be prevented. The acceptance of a new government program does not bring with it acceptance of the belief that it should be empowered to inform the public of its implications. The opposition expresses itself first in legislative budget allocations. But special interest groups in the community are also constantly on the alert to the dangers of government publicity. As an upper level civil servant reported:

Others in the community are also opposed to an extensive public information job. These are people in civic groups like the Chamber of Commerce and Rotary. Suppose your group is businessmen. When you go to give a talk at one of the civic groups on social security quite a few of them will stay away because they do not approve of making such talks. If you use a movie or slide or something like that to illustrate your remarks they don't like it and ask you "who is paying for all that stuff."

In a very real sense the scope and content of government is still evolving in the United States, especially in the areas of metropolitan government and in mass social welfare. Agencies are caught in a cross fire between interest groups opposing or sponsoring administrative legislation. Public officials seem to have to operate with enforced neutrality and with their expert advice hardly sought openly. This enforced neutrality limits their use of the mass media. To a point, neutrality of official and unofficial communications is essential if government agencies are to operate on the basis of consent. This means that official statements in the mass media and at public gatherings are carefully filtered to avoid controversial content. For example, a manager of one of the field offices of BOASI was asked to discuss, on a metropolitan newspaper's television program, the extension of coverage under social security then being enacted by Congress. Although the program operated without a fixed script it was necessary, of course, to discuss the questions and answers in advance. He agreed to speak without a script but insisted in being assured that:

They wouldn't put me on the spot by asking me to defend or criticize the proposed legislation itself but just keep it on an informational "how it will work" level.

The program director recognized the limits within which the civil servant must operate and the program stayed well within the studied boundaries of the currently noncontroversial.

In this process, administrative agency personnel tend to abandon leadership in public information affairs; they tend to give up the tasks of innovation and goal setting, even the technical responsibilities of drawing out the implications of their existing programs. The result is that public information becomes routine or tends to lose much of its interest and meaningfulness to citizen audiences.

Under these circumstances it is understandable that private groups enter into the field of public information in support of administrative agency programs. The activities of private groups become an important service to members and a force in molding the agency's programs. The co-optation of the public information function was to be found in all of the three agencies to varying degree and a full analysis of this process, although beyond this report, is essential for understanding the dynamics of the public administrator and his clients. For example, in the Detroit area, a great deal of effective public information on unemployment compensation and social security is disseminated by the labor unions and a great deal is also done by the employers. The struggle between labor and management involves the supplying of such information services as older conflicts fade and become transformed. The trade unions, especially the CIO-UAW, employ full-time technicians who are well informed on these laws and their administration. The unions develop elaborate information programs to reach their members and the information is presented dramatically and in such a manner as to meet the needs and interests of workers. Much the same is true of management, especially the large auto firms. In the education field, parent-teachers associations and religious and professional groups are active to the same ends.

In a democratic society, it is probably essential that significant aspects of public information for public agencies be carried on by voluntary associations and private groups. But danger arises when the public information function is weakened to the point of ineffectiveness or where the public bureaucracy is denied adequate freedom of action. Clearly, all of the agencies studied have developed an implied concept of administrative neutrality and the philosophy, so to speak, of a "third force" between conflicting groups. But to be an effective third force, agencies must have personnel for interpersonal and mass communications adequate to a positive role in areas where private groups do not and cannot operate.

Note

1. In 1954, at the time of our field work, BOASI had 95 employees within metropolitan Detroit; MESC had 1,183; and for the city of Detroit the Board of Education had 13,316. In selecting respondents among these employees two criteria were used: (1) the employee's official position had to be in the upper managerial and administrative or lower operational level of the agency; (2) he had to be involved directly in the agency's performance of its day-to-day services to the population in the Detroit community. About half of the three agencies' employees (8,487) met these two criteria and form the universe of this special study. For the purpose of securing an adequate number of respondents for quantitative analysis, the entire universe was selected for the smallest staff, BOASI, and in the upper administrative and managerial level of MESC. For the lower operational level of MESC and for the Board of Education, two-stage probability sampling designs were used to select, first, branch offices or schools and, then, relevant employees within

each of these. A high response rate of .92 was but one indication of the general interest and cooperativeness of our respondents.

45. The Master Plan: An Inquiry in Dialogue Form

CHARLES M. HAAR

CHAIRMAN: Will the meeting please come to order? This is a hearing before the Committee on Planning and Zoning of the City Council of Lawnfield on Case No. 276. The City Council is being asked to overrule the action of the City Plan Commission on June 21, 1957, which denied the request of Robert M. Iffucan to change the zoning of an unplatted tract of five acres from Restricted Dwelling to Light Manufacturing. The Plan Commission is represented by Mr. Beauvil, Director of Planning for the City. Mr. Iffucan is here represented by his attorney, Mr. Aeucus. Let me say that the Committee has familiarized itself with the property involved, and with the relevant materials and records of the Plan Commission. Accordingly, there is no need to repeat such information. I think it should be known that, because of the special position of the Plan Commission and the professional competence of its planning staff, this Committee has always recognized a strong presumption in favor of the Commission's recommendations: hence, the burden is on the appellant to demonstrate that the Commission erred. Mr. Beauvil, do you wish to add anything to the recommendation of the Commission at this point?

MR. BEAUVIL: Mr. Chairman, I wish only to reiterate that the Commission found that Mr. Iffucan's application was inconsistent with the Master Plan for the City of Lawnfield, and hence recommended that the appeal be denied.

C.: Mr. Aeucus, the floor is yours.

MR. AEUCUS: Thank you, Mr. Chairman. Since this is a legislative, and not a judicial, hearing my burden is extensive. To place the issues in their proper perspective, I must ask Mr. Beauvil if he is willing to submit to my interrogation on matters relating to this appeal?

C.: Mr. Beauvil?

B.: Certainly. Planning and zoning is my business.

A.: Thank you. We understand the ambiguity of your position here,

From *Land-Use Planning, A Casebook on the Use, Misuse and Re-Use of Urban Land* (Boston: Little, Brown & Company, 1959), pp. 730–44. Reprinted in the *Journal of American Institute of Planners*, "The Master Plan: An Inquiry in Dialogue Form" XXV (August 1959), pp. 133–37, 141–42. Reprinted here by permission of the author and Little, Brown. Charles Haar is a professor of law at Harvard University.

Mr. Beauvil. You are in one sense a defendant to justify the action taken by your Commission in this matter; in another sense, you are an expert in the field of city planning. I trust that you will not find these positions in conflict during this hearing, but if you do, this Committee and my client must rely upon your testimony as that of the objective professional. Mr. Beauvil, will you repeat for the Committee the ground on which the request of Mr. Iffucan was denied?

B.: The Commission found that it was not consistent with the Master Plan for Lawnfield.

A.: I see mounted on the wall over here a map labeled "Master Plan for Lawnfield, as amended 1-1-56." Is this map the Master Plan to which you refer?

B.: Not exactly. That map is only a graphic summary of the Master Plan.

A.: I have here a map labeled "Zoning Map of the City of Lawnfield, as amended by the City Council 12-15-56." Is this a part of the Master Plan of Lawnfield?

B.: No, not directly.

A.: Can you tell us, then, what is the Master Plan of Lawnfield?

B.: Yes. It is the aggregate of all formal decisions made by the City Plan Commission on matters over which it has specific authority as laid down in the ordinance of April 10, 1947, which established the Commission.

A.: And what are those matters?

B.: Mr. Aeucus, you probably can identify them better than I. The statute empowers the Plan Commission to create a Master Plan for the city and environs of Lawnfield. Let me read it: ". . . including, but not limited to, the geographical distribution of systems of transportation and communication, of land uses and population densities, streets, highways, and other facilities for recreation and cultural pursuits, schools, and all other installations for the provision of public services; to determine and recommend proper public measures for the alleviation of slum and blighted conditions and any other circumstances tending to retard the wholesome and efficient development of the city; to determine and recommend any action calculated to improve the economic condition of the community; and to conduct such studies and investigations as are pertinent to any such matters."

A.: Very good. Now let's boil that down. If someone walked into your office and wanted to look at the Master Plan for Lawnfield, what would he be shown?

B.: Probably that map on the wall, unless he had some specific question in mind.

A.: Maybe I'm just a simple lawyer, but I don't see how you can "map" policies and criteria. Now, what if he wanted to know how this plan would affect a piece of property he owned?

B.: Besides that map on the wall we could show him other materials. There are Master Plan reports adopted by the Commission, or amendments specified in the records of the Commission. We would locate his property on the map and find all such references relating to it, and then assemble the relevant documents for him.

A.: Let's take a concrete case. I see by the papers that the Plan Commission has scheduled a hearing next Tuesday to consider certain revisions for the major thoroughfare plan for the northwest part of the city. If after the hearing, the Commission moves to adopt these revisions, what will happen to the Master Plan?

B.: The adoption of the revisions will automatically amend the Master Plan, and after enough changes accumulate we will redraw the map. I have only one draftsman.

A.: Can you tell us what is the nature of these revisions?

B.: They relate to a rerouting and change in the scheduling of construction of the extension of Elm Boulevard. The Commission had previously scheduled this project for about 1960, but the rapid growth of the city in that direction may justify an earlier recommendation to the City Council.

A.: Has this Master Plan or any of its amendments ever been approved formally by the City Council?

B.: No. Approval of the plan by the Council is not required.

A.: Do you know for a fact that all members of the Council are reasonably familiar with the Master Plan?

B.: No.

A.: Is it your opinion that they are?

B.: Well, no.

A.: Is it your impression that the City Council generally goes along with the recommendations of the Commission?

B.: Yes. There have been very few instances in which the Council has not acted favorably on a Commission recommendation.

A.: Do you think that it is a reasonable interpretation of your testimony that the Council has been adopting measures to implement a plan with which they are at best only slightly familiar and in whose making they had no part?

B.: I suppose that is true.

C.: Let me intervene a moment at this point, Mr. Aeucus, to point out that the City Council is extremely busy. They may be asked to vote on anything from a change in the building code to relocation of the municipal airport. I do not think that it is a matter of extraordinary signifi-

cance that the City Council does not know all of the circumstances surrounding the recommendations that its agencies make to it.

A.: Mr. Chairman, it was not my intention to impeach the Council
for dereliction of duty. No one appreciates more than I the difficulties
under which the Council labors and the complexity of the problems with
which it must deal. I simply wish to indicate that the relationship of the
City Council to the Master Plan is one of most peculiar significance. By
your own admission at the beginning of these hearings, there is a presumption on the part of the Council of the merit of recommendations
flowing from the Master Plan. Under these circumstances the Master
Plan becomes a fundamental document; yet it is left in hands of experts
who have no direct responsibility to the community. The very future of
this city, its physical improvements, the rights and obligations of its citizens with respect to the conduct of their property interests are controlled
by it. Obviously, the Master Plan and its recommendations cannot be
reckoned with in the same light as a recommendation from the Sanitation
Department on the scheduling of garbage trucks.

B.: I think you overestimate the policy import of the plan. Policy is
only made when the City Council enacts a recommendation submitted
by the Plan Commission, and at this time full justification of the recommendation is submitted and a hearing is held so that the recommendation can be openly debated before Council action.

A.: I am forced to disagree with you. If what you say were true, the
plan would have nothing to do with directing the application of human
energies in land development. This plan does become the source of expectations upon its enactment by the Commission. Aside from its impact
on other government departments, private decisions, sometimes expensive
ones, are based on the plan, and in this sense, whether formally or not,
aren't they the consequence of policy? Under these circumstances, my
client is placed in a peculiar position, for if you say that a measure is
reasonable or unreasonable by virtue of its consistency with the Master
Plan, he can only attack the plan as it relates to him. Wouldn't you, Mr.
Beauvil, agree that it might be a better arrangement if the City Council
adopted the Master Plan and amended it in accordance with the procedures for adopting ordinances?

B.: No. I think that such a procedure would hamstring planning.
The plan is a dynamic thing, and must be so, because the city is dynamic.
Small events occurring today cast tremendous shadows over tomorrow.
We must be able to accommodate the plan to meet them as we go along,
and at the same time, we must be able to improve it as we detect short-
comings.

A.: I'm surprised that you're even willing to have the Planning Com-

mission adopt your plan. Couldn't you keep up with the times by rec-
ommending amendments to the Council?

B.: I don't say that it couldn't be done this way. But we're after a
flexible working guide, not a rigid design or blueprint. The real problem
is one of perspective. This City Council is concerned about the success
of its administration; it is natural and proper that immediate criteria be
applied to the actions of the political representatives of the citizenry. The
criteria relating to the plan, however, must transcend elections. They
must be related to the long-range objectives of the community, to the
emergent features that are likely to affect the community's future, and
to a continuous re-evaluation of the effectiveness of the plan.

A.: You don't think that a legislative body is competent to apply
such criteria?

B.: I don't think that they should be so compelled. The value of the
plan to the legislature is in terms of how intelligent and useful the consequences of the policy appear to them.

A.: Then you must at least accede to me the right of my client to
refuse to recognize the plan as a closed issue in public policy and grant
him equal footing with it in this hearing.

B.: I would not object to that.

A : Good. I hope that the Committee will so note. Mr. Beauvil, a
moment ago you made some reference to the long-range objectives of the
community embodied in the plan. Did you conduct a poll among the
citizens to determine what those objectives should be?

B.: No.

A.: How then were these objectives determined?

B.: Well, in the early studies for the Master Plan, the Commission's
staff conducted a number of investigations into such things as the future
population growth, the economic base, the character of the land within
the city, the uses of land, the channels of movement, and other aspects
of the city. The objectives were determined as a result of those studies.

A.: Mr. Beauvil, I have had occasion recently to read in the literature
of your profession such writers as Mumford, Wright, and Neutra, and
these people all had very definite ideas about how people should live—
in garden cities, in Broadacre cities, in "biosocial environments." Do you
subscribe to such viewpoints?

B: Subscribe is too vigorous a word. I find such views interesting
and useful inasmuch as they suggest alternatives for the future of cities.

A.: Is there not inherent in such viewpoints some pretty definite ideas
about the objectives of city planning?

B.: There certainly is.

A.: Did you consider any such viewpoints in the determination of
your objectives?

B.: Are you trying to suggest that the objectives of the Master Plan are primarily my own creation?

A.: Are they not?

B.: Only in the sense that there are objectives—orderly change, efficiency of physical relationships, and high levels of public service—on which I think we all agree.

A.: Why were the citizens of this community not allowed to voice their own opinions as to these objectives?

B.: Because it is very difficult to get cogent or meaningful answers in this situation.

A.: Do you mean that the man on the street doesn't have any views on the subject, or can't agree on them?

B.: In part, both. The citizen has all the characteristics of a consumer. Few consumers wanted electric frying pans or ball point pens before they were placed on the market. These wants were inert, in a sense; they came to exist only because the product became available. In the same way, if the citizen is asked to think about the future of the community he generally cofines his attentions to the piecemeal removal of inconveniences and within the framework of the community as it is now.

A.: Are you suggesting then that someone must set his objectives for him?

B.: I only suggest that this is one of the functions of the planning process: the indication of new and bolder possibilities, and their objectification, if you will, in concrete and dramatic form so that your man in the street will have something concrete to think about.

A.: The choice of objectives, however, was determined by yourself or by the Commission?

B.: True.

A.: We lawyers have an expression to cover a case in which a judge states the "facts" in such a way that the outcome becomes "inevitable." Doesn't it seem to you that it would be more in the spirit of the political philosophy of this country if your Commission had derived its objectives from what the residents of this city really wanted out of their Master Plan?

B.: No. I have just mentioned one reason why not. If I asked you whether or not you preferred polarized glass in the windshield of your helicopter, you would answer that you don't have a helicopter, and that the inquiry accordingly doesn't make sense. But another question is raised: how relevant are the wants and needs of today to those of tomorrow? Long-range public policy can't confine itself to today's outlook; things are changing too radically and too rapidly. The biggest mistakes we've made in the past have been through giving longer life than they deserved to limited viewpoints of earlier days by encasing them in steel, concrete, and asphalt. This is the story of the modern city: the expensive straining to break out of the strait jacket carefully designed for it by earlier citizens. If the function of planning is to succeed, it can't be restricted to current viewpoints.

A.: Come now, how do you square this with democratic policy-making?

B.: A very definite program was carried out to tell the public what the plan was all about. Newspapers, radio and television, talks to civic organizations and schools—we utilized every medium of mass communication to say to the public: "Here is a proposed plan, we want you to know all about it. We're going to hold public hearings so that you can be better informed, object to it, endorse it, suggest changes. It is important to you because the future of your city, of your business, of your home is tied up in it." We held two weeks of hearings. In the end the plan was changed in a number of respects and finally adopted by the Commission.

A.: The Commission was not bound by any information from the hearings?

B.: No.

A.: They could ignore them if they wanted?

B.: Yes, in the same way that the City Council can ignore these hearings. They had to depend on their own judgment as to what was relevant and useful.

A.: And you don't think that there were any underlying considerations which influenced you and the Commission in the making of this plan?

B.: Yes, I'm sure that there were. I think the Commission definitely had in mind that a plan should be addressed to improving the quality of living for everyone in the community. I think that they felt strongly about the role of the plan as an instrument to achieve the democratic way of life in our city.

A.: I think that this Commission must comprise a very unusual collection of people if it develops a plan to further the democratic way of life by the autocratic methods you describe.

B.: I'll go along with you that they may be unusual, but I must take exception to your use of the word "autocratic." The Commission was very concerned that this plan should promote a richer and more pleasant life for the citizens of this city.

A.: You spoke of this plan as a dynamic instrument. I presume that you mean that it is subject to constant modification?

B.: Yes.

A.: By the same procedures, generally?

B.: Yes.

A.: Mr. Chairman, this has been a most enlightening discussion on the arcane mysteries of the Master Plan. I would like to point out that Mr. Beauvil's testimony has supported a fundamental contention of my client: that this Master Plan is a document pregnant with policy implications, that it contains objectives and assumptions arrived at in a fashion incompatible with the democratic control of government. Notwithstanding all of the exceptional efforts made by Mr. Beauvil and his Commission to give it an aspect of popular participation, at the heart of the Master Plan is the fact that an employed expert and an appointed body of citizens made and are making decisions with far-reaching significance for the future of this city. My client whose property has been most seriously affected in this process, charges that the Master Plan is unreasonable by virtue of the fashion in which it was engendered and in which it is being changed.

C.: We take notice of your position. But I should point out that the state legislature has apparently decided against you. . . .

Mr. Aeucus. Mr. Beauvil, you have heard the charge that your use of the Master Plan is arbitrary, in that it subjects property to legislative determination by an agency enjoying no delegation of legislative powers. Can you justify this?

B.: Yes, sir. Mr. Iffucan always has the right to request that the zoning of his property be changed. If the Commission responds negatively, he may carry his request to the City Council, which can change the action of the Commission if it seems to be unreasonable. I can't see where the principle of legislative responsibility has been abridged under this condition.

C.: Thank you, Mr. Beauvil. Mr. Aeucus, since your client's property doesn't fall within this case, in what manner do you think that the Master Plan is unreasonable with respect to him?

A.: Mr. Chairman, to date I have merely been interested to show from a number of viewpoints that the utilization of the land-use part of the Master Plan as a kind of extralegislative, superzoning ordinance is unreasonable and certainly not consistent with the common view of governmental responsibility. If this is the case, I am suggesting to you that you should disregard it in coming to a decision about my client's property, and base your conclusions on the simple merits of his application.

C.: And what are those?

A.: That my client is the owner of a piece of property whose size, shape, and location are felicitous for industry; that this Council is on record in supporting industrial development when it is necessary to the future of this city; that my client has entered into an option with a nationally established firm to construct a plant to produce electronic devices under contract to the AEC; that the plant in terms of its design, layout, appearance, and landscaping will not impair the development of surrounding property in accordance with the Master Plan; finally, the plant will substantially benefit the community, not only in terms of the taxable values involved, but also in that it will employ two hundred persons who will spend their payrolls in our city.

C.: Mr. Aeucus, do you think we ought to go along with every such request that comes before us, where a man with a new business enterprise who is unwilling to pay the going price for commercial or industrial property finds a piece of property that he can purchase for a song in a residential district and then asks us to change the zoning for him?

A.: As a rule, if it makes a wholesome contribution to the prosperity of the community, and does not deprive anyone else of the enjoyment of his property, it would seem to me to be unreasonable to deny such uses.

B.: May I interject a comment here? I don't think that Mr. Aeucus realizes that one cannot separate so distinctly the Land-Use Plan from other aspects of the Master Plan. All of these parts are delicately interwoven. For example, last summer, the Water and Sewerage Department undertook to replace an undersized water main from the purification plant. As this area develops, this main will be extended to serve it. They held a series of conferences with us on requirements, and the size of the main was carefully calculated to serve the proposed development of the area according to the Master Plan. Any substantial departure from the plan that would increase the requirements for water would place them in the position of having to replace this main or to parallel it with another for several miles, a very expensive proposition. Two months ago we worked out with the Highway Department the specifications for the development of the Freeway, including the location of a semidirect interlooping directional interchange that would serve most efficiently the planned development of the area. A substantial change in the type of traffic movement would seriously distort this scheme, which has been approved by the State Highway Commission. In other words, to impair the plan at this point would result in substantial and expensive changes in the public sector of the development of the area.

A.: Mr. Beauvil has just supported by contention about the Master Plan. There are a vast number of policy decisions being made about such areas outside of the knowledge of the City Council. I can only answer that such procedures most seriously militate against the property rights of my client. Let me sum up my argument briefly. My client has a piece of property admirably suited to the location of a premium grade of industry; he has that industry in hand, an industry that will be a boon to this community and to the area. He is prevented from using this property by the determination of the Master Plan. The use of the Master Plan in this fashion is a usurpation of the legislative prerogative to make public policy for this community, and the procedures surrounding it are arbitrary and unreasonable. We request that the Council disregard the Master Plan as a criterion for the reasonableness of this application, and that it be examined on its own merits; if this is done, I think you must agree that the proposal of Mr. Iffucan is not only a reasonable attempt to utilize his property to its best advantage, but would concomitantly serve the interests of this community. Thank you.

C.: Mr. Beauvil?

B.: I suggest to the Council that the Master Plan is nowhere as arbitrary as suggested. The zoning ordinance, which is what he really complains against, was properly adopted by the City Council, representing in its eyes a proper distribution of land uses and specifications throughout the city. The Council recognized that the rapid growth of the city and the changing conditions therein might justify changes in the zoning ordinance in the future, and hence provided regulations and procedures for its amendment. With respect to the zoning ordinance, the Master Plan as it relates to land use is merely a complex guide for such changes. It is the antithesis of arbitrariness to set up objective standards for such changes, and that the Land-Use Plan seeks to do. I reiterate, gentlemen, that Mr. Iffucan's request does not conform with the Master Plan for the City, and that Mr. Iffucan has submitted neither a reason for departing from this plan, nor an alternative. Under these conditions, I must affirm the recommendation that the request be denied on appeal.

C.: Thank you, gentlemen, I am certain that the Committee has been most enlightened by the clear discussion of the Master Plan and its relation to this case. We will take this request under advisement and submit our findings to the City Council at its next scheduled meeting.

Chapter EIGHT

URBAN SERVICES

THUS FAR we have given great attention to the democratic process in urban America, but we have paid only scant attention to the substantive issues currently being debated within this process. In this last chapter, we attempt to remedy this deficiency by singling out some of the more important problems of urban government for consideration. No attempt has been made to be comprehensive. Instead, we have endeavored to select representative examples of problems in the various functional areas of urban government.

In considering the politics of these functional areas, it may be helpful to classify the problems involved into several categories. In the absence of any accepted terminology, we shall consider the problems as (1) philosophical, (2) conceptual, (3) technical, and (4) administrative.

The solutions to most substantive problems faced by urban governments depend, initially, on the prevailing public *philosophy;* that is, either the public is or is not willing to spend the necessary resources of time, talent, and money to achieve solutions. In the first section of this chapter, three authors express themselves regarding broad commitments of public resources. John Kenneth Galbraith argues for a greater emphasis on public expenditures within our total expenditure pattern. Henry Churchill, a skeptic, cautions and exhorts us to spell out in large terms just what kind of city of the future we want before we dash headlong into "rebuilding programs." Stephen K. Bailey, a political scientist and former mayor, asserts that our goals are often fairly well agreed upon, that what we need is more imaginative leadership in the private as well as the public sector.

Many political decisions involve financial priorities between the functions of city government. For example, a choice may have to be made between more money for streets *or* for welfare. In many instances of priorities between functional areas, the real problem is a *conceptual* one. Not enough is known about the relationship among land use, transportation, housing, social policies, and taxation. It very well may be that some urban land policies are defeating transportation policies, and that social policies are aggravating taxation difficulties. But there is disagreement among the experts over the interrelations between the policies of these functional areas. It is not surprising that differences among the experts lead to political differences. Alternative solutions favor one group over another. Thus, interests fill the political vacuum caused by conceptual deficiencies.

In other areas, the problems are of a *technical* nature: the need for a better transit vehicle, an improved way to handle waste, or a new means of testing water. While the technical problem may be apolitical, neither the commitment of resources toward finding a solution, nor the implementation of the solution once discovered, is a neutral matter. Witness the difficulties over research for controlling auto exhaust fumes and the fluoridation of city water. The search for a solution is a public expenditure; in the application of a technical solution, the consideration is not only what will work best for least cost but also what will be publicly acceptable.

Given the proper conceptualization of and technical solution to a problem, there remain *administrative* aspects to be dealt with. The application of new techniques or policies are often sensitive matters. Questions of organization, personnel and budgeting may determine the success of the program.

In some functional areas, one type of problem may loom larger than another. Transportation and housing are areas in which the conceptual problems are especially acute. Catherine Bauer, Wilfred Owen, and Coleman Woodbury stress these kinds of difficulties in their writings. Dr. L. E. Burney writes of a technical problem, but shows his awareness of its political dimension. Chief Parker is concerned with the degree to which police problems are administrative problems; their solutions depend heavily on proper personnel recruitment and training. Thomas Eliot discusses the problems relating to education, and Wallace Sayre and Herbert Kaufman those of the judiciary. Most selections do not fall so neatly into any one category, but describe problems in which conceptual, technical, and administrative aspects are present.

Many of the authors raise anew the same questions which were treated in Chapter Four. While all the functions we have singled out for attention are "local" matters, a reading of each of the accounts will indicate that the issues transcend municipal boundaries. The issues are not simply of concern to the cities, but involve the states and the entire nation.

A. THE POTENTIALITY

46. The Theory of Social Balance

JOHN KENNETH GALBRAITH

The final problem of the productive society is what it produces. This manifests itself in an implacable tendency to provide an opulent supply of some things and a niggardly yield of others. This disparity carries to the point where it is a cause of social discomfort and social unhealth. The line which divides our area of wealth from our area of poverty is roughly that which divides privately produced and marketed goods and services from publicly rendered services. Our wealth in the first is not

Reprinted from *The Affluent Society* (Boston: Houghton Mifflin Company, 1958), pp. 251–56, 259–64 by permission of the author and the publisher. Mr. Galbraith is a professor of economics at Harvard University.

only in startling contrast with the meagerness of the latter, but our wealth in privately produced goods is, to a marked degree, the cause of crisis in the supply of public services. For we have failed to see the importance, indeed the urgent need, of maintaining a balance between the two.

This disparity between our flow of private and public goods and services is no matter of subjective judgment. On the contrary, it is the source of the most extensive comment which only stops short of the direct contrast being made here. In the years following World War II, the papers of any major city—those of New York were an excellent example— told daily of the shortages and shortcomings in the elementary municipal and metropolitan services. The schools were old and overcrowded. The police force was under strength and underpaid. The parks and playgrounds were insufficient. Streets and empty lots were filthy, and the sanitation staff was underequipped and in need of men. Access to the city by those who work there was uncertain and painful and becoming more so. Internal transportation was overcrowded, unhealthful, and dirty. So was the air. Parking on the streets had to be prohibited, and there was no space elsewhere. These deficiencies were not in new and novel services but in old and established ones. Cities have long swept their streets, helped their people move around, educated them, kept order, and provided horse rails for vehicles which sought to pause. That their residents should have a nontoxic supply of air suggests no revolutionary dalliance with socialism.

The discussion of this public poverty competed, on the whole successfully, with the stories of ever-increasing opulence in privately produced goods. The Gross National Product was rising. So were retail sales. So was personal income. Labor productivity had also advanced. The automobiles that could not be parked were being produced at an expanded rate. The children, though without schools, subject in the playgrounds to the affectionate interest of adults with odd tastes, and disposed to increasingly imaginative forms of delinquency, were admirably equipped with television sets. We had difficulty finding storage space for the great surpluses of food despite a national disposition to obesity. Food was grown and packaged under private auspices. The care and refreshment of the mind, in contrast with the stomach, was principally in the public domain. Our colleges and universities were severely overcrowded and underprovided, and the same was true of the mental hospitals.

The contrast was and remains evident not alone to those who read. The family which takes its mauve and cerise, air-conditioned, power-steered, and power-braked automobile out for a tour passes through cities that are badly paved, made hideous by litter, blighted buildings, billboards, and posts for wires that should long since have been put underground. They pass on into a countryside that has been rendered largely invisible by commercial art. (The goods which the latter advertise have an absolute priority in our value system. Such aesthetic considerations as a view of the countryside accordingly come second. On such matters we are consistent.) They picnic on exquisitely packaged food from a portable icebox by a polluted stream and go on to spend the night at a park which is a menace to public health and morals. Just before dozing off on an air mattress, beneath a nylon tent, amid the stench of decaying refuse, they may reflect vaguely on the curious unevenness of their blessings. Is this, indeed, the American genius?

In the production of goods within the private economy it has long been recognized that a tolerably close relationship must be maintained between the production of various kinds of products. The output of steel and oil and machine tools is related to the production of automobiles. Investment in transportation must keep abreast of the output of goods to be transported. The supply of power must be abreast of the growth of industries requiring it. . . . If expansion in one part of the economy were not matched by the requisite expansion in other parts—were the need for balance not respected—then bottlenecks and shortages, speculative hoarding of scarce supplies, and sharply increasing costs would ensue. Fortunately in peacetime the market system operates easily and effectively to maintain this balance, and this together with the existence of stocks and some flexibility in the coefficients as a result of substitution, insures that no serious difficulties will arise. We are reminded of the existence of the problem only by noticing how serious it is for those countries—Poland or, in a somewhat different form, India—which seek to solve the problem by planned measures and with a much smaller supply of resources.

Just as there must be balance in what a community produces, so there must also be balance in what the community consumes. An increase in the use of one product creates, ineluctably, a requirement for others. If we are to consume more automobiles, we must have more gasoline. There must be more insurance as well as more space on which to operate them. Beyond a certain point more and better food appears to mean increased need for medical services. This is the certain result of the increased consumption of tobacco and alcohol. More vacations require more hotels and more fishing rods. And so forth. With rare exceptions— shortages of doctors are an exception which suggests the rule—this balance is also maintained quite effortlessly so far as goods for private sale and consumption are concerned. The price system plus a rounded condition of opulence is again the agency.

However, the relationships we are here discussing are not confined to the private economy. They operate comprehensively over the whole span of private and public services. As surely as an increase in the output of automobiles puts new demands on the steel industry so, also, it places new demands on public services. Similarly, every increase in the consumption of private goods will normally mean some facilitating or protective step by the state. In all cases if these services are not forthcoming, the consequences will be in some degree ill. It will be convenient to have a term which suggests a satisfactory relationship between the supply of privately produced goods and services and those of the state, and we may call it social balance.

The problem of social balance is ubiquitous, and frequently it is obtrusive. As noted, an increase in the consumption of automobiles requires a facilitating supply of streets, highways, traffic control, and parking space. The protective services of the police and the highway patrols must also be available, as must those of the hospitals. Although the need for balance here is extraordinarily clear, our use of privately produced vehicles has, on occasion, got far out of line with the supply of the related public services. The result has been hideous road congestion, an annual massacre of impressive proportions, and chronic colitis in the cities. As on the ground, so also in the air. Planes collide with disquieting consequences for those within when the public provision for air traffic control fails to keep pace with private use of the airways.

But the auto and the airplane, versus the space to use them, are merely an exceptionally visible example of a requirement that is pervasive. The more goods people procure, the more packages they discard and the more trash that must be carried away. If the appropriate sanitation services are not provided, the counterpart of increasing opulence will be deepening filth. The greater the wealth the thicker will be the dirt. This indubitably describes a tendency of our time. As more goods are produced and owned, the greater are the opportunities for fraud and the more property that must be protected. If the provision of public law enforcement services do not keep pace, the counterpart of increased well-being will, we may be certain, be increased crime.

The city of Los Angeles, in modern times, is a near-classic study in the problem of social balance. Magnificently efficient factories and oil refineries, a lavish supply of automobiles, a vast consumption of handsomely packaged products, coupled with the absence of a municipal trash collection service which forced the use of home incinerators, made the air nearly unbreathable for an appreciable part of each year. Air pollution could be controlled only by a complex and highly developed set of public services—by better knowledge stemming from more research, better policing, a municipal trash collection service, and possibly the assertion of the priority of clean air over the production of goods. These were long in coming. The agony of a city without usable air was the result. . . .

The case for social balance has, so far, been put negatively. Failure to keep public services in minimal relation to private production and use of goods is a cause of social disorder or impairs economic performance. The matter may now be put affirmatively. By failing to exploit the opportunity to expand public production we are missing opportunities for enjoyment which otherwise we might have had. Presumably a community can be as well rewarded by buying better schools or better parks as by buying bigger automobiles. By concentrating on the latter rather than the former it is failing to maximize its satisfactions. As with schools in the community, so with public services over the country at large. It is scarcely sensible that we should satisfy our wants in private goods with reckless abundance, while in the case of public goods, on the evidence of the eye, we practice extreme self-denial. So, far from systematically exploiting the opportunities to derive use and pleasure from these services, we do not supply what would keep us out of trouble.

The conventional wisdom holds that the community, large or small, makes a decision as to how much it will devote to its public services. This decision is arrived at by democratic process. Subject to the imperfections and uncertainties of democracy, people decide how much of their private income and goods they will surrender in order to have public services of which they are in greater need. Thus there is a balance, however rough, in the enjoyments to be had from private goods and services and those rendered by public authority.

It will be obvious, however, that this view depends on the notion of independently determined consumer wants. In such a world one could with some reason defend the doctrine that the consumer, as a voter, makes an independent choice between public and private goods. But given the dependence effect—given that consumer wants are created by the process by which they are satisfied—the consumer makes no such choice. He is subject to the forces of advertising and emulation by which production creates its own demand. Advertising operates exclusively, and emulation mainly, on behalf of privately produced goods and services.[1] Since management and emulative effects operate on behalf of private production, public services will have an inherent tendency to lag behind. Automobile demand which is expensively synthesized will inevitably have a much larger claim on income than parks or public health or even roads where no such influence operates. The engines of mass communication, in their highest state of development, assail the eyes and ears of the community on behalf of more beer but not of more schools. Even in the conventional wisdom it will scarcely be contended that this leads to an equal choice between the two.

The competition is especially unequal for new products and services. Every corner of the public psyche is canvassed by some of the nation's most talented citizens to see if the desire for some merchantable product can be cultivated. No similar process operates on behalf of the nonmerchantable services of the state. Indeed, while we take the cultivation of new private wants for granted we would be measurably shocked to see it applied to public services. The scientist or engineer or advertising man who devotes himself to developing a new carburetor, cleanser, or depilatory for which the public recognizes no need and will feel none until an advertising campaign arouses it, is one of the valued members of our society. A politician or a public servant who dreams up a new public service is a wastrel. Few public offenses are more reprehensible.

So much for the influences which operate on the decision between public and private production. The calm decision between public and private consumption pictured by the conventional wisdom is, in fact, a remarkable example of the error which arises from viewing social behavior out of context. The inherent tendency will always be for public services to fall behind private production. We have here the first of the causes of social imbalance.

Social balance is also the victim of two further features of our society—the truce on inequality and the tendency to inflation. Since these are now part of our context, their effect comes quickly into view.

With rare exceptions such as the post office, public services do not carry a price ticket to be paid for by the individual user. By their nature they must, ordinarily, be available to all. As a result, when they are improved or new services are initiated, there is the ancient and troublesome question of who is to pay. This, in turn, provokes to life the collateral but irrelevant debate over inequality. As with the use of taxation as an instrument of fiscal policy, the truce on inequality is broken. Liberals are obliged to argue that the services be paid for by progressive taxation which will reduce inequality. Committed as they are to the urgency of goods. . . they must oppose sales and excise taxes. Conservatives rally to the defense of inequality—although without ever quite committing themselves in such uncouth terms—and oppose the use of income taxes. They, in effect, oppose the expenditure not on the merits of the service but on the demerits of the tax system. Since the debate over inequality cannot be resolved, the money is frequently not appropriated and the service not performed. It is a casualty of the economic goals of both liberals and conservatives for both of whom the questions of social balance are subordinate to those of production and, when it is evoked, of inequality.

In practice matters are better as well as worse than this statement of the basic forces suggests. Given the tax structure, the revenues of all levels of government grow with the growth of the economy. Services can be maintained and sometimes even improved out of this automatic accretion.

However, this effect is highly unequal. The revenues of the federal government, because of its heavy reliance on income taxes, increase more than proportionately with private economic growth. In addition, although the conventional wisdom greatly deplores the fact, federal appropriations have only an indirect bearing on taxation. Public services are considered and voted on in accordance with their seeming urgency. Initiation or improvement of a particular service is rarely, except for purposes of oratory, set against the specific effect on taxes. Tax policy, in turn, is decided on the basis of the level of economic activity, the resulting revenues, expediency, and other considerations. Among these the total of the thousands of individually considered appropriations is but one factor. In this process the ultimate tax consequence of any individual appropriation is *de minimus*, and the tendency to ignore it reflects the simple mathematics of the situation. Thus it is possible for the Congress to make decisions affecting the social balance without invoking the question of inequality.

Things are made worse, however, by the fact that a large proportion of the federal revenues are pre-empted by defense. The increase in defense costs has also tended to absorb a large share of the normal increase in tax revenues. The position of the federal government for improving the social balance has also been weakened since World War II by the strong, although receding, conviction that its taxes were at artificial wartime levels and that a tacit commitment exists to reduce taxes at the earliest opportunity.

In the states and localities the problem of social balance is much more severe. Here tax revenues—this is especially true of the General Property Tax—increase less than proportionately with increased private production. Budgeting too is far more closely circumscribed than in the case of the federal government—only the monetary authority enjoys the pleasant privilege of underwriting its own loans. Because of this, increased services for states and localities regularly pose the question of more revenues and more taxes. And here, with great regularity, the question of social balance is lost in the debate over equality and social equity.

Thus we currently find by far the most serious social imbalance in the services performed by local governments. The F.B.I. comes much more easily by funds than the city police force. The Department of Agriculture can more easily keep its pest control abreast of expanding agricultural output than the average city health service can keep up with the needs of an expanding industrial population. One consequence is that the federal government remains under constant pressure to use its superior revenue position to help redress the balance at the lower levels of government.

Note

1. Emulation does operate between communities. A new school or a new highway in one community does exert pressure on others to remain abreast. However, as compared with the pervasive effects of emulation in extending the demand for privately produced consumer's goods there will be agreement, I think, that this intercommunity effect is probably small.

47. Leadership in Local Government

STEPHEN K. BAILEY

Local communities have too often been treated as problems in administrative mechanics. This is unfortunate. Like the human body, the local community is a functioning organism. It lives and breathes, grows and decays, aspires and doubts. Its viability depends not only upon the satisfactory functioning of its economic and administrative muscles, but upon the character of its will and vision; in short, upon its leadership.

In this connection, it seems to me, we need to ask and answer a few questions hoary with age. For it is only in the context of a general philosophy of leadership that the technical questions of taxation, police training, personnel ordinances, public administration, and partisan politics generally take on meaning.

Housekeeping does not make a home. Effective local government depends not so much upon the machinery we employ as the spirit we are of. We can have all the latest IBM systems, all the best personnel rating systems, the best home rule ordinances, all the latest police communica-

Reprinted from *The Yale Review*, XLVI (Summer 1956), pp. 563–66, 569–71 by permission of the author and Yale University Press. Professor Bailey is a member of the Political Science Department of Syracuse University and was formerly mayor of Middletown, Connecticut.

tion networks, and still make a flop of local government. Good municipal government is impossible unless we first discover our goals and unless we think creatively about human resources and human relations. Actually, many of our technical problems are the easiest to solve. The continuing, nagging, frustrating problems of local government involve people and the relationships among people.

Let us start by asking a rather rarefied question: What is it that most people want out of life?

Is this question really so difficult? Do they not want to love and raise their families, to choose freely their occupations and their rulers, to contemplate beauty, to sleep with the security of a child, to be valued by others, to search for truth and meaning without restraint, to laugh with the wind, and reverence the stars? Are these not the values which sages and philosophers of all ages have identified and proclaimed?

If so, then we can say of local government, as we can say of all government and of all human institutions, that they should exist in order to maximize these values. Actually, these values are assumed in the Preamble to the United States Constitution: "We, the people of the United States, in order to form a more perfect Union, establish justice, insure domestic tranquillity, provide for the common defense, promote the general welfare, and secure the blessings of liberty to ourselves and our posterity, do ordain and establish this Constitution for the United States of America." It was the sense of our founding fathers, as it should be our sense, that government exists to achieve values—to establish those conditions within which individuals and groups can achieve the good life. This is the only significant meaning of the phrase, "the good society."

As soon as we put the issue in these terms, we become instantly aware that all too many local governments set their sights too low—far too low. Far too many local governments in America behave as though their only functions were to repair a few hundred yards of streets each year, remove snow, check parking meters, direct traffic, keep vital statistics, and keep out of trouble politically. These activities may keep a treadmill running, but they will never build a civilized community. The main job of local government, like the main job of a housewife, is not to dust under the bed; it is to raise a decent family. Local government must, in short, become an effective instrument of social policy; it must dream dreams about the future, and help those dreams come true.

It is not enough to want absence of disease in our communities; we want the joy of living that comes from a positive sense of well-being. It is not enough to want a high literacy rate; we want educated citizens. It is not enough to want industry or commerce; we want industry and commerce that won't pollute our air or poison our rivers or turn us into little Hobokens. It is not enough to want streets; we want streets lined with trees. It is not enough to have sanitary jail cells; we want those cells to become increasingly unoccupied. It is not enough to double our police force; we want recreational facilities and programs which will cut our police force in half. It is not enough to paint our poor farms; we must give our older citizens something constructive to do. It is not enough to contain the ugliness of our slums; we must destroy our slums, and build new cities in their place.

The "practical" men will say, "Ho, hum," or "Sure, sure"; the cynics will mumble "paternalism," "the welfare state," "socialism," or worse. The so-called realists will say, "Pie-in-the-sky-by-and-by." The members of the taxpayers' leagues will shudder and quietly check their wall safes. And I would agree with all of them if I were talking simply about the possibility of "City Hall" or the "State Capitol" or "Washington" doing all of these things. It is about time that we stopped thinking about social progress as the private preserve of government. It is also about time that we stopped thinking about government as an evil, disease-ridden ogre bent on destroying our liberties. It is about time that we looked at government and private agencies and individuals as useful partners in the common social enterprise of achieving a decent existence for ourselves and our posterity. America was built by this partnership. It was not built by government pretending it could or should do it all; it was not built by private enterprise operating in an antiseptic vacuum of *laissez faire*. As Walter Lippmann has pointed out, "While the theorists were talking about *laissez faire*, men were buying and selling legal titles to property, were chartering corporations, were making and enforcing contracts, were suing for damages. In these transactions, by means of which the work of society was carried on, the state was implicated at every vital point." And Lippmann does not even mention here the governmental grants to railroads, the governmental construction of highways, the governmental regulation of utilities, the governmental issuance of patents, the governmental protection of private property, the governmental training of technicians, scientists, executives, and professional men in our public school system, the governmental protection of public health—and I could go on and on with activities of government that have made our private economic progress possible.

Some of my liberal friends have assumed in recent years that government has done it all—or should do it all. They fail to realize that private economic life makes government financially possible, even if the reverse is in part also true. They fail to recognize that churches and civic clubs and voluntary agencies and dedicated private citizens do more to create civilized communities in America than all the mayors and city managers and first selectmen combined.

What I am talking about, then, is a partnership. When I use the term local government, I am talking about every possible resource, local, state, and national, private and public, which is capable of being mobilized in a common struggle to build a more prosperous, more beautiful, and more humane local society. . . .

In view of the terrifying complexity of modern intra- and inter-govenrmental relations, why complicate life still further by encouraging voluntarism and possible jurisdictional overlaps? Why not streamline administrative channels, firm up gelatinous authority, systematize a clear division of labor between private and public endeavor? Why not single out the tax and the trained administrator as the exclusive twin resource of local government and let it go at that?

The answer, I suppose, comes down to a matter of social philosophy: I am not convinced that efficient government is impossible in a pluralistic matrix. But even if I were so convinced, I think I should stick with some of the inefficiencies in order to maximize the voluntary output of private energies. A sense of community (and may I add a sense of humor) is infinitely more important in our kind of society than a sense of absolute hierarchy.

Furthermore, I am not sure that certain kinds of lateral clientele relationships are necessarily evil. A privately sponsored little league baseball club may do more to keep the maintenance operations of the park department up to snuff than the budget director, mayor, city manager, and general public combined. There are dangers in the parochial demands of citizen's groups directly interested in a part of the total governmental enterprise; but there are also enormous strengths. If local governments can do more than they have done, through charter revision and administrative improvements, to put their internal house in order, to make administrative authority and political responsibility equivalent and unambiguous in the area of formal legal power, private community endeavors can then be encouraged with a minimum danger of confusion and divided purpose.

The maximum and harmonious utilization of the resources available to local communities cannot be achieved by trusting to luck or to some "unseen hand." There is nothing automatic about the process of unleashing and, paradoxically, harnessing social power. The primary resource, without which all other resources are left inert on a centrifugal wheel, is local political leadership, what Woodrow Wilson once described as "the capacity to give sight to the blind forces of public thought." It is the job of those in local politics and administration to give direction and leadership to all the other resources at the disposal of our communities. This is a tremendous responsibility. It means not only that housekeeping functions must be run efficiently and well: police, fire, public works, health, welfare, and the rest; it means that local public officials must become major catalytic agents in stimulating constructive community activity and community planning. It is their job to set goals as well as execute policies. It is their job to harness private energies and federal and state resources in order to create a better society. These things we cannot do unless we brighten our tarnished political instruments and raise our political sights.

In Tolstoi's "War and Peace" the Russian general Kutuzov knew, in Tolstoi's words, "that the leader existed only to give form and expression to the energy of his followers." This is a useful conception of leadership in our society only if a leader understands that he must look for the human, not the animal energies of his followers. There are warring and complex self-interests in all parts of our society, as there are in all parts of us. My own experience in Middletown taught me that people could be appealed to above the level of the belly—and would respond. I am not pretending that I was any great shakes as a mayor. I know that I make a lot of mistakes. But I know also that I was most successful where I was able to make people see the community as a total enterprise, not as a bundle of separate factions to be separately pleased.

What are the obligations of leaders at the local level, or for that matter at any level of govenrment?

We have identified one responsibility already: to take stock of the resources at the community's disposal. A second responsibility of the leader is to search among these resources until he has found what Edmund Burke called the "permanent forces," the most common and the most ubiquitous long-range interests. Leadership involves selection. All groups and all individuals cannot have all their demands satisfied fully and simultaneously. Some demands should not be satisfied at all. The junk dealer who wants a zoning change in a restricted residential zone is defying the "permanent forces," the long-range interests of the community. So is the restaurant owner who asks a health officer to "go easy." So is the real estate entrepreneur who wants to set up jerry-built houses with forty-foot frontages in a new subdivision. So is the slum landlord who defies urban redevelopment. President Charles Eliot of Harvard once identified the prime requisite of an executive as "his willingness to give pain"—not his *desire* to give pain but his *willingness*. Almost every action of government hurts or inconveniences someone in some measure. Unless a leader can identify the "permanent forces" in a community, unless he can mobilize the will to inconvenience the transitory forces which hinder the release of these permanent forces, forward movement is impossible.

48. What is a City?

HENRY CHURCHILL

What kind of a city do we want? An answer to that requires an answer to "what kind of people are going to live in them?" Are they going to be frightened, frustrated people, or "people" abstracted from the census, or human beings living a full life? The answer lies somewhere in the realm of technology, for people are becoming—or are in danger of becoming—creatures of technological function. I do not pretend to know the answer, but every planner should read Norbert Weiner's *The Human Use of Human Beings*[1] and Lancelot L. Whyte's *The Next Development in Man*[2] for some idea of where we may be heading.

What is a city, anyway? It is, of course, a place where people congregate to earn a living. It is also a place in which people are interdependent because of an extreme degree of occupational specialization. It is also a place in which there is an enormous variety of things and people among which to pick and choose. Its essence is gregariousness and anonymity. The small town is the opposite of the city. Its essence is propinquity and nosiness. The suburb is just the bastard of the two.

They should not be confused; they are not just different physically, they are two different ways of life. That has been so ever since there were cities, town, and country, the slick and the hick. They don't mix, except as each serves as a vacation-land escape for the other.

City-planners are generally pretty well agreed about certain things they consider desirable to take the place of blight and slums. More light, although, alas! not in the Goethean sense, more air, more quiet, stabilized land values. Most of them envisage a community of like-minded souls dwelling in well-ordered harmony amid neat community facilities. Most of them, of course, would die if they had to live in one of their own dull Utopias, but they keep talking about them. I believe they do their cause considerable harm, even though it may be the natural reaction to the noise, confusion, and frustration of the cities with which they deal. They forget that what makes them queasy is to many the only reason the

Reprinted from *The Future of Cities and Urban Redevelopment*, Coleman Woodbury, ed. (Chicago: University of Chicago Press, 1953), pp. 45–51 by permission of the publisher. Mr Churchill is a professional architect.

city has for its existence, a vast confusion in the midst of which opportunity, honorable or other, offers its golden charms, and where melting away among other unknown failures is the solace for those who muff their chance. The great novelists, from Balzac to Joyce, better sociologists than the professors of that solemn discipline, have described what the fascination is that brings men and women from the provinces to the city, what it is that makes the city the lure it is, for both good and evil. Any effort to recreate the small town in the city—*rus in urbe*—is foredoomed, since it is a contradiction in purpose.[3]

The city therefore should remain the city, and I say this in spite of the fact that hordes of people are getting out of the cities, turning alleged green pastures into the asphalt corrals of the suburbs. They are looking for sunlight, air, quiet, decent schooling for their children, a place to park their cars—the very things the planners want to give them. But at the same time they try to keep the opportunities and pleasures of the city. They commute. Suggest that they desert the city altogether, find them a home and work in a small town or in the frightening country, there would be small response. Nor would their children be content to stay in such places after they grew up. Indeed it remains to be seen what will happen to the chicken-coop garnishings of the suburban fringe when the present generation attains the age of indiscretion.

People Are Different

So the problem becomes one of making the city tolerable and still keeping it the City. For our big cities have indeed become intolerable, not because they are not like villages but because technological devices have been used to exploit land without any regard for either human needs or human values. If people are deserting them, even for the pseudo-satisfactions of the suburb and the subdivision, it is because of a purely biological will to survive.

It is basically fruitless to think about future city patterns in terms of the present economics that have made them what they are. New patterns, more suited to the use of human beings cannot be evolved under the system of city finances based on *ad valorem* taxes, on the accrual of unearned increment solely to the land-owner, and on the speculative theory of unimpeded growth. There is plenty of evidence that these economic devices are already becoming subject to readjustment. Title I of the Housing Act of 1949 itself is the most notable exhibit.

It should be clear, I think, that if we replan our cities so as to "make them pay" we will only make the most superficial improvements. To overcrowd the land vertically instead of horizontally is no solution at all, since density is a function of total population and not of coverage. There is more open space in the vertical City of Towers, but it is less accessible, and the problems of circulation have merely been transformed, not solved. The social problems likewise: Percival and Paul Goodman have given a most acute analysis of the vertical city in *Communitas*⁴—the only American book on planning I know of that even tries to give an analysis of human use and sees use in the urban sense as not necessarily the equivalent of either Corbusier's totalitarianism or Ebenezer Howard's provincialism.

It seems to me also that certain important segments of people and certain aspects of their livelihood are being overlooked in much of our planning, devoted as it is to the housing ghetto and to industry. There are notable exceptions, but in general little thought is given on how to fit those whom Shaw called "the undeserving poor" into the picture. Public housing is not the answer. Public housing is for the deserving poor, and not for all of them because public housing must not, by any fell circumstance, have a vacancy. There must be a long waiting list of deservers, so that management—and the politician too, perhaps—can have a threat for the recalcitrant tenant. And the undeserving poor do not want to live in a "project" anyway, if they can scratch together enough to go their own unregenerate way. There are people—not counting the "unsocially minded"—who just do not like to live in rabbit warrens. Where, in the bright City of Eniak, are they going to live?

What is also overlooked is that industrial employment is not the only form of work. "Service workers," those who do not work in the basic industries, at least equal the industrial workers in number. And there are a very great many people who live with their work. They are proprietors of small stores, various kinds of small industries such as repair shops, and so on. They don't make much money, but they are independent and they get by. They line the side streets and secondary avenues of every city. Some have come down in the world and are just hanging on; some are on their way up. Our present brand of redevelopment destroys them. Our new plans make no provision for these people, none whatever. They do not belong either to the skyscrapers or the nice little "residential" communities. Where are they to go, what are they to do?

Planning Is Not Statistics

There are many other human problems that must receive thoughtful consideration before any sound pattern for the future can be determined. Is our cultural future going to be wholly one of mass production? For the moment it looks that way, but art is long. Civic art and architecture are arts that traditionally spoke to the masses of people. The city planners who know nothing of architecture and the architects who care nothing for civic art (except the single civic "monument") are doing a grave disservice to our culture.

Will our school systems continue to waste our children's potential by routine mass methods that fail to stir the dull and dull the intelligent? One of the principal reasons for the flight to the suburbs is because there it seemed possible to influence schools and teaching; in any case the smaller classes and better plant seemed to offer better education and care than was possible in the ancient city schools. Will our redeveloped cities go in for smaller schools, scaled to the children both physically and educationally, or will they continue to be "efficient"?

Planners cannot decide these things, but they must know.

What kind of a people are we going to be? Is George Orwell right? Will Wiener's fears be justified? Too much planning thinking leans in the direction of acquiescence. Or perhaps it is planning thoughtlessness, the too ready acceptance of the cliché and "scientific method" in a sphere that is neither scientific nor in possession of a sound methodolgy. The substitution of number for the specific, the curious belief that the statistical average is a reality, make for an easy process of planning, but the easy way may be wrong. The hard way is to take a good look at the statistical process itself and judge whether it is a method of evaluating something in terms of use and human need or a device for eliminating consideration of the individual. It is going to be hard to do this, because we have gotten a quasi-religious faith that statistics "prove" something. This is not so, as any player of the Wall Street averages—or the racing forms—can tell you. Statistics can indicate a probable result based on past performance of a limited number of factors, but can tell nothing about the rightness or wrongness, in terms of human value, of such a result should it by chance come about.

The dilemma of course is that we have to plan now for something and we cannot plan for everyone. But the way out is not—if we wish to keep away from authoritarianism—to plan for averages. We must, I believe, make little plans for little people, lots and lots of plans to human scale. It may mean doing a lot of wrong things and some right ones, but that is better than to do just one thing wrong and no chance for anything right. We need variety and the experience variety brings, not formulas.

I admire the New York Life Insurance Company because it has had the courage to try two totally different concepts of housing. (That is more than either FHA or PHA has ever had.) Fresh Meadows is a highly successful development, yet in Chicago New York Life is going to build its absolute opposite: twenty-three story slab apartments with open corridors, and, even so, a density of only about 20 families per gross acre. The

two structures are spaced widely apart, there will be two-story apartments surrounding the vast court. It would have been easy to repeat the
Fresh Meadows idea; to go to the Chicago extreme takes guts. I happen
to prefer Fresh Meadows; for one thing it provides a greater variety of
living, for another it is more human in scale. Nevertheless, the Chicago
project may prove the better. It will certainly suit many people and it
opens up new possibilities for congested living. But I cannot help wondering, if the example is successful and is widely followed, what will
happen when the buildings become old and decrepit and the area is again
obsolete, and the cost of operation and repair exceeds a "fair return" and
they become vast vertical slums; what then? These wonderful elevators,
these glass walls, these complicated heating systems and miles of pipe
and miles of dirt-swept "sidewalks in the sky," who will maintain them?
Well, it is a long time off, fifty years or twenty, and the investor will be
paid out. It is no concern of ours—now. And, as I said, it may be a step
toward a solution of the problem of how to reconcile compacted living
to satisfy the gregarious instinct with the space needed for the mobility
of the machine. The principal present objection I see is that in order to
escape one's neighbors even for a moment one must depend on a machine
—the elevator—or else jump.

Large-Scale vs. Human Values

There is a very serious danger in the continued emphasis on, and
desire for, "large-scale" action in rebuilding our cities, and in the general
belief that only by large-scale financing and construction can a satisfactory and "permanent" result be brought about. Large-scale building means
mass production for mass consumption, i.e., further steps toward a lowering of standards to the level of the lowest common denominator. It may
be a long first step towards the establishment of an urban feudalism similar in many ways to the rural feudalism of medieval times. It took a great
many hundreds of years to break down the feudalism that was rooted in
the vast holdings of agricultural land; in many countries, notably South
America and China, the system still persists. Urban feudalism would be
different, of course; but the ownership and control of shelter gives tremendous political power, and what begins as well-intentioned paternalism
easily turns to despotism—perhaps benevolent, perhaps not. The individual must be encouraged to retain his individuality, if democracy is to survive. For the planner that means the individual's right to his choice of
a way of life must not be circumscribed by arbitrary physical limitations

imposed in the name of "order" or "efficiency." Within the broadest possible framework of the general good, disorder must be allowed for, lest the people perish. Any form of initiative is disordering of the status quo and so needs encouragement, not suppression, if democracy is to retain vitality.

I believe we can get the carbon dioxide out of our cities, that we can create islands of quiet beauty in them, that we can channel our cars so there will be less congestion and more safety, that the insanity rate can be lowered (unless the psychiatrists set up new standards of "normal" still more exclusive of themselves). We need to give fresh thought to the cliché of the "neighborhood," to the fetish of "stability." The first may turn out to be a sociological absurdity and the latter an economic impossibility. We need to reappraise the use of automotive transportation. We still have two legs and perhaps the private car should only take us *nearly* to where we want to go, like the street car or the subway does. The places in which we live, work, shop might be thought of as pedestrian islands rather than as interferences to a moving vehicle. After all, is not that the basic idea behind the new suburban shopping centers and of the properly designed super-block? It needs to be carried to its logical conclusion, a complete separation of traffic and people. Within some islands there can be as much congestion of people, confusion, life, and noise as is characteristic and necessary for the gregarious anonymity of the city. Within others there can be peace and quiet, and ordered beauty of architecture, the unordered interest of the picturesque. Within a broad frame there is space for community needs, for ample schools, for recreation for the aged. The human scale could be restored, and the human pace, the chance to look and to comprehend. The traffic ways would be designed for a different order of speed, a different kind of receptivity.

Only the public works would need large capital. In other kinds of development large capital investment would be welcome, small capital would have opportunity.

The new technology—Wiener's "second industrial revolution"—can be used for such good purposes if it is not allowed to become the power of the new feudalism, i.e., become the exclusive property of vast capital. The need for physical presence at many functions can be reduced, and traffic thereby reduced. Automatic controls, conferences by television, duplication of documents in several places simultaneously, can reduce the need of people to rush themselves through the streets.

We are at the commencement of a crucial period in city development, and the technician is an important, if not a decisive, factor in the turn of events. It is his responsibility to be aware of where he will arrive once he makes a choice of his road. I have suggested some of the things he should consider, the terms of the alternatives.

I have very little sympathy for those who cry that unless we do things in a Big Way it will all have to be done over again in fifty years or so. I should hope it will be, and with more human understanding than we have now, and with better means for accomplishment. Is not our trouble today that we must undo the work of our grandfathers? What makes us think we are any more prescient than they? Of course, our cities must be rebuilt again in the future, and again thereafter. Our choice now in so far as we can choose, is between the roads that lead to the City of Man or the City of Eniak.

Notes

1. Norbert Wiener, *The Human Use of Human Beings* (Boston: Houghton Mifflin Co., 1950).
2. Lancelot L. Whyte, *The Next Development of Man* (New York: The American Library, 1950).
3. Some sociologists, Svend Riemer, for instance, are coming to the conclusion that the "village in the city" is not socially possible even if desirable—and the desirability has never been sociologically proved.
4. Percival and Paul Goodman, *Communitas* (Chicago: University of Chicago Press, 1947).

B. HOUSING AND TRANSPORTATION

49. *The Dreary Deadlock of Public Housing*

CATHERINE BAUER

Low-rent public housing has not followed the normal pattern for reform movements in modern democratic countries. Every social experiment starts off as an abstract idea, frequently in an atmosphere of violent theo-

Reprinted from *Architectural Forum*, CVI (May 1957), pp. 140–42, 219–22 by permission of the publisher. Catherine Bauer is a lecturer in city planning at the University of California. Her experience has been primarily in the area of public housing. She is currently a member of the Slum Clearance Advisory Committee of the U.S. Housing and Finance Agency.

retical debate. But after it has been tried out for a while, one of two things usually happens. Either it dies off, an acknowledged failure, or it "takes" and is accepted as an integral part of the ordinary scheme of things. The original theories, meantime, become modified and adapted to actual conditions. In the US, public attitudes about social security, collective bargaining and national economic controls have all followed the classic steps outlined years ago by George Bernard Shaw: 1) it's impossible; 2) it's against the Bible; 3) it's too expensive; and 4) we knew it all the time. But public housing, after more than two decades, still drags along in a kind of limbo, continuously controversial, not dead but never more than half alive.

No obituary is yet in order for the US Housing Act of 1937 "as successively [but only in minor respects] amended." It is more a case of premature ossification. The bare bones of oversimplified New Deal theory have never been decently covered with the solid flesh of present-day reality. Even among public housing's most tireless defenders, many would welcome a fresh start if they did not fear that in the process any program at all might get lost.

If the dreary deadlock is to be broken, it is first necessary to figure out what really ails the program. If it is purely a matter of selfish reactionary obstruction, we who want to rehouse slum-dwellers will just have to go on fighting until we win. But if there are inner weaknesses as well, it is high time we faced up to them.

Is the Real Estate Lobby to Blame?

Unquestionably private builders, lenders and property owners have been increasing in political power ever since the mid-thirties, when Uncle Sam rescued them from ruin. And it is equally obvious that they have been all-out in their opposition to public housing.

In general, however, their tactics have been so arrogant, and most of their claims so wild, that they have often tended to backfire. In recent years, moreover, some of the National Association of Real Estate Boards' allies (notably the National Association of Home Builders) have become more sophisticated about the slum problem, and highly vocal about the need to remedy it. The current slogans are "renewal" and "rehabilitation." But gradually it becomes clearer that Operation Fix-Up is no cure-all, and that outright clearance and redevelopment bring relocation problems that cannot be glossed over. The great national spread of antislum propaganda by ACTION (The American Council to Improve Our Neighborhoods) probably tends to favor the cause of public housing, however inadvertently.

The most serious effect of all the controversy has been more subtle. Public housing officials, federal and local, have been kept continuously on the defensive, and the neuroses that come from chronic fright and insecurity are translated into excessive caution, administrative rigidity and lack of creative initiative. Everybody tends to sit tight, clinging desperately to the beleaguered formula, instead of trying to improve it in the light of experience and public attitudes. Sporadic efforts to broaden or modify the program have usually met with as much opposition from professional public housers as from opponents of public housing. Moreover, the hostility has probably tightened management controls, making "project" housing more and more institutional.

But even so, despite the millions they have spent in a vain effort to kill it, the real estate interests can hardly be held wholly responsible for the program's failure to take hold.

Solid Support is Lacking

If the public housing program in its present form had managed to achieve real popularity with the general run of ordinary citizens and their leaders, and above all with the people who live in slum and blighted areas, the real estate opposition would by now have lost its political force. The idea of public housing would be taken for granted, like old-age pensions or FHA mortgage insurance.

But this has not happened. The program has never called forth the kind of pervasive and persuasive popular support that oils the wheels of change in democratic countries. The lot of public housing tenants has undoubtedly been improved in many ways. But the fact remains that only a small proportion of the people eligible for occupancy (by legal definition, low-income families living in substandard homes) actually apply for low-rent dwellings in public housing projects. And of those who do, most appear to be desperate for shelter of any kind: minority families about to be thrown on the street by clearance operations, "problem" families sent by welfare agencies, and so on.

Moreover, general local support by civic-minded groups, such as one might reasonably have expected for such a program, has seldom developed. The US Housing Act has been kept alive by the earnest annual efforts of the Washington offices of national labor, welfare, veteran, municipal, civic and religious organizations, held together by the National Housing Conference and sparked by the genius and devotion of its executive vice president, Lee Johnson. But despite considerable prodding, the local branches and members of these organizations have on the whole been apathetic, sometimes lending their names in a crisis but rarely showing much continuing interest. Where there are established citizens' housing organizations, they tend to be kept going by a few devoted individuals with little general backing.

Why Isn't the Program Popular?

This question has never been seriously investigated, but in general terms, the answer seems quite clear. Life in the usual public housing project just is not the way most American families want to live. Nor does it reflect our accepted values as to the way people should live.

In part the weaknesses are inherent in the physical design. As Architect Henry Whitney said in the first (and still one of the best) critiques by an experienced housing official: "The typical publicly subsidized dwelling is deficient in interior space, in outdoor privacy, and in true American residential character. . . . Families with children generally want to live in individual homes. . . . A yard, a porch or a terrace is almost universally desired." While everybody who had any choice was moving into a one-story home, the housing authorities were busily erecting high-density high-rise apartments, with no private outdoor space whatever. Significantly, perhaps, public housing is most accepted in the one American city where apartment living is also most taken for granted—New York. But even there, opinion surveys show that most tenants would prefer ground-level living if they could get it.

There are also more social reasons for the lack of enthusiastic acceptance. Public housing projects tend to be very large and highly standardized in their design. Visually they may be no more monotonous than a typical suburban tract, but their density makes them seem much more institutional, like veterans' hospitals or old-fashioned orphan asylums. The fact that they are usually designed as islands—"community units" turning their backs to the surrounding neighborhood which looks entirely different—only adds to this institutional quality. Any charity stigma that attaches to subsidized housing is thus reinforced. Each project proclaims, visually, that it serves the "lowest income group."

The resulting degree of rigid social segregation is difficult to align with traditional American ideas. And in addition, if a tenant manages to increase his income beyond a certain point, out he goes, a restriction which also results in the continuous loss of natural leadership among the tenants themselves, and a trend toward problem families as the permanent core of occupants.

On the other side of the ledger has been the considerable success of nondiscrimination and mixed racial occupancy in northern public housing projects. But even this great gain is being lost. Owing to the preponderance of minority families in the lowest income group, and in the areas slated for clearance and relocation, the proportion of minority occupancy tends to rise above the line where mixture is successful, and more and more projects become virtually all-Negro.

And finally, there is the question of management policy and practice in itself. Because of legal requirements, high densities, problem families and sensitivity to continuous political attack, local authority landlordship tends to be rigid and heavy-handed, with all kinds of rules and regulations unknown in ordinary private rental management and unthinkable in a pattern of individual ownership. Sometimes special welfare services are provided which, under these peculiar conditions, may be admirable and necessary. But even at its best, this type of concern by one's landlord seems paternalistic in American terms, and hardly adds to the popularity of project living for normal families.

These are the issues that keep coming up in critical analyses by housers, in conversations with all kinds of people all over the country, and in the few random studies by social scientists. And alongside these criticisms is the patent fact that, with all its drawbacks, the program is so expensive. I doubt that the fact of subsidy in itself is very important in the general public reaction, or in any stigma that may attach to public housing occupancy at present. With all their profound and well-justified faith in private enterprise, Americans have never been purists in the matter of accepting public aid where necessary to achieve something they want. The idea of subsidy is part of the American system, whether for shipping or public education, irrigation projects, redevelopment schemes or housing. Had we not enjoyed a steadily rising market, the FHA-VA system of mortgage aid would have cost the taxpayers far more than the most tremendous public housing program ever envisioned. And certainly no stigma attached to accepting the costly aid of HOLC.* But subsidies must look reasonably sensible in terms of value received. And the fact that high-rise apartments (which no one likes very much anyway), erected by local housing authorities, tend to cost more than the price of a modest FHA-insured tract house, even allowing for a substantial speculative profit, just does not look sensible on the face of it. So the unattractive aspects of the program cannot even be justified on the grounds of economy.

And finally, with all the hullabaloo and all the expense, the program still does not meet even the most obvious immediate need of families dis-

---

* Home Owners Loan Corporation; a federal agency of the 1930's which granted long-term, low-interest loans to home owners threatened with mortgage foreclosures.

placed by clearance or renewal operations, let alone the need in outlying areas for families whom FHA cannot serve. The legal income limits are so low and the other limitations so rigorous, including the territorial jurisdiction of municipal housing authorities, that only a small portion of the need can be met through public housing aid.

Premises: True or False?

How do the assumptions that shaped the public housing program stand up today under quite different economic conditions and in the light of more than twenty years of experience?

Clearly the basic premises are as sound today as they were then. Even after a long period of high prosperity, there are just about as many insanitary, congested and dilapidated homes in the U.S. as there were in the middle of the depression—probably with more people living in them! And today almost everyone recognizes their existence, and admits that these conditions must somehow be remedied. It is also as true as ever (if more reluctantly recognized) that you cannot get rid of slums just by tearing them down, or fixing them up. Somewhere, in reasonably suitable location, there must be better homes available to the slum occupants, at prices they can afford to pay. And although prosperity, FHA, VA and more efficient homebuilding techniques have expanded the effective market for new private housing, it is still true that practically no slum dwellers can afford new, privately built homes, and the few who can are often minority families who would not be accepted. There is some "filtering up," now that the postwar shortage at middle and upper price levels has been relieved. And if there were no vast backlog of outright slums, and little or no urban growth, and no racial discrimination, than a strong program of enforcement and rehabilitation might actually do the job of housing low-income families adequately. But the situation is far different. Millions of existing slum dwellings should be torn down as soon as possible; millions of additional low-income families are certain to migrate to urban centers (a large proportion of them Negroes). And in the light of this, how can filtration possibly be expected to solve the slum problem, now or in a thousand years! Even a slight stepping-up of the process, if it is not merely to produce a lot of new slums by stuffing several families into a dwelling intended for one, would mean a rate of devaluating decent older property that would disrupt the real estate market more than any amount of public housing. FHA financing, also, is geared to steady or rising values for the life of the house, not a reduction in monthly payments that would permit it to "filter down," however gradually.

Apparently it is still as true as it ever was that we need some new housing within reach of families now outside the effective private market. Prosperity only makes the continuance of slum living conditions less excusable, the need for effective solutions more urgent. And the rising significance of the racial aspects of the housing problem adds to the urgency. So does the relocation problem growing from the desire to revitalize central blighted areas and from the tremendous displacement of homes for freeways and other public works.

The basic problem we tried to tackle in the US Housing Act is still with us. What was wrong with our efforts to solve it?

In the light of 1957 conditions, it now seems there were two fundamental fallacies in the original approach, one a matter of basic policy formulation and administration, the other a matter of physical planning and design. The 1937 approach was natural, valid and even necessary at the time, and it represented progress in relation to what had gone before. But it jelled too soon, became too rigid, without allowing for flexible adaptation to American values and conditions.

Two-Headed Housing Policy

The most questionable assumption was the notion that slum rehousing should be established permanently as an independent program, with its own separate legislation and administrative machinery at both federal and local levels, quite apart from other housing policies and the over-all housing picture. This insured the segregation of the low-income slum-dweller, and fortified his isolation as a special charity case by permitting only public initiative and public landlordship, with narrow rules of eligibility, for any form of subsidized housing that might be needed. This also contributed to the segregation of upper-income families in FHA schemes, and to that lily-white suburbia that now presents such a critical problem. And it is just as much public housing's responsibility as the National Association of Home Builders that there is such a vast gap between the two narrow, entirely separate types of federal housing policy, with no real responsibility at any level of government to determine over-all housing needs—whether on a national basis or for any given community—and to see that policies are adjusted to meet those needs.

This came about because federal housing aids were all initiated on an *ad hoc* emergency basis during the depression, with little thought for long-term needs or goals. But depression-mindedness continued too long: it was a fallacious element in much postwar planning, particularly housing. Vested interests grew up and were institutionalized around each separate fragmentary program, with the result that all three major groups

—lenders, builders and public housers—have been about equally opposed to the kind of coordination that would permit more flexibility and realism in meeting the full range of local needs.

Similarly, while the early crusade on behalf of local initiative and responsibility was fine, and the establishment of local housing authorities (or something of the kind) was a necessary step, their permanent role should never have been defined and jelled so narrowly. We now have a proliferation of special-purpose local agencies concerned with slums and housing, with no responsibility anywhere to view the housing picture as a whole, least of all at the metropolitan level where this is most essential. The result is a few expensive, high-density, overcontrolled municipal projects, mostly on central sites, and a vast chaotic flood of middle-class individual homes in the suburbs. With all our complicated housing machinery we cannot solve either the relocation problem in central areas or the equally urgent problem of balanced development out on the fringe.

Viewed in retrospect, it would have been worth-while, for the sake of better integrated, more flexible tools, to make some real concessions. Not the principle of subsidy, for this is absolutely essential to any solution of the slum problem. But if necessary, public landlordship might have been given up and in any case it should have been possible to subsidize various forms of private housing enterprise, including suburban tracts for individual ownership, in order to meet a wider range of need and popular desire (and, incidentally, to bring some private building interests over to advocacy of public housing).

Misapplied "Community Planning"

Having established machinery that could only produce a type of residential development quite alien to any American ideal of community, we then proceeded to dramatize this extreme form of paternalistic class-segregation architecturally, in the name of "modern community planning."

The basic ideas that stemmed from the British garden city planners, and were rationalized by the Bauhaus school of modern architects, contributed vital concepts to American housing. The reaction against chaotic individualism and the wasteful crudity of the ubiquitous gridiron street pattern was long overdue. But in grasping for modern principles of large-scale community design, we embraced too wholeheartedly functionalist and collectivist architectural theories that tended to ignore certain subtler esthetic values and basic social needs. To experiment in this direction was healthy and necessary. The mistake, again, was to jell both policy and practice in rigid formulas that prevented further experimentation to adapt and humanize these principles in suitable terms for the American scene.

The public housing project therefore continues to be laid out as a "community unit," as large as possible and entirely divorced from its neighborhood surroundings, even though this only dramatizes the segregation of charity-case families. Standardization is emphasized rather than alleviated in project design, as a glorification of efficient production methods and an expression of the goal of "decent, safe and sanitary" housing for all. But the bleak symbols of productive efficiency and "minimum standards" are hardly an adequate or satisfactory expression of the values associated with American home life. And all this is, in addition, often embodied in the skyscraper, whose refined technology gladdens the hearts of technocratic architectural sculptors but pushes its occupants into a highly organized, beehive type of community life for which most American families have no desire and little aptitude.

There is no room in such schemes for individual deviation, for personal initiative and responsibility, for outdoor freedom and privacy, for the type of small-scale business enterprise that plays such as an important social role in most slum areas. Management domination is built in, a necessary corollary of architectural form.

How to Reform the Reformers?

A fresh start is badly needed to bring this frustrated effort to effective maturity. And the time may at last be ripe. Until recently there were only a few lonely critics within the ranks of the "housers" themselves. But now some local housing authorities are beginning to question the old formulas. The big push for redevelopment and renewal has also performed an important service in forcing all kinds of civic groups and agencies, including real estate interests and local housing authorities, to face up to hitherto insoluable problems and get together to find solutions. In some areas local and metropolitan planning agencies are beginning to assume some responsibility for determining over-all housing needs, and for fitting the bits and pieces of federal aid and private and public initiative together. In several cities, the mayors have appointed housing coordinators for this purpose. And alongside central redevelopment, a new issue is just coming over the horizon officially in fast-growing regions such as California; how to encourage better balanced communities with a wider variety of homes in the fringe areas, to meet the needs of the lower-income and minority families who are more and more likely to find their employment in outlying plants and offices.

All this broader-based civic effort and sharper awareness tends to make the weaknesses in narrow, overcompartmentalized federal housing policy more apparent. Sooner or later there will be a grass-roots demand for greater flexibility and better coordination, strong enough to overcome the special-interest lobbies, each trying to maintain its own little preserve. And this is the only effective and healthy way to bring about the necessary changes. For it is only when cities and metropolitan areas know what they need and want in terms of federal housing aid that greater flexibility will be justified.

It is not a matter of substituting a new legal-administrative formula for the old one. Under certain conditions the old formula is still the best answer, perhaps the only possible solution. But what is primarily needed, not only for the low-income slum dwellers and minority groups but for the great mass of middle-income families in all their infinite variety of taste and need, is more choice in location, dwelling type and neighborhood character. The kind of home best suited to a given American family can never be decided by officials. Their highest responsibility, rather, is to make sure that public policies keep the "effective market" broad enough to provide some real selection at all economic and social levels.

Freedom and flexibility are probably the hardest things to achieve with public policy. But a country that can devise the insured mortgage (in all its different forms), Fannie May, the modernization loan, the annual contribution, the local authority bond, redevelopment and renewal grants, and ingenious methods for local governments to contribute their share, should certainly be able to find some way to make these excellent tools work more freely and more effectively.

50. *Human Relations and Urban Renewal*

COLEMAN WOODBURY

During the late 1930's, many persons active in urban life and affairs became concerned over the physical blight and deterioration in many parts, particularly the older and more congested residential districts, of American cities. Many of these were persons other than those who, in the preceding years, had been active in public housing. The two groups overlapped, but not very much. The reasons for their interest in this rather melancholy subject were many and varied. I shall discuss them

Reprinted from *The City in Mid-Century,* H. Warren Dunham, ed. (Detroit: Wayne University Press, 1957), pp. 115–27 by permission of the publisher. Mr. Woodbury is a professor of political science at the University of Wisconsin.

briefly a little later. To a considerable degree, however, they shared a common background in the general mood of self-criticism that came with the Great Depression, in the recognized need for new enterprises and outlets for labor and materials, and in the breaking down of traditional taboos as to the proper objectives and methods of public activity. Someone said, with not very much exaggeration, that during the 1920's many prominent citizens liked to boast that "there are no slums in our town," but in the '30's the same persons or their counterparts vied with one another in describing the extent and seriousness of blight in their localities.

This general concern was based partly upon surveys, studies and analyses, some of them rather crude and elementary, made by housers, city planners, sociologists and others. (Many of them, incidentally, were made possible by the W.P.A.) These persons, aided and abetted by civic leaders whose outlook took in both sides of the tracks, local officials, and by religious spokesmen, newspaper editors, labor and business leaders, settlement house directors, and others, also succeeded in making their unpleasant findings, as well as their proposals for action, the subject of considerable public discussion. Sometime soon, someone ought to put together a clear, objective but sensitive account of these efforts and campaigns. For our purposes, however, four or five characteristics of most of these early studies and of the proposals based upon them are pertinent.

First, their focus was largely upon physical conditions of buildings and of neighborhoods or districts. This was not because those who did the work did not care about the human discomfort and misery that went with physical blight and substandardness. Many of them cared deeply. But many of them were temperamentally suspicious of what they considered emotional do-goodism. They believed, rather naively, that if ways and means could be found for wiping out blighted areas and for replacing substandard buildings with good ones, many of the human ills would disappear and other, unidentified people could attack those that remained with brighter prospects of success.

Another characteristic of these early studies and policy proposals is a corollary of the first one: they saw little or no part to be played by the residents of the blighted areas. Often this possibility was not even alluded to, let alone explored. Sometimes it was dismissed in passing with some comment to the effect that those who lived in such areas were disorganized socially and incapable of helping themselves in such matters as their physical environment.

Although physical conditions were the principal object of attention another dimension of the problem was recognized: a narrowly economic one. Asking prices for property in most blighted areas were high—so high as to discourage rebuilding. Besides, reclamation in these areas could not proceed ordinarily on a lot-by-lot basis. Large-scale operations were needed. Sizeable areas, sufficiently large to establish their own character and to resist the effects of surrounding blight, would have to be acquired, cleared, and rebuilt as units. Thus, to the obstacle of high land prices were added the difficulties of land assembly, notably the danger that some owners of key parcels would hold out for exorbitant prices. Clearly, two things were needed: a grant of eminent domain to some agency to aid it in land assembly and some formula whereby the costs of land could be reduced or written down to the redeveloper.

Finally, a fourth feature of these first studies was their static quality. They were snapshots of existing conditions. To be sure, differences in the degrees and kinds of blight were recognized and, in general, the growth of blighted areas was pointed out as one of the inducements to action. But very little attention was given to the *process* of blighting. The assumption seemed to be that only after blight reached a certain stage was it a matter of public concern. Of course, there was some dissent from this. A few public health officers and here and there some student of housing would point out that, after all, cities had certain police powers that might be useful in a broader attack on blight. The prevailing opinion, however, was that these measures had failed to prevent widespread blight and, although they ought to be improved in content and in administration, not much could be expected of them in the anti-blight campaigns of the future.

This is a rough sketch of the conception of urban redevelopment in its early, *i.e.*, pre-World War II days. Essentially it was seen as an attack on physical blight and deterioration. The method was clear: buy up the properties in blighted areas; clear them; if necessary, lay out new streets, parks and other public spaces; write down the acquisition price to encourage new building; sell the land to a redeveloper (or redevelopers) on condition that he (or they) go ahead with the new construction. It was agreed that the write-down of land prices would have to be at public expense. Some persons thought that the land acquisition also should be by a public agency; others favored private agencies that would be given the power of eminent domain under certain safeguards.

The case for public concern, powers and expenditures in such activity was also quite clear. It would improve the physical plant of the community. It would provide new opportunities for builders and developers and more jobs for labor. It would halt and maybe even reverse the outward movement of various groups and classes from the older urban centers, particularly from the central areas of sizeable metropolitan

cities. It would alleviate the financial difficulties of these cities by adding
to their assessment rolls.

Obviously in all this, little heed was paid to human relations in the
usual sense of that term. Many of the early proponents of urban
redevelopment hoped or expected that, directly or indirectly, it would
result in bettering the conditions of human life in cities. A few even
thought that part of that betterment would take the form of encouraging
healthier social intercourse in the rebuilt areas. By and large, however,
all aspects of the matter were defined, analyzed, and proposed in fairly
technical terms—the terms of physical buildings and conditions, of
institutional operations, of business and finance.

Although this initial conception of urban redevelopment has been
modified and enlarged, it is still fairly central to the whole program and
justifies the time I have given to it. . . .

During World War II, of course, no redevelopment could be initiated
and, until near the end of it, relatively little additional thought and
discussion were given to the subject. Then and during the first few
post war years, the arguments were resumed and even a few projects
were planned and undertaken with state aid. The net gain of these years
may be fairly well summarized by looking at a few sections of the federal
housing act of 1949, which included the first provisions for federal aid
to local redevelopment—largely loans and financial aid to the write-down
of high land prices in blighted areas to be cleared and rebuilt.

At least five features of this act deserve our attention. It clearly
recognized different kinds and degrees of blight, including what are
often called "arrested subdivisions," i.e., predominantly open areas in
which normal development has been held back by poor land platting,
bad titles, inadequate public facilities, etc. Rather indirectly it sought to
strengthen local police power codes and ordinances based on standards
of health, sanitation and safety in housing. It limited its financial aid for
land acquisition to local public agencies. It emphasized the importance
of city and regional planning in determining the re-use of blighted areas.
Finally, it faced up to the question of what was to become of the
families displaced by clearance-and-rebuilding operations. In the language of the act (Sec. 105):

Contracts for financial aid . . . shall require that . . . (c) there be a feasible
method for the temporary relocation of families displaced from the project
area, and that there are, or are being provided, in the project area or in
other areas not generally less desirable in regard to public utilities and
public and commercial facilities and at rents or prices within the financial

means of families displaced from the project area, decent, safe, and sanitary dwellings equal in number to the number of and available to such displaced families and reasonably accessible to their places of employment. . . .

It is a matter of record that prominent among those who proposed and backed a provision to this effect were the housing spokesmen of national labor organizations.

For our consideration, this relocation provision is significant. It was one of the first clear, official recognitions that human beings and families were directly affected by redevelopment, and that what happened to displaced families was an important matter to redevelopment agencies and, presumably, to the communities they served. Although this was a notable counter-balance to the heavy emphasis on the physical and financial sides of redevelopment, we should not read into this provision more than is there. In respect to the social problems of large scale clearance, which I will take up a little later, it is really a quite limited statement.

About the time of the passage of the housing act of 1949 and immediately thereafter, a noteworthy change took place in the approach of some of the more thoughtful students and administrators of redevelopment programs. The old dichotomy of blighted versus good urban areas was seen to be an overly simplified and essentially a stultifying breakdown. As a matter of fact, nearly every sizable urban center has areas or sections that ranged all the way from well-located, well-designed, well-built and well-maintained districts to rockbottom slums—residential, industrial, commercial, and mixed. Instead of categories of black and white there was a spectrum or a finely graduated continuum. Clearly, also, mose districts were changing their relative positions in this array— some rapidly, some slowly. From these observations, it was a short step to identifying a *process* of blighting, a sequence or rather a number of sequences through which most districts were moving from levels of acceptableness (or better) toward obsolescence, deterioration, and substandardness. With rather rare exceptions, the shift with increasing age was downward. For various purposes one might draw a line and say, in effect, everything below this is blighted. But fundamentally where such a line was drawn was of less significance than the fact of the continuum and the process of blighting that was going on.

Now, of course, these were not startlingly new discoveries nor towering achievements of the human intellect. They were, after all, relatively simple notions. They had been foreshadowed in much of the earlier study and discussions. But as they took definite shape and clarity, they had practical consequences of considerable importance. Several questions were then in order: What is this process of blighting? What factors lie behind it and contribute to it? Why should intelligent citizens, private organizations, and public agencies stand more or less idly by until it reaches an acute stage in an area before trying to attack it? Why not go after it early in its cycle, try to stop it or, at least, try to slow down its rate of progress? If these be feasible objectives, what tools, powers, and procedures are needed to accomplish them?

Thinking and questioning of this kind produced quite a furor among urban redevelopers, their allies, brain trusters, and hangers-on. It would take more than all my time this evening to trace out the arguments and counter-arguments and to try to unravel the disputes that resulted. Although the terminology became rather confused and some extreme positions were taken, I think it is fair to say (again, with considerable over-simplification) that the outcome has been the recognition of three principal types of urban areas, each needing certain forms of treatment: conservation areas, rehabilitation areas, and clearance-and-rebuilding areas.

Conservation areas typically are well built up, middle-aged, and basically good or, at least, satisfactory districts. They often do show, however, certain signs of incipient blight or deterioration: perhaps here and there a rundown poorly maintained building, or a shortage of open space or play area, or a spill-over of all day parking or through traffic onto minor streets, or a few over-crowded houses or apartments, or unwise or even illegal conversions of large, old houses, or a decline in neighborhood feeling and pride, or obsolete school buildings, etc. The basic problems these areas present are how to maintain or to conserve their basically good features and how to correct the relatively few deficiencies before they become widespread or acute.

Rehabilitation areas are usually well built up but are, on the whole, rather older than conservation areas and show many more pronounced signs of substandardness and deterioration. They are unmistakably threatened with blight or are well advanced in the process. Their problems are to halt the spread of substandardness before it is too late, to enforce all legal standards of repair, maintenance, and occupancy over the whole area, to rally the forces of neighborhood self-respect to bring about widespread property improvement, to plan and carry through a comprehensive, integrated program of public improvements and facilities that will underpin and encourage all other efforts at betterment.

Clearance-and-rebuilding areas are at the bottom of the scale or continuum. Property, environmental, and community deficiencies are the rule, not the exception. They are so bad and so widespread that the only feasible remedy is major surgery—to clear them out and rebuild.

Two additional comments are essential to a proper understanding of this classification of areas. One, the dividing lines between the classes are not sharp and definite. Often they are not lines but bands of considerable width. The three classes do not negate the basic conception of the continuum; they simply subdivide it, more or less arbitrarily, for purposes of explanation, analysis, and treatment. The other, although it would be possible with techniques now available to subdivide a city's land area into these three classes, in fact, this has been done for some localities, the pattern in some districts would be rather complex, *e.g.,* here two or more patches of conservation area, there a larger, irregularly shaped area for rehabilitation largely surrounded by or cut through by strips that clearly need clearance and rebuilding. Thus, when one faces the practical task of planning redevelopment for a sizeable area or sector of a city, particularly an older district, more often than not he will have to apply not the indicated remedies of conservation or rehabilitation or of clearance and rebuilding, but some combination or mix of two or all of them.

Are we getting too far into the intricacies of redevelopment theory and practice and too far away from the subject? I think not. This broadening the scope of redevelopment that I have just sketched has two implications of first-rate import for almost any discussion of human relations in this field. It marks a relative decline in the importance of the earlier conception of the nature of redevelopment. *Urban redevelopment* now becomes the generic term for a wide range of activities with the common objective of doing away with urban blight. What was previously considered to be all or nearly all of redevelopment, namely, the clearance and rebuilding of badly blighted areas, has now become one of three major subdivisions of the whole. More important, it is impossible to describe adequately this broadened conception and particularly the types of treatment appropriate to conservation and rehabilitation areas without using phrases that go far beyond the earlier terminology of physical building, land prices, and finance. And note that these added terms are those of social or human relations—neighborhood feeling and pride, the forces of neighborhood self-respect, environmental and community deficiencies.

The present charter for federal aids to urban redevelopment, title III of the federal housing act of 1954, incorporates many of the changes in conception and approach that I have just outlined. It adds relatively little that is basically fresh or new. Mostly it is concerned with revisions based on experience under the act of 1949 and with broadening the scope of federal aid to include additional assistance to repair and remodeling as well as to new building in rehabilitation areas. Much of this is rather technical material that need not concern us here. At least two features of this act, however, do deserve our notice.

The first is a change in terminology that is simple but has made for some confusion. A new term, *urban renewal,* is used as the generic term for roughly the scope of anti-blight activity that I have just tried to point out as the later meaning of urban redevelopment. Thus, instead of urban redevelopment with three major subdivisions—conservation, rehabilitation, and clearance-and-rebuilding operations—the new language makes urban renewal the inclusive term, and its three principal subdivisions are conservation, rehabilitation, and urban redevelopment. In my opinion, the new phrase, urban renewal, is a doubtful improvement, but inasmuch as most local programs are making use of federal aids or intend to do so, it seems likely in time to become the prevailing usage.

The other feature of the act of 1954 is more significant for our discussion. It is the requirement that as a condition of federal aid, each locality must submit and obtain approval by the administrator of the Housing and Home Finance Agency of a " . . . workable program . . . for utilizing appropriate private and public resources to eliminate, and prevent the development or spread of, slums and urban blight, to encourage needed urban rehabilitation, to provide for the redevelopment of blighted, deteriorated or slum areas, or to undertake such of the aforesaid activities or other feasible community activities as may be suitably employed to achieve the objectives of such a program. . . ." (Sec. 303, c.) After much discussion and some argument, this general notion of a workable progam has been broken down (or, perhaps, built up) by administrative interpretation into seven chief components: (1) codes and ordinances establishing reasonable building and housing standards, (2) a comprehensive community plan, (3) neighborhood analyses of the extent, intensity and causes of blight, (4) administrative organization capable of effective enforcement of codes and ordinances and of carrying through other proposed renewal activities, (5) financing—evidence that local public agencies understand their financial obligations for the proposed activities and can meet them, (6) housing for displaced families, and (7) citizen participation.

In the official explanation of citizen participation the emphasis is heavily on providing "the understanding and support which is necessary to insure success" of the proposed activities of urban renewal. Nevertheless, both locality-wide and neighborhood organizations are suggested and the point is made that "widespread participation should be sought at the time planning of urban renewal activities is initiated, and should continue throughout the execution of each project." To be sure, no intelligent person should be astonished to learn that many localities show a considerable divergence between language in an official pamphlet, even with its limitations, and what actually is going on. But starts are being made; methods and devices are being tried out; competent people are learning from the experiments and the mistakes of themselves and of others.

Enough, possibly more than enough, on this review of the evolving concept and programs of urban redevelopment. I hope what I have said may give some content and meaning to two principal characteristics of this evolution: the broadening scope of both the conception of the job to be done and of the programs—public, private and collaborative—that are being formulated and started in urban centers throughout the country; and the slowly growing appreciation of two related facts. Human beings live in and human groups and associations of many kinds have their existence in blighted and blighting areas. In a basically democratic society, the two-way relations between persons and their groups, on the one hand, and redevelopment programs and activities, on the other, are of vital importance both in shaping and in realizing the objectives of urban redevelopment. . . .

I shall next identify and try to define three of the principal problems of human relations in planning and administering redevelopment programs. On them I have no neat and packaged solutions. If, however, we can agree on their essential nature, then various means for alleviating them or avoiding their unfortunate consequences may be considered and tried out.

The first of these problems is how to minimize the disruption of social life—family, group, and institutional—in redevelopment areas. *Minimize* is, I think, the proper word; clearly the kind of redevelopment required in many districts unavoidably will be more or less disruptive. The questions are how to make it less rather than more and how to help those directly hit to make the necessary changes and adjustments as smoothly and painlessly as possible.

Clearly, one step should be to push ahead as rapidly and vigorously as possible with conservation and rehabilitation programs that will reduce the volume of large scale clearance-and-rebuilding over any substantial period of time. This, of course, won't affect the very large backlog of existing slums and badly blighted areas that need nothing less than drastic surgery. And I hope no one will think that I am suggesting superficial fix-up and paint-up compaigns for areas that are basically substandard and thoroughly rotton. Nevertheless, two long-term objectives should be to reduce the number and size of areas needing clearance and, equally important, to undertake necessary clearance relatively early when it can be done successfully on a smaller scale than when the blighting process in a large area has run its course almost completely.

Probably the most basic remedy is to prepare redevelopment and renewal plans well in advance, to bring into the planning process, as far as possible, representatives of the areas affected, and to give adequate time for discussion of major proposals as well as for the preparation (planning, if you wish) for adjustments that will have to be made by families, clubs, small businessmen, churches, etc. On this crucial point, another common view is that of what might be called the ducks-in-a-row school of thought. Essentially it amounts to this: make your plans as quietly as possible for the area to be cleared; get firm understandings from city departments, the federal agency, and prospective re-developers; prepare the way with key officials and "citizen leaders"—those prominent persons who ordinarily speak up for publication on such matters; then announce the plan, turn on the public relations campaign, hurry through the public hearings and other procedural steps as rapidly as possible. Of course, there are many variations on this theme. It raises many questions outside our present subject. Thanks to some hard experience and the workable program requirements, it does not command as wide assent as it once did among redevelopment officials and prospective redevelopers, but it still has advocates. Even when it cannot be applied *in toto* it can and does influence what is done in local programs and how it is done.

For the purposes of our discussion, the contrast of these two approaches seems to me significant. Certainly for the individuals and groups directly affected in an area the difference is sharp and extreme.

In one case, they are suddenly confronted by a proposal that would force them into rapid, drastic, and unanticipated changes. It is a proposal that they have had no part, direct or indirect, in shaping—apparently because those who made it, including certain public officials, didn't think they were worth consulting. It is backed by public powers, and the indications are that it is to be pushed through. To be sure, the press release says that fair value will be paid for properties taken and that families who wish to apply to a relocation office will be given help in finding another place to live. To these intended assurances, a common response is—so what? What will the money value of old, deteriorated properties buy elsewhere? What good is help in moving when one doesn't know where he wants to go? Besides, why should a lot of little people be torn up by the roots and shoved around so that a few big builders can make some more money? Why should local officials, presumably paid, in part at least, from everyone's taxes, be taking part in this kind of scheme? Yes, the retired president of the First National Bank says this project will be a great milestone in the growth of the city, but what does he know about it? Maybe it looks that way from his downtown office or suburban estate, but it doesn't from here.

To be sure, this isn't the only kind of response, but it is a common— all too common—one.

I won't take the time to sketch out what I think would be the usual reaction to the other approach. Certainly it won't remove all hardship or forestall all opposition. Experience has shown, however, that it does make a difference in both. And, in the absence of careful comparative studies, it seems reasonable to suggest that the two methods would have substantially different effects on class and group animosity, on attitudes toward other local public affairs and agencies, on the reception that the displaced families receive when they move, and on the ease with which they find a place in the life of other neighborhoods or local communities.

The second problem can be put bluntly in this way: In earlier parts of this talk I have made several references to the desirability of broader or neighborhood or community participation in planning and carrying through redevelopment programs. Just what does this mean? Is it more than a pious wish or a rhetorical flourish? If so, how can it be brought about? Take, for example, a man or woman living in a slum or blighted area, limited in formal education, with no training at all in questions of city growth and development, burdened with the cares of raising a family on a small income. How can such a man or woman take part in urban redevelopment?

These are fair and important questions. I can't answer them in every detail, but I hope I can make a fair start toward answers.

First, I do not suggest that this form of participation be limited to any one class or kind of district or neighborhood. Urban redevelopment concerns almost all urban citizens in one way or another. Neither do I believe that all citizens in all neighborhoods can or will or should participate in the same way or in the same degree. The general character and level of participation will vary considerably from area to area. Very seldom will their part be in any sense technical. Much of it will be indirect—through representatives and committees to whom, however, the citizen has ready, uninhibited access and in whose members he ordinarily has confidence. These representatives would work with the technically trained planners—the staff members of planning departments and redevelopment agencies. Part of their training must be in the art of human relations. Finally, I don't look forward to the flower of citizen participation coming to full bloom over night. It will require care, nurturing, and time.

This seems to me also a problem on which the kind of organization or machinery is crucial to satisfactory results. In some cities, Philadelphia for example, the official planning agency has been experimenting with community organizations set up primarily for planning and redevelopment purposes. In others, Cleveland and Kansas City are examples, planning and redevelopment officials are working with and through existing community organizations with much broader aims. Although quite surely more than one pattern will be found satisfactory, this seems to me a wise move in most circumstances. Redevelopment in most localities is bound to move rather slowly. Often it will be hard if not impossible to keep alive a special organization because concrete results will take time, if for no other reason than the greater need of other areas. If the agency or neighborhood organization is broader, achievements, even minor ones on other matters, will help keep interest up until the city's redevelopment program really begins to show results in the particular area.

Although I would not pose as a specialist or expert on community organization, from what I have been told by responsible local officials, I am particularly interested in the Kansas City arrangement. It consists of neighborhood councils for areas corresponding closely to elementary school districts and community councils coinciding in area with high school districts. Each council is served by a community worker, a trained person on the payroll of the city department of welfare, which is *not* a relief agency. The council presidents have an organizations that provides a ready means for comparing ideas, gaining some perspective, and educating local area leaders. Officials in Kansas City have found this set-up a useful two-way communication route—they learn much from the councils and also try to make them see some of the problems of large city planning and administration. The use of public funds, contrary to some people's criticism, has not made the community councils captive organizations. Rather it seems to have given them a feeling of independence and dignity. They are parts of the city-wide governmental organization; city officials recognize their problems, listen to and respect their opinions. Even humble citizens pay taxes, directly or indirectly, and the community workers, therefore, are not their bosses or patrons, but their proper advisors and aides.

Can ordinary lay citizens in these matters make any contribution to planning for and carrying through redevelopment programs? Despite the dogmatically expressed opinions of a minority of planners who suffer from indoctrination in the belief that planning is the prerogative of a small clique, the answer clearly is, yes. Much, although not all of urban planning is concerned with questions of livability, safety for children and adults (indoors and out), space for recreation, lessening congestion, providing more freedom from noise, dirt and general clamor, facilities for retail business, recreation and assembly—all matters on which the non-expert can and often does have ideas and can offer useful criticism. As to carrying through the plans, probably a lively and experienced community organization is the best device yet invented for encouraging conservation and rehabilitation measures by property owners, particularly in maintaining standards above the legally enforceable minima for health and safety. Even on delicate questions of racial and other minorities, such organizations have occasionally lessened tensions and smoothed the way toward mutual respect and more democratic relations.

In my opinion, this is one of the exciting frontiers of urban life. Much, very much, remains to be done on it. Surely our ideas will change and some of our most promising devices may have to be modified or given up. But one thing seems clear to me. The forces of urbanization in this country, with very little help from doctrines or philosophy, have moved city governments more and more into activities that directly affect the conditions of life, physical and social, most urban residents. Redevelopment is one of these activities or, perhaps, a generic term for many of them. In respect to most of these governmental and quasi-governmental programs, the citizen cannot take the part he should, in his own interests and as a citizen of a democratic society, if he has to act solely through the orthodox machinery of government and the usual civic organizations. In forming and expressing his ideas and aspirations in such matters, he must have other means than reading newspapers, voting every two or four years for a mayor and an alderman, and belonging to the Rotary, the Elks or the Sons of Garibaldi. And I hope it is clear that I am not disparaging or denying the importance of newspapers, voting or of existing group organizations.

Maybe local community organizations are one of the devices needed. If not, we must invent, test, and perfect others. The alternative, it seems to me, is growing apathy on urban public affairs, deeper and deeper divisions between classes and groups, and a steeper and steeper path toward attaining even the most modest and unimaginative goals of redevelopment and of other public activities in urban life.

The third problem is closely related. As public action on the structure and functioning of the physical and the social cities increases, so does public responsibility for the results. Very few thoughtful people today believe in laissez-faire in this area of our society. We won't realize the shining city of tomorrow simply by letting realtors, land owners and speculators, builders, architects, mortgage lenders, and promotors make as much money as they can, operating under a minimum of casually enforced rules of the game. As a matter of fact, redevelopment is now engaged in cleaning up, at considerable public expense, the results of earlier sprees of this kind. But redevelopment is a larger and more difficult operation than correcting past mistakes. It requires continuous, thorough and comprehensive planning. But planning implies objectives or goals. For *what* are we planning?

When one asks this question and persists in pressing it, he finds a disturbing weakness. Certainly we want healthful housing, shorter journeys to work, less congestion, more pleasantness, social amenities and beauty in our physical environment. But are these ultimate or near final goals? Don't they depend in some way or other, on more basic values? If this seems likely, what are these values? How can they best be expressed in terms of social organization, the essential nature of man, or something even more fundamental? As matters of practical policy, how can these questions best be raised? By what means can answers most effectively be sought?

Here I believe is the essential poverty of present day urban life— even as represented by devoted workers at city rebuilding. We are spending so much time and energy on repairing the power plant, and improving our skill in navigating, that we have failed to decide where the ship should be going or even in what general direction. Once we have some agreement on that, many other questions will seem less difficult. But we won't approach consensus on this central issue until we raise our eyes from our work benches and begin to ask difficult, delicate and often embarrassing questions.

51. *On Being Urbanized and Motorized*

WILFRED OWEN

Americans have made up their minds to live in metropolitan areas and ride in automobiles. This attempt to be urbanized and motorized at the same time has been less than a complete success. The combination is destroying both the benefits of cities and the advantages of the private car.

Reprinted from *Cities in the Motor Age* (New York: Viking Press, 1959), pp. 3–6, 10–13, 100–113 by permission of the publisher. Mr. Owen is a member of the staff of the Brookings Institution, Washington, D.C.

Cities and their surroundings, designed to bring people together for a better life, are rapidly succumbing to blight and decay. The automobile has fared no better. Designed to get people around quickly and easily, and at reasonable cost, the family car is bogging down in the tangle of an obsolete urban environment.

After fifty years of the automotive age, we are beginning to wonder if cars and crowded highways are really the best possible way to get around. And despite all the centuries that urban concentrations have grown and prospered, we have begun to doubt that the city can survive the automotive age, or even that it should.

The Plight of the Cities

Today much of the population in our older cities is the victim of miserable living conditions by any reasonable standards. Millions of homes are unfit for human habitation. Great areas of the metropolis have become disagreeable to live in or work in, as well as difficult to move around in.

Open space in metropolitan areas is rapidly disappearing. With it have gone the light and air, the natural beauty, and the opportunities for recreation and relaxation that people with adequate incomes and leisure time should be able to enjoy. It begins to look as though the nightmare of megalopolis is really coming true, that someday we will be living amid the brick and mortar of cities a thousand miles long.

For many of us the trip to work and home again is in sharp contrast to other improvements in working conditions. The time it takes to commute has canceled the advantages of shorter hours on the job. It is hard to move and hard to find a place to stop. Transit lines are fighting what appears to be a losing battle, while commuter railroads seem intent on going out of business altogether. The motor vehicle has killed one-third of a million people on urban streets.

The trip from Midway Airport to Chicago's Loop is a good sample of the depth and magnitude of a city's blight. So is the shabbiness of Boston, from the South Station almost as far south as you care to go. Look at Detroit's endless rows of uniform, unimaginative, and boring neighborhoods. Walk through the slums of Brooklyn, Philadelphia, or Baltimore. See how thoroughly Los Angeles has stripped itself of what Southern California had to offer. The big cities that are the biggest sources of America's production and wealth are victims of economic and social deterioration.

Here we are in an age of ever-growing wealth, yet our urban living standards are constantly becoming lower in terms of human values.

Somehow we have failed to apply our wealth to the basic objective of improving our daily lives. With all our productive genius and material possessions, we have been unable to achieve either the conditions of living or the ease of mobility that modern technology should be able to provide.

Flight to the Suburbs

One alternative has been to abandon the city as a place to live, or work, or both. The automobile has made it easy to move away and leave our problems behind. Instead of clearing out the slums, people have been clearing out for the suburbs. In their wake they have left great areas of urban blight, much in the way that earlier generations mined the soil or stripped the forests and pushed on.

But escape from the central city to the fringes has turned out to be no escape at all. In the disorganized retreat made possible by the automobile, we have transported slums to the suburbs. Suburban blight is spreading from the cluttered and unsightly roadsides into once pleasant neighborhoods. The natural beauty of the countryside is being thrown to the bulldozers.

The shape of the slums to come is already delineated on the outskirts. There you can see the disorderly commercial outcroppings along every major highway: the gas stations, the auto dumps, the beer parlors, and the billboards. Life in many suburbs is characterized by the drabness and monotony of mass-produced housing, the disappearance of topsoil and trees, and the absence of public improvements. Because we have been neither assisted nor inhibited by official community plans or adequate zoning, we have met the demand for housing with little concern for the problems of living.

People who have fled to suburbia are beginning to wonder why. They moved out to find more pleasant surroundings, only to be overtaken by thousands of others with the same idea. Their very numbers are depriving them of the life they thought they could find. Thus the suburbs that appeared to offer an answer to the weaknesses of the city have created weaknesses of their own. They are often crowded and disorganized, lacking in public services or adequate play space, monotonous and unattractive. Endless sprawl has made suburbia the negation of the city. The whole process must eventually grind to a halt as those who flee from one disorderly metropolis run head-on into the spreading blight of another.

By 1975 we can expect another fifty million people to be living in metropolitan areas. Twenty million more workers may be added to the morning rush. More people, more jobs, higher incomes, and more leisure time will furnish the ingredients for still greater urban chaos. More than a hundred million motor vehicles will be jockeying for position on the highways.

If these trends are superimposed on today's metropolitan hodge-podge, America will be faced with an absurd paradox. In spite of the world's highest income, the majority of our people may have to endure not only poorer standards of transportation but lower standards of living. The economists' projections of a steady rise in national product may be comforting, but tomorrow's utopias could turn out to be more statistical than real.

Today city and suburb are forging ahead, without adequate plans for their future, toward an inevitable day of reckoning. Many are building for more congestion and blight where the magnitude of the problem has already reached critical proportions. The indiscriminate grab for land has left little time or thought for how to achieve any sort of total community development. Our metropolitan areas reveal few signs of the bold concepts of urban planning and design that are called for by present rates of growth and changing technology. What they do reveal is an almost complete disregard for either natural or man-made beauty. The metropolis has become a jumble of poles and wires, signs and billboards, asphalt and concrete, dust and smog. As one observer puts it, we seem to be hell-bent for Slobovia, Upper as well as Lower. . . .

Problems of the Motor Age

One of the most significant factors affecting America's urban future is the mobility of its people. The automobile and highway have given us a new freedom to live and work and go where we choose. The radius of the city is no longer limited to the distance that can be covered on foot or by streetcar. We are no longer dependent on a central place for working or shopping, or confined to areas easily accessible to a railroad. But the resulting urban sprawl finds us moving on a treadmill. As we attempt at greater cost to increase the speed at which we move, we find we have to go farther and farther to get where we want to go.

Twentieth-century mobility, then, has created a curious paradox. It has enabled a large part of the population to concentrate in cities by furnishing the supply lines that satisfy the appetites of people and industry. In the process, metropolitan districts have become so large and complex that they threaten to strangle the transportation that helped to make them possible.

The biggest effort to cope with the problems of a motorized and urbanized society is the tremendous new federal road program now under way. Altogether, the expenditure of a hundred billion dollars of federal, state, and local funds is probable over the next decade and a half. The most spectacular part of this program will be the construction of a nation-wide system of expressways, approximately six thousand miles of which will be located in urban areas. These urban facilities will absorb approximately half the total outlay for the entire national system.

This is the biggest public-works program in history. It will not only change the faces of the old cities, but will open up vast new areas of rural land for urban settlement. These expressways will become the skeleton of the new metropolis. Their location, and the location of their interchange points, will establish urban patterns for generations to come. They hold out the promise not only of solving critical problems of urban congestion but of setting in motion other related steps that together can help us realize the better urban communities we want.

There is a good deal of evidence, however, that this power of the new highway program to determine the size, shape, content, and looks of urban areas may not be fully understood. In many cases urban expressways are regarded simply as a means of moving traffic. Their role as a basic tool for the restoration of cities and the design of future suburbs is often missed. As a result we may succeed quite admirably in moving ourselves faster through areas of urban decay, only to find that we should rather not be moving through them at all.

In other words, we are in the process of spending tens of billions of dollars for expressways in metropolitan areas with almost no effective effort to decide on the basic outlines of a community blueprint to help guide this investment. How many people will be on the move by the time these roads are built? Where will they be living and working? What density of development are we going to provide for? What kinds of things will be located downtown?

So far the roadbuilders have been left to go it alone. They have had to answer these questions themselves and make decisions that only the community as a whole should be responsible for making. Yet transportation is one of the most potent means to the ends we envision for the urban community. Through lack of simple foresight, we are missing the opportunity of relating the location and design of highways to the design of the community we want.

There is no great difficulty in understanding that better transportation facilities, if they are isolated from other forms of community development, will fail to yield their maximum contribution. But a less obvious point is that transportation facilities alone, without the aid of other aspects of community betterment, are incapable of solving the problems of urban transport.

Evidence of this point lies in the fact that many billions of dollars have already been spent for highways in urban areas with disappointing results. As soon as the additions have been built, their promise of relief has been canceled by the rising numbers of people and vehicles waiting to use them. Even where transit has been highly developed, the greater capacity for movement has promoted a denser development and bigger jams. The difficulties of moving in the metropolis are as great in New York, with its crowded subways, as in Los Angeles with its freeways. Indeed, cities all over the world are struggling with similar problems of urban living and moving, regardless of how they move.

It is now becoming evident that the mechanics of moving people and goods is only part of our problem. We must also provide an urban setting in which transport technology can succeed. The density, arrangement, and planless growth of our cities, together with obsolete government organization, are obstacles that prevent us from solving the problem of movement.

It will take much more than a highway program, then, to adapt our cities to the automobile. It will take still more to adapt urban living to the needs of the human being. A broad program of urban rebuilding will be required to overcome obsolete patterns of urbanization.

Compared to current roadbuilding efforts, however, the magnitude of such redevelopment activities is not impressive. The federal government spends more money on fish breeding and wildlife sanctuaries than it does on conserving human beings through slum clearance. But if, to urban renewal, we add all the home-building and neighborhood developments in the United States, together with the new facilities of industry and commerce, it is apparent that very large forces are being brought to bear on the city and suburb of the future. Actually, our road program over the next decade or two will be dwarfed by expenditures for housing and all the many related community facilities that accompany the construction of homes.

Roads, renewal, housing, industrial developments, and community facilities combined, therefore, will mean a tremendous total effort influencing the course of future urban development. The trouble is that these efforts are actually not combined at all. They are separate and unrelated efforts that will never add up to the great changes in urban living that might be produced by a total strategy of urban development.

The goals of a better urban life, Dean Burchard assures us, are within the skill of planning, just as they are within our economic capabilities. But whether they are within the range of our aspirations is not so certain. He finds it hard to believe that people who listen to the monotonous rhythms of rock-and-roll records while a carhop brings them chicken-in-the-rough and a chocolate malted are not convinced that they already enjoy an abundant life. They would be unlikely to vote for what others considered a better urban environment, even if it were offered. . . .

The Troubles with Transit

The key problem of road versus rail is encountered in the movement of passenger traffic in major cities. Many people hold the view that attempts to accommodate automobiles in densely populated areas are doomed to failure, and that their effect will be to destroy the benefits of urban life.

It is clear that even the current extraordinary roadbuilding effort will fall short of meeting all the transport requirements of the big metropolis in rush hours. Often it seems that the more roads we build the heavier the congestion becomes. By 1975 we may find ourselves with a highway system that can handle more vehicles than ever before, yet one that will be just as overburdened as ever.

The answer to the transportation problems of our densely built-up urban centers does not lie in the private car alone. It is becoming more and more difficult to acquire land for rights of way and parking. Any real effort to make our vertical cities completely accessible by automobile would eliminate much of the downtown development that makes access worth while. In order to preserve the core of the large city, there should be a more balanced attention to all methods of movement—and this means that an adequate public-transit system is essential. Without it the motorist in today's big city may strangle in his own congestion.

Last year nearly nine billion rides were taken on local public carriers. Most riders used buses, but two billion rides were on rapid transit lines, either subways or elevated railways. A lesser and rapidly diminishing number of people still used surface streetcars in some cities commuter railroads played an important role. Many people ride public carriers because they find them the cheapest or most convenient way to get about. Still others are compelled to ride for lack of any other choice. They may be too young to drive themselves, or too old. They may not own a car, either because they prefer not to own one or because they cannot afford it. Some who do own a car may prefer to leave it at home because driving or parking downtown is too much trouble. Others may leave their cars at home for suburban wives who would otherwise be helpless, or would feel that way. The wives may have to shop or serve as chauffeur, or would like to have the comfort of knowing the car is there in case a child needs a doctor.

The question is not whether public transport is necessary, but what kind should be provided and in what way satisfactory standards of service might be assured. Long years of neglect have left many transit facilities in a state of disrepair, and, even where there is modern equipment, the financial burden of transit operations leads frequently to inadequate coverage, poor schedules, and overcrowding. There is a widespread belief that if satisfactory service could somehow be provided, it would be possible to entice more riders into the transit systems and thereby reduce the expressway and parking facilities that would otherwise be necessary to accommodate the increasing number of trips by private automobile. But who is going to pay the cost of providing adequate service? As yet nobody has come forward with a widely accepted answer to this question.

The present troubles with transit have a long historical background. The transit systems of our cities were established by private companies before the auto appeared or at least before its widespread use. They enjoyed a virtual monopoly of the local passenger-transport business. This monopolistic power, together with the companies' aim of earning fat dividends, made public regulatory commissions necessary to protect the public interest. The job of the public-service commissions and other regulatory bodies was to assure reasonable rates and adequate service and to guard against profiteering. Under this system of publicly regulated private monopoly, however, the question always being argued was whether the return on transit investments was adequate or excessive. The importance of satisfactory standards of service was lost sight of in the conflict between public pressure for holding down fares and company interest in pushing up dividends.

When the automobile entered this picture, the monopoly of local transit was broken. The early safeguards established to protect the public now served principally to prevent the abandonment of unprofitable routes and to freeze unremunerative rates. Fares were held to a point that made it impossible to replace obsolete and worn-out equipment. At the same time a variety of burdensome taxes continued to be levied on transit companies despite their financial difficulties. Transit lines were still obliged to perform street repairs along the rights of way they shared with their automotive competitors. The transit industry was expected to subsidize school children by offering them special reduced fares. Under these circumstances it became increasingly difficult to finance standards of service sufficiently attractive to retain riders who had the alternative of driving themselves.

The long period of depressed transit rates and deferred modernization came to an end soon after World War II, when sharply rising costs made it compellingly clear that fares would have to be adjusted to the postwar value of the dollar. By that time, however, the combination of a tremendous increase in automobile ownership and the growth of the new suburbs caused large numbers of riders to shift to automobiles. The change in riding habits was further accelerated by higher fares. Additional revenues obtained by raising fares were hardly enough to compensate for a rapidly declining volume of patronage, and they were less than enough to pay for skyrocketing costs. There was little or nothing left over to finance major improvements in equipment or service, and the transit ride continued to deteriorate.

In 1958, transit lines were carrying ten billion fewer riders than in 1946. The wartime peak was artificially induced by restrictions on driving, but it indicates the volume of business that transit was capable of providing. And the fifty-per-cent cut in patronage that followed the war established a pattern that was more damaging to the industry than the figure itself suggests. Most of the decline took place in off-peak hours, leaving transit companies with much the same high volume of business to handle in rush hours. Transit companies still had to maintain equipment enough to serve the morning and evening peaks, but more and more of the equipment was idle in the hours between.

Use of transit for rush-hour travel has continued on a high level because the congested center of the city has continued to be the principal place of employment. In big cities the heavy movement of traffic from suburb to center does not permit everyone to drive to town and park his car. Moreover, high-density routes in rush hours are well adapted to the provision of mass transport. Service is frequent and transit lines conveniently located. But in off-peak hours, when the commuter rush is over and traffic is lighter, the automobile is best adapted to the helter-skelter of trips in all directions. The automobile is also the preferred means of travel at night and on week ends, when the urban traveler is heading for a great variety of destinations throughout the spreading metropolitan area. Household errands and short trips of all kinds are easily performed in minimum time by automobile.

This is the basic problem by which transit is plagued. It is used primarily for home-to-work travel, concentrated in approximately four hours of the day, five days of the week. This is a costly operation, especially if adequate standards of service are to be supplied. Yet fare increases needed to cover the costs of better service are always followed by a loss of riders, further need for raising fares, and further loss of patrons. The cycle would presumably continue until all motorists had shifted to their own cars, were it not for the fact that in the downtown centers of large cities there is not enough highway capacity or parking space to accommodate all of them.

The Future of Mass Movement

Do the facts indicate, then, that deficits are inevitable in public transportation, and that subsidies capable of financing adequate service are necessary and desirable? The most immediate remedy would appear to be some changes in the rules. Transit would be aided if cities would stop levying special taxes on its operations and imposing street-maintenance requirements that have become burdensome and unfair. Transit operators should not be expected to subsidize schools by hauling students for less than cost. Many people believe, however, that more positive steps are necessary; that high-speed rail service of modern design on a separate elevated or depressed right of way should be financed from general tax sources. They argue that in major cities the choice is either to do this or to assume the very high costs of further expressway and parking facilities.

Many transit systems are already subsidized by municipal governments, and the case for further financial assistance, including federal aid, is being argued in many places. Transit consultant Kenneth Hoover makes the point that, as cities become bigger and bigger, mass transit must be expanded and improved. Obviously this cannot be done with equipment of 1920 vintage. Modern transit will have to be both faster and more comfortable. To supply such service will be costly, but to neglect it will be far costlier in expanded highway requirements and in the destruction of downtown property resulting from the accommodation of more private cars. A downtown office worker requires about 120 square feet of floor space for himself, while his automobile takes 300 square feet of parking space.

Studies of urban transport are beginning to emphasize the need for a complete transportation plan that includes all methods of movement and their relation to urban development. In the reorganization of metropolitan Toronto, for example, it was recognized that mass transportation and automobile transportation are so closely interwoven with other regional problems that it is impossible to deal with them independently. In Boston efforts have been successfully concluded to incorporate commuter railroad facilities into the metropolitan transit system rather than permit the abandonment of railroad lines altogether.

The mayors of Philadelphia, New York, and Chicago have taken a stand in favor of using public funds to help support rapid transit, whether funds are to be obtained from local, state, or federal sources. A recent Philadelphia study concludes that if the center of the city is to be preserved, rapid transit on rails is essential. The attempt to provide all the expressways needed to get Philadelphians into town in their own automobiles would take seventy-five per cent of the ground area in the center of the city to provide parking space.

On the basis of these considerations it is coming to be acknowledged that mass transit is a necessary public service even though it is not a profitable or self-supporting business. The extent to which public funds should be used for such facilities in a particular metropolitan area should depend on a clear-cut estimate of the costs of serving rush-hour traffic by alternative methods now and in the future.

Such a weighing of alternatives leads immediately to the question of the kind of transit facilities to be provided. Where rapid transit or rail commuter lines are already in place, it would seem more economical to modernize their equipment and improve their service than it would be to discourage their use and force passengers to make the costly shift to already congested roads. But in the case of new rapid transit there are still the alternatives of providing the service by rail on an exclusive right of way, or of depending on bus service using the expressways.

The advantages of rail movement on an exclusive right of way are both the high capacity of such lines and the high speed of travel that they provide. The disadvantage is the high cost of an exclusive right of way and the fact that the volume of movement is generally insufficient to justify the investment. Where total travel generated by the central business district is great, as in our largest cities, the density of travel on routes radiating from the center may justify the high capital investment required for exclusive grade-separated rail rights of way. This is particulary true if geographic features restrict the number of possible travel routes. The latter consideration is important in New York, for example, and in San Francisco. Downtown areas themselves may also generate sufficient traffic to warrant a subway network for local circulation.

In many cities, however, densities of central-area development and patterns of new growth do not generate heavy volumes of passenger movement along well-defined routes. In these cases traffic is not sufficient to justify an extensive system of rail rapid transit. This situation is typical of most American urban areas, and it suggests that the most feasible solution of transit problems may be the use of buses operating over expressways. The great advantage of this approach lies in the ability of the bus line to share the cost of the highway with other users. This relieves the transit system of the very heavy investment involved in an exclusive right of way.

The sharing of cost, however, also means the sharing of available space. Resulting congestion may make it impossible for the bus to offer a service sufficiently speedy and attractive to compete successfully with the private automobile. The expressway system is also apt to be poorly located to serve transit patrons adequately. For this reason any extensive development of rapid transit by bus requires that the location and design of expressways be planned with the needs of transit operation in mind, including appropriate stations and access points.

Another possibility is to construct rail transit lines on expressways. An example of this is the Congress Street Expressway in Chicago, where rail transit has been installed in the center mall of the highway. This was done because the elevated railroad had to be eliminated in order to build the expressway. The highway itself is carrying ninety thousand vehicles a day. The potential traffic relief that may be expected from the center-mall transit is an experiment that will have to be carefully observed. But already it appears that the expressway without the rail installation would have been heavily overloaded.

One of the most important advantages of the expressway-bus solution, on the other hand, is that road capacity available for buses during weekday rush hours can be used by automobiles during off-peak hours, in the evening, and on Saturdays, Sundays, and holidays. Rail rapid-transit facilities are not well patronized at these times, and the investment in track and right of way is idle or poorly utilized much of the time. That is why capital costs per rapid-transit ride are high. These costs, regardless of who pays them, have to be related to traffic that moves during only fifteen or twenty hours in a week.

This consideration is likely to be of increasing importance in the future. Transit business was adversely affected by the five-day week, which eliminated much of the heavy volume of travel to downtown areas on Saturdays. It has been hurt in the evenings, not only because of the automobile, but because of television as well. Now it is probable that a further decline in working hours will mean a further reduction in the number of days worked per person per year. Fewer work hours will also mean more hours available for leisure-time travel, mostly by automobile. Frank W. Herring of the Port of New York Authority thinks that eventually recreation travel rather than the journey to work will become the dominant factor determining highway capacity requirements.

The question is whether it is possible to meet both requirements with one system of expressways, or whether both a highway system and a rail network are necessary. From this analysis it may be concluded that even if it were possible by extending rail transit to bring about a substantial reduction in the number of cars being driven to work, the demand for highways might not be reduced at all. Traffic on week ends and holidays may continue to rise until it becomes the basis for designing the highway system. The only effect of providing more rail transit might be to compound transit's financial problems. For a greater volume of patronage would surely add to the peak load rather than bolster off-peak riding.

Commuting by Railroad

In cities such as New York, Chicago, Philadelphia, Boston, and San Francisco a considerable volume of public transportation is being provided by commuter railroads. The financial problems of these lines are generally more severe than those of local transit companies, and for much the same reasons. Rail suburban services are heavily peaked in morning and evening rush hours. Their use in off-peak hours is very small. The result is substantial deficits, which the railroads have been able to withstand over a long period only because commuter losses have been compensated by profits from the transportation of freight.

Railroad commuter travel now represents approximately seventeen per cent of total rail travel in the United States and some fourteen per cent of railroad passenger revenues. In the past several years total travel volume has remained fairly steady, with important increases in patronage on some lines. But when traffic figures are viewed alongside mounting deficits, it is clear that the railroads cannot continue forever to provide a service that incurs such heavy losses.

Philadelphia's Urban Traffic and Transportation Board has recommended one approach to solving the commuter-railroad problem. A new regional transportation agency for Philadelphia would have the authority to purchase commuter-railroad facilities and incorporate them into the transit system. Where the conduct of other passenger and freight services over the same tracks precluded such an arrangement, commuter facilities would continue to be provided by the railroad on a contractual basis. The public transport agency would set the standards and pay the deficit.

The recent rash of petitions for fare increases or abandonment of rail commuter services reveals the growing severity of the problem. Wherever the volume of commuter traffic is high, incorporation of the service into a regional transportation system may be the least expensive course of action. The cost of providing highway capacity to accommodate a shift to buses or automobiles may establish the desirability of providing public subsidy rather than permitting abandonment. In addition, tax abatement and fare systems that actually reflect the cost of service may prove to be the most straightforward solution.

There is little question, however, that in many cases rail commuter lines will have to be abandoned. They no longer go where people are going, and their ability to carry very high densities of traffic is no longer relevant where densities of living and moving are low. Resistance to abandonment by local communities and state regulatory commissions cannot forever withstand the economic pressures in the opposite direction.

The Key Role of the Highways

At this point the relative importance of highways in the urban transport picture becomes fairly apparent. Whatever the balance may be between public and private transportation, the dominant transport need of the urban area will still be its roads. This can be seen first in the fact that the highway system is for all practical purposes the entire passenger transport system of metropolitan areas on week ends and holidays. The same is true of off-peak periods on weekdays, and especially in the evenings. At those times the passenger car is supreme.

Most transit services, too, are provided by buses operating on highways. The possibility of building new rail rapid-transit lines will not change the picture, because such developments will be confined to special circumstances involving rush-hour travel to the central business districts of our largest cities. Even then the highway may be the logical place for rail transit installations. Finally, we have noted that roads are likewise required to meet the extensive demands of motor trucking. A great part of the metropolitan area is entirely dependent on trucks for food and supplies and for transporting the products of urban industry.

The highway obviously holds a dominant place in the metropolitan transportation system, and current trends toward greater dispersal of urban living and economic activity make it likely that this pre-eminence will continue for a long time. It follows, therefore, that mobility in metropolitan areas will depend largely on how effectively we design and build our roads and streets to meet the needs of all users, including private cars, trucks, and public transit. Good transport will also depend on how highway plans are related to various types of land use, to other forms of transport, and to parking and terminal facilities.

The task of accomplishing such an integrated total transportation system, however, runs up against three major problems. First, the creation of a well-rounded total transport system in urban areas has thus become largely dependent upon state highway departments. Their duties, however, do not include responsibility for a total urban transportation solution.

Second, public transit must continue to play a key role in serving the downtown area, particularly in the rush hours. Yet transit service by its very nature cannot be expected to operate without substantial deficits, and there appears to be no ready answer as to how such deficits are to be met.

Third, metropolitan areas must provide guidance to the roadbuilders in the form of long-range plans for urbanized areas, and most metropolitan areas have no such plans. This fact is of key importance; for despite the major role of the highway system, it is now clear that the problem of adapting our cities to the automotive age will mean more than building roads. The problem of moving in cities cannot be separated from the pattern of urban development. It is not merely how we move that creates a transportation problem; it is also the environment in which we move.

That is the reason why, with all the methods of movement at our disposal, the problem in urban areas is still how to move. We have tried to solve the transportation problem exclusively by mechanical means— by highways, railroads, transit, and other physical facilities that add to our capacity to handle traffic. In doing so we have overlooked half the problem. For we have neglected to concern ourselves with how traffic is generated and what we can do to influence the demand for transport services.

Tackling Congestion at the Source

One of the goals of good transportation is to reduce the amount of unnecessary transportation. We need to minimize the need for movement, yet maximize our ability to move.

The field of flood control offers a good parallel. What we used to do was build dikes at the mouth of the Mississippi; and when the river persisted in overflowing them, we went on building the dikes higher. Finally people realized that if they went upstream and stopped some of the water from coming down by afforestation, erosion control, and gully-plugging, the river downstream would not rise so high. In a sense what we used to do with dikes resembles what we now insist on doing with highways. We go on building more capacity, but there is always a flood of new traffic. Our roads will continue to be inundated unless we do what we can to overcome the underlying causes of congestion.

An elevator is the best example of a conscious effort to relate people and goods to transportation. Passenger and freight elevators are designed to carry the loads expected from the volume and type of activity that a building is to serve. But if the building is subsequently converted to a different type and density of use, the relationship between elevator capacity and traffic generated is destroyed. Crowded elevators and poor service are the results.

Actually, then, there are two sides to the transportation problem. The supply side involves the provision of highways, public transit, railroad commutation, terminals, parking, and other related transport facilities. The other side is the demand for transportation—the volume of traffic generated by the various densities and arrangements of urban development. To date, however, attention has been directed exclusively to supplying additional transport capacity.

The futility of this one-sided approach is plain. With so many people living in the suburbs and commuting daily to the center, the problem of accommodating the resulting rush-hour jam is enormous. The typical arrangement is the high-density center for working and shopping, with surrounding low-density residential suburbs for living. This forces large numbers of people to go to the same place at the same times. The pendulum movement from home to work poses a challenge that the best conceivable system of transportation could never hope to meet.

The ultimate solution to this problem is not to build more and more transport capacity. The central city needs to be redesigned to permit more people to live as well as work there. Opportunities for employment need to be decentralized to provide work for suburbanites in outlying locations nearer their homes. Densities of development in the central city need to be reduced, and more open space should be provided there to cancel the effects of adjacent built-up areas.

In today's urban environment the basic problem underlying traffic congestion is too many people and too much economic activity in relation to available transport capacity. We have failed to take into account the traffic-producing potentials of various land uses as an index of transport needs. And conversely we have failed, despite the limitations of transport, to impose appropriate restraints on the types and intensities of permitted land uses as a means of avoiding insupportable transport demands.

The transportation problem, then, is essentially the problem of achieving a reasonable balance between the supply of transport facilities and the demands on available capacity. The task is to make sure that traffic generated in urban areas does not place an impossible burden on roads and streets, parking and terminal facilities, and mass transport.

The big hope for moving around in urban areas is to move the urban areas themselves around. We shall have to attack the congestion of moving by overcoming the congestion of living. Metropolitan mobility depends on a more orderly arrangement of urban living and working. New communities will have to be built and old ones rebuilt in a way that makes it possible for people who live in them to move in them.

Transportation problems could be alleviated, for example, if cities would restore close-in areas and make them fit to live in. It might be possible to reduce the volume and concentration of home-to-work travel if residential areas and places of work were brought closer together. Our new mobility makes it possible to establish new employment centers beyond the radius of maximum congestion.

And so we come back to the goal of redesigning the urban environment. The task cannot be accomplished overnight, but it can and must be started now. In the next decade, with or without plans, we shall be building and rebuilding urban facilities equivalent to fifty cities the size of Boston. This will be necessary simply to provide for new development and the replacement of worn-out structures. It is entirely feasible from an economic standpoint to plan and build the better urban communities we want. Better transportation will be realized to an important degree through better urban communities. The longer we neglect the possibilities, the more staggering will be the task when we finally realize that there is no other choice.

C. PROTECTIVE FUNCTIONS

52. The Police, Minority Groups and the Community

W. H. PARKER

Los Angeles has not experienced an instance of organized group-violence in the past twelve years.

If organized violence occurred anywhere, it should, by all socio-economic standards, have been Los Angeles. In the last decade, the city has

Reprinted from *The Police Yearbook* (Washington, D.C.: International Association of Chiefs of Police, 1956), pp. 157–69 by permission of the author and the publisher. The author was the Police Chief of Los Angeles when he wrote this article. This excerpt was taken from an address given at a convention of police officials.

nearly doubled in size; it suffered the intense dislocation of adjustment to an industrial economy; it has been and still is the focus of one of the greatest migrations in this nation's history. Its two million, two hundred-thousand people, the hub of a five-million person metropolitan area, is a melting pot of races, colors, creeds, and ideas.

Let me cite some examples. Los Angeles is the home of nearly one-quarter million Negroes, an increase of 168 per cent since World War II. It has the largest Mexican-descent population outside of Mexico City. It has the largest Japanese group in the nation; the third largest Chinese group. The number of persons of the Jewish faith at least equals the urban average.

The city is a cross section of the races, colors, and creeds which make up our nation. And, for reasons no one has ever explained to my satisfaction, we are somehow a Mecca not only for strange religious cults, but also for every brand of zealot, bigot and fanatic our society breeds.

This is Los Angeles, not the city colorfully depicted on travel posters —but the one which interests us here today. It has, like other great metropolitan centers, nearly every element which creates community tensions. But its peoples of different background are learning to live together.

The story of that city's freedom from strife is largely the story of the professionalization of its police department. In this respect, I do not discount the efforts of other agencies, particularly those working for community and group betterment. Their progress in the fields of human understanding, education, and welfare, has been remarkable. It holds great promise for the future. But they made one additional contribution. They recognized that there was one thing which would make social tranquility immediately possible. They gave dynamic and unflagging support to police improvement.

I want to approach the subject of police improvement in a bluntly realistic manner. There has been a great deal of discussion about it at this conference, and I am anxious that one serious error be avoided.

As I left Los Angeles a few days ago, I was introduced to a feature writer from another city's metropolitan newspaper. A capable man. His task—analyze the Los Angeles Police Department, study techniques and procedures, and take the story back home. Good journalism—the type which justifies our faith in the Fourth Estate. I hope he won't make the error I'm concerned about. If he doesn't, it will be a rare instance.

Since Los Angeles has achieved its eminence in law enforcement, dozens of citizen groups, city officials, and journalists from other areas have studied our methods. The usual result is a storm of bitter criticism of their department, and a demand that their police adopt Los Angeles' professionalism.

How simple that sounds. And how dangerous it is to assume that a city's so-called police problem stems from the police themselves. These people who demand that their police be more efficient, more honest, more impartial—I invite them to join me in an exercise in realism. Who actually runs a police department? The Mayor, the police commissioner, the chief? The people do! They set its policies, establish its standards, furnish its man-power, and supply its budget.

The police department is not a private endeavor; it has no funds of its own. It is not a legal entity; is has no rights, no vested interests. It is merely a group of citizens employed to exercise certain functions. It is created by the public, shaped by the public, and operated by the public. *And if it operates badly, the responsibility cannot be disowned by the public.*

I have often heard the complaint that the police organization is all right, but the officers just are not producing. And if an employee isn't producing—whose fault is it? The public selected that man—did they select the wrong man? The public furnished the training—was it bad training—or did they neglect to provide funds for training of any sort?

What about the supervisors and commanders? Were they selected by competitive examination on a merit basis—or were they promoted on a political basis? If so, whose politics? If there is a machine in town—a few police votes don't keep it running. But the public vote does!

A recent news report tells of widespread police graft in a Southern city. Officers are "squeezing" merchandise from businessmen, parking fees from truckers, gratuities from other citizens.

The good citizens there, horrified at the exposé, might do well to accept some personal responsibility. The basic salary of their police officer is two-hundred twenty dollars per month. On the six-day week, that runs about a dollar per hour. Carpenter's helpers in the same town earn nearly double that scale. What kind of policemen do they expect to get for a dollar an hour? Their police department costs less than a million dollars per year. Of course, the crime bill, the disorder, the under-the-table pay-offs run fifteen million dollars per year.

A shrewd bargain these good citizens have driven. Of course, they are going to solve their problem. They're replacing the Chief, the seventh in six years.

If a journalist or a citizens' group from that city calls upon Los Angeles for assistance, what should we tell them? They'll want to study our organization, inspect our Planning and Research and Intelligence Division, our strong disciplinary program, observe our cadet school, our continuous in-service training. There are no secrets about these things. They are merely adaptations of sound administrative technique. They are available and understandable to qualified police officials everywhere.

But they cannot be put into effect until competent personnel are attracted by decent job benefits, until an adequate operating budget is furnished; until public cooperation replaces disinterest, shallow-interest, and special-interest. Professional police work will come into being only when the public takes a long hard look at their police, and instead of disowning what they themselves have created, accept full responsibility for the errors of generations.

Returning, then to the Los Angeles experiment—the thing which made police progress and social order there a reality was a public acceptance of these very basic facts. At first, it was understood by only a small group—community leaders such as those represented at this Conference. The job of selling this concept was a different one. Not that it was a particularly new concept—but at some community levels it is an ugly one.

Assuming a community is ready to support the professionalism of its police agency, there are certain techniques which the Los Angeles experiment has proved necessary. The first step is the attraction of proper recruits. Los Angeles policemen draw $440.00 monthly at the end of three years' service. This is probably a minimum figure. Below that, the possibility of attracting sufficiently educated and capable persons is almost nil.

I am of the opinion that the base salary for an experienced line officer should be in the neighborhood of $600.00 monthly, at present living costs. The first city to adopt such a scale will attract high personnel who now select other professions. At the present time, I am trying to convince Los Angeles that we would save money by paying more. Our attrition rate among the most qualified officers is too high.

There must be minimum recruiting standards—and these minimums must be held even though the Department operates below strength. Far better to have to increase unit output than to corrupt your police future with sub-standard men.

In Los Angeles, less than 4 per cent of all applicants meet our rigid police standards. We have been considerably under authorized strength for five years, at one time 10 per cent under an allowed figure which was itself nearly 40 per cent under the recommended population—square mile ratio.

We have managed to do the job only because personnel quality allowed us to steadily improve efficiency. . . .

Recruit selection must be made solely on a merit basis, preferably by an independent civil service department. If a ward boss, an alderman or a councilman can influence selection in any manner, tear up your plans and start over. As a matter of fact if he can interfere in any way other than through official channels, the police improvement plan is doomed.

Categorically, professional police work and politics do not mix—and there are no shades of gray to that philosophy.

A psychiatric test must be included in the recruit selection program. This bears directly on the problem of community relations. The finest training, direction and discipline cannot correct or control serious emotional defects.

Our Cadet Training School runs 13 weeks at present. Again this should be considered a minimum, and then only if the recruit has an education equivalent of two college years. I am personally in favor of a six-month training period, plus a six-months' additional field probation under strict supervision. This should be followed up with in-service and advanced officers' schools, specialist and command school such as are given in Los Angeles. This is, of course, only a sketch of recruiting and training considerations. With it in mind, I would like to consider in more detail some of the training which bears directly on the subject of community relations.

Once the police cadet has received basic technical information, the direction of training pivots to the consideration of human relations. The cadet must be taught to translate his technical background into solutions of field situations—problems which involve people.

In these courses, sociology is stressed more than ethnology. Applied human relations is stressed more than theoretical psychology. The purpose of the training is to provide immediately, usable knowledge. Training schedules do not allow time for building the broad base of theoretical knowledge necessary in university training. The police administrators should not attempt that impossible task under present training time minimums.

The advantages of a college education requirement for police applicants is readily apparent here. Lacking this, colleges do provide upper-level courses, and officers should be encouraged to take advantage of these facilities. In a recent survey, we found that 40 per cent of our officers were engaged in such training.

The cadet learns that people differ—by race, religion, politics, economic status, occupation, and in a thousand other ways. He learns they have a *right* to be different. He learns that we are all minority group members—that each of us belongs to many groups, any one of which can be, and often has been discriminated against.

In other classes, statistical diagrams of the composition of the city are studied. The various peoples are discussed, the movements of groups are traced, the tensions resulting from these movements are pin-pointed and analyzed in detail. The racial composition of police districts is an important lesson here because it must be made clear that there are no "Jim Crow" areas, no "Ghettos."

Every police division has everything found in all other divisions, differing only in proportion. The aim here is to correct stereotyped impressions that the city is divided into clearly defined groups and areas, and that law enforcement differs accordingly. The police department's policy of one class of citizenship, one standard of police technique, becomes readily understandable.

Another class expands this policy. The officer now understands the composition of the community, he has learned how people differ. He is now taught that these variations cannot influence him in the discharge of his duties. His department handles the people involved in incidents *only* according to the degree of their involvement. There is no other measurement. Existing laws are enforced and nothing else. We do not enforce beliefs or prejudices—*including the officer's*. During his hours of duty, he is a composite of the entire community.

Typical course titles are *Police Sociological Problems, Human Relations, Ethics, Professionalism, Civil Disturbances,* and *Public Relations.* Course titles do not reveal the full scope of the 520-hour program. For example, although the *Human Relations* class lasts two hours, that subject is a principal concern in courses such as *Interrogation, Patrol Tactics,* and *Investigation.*

The firearms' class gives more time to "when *not* to shoot" than it does to "How to Shoot."

The entire training staff is constantly alert in the classroom, on the exercise field, and in the locker room to discover signs of disabling prejudice which might make the cadet a poor risk. Conditions of tension are artificially created so that the man's reaction can be studied—and he may never know that the situation was contrived to test him.

At this point, let us consider the subject of racial and religious prejudice. The cadets, of course, reflect a broad cross section of society and bring to us the intolerant attitudes to which they have previously been exposed. The question—what to do about these beliefs?

Recently, a chief of police from a mid-western city made an inspection tour of our Department. He was particularly interested in the extremely low percentage of citizen complaints received alleging prejudicial treatment of minority group members. He was also interested in case studies where so-called minority group organizations defended the Police Department against accusations of such misconduct. . . .

He assumed that such overwhelming public support meant we had somehow erased prejudicial and intolerant beliefs held by police officers.

He was wrong. Those of you who work in the field of education recognize we *do not* and *can not* accomplish this miracle.

Of course, we will not accept an applicant whose intolerance is so high it is a disabling factor. Where it is not too deep-seated, we can erase it, or at least diminish it. In the majority of cases, we must learn to operate equitably despite it. We do that by controlling the results of these beliefs. With policemen, as with society in general, our immediate concern is not in what the man thinks but what he does.

Los Angeles Police policy recognizes only one class of citizenship— Any incident of police action which deviates from this policy is met with swift and certain discipline.

A Police Department's community relations program begins with a training, a firm human relations policy and strong disciplinary machinery to enforce it. It is a departmental application of my second premise—that the immediate issue is conduct, and the immediate solution is enforced order.

For those who question whether that degree of discipline is possible, I have an example. I am thinking of a certain Los Angeles police officer who walks a foot beat in the old section of the city. The street is a racial melting pot. I know the officer personally, he is one of the "old school," recruited long before psychiatric examinations were instituted. If there is a maximum number of racial and religious prejudices one mind can hold, I am certain he represents it. This officer has been exposed to the complete range of police human relations training. He has memorized every maxim, every scientific fact, every theory relating to human equality. He knows all the accepted answers. Of course, he doesn't believe a word of it.

This may surprise you—the officer's eight-hour duty tour is characterized by tolerance, applied human relations and equitable treatment of all persons. Both his division commander and myself have watched his work closely, a little wary that his deep-seated convictions might win out over discipline in moments of stress.

This has not happened during the five years he has patrolled this highly critical district. We are very near an opinion that his intolerance has become a victim of enforced order—habit has won out over belief.

Discipline, enforced compliance with police policy, is a key which is available to every police administrator. If it works in Los Angeles, it will work elsewhere. The entire community relations program is at stake on every officer in the field. It is here that the police department proves itself, or is found wanting.

The second-line community relations effort is handled by specialized police units. One of the most successful of these is our Community Relations Detail working out of the Public Information office. Its mission is to establish and maintain communications between police and the so-called minority segments of the community press serving them, and key individuals in the human relations field. These officers are members of sixty organizations representing a cross section of specialized community interests. Few police details pierce so deeply into the stratifications of our complex society or maintain so many privileged sources of information.

Their first task was at the community press level. Certain of these newspapers were parlaying instances of law enforcement against minority group members into sensational accounts of police prejudice and brutality. Many of these articles were written solely from the unsubstantiated account given by the arrestee. The accumulated result was the fomenting of an hysterical "cop-hating" attitude which rendered suspect every police action involving non-Caucasian persons.

The Community Relations officers went to these publishers and laid their cards on the table. Sensationalism was selling newspapers, but it was hurting the community. They pointed out that sensationalism was actually manufacturing new incidents—feeding upon itself. They offered, with the full backing of the office of the chief, to provide the publisher with exact and complete facts on every inquiry, whether the police action was right or wrong; whether the facts helped us or hurt us.

The confidence I have in the men who publish the nation's newspapers was justified. Community interest won out over self interest.

The Community Relations Detail is, *first*, a public information activity, acquainting community groups with police policies, procedures and tactics. Where necessary, it interprets specific police actions, explaining why they were necessary and how they were taken.

Secondly, the Detail transmits information in the other direction, keeping the police staff informed about minority and inter-group problems and activities. We have found the police are sometimes overly suspicious of a group's militant efforts, seeing in it a threat to order which does not actually exist. The two-way communication furnished by the Detail brings the facts to both sides.

Thirdly, the Detail reports any police activities which are discriminatory, or may appear to the community to be discriminatory. The police staff does not operate under the assumption that it is infallible. Critical comment from this specialized unit often prevents more dangerous and expensive criticism from the public at large.

Lastly, the Detail operates as an advance listening post, alert for rumors which might prelude violent conflict. In a recent instance, these officers were informed that racial violence was brewing at a school. A quick investigation indicated the situation was critical. The Detail flashed the word to citizen groups organized to combat just such emergencies. Affected police field units were placed on a stand-by basis. The result—this Detail, working with citizen groups, contained the situation.

It is profitable to assign to these specialized units, officers belonging to minority groups. They are often more sensitive to the problem, have previously established contacts in those communities, and encounter fewer barriers. However, it must be emphasized that the competency and not his ancestry, is the overriding consideration in making the assignment. Community relations details are not "window-dressing"—they are not publicity gags designed to display non-Caucasians in key positions.

A similar detail works out of the Juvenile Division. In this case, the principal concern is with the actual offenders. One of this unit's primary values is its detailed knowledge of gang members, leaders, and methods. They know their homes, their meeting places, their territories.

They deal with what the law recognizes as children, but do not be mistaken—this is intelligence activity of the highest order. The disheartening message of our crime statistics is all too clear—today's delinquent is often a dangerous criminal—an immediate threat to community order. He is sometimes the innocent tool of intolerant adults, but he can also be a moving force behind community violence.

We are sympathetic with the ideals of juvenile correction—of rehabilitation over punishment. Here, as with other community problems, we invite welfare agencies to work to eliminate causes. Meanwhile, we ask them to remember that *we* are not a social agency. We are bound to read the message in police records and employ protective tactics accordingly.

In Los Angeles, as in other cities, we have a juvenile problem. We do *not* have a problem in mass juvenile disorder, because we face facts, and on the basis of these facts, employ units such as the ones I have described.

Three factors compose the Los Angeles Police Department's community relations program: Training of officers—including training through discipline, *public information* activity, and *efficient* line police work. Unless they are all in existence *and inter-working*, a community relations program does not exist.

Training provides a base, but public information and line officers must forward to training that information which keys it to current needs. Public information is a useless activity unless it is backed up with competent line officers who are enforcing the laws equitably. And the most dedicated line commanders can accomplish little unless training provides well-schooled personnel and public information creates a cooperative public.

I would rather have brought to this Conference, a simple and revolutionary device—some easy way to an effective program. I know of no such device. I *can* promise that to a mutually cooperating public and police department, no problem in community order is beyond solution. The methods are known, they are providing themselves in the Los Angeles experiment—all that is needed is dedicated citizens who will put them into effect.

To this point, this has been a progress report. The Los Angeles experiment seems to justify the philosophy of enforced order as the first step toward improved community relations. Progress of this type can be reported objectively, without seeming to seek praise because law enforcement is absolutely dependent upon the public for any successes it may have. The credit for Los Angeles progress must go primarily to Los Angeles citizens.

I would not want to close, however, leaving the impression that the experiment is concluded. It does not represent the ultimate in community equity and tranquility. Certain factors now at work could bring all the progress crashing down into rubble and violence. I have pledged forthrightness and honesty in this report, and it requires some critical comments, perhaps touching upon activities and attitudes or organizations represented here.

The first comment concerns minority discrimination against the public as a whole. Reaction to police deployment furnishes a good example of this danger. Every department worth its salt deploys field forces on the basis of crime experience. Deployment is often heaviest in so-called minority sections of the city. The reason is statistical—it is a fact that certain racial groups, at the present time, commit a disproportionate share of the total crime.

Let me make one point clear in that regard—a competent police administrator is fully aware of the multiple conditions which create this problem. There is no inherent physical or mental weakness in any racial stock which tends it toward crime. But—and this is a "but" which must be borne constantly in mind—*police field deployment is not social agency activity.*

In deploying to suppress crime, we are not interested in why a certain group tends toward crime, we are interested in maintaining order. The fact that the group would not be a crime problem under different socio-economic conditions and might not be a crime problem tomorrow, does not alter today's tactical necessities. Police deployment is concerned with *effect,* not cause.

When I am told that intense police activity in a given area is psychologically disturbing to its residents, I am forced to agree. And I agree that it can add weight to discriminatory beliefs held by some who witness it, and that it can create a sense of persecution among those who receive it. Is the police administrator, then, to discard crime occurrence statistics and deploy his men on the basis of social inoffensiveness? This would be discrimination indeed!

Every citizen has the right to police protection on the basis of need. The police have the duty of providing that protection, and of employing whatever legal devices are necessary to accomplish it. At the present time, race, color, and creed are useful statistical and tactical devices. So are age groupings, sex, and employment.

If persons of one occupation, for some reason, commit more theft than average, then increased police attention is given to persons of that occupation. Discrimination is not a factor there. If persons of Mexican, Negro, or Anglo-Saxon ancestry, for some reason, contribute heavily to other forms of crime, police deployment must take that into account.

From an ethnological point-of-view, Negro, Mexican, and Anglo-Saxon are unscientific breakdowns; they are a fiction. From a police point-of-view, they are a useful fiction and should be used as long as they remain useful.

The demand that the police cease to consider race, color and creed is an unrealistic demand. *Identification is a police tool, not a police attitude.* If traffic violations run heavily in favor of lavender colored automobiles, you may be certain, whatever the sociological reasons for that condition, we would give lavender automobiles more than average attention. And if those vehicles were predominantly found in one area of the city, we would give that area more than average attention.

You may be certain that any pressure brought to bear by the lavender manufacturer's association would not alter our professional stand —it would only react to their disadvantage by making the police job more difficult. *Such demands are a form of discrimination against the public as a whole.*

For a moment, let us consider this entire problem of group identification. It is one thing for the police to employ it for statistical and descriptive purposes; it is quite another if it is employed to set a group apart from the rest of society.

The question must be brought out into the open and discussed because it represents a conflict of opinion within the physically-identifiable minority groups. Some of these citizens object strenuously to being identified with their background. Others publicly announce it by joining organizations bearing that stamp of identity.

Either attitude can be supported by argument. But I humbly submit that the man, or the group which changes identification at different times and under different conditions, confuses and impedes the social assimilation process. There is no place for dual status in our society, and it is incongruous that the groups with the keenest interest in eliminating dual status should create conditions which perpetuate it.

Organizations which publicly identify themselves with a certain racial group are keeping alive the phantasy that the group is different. By setting it apart from the whole, they help keep it apart.

We need such organizations; they fill a vital role in our changing system; I heartily endorse their good works. I suggest that if a single class of citizenship is the key to social assimilation, then practices and titles which contradict it must be examined and resolved.

Another problem which plagues the police administrator is organized group pressure to promote officers and make command assignments on the basis of race, color or creed. Before a recent Los Angeles election, I encountered tremendous pressure to replace an Anglo-Saxon commander of a detective division with another commander belonging to a certain minority group. I refused to engage in racial discrimination against the Anglo-Saxon commander. He was the most qualified man for the job and, as such he retained the job. Neither do I consider ancestry a factor in making promotional appointments.

The Los Angeles policy is to take the top man from the list. Racial background should not hinder advancement; neither should it help it. Shortly before I left Los Angeles, I had the pleasure of pinning a lieutenant's badge on a young officer born in Mexico. He got that badge because he was the top man, not because accidents of conquest created a national border between our places of birth.

No one is more critical of the American police service than myself. For 28 years I have outspokenly expressed that criticism and have sat in meetings and applauded others who have criticized constructively. Certainly, few other organizations in history have been so unanimously castigated.

I have no complaints to make—it is part of the painful process of growth and improvement.

There is one danger inherent in this process—a point of group-masochism is reached where all other groups become wise and fruitless and self-reproach becomes the total answer. I caution the police against this danger.

I have made the point that discrimination is a two-way street. Those who are most active in combating it are sometimes guilty of advocating that the police practice it. There is nothing shocking in this critical observation—no group is characterized by omniscience. The fact minorities have received intolerant and discriminatory treatment does not automatically lend justice to all of their demands. They are as prone to error as majority groups, and the wiser and calmer citizens within those groups recognize it.

Thoughtful citizens expect the police to stand their ground when they believe they are right. They expect the police to criticize as well as be criticized.

I have tried to steer a course between these extremes this afternoon. I have assessed the situation as forthrightly as I know how. There is always a temptation when speaking on a subject so emotion-laden as this, to skirt issues, to woo friends, rather than court truth.

In my experience with the International Association of Chiefs of Police, I have never felt it necessary to compromise my honest convictions, and I did not intend to dishonor this conference by so doing this afternoon.

53. *Health, Technology, and Water*

L. E. BURNEY

More than half a century ago, at about the time the National Rivers and Harbors Congress was formed, Theodore Roosevelt wrote:

"The Nation behaves well if it treats the natural resources as assets which it must turn over to the next generation increased, and not impaired, in value."

I find it interesting to reflect that in a world of ceaseless change, Man's absolute dependence on water stands as an eternal constant. Our modern jet-propelled, nuclear-powered society is as dependent on water as were the civilizations which developed six thousand years ago in the valleys of the Nile and the Tigris-Euphrates. Now, as then, an adequate supply of usable water is both a biological and an economic imperative.

Virtually every Nation in every age has had a "Water Problem." The characteristics of the problem change as Man's uses of water become progressively more diverse and complex. But the fundamental problem remains the same—getting enough water to the right place at the right time, in usable condition.

Presented at the 47th Annual Convention of the National Rivers and Harbors Congress, Washington, D.C., May 26, 1960. Reprinted by permission of the author and the NRHC. When this address was given Dr. Burney was Surgeon General, Public Health Service, U.S. Department of Health, Education and Welfare.

My talk this afternoon is concerned chiefly with the qualitative aspects—the "usable condition" factor. But so interwoven are the many strands of the water problem that it is impossible to separate considerations of quality from considerations of quantity. Problems of water supply are inseparable from problems of waterborne waste disposal. Economics and health are indivisible.

All of you are well acquainted with the overwhelming statistics on water usage, both today and in the foreseeable future. The volume of fresh water used daily in the United States has increased sevenfold since the turn of the century, and almost doubled since 1945. By 1980, according to the most reliable projections available, our fresh water needs will have doubled again, reaching the astronomical figure of 600 billion gallons, or 1.8 million acre-feet, per day. A week's ration of water, at this rate, would submerge Manhattan Island to a depth of 1,000 feet.

Meanwhile, of course, the bountiful natural supply on which we must draw remains constant over the years. It has been calculated recently by water supply experts that not more than 515 billion gallons per day will be developed for use by 1980, making optimum use of impoundments and other quantity management methods. It is on this fresh water supply of 515 billion gallons that the continued growth and prosperity of the United States depends.

The arithmetic of the situation is elementary. We can develop 515 billion gallons per day by 1980. We shall need 600 billion. A cynic might observe that we are spending water like money. At any rate, something must be done to deal with this "deficit financing" of our water budget.

Of the courses open to us, two have intrigued scientists for ages—desalinization of salt water and weather modification. Both are under intensive study. But in all candor, the likelihood of practical application of either method, in terms of large quantities, is slight, for economic reasons. It appears that we would be unwise to stake our future upon either possibility.

Major diversions between watersheds, to redistribute water according to our needs instead of Nature's whims, offer vast and tempting possibilities. A network of giant power stations and canals fed by excess flood waters from such rivers as the Colorado, Missouri, and Columbia, or by the world's mightiest fresh-water reservoir, the Great Lakes—this is indeed an engineer's vision of Utopia. Parts of the dream have already been realized, and more will become feasible with time. But such diversions carry with them tangled legal, political, and constitutional questions which, as you know, can be more difficult to resolve than engineering problems.

It is apparent, then, that regardless of our relative success or failure with other methods, a great share of our water requirements must be met through reclamation and re-use of water on a much larger scale than has been achieved up to the present. Already, on many of our watercourses, we are using the same water many times as it flows from the hills to the sea. In the years ahead we must do much more of the same.

It is at this point, of course, that the threads of quantity and quality become inseparably interwoven. And it is at this point that considerations of the national health enter the economic equations.

The three controlling trends of contemporary American life are the upsurge of population, the growth of the metropolis, and the expansion and diversification of industry. We are accustomed to dealing with these as the basis for our quantitative predictions. Let us consider them in the context of water quality.

Since I began talking, a few minutes ago, the population of the United States has increased by thirty—not just thirty births, but thirty more births than deaths. At the current rate, we shall have added more than two and a half million people by the time your Congress convenes next spring—considerably more than the entire population of the Washington metropolitan area.

Simultaneously, an ever-higher proportion of us are living in cities. We are already in the age of the metropolis. We are fast approaching the age of megalopolis—super-cities stretching along the Atlantic seaboard from Boston to Washington; along the Pacific Coast from San Diego to Seattle; along the Ohio River Valley and the southern shores of the Great Lakes. Note again, in passing, that civilization follows the watercourses. And then consider with me the impact on water quality, and the implications for human health, of these facts of life.

Increased population and urbanization pose a double-barreled problem. The more people, the greater the quantity of high quality water which must be delivered. At the same time, the quantity of domestic wastes which must be disposed of increases proportionately. In most parts of the country, the same waterways must serve both as sources of supply and as channels of waste disposal.

Thus, water supply intakes and sewage disposal outfalls are wedged closer and closer together. Heavier demands are placed upon both sewage treatment and water purification. And the margin of safety against communicable diseases becomes thinner.

Thus our traditional health problem—protection against waterborne disease—is complicated by population growth and urbanization. In the past several decades, the success of our water and sewage treatment methods has been outstanding. It is clear, however, that our precautions must be redoubled if we are to cope successfully with the aggravated threat of the future. One city's water supply cannot be drawn chiefly from another city's wastes with impunity, unless the highest order of vigilance is practiced.

Moreover, there are still a number of unanswered questions in regard to micro-organisms in water. We know how to deal with bacteria, but we know very little about waterborne viruses. We know that they are present, and that they may well pass the barriers of present water-treatment methods, but much remains to be learned about their actual and potential significance in the spread of disease.

Thus far we have dealt with two of the three conditioners of our time—population growth and urbanization. When we add the third ingredient—the new industrial revolution of the mid-twentieth century—we add a whole new dimension to the problems confronting the health professions.

The growth of American industry in the past two decades is almost beyond comprehension. Industries today are dealing with processes and products which were unheard of prior to World War II. Synthetics, plastics, detergents, pesticides, industrial solvents, high energy fuels—the list of new chemicals in the environment can be extended indefinitely without even mentioning the soaring world of nuclear technology.

Two or three examples will suffice to demonstrate the scale of the problem. Since 1940, production of plastics has increased from 150 million to 5 billion pounds; synthetic detergents from 15 million to 3.8 billion pounds, insecticides and other agricultural chemicals from 8 million to 540 million. It has been estimated that 7,000 totally new chemicals are put to use every year.

The detergent suds and foam which are often visible around sewage treatment plant outfalls are symptomatic of the fact that many of these new chemicals pass unchanged through our treatment process. Some of them actually impede effective treatment. What they do to human beings, cumulatively over a period of many years, is still in the realm of conjecture.

In essence, we are in process of creating a new physical and chemical environment. The water we drink, and the air we breathe, are not what they were twenty years ago. And the challenge to health posed by this new man-made environment differs strikingly from our traditional public health concerns, in several significant ways.

The first of these is the nature of the biological assault. The health professions and the public are accustomed to the microbial disease pattern. The disease strikes; a period of illness is generally followed by recovery and often by residual immunity. The time-span is relatively short between exposure to the disease and onset of symptoms. The cause and effect are relatively easy to detect.

By contrast, the biological effects of chemicals in our environment, or of low-level radiations, may build up over long periods of time. Relating effect to cause is extremely difficult. A single disease may result from a number of causes. The hazard to the individual is related to the cumulative total of radiations or toxic chemicals received throughout his life span, continuously or intermittently, whether their source be water, air, food, or any of several others.

Another way in which the new environmental challenges differ from the more traditional health problems has to do with the complexity of the political, social and administrative structure within which solutions must be found and applied. Traditionally, the responsibility for environmental health protection has rested with the level of government closest to the people. The local community, aided as necessary by the State, has been the first line of defense.

But the growth of the metropolis has greatly complicated the structure of local government and its relation to the State. Many of our metropolitan areas already sprawl across State boundaries. Each of them is in itself a constellation of governmental and quasi-governmental agencies. What is essentially a common water supply, a common air supply, or a common transportation system is dealt with fragmentarily by literally scores of officials and groups. Successful solutions of these problems must be worked out within these new administrative and political patterns.

Finally, and of greatest significance, the nature of our goals is necessarily different. When we are dealing primarily with micro-biological enemies of man, we can in a sense go all-out. We can aim for total eradication. If we can eliminate malaria or smallpox from the face of the earth, everyone gains and no one loses.

But when we are dealing with the possible harmful effects of the by-products of industry or the wastes of nuclear technology, we cannot seek total victory. We must accept a certain amount of deterioration of our environment if we want an urban, industrial society. On the other hand, it would be the height of folly to develop a shining metropolitan, industrialized, nuclear-powered world for a human race whose health had been seriously impaired in the process.

In sum, the Nation must seek a balance which permits maximum development of our economy at minimum hazard to health. The basic decisions in the water resource field, as in many others, are economic and social. But they must be made in terms of biological reality. There is a limit to what we can accept as progress—a limit imposed by the conditions necessary to Man's health and well-being.

Looking to the future, it is plain that we need much more information which can only be developed through research. We need to search for improved, perhaps even radically different, methods of treating sewage and industrial wastes. And in the medical field, we need to accumulate evidence as fast as we can on the long-term biological effects of the new pollutants, singly and in combination.

But these facts, especially those related to health effects over periods of years or even generations, will inevitably be slow in coming. Meanwhile, there is the urgent need to apply what we already know. We cannot afford to wait for final proof before taking action.

In the past few years there has been an encouraging rise in the annual rate of construction of municipal sewage treatment facilities—from an average annual expenditure of $222 million during the period 1952–56 to an average annual expenditure of $360 million in 1958 and 1959. But the cold statistics of population expansion tell us that a still greater annual expenditure—in the range of $575 to $600 million—will be necessary to keep pace with the needs.

Similarly, there have been encouraging indications that a number of industries are becoming progressively more willing to accept their share of the responsibility for pollution abatement. Here, as elsewhere, a tremendous amount remains to be done.

As an indication of the importance we in the Public Health Service attach to these problems, we are presently undertaking a major reorganization of the Service, a principal feature of which will be to give added prominence and stature to our programs in water, air, radiological health, and other environmental fields. Meanwhile, plans are going forward for a National Conference on Water Pollution, requested by the President, to be held in December of this year.

Viewing the vast and complex panorama of the water resource problem, from the standpoint of public health, it seems to me that water pollution control is in a peculiarly strategic position. Pollution control stands at the point of confluence between the rivers of economics and health.

Water pollution control, by reclaiming water for re-use, serves the ever-growing quantitative needs of the economy. Simultaneously, pollution control strengthens the barriers against disease and promotes the conditions favorable to health.

Thus, pollution is doubly imperative. And our efforts to abate pollution should benefit from this double stimulus.

D. EDUCATION AND ADJUDICATION

54. Toward an Understanding of Public School Politics

THOMAS H. ELIOT

Mounting concern over the aims and achievements of American public schools emphasizes the need for continuing analysis of how the schools are run and who runs them. The general theory is simple enough: schools are objects of local control, the people of a local school district exercise that control through an elected school board, and the board appoints a superintendent to act as the chief executive of the district. There are variations from this pattern—in some places school boards are appointed rather than elected, in others the school system is formally a part of the city government, and in a few districts other officials, such as a business manager or building superintendent, share the top executive authority —but it is by far the most common arrangement among the nation's approximately 50,000 school districts.

I

The formal structure is based on state constitutions and statutes, and the latter have tended to confirm the historical development of education in the nineteenth century, especially in one respect: the district system of organization. The desirability of *local* control of the public schools is an article of faith among most trained educators and many other Americans, including President Eisenhower.[1] Laymen assume that local control means control by the people of the district, usually through elected representatives. Professional educators, however, are less clear about this. Their books and journals are rife with intimations that the people and even the school board members should keep their hands off the schools. Even James B. Conant's "report," after echoing the typical

Reprinted from "Toward an Understanding of Public School Politics," *American Political Science Review*, LII (December 1959), pp. 1032–43, 1046–50 by permission of the author and the publisher. Documentation abridged. Thomas Eliot served with the Social Security Administration in its early days. He later was a United States congressman and is now a professor of political science at Washington University in St. Louis.

recommendation that school boards should confine themselves to "policy" as distinguished from "administration," says that they should refrain from interfering with curricular development.[2] But where is educational "policy" made, if not in the development of the curriculum? Doubtless Conant's remark was an inadvertent slip, for his book as a whole deals primarily with the curriculum and is addressed to "interested citizens," a category which surely includes more than educators; but many educators are insistent in urging, in effect, that the schools are the special province of the professionals, the voters being a necessary evil who must be reckoned with because they provide the money. In this view, the school board's primary functions, aside from directing the district's business affairs, are to hire and support a competent professional as superintendent, defend the schools against public criticism, and persuade the people to open their pocketbooks.

This seems like turning representative government upside down. It also reflects a somewhat specialized concept of democratic theory, not unlike that expounded by Walter Lippmann—namely, that the experts should initiate policy and carry it out, with the people's representatives properly confined to the negative function of checking any gross abuse of power.[3] Lippmann was referring primarily to foreign policy, and could argue plausibly that the control of foreign policy—Locke's "federative power"—was a matter for special treatment in an otherwise self-governing society. It seems questionable whether the considerations favoring executive (or expert) direction of foreign policy are equally applicable to the control of school districts. Nevertheless, there are observable reasons for the desire to limit the role of the school boards and the people who elect them. The chief one is the professionalization of public school education.

The professionals consist of three groups. Numerically the largest, and politically today the least significant, are the school teachers. A hundred years ago, school teaching, in contrast to university teaching, law, medicine, and the ministry, was a vocation rather than a profession. A prime purpose of the National Education Association, originated in 1857, was to raise it to a professional status. By a kind of bootstrap operation, this was largely achieved, though it took eighty years to do it. The early normal schools, essentially vocational training institutes, were supplemented by colleges and graduate schools of education; and states were moved to pass certification laws prescribing educational qualifications for teachers. The second professional group is composed of the pedagogues' pedagogues—the faculties of teachers colleges and university departments of education. Their professional status was ready-made, but as the justification of their existence depended largely on the professionalization of school teaching itself, they naturally took a leading part in that process. They also were foremost in creating the third group, the professional school administrators. School administration, as a profession, is a latecomer, but in terms of understanding the politics of the public schools it is perhaps the most important of all. School administration is a decidedly hierarchical and disciplined business and the top administrator, the local school superintendent, holds the key position in each school district. Indeed, there seems to be professional agreement that the most significant duty of the people's representatives on the local school board is the selection of the superintendent.

The thoroughly defensible assumption that school teaching and school administration are the specialized tasks of persons with professional training and status leads inevitably to a professional distrust of lay interference. This distrust has been accentuated by the frequency with which lay demands have conflicted with the convictions of the educators, seeming to them to be destructive of the very purposes of education. Even well meant lay suggestions that more emphasis should be placed on the "three r's" have caused flutterings of alarm, for too often such criticisms have been the softening-up forerunners of assaults on the freedom of the teachers and so on the whole professional concept. Such assaults have caused one writer to describe the politics of public education as "ideological politics," otherwise a comparative rarity on the American scene.

But are we permitted to speak of the "politics" of education? To many educators the word seems abhorrent: not even the admonitions of George S. Counts[4] can overcome their aversion to it. Again, this is understandable. Whole school systems have been blighted by the intrusion of certain aspects of politics, especially the use of patronage in appointments and contracts in apparent disregard of the need to give children the best possible education. Yet because school districts are governmental units and the voters have ultimate responsibility, school board members and school superintendents are engaged in political activity whether they like it or not. The standard professional terminology for this—a semantic triumph—is "community relations"; a successful superintendent, particularly, must be skilled in community relations. Why not say frankly that he must be a good politician?

Surely it is high time to stop being frightened by a word. Politics includes the making of governmental decisions, and the effort or struggle to gain or keep the power to make those decisions. Public schools are part of government. They are political entities. They are a fit subject for study by political scientists.

Yet neither educators nor political scientists have frequently engaged in the examination of public education from this angle. Educators have shied away not only from the word "politics" but from political scientists as well. (The terminology of social scientists who deal with "power structures" and "communications" they find more acceptable.) Their suspicion of political science stems in part from the writings of some public administration professors who have occasionally urged that school systems, being part of local government, should be merged with multi-purpose local units—namely cities and towns—thus losing their "independent" status; and at the state level, that a department of education, like other departments, should be headed by an appointee of the governor rather than a quasi-independent board. These proposals are in direct conflict with the passionate convictions of professional educators, and so have given political science a bad name in the teaching profession.

As for the political scientists, the running of the public schools—except for national defense the most extensive and expensive governmental activity in this country—has seldom seemed worth more than a chapter or two in a text on state and local government. There are honorable exceptions, but they are very few indeed. The taboo has worked both ways, almost as if by tacit agreement: if politics has been anathema to educators, the governing of the public schools has seemed inconsequential to political scientists.

The taboo should be exorcised, for the future of public education, at every level of government, is not only a political issue but an increasingly crucial one. It requires analysis not only in terms of political institutions (almost the only point of contact, and friction, between educators and political scientists in the past) but in terms of voting behavior, ideological predispositions, the clash of interests, decision-making, and the impact of individuals and organizations on nation-wide trends in educational policy. Of these only the first two have been examined at all extensively (and then usually by social scientists whose primary concern is not politics) and even those have not been the source of any noticeable amount of published material. If all the significant political factors are revealed, the people can more rationally and effectively control the governmental process. Such, at least, must be the faith of the political scientist who, devoted to the search for truth, believes that "what can be" is no less the truth than "what is."

II

The most significant subjects for decision by whoever runs the public schools concern the curriculum, the facilities, the units and organization of government, and personnel; and partly shaping them all is the omni-present issue of finance.

Since World War II a war of words over the *curriculum* has been waged at white heat.[5] Because their professionalism seems to lack full public acceptance and because any attack may make it harder to raise the money needed for good schooling, educators tend to object vehe-mently to most lay criticism. The laity, of course, embraces most of us, including school board members and university professors (of everything but Education), so the inference might seem to be that no one but a professional educator has any business criticizing the methods or ideas of professional educators. This was a typical answer to the vigorous attack on the curriculum mounted by Arthur E. Bestor, professor of history at the University of Illinois. However, by stepping carefully even an outsider may win a hearing. Constructive suggestions so phrased as to avoid sensitive toes, especially if preceded by well-publicized and protracted study, are treated with respect: witness the generally defer-ential reception of the report of James B. Conant, who is just as much a "layman" as Bestor. Any citizen who wants to influence the conduct of the schools might be well advised to follow Conant's example. And the person seeking to portray the political process in relation to education must also resist the temptation to be drawn into the controversy over "progressive education," "life adjustment," whether Johnny can read and if not why not, and the curriculum generally. His task is not to say what should be in the curriculum, but how, by whom, and through whose influ-ence that decision is or might be made.

It is hard to read professional pronouncements on this subject with-out concluding that in professional eyes, the curriculum is essentially the school superintendent's business. To be sure, a committee of the Ameri-can Association of School Administrators, in a report addressed to school board members, did say that the school board had "general responsibility" for the curriculum. The emphasis, however, seemed to be on the word "general," as was indicated by the committee's statement that "Curricu-lum planning and development is a highly technical task which requires special training. . . . Board members do not have and cannot be ex-pected to have the technical competence to pass on the work of expert teachers in this field. . . . Nor can the Board pass upon specific text-books."[6] Conant likewise assumes that "the school board will leave the development of the curriculum to the administrative officers and the teaching staff but will be kept informed of all developments."[7] Even this, however, leaves some doubt about the school board's role, or lack of it. Is curriculum "development" something different from educational "policy," and if so, what is the line that separates them?

A school board member, impressively instructed to stick to policy and allow others to develop the curriculum, might well ask this question. But he might also ask why, if the curriculum is of great importance in educating children, he and his colleagues on the board should not take the responsibility for developing it? They are the people's representatives, elected to run the schools. Professional educators may say that they should not run the schools, but the law says that they must. (The law, of course, was made by some more laymen, called legislators.) Of course a strong argument can be made that usually the curriculum stands a better chance of improvement if it is "developed" by knowledgeable experts. But one may also suggest that experts can occasionally be wrong. Even Conant tacitly admits this, in his assumption that the school board will be "kept informed" and, also, that its members will "reserve (and exercise) the right" to question the superintendent and high school principal. One can imagine school board members, reading this, who will snort: "Reserve the right? We have no right to *refrain* from questioning our employees; we're to govern the school district and not to have some one else do it. There has been too much delegation of authority by elected officials lately. The people elected *us* to run things and we're going to run them."

Although recent controversies give the impression that the professionals have made the curriculum "progressive" (whatever that may mean) and want the school boards to keep hands off, there are indications that in many districts the shoe is on the other foot. Through conviction, or perhaps through ignorance and indifference, school boards have often adhered to curricula which the superintendents consider sadly out of date. Neal Gross quotes as typical of a sizeable minority view among Massachusetts superintendents the following complaints: "The selectmen and the town finance committee take the attitude, 'What was good enough for me ought to be good enough for them (the children).' And so do some of my school committee members. How can you run a modern educational program with . . . a classical curriculum when 80% of the kids don't go on to college?" And again: "My committee is primarily interested in keeping costs down. They don't want to discuss or even consider the need to revise the curriculum." The burden is on those who want change: if the Bestors feel frustrated by the insistence on professional domination of curriculum-making, the professionals feel blocked by lay conservatism or apathy.

The question of whether board or superintendent should dominate is important, but nowhere near as significant as what the curriculum contains. The question is reminiscent of the excitement about balancing the Federal budget before World War II. Many people in the 1930s were convinced that to save the country expenditures must be drastically cut—which meant, of course, the reduction or elimination of the relief programs that gave work and wages to millions of otherwise unemployed men and women. Came the war in Europe, and by 1940 many of these same economizers, fervently pro-British and anti-Hitler, enthusiastically favored vast increases in Federal expenditures for defense and aid to Britain. Whether the budget should be balanced was less crucial than what the money was spent for. In the same way, while a certain form of board-superintendent division of authority may, like budget-balancing, seem generally sound, the real question is what kind of school it produces. The basic problem, therefore, is not one of "school administration"; it is the political issue of what is to be taught or read in our schools. We may wish to leave this decision to the experts; we may wish to make it ourselves. This issue is decided chiefly at the local level, and to a lesser extent in the state capitols by legislatures and state education departments. For the last forty years it has also been affected by national legislation granting federal aid for vocational education.

The decisions concerning *facilities*—chiefly school buildings—are made very largely in the districts, with a comparatively high degree of popular participation. The people get engaged in school-building politics more than in any other phase of public school politics, for two reasons. First, a building program requires a major capital outlay, and in nearly all states the bond issues which such capital outlays necessitate are by law subject to popular approval. Second, buildings being tangible and the distance a child must walk or ride to school being measurable, most people feel more qualified to have opinions about the need, nature and location of the schoolhouse than about what goes on inside it.

Closely allied with the location and adequacy of buildings is the issue of *district organization*. Like the former, it is profoundly affected by finance: the Conant report, for instance, calls for reorganization of districts to eliminate small high schools because a really good small high school is, Conant believes, prohibitively expensive.[8] On the other hand, the problems of location cause Alvin Eurich of the Fund for the Advancement of Education to criticize this recommendation: in sparsely populated areas, a large high school would be too far from many children's homes.[9] The decisions on district size are sometimes made directly by state legislatures, or by state departments of education, but more often by the voters in the districts affected. The local voters' capacity to consolidate districts, is, however, profoundly affected by the kind of statutes enacted by the legislature. The internal organization of a district—its system of government, whether its board shall be elected or appointed, its budgetary connection with the municipality—is ordinarily decided at the state level, though some states permit a certain amount of local option.

Personnel decisions include one which, in most districts, is made directly by the people—the election of school board members. Here is politics at its plainest, despite the non-partisan ballot that prevails in the majority of such elections, yet few efforts have been made to analyze the nature of school board campaigns and patterns of voting behavior therein. The educators and such useful publicists for education as the National Citizens Council for Better Schools rightly emphasize the importance of choosing "good" school boards, but their hortatory efforts are seldom buttressed by information as to what factors actually decide school board elections. The next significant personnel decision is the selection of a superintendent by the school board. He is often the key figure (as the professionals wish him to be) on the local educational scene. Indeed, his selection or retention sometimes is the central issue in school board elections; the voters thus occasionally affect the choice directly, and their potential ability to do so influences board action. Also for local decision is the matter of appointment, retention, and promotion of the teachers. Here direct, official popular intervention via the ballot box is rare indeed, although it has happened, and although occasionally a school board election has revolved around the retention of a school principal or teacher rather than a superintendent. In the main the decisions, formally made by the board, are based on the superintendent's recommendations. Chiefly on the superintendent, therefore, beat the informal pressures for appointment, transfer, or removal of a teacher, often in an emotional context arising naturally out of the complex psychology of the teacher-parent relationship.

While these personnel decisions are made locally, in most districts they are constrained by state legislation, particularly laws prescribing minimum qualifications of superintendents, principals, and teachers, and governing the conditions of promotion and discharge. At the state capitols, more than anywhere else, the educators have fought and largely won their fight for professional status. Tenure laws are, in the main, protections against "politics," but a tenure system may enhance status as well as security. More important, as a recognition of professionalism, are the certification statutes. To be sure, state occupational licensing laws hardly confer professional status, in the traditional sense, on every occupation licensed, such as those of elevator operator or hairdresser. In the case of teachers, however, they have been accompanied—indeed, have often been preceded—by state provisions for substantial formal training. This gives an additional justification for the claim of professionalism, especially as certification requirements, which obviously influence teachers' college programs, may also be to some extent geared to the courses offered by the teachers' colleges. The establishment of teachers colleges, furthermore, has created an institutional pressure center which some critics claim has a dominant effect on state and local curriculum decisions and on the selection of superintendents.

Schools cannot be built, equipped, or staffed without money. The problems of *financing* are inherent in virtually all the issues just discussed. Indeed, they are so omnipresent and so grim that if we were required to give one general explanation of the behavior of professional educators, we might frame it in terms of a ceaseless search for funds. Here may well be the basic reason why educators react so emotionally to criticism: any adverse criticism may make it harder to raise money. When school board members are instructed to go out and "support the schools" in the community, it is not because the superintendents and teachers are thin-skinned or prefer praise to criticism. It is because schools, good or bad, cost money, which must be provided by vote of the people or of their elected representatives on the school board, in the city or county government, and in the state legislature. At each level, the issue of school finance is a focal point of several obvious and broad conflicts of interest. The desire for low taxes clashes with the wish for good schools, in a struggle which is waged not only in the community by organized groups but within the mind of the thoughtful householder. A conflict between the owners of real property, on the one hand, and retailers and consumers on the other becomes increasingly important as proposals are made to shift the growing burden from the real property tax to the sales tax. The interests of those who live in wealthy districts with low taxes and good schools clash with the need to provide good schooling in less fortunate districts, through consolidation or equalization formulae. The local taxpayer wants relief which can be provided by state or federal aid, yet fears such aid because it might open the door to state or federal control: he who pays the piper calls the tune. The professionals are apparently less fearful of dictation from distant seats of power, perhaps because what they really distrust is dictation from any lay source, including the local citizenry: the people should pay for the schools but the professional educators should run them.

Financial decisions traditionally have centered in the districts. Studies have consistently shown that citizens who are interested in the substance of education and have some knowledge of what the schools are doing tend to support the educators' demands for money more than do the less informed voters: hence the great emphasis, in the training of the superintendents, on public relations and "communications." But the ways in which decisions are made are fixed by state laws, and often profoundly affect the decisions themselves. Thus in one state a school board may finally approve a budget which increases the property tax rate; in another the tax increase must be approved by the voters; in a third, the budget itself is the subject of a popular referendum. Board issues may be voted by simple majorities in some states but require a two-thirds approval in others. The states, then, play a vital role in the local settlement of financial issues. They are playing a more direct part, for state funds provide now an estimated 39.7 per cent of all money spent for public schools. What new part, if any, the federal government will play remains a matter of conjecture. Today about 3.5 per cent of all school funds spent by school districts comes from federal sources. . . .

Although political power is centered in groups and individuals, its effectiveness and use are shaped by institutions. The institutional pattern of public education may seem firmly fixed, firmly enough, certainly, so that any proposal, to have a chance of success, must appear to conform to it. The pattern, of course, is one of local control through the democratic process. Yet, as we have seen, questions can and should be raised as to the actual extent and nature of local democratic control. If the image is inconsistent with the reality, we should know it, and change one or the other.

The basic public objective is to have American school children taught what they should be taught by able and dedicated teachers. As to what they should be taught, the broad conflict seems to be chiefly between most of the professional educators and some articulate laymen. General public knowledge about school curricula is hardly less than general public interest in the subject—both are small. But the launching of the first sputnik did stir the people—including educators—more than had the books of Lynd and Bestor, Keats and Smith. A typical professional response was to start teaching algebra in the eighth grade—as an "answer to the Russians" and, more realistically, as a defensive move against possible public criticism. The question remained as to what affirmative role, if any, the layman should play in curriculum development.

The pressures for changes in the curriculum seem to have come from three sources. First is the professional viewpoint itself, shaped largely in teacher-training institutions and often reflecting or adapting the ideas of individuals of almost prophetic stature, such as John Dewey. Second is the need for money causing modifications of the program designed to anticipate public demand—a minimum obeisance to the sovereign people. Third is the activity of organized lay groups. At the local level, the "citizens' committee" usually lacks any real power base and hence is stalemated by the disciplined ranks of the professionals if it tries to engage in curricular reform. Other lay groups, however, such as industrial associations, unions, and patriotic organizations often seek to influence

the content of the curriculum; if they have electoral strength in the community, they may be hard to resist. At the state level they may have an
easier time, for the legislators are not professional educators. In the
legislature, the educators' professional associations constitute pressure
groups competing with the lay organizations, in the familiar fashion of
American politics. Perhaps the very fact that the legislature constitutes a
battleground which educators cannot dominate is a basic reason for the
professional insistence on local control. By making local control a virtual
article of faith to which all good Americans, including state legislators,
should subscribe, the educators have gained an advantage at every
capitol. They can always argue politely and persuasively that regardless
of the possible merit of any legislative proposal to require the teaching
of particular subjects, discretion must be left to each school district.
Compulsory uniformity would be a departure from the American way.

As for the quality of the teachers, it may be true, as Bestor and
others have implied, that the kind of training prescribed as a prerequisite
to entry into the profession discourages able men and women from becoming school teachers. It is a reasonable hypothesis, too, that the vested
interests of the teacher-training institutions impose overwhelming obstacles to any radical reform, for the laymen who would like to substitute
subject-matter scholarship for courses in pedagogy have two or maybe
three strikes against them before they begin. They lack political power,
they lack the experts' status, and they can find no short and simple
answer to the question: "As teaching is a profession, why shouldn't
prospective teachers be taught how to teach?" If the reform of teacher-
training must precede the recruitment of an adequate number of new
and highly competent teachers, it must be sparked by the profession
itself—or so, at least, the political realities seem to suggest.

The profession by itself cannot, however, gain the other objective
which must be reached if first-class teaching is to be the rule: it cannot
raise the money needed to hire and retain excellent teachers. Good
salaries, by themselves, do not produce good teachers, as Eurich has emphasized, but bad salaries certainly are a factor in driving able teachers
into more remunerative pursuits and in keeping potentially fine prospects
out of the schools. Here, and also in the matter of school buildings, the
educators have taken the lead and have sought to stimulate organized
lay support. Their professionalism does not greatly enhance their per-
suasiveness, for salary scales and classrooms are not occult mysteries. In
fighting for financial support, therefore, their influence must stem less
from their specialized knowledge than from their dedicated concern or
their political power.

As a working hypothesis concerning the political system of public education, the following summary might be useful in facilitating analysis and putting the emphasis on the significant spots: As to what should be taught, generally the professionals are dominant, and this may be altogether necessary and proper. Their financial dependence on public approval makes them somewhat responsive to reasonable public demands, tactfully presented, although their very professionalism forces them to resist proposals of which they disapprove and causes them to react adversely to most lay criticism. Professional influence is usually preponderant in local districts where the school superintendent is, or can be, the leader of the school system. It is much weaker in the state legislatures, but even there it is aided by the tradition of local diversity and the easy access afforded by the presence of professionals in official state positions —the heads of teachers colleges and state departments of education. As to who should teach, the profession has generally sought state protection against pressures for local personal and partisan patronage. This protection, as a by-product, has solidified the position of the teachers college where most prospective teachers must be trained and which increasingly influence boards of education in the selection of superintendents. As for the acquisition of sufficient funds to build and run adequate schools, the decision-making authority rests partly in the school boards, partly in the local electorates, and partly in the state legislatures. To these lay groups the profession comes as supplicant, its demands competing with other demands (for highways, hospitals, etc.) and meeting the inevitable resistance of the taxpayer. If there are to be good schools, the competition must be largely won and the resistance broken down. To achieve these ends at the local level, the professionals seek to stimulate public interest in education, at the risk of lay interference with the schools. Their achievement at the state level depends more on the effectiveness of the professionals operating as pressure groups, with lay support which is less likely to involve lay dictation in curricular and personnel matters. At the federal level they have not yet been achieved. Unsuccessful drives for federal financial aid have been sparked by the largest professional pressure group and have been balked by a combination of three factors: the peripheral but highly charged issues of religion and race, the pocketbook interests of taxpayers in relatively wealthy states, and the traditional fear of central dictation. Perhaps only the passage of time can overcome the first of these obstacles, though acute public awareness of a national need for better schools might be enough. Such awareness is obviously needed to overcome the second. The third is not likely to be overcome without a more thorough, comprehensive analysis of its validity or unsoundness than has yet been forthcoming.

The fact that the professionals, who have the greatest power stake in local control, are the people least afraid of federal aid may be an indication of the needlessness of any fear of federal control. But it may also indicate something more basic. Is it conceivable that national financial aid and its concurrent possibility of national standards is acceptable to a national professional organization because that organization itself believes in or recognizes the existence of national standards? Perhaps we have been tending for a long time toward a greater degree of national educational uniformity than the old theory of local discretionary control implies. The professionalization of the school superintendency surely pushes us in that direction. The superintendent, like a city manager, moves from district to district. His methods may alter to conform to the local mores, but his basic educational philosophy remains the same. And, by all appearances, one modern superintendent's educational philosophy is likely to be much like another's, for more and more of them qualify for the position through studies at teachers colleges of largely similar outlook. The profession is certainly not intellectually monolithic, as the debates and disagreements in journals and conventions show; but it may well be growing more unified in its devotion to agreed-upon professional standards and goals.

If this is so, what is the future for the "diversity" which justifies unimpaired local control? If local control in the most fundamental matters —curriculum and teaching—is largely in professional hands, are there even now fewer significant differences between districts than was formerly the case? Granted that state requirements differ, that local interests may differentiate programs in rural districts from those in urban districts, and that the curricula and teaching in particular schools or districts take account of the varying backgrounds and objectives of the student population; still, the classifications are broad. In thousands of districts the educational needs are similar. Conant may disclaim any intention to provide a blueprint, but his recommendations are not intended as the basis for a single district's experimentation: they are aimed at innumerable American high schools. And, significantly, the professional reaction to the Conant report has included little, if any, objection to the basic curricular uniformity which it implies. Perhaps, then, at least within broad urban-rural or socio-economic categories, local diversity is or will soon be significant only with respect to those matters where professional domination is weakest: school buildings (including site selection), transportation of pupils, and finance. Decisions as to the last, assuming any real public desire for improved schooling, will continue gradually to move out of local hands and into the state legislatures. Certainly the extent and nature of inter-district diversity in basic educational processes need prompt analysis. If, indeed, they are minimal, then the lay proponents of complete local control must be prepared to defend their position in terms of their convenience and their pocketbooks rather than their concern for educational content. . . .

Notes

1. When President of Columbia University, Mr. Eisenhower, in a letter to Representative Ralph Gwinn, pictured general federal aid for education as "another vehicle by which the believers in paternalism, if not outright socialism, will gain still additional power for the central government." *Congressional Record,* Vol. 95, Pt. 14, p. A3690, June 14, 1949.

2. James B. Conant, *The American High School Today* (New York, 1959), p. 43.

3. Walter Lippmann, *Essays in the Public Philosophy* (Boston, 1955).

4. "The profession should seek power and then try to use that power fully and wisely and in the interests of the great masses of the people." George S. Counts, *Dare the Schools Build a New Social Order?* (New York, 1932), p. 29.

5. The best-publicized attacks on the curriculum, aside from those of "superpatriotic" groups, include the books of Arthur E. Bestor, especially *The Restoration of Learning* (New York, 1955); Mortimer Smith's artistically written *And Madly Teach* (Chicago, 1949); John Keats, *Schools Without Scholars* (Boston, 1958); and the recent call to arms by Vice Admiral Rickover, *Education and Freedom,* . . . . The educators' defense and counterattack have been confined almost wholly to articles in professional journals: a number of them can be found in Scott and Hill, ...

6. *School Boards in Action,* . . . p. 178. For a less guarded professional viewpoint, consider the implications of an "opinion survey" of a sample of teachers from eighteen scattered states. Asked who they thought should make various kinds of decisions, they were in substantial agreement on the curriculum-making process, as follows; "Determination of the objectives for the total instructional program of the school: principal, groups of teachers, and superintendent." Chiranji Lal Sharma, "Practices in Decision-Making as Related to Satisfaction in Teaching," unpublished dissertation, University of Chicago (1955), quoted in The Midwest Administration Center's *Administrator's Notebook,* Vol. III, No. 8 (University of Chicago, 1955). See also E. M. Tuttle, *School Board Leadership in America* (Danville, Ill.: Interstate Printers and Publishers, 1958), pp. 31, 40, wherein the first secretary of the National School Boards Association, Inc., says that the board's "policies on the educational program should set forth clearly the goals which the community is seeking" and that the board should "interpret, defend and support constructive educational programs when the need arises." Mr. Tuttle does, however, also imply that some more direct board participation is desirable, including meeting with the superintendent and "professional educators and consultants" to consider "new ideas and concepts of instruction and curriculum planning" (p. 66). A teachers college professor expresses his assumption that in fact, the curriculum is largely shaped by what the professionals believe to be local lay opinion: he believes that this inchoate lay influence is highly unfortunate. Myron Lieberman, "Let Educators Run Our Schools," *The Nation,* March 7, 1959, pp. 206–209.

7. Conant, *op. cit.,* p. 43.

8. Conant, *op. cit.,* p. 37.

9. *New York Times,* Feb., 1959. Evidently, the question depends in part on how much the district is willing to pay for bus service.

55. *Municipal Justice*

WALLACE S. SAYRE AND HERBERT KAUFMAN

(This account of municipal justice is taken from a study of New York City.)

In particular, judges settle disputes—disputes involving money, services, office, reputations, and even life and liberty, disputes between litigants invoking governmental powers to implement their claims upon each other, upon the parties, and upon governmental officials and employees. Judicial decisions thus determine, in part, who gets what. Private citizens and nongovernmental groups may be contending with one another, or they may contest the action, or inaction, of officials or employees at any level of government. Government officials often bring suit against one another, or, when this is precluded by existing law (the city, for example, is unable to sue the state) may achieve the same effect by staging tax-payer suits. Law enforcement officers of all kinds represent the state in litigation with alleged law violators. Public officials and employees some-times bring actions against their employers; the city, being a corporation rather than a "sovereign" power, is especially vulnerable to attacks of this kind. Voters, candidates, and party members frequently challenge party leaders—sometimes within their own parties sometimes in other parties —in the courts. At one time or another virtually every possible combination of those identified as contestants for the rewards of governmental action appears in the courts. And the judges, in deciding the questions at issue, in effect employ governmental authority in such a way as to allo-cate some of the prizes. Most of the time, judges are umpires rather than players. But, after all, how a contest comes out depends in large measure on what the umpires do.

As Interpreters of the Rules

Judicial decisions often do much more than settle the immediate question in litigation. They often determine the content and scope of the constitutional and statutory provisions earlier characterized as "the rules of the game," and they may sometimes upset state legislation, local

Reprinted from *Governing New York City* (New York: Russell Sage Founda-tion, 1960), pp. 528–31, 536–38 by permission of the authors and the publisher. Authors' footnotes omitted. Wallace Sayre is professor of political science at Columbia University. Herbert Kaufman is professor of political science at Yale University.

legislation (far more frequently), or administrative rules and regulations, instead of merely invalidating a specific governmental act under a particular rule. The way in which judges dispose of election cases has far-reaching effects on the relationships among the parties and especially among the factions within parties. Judicial attitudes and actions of both kinds generally strengthen the positions of some contestants seeking to influence governmental policy and reduce the leverage of others—rarely does an interpretation of the rules of the game affect equally all who are concerned with them—sometimes regardless of what the judges intend or prefer, but effectively just the same. Thus, for example, when the courts construe narrowly the meaning of the phrase "government, property, and affairs of the city" in the Home Rule Act, the Home Rule Law and the home rule provisions of the constitution... they permit state officers to intervene more extensively in the governance of the city than a different construction of the language would allow. When they ruled that the principle of separation of powers does not apply to governments of cities, they denied to the Mayor powers and immunities associated with the chief executives in Albany and Washington, particularly in his relations with the City Council. When they refused to invalidate inequalities of representation growing out of failure to reapportion the lines of the old aldermanic districts, they buttressed the Democratic majority that benefited from the prevailing situation; when, on the other hand, they refused to hold proportional representation unconstitutional, they strengthened the hands of the minority parties in the city. When they upheld the power of the city, under permissive state legislation, to enact rent control laws, they won the plaudits of the tenants and the condemnation of the landlords, and the net result was to increase the popularity of the Democratic officers who were responsible for the measure. When they declared municipal employees were subject to the federal income tax, the result from the point of view of these persons was a reduction in salary. It has been said the law is what the judges say it is; while this assertion, without qualification, is unquestionably an exaggeration, it reflects the fundamental truth of the proposition that the distribution of rewards among the contestants striving to influence governmental decisions is shaped to a large extent by what judges say the rules are.

As Appointing Officers

The 315 judges in or from the city are the formal appointing officers for several thousand employees constituting the nonjudicial staffs of the court system. The exact number of such appointees outside the competi-

tive civil service is difficult to ascertain, but it apparently amounts to
some four or five hundred. A relatively small number of appointees, in
turn, are themselves appointing officers who formally name staffs of their
own.

From the standpoint of salary, prestige, responsibility, and prominence, the most important of the judicial appointees are the County
Clerks and the Public Administrators. The County Clerks, appointed and
removable by the Appellate Division of the Supreme Court, receive
$15,000 a year, except in Richmond, where the County Clerk gets
$10,500; as custodians of all the books, records, and papers of their re-
spective counties, and as clerks of their respective County Courts and
of the Supreme Court when it sits in their counties, they have substantial
staffs of their own. The Public Administrators are appointed by the Sur-
rogates; they administer estates for which, for one reason or another,
no other executor is available, and they have employees to assist them.
The Public Administrator in New York County is paid $15,000; in Kings,
$10,750; in Queens, $8,750; in Bronx, $4,000 and fees; in Richmond,
$5,925.

Even the less visible positions, however, are frequently highly remunerative. The Chief Clerks of some of the courts receive as much as
$20,000, while many fall in the range from $9,500 to $11,500, and their
deputies normally are not far behind. Individual judges frequently have
clerks who earn as much as $10,500, and some have confidential attend-
ants in addition who get from $5,000 to $7,000. Three courts have Commissioners of Records in the same salary bracket as the clerks, and the
Commissioners' deputies are proportionately well paid. There are also
secretaries and law assistants who may be paid from $5,000 to $15,000. At
the lower levels stand the clerks to the Justices of the Municipal Court,
whose salaries are about $3,800 a year for each, and some courtroom
personnel. Many of these salaries are set by the judges themselves, and
are mandated upon the city by state legislation. Furthermore, there are
numerous appointments as commissioners in mortgage foreclosure which
yield substantial fees, as administrators of the estates of persons who die
intestate, as guardians, and as referees, all of these quite apart from the
appointments to positions on the public payrolls. The judges are thus
formal dispensers of jobs and benefits, many of them highly rewarding.

Not all the appointments to public positions are wholly at the discretion of the judges. Most are under the jurisdiction of the city or state
personnel agencies, and the appointments must be made from lists of the
names of people who have passed a competitive, or at least a qualifying
examination. Party considerations play significant parts in the selection
of personnel for some posts. And the necessity of having competent

personnel to perform many of the duties incidental to the judicial process
is an imperative which cannot be ignored; hence, as a matter of common
practice, law clerks in the federal courts, the Court of Appeals, the
Appellate Division, and many parts of the State Supreme Court are
selected by the judges from the top law school graduates without
reference to political recommendations. So the judges are not without
restrictions, both legal and practical, on their range of choice. But they
are the formal appointing officers in all these instances, and their discretion, if not unlimited, is still quite broad. Their appointing authority
places them squarely and prominently in the political struggle.

Differences Between Judges and Other Contestants

While judges, since they share in the distribution of the stakes of
politics and can use their control over the distribution of other prizes to
buttress their own claims and those of their allies, may thus be treated
in much the same fashion as other governmental participants in the
contest for these stakes, the distinguishing features of the judicial process
and judicial institutions must not be overlooked. On the whole, the
distinctions between the courts and other governmental institutions and
practices are differences in degree rather than in kind. But the differences
are sufficiently pronounced to warrant particular attention.

Take, for instance, the Anglo-Saxon juridical principle of judicial
independence. This tradition is reflected in the deliberate insulation of
judges from many types of control exercised by legislatures and chief
executives over other public officers and employees; hence, the security
of tenure, the unusually strong safeguards against suspension or removal,
the constitutional and statutory bans on reductions in the salaries of
sitting judges, and the weakness of overhead agency controls upon the
courts. The procedures that keep the other agencies of government
responsive and "accountable" to elected legislators and executives have
purposely been rendered inapplicable to the courts; they contravene the
principle of judicial independence. Some administrative agencies, it is
true, achieve substantial autonomy, sometimes by the way they are
structured (as, for example, in the case of regulatory commissions, public
corporations, and public authorities), sometimes by accident, and sometimes by virtue of the personalities and strategic skills of their leaders.
But no other agencies are shielded as are the courts by so many built-in
protections, by such strong constitutional and statutory and traditional
bulwarks. Even judges are not totally immune to pressure and retaliation,
but successful assaults on their redoubt are less frequent. Figuratively

speaking, they can follow the dictates of conscience almost to the extent of thumbing their noses with impunity at those outside the judicial hierarchy. Other things discussed in this chapter make it most improbable that they will feel so inclined, but the fact that they could conceivably do so sets them apart from most of their governmental colleagues.

In addition, the formality of judicial procedure, the weight of legal traditions, the ethical norms instilled through professional training and policed in a general way by professional organizations, and supervision of lower courts by higher ones appointed by other chief executives or elected from other constituencies, all combine to restrict the avenues of access to judges and to limit both their opportunities and their willingness to use their decision-making powers for bargaining purposes. Again, this is only a relative proposition; it is not impossible to negotiate with, or bring pressure to bear upon, a judge, but it is rather more difficult to reach a judge this way than to reach other public officials who are regarded, and who regard themselves, as having a primarily "representative" function in contrast with the emphasis on judicial independence.

Taking account of these qualifications (which apply primarily only to the processes of judicial decision and less to appointments by judges), it may be said that the factors identified in the foregoing paragraphs tend to reduce the vulnerability of judges to the pressures of other claimants on the prizes of politics, and to limit (but by no means to eliminate, particularly in the lower courts) the responsiveness of judges to some influences from outside the courts and the legal profession.

The distinctions between judges and other participants in the contest for the rewards of politics can easily be overdrawn. All the participants have much in common, and judges are participants. But it is important to bear in mind that the independence of the judiciary is one of the central values around which our court system is organized, and that judicial procedure is less flexible, less hidden from scrutiny, more circumscribed by expectations of neutrality and impartiality and by the traditions of the legal profession, than most of the other institutions involved in the governmental process.

INDEX OF PERSONS

INDEX OF CITIES

PRINTED IN U.S.A.